THE ONENESS/OTHERNESS MYSTERY

To Sebastian
Aronowitz
from
Sutapas
Bhattacharya

The Oneness/Otherness Mystery

The Synthesis of Science and Mysticism

SUTAPAS BHATTACHARYA

MOTILAL BANARSIDASS PUBLISHERS
PRIVATE LIMITED • DELHI

First Edition: Delhi, 1999

ISBN: 81-208-1654-4

Also available at:

MOTILAL BANARSIDASS

41 U.A. Bungalow Road, Jawahar Nagar, Delhi 110 007
8 Mahalaxmi Chamber, Warden Road, Mumbai 400 026
120 Royapettah High Road, Mylapore, Chennai 600 004
Sanas Plaza, 1302, Baji Rao Road, Pune 411 002
16 St. Mark's Road, Bangalore 560 001
8 Camac Street, Calcutta 700 017
Ashok Rajpath, Patna 800 004
Chowk, Varanasi 221 001

PRINTED IN INDIA
BY JAINENDRA PRAKASH JAIN AT SHRI JAINENDRA PRESS,
A-45 NARAINA, PHASE I, NEW DELHI 110 028
AND PUBLISHED BY NARENDRA PRAKASH JAIN FOR
MOTILAL BANARSIDASS PUBLISHERS PRIVATE LIMITED,
BUNGALOW ROAD, DELHI 110 007

Dedication

To my two mothers, Shima and *Bhārat*

CONTENTS

PREFACE

Sarvam idam brahma eva
(Verily, all this is Brahman.)
(*Upaniṣads*)

They reckon ill who leave me out
When me they fly, I am the wings
I am the doubter and the doubt
And I the hymn the brahmin sings
(R.W. Emerson; *Brahma*)

This is a work about our very existence, about Reality. This is a work about the relationship between the individual personality and the cosmos in which that personality exists, showing how the person is a microcosm, a little part of the cosmos, subtly reflecting his or her 'world' however autonomous or independent (s)he may believe (s)he is. As such, nothing is beyond the scope of this work which is intended to restore *metaphysics* to the study of the "world as a whole". While writing this work, I came to resolve the central problems of Eastern and Western philosophy, the question of the meaning of the mystical union and the question, which has arisen in the modern West, of the relationship between Consciousness and the so-called "physical world". Both are clearly resolved as I shall begin to synthesise Science and Mysticism through my identification of the physical correlate of the Divine Light (*chit*/Pure Consciousness). From this fundamental identification, many of the great questions regarding the nature of the transcendental and the mundane, and regarding the individual and the Absolute shall be resolved, doing away with a large part of what has been the subject matter of "philosophy" over the last three thousand years. Using knowledge from Science, authoritative yogic traditions, my own theory of consciousness, history and Western philosophy, I shall begin to affirm what has been called the "Perennial Philosophy", derived from the phenomenological knowledge of mystics from all over the world in all ages.

I will establish beyond any reasonable doubt the validity of my identification of the physical correlate of the Divine Light and we shall see that remarkable concordances are revealed with yogic knowledge that has been established over thousands of years. Given the central position of the Divine Light in Mysticism and its equally central position in theology, where it is referred to as the Godhead, we are, for the first time ever, placed on a secure footing from which we may proceed to examine all aspects of Mysticism, cutting away at the chaotic growth of religious superstitions and dogma and the mythological distortions to reveal the great, essential truths beneath the clutter and confusion of competing traditions, the arcane terminology, and the often misunderstood doctrines of the great Indian yogic traditions.

Indeed the structure of the final essay, presenting the Science-Mysticism synthesis, provides a convenient basic framework for categorizing the various aspects of yogic mysticism which are often jumbled together haphazardly by uneducated holy men and commentators who often have little appreciation of the real significance of the various mystical realisations. Those who thought that scientific encroachment onto the 'territory' of Mysticism would lead to Science explaining away outdated superstitions will be in for a rude awakening. Rather than materialist science swallowing up and explaining away yogic mysticism, we shall find that the entire modern, materialist picture is swallowed up and can be truly understood only from the perspective of the core yogic understanding of Reality which may be called the *Sanātana Dharma*. The understanding of the true nature of Consciousness and of the transcendental shall provide us with numerous insights, not only in regard to the mind, but also in regard to physics, cosmology and biology. Many of the constructions of modern science will be exposed as mythologies, often animistic projections, the products of the most basic epistemological errors and immaturity displayed throughout history by some of the most revered 'great minds' of the Western world. We shall also see that modern science remains to a considerable extent the product of Christian (especially Catholic) superstitions. Furthermore, the bigger, deeper picture of the *Sanātana Dharma* will allow us to begin to understand issues precluded by reductionist, materialist science such as creativity, insight, paranormal phenomena, mind-body interactions, the source of the universe and also some of the seemingly intractable paradoxes which Western science has brought upon itself through its dogmatism and ignorance of basic epistemology.

I shall present my ideas in a manner both comprehensible to any educated layman while at the same time capable of persuading 'hard-nosed' sceptics indoctrinated into the modern scientific world-view, given they open their minds for a change, using arguments which I have used successfully to convince numerous scientifically-educated people, many of whom were once sceptical. When one has a correct orientation to Reality, the basic arguments become remarkably simple; it is only the speculative philosopher, manipulating abstractions, who needs to complicate matters in order to try to impress or simply because he has, through his own confusion, got himself into some abstract tangle and presents the product of his own confusion as profound mystery. In order to fully appreciate my argument, I urge the reader to tackle the work in the sequence in which it is presented even though the actual synthesis will be presented in the final essay as the preceding essays and the verse work will give one the necessary acquaintance with the overall historical picture, relating to the philosophical and politico-economic encounter between Indian civilisation, now known to be the world's first civilisation, and the modern West.

As I discuss in this work, the idea of fusing Indian Spirituality with European science was originally propounded in nineteenth century Calcutta by Bankim Chandra Chattopadhyay who is generally considered to be the "Father of Indian Nationalism". It was the core element of the notion of the East-West Synthesis, the idea of synthesising the positive features of both Eastern and Western civilisation and discarding the "rubbish" from both to create a higher civilisation. Indeed, India's first great modern scientist, Jagadis Chandra Bose, had hoped to challenge the Western dominance of Science using holistic Vedantic concepts. As this work stresses, the metaphysical and the mundane cannot be totally separated and this work itself is not merely a metaphysical work but, more generally, a reinterpretation of the original ideals of Indian Nationalism faced with a vastly changed world situation and the rise of sectarian "Hindu" Nationalism as India gears up towards economic "take-off". The metaphysical East-West Synthesis presented in this work has clearly come to be as a product of this historical encounter between India and the modern West.

All metaphysical thought, indeed all systems of knowledge,

reflect the socio-economic, cultural perspectives of the societies within which they were constructed even though the source of metaphysical knowledge is universal. I shall show the relationship of all domains of human enquiry to the complete picture of human knowledge, showing the domains in their proper relationships to the Whole. In response to the argument presented by Karl Popper and his acolytes that the theory of evolution is not science but "metaphysics" because it is not testable, scientists argue that it is correct picture because everything falls into place within the framework. Similarly, as I show the falseness of materialism, religion, and language-manipulating philosophy, etc. which make their symbolic constructs, the "physical world", personal gods, language, information, etc., to be the Ultimate Reality, the ultimate frame of reference, it is worth keeping in mind that within my scheme of things, grounded in *Brahman*, the Ground of all Being, everything falls into place. To those seekers of Truth who remain open-hearted and free themselves from the indoctrinations of the modern world, I say, "welcome to the New Age".

Sutapas Bhattacharya

ACKNOWLEDGEMENTS

There are those who are taught from without by human teachers and those who are taught from within by the deeper Self which communicates its instructions through many means and controls our destinies. I was privileged to be chosen for special tuition from within although the lessons were often in the form of ordeals testing me to breaking point. I continued to follow the guidance of the Inner Voice even when the world outside laughed at me and it appeared that I was being driven into wasting away my life. Yet the inner guide leads us to our destinies without revealing exactly what these are and this work bears testimony to the superiority of the path of inner tuition, the guidance of the deeper Self, which, through compulsions and synchronicities, led me progressively towards fulfilment of this project. Thus, first and foremost, I must acknowledge that the inspiration and the tuition which provided me with the creativity and insights to produce this work came from my deeper Self, the impersonal Spirit within, which we Indians call the *Ātman*.

It seems as if my *Ātman* determined that my long course of higher learning must be undertaken in a reclusive mode of existence so that I would not be disturbed by the nay-saying of others who, trapped in the littleness of the mundane plane of material existence, would have thought my task an impossible one. Thus, I acknowledge no teachers or advisors as I had none. My formal qualifications have nothing to do with this work which was completed without any sponsorship or even the use of any libraries. None the less, I must acknowledge the encouragement given to me by certain people at various points in my development although I have never met any of these people in person. My thanks go to J.J. Williamson, DSc., President of the Society of Metaphysicians, Hastings, who published my first immature article on the nature of consciousness in 1983; to Professor D.W. Hamlyn, editor of the journal *Mind* in 1983, who responded most positively and generously to the teenage boy who wrote to him; to Dr Beulah McNab of the University of Amsterdam who, in 1992, generously offered to help me to find a publisher for my 1987 paper on consciousness and who, in 1994, was the first person to agree with my seemingly outrageous claim to have identified the physical correlate of the Divine Light; to Dr J.J. Clarke, academic and writer, who responded most positively to the first half of this manuscript which I sent him unsolicited in 1995; to the late Professor Willis Harman, President of the Institute of Noetic Sciences, Sausalito (1978-96), who responded most positively to the synopsis of this work in 1995 but who, sadly, did not live to see it and realise that his predictions for the future incorporation of the scientific picture into the Indian cosmology would begin to come true so soon. A special thanks must go to Narendra Prakash Jain of Motilal Banarsidass, who offered to publish a most unconventional manuscript sent in by a complete unknown which most publishers would have ignored and, had they perused the covering letter, out of ignorance would have dismissed my claims as nonsense. It was my Inner Voice which told me to try Motilal Banarsidass even though they were not listed in the *Writers and Artists' Yearbook*. Last, but not least, I must acknowledge the countless yogis of India who have revealed to the world the *Sanātana Dharma* towards which my *Ātman* relentlessly guided me.

INTRODUCTION

Aristoxenus the musician tells us the following story about the Indians. One of the men met Socrates at Athens, and asked him what was the scope of his philosophy. "An inquiry into human phenomena", replied Socrates. At this the Indian burst out laughing. "How can we grasp human phenomena" he exclaimed, "when we are ignorant of the Divine?"

—Eusebius

THE LYRICISM OF A PHILOSOPHER

The creation of the sūtra

I have written this introduction to my work in order to help the reader appreciate the integral nature of the work, highlighting some of its intentional and emergent themes. I also wish to state my position in regard to some of the possible interpretations of this work, which is prone to considerable misrepresentation. In life, as well as in writing, the fact that I tend to baldly make certain assertions which may break the taboos of 'politically correct' public expression in 'postmodern' liberal society has led to much misunderstanding of my actual views on various matters. I am all too aware of the idiosyncrasies and mood-dependent variations in my outlook permeating this work.

Although the verse may come across as the painting of a substantial portion of my world-view, it in fact represents a rather selective window on the world-view of a twenty-six-year-old, a young man, a boy to some, whose plasticity of mind has led to some changes in his political outlook and who has, since writing the verse, pursued its philosophical ramifications to their limits leading to remarkable developments which extend the scope of the overall work way beyond the limits of the verse. Given that I now claim to have resolved the central problems of Eastern and Western philosophy (the problem of the 'mystical union' and the so-called 'mind-body problem'), directly linking together and beginning to synthesise Science and Mysticism, the state of my thought leading up to these developments as represented in the verse will obviously be of some significance. The broader development of my thought since writing the verse is given in the two essays of the Postscript following the verse work.

Written in the summer and autumn of 1991, the verse is partly the product of a peculiar historical situation with the rapid dissolution of Cold War geopolitics and the latest spate of pipe dreams about a 'New World Order' emanating from the Anglo-American West after an almost mercenary war over the control of oil resources. This war seemed to hammer home the message that the historical legacy of Western military technological supremacy and its use in dictating the flow of the world's resources (the new imperialism known as neo-colonialism) was alive and kicking. Of course, there were mitigating factors such as the neutralisation of a brutal, warmongering dictator and the restoration of oil prices, but what stuck in the mind of many people across the world was the shameless display of double standards over reprimanding outlaw states and the disturbing display of overwhelming military power used with considerable disregard for any countervailing opinion as to the appropriate means of resolving the dispute. This was set against the death throes of the Soviet Union which had posed the only serious challenge to Western imperialistic domination of world affairs. The Soviet Communist system, albeit a futile system best done away with in most respects, represented the only concrete challenge to the Western-dominated economic system and its dissolution had a remarkable effect, causing a concomitant dissolution in the cognitive structures of people around the world whose geopolitical outlooks had been framed in relation to the Cold War. This affected me even though I had largely agreed with the Non-Aligned Movement's assertion that the real polarization of the globe was, not between so-called East and West, but between so-called North and South. The gurus of the so-called 'free market' system were in triumphalist rapture with the liberalisation of state-controlled economies and India's new government had just embarked upon this road in earnest as I began to write the verse. The verse also reflected what one may call a search for my roots in that I had read a number of books on Indian history, especially in 1990, and had begun to investigate Indian philosophy with which I had only a brief acquaintance at the time I wrote the verse.

Now I am not so young a man, less angry about such geopolitical issues where the prospect of an Asian resurgence is looming ever larger on the horizon. Destiny deemed that I should not progress in a formal career and, following a nervous breakdown in 1993, I turned my energy towards my philosophical work which, deep down, I always saw as my 'true vocation'. Indeed, on my school-leaving form, which asked what I wanted to be when I grew up, I answered, "poet, priest, philosopher". As I proclaim in the opening quatrains of the verse, I am what is called in the modern world an 'outsider', a reinterpretation of the type traditionally associated with prophets and mystics. Indeed in 1993, when I looked at the poems I had written as a schoolboy, I was struck by the fact that this 'outsider' character of my personality was clearly manifest around the age of fifteen and sixteen when last I put my thoughts to verse. I consider the verse work that emerged from my naïve, seemingly whimsical attempt to write a grand poem for a poetry competition as a *sūtra*, an exposition of one's philosophy written in aphoristic verse. As with the ancient Indian *sūtras*, the aphoristic verses (useful for mnemonic purposes during the age of oral transmission) required a commentary in order to explain their meaning and this I had to provide in 1991 (included in this work as the "Commentary" which explains terms and ideas on a line by line basis where appropriate, especially for Western readers). However, whereas the development of the philosophical questions raised by ancient Indian *sūtras* took place over hundreds of years with the commentaries of generations of philosophers, the further development of the philosophical questions in my *sūtra* of 1991 was undertaken by myself from 1993 onwards as the brief Commentary was insufficient explanation of the overall *raison d'être* of my *sūtra*. The discussion of the metaphysical contents of the verse led way beyond my original plans and the final metaphysical essay now constitutes the 'centrepiece' of the book.

As I consider this work to be a continuation of the Indian tradition, although written in English in London, I also like to look upon my role in writing the verse as that of a *kavi,* where the poet is a sage or philosopher rather than just the creative writer that is the modern Western *poet.*

I certainly do not identify with the writings categorised as 'poetry' by the British poetry establishment with their emphasis on the most mundane lyricism and lack of formal structure. Thankfully, I remained ignorant of the modern world of British poetry with its clique-ridden self-congratulation and its rather Maoist 'cultural revolutionary' attitude when I decided to enter the competition having received, unsolicited, an entry form following a previous entry while I had been at school. Indeed, nearly all the prize winners had attended courses, out in rural England, run by the organisers. The 1992 British *Writers and Artists Yearbook* even suggested to would-be poets that they copy the style of such poets! I have no intention of going back to the land to be brainwashed by the Red Guards. I was much amused to see the letters in the competition's sponsoring newspaper, from those who felt that such formless work was not *poetry,* stating that the winning works were devoid of any lines which invoked higher sentiments or which stirred the heart; something that clearly cannot be said of my verse. Such ultra-modern, formless verse about the very ordinary problems of very ordinary people favoured by the organisers was certainly not the "poetry" referred to by Nobel Laureate physical chemist, Ilya Prigogine, inventor of the new thermodynamics and admirer of Tagore, who has asserted that the 'new science' was beginning to confirm the great truths affirmed by the *poets* and mystics of all ages. The modern minds which wax lyrical about little things clearly cannot connect to the depths of their being from which the great truths arise. None the less, without the existence of this competition, I would not have embarked upon this project. Therefore, I owe something to it in much the same way as Columbus owed something to his mistaken view of reaching the Indies by sailing West which led to the supposed European discovery of the 'New World'.

But as we now know, Columbus had prior knowledge of what he was about to find across the Atlantic. With hindsight, I feel that my strange burst of poetical outpourings were guided by the secret knowledge of my 'deeper Self'. Indeed the primary conscious motive behind the creation of the verse was the hope that it would help publicise my panpsychist theory of consciousness which was contained within it (Section XV) as I clearly was not going to be allowed to air my views by the Western academics who called themselves 'philosophers' and to most of whom, blinded by science, language and logic, panpsychism was anathema, primarily because of its close association with mysticism.

Logicians, haughty, in esteem held
Looked like blind men tapping lathis
Was blinded not by science this schoolboy
Saw the whole beast as a hathi

(When I first scribbled down this verse, the first line read, "The great professors of the West".) Now, as the project has led to my identification of the physical correlate of the Divine Light/*chit*/Pure Consciousness, confirming my basic panpsychist tenets and the beginning of the synthesis of Science and Mysticism, it will be my extended views on Consciousness which will take the lead in giving the rest of the work an airing. For years before I wrote the verse I had had premonition-like fantasies of writing a book of essays which, in itself, would arouse interest and thus publicise my theory which I would include as an appendix. In 1991 I was surprised that this seemed to have been fulfilled in the form of a verse work as I had had no intention of writing in verse again after leaving school until I received the entry form in 1991, and I have not written anything in verse since 1991. Now my premonition is truly becoming fulfilled as the verse work takes a back seat beside the essays of the Postscript. The final essay shall contain the metaphysical synthesis which constitutes what many people have been predicting as the basis of the 'New Age'.

Traditional elite transcendentalism versus superficial mass culture

If my work is seen as being pretentious, I believe it says more about the diminution of learning, and derision of higher intellectual aspirations in today's cultural tyranny of the majority with its emphasis on catering for teenagers and those who have not progressed beyond teenage mental ages, with its conspiracies of mediocrity apparent in so many spheres of endeavour. Those incapable of 'higher' things like to prevent others from aspiring to higher things which show up the shoddiness of their own efforts with accusations of elitism, etc.

> *Ours is an age of systematized irrelevances, and the imbecile within us has become one of the Titans.* —**Aldous Huxley**

The West may have given universal literacy to its masses but it has failed to make them truly *educated*. The mind does not mature fully in terms of intellectual development even with good schooling up to the age of twenty-one (which very few actually receive). Indeed, although I was regarded considerably more advanced intellectually than most of my classmates at school and university, my mind has made remarkable progress since leaving formal education. The development of my understanding in the six years between writing the verse in 1991 and the synthesis of the disparate realms of knowledge alluded to within it in 1997 marked a remarkable leap forward from an already fairly advanced position. Given that my mind naturally seeks the 'deep structure' of knowledge and roams across such terrain during idle moments and that the 'holistical' contextualization of the raw data into its broader 'philosophical' nexus is my natural mental predisposition, however inappropriate this may be at times, the grandiosity of my verse, far from being pretentious, may be interpreted as the lyricism of a philosopher.

Similarly, due to my philosophical disposition and my scientific education, I have never identified much with the literary approach to great questions through the telling of stories which ramble roundabout the issues without ever penetrating into the heart of the matter. To me, reading stories or poetry is merely for little minds seeking a bit of entertainment, no true seeker of knowledge would waste his time trying to glean some vague snippet of wisdom in such a roundabout manner. Such an approach to "broadening one's mind" is for those who would shy away from any serious examination of the questions, content to live with simple truisms, like those who believe in religious traditions with their misleading symbols and their personality cults. I find it quite amusing to consider some of the grander arguments of most of the literary figures considered to be 'thinkers' by the pseudo-intellectual literati dominating the Western media as their understanding of issues is often actually very shallow (see my responses to V.S. Naipaul's rantings) yet their friends in the circles of reviewers laud these inchoate and often obviously nonsensical thoughts as profound. I recall reading on the back cover of Salman Rushdie's, "Booker of Bookers" (Best of all the Booker Prize Winners) *Midnight's Children*, an excerpt from a review which asserted something along the lines of an entire subcontinent having found a voice. Having ventured in 1989 to see what all the fuss was about, I took the reviewer to be insulting the Indian people. As if all the subcontinent had to tell the world was some little story full of the usual 'India for idiots' trivia which is forgotten almost as soon as it is finished with nothing memorable to store for posterity. Where were the "oum-boum" echoes of Forster's cave, representing India, which shook the Westerners' deepest beliefs. The ephemeral memory of *Midnight's Children* brings to mind the phrase "wham bam" rather than "oum-boum".

In 1993, I read an essay by a literary critic style academic 'philosopher', Richard Rorty, which was presented as the first essay in a volume of papers presented at the Sixth East-West Philosophers' Conference held in Hawaii[1]. Rorty stated that, in regard to intercultural comparisons, the focus on philosophy was likely to be misleading as philosophers from East and West tended to be a certain type of person found in all cultures, the 'ascetic priest', "the person who wants to set himself apart from his fellow humans by making contact with what he calls his 'true self' or 'Being' or 'Brahman' or 'Nothingness' ". He noted that the ascetic priests are the main producers of high culture and that the spin-offs from their private projects often turn out to have enormous social utility:

> *Ascetic priests are often not much fun to be around, and usually are useless if what you are interested in is happiness, but they have been the traditional vehicles of linguistic novelty, the means by which a culture is able to have a future interestingly different from its past. They have enabled cultures to change themselves, to break out of tradition into a previously unimagined future.*

Rather than compare philosophers from East and West, Rorty compares the philosophers' taste for theory, structure, essence etc. with the novelists' taste for detail, diversity, accident etc. In doing so he focuses upon the views of Martin Heidegger as contrasted to those of Charles Dickens and Milan Kundera.

When I first read Rorty's essay, it immediately struck me as being particularly relevant to my verse with my emphasis on my 'outsider status' and my ideal of the 'true brahman' corresponding somewhat with the type described by Rorty as the 'ascetic priest'. There are some parallels to Heidegger's disdainful attitude in my verse with its condescension towards mass culture and the mercantilist mentality. Again, Heidegger's emphasis on 'Being', which the West seemed to have forgotten resembles my emphasis on *Brahman* (although Heidegger's first step was to query Husserl's assumption that Being is correlative to Consciousness[2]). However, as Rorty notes, for Heidegger all human phenomena are equivalent metaphysically, just surface perturbations which distract one from understanding what is *really* going on. Rorty refers to Habermas' descriptions of Heidegger's "abstraction by essentialization" which saw Stalin's Russia and Roosevelt's America as metaphysically the same and viewed the Jewish Holocaust as equivalent to far lesser outrages. Such an approach might have appealed to Shankara with his *māyāvāda* (doctrine of *māyā*) which downgraded temporal phenomena (*saguṇa Brahman;* the Reality with distinctions/form) to non-real superimpositions on an eternal Ground (*nirguṇa Brahman;* distinctionless/formless Reality) that didn't *really* change at all but it is not to be found in my work which discusses both human phenomena and the nature of Being/Consciousness. Rather, as the quote from Eusebius indicates, to me at least, there is a need to relate human phenomena to knowledge of the Divine ('transcendental'), to see beneath the surface phenomena but not to ignore their particular relevance within the realm of the mundane. The need to see both the transcendental and the mundane in relation to each other was stressed by Rāmakrishna *Paramahaṁsa*[3]:

> *Supreme Reality alone exists — as* ***brahman****, the Pure Consciousness within and beyond all forms of consciousness, and as* ***shakti****, the primordial, evolutionary Divine Energy. They are*

> *not two.* ***Brahman*** *and* ***shakti*** *are like the snake and its smoothly flowing motion. . . Precisely the same is true of the Absolute and the relative, which are indifferentiable in essence. The Absolute is inevitably expressed by the relative, and the relative is inevitably contained by the Absolute.*

I do however point out in the verse that, when the West berated the Soviets for having built their system on Stalinist terror, it chose to ignore the fact that the capitalist global market system was itself the product of genocide, slavery, deindustrialization and 'plantationisation', and resource parasitization by the Europeans as they conquered the world by brute force. I also point out the well-known thesis that Nazism took European colonialism to its logical conclusions. This is not a pointless metaphysical obliteration of differences between particulars, but a perfectly valid exegesis of the historical testimony, countering the selective focus of Western establishment propaganda which would avoid too close a look at the true nature of the West while it castigates the rest of the world.

The true brahman and Western academic mythologies

Having distanced myself from Heidegger, I would none the less take exception with Rorty in his general characterization of philosophers of whom Heidegger is only one very particular example. Rorty says:

> *My description of the ascetic priest is deliberately pejorative and gendered. I am sketching a portrait of a phallocentric obsessive, someone whose attitude toward women typically resembles Socrates'. . . shares Nietzsche's endlessly repeated desire for, above all else, cleanliness . . . same attitude toward sexual as to economic commerce; he finds it messy . . . and to favor a caste system . . .*

Although there are references to caste and to the "true brahman" in my verse, this does not mean that I favour a caste system. My "true brahman" is not conceived as being of hereditary caste or a male. Indeed, I am proud to be considered by relatives as not resembling my (Sanskrit-literate) father in personality, as I despised him. I certainly do not see my equally hereditary *brāhmaṇ* brothers as my "true brahmans". My "true brahman" refers to anyone who is inclined towards the *via contemplativa* (or the *jñānamārga* the "path of knowledge" (*jñāna* actually means gnosis) as I call it in the verse, shunning the vulgar excesses of modern popular culture although it tends more towards the "ascetic priest". My attitude towards women is discussed both in the verses and in the Postscript. I see myself as a 'hermaphroditic' character in terms of my mental faculties and certainly in regard to aspects of my personality in relation to the generally repressed personalities of British males. As stated in the following essay, the label 'Indian' overlaps considerably with the label 'feminine' and thus I would like to see a growing Indian/feminine influence in the world. Although I have stated above that my natural predisposition is towards abstracting 'deep structures', I also stated that my mind tends towards 'holistic' contextualizations of the raw data, thus, as is clearly apparent in this work, my writing is not a simple search for essences but an attempt to weave together an elaborate tapestry showing the world as an interconnected whole. Coming from the Indian tradition, I do not accept the "either, or" categories of Western thought, both contrasting approaches are usually equally valid in describing reality. Even the description of the ascetic priest as being not much fun to be around would not apply as to anyone who has witnessed my behaviour will testify. Although there is a stereotypical image of the 'philosopher' as usually bearded, rather rugged old man etc., and many a modern self-proclaimed 'philosopher' tries to play to this stereotype hoping that such posing will make up for a lack of true metaphysical insight (a recent photograph portrait book of so-called 'philosophers', including that pandering, Neo-Orientalist Nirad Chaudhuri!, illustrated this posing; a recent advertisement for publishers Jonathon Cape featured the same serious-minded posing in black and white by best-selling novelists). Today's academic self-proclaimed 'philosophers' will accuse non-professionals who trespass on their self-proclaimed 'territory' as being "out of their depth" as was the case recently with journalist Brian Appleyard who wrote a book *Understanding the Present* which challenged the orthodox view that scientific truth was the only truth, moving tentatively towards mysticism[4]. I have not read the book or the critiques but it seems as if the academics' "out of his depth" comments refers to an inability to play with words or abstract scientific models as well as they could and seeking to actually go deeper than their deeply unsatisfying, self-congratulatory superficialities. I, claiming to have actually resolved the central problems over which the word-players merely speculate in the dark, still look rather boyish, am a spontaneous joker and prankster who loves to burst into song, flirt, brag, brag about bragging, and am not at all afraid to make a fool of myself unlike those whose reputations depend more on image than substance (which would certainly account for Wittgenstein and many, many others held in esteem by academia). I like to cite an aphorism, whose exact source I am not sure of: "And God made the fool to confound the wise men".

However, leaving such trivia to one side, my main bone of contention with Rorty rests with his, admittedly pejorative, description of the ascetic priest as a phallocentric obsessive who considers himself more manly than the warrior caste because he, "penetrates through the veil of appearances and makes contact with true reality". If one recalls, I wrote above in regard to the literary approach to the 'great questions' that the literary types rambled roundabout the issues without penetrating the heart of the matter. I find Rorty's reliance on Freudian notions of obsessions with cleanliness leading to philosophical simplicity and essentialism, and sublimation of Freud's sexual 'libido' to be absurd nonsense. Perhaps Rorty sees everyone in his own image, projecting his own psychical constitution onto others (which Freud was probably guilty of). Given Rorty's use of the pejorative term "folk psychology" (see below), one could call Rorty's approach above "joke psychology". What about toilet training? How the quest to penetrate the veil of appearances to seek the underlying reality could be the product of a phallocentric obsession defeats me when so many women share this same desire to look beneath the superficial phenomena to understand the deeper nature of things. I would argue that the desire to go beyond appearance stems from the very biological function of the mind which has evolved to make sense of the flux of perceptual information; it is simply taking this basic mental *raison d'être,* to make sense of diverse phenomena, to its very limits. Coupled to this is the rather neotenic retention of curiosity in fully developed humans. There may also be other more 'spiritual' reasons related to knowing one's 'true self' as put forward by mystical traditions and the likes of Jung which cannot be dismissed by such ridiculous sublimation of the sex drive arguments. Indeed, in the final essay we shall see that my synthesis of Science and Mysticism confirms Jung's view of *libido* as a general psychic energy as against Freud's nonsensical, unscientific notion of a sexual energy.

Incidentally, in 1994, I discovered that the same Richard Rorty had in 1965 put forward a 'classic' paper in regard to consciousness supporting the notion of 'eliminative materialism'.

> *Its basic idea is that our mental vocabulary and our ordinary ways of using it embodies a theory of the mental called "folk psychology", but a theory that is systematically misleading. What is needed, according to the eliminative materialist, is a radical revision of our folk psychology, or even a total elimination of our mental vocabulary . . . . every ordinary mental occurrence is strictly identical with a physical occurrence in a human brain.*
>
> **G. Svensson**[5]

Rorty does not seem to have changed his views. He was quoted by a leading neurobiologist in a 1991 book on the neuropsychology of consciousness.

> *Alternatively, it may induce outright denial of the subjectivity of consciousness, as exmplified by Rorty's statement, "The problem is not to take account of the special difficulty raised by the 'inside'-character of consciousness, but to convince people that there is no reason to grant that persons have more of an inside than particles" (Rorty, 1982, p.183). Not many people, I surmise, are likely to be persuaded by Rorty.* **E. Bisiach**[6]

So, if we just stop using our outdated language in relation to our experiences, we will, according to Rorty, stop misleading ourselves as to our own subjectivity which, in itself, is a misleading notion evoked by "folk psychology" based on old prescientific mythology about the nature of mind. All that really exists are physical brain states. I will not go into detail here why this is such a preposterous position, it will no doubt be apparent from the rest of this work if it is not already apparent. However, I would like to note here that, in attempting to "eliminate" the reality of subjective experience, by saying that it is merely a distortion produced by the way we are used to talking, tends towards making Language the ultimate frame of reference, the Ultimate Reality. No matter what the Anglo-American 'Analytical School' might say about Language being prior to Thought, languages are merely systems of conventional symbols, representations, used for abstracting some parts of our subjective experience and communicating these abstractions. Clearly these abstractions are not the ultimate frame of reference. The yogi who has experienced the interconnectedness of conceptual constructions in his insight meditation practices and progressed to deeper levels, cleansing the mind of word-labels is hardly likely to be taken in by the, seemingly profound, yet actually naïve pronouncement of Wittgenstein that whereof we cannot speak, thereof we should remain silent. The transcendental planes of existence can of course be experienced and, although our language is imbued with spatio-temporal categories, we can attempt to discuss them within the limitations of Language as I do in the final essay. Rather than being outdated nonsense, the "folk psychology" based on traditional phenomenological knowledge is closer to the truth than the fraught attempts of abstract symbol-manipulating scientists, and their word-manipulating apologists, to justify materialism by magically wishing away subjectivity. Clearly Rorty cannot read between the lines when it comes to serious metaphysics. The word-manipulators should stick to literary criticism and let the 'big boys' penetrate the veil of appearances cast by words, mathematics and other symbols over Reality.

While on the subject of language and academic philosophers, we should address the fashionable notion of incommensurability that so fascinates the self-proclaimed 'philosophers' in today's universities, especially in regard to comparisons between East and West. Again, there is a wish to copy the 'big boys' in Science here as the current infatuation with this notion stems from the over-importance given to Thomas Kuhn's notion of Science operating within autonomous conceptual frameworks or 'paradigms'. I grant that in certain spheres, such as social concepts etc. the use of the notion of incommensurability is perfectly valid especially as Westerners have constructed false images of the

East by applying their own conceptions to Eastern terms framed in an entirely different context. But this notion cannot be valid when it comes to the examination of metaphysical systems which are all derived from a common phenomenological source. This again stems from an over-regard for symbols over Reality and the failure to press beyond various symbolic conceptual frameworks to the universal Ground beyond them.

> *Turning from the body of the book to the preface, we find an even more striking example of that literally preposterous over-valuation of words and notions to which the cultured and learned are so fatally prone. "I do not know," Mr Eliot writes, "whether she (Simone Weil) could read the Upanishads in Sanskrit —or, if so, how great was her mastery of what is not only a highly developed language, but a way of thought, the difficulties of which become more formidable to a European student the more diligently he applies himself to it." But like all the other great works of oriental philosophy, the Upanishads are not systems of pure speculation, in which the niceties of language are all important . . . . concern was to teach a doctrine which could be made to "work"*
>
> ***Aldous Huxley***[7]

In the final essay I shall prove wrong all those who staunchly maintained the incommensurability of Science and Mysticism, including those 'New Agers' who were frightened by the criticisms, like those of physicist Jeremy Bernstein[8], that, if you 'hitched' your mysticism to today's physics theories, then what will you do when today's physics theories ("paradigms" even) are discarded in the future as inevitably they will be. My work does not involve an infatuation with Quantum Theory and completely bypasses this argument just as it completely bypasses the argument, cited by Jones[9] and others, that the different mystical traditions all say different things. This is because I identify the central element of <u>all</u> mysticism with a <u>known</u> physical process which is constituted by the central 'groundstuff' of all physical processes, energy, the conception of which is not dependent upon particular scientific theories. The scientific concept of energy plays a role remarkably like that of Spirit and, indeed, the principle of the Conservation of Energy was originally propounded by German physiologist J. Robert Mayer (who knew little physics), saying that the idea came to him in a sort of mystical experience of the 'ground of all Being' which is maintained through all transformations of phenomena[10]. The scientific concept of energy (whose roots are discussed in the final essay) is derived partly from the earlier concept of a 'force' (Newton's abstract $f=ma$ is isomorphic to Einstein's $e=mc^2$ as a velocity squared is an acceleration) which seems to ha\ e have been derived from the projection of the subjective act ot volition onto the external world.

> *Both Reid (1710-1796) and Maine de Biran (1766-1824) emphasized our experience of the mind (the will) acting on our body and producing effects in the material world as the source of our universal notion of force (Jammer, 1957:230-231).*
>
> **B.I.B. Lindahl and P. Arhem**[11]

The true 'philosopher' and social concerns

In his essay on philosophers and novelists, Rorty went on to empathise with Milan Kundera's comments about the novelists being the spokespeople for the 'vulgar', unweaving the tapestries woven by the ascetic priests who are indifferent to the utilitarian ideal of the greatest happiness of the greatest number. Rorty also berated the philosophers who saw the logic of European Enlightenment rationalism and of scientific mechanization woven into the historical phenomenon of the Nazi death camps.

> *We want to relate our private obsessions, our private fantasies of purity, novelty and autonomy, to something larger than ourselves, something with causal power, something hidden and underlying which secretly determines the course of human affairs.*
>
> **Richard Rorty**[12]

He went on to mention Kundera's rough equation of "the novel" with "the democratic utopia" where nobody would "dream of thinking that there is something more real than pleasure or pain". Leaving aside this amusing conception of humans as mere stimulus-response Skinnerian pigeons coming from a man dreaming of democratic utopias whilst living under Soviet totalitarian thought control, and leaving aside Rorty's views on philosophers seeking to find underlying 'logics' to historical phenomena (as we have seen, Rorty's opinions are, at best, entertaining), it is most interesting to note, that Friedrich Meinecke in his *The German Catastrophe* (1950; discussed by Ashis Nandy) located the origins of National Socialism in:

> *the ancient "bipolarity extending throughout life of the Western Man" between the utilitarian which was stressed and the spiritual which was suppressed, to the excessive emphasis on the "calculating intelligence".*
>
> **Ashis Nandy**[13]

So we see that, when it comes to Nazi outrages, the deeper analysis seems to link Rorty's and Kundera's favoured utilitarianism (which, if one recalls, originally had a 'felicitic calculus' for quantifying the maximum happiness of the maximum number!) with the development of the Nazi phenomenon, whereas it was the very spirituality which Heidegger lamented had been lost which might have mollified German behaviour. Clearly, Hitler's "Final Solution" involved a sort of utilitarian, calculating logic in which only Hitler's so-called Aryans counted in the felicity maximization. Nevertheless, Rorty, whom I understand is generally perceived as an apologist for American liberal bourgeois values, maintains his faith in utilitarianism and the so-called "pursuit of happiness". This question of utilitarianism will be relevant later in this work in relation to my identification of the Indian *nation* as much with Indian *civilisation* (closely associated with 'high culture') as with the Indian *people* in my hopes for its future. Incidentally, the Czech playwright Vaclav Havel, as President of Czechoslovakia, told the United States Congress:

> *As long as people are people, democracy —in the full sense of the word —will always be no more than an ideal . . . . We too can offer something to you: our experience and our knowledge that has come from it. The specific experience I'm talking about has given me one certainty: Consciousness precedes being, and not the other way around, as the Marxists claim. For this reason, the salvation of the human world lies nowhere else than in the human heart, . . .*
>
> **Vaclav Havel**[14]

Of course the ascetic priest type would hope that his ideas will have causal power, subtly influencing the course of events. The mind interprets the world, not only in order to predict events, but also to reshape the world, hopefully to the individual's perceived advantage. True, the philosopher distances himself from his fellow human beings concerned only with mundane and superficial matters (the pleasures and pains of the sensorimotor plane); and why not? Why is it wrong to aspire to something loftier than the level of the vulgar masses who may behave like Skinnerian pigeons as Kundera thinks everyone should. Did not Danton say to that ascetic priest Robespierre, attached to his utilitarian notion that the greater good of the people came before the good of individuals, something along the lines of, "if any citizen sticks his head out, above the level of the mob, you will cut it off". Heidegger asserts that, unlike ordinary folk, a Thinker or a Poet makes contact with something Wholly Other. In contrast to the simple humanistic assumptions underlying utilitarianism, if there is any truth in the doctrine of *līlā*, that the phenomenal world is spontaneously created for sheer sport by *Brahman*, then one is entitled to ask as to whether the suffering or the happiness of the countless masses the world over, whose monotonous existence involves little other than the basic biological functions we share with animals, add anything to the *Brahmalīlā*, or does the Divine Ground have a partiality towards the rarified achievements of a few individuals who add novelty to the Creation. If creativity springs from this spontaneous creativity of this Divine Ground, then is it the inspired few who are the blessed and beloved of the Divine? If there is any truth in the fanciful notion of the cosmos evolving higher forms in order for them to unravel the secrets of their own creation, or simply to work out the full potential ramifications of the Creation then the creative individuals who reveal new insights into the nature of our existence or those who open up novel vistas of development through their creativity may be the stars in this act of the cosmic drama. It is the primordial relationship faced by the individual, the great mysterious relationship which arises with the awakening of self-consciousness in the child, between the individual and the rest of the Cosmos as a whole, my "primal bondage" in the verse, which, in my opinion, should be of central importance to the philosopher rather than becoming infatuated with the words and symbols of modern scripture. Indeed this statement somewhat resembles the assertion of St Augustine that "the true philosopher is a lover of God" although, as we shall see, the dualistic Christian conception of a personal god is itself a mental construction resulting from the failure to go deeper and literally lose oneself in identity with the Godhead. We shall see that the penultimate state of meditation, prior to mystical union (corresponding to the Christian 'Passion with Christ' or the popular Hindu *bhakti* experience of loving embrace by the *ishta devatā* or chosen deity) can be the source of supreme insights into Reality for the true *lover of wisdom.* We shall also see that the Divine Light is the true alchemical "philosopher's gold". All the other relationships, the 'bonds' to the other 'greater beings' in my 'oneness/otherness mystery' are secondary to this fundamental, mysterious relationship, and no other person, however intimate, can truly share in the intimacy of one's fundamental sense of existence as an individual, distinct from the Whole.

Human variation and the pursuit of so-called happiness

What the vulgarians think of the philosopher's reclusion should not bother him. If one has the privilege of a well-developed intellect and the satisfaction that is derived from a deeper understanding of the world, why should one want to be associated with the vulgarian herds like those who have not grown out of the pubescent boy's obsession with seeking vicarious glory in the fortunes of a football team.

I see the sons of unschooled fathers
With whom as child I talked and jested
Lost in worlds with short horizons
In adolescent minds arrested

In the verse, I stress the evolutionary principle of *variation* which belies the Lysenkoist tendency that holds sway amongst certain Marxist and trendy liberal circles (at least in their public pronouncements). The fierce socialist, republican, anticlerical campaigner and opponent of inherited privilege, Emile Zola, none the less wrote his Rougon-Macquart novels to show that an individual's life was largely a result of the unfolding of a hereditary predisposition[15]. When one is embroiled in a revolutionary struggle with its one-sided self-justifying ideology being trumpeted loudly, there has to be some outlet for voicing the repressed side of reality, just as much literature today, with its support of mysticism, functions as a corrective to the dominant scientific world-view (this resembles Jung's view of dreams as 'compensation' by the repressed part of the psyche). The fact is that human beings are born with different levels of intellectual potential and different predispositions (I am <u>not</u> arguing against better education for everyone or for inherent group-specific differences, I am talking about *variation*) and some individuals, through both nature and nurture will have higher intelligence and a better understanding of the world than others. The principle of variation involves the random reorganisation of the chromosomes at meiosis and the vital evolutionary requirement for populations to maintain variation if they are to survive environmental challenges. Variation thus works against any simplistic notion of hereditary transmission of superior qualities or group-specific traits as there is always random reorganisation between one generation and the next and each group contains within itself a vast amount of genetic variation which is not always explicitly manifest.

> *Were all men same, Man would be dead*
> *We live as variants on one theme*
> *Within the pale, most born in blindness*
> *Few at the margins, men of dreams* (Section I)
>
> *Prophecy self-fulfilling beckons*
> *When the schoolteacher then forgets*
> *These differences but norms, statistics*
> *Not essences by Nature set* (Section VII)

Knowledge such as that of the evolutionary basis of our psychological drives, the broader consequences of our actions, the ephemeral satisfaction derived from superficial cultural activities etc. clearly affects the behaviour of those intelligent enough to understand the causes and consequences of their behaviour. Coupled with this will be a degree of conditioned refinement which further inhibits the more intelligent from behaving like the vulgarians enslaved by the childish desire for instant sense-gratification and the herd instinct of those who are not sure of themselves, unable to stand alone if need be, unmoved by the derision of the herd. Such knowledge also leads to a greater prudence in the management of one's affairs, leading to avoidance of avoidable problems and to relative prosperity. This naturally leads to a degree of self-justifying disdain over those who, although born to the same opportunities, squandered those opportunities through childish enslavement to the uncivilised mentality of attachment to mere pleasures and pains.

Of course the vulgarian will argue that he has much more fun but it is ridiculous to think that everyone, deep down, enjoys the sort of 'fun' craved by the vulgarians. The combination of alcohol and drivel that constitutes 'fun' for the barroom 'philosopher' really is a pitiable waste of life potential. I have had the personal experience of seeing a young, very immature, man of working class background, who, although university educated had not succumbed much to embourgeoisement. Used to imitating the vulgar behaviour of working class friends and captivated by the escapist mass media images of what "having a good time" should be, unable to come to terms with the restrained and refined behaviour of a middle class environment, retort, with such articulate sophistication as his limited vocabulary would allow, that the restrained people were "sad", a fashionable popular culture buzzword for those who refrain from juvenile 'fun-seeking' behaviour. It was apparent to everyone else that it was the very immature young man ('boy' would be more appropriate), constantly projecting his insecurities and failures onto others, who was the pitiable one for whom the word *sad* truly applied. The infatuation with the glittering icons of the popular media smacks of the primitive's captivation by shiny baubles and bangles, and of the need to seek vicarious glory in an otherwise unfulfilling life. (It is not only the ascetic priest who seeks glory, but at least the ascetic priest seeks glory through his own achievements). The current spate of mass drug-crazed frenzies known as 'rave parties' may be viewed, not only as cultural degeneracy, reverting to the behaviour of uncivilised tribes, but also as desperate escapism from vacuous lives. The pursuit of happiness is very often just a pursuit of behaviour patterns conditioned by the society in which the individual is expected to oblige, not because he or she necessarily gets great happiness from it, but because he or she knows nothing better. In regard to what constitutes 'happiness' for the vulgarian and for the ascetic philosopher, the notions of incommensurability and cultural relativity are particularly relevant.

The fickle fashions, childish zoetropes
Like glass beads captivate the apes
Apes not the apes, the would-be human
But from their world he can't escape

The reclusion of the ascetic priest may be forced upon him by forces beyond his control, linked to his 'true self', which are associated with the notion of *destiny*. Indeed, this ascetic philosopher, whose name includes the Sanskrit *tapas*, which literally meant 'burning' but also means 'creative ardour', 'psychophysical energy' and the 'ascetic sacrifice' which elicits divine boons, sees himself fulfilling his destiny in that the vague childhood fantasies he held about his future are beginning to materialise, after tremendous sacrifice and psychological suffering which seemed to have been the forced upon him.

Why shape me, make me full of promise
All the fruits of Earth to merit
Then shape my world so to negate me
All my birthright disinherit *(Section XVI)*

The word waste, Nature knows no meaning
My discontent, she sees a role
By my feet scorching, makes me dance
Man's restless spirit, the burning soul *(Section I)*

I have known pleasures and pains but nothing can match the remarkable sense of satisfaction that comes from a sense of fulfilment which makes all the enormous suffering and sacrifice of the past seem to have been worthwhile for they were driving me towards my true vocation, my destiny. Kundera's "democratic utopia" in which nobody would dream of thinking that there is anything more real than pleasure or pain also precludes attachment to some greater or nobler cause requiring a degree of sacrifice such as the sacrifice of those fighting for the end to some great injustice.

Those born in freedom struggle, between
Bullets and jails, no time to pause
Their life stories are simply written
The meaning of their life their cause

The social utility of the philosopher

Yet it would be very wrong to think that the disdainful philosopher does not have any concern for the fate of the masses; Heidegger may not have done but he is hardly representative of philosophers in general. Rorty correctly identifies philosophy as a genre closely associated with the quest for greatness and, as noted above, points out the social utility of the private projects of the ascetic priests which have, for instance, allowed traditional cultures to break out into "unimagined futures". The second part of this Introduction is entitled *The Reassertion of the Indian* as this work, overall, represents the Indian challenge to the dominant Western point of view, both geopolitically and metaphysically. I see the undermining of the dominant Western metaphysics as a vital part of India's self-affirmation, breaking free from the collective inferiority complex resulting from Western colonialism towards self-belief and self-confidence, essential factors required for India's quest to lift herself out of poverty and impotence towards prosperity and global self-assertion concomitant with her huge population and her status as a great civilisation.

India probably has the world's largest number of truly abject poor and thus to align oneself with the cause of uplifting India is, in a sense, to align oneself with utilitarianism as Rorty himself does. In other essays of this work, I discuss the concept of the Indian Nation which includes the notion of the *nation* as the *people* and the notion of the *nation as self writ large*. The latter introduces a socialistic element into nationalism as the poverty-stricken state of the Indian masses reflects badly upon one's own self-image. The concept of the Indian Nation also includes the notion of *Indian civilisation* and the *nation as a substitute personal god*. In contrast to the notion of the *nation as the people*, the latter two may appear more in keeping with the interests of Rorty's supposedly indifferent ascetic priest, as I have stated above in regard to utilitarianism, in that *Indian civilisation* here is closely associated with Indian high culture. However, for Indian civilisation to fully flower in, a modern form, in the near future, the full potential of all Indians must be developed. This is related to the notion of hereditary variation stressed above in that the talents hidden amongst the less privileged strata must be brought out by creating the conditions which allow everyone to attempt to fulfil their potential. As I stated at the beginning of this essay, people often misrepresent my views in regard to, for instance, class and heredity by putting their own limited interpretations onto particular statements without comprehending the *whole picture.*

I may show disdain towards the vulgar masses but this is in relation to the degenerate aspects of Western mass culture and nothing to do with the plight of the poor. One can hardly read this work and come away with the conclusion that I have not given much time and thought to the question of the suffering of the world's poor. The literary types may admire the saintly individual who can go and live amongst the poor and do his little bit to alleviate their suffering but I do not believe that the tinkering of the saintly types can do anything significant to solve the real, underlying problems. The philosopher like myself is not interested in such unsustainable drops in the ocean, he wants to find a way to lift the whole of India's masses out of their miserable condition. And it is here that Rorty is so very, very wrong in his attitude toward philosophers seeking the 'logics' underlying historical phenomena. A Chinese proverb about leaders ends with the best leader being the one of whom the people say, "he did nothing, we did it all ourselves". It is only through developing these underlying 'logics', these frames of mind, through putting the ideas in the minds of individuals, and through developing national self-esteem and self-belief that the whole nation can be lifted up and the utilitarian goal fulfilled.

Indeed, the very alienated 'outsider' personality of the ascetic priest allows him to break the bonds that tie him to his class interests, his very misanthropy stems partly from a sense of deep frustration with the preoccupation of the vulgarians with their materialist 'pursuit of happiness', their consumerism and their wasteful consumption, when so many people in the world are forced to live in such abject poverty. Does Rorty not want us to *penetrate the veil of appearances* and see that the two are linked through the nexus of international unequal relations and the subtle imperialist means by which the underlying world order reinforces those inequalities associated with the term "neo-colonialism" for such philosophical insight into the *underlying realities* undermines Rorty's simultaneous espousal of the 'pursuit of (so-called) *happiness*' and of utilitarianism (the maximum happiness of the maximum number).

I do not share the saints' empathy with the poor as individuals, my mind attaches itself to grand abstract notions like justice and fairness rather than following existential avenues. There is a tendency to romanticise the poor as merely the victims of the better-off classes, ignoring the many inertial factors inherent within certain subcultures which perpetuate suffering. Of course, cultural relativity has taught us that what the higher classes perceive as wasteful behaviour is perfectly rational behaviour within context of the 'life-world' of someone trapped in poverty. But the influence of cultural relativity sometimes provokes derision towards those who would 'uplift' the poor for their own long-term good by transforming their subcultures. This is not to say that I identify at all with the rich. I was raised in relative poverty by a poor, little educated, widowed mother who had to do an almost manual, low-paid job whilst bringing up a four children and paying off an uninsured mortgage which had 22 years to run when my father died. It is not without reason that I state in the verse that Lord Beveridge played the role of my father for, without the support of the welfare state, my family's situation would have been unbearable. Furthermore, as a 'non-white' immigrant in British society, still steeped in racial discrimination, I know what it feels like to be poor and discriminated against and to sometimes feel trapped in a miserable situation far removed from my actual potential.

Recently, in relation to my work on Science and Mysticism, I have begun to understand the Modern Mind's separation of Thought from Feeling. Faced with human suffering *in person*, I am filled with sympathy and concern whereas, writing about it from a distance, I can treat mass human suffering as an abstraction, numbers, to be dealt with in grandiose strategies. This clearly stems from the spiritual distinction between the individuated ego, which is concerned mainly with perceived self-interest and the 'deeper Self' or 'true Self' (ignoring Rorty's disbelief of such "folk psychology") related to the transcendental ground (or the 'Divinity'). It seems as if I have been possessed in part by resonances from the collective levels in the depths of our being. The suffering of the Indian masses experienced at first hand or on television would send me into deep emotional crises which bore little relationship to my personal circumstances. Although I state that the nation is partly the self writ large, implying a projection of our personality, it will become clearer from the discussion in the final essay that the deeper Self, at a certain level, is in a certain sense one with the 'nation' as the people. My intuitive grasp of arcane yogic philosophy seems to stem from such resonances with collective racial resonances. My criticism in the verse of the film version of the book *City of Joy* was prompted by the philospher's concern that the members of the literary camp, aroused into some sense of outrage by such superficial stories, failed to see the deeper and broader picture, being captivated by the romanticised plight of a few fictional individuals. The director Roland Joffe, on a television programme attacked the attitude of the West Bengal government which he naively perceived as being indifferent. His attitude seemed to be that, unless you show a supposedly *Christian* sense of outrage at every case of human suffering, like some Western tourist who can run away from it all when he chooses, you don't *really* care about the problems! My response was given in the commentary to the verse.

The increasing self-consciousness of the individual that develops with the modernisation of society and expresses itself in novels and similar media such as cinema clearly has many a role to play and, during periods of social transformation, a few works like some of Dickens or an *Uncle Tom's Cabin* might serve great social purposes. Bankimchandra Chattopadhyay, honoured in this work as a 'Father of my nation' was one of India's first successful novelists and his novel *Ānandamath*, containing the 'hymn' *Bande Mātaram* (both mentioned in the verse) inspired future Indian nationalists and revolutionaries. None the less, it was his philosophical writings rather than his popular stories that really counted in helping to lay the ideological framework of the emerging Indian Nation. His dream, in his *Dharmatattva*, of the synthesis of Indian spirituality with European science has at last begun to come true with my own philosophical work presented in the final essay. Let so-called 'postmodern' Westerners chastise the philosophers and let them write about all the banality, human degradations and trivia under the sun; this is a sure sign of historical decline.

Narrow-minded dogmatism in modern scientific scholasticism

Coupled to my philosophical disposition is a scientific educational background. The influence of this is clearly manifest throughout the verse. I am well aware of the limitations of scientific interpretation, the problems of the misuse of science and the inappropriateness of Western technology and modes of research in certain contexts. None the less, Science still provides us with the most useful corpus of knowledge about the world and the best ways of understanding the behaviour of a vast range of regular phenomena. Added to this is its omnipresent socio-economic influence through technology and the 'rationalisation' of our socio-economic activities. Although I used to criticise the 'literary camp' for their failure to truly understand Science, I have come to appreciate that they are generally more open-minded as regards Mysticism and the limitations of Science than those who have had a scientific education which tends to close the mind to alternative modes of interpreting the world.

In relation to Science I reserve my respect, however, for the *understanding* of the world in terms of the behaviour of regular phenomena and the interrelations between the various scientific models gleaned by the collective labours of the glorified technicians and for the few creative individuals amongst them who make the important advances. It is perhaps a sad reflection on the naivety of laymen that the possession of a doctorate is automatically held to indicate intellectual prowess when, in many cases, it signifies an incapacity for independent thought and the retreat into the security of the endless permutations of the paucity of concepts which form the basis of the narrow speciality. The narrowing of the scope of the modern mind is perhaps best highlighted by the case of these technicians, called scientists, often unable to think beyond the tramlines of their field or easily see the broader context and the ontological and epistemological presuppositions of their own work. Indeed in an article entitled "How to be a PhD student" in *New Scientist*, Simon Wolff[16] stated:

> *You have to kid yourself. You have to hypnotise yourself. You have to talk yourself into a state of religious fervour. You have to get yourself into that peculiar state of mind where you can go to an issue of* **Nature** *and read a paper entitled "Glucose is an essential cofactor for function of the glucose porter* **in vitro***" from top to bottom and think "Wow" and then aim for similar lofty heights.*

There are of course a number of admirable exceptions. Clearly, the scientific method forces one to follow such a narrow field of research, to think reductionistically and to accept the conventional wisdom in order to pass peer review of one's work. This peer review system, although vital for various purposes and although it applies only to specific publications, is none the less indicative of the conservative pressures that operate upon the scientific community steering people to accept an orthodox view and not to question underlying presuppositions for fear of destroying their reputations. With such pressures forcing most scientists into line with the orthodoxy, further reinforcement of orthodox opinion occurs because people feel that the orthodoxy must be right because so many of the community agree with it.

I kept outside these mental prisons
In which dead habit casts a pall
In which the mind and world is broken
Fragmented by these cloistered walls

Recently we have seen one of the central tenets of immunology, the Self/Non-self distinction supposedly made by the immune system in regard to alien bodies which was propounded by Burnet and Medawar, seriously challenged by the more realistic 'Danger model' propounded by an extravert female immunologist who went to university late after having worked as, amongst other things, a 'bunny girl'. In spite of some remarkable experimental evidence in support of the Danger model, involving acceptance of cross-species transplants without the need for constant immunosuppression, it has provoked some vitriolic attempted 'put-downs' by members of the scientific establishment including nonsensical arguments that it cannot be tested. Thomas Kuhn's point that scientists rarely change their views when new ideas come along, rather the older generation dies out, seems to be clearly in evidence with the older generation of immunologists showing the most hostility and the younger generation the most support. I found it amusing to listen to a scientist, whose work helped form the basis of the new model, lament that he had not thought of it himself as his mind had been restricted to a narrow framework and because of the authoritative status of the Self/Non-self model[17].

Even though I quickly abandoned a materialist ontology at the age of eighteen (1983) in favour of a panpsychist view linked to modern scientific knowledge based on Spinoza's views and my own insights and analysis, my scientific background still exerted a conservative pressure upon me right up to the moment I identified the physical correlate of the Divine Light as I turned thirty (1994). My original ideas had only dealt with normal states of consciousness because I couldn't imagine any other states. My scientific background and my wish to be taken seriously by scientists forced me to steer clear of mysticism as far as I could for fear of being considered a fool. Mysticism was virtually taboo. I only began to think about the broader and deeper meaning of my own model for consciousness when I began to write the first draft of the metaphysical essay of the Postscript in 1993, suggesting that energy was the physical correlate of *chit* (Pure Consciousness). I became drawn towards the yogic sources of Eastern philosophy by way of looking into near-death experiences as the latter remained more amenable as they usually occurred in modern hospitals, closer to scientific enquiry. As I stress in the verse, my own views do not support certain mystical doctrines such as the notion of a soul and of reincarnation (although my ideas make it is possible to understand why people have mistakenly developed such notions rather than dismissing them as derived from mere fantasy). I am sure that certain advocates of mystical traditions will still find my views too 'reductionist' and 'psychologising' for their own likings but this is of no concern to me. The inconsistencies of the mystical traditions do not help in allowing one to take them seriously. Right up to my final breakthrough in 1994, surrounded in synchronicitous experiences, I maintained a very sceptical attitude to what is called the "Perennial Philosophy" until the actual breakthrough had a profound effect upon my mind, sending my cognitive structures into turmoil as if in a mild nervous breakdown, before restoring me to psychological stability as a new man, whose disparate cognitive structures, reflecting different fields of knowledge, had been fused into one integrated whole picture. In spite of my own panpsychism and my knowledge of Vedantic teachings that *Brahman* was *chit* (Pure Consciousness), the spiritual importance of consciousness had never really sunk in due to my scientific indoctrination leading to a fundamental antipathy towards anything associated with spirituality.

History will no doubt mock the high priests of materialistic dogma who refused to even acknowledge the counter-evidence and concerned themselves only with the consideration of mental constructions representing the behaviour of stable, regular phenomena. As will be clear from my own work, the history of Science's famous series of 'despiritualisations' of Nature actually turn out to be but a history of abstracting the regular features of natural phenomena and then beginning to consider this vast corpus of abstractions to be Reality itself. Arthur Eddington, who helped confirm Einstein's theory of General Relativity, in his *The Nature of the Physical World,* pointed out that, if one looked carefully at the epistemology of Science, then it was clear that the 'fundamental particles' only existed as "schedules of pointer readings" arrays of indicators (even the tracks in so-called 'cloud chambers' etc. are open to alternative interpretations), abstracted from the actual reality, which he, a Quaker, held to be like consciousness. The Evangelical Christian, Michael Faraday, had tried to demonstrate the underlying unity of electromagnetism and gravity back in the nineteenth century driven by his conviction of the underlying unity of all phenomena. In attempting the grand final despiritualisation of Nature, the materialist interpretation of consciousness, scientists have found themselves in a quandary. Few would go as far as the 'philosopher' Rorty and openly "eliminate" consciousness, but, even when scientists do accept its existence, they can only cope with it by tacitly eliminating it, pretending that somewhere along the line of their confused arguments about complex systems, information processing and emergent phenomena they have dealt with it. But consciousness cannot be magically wished away. The actual understanding of consciousness shows why Science cannot come to terms with consciousness; far from Science achieving its final despiritualisation, Nature has the last laugh, revealing that it was Spirit all along!

Although I attained an outstanding first class degree in molecular biology, I realised that I was a thinker and not a technician, having been attracted to the field by intellectual curiosity in regard to the philosophical questions associated with living phenomena (coupled with a naïve youthful faith in reductionism). Much of molecular genetics research these days is best left to automata and increasingly is so, even some experimental strategies tend to be so predictable that they can be determined by computer programs. My creative mind could not discipline itself into such narrow fields of enquiry requiring such pedantic modes of thought. Nor were there any important problems on the horizon where it seemed a good dose of creative thinking could provide solutions which no amount of experimental drudgery could resolve; the technicians were all working within paradigms which had only recently been defined and were satisfied with simply pursuing the ramifications of the original creative work. My deeper Self wanted to tackle the deepest and the broadest questions. In fact, when I made my important breakthrough in 1994, I realised that I was able to make it due, not only to the depth of my thought, but also my breadth of mind which allowed me to see the parallels between diverse conceptual frameworks.

One of the definitions of *metaphysics*, albeit a rather outdated one, is *the study of the world as a whole.* Of course it was only by rejecting this old metaphysical approach and limiting enquiry to specific problem domains that modern science achieved its great breakthroughs and the emergent whole arising from its vast and varied domains remains, as I stated above, the greatest corpus of knowledge available to us. I have few regrets about having pursued a scientific education as I acquainted myself with nearly all the philosophically interesting areas of the sciences which offer ways forward for our understanding of the deeper questions in contrast to the sterile linguistic nitpicking and literary criticism of much of Western academic 'philosophy'. The creation of the verse work represented a major shift away from my scientific, rationalist education, away from the need to present my ideas in a clear and unambiguous manner with a logical structure of argument and a rigid presentation, back towards a more *native* state. Indeed I had not written 'poetry' for ten years prior to this work and had no plans to do so just before I suddenly decided to embark upon this project, mainly because the rationalist in me could not comprehend such an imprecise and ambiguous mode of expression (this is one of the reasons why I have so much in the way of prose explanation associated with the verse). Whilst Darwin found that he could no longer read Shakespeare as he grew older because his mind had turned into a machine for abstracting generalisations from masses of data, my mind between the age of 21 and 30 went in the other direction, slowly opening up again after having been so restricted by my youthful infatuation with Science and Rationalism. I have stressed the word 'native' as I believe that this reversion is not only a reversion to the modes of expression I had before my ultra-rationalistic phase but is also related to the reversion to my underlying 'Indianness' which has been masked by this extreme form of Westernisation. It was perhaps not surprising that although I conceived the verse work as a *poem*, it actualised itself into something like a *sūtra*.

THE REASSERTION OF THE INDIAN

Āchārya: The day European science and technology unites with the spiritual self-control of India, Man will turn demigod. Thereafter such science and technology will be put to more positive use.

Pupil: Will Man ever see such a day?

Āchārya: Why certainly! You Indians are eminently suited for this purpose. It is all in your hands. If you so desire, you could be the masters and leaders of this world. However, if you do not aspire to this, then all my words have been in vain.

Bankim Chandra Chattopadhyay[18]

Neo-Hinduism, Brahmanism and Indian Nationalism

One way of interpreting the overall content of this work, though far from providing a full perspective, is to view it as a counterblast to Western ideological triumphalism. As with the birth of Indian Nationalism, which the verse touches upon (and which is discussed further in the Postscript), this work is a product of the 'Indian Mind' encountering the overwhelming presence of the West. In this case, this particular Indian has been transported to the West as a child whereas in the past the West, in the form of the British, forced itself through conquest upon India. After the initial phase of infatuation with everything Western and denunciation of the Indian, the underlying 'Indianness' begins to reassert itself and question the once unquestionable supremacy of Western thought. The once repressed part of the Self which had always been there in the background begins to make its presence felt for it is vital for the restoration of one's wholeness, one's peace of mind. Indeed, the very form of the verse work, resembling in its terse, aphoristic pronouncements the ancient Indian *sūtra* form, represents part of the reassertion of my own Indianness, after my Westernisation and scientific and rationalist mental development had made me averse to vague and imprecise modes of expression. The verse work had not been planned as a *sūtra*; rather it arose from the unconscious depths of my mind in a period of intense, inspirational activity. The presentation of my thought primarily in the form of a *sūtra* may be viewed as a rejection of conventional modern Western modes of philosophical expression.

Soon after writing the verse work, I read Wilhelm Halbfass' encyclopaedic but rather Eurocentric work on the intellectual encounter between India and Europe entitled *India and Europe: An Essay in Philosophical Understanding*[19]. Halbfass notes the special status accorded to 'philosophy' in Indian Nationalism:

> *visionaries, reformers, and national founding figures — and in general personalities who stand for the cultural and national identity and the international resonance of modern India — are depicted as "philosophers" . . . modern India is portrayed as a country whose national and cultural identity bears the stamp of "philosophy", with philosophy itself being assigned important tasks for the future shaping of national and international life.*

Halbfass discusses what he, following Paul Hacker, calls "Neo-Hinduism" the rather apologetic, liberal reinterpretation and transformation of traditional Indian thought using Western concepts and responding to Western expectations. Section XI(c) of the verse, entitled, *A Nation Born Through Synthesis,* touches upon this especially in regard to the resistance to Christian proselytization in early nineteenth century Bengal. The later 'Hindu Revivalism' of the late nineteenth century in Bengal, a return to more traditional forms of worship, was closely associated with the birth of Indian Nationalism, in the face of the glaring racism of the British administration as Indian petitioning led the British government to concede Indian entrance into the upper echelons of the Raj bureacracy[20] which is also mentioned in the verse of Section XI(c). Numerous reform movements transformed the character of traditional Hinduism and Islam across India during the nineteenth Christian century[21]. Prominent Indians have tended to present so-called 'Hinduism' to the Western world in the form of this so-called 'Neo-Hinduism'. It is not an altogether false representation of 'Hinduism', rather a selective one, usually taking the *Vedānta* (especially Shankara's dominant interpretation of *Advaita Vedānta)* and presenting it as the 'true essence' of 'Hinduism' and discarding the 'superstitious rubbish' that had accumulated over years of degeneration.

This emphasis on Shankara's *Advaita* is misleading as this has come to be taken by many as *Vedānta* as a whole, ignoring the many other interpretations of the relationships between the Individual and the Absolute, and the Transcendental and the Immanent *Brahman* in the numerous schools of *Vedānta*. I only began to understand the true nature of Indian spirituality once I had cast off the shackles of the Neo-Hindu emphasis on *Vedānta*, which says little in its commentaries about the actual yogic sources of the Vedāntic philosophies, and encountered the meditation texts. The various Hindu systems of philosophy have of course influenced each other and Patañjali's *Yoga Sūtras* are themselves influenced by *Vedānta*, the dualism of *Sānkhya* metaphysics (with its *Puruṣa* (Consciousness/Spirit) and *Prakriti* (Nature/Matter) underlying the older *Yoga* philosophy having been largely rejected by Indians in favour of Vedāntic monism based on the unitary *Brahman*[22]. The emphasis on *Vedānta* should also be understood within the context of the distinction between 'Brahmanism' and popular 'Hinduism', a distinction which European scholars like the famous Sanskritist H.H. Wilson began to make[23]. The Neo-Hinduism which Halbfass talks of is largely the reformulated 'Brāhmanism' of the predominantly *brahman* elite, who over the centuries had become more and more associated with the popular local traditions such as the cults of the Mother Goddess Durgā and the Vaishnavite icon Krishna in Bengal. What is rather false in so-called 'Neo-Hinduism' is a tendency to suggest that liberal and open-minded values were always present in 'Hinduism' although there is much truth in the well-worn assertion of Hindu tolerance towards other faiths; 'Hinduism' itself not being a 'religion' (a product of Semitic civilisation) but a Western generic term for India's panoply of divergent sects embracing virtually every school of philosophical thought.

In regard to the 'high' Vedāntic Brahmanism, Halbfass notes that early Christian visitors had lauded it as the 'natural light' or a natural conception of God devoid of the ritual trappings and superstitious distortions. The Jesuits had hopes of applying such ideas to Christianity and indeed such ideas from India played a key role in the development of European Deism during the Enlightenment (e.g. the Cult of the Supreme Being in revolutionary France). Interestingly the very religious experience of being 'born again' sought by the English Evangelicals of Wilberforce's highly influential 'Clapham Sect', which pressed for the opening of India to missionary enterprise (holding the conversion of India to Christendom as a greater priority than the abolition of Slavery), was one of the soul turning in on itself, stripping itself of habit and becoming aware of its thraldom[24]. Thus the very source of the Christian proselytizing incursion into India, which provoked much of the reinterpretation of 'Hindu' ethical thought, itself had a degree of similarity with the mystical essence of 'Hinduism' and could well have developed through Indian influences.

Given the opportunity to look back upon the major contours of my mind, manifest in the emergent themes of my verse, I became aware of the underlying 'Hinduism' apparent in my basic orientation to the world. This 'Hinduism' was an almost inseparable part of my underlying 'Indianness'. The 'Hinduism', or more specifically Brahmanism, manifest in the verse written in 1991 is now much more pronounced given the fact that, during 1993 and 1994, whilst writing the Postscript to the verse, attempting to elaborate upon its philosophical content I finally came to understand the parallels between my speculative panpsychist theory of consciousness, based on scientific knowledge, and the Vedāntic view of *Brahman* as *saccidānanda (sat chit ānanda*), as I identified the physical correlate of the Divine Light (Pure Consciousness) and began to appreciate the validity of the Indian mystical, existential approach to understanding Reality. The underlying 'Hindu'/Indianness had been lying hidden within my theory of consciousness as well. In fact the mutuality of Science and Brahmanism that became manifest in my own work, was apparent in a less clear manner in the development of Neo-Hinduism in nineteenth century Bengal, where the Brahmanical elite openly accepted Western scientific knowledge without abandoning their Brahmanism. This 'non-secular' modernisation of elite culture and Gandhi's reaction to it are briefly discussed in *In this Age of Falling Curtains*.

Clearly such an identity thesis between 'Hinduism' and 'Indianness' is not devoid of political connotations in the light of Ayodhya and the rise of sectarian 'Hindu' Nationalism in the form of the Bharatiya Janata Party (BJP). As stated in the verse, I do, deep down, hold to a conception of a *Hindu Rāshtra* (nation state), as clearly did most of the founding fathers of modern India. However, this should not be interpreted as giving succour to the BJP and its ideological mentor organisations although some of my views will no doubt converge with some of theirs and thus I openly admit to sympathising with some of their views, as, I am sure, do many self-professed opponents of the BJP. Attempts by reactionary elements within the Indian *ulema* to make Indian Muslims abide by *shariat* law rather than National law cannot but provoke anger amongst non-muslims. There is much to be said for seeking to preserve positive elements of the Indian heritage from the pernicious influences of Western cultural imperialism. There is also a pressing need to seek a national identity that transcends the petty divisions of region and caste with so-called 'Hinduism', which united countless divergent sects under the brahmanical umbrella appearing to provide the only solvent in this context. The famous saying that there are as many Hindu gods as there are Hindus reflects the openness of the 'Hindu' tradition with its emphasis on direct access to the Absolute. The brahmanical understanding of the relativity of each of the various paths to the Absolute, manifest in the modern Neo-Hindu doctrine of the Unity of Faiths can accommodate Islamic minorities which seek to modernise for the betterment of everyone. My interpretation of the mystical union involving its direct linkage to scientific knowledge as presented in this work confirms the doctrine of the Unity of Faiths; *Brahman, Al Haq,* the Tao and the Holy Spirit are only cultural labels for the same Light. Whereas the BJP would semitise 'Hinduism' giving it a holy city in Ayodhya and a prophet-like figurehead in Rāma, viewing this as a positive development in mobilising Indians to higher things, I am certain that my new interpretation of the mystical union will provide a universally acceptable basis for spiritual understanding amongst educated people and eventually force all religious and mystical traditions, including *Vedānta,* to re-examine and re-interpret themselves in the light of the new understanding.

In due course, sectarian forces from any tradition will have the ground taken away from under their feet although they will not readily admit this. In the struggle for the heart and soul of the Indian nation, rather than letting the sectarian forces claim to be champions of the Indian tradition, the cause of tolerance and progress is served by reaffirmation of liberal Neo-Hinduism and the grand ideals of Indian Nationalism. The grandest of these ideals, the East-West synthesis, as indicated in the quote from Bankim above, has now been achieved in terms of uniting the metaphysical grounds of Indian spirituality with European science and opens the way for a truly universal, global civilisation for the future. Liberal Neo-Hinduism must, like Arjuna on Kurukshetra's plain, fight its sectarian kinsmen on the spiritual as well as on the temporal plane on the Gangetic plain. But I would suggest that, true to the Indian tradition, liberal Indian Nationalism, rather than simply presenting the antithesis to the BJP, prepares a new political synthesis appropriating the positive values espoused by the BJP and thus helping to undermine its very *raison d-être* and leaving it, distinguished only by its negative features, to wither away.

A continuation of the Indian approach to philosophy

The general eclecticism of my work can itself be interpreted as typically 'Neo-Hindu' and indeed 'Indian' as such inclusivism is held to be characteristic of Indian thought, firmly grounded in the Absolute and thus capable of beholding the relative validity of all forms of partial knowledge rather than holding some conceptual system to be the Ultimate Reality and arguing that others' views, as they are contradictory, are, of necessity, false as is so common in Western thought. My use in the verse of notions and terms such as 'greater beings', 'oneness/otherness mystery', 'primal bondage', etc. unwittingly paralleled the existential nature of Indian philosophy with its emphasis on Being and the Vedāntic emphasis on the relationship between the individual 'self' and the 'Cosmic Self'. As stated above, although at the time of writing I hardly understood Indian philosophy at all, I have now come to harmonise such notions with my scientific understanding of the world. My emphasis in the verse on the limitations of logic (and language) and the championing of visionary insight is in keeping with the Indian philosophical tradition which relegated logic to an inferior position as the ultimate existential questions, as is now widely recognised, fall beyond the limited scope of the logical analysis of conceptual abstractions.

It is clearly misleading to stereotype Indian thought as purely 'intuitive', 'introspective' etc. and, conversely, to stereotype European thought as 'logical' and empirical. One of the six major 'Hindu' systems, *nyāya,* is a system of logic. Willard V.O. Quine, the eminent Harvard logician was most surprised to discover that ancient Indian logicians knew, for instance, De Morgan's law although formal logic never developed to the extent it did in Western thought[25].

> *The Indian philosopher, even the logician, was concerned not with propositions but with knowledges* ***(jñānani)****. Bare possibilities, not capable of being fulfilled in experience, did not interest him. Mathematics never bothered him. The distinction between analytic and synthetic truths, between truths of reason and those of fact, never weighed on his mind. The issue between rationalism and empiricism cannot be stated in his language....Indian philosophical thinking has been predominantly phenomenological and not speculative, concrete and not abstract.* ***J.N. Mohanty***[26]

As Mohanty notes, the Sanskrit word *darśana* which is used for a system of Indian philosophy is etymologically derived from 'seeing'; it is a way of seeing the truth. Although based on phenomenological insights, the *darśanas* none the less all attempt to conceptualise the intuitions and support them with logical arguments. Indeed this process resembles modern understanding of the creative process in Western science where insights, visions and intuitions are later formalised into hypotheses. The theoretical physicist David Bohm, himself much influenced by Indian thought, has noted how modern physics has moved away from the notion of insight into Reality towards a view of simply understanding the nature of abstract mathematical models without asking deeper questions about their actual relationship to Reality, a misguided trend in his view[27].

In his recent biography of the remarkable mathematical genius, Srinivas Ramanujan Aiyar, Robert Kanigel[28] has noted that many mathematicians do not consider Ramanujan to be a mere genius, but a magician. With a normal genius, given *hindsight* you can *see* where he is coming from (I have emphasised the words associated with seeing here). For instance, with the benefit of hindsight, a modern physicist can see the basis of Special Relativity in the Lorentz transformations although it took the genius of Einstein to see this at first. Ramanujan often put together mathematical functions from such disparate fields that it appears as if he plucked them out of thin air. True to Indian form, Ramanujan lacked an inclination for rigorous formal proofs of his mathematical insights. He did lack a full Western style education and formal proofs often took years to deduce; people are still working out proofs of his theorems decades after he died. The East/West dichotomy is shown in the fact that in Britain, faced with the skepticism of his atheistic patron, G.H. Hardy, Ramanujan kept quiet as to the true source of his inspiration. In India he was not so reticent, explaining that his amazing insights came to him in meditative absorption upon his village deity, Namagiri (he was in fact a brahman). Kanigel notes that in the ancient West, the Greeks and Romans knew of the link between the 'unconscious' and the transcendental realm.

In their recent biography of Tagore, Dutta and Robinson[29] tell an interesting story about the encounter between the high priests of Logic and Language, Bertrand Russell and Ludwig Wittgenstein, and the mystical philosophy of India. Russell was shaken by Wittgenstein's critique of his 1912 article *The Essence of Religion*. Wittgenstein accused Russell of being a traitor to the gospel of exactness, indulging himself in vague terminology. In sharp contrast, Tagore sent Russell a letter congratulating him and citing the famous lines from the *Upaniṣads* about words and mind drawing back in fear and coming back baffled, faced with the ineffable nature of *Brahman*. Russell published Tagore's letter in his 1967 autobiography but when questioned about it said that Tagore's "talk about the infinite" was "vague nonsense". He continued, "The sort of language that is admired by many Indians unfortunately does not, in fact, mean anything at all". Dutta and Robinson note that, in contrast, Wittgenstein, who had so shaken Russell in 1912, in the 1920s and 1930s became a devotee of Tagore. At the Vienna Circle meetings, he would turn his back on the Logical Positivists, so certain of themselves, and read from Tagore's poetry. I would add that many of the physicists, whose supposedly objective and exact theories the Logical Positivists were trying to emulate in their philosophical systems, frowned upon the closed-minded approach of these 'philosophers', who did not really understand the metaphysical problems underlying the seemingly exact theories of physics.

> [Neils Bohr] *"they [Positivists] think that many of the questions posed and discussed by conventional philosophers have no meaning at all, that they are pseudoproblems and, as such, best ignored . . . . this same ban would prevent our understanding of quantum theory".*
>
> [Heisenberg] *"Positivists . . . are extraordinarily prickly about all problems having what they call a prescientific character. I remember a book by Philipp Frank on causality, in which he dismisses a whole series of problems and formulations on the grounds that all of them are relics of the old metaphysics, vestiges from the period of prescientific or animistic thought."*
>
> ***Werner Heisenberg***[30]

I also like to note that Wittgenstein, who gave away his inherited wealth and lived like a hermit was clearly a Western 'holy man' who had, through his cult of personality, captivated many leading Western thinkers with his half-baked, puerile utterances. These same Westerners would go around accusing Indians of falling for the personality cults of their holy men who uttered vague nonsense.

Harvey Cox, in an essay on Science and Religion in the West[31], has discussed the difference in emphasis between the two great philosophers of thirteenth century Europe, the Aristotelian Aquinas, who held that we can only know God indirectly through divine 'traces' in the phenomenal world, and the Franciscan Bonaventure who emphasised the action of the mind and introspection, leading to union with Divine Reality. Christian theology, with its emphasis on book learning, largely followed Aquinas who became the official Roman Catholic theologian in 1879. It should also be noted that whereas the Western Church has followed the Roman tradition of seeing God as the Roman Governor writ large, laying down the laws, whereas the Eastern Church has maintained the spiritual tradition, including meditation. As I noted in the verse, the Christian conception of a God separate from Nature (*supermundanus*, implicit in the Doctrine of Creation *ex nihilo*), laying down fixed laws, led to the scientific search for these supposed laws.

Trying to teach postgraduate students at Benares Hindu University, A. Bharati[32] noted, "It was almost impossible to introduce modern analytic, linguistically oriented philosophy". They showed a marked preference for holistic Western thought. Clearly there have been different emphases between traditional Indian thought and that of the West, especially the modern West. The likes of Hegel saw the 'Hindu' mind as incapable of anything beyond creative imagination or fantasy, accusations which have also been thrown at females. Of course, in spite of my use of the 'Indian Mind', the notion of a specific mind-set associated with a particular civilisation is a gross generalisation based on the dominant modes of thought determined to a large extent by history and socio-cultural conditioning. The individual, as this work stresses with its use of the notion of 'greater beings' really is sort of 'microcosm', reflecting his or her 'world' which structures his or her perceptions and modes of understanding. The Indian tradition has always had its materialists, such as the ancient *Chārvākas* but the spiritual tradition has dominated Indian thought, successfully pointing out the limitations of materialism and 'atomising' logic faced with the possibility of knowledge of the Absolute. Being both a brahman and a *bhadralok* (a member of the high-caste Bengali 'intelligentsia' of the same name), I can identify clearly, both with the dominant traditional 'Indian Mind' of the brahmanical ideology and with the mind-set of modern Indian elite nationalism as this ideology was formulated to a large extent by *bhadralok* intellectuals (as discussed in this work). The Indian way of understanding the world, both politically and metaphysically, strikes a chord deep within me and thus, for all my Westernisation, this work, the verse part of which especially arose largely unconsciously, is very much a product of the modern Indian Mind.

Western attitudes to Indian thought

At a time when many small-minded Indian academic 'philosophers' see the way forward for Indian philosophy as being in copying the contemporary Western fashion for sterile language analysis and when small-minded academic philosophers in the West focus on the fashionable notion of 'incommensurability' of philosophies from different cultural worlds, I will begin to present in this work, the direct synthesis of Eastern and Western philosophy, in the form of the synthesis of Science and Mysticism at the most fundamental level, showing the universal reality that underlies all conceptual schemes, however different they appear superficially. Reading the works of academic philosophers it usually seems as if the comparison of texts and the logical analysis of writings is more important to them than actually tackling the basic problems of philosophy. Stuck in their own little world of academia, they cannot break free to see that the approaches to resolving the great perennial questions which they belabour to little avail lie outside the realm of logical analysis. No amount of logical reasoning and intellectual wrangling can bring one to resolve the fundamental questions relating to consciousness. I had opted early on for the universalism of scientific enquiry. But this also led to barriers which Western philosophy simply could not break through. It was only when I broke through the psychological barrier that my Western upbringing had put between myself and mystical knowledge and began to look at the phenomenological knowledge of the yogis did I finally resolve the central problems of Eastern and Western philosophy. The fact that Indian philosophy had been created by men like myself and my nationalistic outlook both played a role, as I myself had been more than a match intellectually for my European counterparts at school and university and the fact that Vedānta was the epitome of Indian thought led me to take a far more lenient attitude towards it than I would have taken towards non-Indian spirituality although the very non-theistic and rationalistic approach of Advaita Vedānta appealed in itself to me. Thus the subliminal racial barriers which prevent many a Westerner from taking Indian thought seriously could not be maintained as I was a self-respecting Indian.

The bigotry of the scientific establishment

Of course a significant shift has occurred in more popular Western attitudes towards Indian thought and Eastern thought in general although this has not really permeated the Western intellectual establishment. The prestigious British cancer research charity, the Imperial Cancer Research Fund (ICRF), which finances much orthodox scientific research was recently involved in trying to rubbish a well-known centre for cancer patients in Bristol which used a mixture of conventional scientific therapy augmented by 'alternative' techniques, especially yoga. The widely publicised study of the Bristol centre purporting to show patients were actually more likely to die by going there turned out to be based on clearly false statistical comparisons which were not subjected to the scientific establishment's own peer review procedures and a leading cancer specialist, Karel Sikora, who had agreed to speak out at the press conference hastily organised by the ICRF to publicise the study, suddenly pulled out following alleged political pressure by the ICRF. In the 1980s Jacques Benveniste and coworkers at the University of Paris, using an immunological system involving anti-sera to immunoglobin E, produced some results which seemed to support the claims of homoeopathy. Biological effects remained in solutions which had been diluted so many times that no biologically active molecules would be likely to be present in a given sample. John Maddox, the editor of *Nature*, pressed for replication of these results by other laboratories before accepting Benveniste's paper for publication in the flagship of the British scientific establishment. However, Maddox also included an editorial comment calling for "prudent people" to "suspend judgement" as the data violated the present laws of physics such as the principle of mass action. Furthermore, Maddox and a couple of self-appointed scientific fraud investigators (one of whom was the notorious James "The Amazing" Randi, who has no scientific qualifications and purports to debunk claims of paranormal phenomena) subjected Benveniste's laboratory to what Benveniste described as a witch hunt[33].

We shall see in the final essay how the notions of some sort of memory trace left in the solution are related to Indian yogic notions associated with terms like *ākāśa* and *karma*. Such notions have been reformulated in a biological context by Rupert Sheldrake in his books *A New Science of Life* and *The Presence of the Past*. *Nature's* view of the former book was that it was "the best candidate for burning there has been for many years" (witch hunts again!). Developmental biologist Lewis Wolpert stated that 'Sheldrake's ideas are just nonsense". Wolpert seems to be one of Britain's two ubiquitous media commentators on matters biological. In recent newspaper reviews I have found him staunchly defending the orthodoxy against the increasingly popular New Age style ideas in complementary medicine. I read a review of his book *The Unnatural Nature of Science* a few years ago. The main point of the book, as portrayed in the review at least, was that only the Greeks had invented *Science* and that today's popular claims of Science existing in ancient China and India missed the point of what Science was. This Eurocentric defence of the uniqueness of the Greeks myth is ironic in that the Greeks were extremely open-minded towards Eastern ideas as is clear from our knowledge of the influences upon the thought of Plato and Pythagoras and similar Greek thinkers. Itinerant yogis known as 'gymnosophists' were found throughout the Hellenistic world. Plotinus attempted to reach India to find out more about the Truth. The negative attitude towards Eastern knowledge is in fact a product of the tribalistic, territorial, bigoted mentality of the Semitic religions which snuffed out the old Hellenistic open-mindedness as is clear from the narrow-minded attitudes of the defenders of the scientific orthodoxy. Such thinkers tend to think that, just because the Semitic religions permeating Western culture are based on blind faith and superstitions, Eastern spiritual knowledge must be the same.

The other seemingly ubiquitous commentator in the British media is Richard Dawkins, famous for his populist books on Neo-Darwinism and currently, I think, holding a position of Professor for the Public Awareness of Science. Dawkins seems to be pursuing a one man crusade against Religion. Unfortunately he seems oblivious of the fact that he is like the alter-ego of Western religion, with the same closed-minded and zealous approach which any religious bigot would be proud of. Mathematical biologist Brian Goodwin[34] has even pointed out that Dawkins' well-known 'selfish-gene' views are a modern reformulation of the Christian myth of Original Sin where, although humans are born into sin (or DNA is basically 'selfish' in Dawkin's version), by faith and moral effort humanity can be saved (or humans can develop altruistic qualities that contradict their inherently selfish nature). Speaking at the Publishers Association

Centenary Conference, Dawkins[35] quoted Wolpert's view of the unique invention of Science by the Greeks with approval. Dawkins also asserted that, if Shakespeare were to return from the dead, even the best modern writers would be obliged to sit at his feet. However, as Science was progressive, even an averagely bright school child studying physics or biology could tell Aristotle why he was wrong in almost every single thing he said about either subject. This attitude towards traditional knowledge is most revealing. The fact of the matter is that many open-minded scientists are beginning to realise that Science is mistaken in focusing exclusively upon certain aspects of Nature and that we can learn a thing or two by reconsidering the broader approaches of traditional thinkers like Aristotle in regard to, for instance, formal causation. Dawkins, speaking about publishing, referred to "mystical rubbish" and hoped that for the next millennium, the publishing of mystical pseudo-science will wither away and be replaced by astronomy and other genuine sciences. On a recent radio report about the survey published in *Nature* which showed that forty per cent of US scientists believed in a personal god (and immortality of the soul) Dawkins was quoted from a newspaper rubbishing views of some 'mystical life force'. He also asserted that Life was nothing more than bytes of self-replicating information. We shall look at scientific and mystical views of Life in the final essay. Although I must admit that Dawkins' *The Selfish Gene* influenced me when I read it as a teenager, hence the odd references in the verse, I have since grown up as will be apparent in the rest of the work.

Jung as a bridge between East and West

The influence of Indian thought is growing none the less with an upsurge of interest in the writings of C.G. Jung which have played a significant role in fulfilling Jung's wish to build a bridge between Eastern and Western thought. J.J. Clarke, in his introduction to *Jung on the East*[36], notes that, "the role which the East has played in the formation of the modern Western mind has been, if not actively censored, at any rate conveniently marginalized". Even Jung's own followers have been reluctant to take his work on Eastern thought seriously and Jung's own work was coloured by the prevailing Orientalist notions of his day.

Clarke notes that, contrary to the oft-cited suggestion that Jung's involvement with the East began in 1928 with his commentary to Richard Wilhelm's translation of the Chinese meditation text, *The Secret of the Golden Flower*, Jung's interest started much earlier and continued right up to his death. Clarke writes that Jung discerned important affinities between his own thinking and Indian yoga and that his insights reflected the age-old theories and practises of India. The central Jungian concepts all have their counterparts in Eastern thought as we shall see in the final essay.

In 1983, the year I left school, first put forward my Panpsychist interpretation of consciousness (based on Spinoza's basic view and Western scientific knowledge) and started my BSc course, I had read parts of a book of Jung's selected writings edited by an English psychiatrist[37] who, with hindsight, I have noted avoided Jung's association with the East (the influence of Schopenhauer was mentioned) and did not even mention clearly that *The Secret of the Golden Flower* was a meditation text. At the time, as I was in my ultra-rationalistic phase (in spite of my insightful conversion to panpsychism) and lacking any background knowledge, it meant little to me although I picked up a very vague notion of 'archetypes', as manifest in the verse:

You live in me through archetypes
In me you resurrect your themes
Oh land surrounded in memory
Oh patchwork land made up of dreams

which reflects the theme of this essay in that I saw India 'resurrecting' itself in my own being in the remarkable concordance between my own orientation to various issues, primarily political, and what I later learnt about Indian national ideology. The parallels between my metaphysical outlook and the Indian tradition which I discerned after writing the verse have been mentioned above. I see a strong hereditary component in my microcosmic reflection of the 'Indian Mind'. I also picked up from Jung in 1983 the notion of synchronicity which was to play an important role in my own life especially in the critical periods. In 1994 I looked at the Jung book again in order to consider the notion of synchronicity and read the whole book as at last it began to make sense. The initial breakthrough in linking my theory of consciousness to yogic ideas in 1994 was mediated by a book by a Swiss Jungian who used Jung's psychological concepts in relation to Zen meditation. As with Jung, who found that his radical ideas, partly derived from the study of schizophrenia, were largely supported by Eastern knowledge and philosophy, so I found, after years of feeling isolated, that my own radical ideas on the nature of consciousness and mentation were largely supported by the East. At first I largely agreed with him in his refusal to take the metaphysical theories of the East (as well as those of the West) too seriously, but I have since come to see the limitations of Jung's understanding and to appreciate the validity of Eastern metaphysical claims as we shall see in the final essay. Jung failed to come to terms with the egoless nature of the final state of meditation, egoless Pure Consciousness, and failed to appreciate the deeper spiritual planes[38]. Although Jung imbibed some of the colonialist attitudes of his day, he remained very sympathetic to Eastern civilisations in general and has had a positive influence in the coming together of East and West.

> *But if the white man does not succeed in destroying his own race with his brilliant inventions, he will eventually have to settle down to a desperately serious course of self-education. Whatever the ultimate fate of the white man may be, we can at least behold one example of a civilization which has brought every essential trace of primitivity with it, embracing the whole man from top to bottom....India represents the other way of civilizing man, the way without suppression, without violence, without rationalism.*
>
> **C.G. Jung, *What India Can Teach Us*[39]**

Metaphysics as the study of 'the world as a whole'

I have noted above that the presentation of my thoughts in verse form, resembling a *sūtra,* reflected an unconscious return to my 'native' state, rejecting the conventional modern Western mode of presentation. I see myself as a metaphysician but the presentation of ideas in this work, both in the verse and the prose, will not involve the manipulation of abstractions. My intention is to return metaphysics to the study of 'the world as a whole' in contrast to the secular compartmentalization of modern Western thought. Metaphysical ideas cannot be taken apart from the mundane contexts in which they originated and this shall be particularly apparent in my resolution of the mind/body problem which, as we shall see, was largely a cultural artefact of the modern West. I have none the less divided the Postscript into discussions of the 'mundane' (socio-political) and the 'metaphysical' content of the verse (and the later developments of my thought) for convenience whilst emphasising the importance of the metaphysical base in understanding the mundane matters. In the metaphysical essay of the Postscript, entitled *The Oneness/Otherness Mystery*, I shall describe my subjective experiences associated with the development of my ideas, in contrast to the supposedly impersonal objectivity of 'hard-nosed' modern Western metaphysical thought which attempts to emulate the supposed impersonal objectivity of science. This presentation actually strengthens my case as I wish to illustrate the actuality of synchronicitous and related mystical experiences, involving subjectivity, surrounding such insights into Reality (these are also experienced by many creative scientists but the dominant culture expects them to record these events only in their private diaries). Of course, in its attempt to eliminate subjectivity from scientific experimentation, Western metaphysics has rejected the paranormal phenomena which depend upon subjective factors for their generation (as will be discussed in the final essay). Following on in the Indian tradition, I certainly do not see the ultimate goal of philosophy as being logic-chopping or categorizing everything into neat classes and manipulating these abstractions. Rather, I see the goal of philosophy as showing how everything relates to everything else and how such knowledge constitutes an integrated, whole picture which can account for all the facts of experience which Western metaphysics certainly cannot do. One intuitively knows when one has interpreted things correctly as everything falls into place, fits together, in relation to the whole. Indeed, this is the very argument that scientists would use to defend the theory of evolution against the charges of the Popper-style argument that it is merely metaphysics as it is not open to falsification. This is my interpretation of metaphysics as 'the world as a whole'.

> *If we can judge what philosophy is by what great philosophers have done in the past, its business is by no means confined to*

> *accepting without question, and trying to analyze, the beliefs held in common by contemporary European and North American plain men. Judged by that criterion, philosophy involves at least two other closely connected activities, which I call* ***Synopsis*** *and* ***Synthesis.***
> ***C.D. Broad***[40]

The feminine aspects of the Self

My so-called "Reassertion of the Indian" may be interpreted more broadly as the reassertion of some aspects of thought common to most traditional societies, not just Indian society. Furthermore, the fact that Indian thought emphasises experience ('feeling'), intuition, insight and holistic modes of understanding places it clearly in a position overlapping the convenient label of the "feminine" in regard to the dominant Western cultural categorization of mental faculties. Indeed India has been seen as the most 'feminine' of the great civilisations and some of the links between the notions of the Indian or the Hindu and the 'feminine' are touched upon in the verse and discussed further in the Postscript especially in relation to the 'hypermasculine' colonial culture which subconsciously categorised subject peoples as 'feminine'. The likes of Hegel and Jungian students of myths have depicted 'Hinduism' as feminine, linked to psychical principles which are considered to be feminine[41]. According to Indian psychologist Sudhir Kakar (whose neo-Orientalism appeals to V.S. Naipaul in his put-downs of India), the "female layer of the unconscious" is most in evidence in Indian civilisation. The 'Hindu' ideal has always been a somewhat hermaphroditic character (note Krishna) and the masculine and feminine principles have been combined in the mythological dyads of Radha/Krishna and Sītā/Rāma. India is also where the cult of the Mother Goddess still has a powerful influence and the modern nation is itself held by nationalists to be a substitute mother goddess, *Bhārat Mātā* (Mother India). The feminine aspect also enters the discussion of what Ashis Nandy[42], following Freud, calls 'isolation', meaning the separation of thought from feeling which underlies much of the development of modern Western civilisation. Nandy notes that the refusal of Asian civilisations to think in terms of clearly opposed, exclusive Cartesian dichotomies was held by Europeans to be the final proof of the cognitive inferiority of non-white races. This 'isolation' stems from the metaphysical separation of matter from spirit and, taken to its extremes, results in the reification of suffering and moral issues as matters to be dealt with in a detached scientific manner (i.e. the exclusion of subjectivity again). The role of isolation in Nazism has been discussed by the likes of Adorno who also lamented that vulgar materialism, resulting from the denial of Spirit, has led to the thought of money entering the most intimate and spiritual relationships and also to the exalted status given to political economy[43]. Nandy quotes Erich Fromm[44]:

> *'Logical thought is not rational if it is merely logical . . . Logic does not exclude madness. On the other hand, not only thinking but also emotions can be rational . . . Reason flows from the blending of rational thought and feeling.*

From my own personal experience it seems as if the infatuation with logic is something that captivates the adolescent male who, hopefully, then matures to see the error of his ways. We saw something of this in Wittgenstein's puerile *Tractatus Logico-Philosophicus* which he later saw for what it was. However, many a scientist and Western 'philosopher' does not mature intellectually and remains arrested in this adolescent frame of mind which worships logic and abstractions and chastises as vague, irrational and unscientific rubbish all those things which he represses because they do not fit his world-picture (his little 'whole') or because he has never experienced them and cannot imagine that they exist.

Scientific modernisation and Indian Nationalist aspirations

My scientific educational background also has its nationalistic connotations. The founding fathers of modern India generally shared a commitment to the 'scientific frame of mind'; part of the overall European Enlightenment outlook adopted from the contemporary West with Comte's Positivism having a strong influence on them. Later on in the history of Indian Nationalism, Gandhi would take a rather anti-scientific stance but this in itself partly reflected Gandhi's political position of challenging the authority of the Brahmanical elite. It was the successful accommodation of modern science alongside the Neo-Vedāntic

Brahmanical world-view by the elite founding fathers (whose implications for Indian secularism are noted in the Postscript) which helped to make Gandhi suspicious of a science that seemed to help legitimise the social orthodoxy he was challenging[45]. In contemporary India, the debate continues over the relationship between the scientific modernisation programme and social disparities, with the elite seeming to gain by far the most from the unquestioned status of Science as a 'Reason of State'.[46]

For all the West's laws, social institutions and administrative skills, lauded by the Victorian Whigs and Utilitarians as the panacea for India's ills, it was ultimately its technological superiority which determined who was master and who was serf in the colonial world. Indeed the Western developments in political and economic theory around the eighteenth century were based on the success of the new science with social thinkers attempting to develop the supposed 'sciences' of government and political economy by imitating the mechanistic picture. A few months before I wrote the verse, the overwhelming technological superiority of the West was displayed to full effect against a 'Third world' country which, although armed to the teeth (partly by the same Western powers through covert deals), remained defenceless against the computer-guided cruise missiles (the real end-product of the original American university research into 'artificial intelligence'; the pioneers of which were quietly funded and 'steered' in the desired direction by the Pentagon), radar-evading Stealth warplanes, spy satellites and the rest of the 'high tech' arsenal arrayed against it. The British news broadcasts brazenly eulogised the new computerised short range missile system being used in earnest for the first time. As many people have noted, the savage reality of warfare was presented to the public by the official Western media as a 'video game', devoid of the brutal imagery which inflamed public opinion during the US invasion of Vietnam. The sense of the almost magical power of Science and modern technology, as demonstrated in this conflict, had been with me since childhood and my pursuit of a scientific education came partly from a desire to partake of this modern magic but also, in part, a subliminal manifestation of my nationalistic orientation, recognising that the mastery of Science was crucial for India to rise out of poverty and impotence.

Saddam Hussein was clearly guilty of numerous brutal crimes, including the invasion of Iran on the pretext of righting the wrongs done by the previous US-backed regional warlord, the Shah, and brutal atrocities against the Kurds (the Western demonisation of him over the use of chemical weapons failed to mention that the precedent of chemical warfare had been set by the British against Iraqis in British Mesopotamia and that Winston Churchill had pressed for the use of chemical bombing of rebellious Kurdish villages). The innocent Iraqi conscripts used by Hussein as cannon fodder and often portrayed by the West in terms of 'Oriental despotism' are little different from the European conscripts of the 1914-18 war, led by Hussein-like warmongers. The Dardanelles fiasco, costing 100,000 British Empire troops was the bright idea of Winston Churchill who had hoped to gain tremendous glory for himself by the opening up of a second front. The Western news media, ever keen to boast of its independence, continues to present the pictures of other societies which serve the interests of the state, just as Western scholarship in the nineteenth century dehumanised the societies which were being attacked and plundered. Iraq clearly has a justifiable sense of grievance over the earlier Western neo-colonialist preservation of the reactionary principality of Kuwait which clearly fell within the 'natural borders' of the newly created state of Iraq. The Indian Union marched into the 'collaborator' princely states which refused to join the union but Western control of oil resources were not threatened by this. Regardless of the ugly nature of Hussein's fiefdom, the sheer one-sidedness of the conflict and the brazen steamrollering through of the US intervention over the heads of the supposedly "United Nations", ignoring veto power China's objecticns, highlighted the appalling double standards in regard to the responses to aggression by various states such as Israel and Indonesia and the total disregard by thc US for UN resolutions against its client states based on the maintenance of Western neo-colonial interests.

I was at one with the general feeling in India, where there was outrage at the West's attempts to prevent India sending food to the Indians stranded in Kuwait, and a general feeling of national impotence. It left a clear and disturbing message in regard to 'who calls the shots' in the supposed "global village", especially as the Soviet Union was disintegrating and the West was using

Iraq as a pretext for strengthening its nuclear Non-Proliferation Treaty (recently extended indefinitely!) which, as with the UN Security Council, maintains the ridiculously outdated great power status of the old colonial powers, Britain and France, and which clearly smacks of an attempt to monopolise the one power that could allow non-Western states to deter such overwhelming superiority in conventional firepower in case of Western neocolonialist interventions against them. Indeed, given Europe's history of brutal aggression and plunder across the world, it is just as reasonable to fear that a Europe, finding its ill-begotten position in the world declining due to globalisation of industry, will pose as much of a potential threat to world peace as any other power in an unpredictable future.

Although great technological leaps have been made by authoritarian regimes (let us remember the authoritarian nature of most Western governments not so long ago), there remains a correlation between prosperity achieved through scientific progress and the development of liberal democratic social structures. The great technological showpieces of the Soviet Union were largely reminiscent of ancient pyramid or medieval cathedral building, failing to feed through into improving the lives of ordinary people. The full awakening of the scientific potential calls for a degree of openness and freedom. Thus technological modernisation tends to create around itself more democratic social structures without which creative technological progress would be stifled. Although in economic terms the authoritarian regimes of Eastern Asia have raced ahead apace (and there is a lot to be said in regard to the benefits of mildly authoritarian rule for developing societies), liberal democratic India, forced to take heed of fractious vested interests and other inertial forces, could in the long-term prove to be the sustainable tortoise besides the 'slash and burn' hare of China. India's open institutional structures already allow Indians to take more heed of the vital environmental concerns related to modernisation and they could help foster the creativity needed to provide new ideas to allow for development whilst maintaining a healthy environment and to make India the future scientific superpower.

Western humanistic rhetoric and Indian Nationalism

Of course democracy itself is something of an out-of-place Western institution hastily transplanted onto an Asian context and has its negative aspects which the verse touches upon. India's strategic priorities would perhaps benefit from a period of benevolent authoritarianism. This could only be tolerated if a new sense of national consensus, transcending petty vested interests, could be attained. Westerners berate authoritarian regimes for violations of so-called 'human rights', as defined only very recently by Westerners, whilst Western financial institutions keep pouring investment money into those same countries as authoritarian regimes are viewed as providing stable environments for investment profits.

In spite of my criticism of the Western control of the global media in the verse, the technological revolution which has brought us almost immediate coverage of world events has clearly led to a more optimistic scenario in regard to international relations although the images of atrocities against (non-oil-rich) Muslims in Bosnia did not seem to move the European politicians who presumably harboured notions of Europe as Christendom beneath their pseudo-humanistic rhetoric. Once again it was the USA which sorted out Europe's internal problems, the nation of immigrants taking such humanistic concerns far more seriously than the Old World old guard who did nothing but stall to prevent action with each new Serbian outrage. Had Europe faced a new plague of Muslim fundamentalist terrorism, as the Russians faced with Chechnia, in the 'heart of Europe' it would have been of its own making through refusing to come to the aid of the extremely secularised Bosnians. Martin Bernal[47] tells an interesting story about how Egypt became the country with the world's second largest industrial capacity in the 1830s following its modernisation under Mohamed Ali, an Albanian General in the Turkish army. Egyptian forces helped suppress the Greek bid for independence from the Turks in 1825 but the British, French and Russians combined to destroy the Turkish and Egyptian fleets at Navarino in 1827. The European resistance to the arming of the Bosnian government smacked of anti-Islamic prejudice; instead the so-called UN 'peacekeeping' forces seem to be in Bosnia as part of a pseudo-humanistic sham to ensure that the Bosnian Muslims had no control over their own destiny, preventing the Arab oil wealth that was demanded by the USA to fund the almost mercenary intervention in Kuwait from helping the

Bosnians and thus maintaining Christian control. One could not have imagined such resistance by the Europeans had the situation been reversed. Although the 'non-aligned' Serbs, for long ruled by Turkic Muslim invaders arouse a good deal of empathy amongst 'Hindu' Indians like myself, who share a similar historical experience and face Muslim separatism on our borders, one reaches a point where Feeling has to triumph over cold, calculating Reason and say that enough is enough. President Bush's trumpeting of a supposed New World Order in 1991 aroused fears of Western imperialist revivalism unchallenged in the post-Cold War era. With even Margaret Thatcher, who shamefully stood out against sanctions against South Africa, amongst other neo-colonialist stances, for once speaking out on the side of the oppressed, the hollowness of the Western humanistic rhetoric was clearly exposed two years later faced with Serbian barbarity in Srebrenica.

In this disturbing post-Cold War period of re-emerging nationalist conflicts in Eurasia (Eurocentrism infected geography as well, making the subcontinent of Europe a supposedly separate 'continent'; indeed India is more distinct geologically from the Eurasian landmass) and tribalism in parts of Africa, it might appear a little foolhardy to champion one's own national ideology (or one's own perception and interpretation of it). For me, the idea of Indian Nationalism, especially in regard to the question of what India's role in the world should be transcends any petty tribal affiliation. It turned out that my own personal view of Indian Nationalism reflected the actual nature of Indian Nationalism as is discussed especially in *In this Age of Falling Curtains*. The recurring reference to *Bhārat Mātā* (Mother India) in the verse indicates something of the 'feminine' qualities attributed to 'India' in contrast to the aggressive tendencies of petty European-style tribal nationalisms. Indian Nationalism represents inclusivism in having to accept all the diverse communities of India, historically separated by race, caste, creed, and region as one united family, a microcosm of the new global inclusivism which at present exists largely in rhetoric. Indian Nationalism also represents the ideal of religious tolerance and the Neo-Hindu doctrine of the Unity of Faiths. In spite of the *de facto* exclusivism of caste, it should be noted that newly independent India introduced positive discrimination for the 'Scheduled Castes and Tribes' (the untouchables and the tribal populations) long before such notions became fashionable in the West. It is perhaps worthwhile contrasting India's diverse ethnic mix with the rather homogeneous populations of Japan and China which, although highly beneficial for internal cohesion and authoritarian control, tend to lead to exclusivist attitudes in relation to foreigners, be they even of the same ethnic origin, as the Koreans are to the Japanese. As stated above, I found that my interpretation of Indian Nationalism and my analysis in the Postscript, which tended towards the Nation as a *civilisation*, was not new. Tagore rejected Nationalism as a post-medieval European phenomenon in favour of a widely held Indian view of India as a civilisation, rather than a nation, where the notion of 'unity in diversity' played a prominent role[48].

> *Despite occasional attempts to base Indian Nationalism on unalloyed self-interest, 'pure' nationalism had never been able to mobilise even the Indian middle classes fully. Indian Nationalism still vaguely reflected, in however distorted a form, what could be called the ultimate civilisational goal of India: to be the cultural epitome of the world and to redefine or convert all passionate self-other debates into self-self debates.*
>
> **Ashis Nandy, *The Illegitimacy of Nationalism*[49]**

This view of Indian Nationalism representing something much higher than just tribal affiliation and patriotism was further extended by Gandhi with his 'Hindu' emphasis on the individual's own personal 'liberation' taking precedence over collective aspirations. The more westernised Indian Nationalists, especially the Radical wing of the Congress (mainly Bengalis), could not understand how, in February 1922, after forcing the British onto the defensive with his nationwide civil disobedience movement, Gandhi could draw back from the kill due to a minor incident involving the killing of some policemen in a heated confrontation in the unheard of village of Chauri Chaura. As Gandhi explained after another calling off of civil disobedience in 1931, the aim of *satyāgraha* ('holding firmly to the Truth') was to convert your opponent by love[50]. This inward looking approach of *satyāgraha* reflects the traditional ideals of converting the drive to power to a drive for power over one's self, especially over its unacceptable aspects[51]. One is reminded of the famous conversion of Aśoka to Buddhism, mentioned in the verse, following the bloody conquest of Kalinga (Orissa) which completed the conquest of all of India begun by his grandfather and his implementation of social welfare schemes. Nandy notes that Gandhi's view of the aim of the oppressed was that it was not to become a first-class citizen in a world of oppression instead of a second- or third-class citizen but to build an alternative world where he can hope to win back his humanity[52]. In 1931 Tagore told an American audience that they had not responded to India's appeal for freedom because they only responded to power. They had responded to Japan because, by copying Western-style nationalism and colonialism, Japan proved that she could make herself as obnoxious as the West[53].

Indian Nationalism and Neo-colonialism

Indian Nationalism also represents the historical struggle of the ex-colonial subjects to obtain economic justice in the post-colonial world whose major currents of resource flow were determined to a large extent by the 'parasitic' relations laid down in the colonial era. Such concerns are reflected in the verse. Kenneth Kaunda stated in 1975 that Mahatma Gandhi and 'Pandit' Nehru were heroes of the entire oppressed peoples of the world[54]. When India attained political freedom, the rest of the colonised world where the natives had not been exterminated and replaced by the Europeans knew that their time would be coming soon. These aspirations are still reflected by the Non-Aligned Movement in which India has played a leading role. In a fast-changing world, I accept that the neo-colonialism thesis is becoming somewhat outdated as drastic changes in the world's economic order are underway with a huge shift of industrial and economic power to Eastern Asia which will hopefully spread westwards in the near future. The New International Economic Order was never going to come about by appealing to the West; it will be created by the ex-colonised world as the economic power imbalance is reversed. Indeed, recently there has been much talk and some signs of India's economy being on the verge of self-sustaining 'take-off'.

In spite of these very positive developments, the neo-colonialism thesis is certainly not an effete notion best left for the whinging good-for-nothings. Not only do we still live in a global political order rooted in the legacy of European colonial domination where Western interests override any conflicting issues of justice, but the whole thrust of current market-driven changes seems geared to the philosophy of export-oriented developments which place the emphasis on catering for the wealthy world's latest fancies rather than putting the emphasis on raising the living standards of the poor and catering for their more basic needs. Of course, exported-oriented growth, raising 'hard currency' (itself a subtle component of the system of Western economic domination), may be seen as a first step in accumulating wealth but the whole economic order based on shallow principles of purportedly 'free' markets and the imperialistic imposition of financial austerity packages upon developing nations by the West enforcing export-oriented changes reveals the underlying neo-colonialist order. As with the Bosnian Muslims, prevented by the Europeans from freely purchasing arms to defend themselves, such impositions of economic policies are not necessarily in the 'best interests' of the developing nations. The advice given to many developing countries to grow the same export crop has led to crashes in the world price for the commodity, leaving the producer nations with a worthless crop which may have replaced the staple food crop and the rich world with a big reduction in the price of some luxury produce. As with the origins of 'artificial intelligence' noted above (one could also mention the CIA's funding of the new academic discipline of 'Cognitive Science' in the 1950s to learn about 'brainwashing') no expert knowledge is free from subtle political considerations, even though the expert may not be totally aware of the subtle political conditioning framing his thought through the very institutions he works for and his cultural background. The 'free market' gurus may believe that they have the interests of the whole world at heart but, upon analysis, this usually boils down to a vision of the 'world' as their own perceived national interests writ large.

The current round of GATT negotiations on world trade has shown how the 'haves' continue to lay down the rules to disadvantage the 'have nots' with some marginal concerns of countries like France taking precedence over far more fundamental concerns of large numbers of developing countries. Recently, the US has tried to block the sale of Russian cryogenic rockets to India using the 'dual purpose', potential military application, argument. India's development strategy includes the vital use of remote sensing of natural resources and weather forecasting satellites. Letting pass for the moment the outrageous US attitude of trying to dictate defence policies to other countries, the fact is that no advanced industrial country has used this type of rocket for military purposes since the 1960s as loading the fuel takes a whole day! The only motive one can seriously discern behind this, given that India is as wary of Islamic radicalism as the US, is one of stifling competition in the space sector. There are clearly similar ulterior motives behind the nuclear Non-Proliferation Treaty and India correctly rejects such neocolonial impositions. The rising concern over the environment has led to a sharper debate in relation to the injustices of the international economic order but it remains the case that the rich world, which brutally plundered the resources of the rest of the world to attain its current position (the verse notes the extreme example of the US government's deliberate slaughter of millions of buffalo a century ago in order to destroy the Plains Indians livelihood and steal their land) and which has largely created the mess, tending to try to put the blame, reductionistically, on the poor world's attempts to raise themselves and thus appears to be hindering their prospects for development.

> *To this terribly important task of representing the collective suffering of your own people, testifying to its travails, reinforcing its memory, there must be added something else, which only an intellectual, I believe, has the obligation to fulfil . . . . For the intellectual, the task is explicitly to universalise the crisis, to give greater human scope to what a particular race or nation suffered, to associate that suffering with the sufferings of others. This does not at all mean a loss in historical specificity, but rather it guards against the possibility that a lesson learnt about oppression in one place will be forgotten or violated in another place or time.*
>
> ***Edward Said***[55]

Indian spirituality and Western social materialism

A rejuvenated India, rising to economic power and global influence must recognise that, just as it was in the vanguard of the anti-colonial struggle, it should utilise newfound power to help restructure the world economic order away from its current neo-colonial basis towards an order benefitting other colonially dispossessed and developing nations in India's own long-term interest. So-called 'South-South' cooperation, including the barter of produce, bypassing the use of Western 'hard currency' systems etc. has already been in operation amongst non-aligned countries to some extent. Of course, such long-term interests do not rule out a period of playing the game according to the existing rules when this is the best available option for national development but there must be an underlying recognition of the sheer aimlessness of the so-called 'free-market' approach which is likely to lead to tremendous social disruption in all parts of the world. The ridiculous over-emphasis on the market mechanism, a manifestation of the underlying materialistic culture, is already leading to the degeneration of the public educational and healthcare systems in Britain under the sleaze-ridden Conservative administration full of brazen 'climbers' who view politics merely as a means to personal financial gain. In early 1997 about three quarters of the parliamentary Conservative party, claiming to represent the concerns of all the British people, had personal fortunes of over one million pounds. After being deposed as Prime Minister, monetarist Baroness Margaret Thatcher had no qualms about serving tobacco giants Philip Morris as an international lobbyist campaigning against curtailment of cigarette advertising in East Asia. The cocaine barons of Columbia are demonised by the West but their own tobacco baroness, in much the same way as opium barons Jardine and Mathieson did before her, passes herself off as a guardian of 'free trade'. The Conservative right wing's hostility to European integration stems partly from their revulsion at the fact that countries like France recognise the need to maintain a stable society and make economics serve society rather than *vice versa*. Indian civilisation, whose ruling elite adopted modern ways without the European-style secularist split from spirituality, must challenge such shallow materialism to the benefit, not only of developing nations, but also the best long-term interests of the advanced industrial nations themselves and especially the marginalised within them. The holistic 'Hindu' frame of mind cannot be satisfied with such one-sided development, and must seek to 'transcend the opposites', taking what the market system has to offer in terms of efficient material production and distribution whilst maintaining the goals of social justice, harmony and stability in new interpretations of the *dharma*.

India has followed a pragmatic middle road between Capitalism and Socialism and was the non-communist state most friendly towards the Soviet Union. In spite of all the intrinsic contradictions and manifest failings of Communism, there was none the less a noble ideal behind it, however distorted the reality became. I would hope that India will maintain the ideals of the Gorbachev-Gandhi 1986 'Delhi Declaration' which envisaged international relations shifting towards a basis of mutual friendship and cooperation rather than mere mutual economic back-scratching between the world's mercantilist classes. The market mechanism has a great role to play in the production and distribution of material commodities but it cannot play the role of the god 'Invisible Hand', the term used in the verse, for its apotheosis as the solvent for all socio-economic ills.

Indian Nationalism has its roots partly in the central notion of a synthesis of the best aspects of 'Eastern' and 'Western' cultures in an effort to create a higher civilisation. More specifically, as the quote from Bankim at the head of this essay indicates, the synthesis involves, at base, a counterbalancing of the one-sided materialistic development of Western civilisation through the fusion of Indian spirituality with European science, leading to a better use of Science and modern technology. In regard to the microcosmic "reassertion of the Indian" in myself, it is interesting to note that I, like the nineteenth century founding fathers of modern India, managed to accept the scientific world-view without abandoning Indian spirituality, even though I did not really understand the latter. Although over a century later, this notion of synthesis has been obscured by the mundane realities of domestic politics, it still holds enormous potential, not only for India, but for a world realising the limits of Western-style industrial development with its emphasis on 'formal rationality', the ever more efficient running of the economic machine with ceaseless 'growth' in output, regardless of the environmental damage and unsustainability of the enterprise and the dehumanising effect it has on individuals who become construed, following the materialistic approach, as mere abstract, mechanistic components in the formal system of mechanistic abstractions. I have mentioned above Adorno's criticism of the vulgar materialism in which money entered the most intimate and spiritual considerations and which gave political economy such an exalted status. The need for a shift towards a less wasteful, less materialistically inclined yet sophisticated lifestyle, emphasising individual fulfilment with a more stable civilisation capable of self-preservation whilst accommodating rapid technological advances calls for a closer look at the positive features of Indian civilisation in the search for new modes of living in all parts of the globe. Interestingly, in 1952 Arnold Toynbee prophesised that, in the 21st century, "India would conquer her conquerors"; not politically but culturally[56]. The growing influence of Indian philosophical thought in the West is part of this process.

Pernicious Western relativism and universal degeneration

And the synthesis of Indian spirituality with European science, far from being a romantic dream, has actually come to be. In analysing the metaphysical content of my verse work, I eventually managed to link together Science and Mysticism at their most fundamental levels. Given the close association between the rise of scientific materialism and the mercantilist capitalist world order, the fact that my metaphysical breakthrough restores the world to a grounding in *Brahman* ('Spirit') must eventually work its way through to have a transforming effect on the politico-economic superstructure. The 'New Age' will not be as simple as many of the wishy-washy counterculture people in the West may wish but, in essence, the dissolution of the materialist picture of discrete entities as the substantial Reality must work its way through the systems of thought to a dissolution of the picture of the transactions of material entities (or even the new, more subtle, materialistic 'Reality', *information*) as the fundamental basis of the social order towards a more 'holistic' view in tune with the need to cater for the needs of the whole world and the growing environmental concerns. It is interesting to note that the scientific focus on the 'material' has perennial roots in the Latin *materia* which is etymologically related to *mater* and thus is the symbolic representation of Nature as the Mother. The reconnection to the depths of our being can help us to re-examine and control the juvenile cravings so cynically exploited by mass marketing with its consumerist culture and turn back the tide of hyper-individualistic, hyper-materialistic social degeneration. I certainly do not espouse the 'anything goes' pernicious relativism often associated with popular neo-pagan Western counter-culture. Clearly a lot of popular New Age writing is patent nonsense with UFO mythology, astrology and revamped religious superstitions all juxtaposed with more serious works on spirituality under this 'New Age' label by the media and some popular publishers. It should however be remembered that today's natural science itself has some of its roots in alchemy and the occult:

> *"Witchcraft, astrology, and magic" point better to the general climate of thought and belief in which modern science arose than do the antiseptic details of the Democritan-Archimedean tradition. And they remind us of the context in which it is natural to find references to the writings of Hermes, Orpheus, Moses, and other pseudo-priscine authors scattered through Copernicus, Gilbert, Kepler, Wallis, and Newton, to find More immersed in the Cabala . . .*
>
> ***Mary Hesse***[57]

Although I am not against 'letting a thousand flowers bloom', I am wary of the anarchic and degenerate tendencies which are let loose when people lose sense of civilising values. There is a real need to curtail the pernicious influence of numerous decivilising tendencies unleashed by mass culture, mass marketing and uncritical relativism.

This pernicious relativism is most apparent in the 'universal degeneration' fostered by the global market-place with its lowest common denominator 'Cola Culture' as I refer to such simplistic mass marketing gimmicks. The common denominator in the forces behind such degenerative tendencies is mental immaturity, the sort of puerile rubbish that appeals to those in their early teens is amalgamated in the Cola Culture with its 'pop' music, brand-name clothing, glorification of sport and infatuation with sex, treating the orgasm as if it were the ultimate absolution. In London recently, a gang of fourteen-year-olds from about four different ethnic minorities, brutally gang-raped an Austrian tourist and threw her into a canal hoping to drown her. Only one of the eight, a Filipino, denied the charges and was tried in court. The newspapers carried a picture of him dressed in a baseball cap worn backwards, brand name trainers and other designer clothing sticking up his middle finger in a gesture of defiance to the photographers outside the court. The victim had stated that she had not felt in danger when the boys first surrounded her as they were only 'kids'. None of the rapists were of South Asian origin but a short while later I personally saw some Hindi-speaking youths dressed in the same American ghetto gang clothing brazenly cheating their way onto a London bus. On the bus they talked rowdily in Hindi until they spotted a friend on the street outside. They then broke into a sort of 'jive-talk' English seeming to know only the two words, "f..k you", and spitting out of the window. A friend told me that numerous working class Indian/Pakistani boys in Britain's schools now dress and speak in the same way, refusing to speak English. The trash-peddling sections of the media and their sociology professor apologists who deny that the media plays a role in stimulating youth crime and general rowdiness have a lot to answer for. It should also be of concern that, recently, the President of India gave an award to a singer of Indian origin who had had some success in the British popular music charts with American ghetto culture style songs. This was not only uncritical relativism but a hangover of the colonial subjects' inferiority complex that assumed that any sort of success in the West was the height of achievement.

Hopes for a future Universal Civilisation

The synthesis of Eastern and Western thought, de-repressing those aspects of Reality suppressed in the development of the modern West and beginning to explain the mystical union and the 'Godhead' which underlies all the cultural constructs called 'religions', opens the way for a truly universal, global civilisation for the future, the 'One World'.

I have just read Samuel Huntington's *The Clash of Civilisations and the Remaking of World Order*[58], the book based on an extremely influential article published in the journal *Foreign Affairs* in 1993. Huntington asserts correctly that the West is in decline and laments the increasing multiculturalism in the USA which is undermining the West's traditional ideological cohesion, hoping the USA can lead some sort of Western revival. He also asserts correctly that in the post-Cold War era countries and groups within countries are realigning themselves on the basis of civilisation affiliations leading to 'fault-line conflicts' such as that in Bosnia where people from three major civilisational groupings (Western Christianity, Orthodox Christianity and Islam) lived together. He focuses on the aggressive tendencies displayed by Islamic countries and by China which could threaten the Western dominated world order. The sinister military and nuclear collaboration between China, Pakistan and Iran clearly poses a threat to India as well as to the West. In this regard Huntington foresees India and the USA coming closer together and states that the expansion of Indian power in Southern Asia cannot harm US interests and could serve them. He dismisses vacuous Western pretensions to universalism and the various popular notions of an already emerging Universal Civilisation such as those put forward by the likes of V. S. Naipaul (as discussed later in this work) and the so-called 'Davos culture' of a tiny, jet-setting Westernised elite of agency officials and businessmen.

Huntington has been criticised for focusing on human differences and not seeing underlying commonalities and thus painting a very negative picture. Huntington also stresses the role of Religion as the key factor in determining civilisational differences, tending to view these all as being like the Semitic religions and seemingly as immortal institutions which never become extinct. He obviously does not foresee the undermining of Western materialism and the dharmic implications that will follow as society and culture slowly transform in line with the new metaphysics. However, he does note at the end that the "real clash" is between Civilisation in the singular and barbarism although he overlooks the fact that it is the USA which, through Hollywood and other media, is promoting the 'decivilisation' being berated by the elites of East Asia as "degenerate culture". He also states in regard to common moral values:

> *the world's major religions . . . also share key values in common. If humans are ever to develop a universal civilisation, it will emerge gradually through the exploration and expansion of these commonalities.*

We shall see later in this work how limiting our focus metaphysically also leads to distorted views of Reality. The synthesis of Science and Mysticism allows us to truly account for everything, material and spiritual, grounding our metaphysics on the true Ground of all Being. The socio-economic *dharmas* of all civilisations will have to adapt to this new understanding, ridding themselves of materialist and religious mythologies and integrating philosophy, science and spirituality into a coherent whole. The One World cannot be attained within the current neo-colonial world order as the One World will not come about through some superficial Western marketing rhetoric of a 'global village', nor by the imposition of integrated international structures upon the rest of the world by the West. The One World can only come about through the willing participation, on equal terms, of all the great civilisations, including the great civilisation of India.

My bonds to Bhārat Mātā

I, the outsider, the alien spirit, not feeling 'at one' with humanity, none the less possess this powerful mystical bond to this greater 'whole', my civilisation, conveniently called my 'nation', with which my mind seems to be in considerable harmony. Long before the French Revolution, Spinoza had foreseen that if a personal god is no longer worshipped, then people would worship the state (which the French *philosophes* and revolutionaries transformed into *la nation* or *la patrie*)[59]. Clearly, Bankim and Aurobindo were aware of the human need for a personal god in their identification of the Great Mother Goddess with the Motherland, creating the notion of *Bhārat Mātā,* Mother India. My bond to my 'nation' is not merely the filling of this deep mental vacuum with a god-substitute. A scion of the *brāhmaṇa* caste and the Bengali *bhadralok,* who thinks deeply about the nature of his being cannot but feel a deep resonance in his mental 'archetypes' with the great civilisation whose traditional and modern cultures were largely shaped by men like himself. However, this bond also stems from the need for a hopeful ideal to stand for faced with a somewhat hostile reality in a foreign land where, in spite of the superficial equality under the law, the underlying reality of discrimination and second-class citizenship is never far from the surface. The customs officers at British airports are only too keen to make sure that a non-European UK citizen does not feel 'at home' when he re-enters Britain from abroad. The non-European name on a *curriculum vitae* will very often stop you getting an interview for a job for which you may be ideally suited. Racial discrimination remains alive and kicking, sometimes manifesting itself as cultural exclusion of those who don't take part in 'normal' social activities such as the over-consumption of alcohol and the concomitant rowdiness which British society finds so amusing. It may be that drunkenness is the only outlet available to Britons brought up in a culture which generally represses expressions of deeper feelings. However, all it generally brings out is the loutishness, wife beating and road deaths which civil society can do without. It is also interesting to note that, apparently, when British companies take over American ones, the first thing that often goes is the positive discrimination scheme for the minorities. My bond is thus also the emigre's dream for a homeland which could provide suitable economic opportunities, avoiding the marginalisation he faces in a foreign land.

I dream great dreams of ***Mahā Bhārat***
High culture, Science bejewel Her Crown
Not drained, our brains reach for the sky
No ceilings glass, to hold them down

In the verse following the one above, I draw the parallel with pre-Holocaust Zionism, which reflected similar concerns. I had hoped that with the first steps towards peace in Palestine underway, the European Zionist settlers would cast off their racialist attitudes towards the Arabs, and indeed the Sephardic Jews, and start perceiving themselves as part of the Middle East rather than remaining as the colonially imposed thorn in Arabia, a satellite of the West propped up by US taxpayers' money that, they have been so far and start using their scientific and technological skills for the benefit of all the peoples of the region as, I believe, was part of the original pre-Holocaust Zionist ideal. I must add that I have found great understanding for the predicament of Indian immigrants amongst British Jews whatever our differences on the Palestinian question. One can add to the Jews, the British Celts who still retain the folk memory of oppression and marginalisation by the dominant English establishment. James Morris[60] writing in regard to the British extermination of the Tasmanians and other colonial outrages says:

> *even in the most ferocious episodes of Empire, there were honourable exceptions — men to whom race really was irrelevant, and colour added only variety to the human scene. Some were practising Christians. Many more were just people of decent instinct — sometimes tempered, especially in Irishmen, Scotsmen and Welshmen, by hereditary experiences of their own.*

One should add the identification of the English working classes with the plight of the oppressed and of course there is the sympathy shown by women in general. The link between hypermasculine culture and imperialism is stressed in this work, and I have noticed all the seeds of what I criticise in such imperialism lurking within myself. I do, however, point out some of the positive aspects of 'masculine' behaviour and imperialism in *In this Age of Falling Curtains.* During the Empire, British women played a leading role in such progressive causes as the abolition of slavery and India remembers with pride the prominent roles played by Margaret Noble (Sister Nivedita) and Annie Besant (founder of the Home Rule League and Indian National Congress *rāshtrapati* (President — literally "Father of the nation") for 1905). Along with the unleashing of the wasted potential of the lower castes, we must strive for the unleashing of the potential of women as this, as I have noted above, is closely associated with what I have called "The Reassertion of the Indian", in that the label *Indian* overlaps with the label *feminine.* I have noticed how women in Britain, generally, take naturally to Eastern philosophies whereas the 'territorial' resistance is largely amongst males, especially those identifying closely with the establishment. Christian Europe, after all, burnt millions of women for being blessed with the natural gifts of the psychic which are accepted by Indian philosophy and which seem to come more easily to women (perhaps related to the bilateral functioning of the cerebral hemispheres). Aurobindo's *The Life Divine* was nominated for Europe's Nobel Prize for literature by Pearl Buck and Gabriella Mistral. The Europeans stuck to their own culture and gave the prize to the logician

Bertrand Russell who, as we have seen, thought that Indian philosophy was vague nonsense. In regard to male-female relations, it is worthwhile noting here that Russell's wife Dora said that Russell was just all "brains and balls" with nothing in between. The verse includes a section on the historical oppression of women and another on the psychological roots of the problem of male dominance which I am aware of in my own being. Women are, in general, nicer, more sociable, more open-minded and accommodating than men and their general, natural tendencies towards nurturing which is manifest in, for instance, their tending to care for plants does, as Gandhi noted, accord naturally with the Indian notion of *ahiṃsā* (non-injury to all living things). We must contrast this to the aggressive baboon-like behaviour of many young males, condoned by the pernicious relativism of the Western media. The rise of feminine influence must eventually feed through to transform the imperialistic international structures created by thousands of years of patriarchy.

What if we would extol the Female
The Woman that's within us all
Could we transcend this manly conflict
Would everyone then have a ball

My sense of alienation in Britain arises, not only from the underlying racial discrimination, but also from my complete inability to identify with the philosophical orientation of the dominant culture. The British establishment is of course noted for its emphasis on supposed 'hard-nosed' empiricism and positivism. This is after all the land of Dr Johnson whose ridiculous kicking-of-the-stone argument to counter Berkeley's idealism still strikes a chord amongst many. This is discussed further in *In this Age of Falling Curtains* in relation to the influence of Indian thought upon the West. Anglican Christianity seems to be even more intolerant of other faiths than Christianity in general, with a widespread 'God is an Englishman' type attitude (incidentally, the Spanish Inquisition, undertaken by professional lawyers and whose official records are well preserved, was far less brutal, both in terms of severity of punishment and numbers persecuted, than the religious persecutions in the Protestant countries which held to the myths about it[61]). My personal experience reflects the historical encounters, with continental Europeans seeming to be far better acquainted with Eastern thought, or far less sarcastic towards it, than their British counterparts. This stems in part from the islander mentality of the British, something they share with the Japanese, and also in part from colonial self-justification which rubbished the cultures of the colonised. There is also the strong mercantilist tradition, the "nation of shopkeepers" as Napoleon called them. This was manifest most prominently in the recent premier, Margaret Thatcher, the grocer's daughter who saw the nation as a shop writ large. Also, in spite of being the first woman Prime Minister, her political character seems to have been formed by trying to be more of a 'man' than the men within the boys' club of the Tory Party and thus was not truly representative of feminine influence. The post-war British attempts to seek vicarious imperial glory in terms of the so-called 'special relationship' with the English-speaking USA has led to a greater American influence on British society than on continental European society, including the more prominent presence of superficial mass market culture and perhaps some of the other pernicious influences subsumed under the label of Americanization. Thus the encounter between the 'Indian Mind' and the West has to be clarified as the encounter with the West primarily as represented by the dominant British culture. The verse reflects the Indian empathy with the thought of republican France, metaphysically-inclined Germany and revolutionary Russia which are also manifest in my own thought.

I am well aware of the fact that many recoil from what they perceive as 'disloyalty' to Britain; the more liberal amongst them on the basis that this will only further marginalise Indian immigrants. My views come as more of a shock to them as I appear to be the sort of Indian patronisingly referred to as the 'brown Englishman', who has taken Western elite civilisation on board more so than most Westerners and who speaks English better than most of the English. There is the condescending assumption that he must be a total convert to our way of thinking. This is a very mistaken view as Ashis Nandy has pointed out in regard to the psychology of colonialism[62], for the reality tends to be an Indian adopting only those attributes of Englishness which suit his own sense of modern Indian identity. The use of the English medium in modern Indian culture is discussed in *In this Age of Falling Curtains.* I am not suggesting that my position in regard to national affiliation (as expressed mainly in Section III: *Rāshtra is My Word for Nation*) is appropriate for every member of the Indian diaspora. But I do feel that those Indian immigrants, or their offspring, who are most keen to be called 'British', as with the ultra-Nationalist thugs in Japan of Korean origin, display a shocking sense of inferiority, holding neo-Orientalistic superficialities in their minds, afraid to be tainted by Indianness. The same is true of a number of well-known writers of Indian origin who pander to the presuppositions of the largely ignorant Western public by rubbishing Indian civilisation (this is discussed further in *In this Age of Falling Curtains*). I recall that the late Czech-born Jew, Ludwig Hoch, (known as Robert Maxwell) who tried to out-British the British in his supposed loyalty, printing 'Forward with Britain' on his tabloid newspaper mastheads, had bought his burial 'plot' on the Mount of Olives long before his death. At least I do not pretend to be what I am not.

I laugh at all these ersatz Westerners
Ashamed to claim their names of birth
Feel not the shame of tame subaltern
Know not what dignity is worth

The above verse ends the Section entitled *Rāshtra is My Word for Nation* in which I refer directly to the right-wing British politician, who inflamed racial tensions in the 1960s with his "rivers of blood" speech in regard to non-'white' immigration, Enoch Powell's view that being British (he may have said 'English') meant identifying deeply with the people who won the Battle of Waterloo etc.

How right you were evil-eyed prophet
Waterloo to me means station
Agincourt to me some road name
***Rāshtra** is my word for nation*

Powell's view is of course a very 'romantic', old-fashioned view with which many English people disagree for various reasons. With increasing Western European integration, the situation changes and there is a danger of increasing European racial identification. Concomitantly, the smaller nations, such as Scotland, historically forced into union with more powerful neighbours are beginning to voice separatist feelings within the framework of a European Union in which the old nationalities will become outdated. In response to such devolutionary pressure, the constructed nature of 'Britishness' has been debated especially in regard to the immigrant 'British' who cannot claim to be English, Scottish or Welsh. The Indian style 'unity in diversity' seems the only way forward. In regard to Indian Muslims, I state in *Bande Mātaram:*

> *Though they may turn their heads to Mecca*
> *And disparage* ***Dharma Sanātan***
> ***Īśvara, Allah te re nam***
> ***Shobake sanmity de Bhagavān***

quoting Tagore's national hymn which appeals to the Lord, who is the same despite the different names given to him by Hindus and Muslims, to whom everyone should pay respect. I certainly do not expect the diverse peoples of India to have the same affinity to the idea of India that I possess. As stated in *In this Age of Falling Curtains,* India has to hold together its fractious coalition of communities by accepting the holistic approach of 'unity in diversity' and highlighting the benefits accruing to everyone from unity.

In essence, the powerful bond to one's 'nation' boils down to one's own self-image and self-respect. One's sense of one's capacity to fulfil great achievements is shaped to an extent by one's perception of the historical achievements of one's 'nation', especially in the ethnic sense of the term. Indeed, the reconstruction of the great history of ancient India was a major impetus for the emerging (Hindu) Indian Nationalism of the late nineteenth century, filling Hindus with a newfound sense of pride and self-belief. The great achievements of early modern India's scientists and writers came as great confidence boosters to all Indians subjected to racialist colonial ideology, inculcated in the colonial schools. Narayana Menon[63] has said of Nirad Chaudhuri, born in Bengal in 1897 and now living in his beloved England, who has pandered to the British with derogatory Orientalist views of India, that (Chaudhuri is) 'like a dog trained to wag its tail when its master said "England"'. Referring to modernising Islamic states, Gustav von Grunebaum[64] says:

> *A self-image apt to facilitate the realization of collective ambition must be perceived or, if need be, created to assuage the pains and anxieties of acculturation.*

Grunebaum regards the apparent inability of many 'third world' countries to 'self-construct' themselves in the light of the Western phenomenon as a serious impediment to their development, in view of the linkage between self-image and subsequent historical action[65].

Brought up since child in little England
In ways of West my mind was schooled
Taught myths about colonial rulers
Still saw the world through eyes of ruled
(*Rāshtra* *is My Word for Nation*)

Though sign of cross knots round my neck
Schools glorifying Greece and Rome
Britannia rules the surface waves
In depths of heart ***Bhārat*** *my home* ***(Bande Mātaram)***

A black popular musician recently lamented the fact that black children in Britain read in history books that the Greeks and Romans, and to a much lesser extent, the Arabs, the Indians and the Chinese did this, that and the other whilst Africans do not appear and this leaves them feeling impotent in relation to mainstream cultural activities. There has recently been much effort to emphasise that Ancient Egypt, from which the first European civilisations evolved through Egyptian (and Phoenician) colonisation and from the later borrowing from Egypt by the Greeks in many spheres, can be considered the true source of Western civilisation. Europe also tends to overlook the Afro-Asiatic roots of Christianity, closely associated with 'European identity', which was, after all, an Oriental religion adopted by the Romans who civilised the Western European tribes. Martin

Bernal stresses the African sources of Egyptian civilisation, tracing its roots to ancient Abyssinia[66]. Such arguments can however be taken to ludicrous extremes as was the case on a television programme for British Afro-Caribbeans, in which Bernal made an appearance, where some people were extending the claims from purportedly black pharaohs to a black Buddha on the basis of one or two images of the Buddha! Another television programme discussed scholarly views of Bernal's book and an Egyptologist pointed out that the Egyptians made a clear distinction between themselves, whom they portrayed as brown, and the black Nubians. Recent Egyptological research has shown that the conventional dating for the Pharaonic dynasties deduced by the nineteenth century Orientalist scholars (based on a phonetic resemblance to a name mentioned in the Bible!) is wrong. The Biblical conqueror of Jerusalem known as 'Sishak', whom Orientalist scholars had identified with Pharaoh Shoshenk, turns out to have been Rameses II (also known as Sishak) who conquered 'Salem'. A more realistic assessment based on numerous pieces of sound evidence and argument shows that the Pharaonic dynasties are many hundreds of years younger than the supposedly 'scientific' Orientalists thought.

As stated above, in managing to link together Science and Mysticism, resolving the central problems of Eastern and Western philosophy, I had to overcome the psychological barriers imposed by my Western indoctrination and take the knowledge presented in Indian philosophy seriously; after all, it was created by men like myself and I had surpassed my European classmates and colleagues in intellect so easily. Inside the copy of his book, banned by the British in India, *The Case for India,* which he presented to his friend Tagore, American Will Durant wrote that Tagore alone was reason enough for India to be given independence[67]. While Tagore was taking the literary world by storm in 1913 (the Europeans did not give their Nobel Prize to an Asian writer again for fifty five years), compared by Ezra Pound to Dante, in Cambridge, Srinivas Ramanujan Aiyar, the genius brought over to England from Madras, towered over all the Western mathematicians of the day in terms of natural genius. His Cambridge patron, G.H. Hardy, perhaps Britain's greatest mathematician at the time, suggested that on a scale of zero to one hundred (note that both the zero and the place value decimal system are of Indian origin), in terms of natural creative ability, Hardy himself would score about 4 besides 100 for Ramanujan[68]. In 1941, the Cambridge mathematician E.H. Neville broadcast a radio lecture on Ramanujan but had to omit the following passage from his prepared speech:[69]

> *Ramanujan's career, just because he was a mathematician, is of unique importance in the development of relations between India and England. India has produced great scientists, but Bose and Raman were educated outside India . . . India has produced great poets and philosophers, but there is a subtle tinge of patronage in all commendation of alien literature. Only in mathematics are the standards unassailable, and, therefore of all Indians Ramanujan was the first whom the English knew to be innately the equal of their greatest men.*

THE BIGGER, DEEPER PICTURE

As I have indicated, the discussion of the metaphysical content of the verse work led to the critical breakthrough of my identification of the physical correlate of the Divine Light. The actual development of my metaphysical thought from about age twelve to this breakthrough in 1994 at the time of my thirtieth birthday is presented in the first part of the final essay entitled *My Path to the Light.* This breakthrough has led to remarkable progress in my understanding of the relationships between Science and Mysticism allowing me to begin to synthesise the two. I will not reveal the details of the synthetic work here as the argument needs to be developed gradually in a step-by-step manner as I do in the final essay. What I will consider here are some of the general aspects of the emerging synthesis in regard to the overall character of this book.

The materialist creed

I have mentioned how the success of modern materialist science has resulted partly from the rejection of the traditional metaphysical approach of considering the 'world as a whole' and focusing on particular problem domains for which grossly simplified, idealised models predicting the behaviour of limited aspects of the system under consideration have been constructed and developed. Science thus presents us with a number of largely self-contained paradigmatic structures which conform to the basic metaphysical assumptions of materialist science and general unifying frameworks such as the currently accepted Laws of Physics and the Theory of Evolution. Through the construction of such interlocking paradigmatic structures, materialist science purports to account for all aspects of Nature and even claims that it will eventually account for the supposedly few mysteries such as consciousness (misconceived as just a product of physical processes in the brain) and the nature of the mind. Of course, certain mysteries such as paranormal phenomena tend to be dismissed as nonexistent, as their characteristics, such as transcendence of normal space and time causality, totally defy the limited scope of materialist, reductionist models. This denial of the evidence by many materialists is a form of the psychological 'denial mechanism' people often display when faced with traumatic news which they do not want to believe is true as it will upset their whole 'world'. The universalist pretensions of the materialists are manifest in the search for so-called 'Theories of Everything' and, for instance, in the claims made by the *Scientific American* staff writer John Horgan in his recent book *The End of Science* that, as all the 'big questions' have been answered, all that most scientists do nowadays is simply tinker with the existing theories like the scholastic philosophers of old who proverbially debated the number of angels which could be balanced on the head of a pin. I have already pointed out that most scientists, being 'glorified technicians', have always just tinkered within the existing paradigms, feeling safe in reaffirming the dogmatic views of the establishment. Indeed, Harvard physicist Sheldon Glashow[70] has proposed an "article of faith" shared by scientists that our sense-organs can discern the one full and unique true theory of the world and that Science will lead to this one correct theory which will rule out all alternative views. Horgan's analogy of the scholastic nitpicking is of use, not because Science has answered all the real, big questions, but because reductionist, materialist science has replaced Christian scholasticism as the new dogmatic creed which is accepted by the initiates without serious question. Indeed, far from having totally eradicated the superstitions of the Christian past, we shall see that the paradoxes and mysteries which Western materialist science cannot cope with have arisen because, as it is a product of Western Christian culture, materialist science remains rooted in Christian mythology.

When one begins to question seriously the epistemological assumptions of materialist science and when one begins to consider those aspects of the natural world and our basic sentient existence which materialist science denies or sweeps under the carpet of its obfuscating scripture, the universalist pretensions of materialism are quickly swept aside as the immature mythology of modern Western secular society which, captivated by its own technological prowess, perpetuates the most puerile metaphysical errors as long as the simple prediction of the regular behaviour patterns of natural phenomena continue to yield technological advances and ever more elaborate mythological constructions based upon such naïve metaphysics. The technological successes of the predictive physical models has resulted in the often ridiculous attempts to emulate the 'big boys' in the 'hard sciences' by the 'little boys and girls' in academic disciplines such as philosophy, as we have seen, and also in biology, psychology and social sciences where, often the mass production of simple graphs displaying rather obvious relationships between parameters gives the false veneer of pursuing scientific studies equivalent to those which have yielded such dramatic results in the physical sciences.

Idealism and the transcendental realm

There are some scientists who have questioned some of the more naïve, reductionist approaches taken for granted by mainstream scientists and have shifted towards more mature, holistic views involving notions of emergent materialism. Although a step in the right direction in regard to certain limited issues, such half-hearted holism cannot hope to account for the deeper problems although some, like Nobel laureate neurologist Roger Sperry, have made exorbitant claims in regard to such simplistic, holistic revisionism as being the key to answering the questions of consciousness, life, the universe and everything as we shall see in the final essay. Mature consideration of the epistemological assumptions of materialist science reveal reductionist materialism and emergent or holistic materialism to be products of empirical focusing at different levels of regular phenomena in the external reality. A deeper analysis reveals that beyond these limited abstractions of stable aspects of phenomena, a comprehensive understanding of Reality requires us to adopt an approach which is transcendentalist, holistic (in a deeper, transcendental sense associated with "holy" rather than the superficial holism of emergent materialist revisionism), panpsychist and idealist. The term *idealism* is often misunderstood and taken to mean that the mind somehow magically creates the external world every time one opens one's eyes. By idealism, I mean that the supposed 'physical world' is in fact a perceptual abstraction of regular features of the environment and is thus a 'mental construction' or limited representation of the external reality which is, in actuality, far more complex. Similarly, the term *transcendental* is widely misunderstood. I use it to mean beyond the realms of our ordinary perceptions involving normal spatio-temporal categories of organization as shall be explained in the final essay. Even simple contemplation of the modern scientific understanding of sensory reception of information from the environment can reveal to us the seemingly paradoxical issue as to why we perceive the world as moving smoothly through normal space and time when, clearly, the information from past states of entities must still be present in some form in the environment as it cannot simply be disappearing into total nonexistence as soon as our sense-organs are finished with it. Indeed, such a ridiculous epistemological view is conventionally assumed by many who ridicule idealism as involving the external world appearing and disappearing at the whim of our sense-organs. Such materialists are unwittingly espousing an epistemology resembling the Buddhist ontological mythology of Impermanence (*anitya; anicca*) and Momentariness (*kṣanika*) where momentary events just appear and disappear out of nothing. In altered states of consciousness the mind can begin to perceive transcendental aspects of the world which are vastly different from the limited experience of everyday perception (the 'mundane' or 'material' realm) upon which the naïve reductionist, materialist metaphysics, which views such limited abstractions as the actual Reality, is based.

The Sanātana Dharma

Such transcendental realms have been perceived since time

immemorial by shamans, *riṣis* (seers), yogis, and mystics and their realisations, often cloaked in mythology, form the basis of the world's great spiritual traditions. The transcendental realms have also been experienced by natural born psychics and by others whose minds have on occasion shifted spontaneously into altered states of consciousness. One such person was Richard Bucke, elected President of the Psychological Section of the British Medical Association in 1888 and elected President of the American Medico-Psychological Association in 1890. Bucke's well-known little book *Cosmic Consciousness* was published in 1901. The common underlying structure of these various revelations, stripped of the various cultural mythological overlays, constitutes the so-called Perennial Philosophy in which the 'physical world' is understood to be an emergent manifestation within the transcendental Reality constituted of *Brahman*, Pure Consciousness, Divine Light, Spirit etc. These are merely cultural labels for the one Ultimate Reality. This common structure has long been recognised within the various Indian yogic traditions whose various schools and sects argue over the details whilst accepting that they are all attempting to interpret correctly the same Reality. The underlying commonalities of the Indian yogic traditions is what really constitutes the so-called *Sanātana Dharma* (the Eternal Order or the Eternal Truth). Continuing this longstanding Indian tradition, the aforementioned Doctrine of the Unity of Faiths was propounded by the great Bengali 'saint' of the last century, Rāmakrishna *Paramahaṁsa* who meditated upon the world's great religious icons drawn from the major religions and found that all led to the one true Ultimate Reality, the Light of Pure Consciousness, the Godhead whose energetic activity manifested the entire universe.

The question as to how it is possible to make such grand cosmological claims through introspection (or how ontology can be derived from phenomenology) will be discussed in the section entitled *The Interface of Mind and Cosmos (Phenomenology and Ontology)* in the final essay. The fact that elements of the perennial wisdom can be found in all religious mythologies does not, however, give credence to religious mythologies as elements of the perennial wisdom, reflecting the structure of perceptual and conceptual 'world-construction' in the human brain, can be found in any system of human knowledge including the theories of materialist science. Indeed, we shall see how Einstein's four-dimensional space-time continuum and quantum mechanics reflect the structure of perception as much as they reflect aspects of the external world. My synthesis of Science and Mysticism shall thus proceed utilising the knowledge of the authoritative Indian yogic traditions which have developed rational philosophical systems based upon the collective testing and verification of their phenomenological revelations by countless yogic initiates over thousands of years. This distinguishes them from the lesser, popular yogic traditions which appeal to the simplistic fantasies of the uneducated and the religious theistic traditions which are based on blind faith in superstitious dogmatic creeds and personality cults which satisfy only the unthinking masses who require a simple, reassuring myth telling them of their place in the supposed great scheme of things. The Semitic religions have also branded as heresy the testimony of mystics who challenge their dogma with perennial insights and have put them to death in the past. Indeed, the Christians suppressed the Gnostic tradition (which developed under Indian influence) in which it has some of its roots because the Gnostic's assertion that direct knowledge or gnosis of Divine Reality is available to everyone through meditative contemplation does away with the need for a Church to supposedly mediate between the Divine Reality and the general population.

As stated above, in spite of the differences between the various yogic traditions, based on their particular focuses leading to abstraction of differing aspects of the one Reality, there is general agreement on the underlying commonalities and that the traditions are each only relative viewpoints. This was most clearly shown by Sri Aurobindo, India's foremost modern philosopher, in his *Synthesis of Yoga* which I shall use alongside knowledge from the great ancient traditions. We shall see that when we press on beyond the superficial differences in the various approaches, the underlying picture that emerges is one of the manifestation of the phenomenal world, the Creation, through the myriad energetic vibrations arising within the underlying Ground of all Being, the Light of Pure Consciousness which is most commonly referred to in India, following the Vedāntic tradition based on the *Upaniṣads*, as *Brahman*. Buddhism, which emerged within the ancient Indo-Aryan context dominated by Brahmanism, rejected the notion of an underlying Ground of all Being in its Doctrine of Impermanence which, as we shall see in the final essay, results from the selective focus of Buddhist yoga and the abstraction of only the superficial discontinuous events which the orthodox Indian traditions recognise as arising from the continuous substratum, the *ekatattva* (one principle). It seems clear that this selective focus on the superficial, discontinuous aspects of the vibratory activity served the Buddha's socio-political purpose of challenging the Brahmanical domination of Indian society by challenging their metaphysics as the two are interwoven in the notion of *dharma*. Such political distortions of true knowledge continue today with Marxian distortions of biological knowledge of heredity etc. and many a naïve Westerner is attracted to Buddhism on the basis of its appeal to egalitarianism, as against elitist Brahmanism, rather than through any concern for the Truth. The orthodox Indian traditions hold Buddhism to be but an unorthodox form of the *Sanātana Dharma*. Ananda Coomaraswamy, a leading Sri Lankan Buddhist scholar, stated[71]:

> *The more superficially one studies Buddhism, the more it seems to differ from the Brahmanism in which it originated; the more profound our study, the more difficult it becomes to distinguish Buddhism from Brahmanism, or to say in what respects, if any, Buddhism is really unorthodox.*

We shall see that Buddhism, although it rests upon this fundamental error and, in appealing to the masses, introduced childish mythologies relating to transmigration into the mainstream Indian tradition, does provide us with some doctrines which accord best with Reality.

Understanding Science from the deeper perspective

Contrary to naïve assumptions that materialist science will swallow up and explain all mystical phenomena in its own terms, my identification of the physical correlate of the Divine Light and the ensuing synthetic work actually involves the whole of the modern scientific picture being swallowed up into the bigger, deeper picture of Indian yogic mysticism which we may term the

Sanātana Dharma. The real issue then becomes one of explaining the superficial scientific paradigms and all the other aspects of Reality, inexplicable to or denied by materialist science, within the universal metaphysical picture of the *Sanātana Dharma*. We will see that questions such as, what is the universe created from in the first place and how an infinitesimal singularity could magically become the near-infinite expanses of the known universe, as suggested by the Big Bang hypothesis, begin to make more sense to us when considered from the perspective of the bigger, deeper picture of the *Sanātana Dharma*. The magical injection of a supposed 'consciousness' into the insentient material world of materialist science and the projection of technological mechanistic notions onto the workings of the mind are shown to be the inevitable outcome of modern materialist mythology which, due to the peculiarities of Western Christian history, has become the dominant metaphysics of the modern West. We shall see how the experimentally confirmed paradoxes of Quantum Theory indicate that the physical world is manifested from a space-time transcending realm of potentialities consisting of energetic vibrations as indicated by the *Sanātana Dharma*. The naïve reductionist, materialist pictures of the living organism as an automaton or the vehicle for the transmission of 'selfish genes' shall be shown to be the products of the extremely selective focus, the animistic projection of anthropomorphic Christian myths and of computer metaphors onto the true nature of the organism which may be understood as a manifestation of the creative play of the transcendental spirit becoming constrained by the emergence of self-limiting spatio-temporal structures at various levels of spatial order. As stated above, the limited revisionism of the emergent materialists is shown to be an insufficient broadening of focus to allow a full description of the sentient and transcendental aspects of the organismic reality just as it fails to come anywhere near to giving a full description of mental phenomena.

Not only does the *Sanātana Dharma* allow us to explain the scientific paradigms relating to the mind, physics and biology but it also allows us to begin accounting for all the other aspects of Reality which cannot be included within the materialists' narrow systems of abstractions. I shall show how human creativity and insight, paranormal phenomena, mind-body interactions and phenomena relating to the notion of *Karma*, including the modern Western reformulations of old yogic notions by the likes of Carl Jung and Rupert Sheldrake, all indicate that the Reality underlying our relative models is that described by the *Sanātana Dharma*. The jungle of confusion surrounding such mysterious notions as *Karma* and *Māyā* shall be hacked away to reveal the essential truths underlying the chaotic growth of mythologies surrounding the perennial realizations upon which such notions are based.

Knowledge from the authoritative yogic traditions shall be supplemented with knowledge from the limited scientific studies of meditation-related phenomena and from semi-speculative explanatory models developed by some distinguished scientists in order to go beyond the superficialities of conventional materialism towards an understanding of the transcendental. In spite of the bewildering array of terms (often in Sanskrit) and the countless variations upon common themes, we shall begin to deduce how such variations have been arrived at and thus we shall be able to select the best particular hypotheses in regard to particular questions by considering the compatibility of the hypotheses with the actual hard evidence and the overall framework of understanding that begins to emerge. Approaching these issues from the Indian philosophical perspective, we shall not be limited to naïve Western-style dichotomous thinking which pits one relative abstraction against another and bogs itself down in countless contradictions as is manifest in the modern arguments between Western materialist science and Western religions. Rather, we will attempt to glimpse as much of Reality as is possible, using the limited medium of language, by considering the positive distinctions of each rational, relative system of knowledge as each contains some elements of truth reflecting the actual state of affairs in the One Reality.

REFERENCES

1. Rorty, R.L. (1991) Philosophers, Novelists, and Intercultural Comparisons: Heidegger, Kundera, and Dickens. In Deutsch, E. (Ed.) *Culture and Modernity: East-West Philosophic Perspectives*. University of Hawaii Press.
2. Ayer, A.J. (1982) *Philosophy in the Twentieth Century*. Wiedenfeld and Nicolson.

3. Ramakrishna Paramahamsa. Cited in Hixon, L. (1992) *Great Swan: Meetings with Ramakrishna*. Shambhala.
4. *The Bookseller*. (London). 3rd December 1993.
5. Svensson, G. (1994) Reflections on the Problem of Identifying Mind and Brain. *Journal of Theoretical Biology: Special Issue: Mind and Matter: Essays from Biology, Physics and Philosophy*. Volume 171, No.1.
6. Bisiach, E. (1991) Understanding Consciousness: Clues from Unilateral Neglect and Related Disorders. In Milner, A.D. and Rugg, M.D. (Eds) *The Neuropsychology of Consciousness*. Academic Press.
7. Huxley, A. (1956) Knowledge and Understanding. *Vedānta and the West*. Reprinted in Bridgeman, J.H. (1992) *Huxley and God: Essays*. Harper Collins.
8. Wilber, K. (Ed.) (1982) *The Holographic Paradigm and Other Paradoxes: Exploring the Leading Edge of Science*. Shambhala.
9. Jones, R.H. (1986) *Science and Mysticism: A Comparative Study of Western Natural Science, Theravāda Buddhism and Advaita Vedānta*. Associated University Press.
10. Jung, C.G. Cited in Storr, A. (1983) *Jung: Selected Writings*. Fontana.
11. Lindahl, B.I.B. and Arhem, P. (1994) Mind as a Force Field: Comments on a New Interactionist Hypothesis. *Journal of Theoretical Biology*. Vol.171. No.1
12. Rorty, R. (*ibid.*)
13. Nandy, A. (1992) *Traditions, Tyranny and Utopias*. Oxford U.P.
14. Havel, V. (1990) quoted in Palmer, P.J. (1996) Leading from within. *Noetic Sciences Review*. No.40.
15. Rose, S., Lewontin, R.C. and Kamin, L.J. (1984) *Not in Our Genes: Biology, Ideology and Human Nature*. Penguin.
16. Wolff, S.P. (1992) *New Scientist*. 6th June.
17. *Horizon*. BBC Television. 17th April 1997.
18. *Dharmatattva*.
19. Halbfass, W. (1988) *India and Europe: An Essay in Philosophical Understanding*. Indian Edition, 1990. Motilal Banarsidass.
20. Sen, A.P. (1993) *Hindu Revivalism in Bengal 1872-1905*. Oxford U.P.
21. Jones, K.W. (1989) *The New Cambridge History of India: III. 1. Socio-Religious Reform Movements in British India*. Cambridge U.P.
22. Taimni, I.K. (1961) *The Science of Yoga*. The Theosophical Publishing House.
23. Inden, R. (1990) *Imagining India*. Blackwell.
24. Stokes, E. (1959) *The English Utilitarians and India*. Oxford U.P.
25. Mohanty, J.N. (1993) *Essays on Indian Philosophy: Traditional and Modern*. Oxford U.P.
26. *Ibid*.
27. Bohm, D. and Peat, F.D. (1989) *Science, Order and Creativity*. Routledge.
28. Kanigel, R. (1991) *The Man Who Knew Infinity: A Life of the Genius Ramanujan*. Scribners.
29. Dutta, K. and Robinson, A. (1995) *Rabindranath Tagore: The Myriad-Minded Man*. Bloomsbury.
30. Heisenberg, W. (1950) *Physics and Beyond*. Reprinted in Wilber, K. (1985) *Quantum Questions: Mystical Writings of the World's Great Physicists*. Shambhala.
31. Cox, H. (1987) A Lovers' Quarrel: The Story of Religion and Science in the West. In Singh, T.D. (Ed.) *Synthesis of Science and Religion: Critical Essays and Dialogues*. The Bhaktivedanta Institute.
32. Cited in Philip, D.S. (1986) *Perceiving India Through the Works of Nirad C. Chaudhuri, R.K. Narayan and Ved Mehta*. Oriental U.P.

33. Becker, R.O. (1990) *Cross-Currents*. Tarcher Putnam.
34. Goodwin, B.C. (1994) Towards a science of qualities. In Harman, W. and Clark, J.(eds) *New Metaphysical Foundations of Modern Science*. Institute of Noetic Sciences.
35. Dawkins, R. (1996) In *Bookseller* 12th April.
36. Clarke, J.J. (1995) *Jung on the East*. Routledge.
37. Storr, A. (1983) *Jung: Selected Writings*. Fontana.
38. Clarke, J.J. (1994) *Jung and Eastern Thought: A dialogue with the Orient*. Routledge.
39. Cited in Clarke, J.J. (1995) *ibid.*
40. Broad, C.D. (1953) from *Religion, Philosophy and Psychical Research*. Harcourt Brace. Cited in Murphy, M. (1992) *The Future of the Body*. Tarcher Putnam.
41. Inden, R. (1990) *ibid.*
42. Nandy, A. (1992) *Traditions, Tyrannies and Utopias*. Oxford U.P.
43. *Ibid.*
44. *Ibid.*
45. *Ibid.*
46. Nandy, A. (Ed.) (1988) *Science, Hegemony and Violence: A Requiem for Modernity*. Oxford U.P.
47. Bernal, M. (1987) *Black Athena: The Afro-Asiatic Roots of Classical Civilization. Volume 1. The Fabrication of Ancient Greece 1785-1985*. Free Association Books.
48. Nandy, A. (1994) *The Illegitimacy of Nationalism: Rabindranath Tagore and the Politics of Self*. Oxford U.P.
49. Nandy, A. (1994) *ibid.*
50. Nanda, B.R. (1985) *Gandhi and his Critics*. Oxford U.P.
51. Nandy, A. (1992) *ibid.*
52. Nandy, A. (1992) *ibid.*
53. Dutta and Robinson (1995) (*ibid.*).
54. Nanda, B.R. (1985) *ibid.*
55. Said, E. (1993) Representations of the Intellectual. The Reith Lectures. *The Independent*. (London) 1st July 1993.
56. Cited in Swami Prabhavananda (1979) *The Spiritual Heritage of India*. Vedanta Press.
57. Hesse, M. (1970) Hermeticism and history: An apology for the internal history of science. In R.H. Stuewer (ed) *Historical and Philosophical Perspectives of Science*. University of Minnesota Press.
58. Huntintdon, S.P. (1996) *The Clash of Civilisations and the Remarking of World Oder*. Simon & Schuster.
59. O'Brien, C.C. (1988) Nationalism and the French Revolution. In Best, G. (Ed.) *The Permanent Revolution: The French Revolution and its Legacy*. Fontana.
60. Morris, J. (1973) *Heaven's Command: An Imperial Progress*. Faber and Faber.
61. The Inquisition. *Timewatch*. BBC Television. 1994.
62. Nandy, A. (1983) *The Intimate Enemy: Loss and Recovery of Self Under Colonialism*. Oxford U.P.
63. Cited in Philip, D.S. (1986) *ibid.*
64. Cited in Philip, D.S. (1986) *ibid.*
65. Cited in Philip, D.S. (1986) *ibid.*
66. Bernal, M. (1987) *ibid.*
67. Dutta and Robinson (1995) *ibid.*
68. Kanigel, R. (1991) *ibid.*
69. Kanigel, R. (1991) *ibid.*

70. Glashow, S.Cited in Nelson, L.H. (1994) On what we say there is and why it matters: A feminist perspective on metaphysics and science. In Harman, W. and Clark, J. (eds.) As for Ref. 34.
71. Coomaraswamy, A. K. Cited in Versluis, A. (1993) *American Transcendentalism and Asian Religions.* Oxford U.P.

THE *SŪTRA*

I. This Oneness/Otherness Mystery

I walk these streets as if in blinkers
As if born of a noble breed
The madding crowd mill round the stalls
Look at these wares I do not need

Why maketh me this alien spirit
Ghost in this world of humankind
This pen for sheep, Society
These earthworms blind, led by the blind

They hide as one within the herd
And hear the things they want to hear
The bubbling froth of cola culture
Egregious to egregious ear

Ignorant of their own ignorance
But in their own esteem so wise
On premises false, great mansions build
Fed by their oracles with lies

These sheep they think they live so freely
When everywhere they live in chains
Scratch neath the sleek veneer of progress
Deep down the order old remains

Born true to my *twiceborn* inbreeding
Semi-detached, full of disdain
In civil world where saneness madness
'Tis best to stay somewhat insane

The meek they seek the crowd's approval
To 'prove' themselves to be of worth
In world where honour has no meaning
The meek shall come to rule the Earth

Submerged in crowd I feel sequestered
See not the things they see with eyes
I grant my green and blue are theirs too
Beyond raw feels what to surmise

Like tree which falls without perceiver
For me this bustle makes no sound
This noise but noise to my attention
Outside my field this noise impound

I walk upright, my sounds form language
My nakedness in clothes I hide
I live at once within this jungle
And in another world reside

But can I truly claim myself
Free from nation, race and history
Clan, class, sex, species, cosmos, fate
This oneness/otherness mystery

Were all men same, Man would be dead
We live as variants on one theme
Within the pale, most born in blindness
Few at the margins, men of dreams

The word 'waste' Nature knows no meaning
My discontent, she sees a role
By my feet scorching makes me dance
Man's restless spirit, the burning soul

She frames the eyes of the outsiders
She casts them in a foreign mould
To see beneath the surface civil
See all that glitters is not gold

The specious reas'ning of the *baniās*
Who whole world in their hands now hold
Economise with truth their salesmen
Utopia made of tinsel sold

This Lucifer reversed, this angel
Exhorting all to see its light
Exalting windows where it shines now
Though most of sky remains in night

This seemingly the least of evils
This selfish devil that we know
Presents himself as benign blessing
Though as a parasite did grow

Is selfishness our truest nature
Could not a caring human side be found
If in a world we need not struggle
Where all the fruits we crave abound

What if we would extol the Female
The woman thats's within us all
Could we transcend this manly conflict
Would everyone then have a ball

But creatures shaped in Nature's jungle
Could not so simply natures change
We'd seek false values and false status
In pecking orders all arrange

Perhaps we are some sort of virus
Set to devour Mother Gaia
Fore thundering off to foreign worlds
In chariots blazing trails of fire

Will Gaia the greedy gall garotte
Her gentle aura wearing thin
To leave the 'wonders of the world'
Mere pockmarks on her fragile skin

Of course I hear the growing chorus
Which every would-be prophet joins
To spare the fruit upon the trees
To feed our future fruit of loins

No progeny to live beyond me
I sing unchained my solo song
My verse the verse of the bystander
Perhaps in time I'll join the throng

No monad in itself has meaning
For meaning lives within the wholes
Its meaning is its greater beings
In which it plays so many roles

Where stand I midst my greater beings
No mere abcissas, ordinates
Can map me out, can give me bearings
No system gives coordinates

I turn to thee my greater beings
You dwarf me in both Time and Space
Your bonds of being all create me
And in you I create my trace

II. And Born Was I

They say that given time infinite
A chimp by chance types Shakespeare's plays
But chimp beholds no work of art
Upon its play cares not to gaze

A thing alone, thing without meaning
Torn apart from its relations
Just random noise would be such typing
Nothing stands in isolation

A beast that rises up within us
When with two backs that beast we make
I'm told that when we go to bed
A horse and crocodile we take

Vestiges of brains ancestral
Hide deep beneath our hemispheres
My greater being extends in time
Way back into primeval years

I looked upon the frontispiece
Of Wilson's controversial thesis
Became one with those savage apes
The fathers of our savage species

Shielding their own from hunting pack
Four-legged hunters on the prowl
Erect on haunches wielding sticks
With snarling grimaces and growls

Became one with those mole-like mammals
In reptiles' domain hid in holes
Till revolution razed the manor
Out came the serfs, filled masters' roles

****

If thinking minds to lizard kind
Had one day found themselves attached
Society shaped by alien rhythms
Cold-blooded ones who from eggs hatched

The cosmogony of the egg
The universe within a shell
The raging fires in heavens burn
The icy coldness of their hell

Their females not with wombs encumbered
'Tween males and females balance scales
On two legs stand the thinking reptiles
With but a vestige of their tails

Legends retold of lizards bold
Rebels who got themselves in scrapes
In epic scenes saved virgin queens
From paws of monster hairy apes

Satellites shooting to the stars
Seek out those born of foreign suns
They bear the image of Earth's firstborn
With greetings from the green-skinned ones

Thanks to some ancient cataclysm
That mammal *sapiens* first appeared
And God is not some green-skinned lizard
But aging ape with flowing beard

****

Beyond the bonds of fur and wombs
I once was one with stranger creatures
Like slimy things that crawled with fins
From water onto ancient beaches

And back down into slimy water
Way back into primeval time
In zeolites and carbon soups
Was I the clay, was I the slime

To primal times my being extends
We are stardust, we are glowing
Exploding suns in distant aeons
Seeds of Mother Earth were sowing

When *Brahman* was reborn of *Purush*
New *AUM* in newborn heavens rang
Twins Space and Time reborn through *yajña*
And born was I in this Big Bang

Oh sweet crescendo song of love
Which brings to me some absolution
Am I at one with Cosmic Will
Which fuels this cosmic evolution

Is this the joy of *līlā*, *Brahman*
I forge a link in Thy Great Chain
Art Thou like king, born with no needs
By sport his being entertains

When into Thee I am reabsorbed
Sun's rays no more shall catch my face
Amidst the ocean of *saṃsāra*
How faint the ripples of my trace

My greater being surges onwards
From milky ocean, new forms churning
Reflecting on their own creation
Then to *pralaya* all returning

I speak not to you of Superman
Man-made conscious forms I see
New phase of self-realisation
Lifeless fruit of living tree

Man constrained by Nature's tinkering
In frugal concepts all does class
New beings with new modes of thinking
Man's meagre mind shall match, surpass

But then, new modes of simulation
Want of abstraction still constrains
But one Mind grasps reality
That One Reality contains

III. *Rāshtra* is My Word for Nation

Foreigner's footsteps fall so heavy
Rastai hati, walk in street
One foot in *Bhārat,* one in Britain
With no sure ground beneath my feet

How quaint you paint this land of England
Trim hedgerows, plush these pastures green
To my imagination barren
Godmen walked not amidst these scenes

Sacred the ground where once walked Buddha
Traversed by Shankar, corners four
Endowed with legend, Krishna, Rāma
And epic poets wrote its lore

Where Indra's children came across
The Indus culture's dying trace
And learnt the ancient yogic rites
Long practised by this ancient race

Where Aryan chariots thundered East
And claimed the land along the *Gangā*
And brought the *dharma,* my forerunners
Into the deltaland of *Vaṅga*

You live in me through archetypes
In me you resurrect your themes
Oh land surrounded in memory
Oh patchwork land made up from dreams

I'll wave not the gunboats' ensign
Shipped plunder, slaves, and ruled the waves
Drake's nationalised skull and crossbones
Drapes now the crew-cut misbehaves

Degenerate, soft underbelly
Donkeys by the donkeys led
Question not the Queen's few shillings
As long as by the press gang fed

Like Hitler's last-ditch cannon fodder
Conquering days long gone before
Their captors asked, was this the *wehrmacht*
Did rabble such wage lightning war

Standard I'll bear bears chariot wheel
Of Asok, greatest of the Mauryas
Turned *ahiṃsā*, when Kalinga
Turned red with blood of conquered Oriyas

Oh *Bhārat*, always land of dreams
Ancient Otherland of magic
Turn my mind from tunnels grey
Piles of paper, dramas tragic

Not born or bred for world of *baniās*
Jñānamārga, path I follow
Quaker to my cohorts, legion
In false idols' *bhakti* wallow

No haven found in new Nālandā
Place values *hathi's* hollow tusks
Kernel I'll eat of any fruit
Not waste my time with empty husks

I kept outside these mental prisons
In which dead habit casts a pall
In which the mind and world are broken
Fragmented by these cloistered walls

Two strong men, face to face at my place
The best of both worlds I can host
But man of two worlds lives in limbo
Belongs to neither, lives a ghost

Cast out by modern *varṇadharma*
Cast out as too true to his caste
This *brahman* true, born of pariahs
Misfit, misplaced and so miscast

Refujis from world-market's downside
Up to the brighter side of town
Uprooted, gelded, gilded ghetto
As if in world turned upside down

Yet still I bonded *Mātā Bhārat*
Dug deep my roots in *Āryāvarta*
While father's sons born in *avidyā*
Know Manu not but Magna Carta

How right you were evil-eyed prophet
Waterloo to me means station
Agincourt to me some road name
Rāshtra is my word for nation

Find foes at whom to stick two fingers
On Crispin's day pulled longbow's chord
I find my kin like archer Arjun
For whom was sung Song of the Lord

Expect me not to do your duty
I'll sanction not slaughter of kin
I see through double standard *dharma*
Blur vision with dust-veil *khamsin*

Brought up since child in little England
In ways of West my mind was schooled
Taught myths about colonial rulers
Still saw the world through eyes of ruled

While still not out of single figures
Howzat! Such joy from heart would well
As peasants poor from pockmarked paddies
Sent Rāvan's *vimān's* down to hell

Evolves my mind upon small island
Drifts not from species left behind
Knew not Nehru, Nasser, Nkrumah
But knew my heart was non-aligned

I laugh at all these ersatz Westerners
Ashamed to claim their names of birth
Feel not the shame of tame subaltern
Know not what dignity is worth

IV. Bonds of Kinship

The unborn child's not blessed with choice
Its parents chosen by sheer chance
Their fortunes, failings shape its world
This victim of birth's circumstance

Ask unborn child what sort of world
If she could choose, she would be born in
She answers where her day and night
Aren't shrouded in the veil of morning

Von Humboldt had bold dreams of *bildung*
Of building new world here on Earth
Where all could fill out their potential
Not pruned to take their place at birth

The nepotists, the lechers, cliques
The *apparatchiks*, bigots, guilds
Those frightened of young blood beneath
Lay waste to what the dreamer builds

Self-images, false gods of merit
This 'Mythras' of progress through lights
But then why should unequal talents
Give unto some unequal rights

The angry young man counts his burdens
As blessings hidden in his pen
The progeny of much injustice
Meted 'by meiosis and men

****

Why bear me of these wretched beings
When all we have in common's name
Why brother me with sons prodigal
Who seem their *daitya* to disclaim

Like chicks in nest on that book cover
With empty gizzards, gaping beaks
As mother bird brings home the worms
And feeds first that which loudest squeaks

My father knew not life *grihastya*
I grew in darkness, in his shade
Wept not a tear at his good riddance
Lord Beveridge my true father played

Oh Bankim, Father of my Nation
Like me by carefree father cursed
You paved the way for lesser sons
And all his lenders reimbursed

Mine left us only debt and hardship
Mem'ries of life beneath his yoke
Though child I sensed a great weight lifted
When death paternal bondage broke

Small price to pay was poverty
My prizes money could not buy
Mind free from fear in freedom's heaven
And walking with one's head held high

The saving grace of early days
Which falsely gives them rosy tinge
The real world of which I knew naught
Did not upon my dreams impinge

Though we were poor and times uncertain
I'd hide away in story books
The far off land of adulthood
In child's eyes such adventure looks

Homely sights that once gave bearings
Now taunt me with their stagnant stares
Class, race and worldly expectations
Pollute my once clear childhood airs

I see the sons of unschooled fathers
With whom as child I talked and jested
Lost in worlds with short horizons
In adolescent minds arrested

I had the gifts of pen and paper
The hallmark of my *brahman* stock
Full sail ahead through learning's ocean
Then floundering on earning's rocks

And earning values not true knowledge
Like peasants in its mud we toil
Nursuried in such fertile compost
Replanted in such barren soil

This worldly soil in which weeds flourish
Their *raison d'être* vegetation
Saps the soul of sapling, Peepul
Which gives itself for contemplation

The man-made forest prunes the shoots
And all that grow are narrow Pines
In sunless shade, the creepers climb
Up rotten trees, the rotten vines

And chained to ground by roots unchosen
That nourished me but hold me down
Wouldst I were born a footloose being
Born free to find my own true ground

Now as I ripen into manhood
And start to loosen childhood straits
I come to see in my behaviour
The traces of my parents' traits

Enslave me with these bonds of kinship
Which even death can't tear apart
Make me perform such sacrifices
And pin me down through my soft heart

V. Two Two-Legged Human Races

Fate brought this child across the waters
To live in this privileged clime
And History shaped new world around me
I live in this privileged time

My parents born into a world with
Two two-legged human races
The white men who called all the shots and
Natives taught to know their places

Times when the Morning Post had readers
Raising funds for General Dyer
Twenty-eight thousand pounds for him
Who at Amritsar opened fire

Remember times, lest we forget
In France and Flanders millions fell
Young men my age dreamt not of heavens
Just dreamt of getting out of hell

Brave new worlds built for war heroes
Confidence lost turned to rubble
When in the booming, busting cycles
Burst the booming Twenties bubble

Though in my world of 'full employment'
The countless jobless still remain
There still remains a world of difference
Which shields us from the Thirties' pains

Built in one country, 'Socialism'
World marvelled at industrial surge
Post-Fordist world commands its ruin
And reins the nightmare reign of purge

Then burst the boil of total warfare
With countless million lives cut short
Century's great watershed of bloodshed
For us such welcome changes brought

And I who hurt at simple taunting
Inadequates who vent their 'views'
Cannot in my new world imagine
What life was like for Gypsies, Jews . . .

Austerity amidst the ruins
And Welfare State, cradle to grave
Reactionary world of Eden
Britannia dreamt she ruled the waves

The affluent society bought
Effulgent times for Western youth
Stormed Darkness' Castle with their swords
To free the *fellah*, free the truth

Fiery blast from Fanon, "Leave this Europe . . ."
Resounded on Left bank of Seine
The slaughterers-of-Setif's children
Cried, *"Algerie algerienne"*

Les Temps Modernes reflected Sartre
Simone de Beauvoir by his side
Who taught the once-dutiful daughters
Not to become dutiful brides

A century after Sherman marched
From old Atlanta to the sea
Sang as they rode the Freedom Riders
Through Pharaoh's land to set slaves free

Then Mao Zedong was Prometheus
Across the world his red sparks flew
Each place they fell, found tinderboxes
The reddish fire arose anew

Red sparks flew into Naxalbari
India's "Spring Thunder" Beijing hailed
While in the late spring May in Paris
The new Bastilles young France assailed

From Vietnam resounded Tet
From trail of ho ho Ho Chi Minh
Cambodia, Laos like Vietnam
Heard Rolling Thunder's hellish din

And born was I amidst this thunder
Decolonialising youthful thought
From Eurocentric superstition
Ancien regime's mental support

For in the Old World Humanism
Alone in Europe true Men born
To treat the natives as subhuman
To keep them in a state forlorn

White myths of how the world's great wonders
All had their roots in Ancient Greece
Though Egypt Danaos brought to Argos
Kadmos who brought true 'Golden Fleece'

Born of Phoenicia, Prince of Thebes
Barbarians taught, taught Greeks to write
Whilst Danaos was kin to Aegyptos
Like Kekrops, Athens built for *Nēit*

Europa, Princess of Phoenicia
Mother of Minos, King of Crete
In ancient time, in uncouth Europe
Walked cultured Afro-Asian feet

Eusebius claimed that Socrates
With learned Indians conversed
It seems with such old Indian thought
Student of Socrates rehearsed

Now sun it rises East in *Nihon*
So gone technic'lly unfit man
The slogan old "Look West" no longer
Now say, "Look East, learn frsom Japan"

****

I hear them moan, problems of plenty
My affluent cohort born so blind
Though I too share in spoils of Europe
I see through the postmodern mind

Yes I plead guilty to averting
My eyes from facts of world so cruel
If rich want richer cakes to gobble
Poor masses must make do with gruel

The tadpoles, large, in crowded ponds
Substance secrete which growth can stunt
Not in themselves for they grow faster
By keeping down the little runts

I see neocolonial suckers
Sucking in the world's resources
Diplomacy of flying gunboats
With bombs the Open Door enforces

Plan of the world it differs little
From the old maps made by Mercator
Designed so Northern states inflating
While shrinking those near the Equator

Though blurred, the two worlds still remain
Not spoken, seen by Western eyes
Reflection sees Narcissus media
The sophists, blind to hidden lies

Those holding nations whole as hostage
With terrorist machines of state
Then sermons preach on barbarism
Over their individual's fate

Death squad dictators' puppeteers
Shareholders in modern day slaves
Scream "Violence!" when victim fights back
Of law and order rant and rave

I ask why is it decent people
Stop not such deeds done in their names
Part powerless, emergent forces
And part misled from real aims

Some show outrage at great outrages
But question not the 'quiet violence'
Worst of all the loudmouthed liberals
Who know on what to keep their silence

VI. Thou Art the Reason

Some say we live for procreation
As vehicles for selfish genes
Programmed to act for kin selection
Increase our alleles in the demes

And so arise the bonds of kinship
Through subconscious self-selection
And to ensure the genes' survival
For other sex this predilection

After those lust who speak through bodies
Yet long for her who speaks through head
Where hideth thou Śakuntalā
You in whom all at once is said

Perhaps I've passed you by unknowing
Dull urban drone it drowns our calls
May be so near me, lying hidden
In this dense undergrowth of walls

Oh wouldst I had your luck Pygmalion
Wouldst I my ideal partner make
Or wouldst I had the eye of eagle
Like *Brahman* of each soul partake

But born am I a mortal being
Partake of what my world does yield
No time have I this Earth to scour
This cup of dice my playing field

Of heavens dream not cursed by Time
World of ideals, eternal youth
Sterile this world my mind creates
Monotony, infernal truth

The sweetest love both sword and shield
With us in lions' pit is hurled
For when we turn to face each other
No face does face sad facts of world

This love, this need to share one's being
Part born of lust yet lust transcends
Gives purpose to two pointless monads
When on the other each depends

And you whom once I'd pass unnoticed
Appear anew before my eyes
Was I so blind not to have noticed
Or were you wearing a disguise

I was so taut, so full of tension
Restless my quiver, arrows full
Oh now at last I find my archer
Who can this highstrung bowstring pull

I was so taut, so full of tension
A careless stroke and I would break
Oh now at last I find my fiddler
With whom I'll wondrous music make

****

Oh gliding grace, curvaceous face
Slight, silky, slender-contoured being
Born is this vision to behold you
Thou art the reason for all seeing

Soft songbird voice, melodic noise
Dancing on air, spring from lips glistening
Formed is this memory to enrol you
Thou art the reason for all listening

Flow wispy locks, flow teasing frocks
Hints of heavenly form concealing
Born is my body to enfold you
Thou art the reason for all feeling

Transfixing smiles, womanly wiles
Each moment with you pleasure giving
Worn is this ring for I betroth you
Thou art the reason for all living

Playfully coy, gasping in joy
Clasping me yet my spirit freeing
Sworn is this union, I behove you
Thou art the reason for all being

* * * *

Awakes perception of each trait
Subjected to acute dissection
Each tiny morsel of your being
I eat as breakfast of perfection

I ponder hours upon your past
Detective delves in mystery
What factors played to form you such
You are my era of history

Each curl of your hand-written letter
Perused to find its hidden meaning
You are the medium and its message
You are the wisdom I am gleaning

Your gentle pull on silken locks
I'd feel if in antipodes
You are my action-at-a-distance
Mysterious pull between bodies

My ears discern each small inflection
My mind replays each of your sighs
You are my *AUM* of meditation
You are the truth I realise

VII. We are Two Branches of One River

We are two branches of one river
I am the Wye, you are the Exe
And I am Man and thou art Woman
Thou art my fairer, gentler sex

I am the raging, roaring torrent
I cut the path of least resistance
You are the fertile flow of delta
You share your load for our subsistence

I am your fugue composed by Nature
My countless seed my one true asset
The cutting edge of variation
The species' jewel I multifacet

Our forms unfold in common fashion
Choreographed to the same tune
Yet I prance Man and thou dance Woman
Like ray of sun and ray of moon

Thou art the ground of human being
Thou art the pattern of default
Would-be Man would be born 'Woman'
If impulse-male came to a halt

* * * *

These differences of dimorphism
Born of this simple impulse-male
So much the same yet somehow not so
What secrets hide behind the veil

How much of us is shaped by nurture
How much of us is fixed, ingrained
Are we the products of tradition
Or truly by our sex enchained

For we who boast that mind demarcates
Above the beasts, mind Mankind raises
Have kept you down through our brute muscle
Louder voices, selfsame praises

As Nature's whims had made you Mother
And gave you milk to feed the young
We kept you home and kept you captive
And kept your noble deeds unsung

You who have borne the countless labours
Of every would-be Hercules
Of Alexander and Lysander
And all the other men like these

He spun such yarns, the chronicler
The patron's pleasure swayed his pen
Hero worship, hagiographer
But 'biographies' of great men

Within the *Gītā* women classed
With base-born serfs and artisans
We named the womb of all creation
Purush, the Male, primeval Man

Once born *twiceborn* from body *Purush*
Born status from status of part
What status bears the rib of Adam
What caste was cast from cage of heart

No good was fertile Mother Goddess
Sought warring nomads, victory
So sky too filled with warring chariots
In Bronze Age epic history

When Aryans entered Tantric *Vanga*
With *devīs* the *brahmans* at odds
Soon made them spokes in cosmic *chakra*
By making them wives of our gods

For laws and 'progress' Europe lauded
Its ancestors, Athens and Rome
Far cry from code of Hammurabi
Hellenes held Helens *homer* home

French men and women stormed the Bastille
Much of the Rights of Man was said
When sisters questioned *patrie*-archy
The brothers said, "Off with their heads"

When women worked down mines and in mills
Words stirring new Isaiah writes
You have nothing to lose but your chains
Working men of all lands unite

World's work you bear two-thirds of burden
Come home and work again when spent
Underpaid for equal labour
World's property own one per cent

****

I who feel one with oppressed peoples
Like victims of colonial crime
Still cannot truly share your feelings
Oppressed since birth since dawn of time

I bear the burden Oriental
Held down by white men below par
Though gone the overt subjugation
My *weltanschauung* still bears the scar

I know too well of smug self-sureness
Sophistry of Western power
Knowing too well its own injustice
Makes its victims' truths sound sour

I know the subtle power of media
Selecting Muslim stereotype
The anguished cries of dispossessed ones
Distorted through the media hype

Such empathy is asymptotic
I cannot see through female eyes
I see too well the contradiction
For within me the 'problem' lies

My conscious mind may think with reason
But *homunculi* lurk behind
Irrational, unthinking bigots
Hide deep in my subconscious mind

I subdue little men with reason
In my world of conscious living
Subconscious subtext of behaviour
Submerged messages still giving

Perhaps my genes are shaped to 'see' you
Vessels for their reproduction
Though human minds disengage *kāma*
See mere objects for seduction

Perception discriminatory
Selects your curves for my attention
Blind to the *gestalt* of your being
Abstracting only one dimension

But this, it seems, is natural process
Inbuilt for seeking out our mates
But carried into social discourse
False concept now discriminates

The misogynous fear of 'upstarts'
Like all old forms of privilege
Acts subtly to maintain injustice
By making sure men have an edge

Injustices not solved so simply
Who would partake of labour menial
If foreign migrants not exploited
For jobs that no one finds congenial

And so the case with woman housewife
Domestic servants yoked with ring
And even more with woman mother
For who can migrant mothers bring

Few truly hold such views unseemly
But matters not what people say
For higher forces shape Society
Emergent systems act this way

Male mind may be so atomistic
Blind to continuous work like waves
Like 'quiet violence', household work
Unjust, unspoken, fortune saves

And now it seems perhaps the impulse
Plays different games within our brains
But fools see sport as gains and losses
Why not both outcomes equal gains

And here again meaning of meaning
In social nexus values stand
If variants are given values
They are thus scarred with mental brands

Prophecy self-fulfilling beckons
When the schoolteacher then forgets
These differences but norms, statistics
Not essences by Nature set

* * * *

In Kipling's day when Orient 'female'
White men were schooled to be 'real men'
To conquer, subjugate the Other
To master 'womanlike' heathen

If you could show no true emotion
And do what Empire wanted done
Obey all orders without question
Then you would be a Man my son

If this is Man, thank God for Woman
Thank God for our feminine side
Conquers by caring and concurring
Behind those Graecian masks won't hide

Is not my Nation-God a female
Bankim saw Durgā, many-limbed
She bore her arms with *shakti* power
Wrote *Bande Mātaram*, her hymn

My *Bhārat Mātā* not Britannia
No pompous, overbearing song
The symbol of long-suffering Mother
Shakti, both feminine and strong

VIII. Bande Mātaram

In this age of falling curtains
False prophets final triumphs portend
One true invisible-handed god
As if 'History' were near its end

Species born of mortal mind
Immutable, at the mercy of Time
Tigers on paper leapt not from page
Though noble cause and words sublime

No brainchild bold the world bazaar
Its creepy growth as grows a mould
On rot it feeds, organic, civil
Now whole world has in hyphal hold

'I worship no idol', the prophet proclaims
'My God no creature of my mind
None may behold Invisible Hand
His labour's fruits though all will find

'Omnipresent, omniscient
His fruits fulfil all human needs
New needs we know not that exist
To them the shepherd His flock leads

'His temples scrape the city skies
In all our homes his unseen waves
Adorned His youth in sacraments
New subject nations' souls he saves'

****

Though sign of cross knots round my neck
Schools glorifying Greece and Rome
Britannia rules but surface waves
In depths of heart *Bhārat* my home

I journeyed East above the clouds
To tread once more my Motherland
Half-hearted though her love for Him
In tightening grip of Unseen Hand

Plentiful crops painted *Gangā's* plain
Buffer stocks bulged in government keeps
Pushing up prices in the bazaar
Near half the nation went hungry to sleep

Push exports, grain, while half go hungry
Sing praise of Revolution Green
Push, expel poor to bursting *bustees*
Dark traits transplanted social gene

Oh wretched *ryot*, Son of the Soil
Could we ever as true brothers pass
My Rām, 'high' Rām of Vālmīki
Your Rām, 'low' Rām of Tulsīdās

My Rām he speaks in noble Sanskrit
Your Rām he speaks in common tongue
Can we two dream same *Rāmarājya*
Could we one day sing the same song

I dream great dreams of *Mahā Bhārat*
High culture, Science, bejewel Her crown
Not drained, our brains reach for the sky
No ceilings, glass, to hold them down

Adrift since babe by London's river
Dream of home, shoulder to cry on
By *Gangā* find another nation
Live the lie of my New Zion

No mortar bombings, forced expulsions
Just market forces dispossessed you
You who 'make bomb' from fertilisers
Unseen Hand's green fingers blessed you

You dream dreams born of half-filled stomachs
Dreams, gaudy, framed in *masala* mill
We took the books you should have opened
Ope bootleg bottles, time to kill

What means to you our sense of history
Our dreams to be a superpower
Was *Bhārat* ever 'Great' for you
What meant to you the Midnight Hour

What means to you our notion *Bhārat*
What far horizons do you chart
Live day-to-day and cross your world
In national vehicle, bullock cart

What good do you these atom-smashers
New symbols of our nation's pride
What good to you our talk of Space Age
For who's being taken for a ride

You sit on ground in dusty *grams*
Where lights still burn with kerosene
Watch pictures from another world
Beamed down from space to TV screen

The glossy goods and gadgets new
Imported from much richer lands
For status prized by city folk
New marks of caste, the Western brands

As meek now speak through ballot boxes
Who stops to question, who asks why
Who makes the most from modernising
Guardians Aryan speak Aryan Lie

Here the Song of Democracy
Is truly this the anthem for us
For we have written every verse
Letting you just hum the chorus

****

Oh *Shūdra, Dalit, Ādivāsī*
'Twas always 'Brahman Congress' *bhai*
Swarāj my birthright, I will have it
Now *Hindūstān hamara hai!*

The *satyagrāhi* brought you out
All *khādī*-clad, we stood as one
His simple dreams of *Rāmarājya*
Forgotten when our need was gone

The brahman *rājā* bought them out
The *zamīndārs* with *lakhs* for land
Wrote paper laws, put ceilings down
Waived paper laws, no *lathi* hand

When Indhira said *garibi hatao*
Then brahman stood by *harijan*
But those between us, turned against us
Turned 'Kaṃsa' out, new Nārāyan

And now we see the rise of Backwards
Like *kisāns* born of Krishna's clan
What vision have these uncouth upstarts
What heritage, far-sighted plan

Progress I greet with reservations
New power for those long kept down
But fear their dreams to me a nightmare
Culture Cola on which I frown

But fear I more this new Rām mania
This *Hindutva*, Army of Shiva
Ayodhyā, *kar sevaks, rath jatra*
Stoking up this saffron fever

Deep down I too hold *Hindu Rāshtra*
Like author of *Ānandamaṭh*
But with Ramkrishna, hold all faiths
To the same goal but various paths

Though they may turn their heads to Mecca
And disparage *dharma sanātan*
Īśvara, Allah te re nahm
Shobake sanmity de Bhagavān

But those who disclaim *Bhārat Mātā*
And seek one of her arms to break
Shall find I claim their home as sacred
And not an inch I'd let them take

I too am torn 'tween state and union
To *Āryāvarta* bond by caste
But mind of Bengal nonconformist
Shaped by non-Aryan *Shūdra* past

A shadow empire, 'wolf' as 'sheep'?
Shaped by the swords of empires old
But unity our path to greatness
Together *Bhārat* we must hold

Half-heartedly condone repression
Of rebels who'd disrupt our dreams
Comes a poor second sometimes, Justice
When it conflicts with our grand schemes

Oh natives of Narmada valley
With you I'm not sure where I stand
You stand, some say, in way of progress
Our dams would stand to drown your land

* * * *

Our neighbours great, beyond the mountains
Who lived by Buddha's *Ārya Dharma*
By *dharma* communal live now
And not by rich men's myths of *karma*

(*Borolok* in his big *bhavan*
Chotolok crammed into *bustees*
Karma made them high and lowly
And made brahmans estate's trustees)

And while beloved *Bhārat Mātā*
Pales in public squalor, private greed
The Middle Kingdom's Iron Rice-bowl
One billion hungry mouths does feed

Some mourn but thousand angry young ones
The well-schooled mouse like lion roars
Half *crore* each year we feed to Moloch
Their feeble cries *Mātā* ignores

Despite/because of this great *yajña*
No holding back this human ocean
This rising tide that might engulf us
This silent growth, this huge explosion

What is the value of this 'freedom'
From what the wretched poor unfettered
Freedom to go through life malnourished
Freedom that keeps two thirds unlettered

That famous line in *Mother India*
'What do you want, food or mother?'
The hungry son spat out his mouthful
Followed by his hungry brother

The angry son shot usurer down
And tried to abduct usurer's daughter
But shot, himself, by his own mother
What's right's what Hindu *dharma* taught her

Once-fiery reds and Naxalites
Now lay their hammers, sickles down
As Mother marries Unseen Hand
And prays that manna trickles down

His face adorns a million *pān* shops
The angry son 'Mahātma' spurned
Some dream that he'll return to save us
Our *Neta* Subhas who never returned

We look back on his 'brother's' kingship
Look back on all those chances missed
Look back through tomes of *Bhārat's* history
Where in them lies Destiny's tryst?

Spoke flowery words, vague global rambling
Toothless reforms, half-hearted wool
The *soma* Freedom's drunk half measure
Will *Bhārat* ever drink it full

IX. Satanic Mills

Come hither oh prophets of the bazaar
See the Unseen One *Bhārat Mātā* embrace
Come hither and see how the other half dies
On seeing Unseen's unmasked face

'Follow our footsteps', the prophets replied
'All you need do is open your doors
Do as we do and you too shall find
The forbidden fruit will one day be yours

'Worship with your heart Invisible Hand
And homespun idols false destroy
Though at first you'll find the going rough
We bring good tidings, comfort, joy'

Religions, gods legitimate orders
Thus of such gods the privileged preach
Can we by following Christians' progress
The same Celestial City reach

We see through words of noble missions
We who spoke out through Krishna Menon
Know public words like Kennedy's
And secret words like those of Kennan

Those forcing others' doors to open
So freedoms theirs' we don't restrict
Are like ex-harlots, now retired
Now closing down red light districts

The Cold War countries now called Tigers
Those who fed off neighbours' slaughter
Compare the funding of Bhilai
To the funding of Yawata

For foreign money, cash crops grown
On Western gurus' good advice
Less food at home, but lux'ry foods
For rich world at a bargain price

And all enjoined to grow the same
Watch prices fall for produce raw
While finished goods from those who gain
In real terms costs even more

But centuries old, world market system
For which the bazaar prophets spoke
They only show its mature manhood
It's bastard birth 'neath history's cloak

* * * *

I thus consulted kindred spirits
From near and distant lands and ages
Who spoke to me as I sat, listened
As danced my eyes across the pages

Behold communication magic
With those afar and those unborn
Together brings those of an ilk
Whom Space and Time apart have torn

I turned the pages of the books
Turning over unturned stones
Opening up a dingy cupboard
Which was full of human bones

As danced my eyes, was tranced my mind
By things that I did read
I heard faint voices 'tween the lines
Of which I soon took heed

'Go tell the Christians, Stranger
Tell them that here we lie
In obedience to their orders
Hidden from History's eye

'Read you true book of History'
Lamented voices faint
'Writ large across the world in blood
Which soul of Europe taints'

From pages rose ancestral voices
In lilting tone of mother tongue
For children of my foster parents
The Ballad of Bengal they sung

'You paid us first for goods in silver
Which Spaniards paid for negro flesh
But longed to save your slavers' bullion
Like cyclone came to Bangla *desh*

'Calico, silk, our finest muslin
Across old Europe highly prized
So your Satanic mills could flourish
India you deindustrialised

'Preached 'free trade' and raised huge tariffs
Fabric walls we could not breach
Broke weavers fingers, cut their thumbs
India's plains their bones did bleach

'The thriving trade of Bengal's textiles
Just like her cloth you tore asunder
Your *Nabob* parvenus brought *loot* home
The Hindi word to rob and plunder

'Too much *loot* for lives of luxury
So *loot* found work through speculation
Primed forge and clanking loom and engine
World's first industrial revolution

'And what of India's richest province
Left pauperised once-gold Bengal
What tribute paid to your great tribute
Built grimy mill and Taj Mahal

'You blacken name Sirāj-ud-Daula
Upon whose sceptre you impinged
Mere forty died from his neglect
The Lion's tail was barely singed

'No cricket played on Plassey's field
The Lion tried to fix the match
No cricket game, but saved by rain
A thunderstorm did India snatch

'Still rung in mem'ry, cannonade
You wrung Bengal, to the last drop
Her blood you sucked like thirsty leeches
We dropped like flies when failed the crop

'While locked in famine was Bengal
Company locked grain in magazines
Count to ten million, then count forty
To see what 'Plassey' really means'

****

Some think that they lie far-removed
Casualties of colonial crime
My people still recall with horror
What happened in my parents' time

When Rising Sun and Springing Tiger
Seemed set to cross our Eastern border
The healthy harvest was exported
Came famine through colonial order

'A *kathal* bought his last few *paisa*
To quell his hungry children's cries
He disappeared whilst they devoured it
Than see them die before his eyes

'They haunted doorways in Calcutta
For *fanna* begged, not even rice
Begged the wastewater from the ricepan
The death toll was a million thrice'

X. *Lebensraum*

Apartheid or our *varṇadharma*
Lets those we conquered rise again
Less evil than extermination
Though generations bear the pain

Condemn outright the great Red Terror
On which the late red system built
Red purges born of settlers' urges
Let History also judge their guilt

Red spirits haunt Protestant Ethic
New Europe in New World you build
Old World germs cleared Pilgrim's conscience
But terror *terra nulles* filled

'When White Man first crossed the wide waters
He was but a very little man
His legs were cramped, sat long in boat
To light a fire he begged some land

'He warmed himself before our fire
Our hominy ate and huge became
Bestrode the mountains with one step
Feet covered valleys and the plains

'On moon head rested, became our Great Father
Hand grasped the Eastern and Western seas
I heard his talks, all begin and end thus
"Get a little further, you're too near me"'

****

Talk not of 'Wild West', Connecticut Yankee
Or chivalry at King Arthur's court
I hear the screams of burning Pequots
Your savagery at the Mystic fort

As lawless settlers rout the Redcoats
Appalachian Frontier Westward rolls
Quill of Common Sense of what Man writes
These times that tryeth Red Men's souls

Your greed knows no frontiers, white settler
You scalp for bounty, rape and ravage
As Blackfoot signs your gunpoint treaty
Hear noble words of noble savage

'Our land is worth more than your money
By flames of fire it shall not perish
While shines the sun and waters flow
Both men and beasts our land shall nourish

'We cannot sell lives of men or beasts
To sell this land is more than wrong
Great Spirit put it here for us
To us this land does not belong

'You can count your money and burn it
Within the nod of a buffalo's head
Great Spirit alone can count blades of grass
Of these plains on which you tread

'We will give to you as a present
Any thing you can take with your hands
Your wagon carts, your iron-horses
But never shall you take the land!'

Now hear the White Man's verses blank
A heart as cold as frost is white
The land was ours fore we the land's
This land to us 'The Gift Outright'

First man to put a fence 'round land
And claim the right proprietary
And find some fools so taken in
The founder of Civil Society

The Cherokees were 'civilised'
They learnt to live as lived the Whites
When gold was struck, Whites craved their land
They took their case to court to fight

They took their case to capital
And White Chief Justice did endorse it
But Jackson, 'General Genocide'
Laughed, 'Now let him try to enforce it'

Hear you White Chief's words civilised
To his own laws he turns deaf ears
Turned out of home to Oklahoma
They perished on the Trail of Tears

The satrap White of California
Upon such issues words succinct
'Goes on war of extermination'
Until the Indian race extinct'

Where now they make cowboy pics, programs
Once pogroms sealed the Indians' fate
Wiped out villages, vigilantes
Soon after Polk seized Golden State

Of Church of Christ, John Chivington
Black Kettle not his cup of tea
Smoked pipe of peace with Washington
Flew Stars and Stripes above tepee

They rallied round the flag, Cheyenne
And waved flags white, mercy to seek
Baptised them, John, into 'good Indians'
Ran red the water of Sand Creek

Cut dead squaws wombs you sons of Caesar
Unborn left tossed by mothers' sides
Cut private parts from redskin women
Worn stretched on hats in ranks you'd ride

Their wardance danced, tribes of the plains
Red Cloud rained blood on soldiers blue
Forced forked-tongue snakes to sue for peace
And leave the sacred land of Sioux

But White Man's paper counts for naught
And gold he craved in Sioux's Black Hills
Why throw greenbacks on soldiers blue
His ends he met with Buff'lo Bills

Great rumbling cloud of sirloin sinew
Across the trembling plains you thundered
Your surge oceanic, sixty million
Hunted down to just one hundred!

Starved into camps of concentration
Kept like two-legged beasts or game
Stole nineteen-twentieths of your homelands
But kept for half their states your names

Dance the Ghost Dance of Wovoka
Once spirits free, now caged in pen
Oh roll up ground like a great carpet
And rid us of these pale-skinned men

Oh swansong sad of murdered race
How could this mad dream come to be
Still shot you as you sang and danced
In carpet white at Wounded Knee

****

South of the river Rio Grande
Lived Indians, million times four-score
Million times four in Sixteen Fifty
Cut down by the conquistadors

Oh settler, grave is your dilemma
You turn hosts homes into their graves
Yet also want to steal their labour
To build your Europe New with slaves

So sailed the ships across Atlantic
Trade which then made greatest profit
Ship crammed with negroes like sardines
Chained so they could not jump off it

Before the Century Nineteenth opened
Far fewer saw America
Of freemen settlers leaving Europe
Than men in chains from Africa

They speak of spirit pioneering
And of the plough that broke the plains
Not of the blacks who broke their backs
And built America in chains

Condemn misdeeds of failed great systems
The terror centralised by state
Yet keep mouths shut on diffuse terror
Which served to fill the Western plate
The poisoned flour left in Tasmania
Wiping out the vermin human
The murder mass of wretched peoples
In the name of Doctrine Truman

And on they went these threnodies
From each enslaved and murdered race
Who paid for Europe's luxury
Who died for Europe's living space

****

After the cuckoos' war of trenches
The vanquished nation at Versailles
Deprived of distant *lebensraum*
Upon her neighbours cast her eye

Wrote future *führer* in *Mein Kampf*
How British Empire he admired
His nation would find its own India
So parts of Europe he acquired

Brought home to roost Colonialism
And Europe finally got a share
Of bitter-tasting medicine
Prescribed for patients born elsewhere

Swallow your words you hypocrite Europe
'Freedom, self-determination'
Faced with your own true alter-ego
Slavery and extermination

Saved from herself by comrades' blood
And wealth built on Red genocide
For crimes against humanity
Just a few axis-men were tried

XI. Indo-Europe

XI(a). *Chol Dilli*

Our M.N. Roy sought help from Kaiser
In Berlin during first Great War
Sent ships of arms to help free India
Got seized before they reached our shores

Again Bengal had son in Berlin
Moscow would not help our *Neta*
'Our enemy's enemy is our friend'
Subhas fared a little better

In Mozambique from U-boat surfaced
Again in Lion City's port
Rallying on his Springing Tiger
'*Chol Dilli* ! On to the Red Fort'

They marched as Indian Freedom Fighters
Though fighting with the Rising Sun
Through jungles of Malaya, Burma
They had the British on the run

But overstretched and way outnumbered
At Imphal came the sure defeat
But barely inside India's borders
They had to turn and beat retreat

As *sahebs* hunted down the Tiger
The jungle war was all but lost
He read again of Ireland's struggle
And all the noble lives it cost

Though Ireland's heroes brave died fighting
Their spirit lived for all to see
Spirit of Freedom undefeated
Ensured that Ireland would be free

And in defeat *Neta's* lieutenants
At last appeared at the Red Fort
Which for the purpose of show trial
The *sahebs* turned into a court

How loudly Churchill ranted, raved
Would fight on, Britain, to be free
Even Nehru dusted down his robes
It's right for you, why wrong for me?

Had been a house divided, *Bhārat*
As Jinnah pressed for Pakistan
But stood as one as stood the three
A Sikh, Hindu and *Musulman*

Brown troops refused to leave their barracks
The brown-skinned sailors mutinied
White troops shot down our striking workers
Demanding that three men be freed

Morrison's men came midst the mayhem
Saw insolence of soldiers brown
And understood on bankrupt Empire
The sun must finally come down

XI(b). *Old Indian Air*

Third Reich that broke the British Empire
Talked 'Aryan Race', wore *swastikas*
Familiar words, familiar symbol
In *Bhārat's* books and *patrikas*

How was it that this old *Hindūtva*
Had in this way become transformed
Inverted our gammadion
Beneath this standard troopers stormed

Old emigre our ancient culture
Preceded Roy to Germany
Played part in shaping cataclysm
Reshaped the world, set *Bhārat* free

To thee I pay homage, William Jones
Āchārya of Sanskrit translation
You helped reclaim our heritage
Oh midwife to the Indian Nation

You found the language of the Aryans
To Latin *dada*, same with Greek
Deduced before we went our ways
A common tongue we used to speak

Enlightened lover of Kālidās
Your countrymen still find it hard
To contemplate that darkie poet
Surpassed or even matched their bard

But not so in the land of Prussia
Not *sahebs* keeping up appearance
Our ancients their 'ancestors, brothers'
Their moderns our ancients' adherents

Old Indian air surrounded them
And Schopenhauer took full breath
It was the solace of his life
It was the solace of his death

Early engrafted superstition
Choking Bible-milk, mind weaning
Unbridled thought of kindred spirits
So thoroughly his mind was cleaning

Wilhelm von Humboldt who Berlin's
Great university had founded
Thanked God he was alive still when
The *Gītā* in his land resounded

Great tuba blasts, so deep, profound
Bellowed forth from Rhine *Valhalla*
Composed in notes of *doh re mi soh*
With hints of ancient *rāga, tāla*

Was *noumenon* born née *nirguṇa*
Jagati jog the mind of Hegel
Who lectured with the new *vedāntin*
While championing the Aryans, Schlegel

And when the smoothest stones of Newton
Roughened by new quantum reasoning
Said Heisenberg his own subconscious
Had a trace of Vedic seasoning

Schrödinger did without the matrix
Made new wave function cloud the quanta
He fled the Nazi cloud o'er Europe
Wrote *What is Life* with the *Vedānta*

At Nuremburg the *führer* raved
He'd 'purify' the Aryan Race
At Auschwitz far from *Āryāvarta*
The ancient *Manusmriti's* trace

XI(c). *A Nation Born Through Synthesis*

Said Bacon that these three inventions
Gunpowder, the compass magnetic
And printing changed the face of world
Of course all three were Asiatic

The mechanical clock had also
Come to Europe from far China
Christian cosmos became clockwork
Fashioned by the Grand Designer

Yet in their ancient birthplace, China
These wonders caused no great upheaval
But when transplanted into Europe
They dragged her from Age Medieval

For China, world by Tao self-governed
While Europe's God external cause
Who lays down rules which Nature follows
Her scientists strove to find these laws

With compass, bullets, cannonballs
So Europe won the world's compliance
And in the wake of cannonballs
The world awoke to Europe's science

As Orient does live in Europe
So too does Europe live in me
Transplanted into India's thinking
So much of West's philosophy

Idea of Progress, Humanism
The scientific frame of mind
Such useful notions, Nation's fathers
With *Hindūdharma* soon combined

We follow great Shankaracharya's
Upanisadic exegesis
Reclaiming *Bhārat* from the Buddha
By conflict not but by Synthesis

Your men of 'God' tried to convert us
Laughed at our idols, Reverend Duff
We synthesised your ways with Vedas
And so his onslaught did rebuff

Fools shaping 'God' in their own image
Found no audience for their lecture
Our idols we knew were just symbols
For that which we cannot picture

The *bhaktimarga* for the simple
Uneducated laity
The high *Vedānta* for those grasping
'Ungraspable' through *naiti*

Before the reign of Queen Victoria
When Britons ruled by landed gentry
In India followed Indian customs
Refusing missionaries entry

But came to power middle classes
Reformist Whigs, evangelising
In India came the *pukka saheb*
Through such bourgeois proselytising

Transformed into a race apart
Thought born to 'civilising' mission
Translated possessions of plunder
Into a grand imperial vision

They would 'uplift' us, 'educate' us
Colleges they would establish
Wrote Rammohun Roy to Lord Amherst
Teach not Sanskrit, teach us English

We learnt the wisdom of the West
Took Newton, Shakespeare to our hearts
Yet Kipling called us *bandor lok*
The monkeys aping White Man's parts

Oh Rudyard you who dreamt in Hindi
As Indian White in India born
Outcast when sent to school in England
On us you turned self-hating scorn

The *babu* fought not like the martials
Yet in the Lion's paw stuck thorn
By spreading word to far-flung districts
That a New *Bhārat* would be born

At first we welcomed Western Progress
Fine talk of fairness, equal rights
But blocked was progress up the ladder
On new horizons set our sights

The first English-taught generation
Had the watchword, Rationalism
But came the second generation
With new watchword, Nationalism

When first he heard of Revolution
Of nothing else he'd think or speak
All that day spent Vivekānanda
Shouting out *Vive la Republique* !

Said Nehru this to Monsieur Malraux
Display here not your sculpture, dance
Do you not know that here in India
La Revolution, c'est la France

When the Red Star first shone in Russia
And Lenin spoke out for our cause
Oh Sister to our Mother, Russia
You stood for ours, we'll stand for yours

We heard the words of Sultan Galiev
Of the Muslim Commissariat
Colonial subjects of all classes
Formed one great world proletariat

We did not think so ill of Hitler
Till Eastward his attention turned
Our hearts were one with Russia where
For us the light of Progress burned

Tagore, our guru, on his deathbed
For his great self he had no want
Soon one with *Brahman*, first with Russia
'Bring me the news from Eastern front'

New India sought *tabula rasa*
Both in its mind and in its speech
But all the top schools in our country
Still through the English medium teach

With alien tongue we speak our minds
In some ways cursed, in some ways blessed
A nation born through Synthesis
To take the best of East and West

XII. No Sure Ground

Some say why stand for Mother Nation
Why not the whole world represent
I'll not wear false united colours
Cheap village garb, global peasant

Some zealots quite sincere in preaching
As if the global answers known
For complex problems, simple answers
With green philosophers new stone

No mind can hold the whole world's problems
Can hold the factors all involved
If all involved in small-scale action
Still would the problem be half-solved

What good such good-intentioned tinkering
When polarising market forces
At macro-levels work negating
By creaming off the world's resources

Although the Earth's a finite system
I know the game's not zero sum
As science changes needs and usage
But can such technofixes come

If they were born, who would control them
Ensure good uses implemented
And not abused to make a killing
So people say best uninvented

What good in truth one's good intentions
How does one's conscience reconcile
Altruism feeds not through system
Oft good intentions bring ends vile

The hazards of industrialising
Spelled out by greenbeard loons so solemn
From rich world blindly playing role of
Neocolonial fifth column

The global media gets the scent
And poor men's plans for progress foils
With pious cant their forebears scorned
For poverty the Earth despoils

What counts in all this counterculture
Do-gooders green or truly *green*
Feel good in thinking doing something
Do something good their soul to clean?

Mass pressure, yes, helps change the 'climate'
And yes, we need more 'global thinking'
Not simply empty global gimmicks
But macroeconomic linking

****

Now conscience sold within a package
And fashion dictates what to buy
Exotic flavours, Third World problems
Packaged outrage, *City of Joy*

Sense bites for those with short attentions
Prepared before the screen with tissues
Sanitised squalor, simple visions
Not questioning the wider issues

I too consume this distant suff'ring
Spiced food for thought brings my mind colour
And brainteasers my mind to play with
My humdrum problems seem much duller

Who truly cares for other's suff'ring
Especially when so far away
Far from their world of common problems
Which fill their senses everyday

Who keeps in mind the higher motives
Beyond approval from their peers
And cares to shed the wasteful lifestyles
Behind the crocodilian tears

What truth fine talk of common future
'Our wastes for borders no respect'
While Common Market, Fortress Europe
The outside world seems to reject

Far from great moves to common future
This jostling into trading blocs
Like Old World empires' spheres of influence
Which often into conflict locked

* * * *

What is this common human motive
Beyond ensuring 'gainst our death
I see but seedy LCD things
I see no moves to HCFs

I feel submerged in tides of progress
This cultural diktat of the proles
These great great grandchildren of peasants
Transmigrate not their peasant souls

Tyranny of the mediocre
Against the Old the Youth rebels
No need to strive for higher meanings
The vacuous the one that sells

Philosophy now futile wordplay
And chopped-up prose as poems pose
The 'giftedness' of every pupil
Banal the best, anything goes!

Attraction of Americana
Its circus gallery of freaks
Play to the gallery of morons
Which in this new world language speaks

Is it because they lack good schooling
They transmute not'from lower forms
Debase a once discerning culture
To mass degenerative norms

To small avail, I fear, their nurture
Though clearly hides much grain, this chaff
We are all seeds of variation
Most good for feed, for fodder, raff

Yet from such dross arises pearlstones
In sky of darkness, points of light
That mark out the forlorn endeavour
To make a new day of this night

The noblemen born of nobodies
Like grinder of the glass for lenses
Shine forth in the polished reflection
Which short-lived surface filth soon cleanses

This aimless, drifting smog, it chokes me
Whilst most contented to be led
Conditioned 'happiness' pursuing
Thankful for circuses and bread

Those born in freedom struggle, between
Bullets and jails, no time to pause
Their life stories are simply written
The meaning of their life their cause

But in my world of modern magic
I face this foe without a face
Impersonal, emergent forces
Enveloping the human race

And in this wretched world of *baniās*
True brahman shows much abnegation
To debase his currency too proud
Yet bearing such humiliation

But still unbowed and unretracting
By hemlock modern undeterred
To speak his mind when all stay silent
Contemptuous of the grov'lling herd

Unmoved by judgement of contemp'ries
Judged only by the chosen few
Beyond the bonds of blood and nation
A higher bond of brethren true

Deep down so lonely, manchild Mowgli
Who longs to live amongst his kind
At home in jungle creatures scurry
In world of darkness, best born blind

* * * *

We live our lives in such illusion
Which our uncertain passage smooths
To give us bearings in this jungle
These noble lies, these common truths

Without such lies no civil order
Without one's lies no mental peace
The highest science on half-truths built
Each theory holds a temp'ry lease

We dearly cling to myths, to *māyā*
As if on them all things depend
Though well aware of contradictions
We feel we must these lies defend

And yes, some lies well worth defending
To death worth fighting for some lies
I speak not for life abnegation
I speak for opening of eyes

Come walk with me on sands a shifting
Pick pebbles rough that complicate
To cast upon your seamless ocean
And see the ripples imbricate

The patchwork quilt of human knowledge
The bubbling broth of contradictions
An Ancient Greece of *polis* states
Untamed by nationalist fiction

Come walk upon these red-hot pebbles
And find there is no surefoot stance
No choreography prepares you
To be the Shiva, Lord of Dance

No system stands upon these pebbles
No plodding logic stands the heat
To stand upright we must be nimble
With no sure ground beneath our feet

XIII. That One

XIII(a). *Tad Ekam*

Perhaps its all just solipsism
What proves that the outside's out there
In truth there is but one true given
I am because I am aware

Grant that there is a world around me
Why feel I not one with the whole
If all is One, That One in all then
Why feel I this monadic soul

I feel like bull so trapped and taunted
Only this beast commands my mind
What moves this world which turns against me
Or does this matador run blind

Wouldst I could will this world around me
Much as I will these monkey limbs
But bound am I to rhyme and reason
Of that Great Other's heartless whims

These worldly bonds may wither away
If one can cut *avidyā's* tether
But bonds to That One that one can't break
That One that holds all things together

The prayers that rise from desperation
Address That One by many names
But who That One ? But why That One?
But what That One and whence it came?

What makes it that the mystic visions
The ancient verse of Vedic sage
Converges with the rhymeless reasoning
And blase quips of Quantum Age

'There was not then what is or is not
No heavens then, nor even space
What latent potent lay there, where?' There
In that unfathomable place

'There was no hint of day or night then
No immortality nor death
By intrinsic power breathed That One
And breathed That One with windless breath

'All this was fluid, formless ocean'
No wave nor ripple, just one flow
'Out from this void, where dark hid darkness
Arose That One through tapas' glow

'Who truly knows whence came this cosmos
Was it born, perhaps it wasn't
He who surveys from Highest Heaven
Does He know, perhaps He doesn't '

Some call this formless ocean, *Purush*
Potent sea beyond Creation
That One who rose out That One, *Brahman*
Born of its self-limitation

In *Purush*, Time and Space, no meaning
Devoid of form there is *no thing*
Space, Time and differentiation
Into existence *yajña* brings

Part only of His boundless being
Into the cosmos actualises
A drop pinched off from formless ocean
Itself from Its true Self disguises

Born Bursting Forth is *Brahman, shristi*
Brahman, The Word or Growing Great
All things in essence born of *Brahman*
All things in *Brahman* have their fate

When *kalpa, Brahman's* day, is over
Back into *Purush* He dissolves
To rise again in a new *shristi*
The timeless time *Purush* resolves

They say that in the quantum cosmos
Energy vast this vacuum fills
The matter but a tiny ripple
This formless ocean's overspill

This void it still exists in Space-time
While *Purush* free of all dimension
Like 'nothing' from which Space and Time born
In singularity's extension

This bursting forth primeval atom
It shifts away this huge free lunch
In darkness hides the night of *kalpa*
Which pulls *pralaya,* the Big Crunch

XIII(b). *Tat tuam asi*

They sat down near the sage in forest
On *Brahman* nature they conferred
When student asked the sage about Him
The sage spoke not a single word

They sat down near the sage in forest
Enquired into reality
Was it like this or like its other
Said sage, *'naiti naiti'*

They sat down near the sage in forest
Of *AUM* the *śabdatattva* heard
Expression creative of cosmos
The underlying cosmic word

They sat down near the sage in forest
And pressed on with what *Brahman* is
They heard the words *sat chit ānanda*
Pure Being, Raw Awareness, Bliss

They sat down near the sage in forest
The sage this wisdom did impart
The Self, *ātman*, is one with *Brahman*
'Tat tuam asi', That thou art

****

Where from this AUM, this *śabdabrahman*
From mantra chanting AUM the ground
Breath drone by mouth into words broken
The metaphor of speech or sound

Thus spoke the sage by speaking nothing
This from that silence wise ones learn
Beyond the reach of words is *Brahman*
They go towards Him but return

And so 'not this, not that' is spoken
No words may *Brahman* predicate
Said Shankar that these *mahāvākyas*
To *Brahman* only indicate

No thought can grasp *nirguṇabrahman*
Beyond all forms, beyond all tokens
But in the mindless state of *mokṣa*
The formless Self in us awoken

Chit, ground of consciousness is *Brahman*
That thou art, Seer of Seeing
The essence of thy Self is *Brahman*
Sat Thou art, Be-er of Being

And those who reach this state of *mokṣa*
Speak of *ānanda*, boundless joy
The freedom unconstrained of Being
Free from all wants, free from all *bhoi*

XIV. Mind Games

The whole bestows on part its meaning
Born of nexus of relations
Do we demean by seeking meaning
Of That One that's all Creation

Be it 'nonbeing', be it 'no-thing'
Beyond That One no bonds we find
Devoid of form, devoid of 'meaning'
We look far out into our mind

The mind is born to bring out order
Feeds on percepts without weaning
For meaning baby still cries out where
Meaning cannot have a meaning

The parallels modern and mystic
Mental tramlines that constrain us
As do the Idols of the Market
Thought and Language, bonds that chain us

Know not the Analytic Schoolboys
We thought in vision fore we talked
Mother of Thought was not word-language
Pure thought was born when two-legs walked

For when we stood up on our hind legs
To toil with tools our fingers free
'Tween touch and sight in brain were bonds made
Pure thought through standing came to be

Built tool-sight trusting empire, Science
But human brains stay same way shaped
Beyond horizon metaphoric
Imprisoned thought has not escaped

Composed with occult symbols, symphonies
'Mahāvāquations' hide import
Which mind can map as maps terrain
Dimensions lost, flattened by thought

Mahāvākya of pebble-picker
Who Leibniz framed, from jealousies
Asked of this long-armed force so spooky
Said, 'I frame no hypotheses'

These models made with symbols playing
Within the mystic realm of number
Describe the dancing dream of *māyā*
But disturb not *Puruṣa's* slumber

Is His great *yajña* born of speaking
Is *Purush* Mind as *Brahman* Word
The *AUM* created, Mind reflecting
Is *Brahman* how *Purush* is heard

Perhaps there lies some truth in *līlā*
Purposeless play, sheer aimless sport
No course of action rules His Being
For *Brahman* no desire does court

Not His intrinsic need, Creation
Niṣkāma Karma through His Will
His very Being is creative
No final goal left to fulfil

Mind games upholding His 'perfection'
Perhaps this 'Great Chain' has a goal
Evolving higher sentient beings
Monads reflecting on the Whole

But we misread such evolution
As for anamorphosis striving
When all but constant adaptation
All forms are equal in surviving

The grubby germs that grace our innards
Evolved as highly as is Man
Selection fills potential niches
And pursues not preordained plan

The complex beings follow simple
As anamorphosis takes time
No leading shoot of late arrivals
Mere adaptation to new climes

Perhaps in countless variant *yajñas*
Mere chaos from the *AUM* evolves
No monads look back on Creation
Before the barren Word dissolves

May be the *yajñas* run in cycles
And may be countless cycles run
Or may be countless random *yajñas*
Within that greater Unknown One

* * * *

Behold this option quite bizarre
Propounded by Everett the Third
Which saves his God from playing dice
When no one outcome is preferred

Faced with that dog of a conundrum
Of Schrödinger's *gedanken* cat
Does it go one way or the other
Answers Everett both this and that

Each time there is no certain outcome
The quantum system bifurcates
And two worlds born of indecision
Part ways to meet their separate fates

We live in one of many worlds
Which breed through quantum splits, disjunction
All options open actualised
In this great cosmic wave-like function

What cruel thinking Cosmic Mind
To have branched me into this
And not into another world
Where my double lives in bliss

XV. This One

How then That One becometh this one
What is my Self, my conscious mind
How could I sleep, all was awake when
Saw 'Mind' and Matter disentwined

Logicians haughty, in esteem held
Looked like blind men tapping *lathis*
Was blinded not by science, this schoolboy
Saw the whole beast as a *hathi*

Like boys they bicker amongst themselves
And think their superstructures sound
Yet flimsy are these cheap brick houses
On flimsy myth of concrete ground

But spatial patterns Science pictures
To smaller patterns all reducing
Emergent pattern, Life succumbed as
Now Consciousness they try seducing

But if new life were made *de novo*
Meas'ring patterns, we would know it
But consciousness if born anew then
Pattern meas'ring cannot show it

Negating ways called Positivism
What's measured not does not exist
But how to measure this awareness
Flux patterns' ground is always missed

In triangles, circles, symbols, shapes
Book of the Cosmos not all writ
I came to see where there is *sat*
There we must also posit *chit*

But in itself this nothing novel
The *ṛṣis* such had long proposed
But none could say how raw awareness
To conscious minds metamorphosed

I got no farther than Spinoza
With two attributes, matter, 'mind'
But why alone in higher creatures
Should we both the attributes find

I gave up in despair exhausted
Convinced that Man could say no more
Saw no way forward, openings barred
But came a vision, opened door

A vision vague of living brain cells
Which somehow came to be translated
Into a many-levelled cosmos
In whirlpools individuated

Each level of *saṃsāra's* order
Like whirlpools, processes revealed
Which folded back upon themselves
Secrets from higher whirls concealed

Each cell in body like a whirlpool
Body itself such a closed field
Thought through this hi'rarchy of whirlpools
And, of my being, ground did yield

Appear apart, physique and psyche
But in some hidden way are joined
As parallels alone we grasp them
As if two sides of the same coin

And every whirlpool in the cosmos
Each moment feels its patterns changing
Of Self and Time most have no notion
Just meaningless, mad rearranging

Anamorphotic evolution
Forever with surprise arriving
To steer its mobile legged creatures
Made Mind, a method new for driving

To steer safe path through world of danger
Grew foresight, in-brain simulation
Of body and its key surroundings
The world we know, our own creation

This carefully ordered world of patterns
A whirlpool, 'closed' electric field
Its meanings born of strict relations
Thus *Consciousness* from *chit* congealed

Our Self aware alone of itself
Phenomena, internal flux
Born in ourself through outside influence
From them World Physical constructs

Though grasp we Self and feel Time passing
In essence all we have is *chit*
In brain's unwiped slate, Self and Time frames
Regenerate what fades and flits

When we lie lost in dreamless sleeping
We are in truth annihilated
But feel all fields though new the same field
Through memory regenerated

Like *Brahman* reborn of *Puruṣa*
From the potential state *pralaya*
Potential Self lives on in mem'ry
New fields are fooled through mem'ry's *māyā*

Perhaps our dreaming sleep's a being
Born in the other half of brain
In vision strong but weak in reason
But same life-history retains

So we are one, may be two series
But fooled to feel one episode
This our only reincarnation
Within the brain our sole abode

Thus we are as is all of Nature
But *meaningfully organised*
In this panpsychic flux called Cosmos
We are whirlpools I realised

XVI. The Web Intricate

What point in saying things are wrong
When things have never once been right
Like fly trapped in a web intricate
Each way I pull it pulls more tight

My mind weeps from this silent torture
But no response show mouth or eyes
Stolen from me my true expressions
I live this public world of lies

Why shape me, make me full of promise
All the fruits of Earth to merit
Then shape my world so to negate me
All my birthright disinherit

I know not if these gifts of God
Have made me cursed or made me blessed
What torture matches torment cruel
Potential wasted unexpressed

Born into fire of sacrifices
Faced full the flames for little credit
Those opening chapters can't be altered
The Moving Finger doesn't edit

My memories are uninvited
Though innocent and sweet some scenes
Invite the question that cuts deepest
How much more full life could have been

Curse will to live and fear of dying
Instinct to fight ignores defeats
So hard to give this world a beating
Within the length of these heartbeats

And curse imagination magic
Much happier worlds through my mind fleet
Small changes could have brought such joy but
Fate keeps them from my world concrete

Rare glints of hope set soul afire
But failure's not just chances missed
The punch is laced with irony
Which always adds some cruel twist

Prospects of hope that raise my spirits
Infect like mould, ferment and leaven
My amplitudes like liquor steepen
And bring me hell from dreams of heaven

False calm reigns over sea of being
Before by sudden storm its lashed
Unleashing all the rage kept hidden
When heightened hopes on rocks are dashed

Stay deaf to all the warnings, sirens
Raise self-esteem although they tease
And shake me out of stagnant slumber
Though battered by these restless seas

How disengaged this evolution
Puts higher minds in beastly forms
Ill-fitted by these monkey bodies
Ill-suited to these monkey norms

Yet still enchained by monkey instinct
Strong waves upon which float the foam
Of higher thoughts and higher vision
So alien in this monkeys' home

And in this world of monkey business
The would-be human at a loss
What monkeys hold as gold and silver
The would-be human sees as dross

The fickle fashions, childish zoetropes
Like glass beads captivate the apes
Apes not the apes, the would-be human
But from their world he can't escape

Like brothers Hesse and Bhartrihari
'Tween flesh and spirit vacillate
'Tween monkey and the human being
Live in a schizophrenic state

Thus of my Self, I am not sovereign
The ape of ape world needs a share
Torn by this internecine struggle
Pulled this and that way get nowhere

Sometimes I envy simple monkeys
Devoid of higher human trace
Know what they want and go and get it
See but the jungle, know their place

And even were my luck to alter
If suddenly things turned around
I fear my bonds would undermine me
As things looked up would drag me down

Torment me not with talk of reason
I know full well coincidence
A mask for matters unexplained
The hidden hand of fate I sense

This fate surrounds me with an aura
Which from my star-crossed being wells
It makes me in this world a magnet
Which this thing happiness repels

I know what causes this inertia
How right you were Professor Mach
Cosmos against me is contriving
It drags me down, it holds me back

And this I know the primal bondage
Between my Self and cosmic Other
This fire of Self like snuffled embers
Just flickers as entropy smothers

This minute apperceiving monad
This moments glimmer on the ocean
Olympian intrigue, casts itself in
And sees its role in tidal motion

In wonder gasp at my minuteness
Beside uncharted ocean wide
Like speck of sand on island stranded
Submerged in such emergent tides

When milky ways collide oh *Brahman*
A billion worlds come to an end
One seed succeeds out of a million
Into the egg to weave and wend

Oh *Brahman*, You who play with planets
Our wretched lives at will You waste
To You our joys and suff'ring same
Just spices of the life You taste

COMMENTARY

Line numbers are given in **bold type.**

I. THIS ONENESS/OTHERNESS MYSTERY

4 Socrates: 'Look at all these wares that I do not need'. **8** *Muṇḍaka Upaniṣad* Part I(2)8 'Like the blind led by the blind' **14** *Muṇḍaka Upaniṣad* Part I(2)8 'Ignorant of their ignorance, yet wise in their own esteem' — the passage refers to those who concern themselves with the rituals of 'lower knowledge'. **18** Rousseau: 'Man is born free, and everywhere he is in chains' (opening words of *The Social Contract*) **21** *Twiceborn* — The three upper castes, in the traditional Hindu caste system, who were drawn from the Aryan ethnic group. The traits hinted at in line 22 are supposed to be associated with my own brāhmaṇa caste rather than with all twiceborn castes; a degree of other-worldliness and the haughtiness associated with the educated and 'priestly' caste. **32** Raw feels: the elements of conscious experience, i.e. the raw feel of redness is that which is common to the perception of all things which one experiences as being red in colour. Line 31 is parodying a famous philosophical question concerning the common experience of raw feels. **36** Field: Field of attention — unimportant background noise is filtered out by preconscious perceptual processes so only the potentially important information reaches the 'field of attention' (or reaches consciousness). **46** A species must maintain a wide range of variation in the characteristics with which its individuals are endowed in order to avoid being wiped out by epidemics and other catastrophes and to have the potential to adapt to changing environmental circumstances. **49-52** It has been suggested that the human species has maintained a high proportion of certain types which would normally be considered deleterious, such as depressives, due to the creative potential associated with such psychological traits. (Line 52 'burning': see note to XIII(a) (40)). **57** *baniās* merchants/middlemen **82** Gaia — nowadays popularly associated with James Lovelock's so-called Gaia hypothesis in which he views the Earth as sort of self-regulating organism — a living cell perhaps to Man the virus in my verse (it is interesting to note that viruses are now known to have originated from normal living cells; they are packets of 'rogue genes' which break free from cellular control and replicate themselves by hijacking the cell's 'machinery' — a worrying parallel with Man's relationship to the environment).

II. AND BORN WAS I

4 The word *play* here does not mean that the chimp has written a play, rather it means that the chimp has been playing, tying us in with *līlā* (see line 73). **11-14** Refers to MacLean's notion of the triune brain where the cerebellum (the smaller 'brain', behind and below the cerebral hemispheres, which controls automatic repertoires etc.) is taken to be equivalent to the level attained by a horse's brain whilst the brainstem is taken to be equivalent that of a reptile. The value of this notion lies in its highlighting the presence within our head of vestiges of our evolutionary past which once played more prominent roles (maybe with some relevance to VII.(98-100) and almost certainly to lines 9-10 here). **18** E.O. Wilson's *Sociobiology* which caused quite a stir when it was first published in 1974. My verse is based on a true momentary experience of identification with the 'ape-men' in the cover picture (rather than the frontispiece). **25-28** Based on momentary identification experience with the small shrew-like mammals mentioned at the end of the BBC *Life on Earth* episode on the dinosaurs. Without the 'removal' of the dinosaurs, the 'higher' niches would have remained filled and these small mammals would not have radiated out to create the higher mammalian forms. **29-30** It has been suggested by some that a large brain is incompatible with a reptilian metabolism etc. but I believe this is a minority opinion. **39** See XIV(20-24) for the link between the bipedal posture and the capacity for thought. **41-44** Given lines 37-38, if the female is not burdened by child-rearing etc., in a consistent world this would not hold; nor would the evolution of apes given lines 27-28. **55** *The Rime of the Ancient Mariner:* 'And slimy things did crawl with legs upon the slimy sea' **59-60** Refers to the possible role of inorganic clay structures (esp. zeolites) in the origins of life on Earth. Although the conventional wisdom of the 'primeval soup' of organic (carbon-based) molecules explains the synthesis of the basic organic building blocks; the peculiarity of the presence of only certain optically active forms has led to speculation about the role of zeolites in early living systems. Some have even suggested that the first 'living' systems were inorganic clay systems. **62** 'We are stardust, we are glowing': from the song *Woodstock* by Crosby, Stills, Nash and Young. **63-64** Iron and heavier elements in the universe were created by nuclear fusion in extremely high energy supernovae events. Iron of course forms the basic core of the Earth. This fact with its mystical connotations of earlier generations of stars being necessary for the evolution of the elements necessary for our own existence has had a profound influence on the thoughts of many people (but see XIV(65-68)). **65-68** The ideas alluded to in this verse are dealt with in Sections XII and XIV of this work, suffice to say here that there exists a parallel between the ancient Vedic ideas and the Big Bang theory. **69-72** See also VI(1-4) I am comparing the orgasm here to *līlā* (see below) or to a Cosmic Will; in some Hindu thought, the orgasm has been viewed as a very weak form of *Brahman's* 'bliss'. **73** *līlā* (sport) the doctrine propounded in the *Brahma Sūtra* (a summary of the *Upaniṣads*) which, as in lines 75-76, sees Creation as being the mere sport of *Brahman* (the Ultimate Reality/Ground of all Being) (see Section XIII) and not directed towards any goal (see Section XIV). **74** Great Chain (of Being) is actually a symbolic, religious term for the states of consciousness with the Ground of all Being and a hierarchy of lesser levels of being (see Postscript). This phrase has become associated with a cluster of ideas relating to cosmic evolution since A.O. Lovejoy discussed the tension between 'Being' and 'Becoming' in Western metaphysics in his *The Great Chain of Being*. Lovejoy saw Bergson's 'creative evolution' to be basically a reworking of Schelling's ideas. Schelling was strongly influenced by Indian philosophy. This Great Chain of Being idea involves the gradual realisation of (all) the possibilities inherent in the cosmos. (See XIV(77-96) for an extreme form of this notion, the Many Worlds interpretation of Quantum theory). **79** *saṃsāra* (literally, "without ceasing") here means the ceaseless flux of phenomena **84** *pralaya*: the dissolution of the cosmos at the end of one cosmic cycle and the state of formlessness into which the cosmos returns upon dissolution (see Section XIII). **85** 'I speak to you of Superman, Man is something to be surpassed' (Nietzsche: *Thus Spake Zarathustra*). **86-88** Line 86 is in fact alluding to a logical conclusion from my own theory of consciousness (see Section XV) that consciousness can exist in future human artefacts (lifeless fruit) — I have left the full explanation until the notes for that section. 'Self-realisation'; here meant in the sense of the cosmos creating higher sentient forms in order to look back upon its own creative work/play. **93** 'modes of simulation' here means modes of perceiving and conceiving the world through dynamic representations (simulation) (see XV(65-68) and notes).

III. *RĀSHTRA* IS MY WORD FOR NATION

2 *rastai hati* I walk in the street (Bengali) **3** *Bhārat*: India **8** The parallel with Blake's, "And did those feet in ancient time/Walk upon England's pastures green" was not intentional although I used 'pastures green' in line 6. **10** Shankar (Shankara or Shankaracharya: see also XI(c)(29)) Keralan brahman *c.* eighth century, greatest philosopher of the *Advaita* (Nondualistic) school of *Vedānta* philosophy, author of the *Brahma Sūtra Bhāṣya* (commentary on the *Brahma Sūtra*). He set up four 'missions' in the 'four corners' of India. **13-16** 'The Harappan civilisation' and ending 'other oldest civilisations'. 'Indra's children' — the Aryans (Indra being the primary god of the *Rigveda*) — entered India *c.*1500 BC (according to the conventional view). The Aryan invasion is now known to be an Orientalist myth (see Feuerstein, G., Kak, S. and Frawley, D. (1995) *In Search of the Cradle of Civilization: New Light on Ancient India*, Quest Books, and Postscript p. 222). The Harappan civilisation of the Indus valley and Western India is now known to have been built by the Vedic Aryans themselves and was probably the world's first civilisation (*c.* 7,000 *BCE*). Essential features of Hinduism, such as *yoga* (e.g. images of Shiva *Yogeśvara* (Lord of Yoga)) and communal baths have been found in Harappan sites leading to the mistaken view that the invading Aryans adopted these practises. **19** *dharma* the ubiquitous term associated with lawfulness and regularity which intertwines the metaphysical and the mundane is here used in the sense of the Indo-Aryan social order **20** *Vangā* Sanskrit name for Bengal **22** See III(96), XII (151-168), XV(30) for Indian themes manifesting themselves in my own thought. **23-24** these lines are based on the the words *O shé shopno diyé toiri shéjé, smriti diyé ghera* (Oh which is made up of dreams, surrounded in memory) from the Bengali nationalistic song by D.L. Ray known popularly as *Amar janmabhoomi* (The Land of My Birth). **37-40** The symbol on the Indian tricolor is Ásoka's *chakra* (chariot wheel). Ásoka (grandson of Chandragupta Maurya) completed the Mauryan conquest of the subcontinent with the conquest of Kalinga (modern Orissa) — appalled by the bloodbath, he turned to Buddhism with its doctrine (adopted from the Jains) of *ahiṃsā* (non-violence to living creatures) and implemented social welfare programmes. (Congress leaders actually rejected Gandhi's choice of the spinning wheel in favour of Ásoka's *chakra*). **42** From the time of Herodotus, India has been perceived in the West largely as a land of the 'Other' with contradistinctions made between the two, serving the purpose of Western self-affirmation. It has also been the 'Otherland' in the sense of the fabulous land of strange creatures, great wealth, strange religions etc. **45** *baniās* merchants/middlemen **46-48** *jñānamārga* one of the three Hindu paths (*trimārga*) to *mokṣa* ('liberation': see Section XIII(b)(41)). It is the path of contemplation/'knowledge' (actually *jñāna* means gnosis) similar to the Western *via contemplativa. Karmamārga* is the path of works which presupposes high caste standing. *Bhaktimārga* is the path of 'loving devotion' (terms such as 'God intoxication' through ritual chanting etc. are often used), open to all, it is the popular Hinduism of the temples, idol worship etc. I have used the term 'cohort' to mean 'generation', extending upon its use in population biology for one breeding season's progeny of a population. **49** Nālandā — the ancient Buddhist centre of learning near Rajgir (capital of ancient Magadha); Indians tend to refer to it as an ancient 'university'. **50** Place values — the allusion is to the invention of the decimal 'place-value' arithmetical system in ancient India (leading also to the Indian invention of the 'zero'). G.G. Joseph (*The Crest of the Peacock: Non-European Roots of Mathematics,* (1991) I.B. Tauris/Penguin) notes that the Babylonians had a place-value system based on 60 (the number we now use for angles and time-keeping; but too cumbersome for most purposes). The base 10 was used in the Harappan civilisation (famous for its standard units of measure) and is the only base used in the whole of Sanskrit literature. *Hathi* — elephant the allusion is to 'ivory towers') **54-56** 'Where knowledge is free/Where the world has not been broken up into fragments by narrow domestic walls' (Tagore: *Gītānjalī* XXXV). **67** 'Where two strong men stand face to face, though they come from the ends of the Earth' (Kipling *The Ballad of East and West*). **61** *varṇa-dharma* the caste laws. The term *varṇa* means 'colour'. **75** 'ji' is a term of enderment suffixed to Indian names (e.g. Ghandiji). **68** There is a rather unintentional allusion here to 'The world turned upside down', the title of a well-known book (I think the title comes from a song title) by C. Hill on the radical (materialist/socialist) English sects in the seventeenth century. **69** *Mātā Bhārat* (*Bhārat Mātā*) Mother India **70** *Āryāvārta* (the Aryan homeland) name given to the region of Eastern Uttar Pradesh and Bihar (Eastern Gangetic Plain) where a number of Aryan kingdoms sprang up early in the first millenium BC following the Aryan migrations Eastward. My ancestors moved on Eastwards (in much more recent times) to the Gangetic deltaland of Bengal. In the past, brahmans were sometimes 'imported' into peripheral kingdoms to introduce a 'Hindu' (aryanised) social order. **71** *avidyā* (ignorance (literally 'non-seeing') **72** Manu legendary author of the ancient 'Hindu' law book, the Code of Manu (*Manusmriti*). **77-78** The origin of the British two-fingered insult sign apparently lies in the Hundred Years war when the French would cut these two longbow-pulling fingers off English prisoners. Agincourt was fought on St Crispin's day. **79-80** Arjun (Arjuna), the greatest archer/warrior amongst the sons of Pandu in the *Mahābhārata*. The *Bhagavad Gītā* (Song of the Lord) is the book of the Mahābhārata in which, as the two armies meet on the field of Kurukshetra, Arjuna refuses to take part in the battle, seeing so many kinsmen and old friends in the enemy ranks. Krishna, the enigmatic figure acting as Arjuna's charioteer, responds to Arjuna's doubts by voicing what is probably an attempt at a synthesis of various schools of Hindu thought with a strong emphasis on *bhakti* which was inserted into the great epic at this critical juncture in the story. The famous advice to Arjuna includes the Doctrine of *Niṣkāmakarma*, to undertake one's worldly duties without any selfish attachment. **84** *khamsin* an

Arabian Desert storm **92** *Rāvan(a)* the demon king in the *Rāmāyana; vimāna* flying ship(s) in Hindu legend (the reference is to B52 bombers). **93-94** Refers to Genetic Drift (or the Sewall Wright effect) in evolutionary theory whereby traits are lost in a small isolated population (usually on a small island) as the traits are not transmitted genetically to the offspring due to purely random effects due to small sample (population) size.

IV. BONDS OF KINSHIP

9 Wilhelm von Humboldt, who as Prussian Minister for Education (late eighteenth century) propounded his philosophy of *bildung* (formative education) which meant for him the fullest development of the potential of individuals, communities and of humanity. (See also XI(b)(37-40), XII(92-100), XVI(13-16). **18** lights — a person's ideas, knowledge, understanding **24** meiosis — the cell division that produces the sperm and the eggs. It involves random recombination of genes in order to generate variation (see also XII(99). **28** *daitya* familial responsibilities **29** Refers to the cover picture of a paperback version of R. Dawkins popular exposition of modern 'gene-centred' evolutionary thought *The Selfish Gene* (see also VI(1-8)). **30** the second Vedic 'stage of life' for the ideal high caste man is *grihastya* which involves the duties associated with the care of one's family (*grihasta* 'householder'). **37-40** Bankim Chandra Chattopadhyay, early Nationalist thinker (see also VII(171-174), VIII(121-122)). He always resented the fact that he had had to make great sacrifices due to his father's debts (T. Raychaudhuri, *Europe Reconsidered: Perceptions of the West in 19th Century Bengal*, Oxford UP, 1989). I note that in the *Rig Veda,* the term *riṇacyuta* (one who removes debts) has been used for 'son'! **47-48** 'Where the mind is without fear and the head is held high . . . . Into that heaven of freedom, my Father let my country awake'. First and last lines of Tagore's *Gītānjalī* XXXV. One could describe this as a wish to be free from a sometimes 'paternalistic' bondage (see also X(21)). **75** Peepul (Peepal or Pipal) tree, similar to the Banyan. Buddha attained enlightenment under a Peepul tree near Gaya in Magadha. **78** See also III(55-56). Much of Britain's Northern forest land has been replaced by managed forests with fast-growing pine trees grown for timber. The Peepul is of course a tree that spreads itself out broadly, in keeping with this tree metaphor for the narrowly educated products of today's educational system.

V. TWO TWO-LEGGED HUMAN RACES

21 The post-war goal of Keynesian 'full employment' seems to have been abandoned in practise by the British Conservative government. **27** Refers to the notion of the decentralised decision-making processes (achieved partly through technological progress in communications and control) which have characterised the Western economic systems allowing technological innovation and product differentiation. It should be remembered that back in the thirties the Stalinist command economy was in keeping with the sellers market situation which allowed Henry T. Ford to give the consumer any colour he liked as long as it was black. We are now seeing Post-Fordist effects destabilising Western giants such as IBM and General Motors. (See VIII(6)). (VIII(40) refers to another notion whereby technological change affects society). **32** Along with the enormous technological strides made during the war, I am referring to the break-up of the old colonial world and the trends towards greater democracy occurred in the aftermath of the war. **43** 'And let me set free with the sword of my youth; From the Castle of Darkness, the power of the truth' (from the hymn *When a knight won his spurs*). **44** Now the *fellah*, the unemployed man, the starving native do not lay a claim to the truth, for they are the *truth*. (F. Fanon, *The Wretched of the Earth*, 1961). **45** 'Let us waste no time in sterile litanies and nauseating mimicry. Leave this Europe where they are never done talking of Man, yet murder men wherever they find them, at every corner of every one of their own streets, in all the corners of the globe.' (ibid.) (see also X(62), XI(c)(63-64)). **47** Fanon (ibid.) writes, 'In 1945, the 45,000 dead at Setif (in Algeria) could pass unnoticed, in 1947, the 90,000 dead in Madagascar could be the subject of a single paragraph in the papers'; (see also IX(53-60), (107-114), (115-130) and Section X). **49** *Les Temps Modernes* — the monthly review founded and edited by Sartre and de Beauvoir. Sartre wrote the famous preface to the French edition of Fanon's *The Wretched of the Earth*. **56** 'Go down, Moses, way down in Egypts land; Tell old, Pharaoh, to let my people go'. I believe that these lines are from a negro spiritual from the American 'Deep South'. The freedom riders were mainly protesters from the North travelling through the segregationist South. **61-62** The famous uprising amongst mainly landless 'tribals' in Naxalbari district of northern West Bengal in 1967 was immortalised in revolutionary legend by the Radio Beijing broadcast which hailed it as the 'spring thunder of the Indian revolution' although much more serious Maoist inspired disturbances occurred elsewhere in India. Naxalbari led to large-scale student/worker disturbances in West Bengal (esp. Calcutta), hence the term 'Naxalite' (see also VIII(181-182). Maoist 'Naxalite' activity is still around in parts of India, especially around Gaya in central Bihar (the Bodh Gaya) of Buddha's enlightenment as noted above (IV(75). **68** Operation Rolling Thunder: the US carpet-bombing of Indo-China, escalation of the war that led to the ongoing tragedy in Kampuchea (see also III (89-92). **79-88** Based on Martin Bernal's *Black Athena: The Afro-Asiatic Roots of Classical Civilisation.* Vol. I: *The Fabrication of Ancient Greece.* Bernal associates the Danaans who colonised Argos with the Semitic Hyksos who were expelled from Egypt after a period of rule there. Danaos was supposed to have come from Egypt or Syria (his half-brother was called Aegyptos) and he introduced irrigation into Greece. Kadmos, founder of the second city of Thebes was probably a Phoenician and is accredited with introducing the alphabet (and certain weapons) to Greece. Kekrops (Cecrops), legendary founder of Athens, according to some sources was of Egyptian origin. Bernal associates Athena with the Egyptian goddess *Nēit* associated with the Egyptian city Sais with which Athens had strong links. Europa was daughter of Pheonix (Phoenicia) and mother of Minos. The Minoans are generally regarded as Europe's first civilisation thus Europe's first civilisation was most probably created by Egyptian and Phoenician colonisation of Crete; the famous Bull culture of the Minoans may be traced back to Egypt. Such Afro-Asiatic roots for Greek civilisation were recorded, not only in legend, but also by the likes of Herodotus and was the conventional view until revisionism associated with the development of 'Classics' appropriated Ancient Greece as the cradle of European civilisation and omitted the references to non-European influences. In regard to the milieu and world outlook of the Greeks one only has to ask, where did Alexander go when he sought to conquer the world. The achievements of the Greeks (clearly there were many novel developments, particularly in methodology, which were dramatic advances on what existed previously) were less of a 'miracle' and more of what the Egyptian intellectual Samir Amin has associated with the lack of inertial constraints in what he calls 'peripheral tributary cultures' (*Eurocentrism*, Zed, 1989), which highlights the similarity of the Greece phenomenon to that of Britain in relation to Europe and Japan in relation to E. Asia in more recent periods of history. In regard to Bernal's basing a lot of his arguments on legendary associations, I will note that the other great 'ancestors' of Europe, the Romans, claimed ancestry from Aeneas. Aeneas would almost certainly have been related to the Hittites (like the Trojans) of Asia Minor. Given the close kinship between Sanskrit and Latin, and given the modern knowledge (see C. Renfrew, *Archaeology and Language: The Puzzle of Indo-European Origins,* Jonathon Cape, 1987) that the Hittites were also Indo-Europeans, it seems that there is more to legends than mere delusions of ancestry from epic heroes. **89-90** Eusebius, preserving a tradition attributed to Aristoxenus (a student of Aristotle) says that learned Indians visited Athens and that one of them discussed philosophy with Socrates. The visit is also mentioned in a fragment of Aristotle's dialogues preserved in Diogenes Laertius. The story goes that, when asked by the Indian what was the scope of his philosophy, Socrates replied, 'an inquiry into human phenomena'. The Indian burst out laughing and said that it was impossible to understand human things without considering the Divine. (S. Radhakrishnan, *Eastern Religions and Western Thought,* Oxford U.P., 1939). W. Halbfass comments that the story is used by the church father Eusebius to challenge the concept and project of philosophy as a rational, merely human enterprise in favour of the idea of an 'original wisdom' which leaves religion and philosophy, metaphysics and ethics, God and man, undivided. (*India and Europe: An Essay in Philosophical Understanding,* (Indian Edition), Motilal Banarsidass, 1990). One would note that such divisions by the Greeks and, later, the Europeans were part of the reason for the success of their scientific investigations (see also XI(c)(9-16)). **91-92** Various scholars have noted the considerable similarities between the writings of Plato and older Indian (and other Eastern) ideas.

None the less, it is still common in the West to cite Plato as the original source of half the ideas under the sun. (See also XI(b) for the Indian influence on German philosophy). **93-96** This verse is based on an ironical anecdote told by some famous American and retold on a radio programme that when he served in the Pacific war against Japan in WWII, the US troops were told that the Japanese, being racially inferior to the Europeans, were inept at using technology. With Japan's 'sunrise' industries proving the Americans wrong with such a remarkable vengeance, the old Asian slogans of looking to the West to seek models for development (see also note to IX(28)) have largely been replaced with that in line 96. For the first time in at least five centuries, an Asian power has surpassed the once-invincible Westerners in strategic technologies, a matter of enormous future historical import in regard to Western hegemony (see also XI(c)17-20). The USA, rather than looking East across the Atlantic is looking West with President Clinton talking of the coming American Pacific Century. **98** cohort: generation (see III (47) note). **105-108** Emergent forces: the metaphysical notion of *emergence* appears throughout this work without always being named as such. Loosely, emergent phenomena are processes that appear at 'higher levels' (i.e. at larger scales), and they are not wholly predictable from their constituent processes. Here higher-level economic/geopolitical forces beyond the control of individuals and even governments (not always cynical strategic manipulators, often carried along by the tide of events and irresistable forces) are being referred to. Adam Smith's Invisible Hand used in Section VIII to represent market forces is another set of emergent processes. (see also I(98-99), VII(131-132), XII(11-16, 27-28, 119), XV(15), XVI(104). **134** Quiet violence: suffering and death (including premature deaths) caused through slow, continuous processes of direct or indirect economic exploitation (and associated neglect). (See also VII (133-136), VIII(163-164).

VI. THOU ART THE REASON

1-4 This verse is based on the popular expositions of the modern way of looking (rather abstractly) at the mechanisms of biological evolution in which our bodies (or organisms in general) are viewed as temporary vehicles created by the genes for means of perpetuating the genes through time. No actual motivation is posited; it is simply because those combinations of organic self-replicating variants which evolved to act in this 'selfish' way are the ones which survived early in the history of biological systems. It is not as if the very same molecules are surviving through generations of evolving organisms, rather the same variants of the particular genes (the alleles) and more realistically, combinations of these which generate advantageous features in the organisms. The old-fashioned way of stating the mechanism of biological evolution is to say that it is the action of Natural Selection on heritable variation. Implicit in this is that the mechanism of evolution involves a dialogue between the environment and the heritable variation (now known to be DNA/genes) in which our bodies are just the particular expressions of a set of genes through which the environment gauges the fitness of that particular set. As the environment keeps changing unpredictably, organisms have evolved to generate varied populations of individuals which need to keep breeding and dying etc., hence the view that they are 'vehicles'. (See also I(45-46), II(69-72), IV(24) notes, VII(10-12, 105-106), XII(99)). Kin Selection involves behavioral favouritism towards those more closely related to the organism as the closer the relationship the more alleles are shared. Alleles are the particular variant forms of a particular gene. A deme is a population of interbreeding organisms. The organism is seen as attempting to increase its particular set of alleles in the gene pool of the deme by leaving the most viable offpring; hence line 1. **11-12** Refers to Goethe's well-known epigram written in honour of Kalidasa's play *Śakuntalā:* "Wouldst thou the young years blossoms and the fruits of her decline?/ And all by which the soul is charmed, enraptured, feasted, fed?/ Wouldst thou the Earth and Heaven itself in one sole name combine?/ I name thee, Oh Sakuntala, and all at once is said. (See also XI(b) (21-24)). **17** The Pygmalion referred to here is the one from Ovid's *Metamorphoses,* the sculptor whose statue of his ideal woman was brought to life by Venus. **20** See Section XIII(b). **35** The reader acquainted with philosophy may note the vague allusion to Leibniz's monads, playing on the word 'pointless' in relation to the problem of infinitesimal mathematical points. Leibniz's monads were of course rather lonely entities as they had no actual causal relationships with each other, rather mirroring the rest of the monadic universe in itself. (See XV(73-76) for a partial parallel between this 'mirroring' and my own theory of consciousness). **83-84** Refers to the problem of gravity in Newton's model being a 'spooky' action-at-a-distance (see also XIV(33-36)).

VII. WE ARE TWO BRANCHES OF ONE RIVER

2 In human development, the sex is determined by the presence of the so-called Y chromosome which differs in shape from the other X-like chromosomes. The Wye and the Exe are English rivers. **10-12** Males are thought to have evolved in order to increase the potential for variation (see I(46) note). Males produce vast numbers of gametes (reproductive cells) through meiosis (see IV(24) notes) containing a vast range of genetic variation (different combinations of alleles (see VI(1-4) notes)). **17-20** The human embryo will, by default, develop into a basically female form unless it is switched into the male programme of development by the action of testosterone (the word *hormone* comes from the Greek for *impulse*); the Y chromosome's presence is related to testosterone production. (see also VII(137-138)). **21** Dimorphism: (Sexual Dimorphism in this case), the presence of two distinct forms of a species. **33** In the 'selfish gene' view of evolutionary cost/benefit analysis of behaviour in relation to gene transmittal, the female invests a huge proportion of its resources in gestating the young, whereas the male's basic contribution is minute, hence the difference in maternal and paternal behaviour. The female has a far greater investment to protect. **38-40** "Some speak of Alexander, and some of Hercules/ And some of brave Lysander, and other men like these" (opening lines of the British Grenadiers' song). **44** "History is but the biography of great men." (Thomas Carlyle, *On Heroes and Hero Worship*) (see also VIII(4) note). **48** *Purush (Puruṣa). Puruṣa* appears in various hymns of the *Rig Veda*, in line 7 I am referring to the use of the name *Puruṣa* as in Section XIII(a)(45) for the void from which the universe emerges (based on the creation hymn *Nāsadīya-Sūkta* (The Hymn of 'Non-Being'). **49-50** The *Puruṣa* referred to here is the very different notion from *Rig Veda* 10.90, *Puruṣa-Sūkta* (The

Hymn of Man). In this famous hymn, we have the oldest recorded reference to the four *varṇas* (traditional castes). The universe is created from the body of *Puruṣa*. The *brahmans* originate from his mouth, the *kshatriyas* (warriors) from his arms, the *vaiśyas* (commoners) from his thighs, and the *shūdras* (serfs, cultivators) from his feet. **53-56** This verse is based on the idea that, prior to the Bronze Age (of warring heroism), the settled communities worshipped fertile Mother goddesses. There is clearly a degree of truth in this assertion (see next verse, for instance). Female terracotta figures found in Harappan sites resemble the *devī* images found throughout modern India. Some have suggested that the Harappan culture was part of a greater culture spreading from the Mediterranean to central India, in which the Great Mother was the creator. (See also III(13-16 note). (See also XI(c)(4-8) for another example of new technology changing the metaphysical outlook). **57-60** As previously mentioned in III(17-20), *Vangā* is the Sanskrit name for Bengal. *Chakra*: chariot wheel. The Bengali natives worshipped mother goddesses (*devī* — goddess) usually with village deity cults. The Tantric cults in which the *Shakti*, (*Śakti*) the female principle is the dynamic, creative life force of the universe (identified with *prakriti* (matter)), as opposed to the passive male *Śiva* (identified with *puruṣa* (spirit). This is based on yet another Vedic myth in which *Puruṣa* divides equally into the passive *Puruṣa* (spirit/consciousness; male) and *Prakriti* (matter/Nature; female). The female goddess is supreme in Tantric Hinduism. The Bengali *Durgā pūjā* apparently bears traces of an ancient matriarchal society. As with most non-Aryan deities, the Aryan conquests resulted in aryanisation into the complex 'Hindu' pantheon. The influence of such cults is still strong in Bengal (as in many parts of village India) and the Bengali *devī Durgā* manifests herself at the very heart of Indian Nationalist symbolism (see VII(171-178). **61-64** The West has long portrayed Greece and Rome as the birthplaces of progressive social institutions; slave-owning Athens (like the slave-owning United States) exalted for their 'democratic' institutions. In Athens women were mere chattels, whilst in older Roman law, women were classed as imbeciles, unfit to give testimony. In the Code of Hammurabi (Babylon, eighteenth century BC), numerous rights, 'progressive' by the standards of much later societies, were conferred upon women, such as divorce on the grounds of cruelty and adultery, return of the dowry if their husbands divorced them, retention of the bride-price as the wife's personal property etc. In Ancient Egypt, the status of women was higher still with women holding public office. The name *Homer(os)* meant hostage. **65-68** Early women's rights campaigners in revolutionary France met with the same fate as other dissidents during the Reign of Terror. As line 65 indicates, women had played a very active part in the Revolution and prominent females campaigned for equal rights. *La patrie* was equivalent to *la nation*. **73-76** According to an International Labour Organisation report from 1980, women do two-thirds of the world's labour, receive ten per cent of the world's income, and own less than one per cent of the world's property. **90** I have chosen 'Muslim' to represent oppressed non-Westerners here as Muslims have tended to bear the brunt of the Western media's negative image portrayal mechanisms, concentrating on riotous anti-Western hordes burning flags etc. rather than allowing articulate individuals to put forward their reasoned arguments (see also IV(121-124). It was noted in a television programme on British television on the life of Gengis Khan, the archetypal, bloodthirsty heathen, that his contemporary, Richard I the Lionheart was a vicious anti-semite, initiating the anti-semitic disturbances that led to the burning of the Jews at York (and later their expulsion from England). Richard's own Plantagenet chronicler boasted about the crusader's barbarous atrocities against the Muslims in the Holy Land, murdering thousands using methods such as boiling in oil and roasting on spits. **105-108** See also notes to VI(1-4). *kāma* desire/pleasure — it is perhaps worth noting that our capacity for thought does free us from the tyranny of the 'selfish genes' (see also XVI(49-72)). **110** It was of course the Gestalt school of psychology which undertook the famous work on how the mechanisms of perception tend to seek out the more 'perfect' forms that can be generated from the sense data. **128** I am aware that there are men who 'import' submissive wifes from South-East Asia. **131-132** See V (131 notes. **133-134** The likes of the narrow-minded Freudians would tend to associate such notions with the differences between the male and the female orgasm. If there is any truth in this it is related to the first two lines of the following verse. The 'feminine mind' has, like the 'Hindu mind' been associated with holistic modes of thought which are probably related to right hemisphere-linked brain activity. **135** Quiet violence: see V(134) notes. **137-138** Refers to recent research suggesting that testosterone is responsible for inducing slight differences in the development of the male human brain leading to differences in mental performance between the sexes. These may be related to the well known differences in the general modes of information processing between the left and right cerebral hemispheres where the male/female emphasis has often been suggested. **145-148** The danger of overplaying the significance of such testosterone-induced differences is that it leads to false expectations of capabilities. Unthinking teachers will push girls towards 'female' subjects, failing to realise that, even if testosterone does actually affect mental aptitudes, the male/female difference is a statistical one. Within the norms of the population distribution, there will be a noticeable difference. However, an individual, due to our inherent variation (see I(46), VII(9-12), XII(99) etc.), can easily fall outside these norms, and many females will be inherently better at supposedly 'male' subjects than most men. **159-162** As Ashis Nandy notes, the British colonial rulers developed a 'hypermasculine' culture and perceived the natives (especially the intellectual Bengalis) as being effeminate. This 'hypermasculinity' and anti-intellectualism being inculcated in the 'public' (private) school system. (A. Nandy, *The Intimate Enemy,* OUP, 1983). **163-166** Parodying Kipling's poem 'If'. **171-174** Bankim Chandra Chattopadhyay (see also IV(37)) in his novel *Ánandamaṭha* (see also VIII(122)) about a secret society of 'devotees' dedicated to freeing their country from foreign rule, wrote the hymn *Bande Mātaram* (Hail to the Mother) which became an anthem and the phrase *'Bande Mātaram'* a Nationalist salute. The Mother was *Durgā,* the warlike goddess associated with Hindu Bengal. *Durgā* is associated with *śakti,* the female, creative power principle (see notes to lines 57-60). **175-178** The Mother (above) became transformed, partly through the influence of Aurobindo Ghose's 'Mother' notion, into *Bhārat Mātā* (Mother India) an abstract notion without symbolic representation. Spinoza's view that men, devoid of a personal God, would substitute the state ('nation') is clearly manifest here.

VIII. *BANDE MĀTARAM*

3 I have used Adam Smith's immortal phrase 'invisible hand' (the processes regulating the economy resulting from competition between individuals — turned into a beneficial agency) to represent the glorified conception, most prevalent in the 1980s, of emergent market forces as the solvent for all economic ills. **4** The allusion is to Francis Fukuyama's much hyped thesis *The End of History* which, if I recall correctly, stated that, with the collapse of Communism, the dialectical struggle which Fukuyama identifies with 'History' was over, the only option left being American style liberal democracy. Of course the Hegelian-Marxian conception of History as a single trajectory totality identified more or less with Western developments was a nonsense from the start. It has been noted that Marx, like countless others, misinterpreted Darwin's 'evolution' as being teleologically oriented towards the perfectly adapted creature (see XIV(57-64)) and thus saw 'History', in parallel, evolving towards the perfect society. **5-12** Continuing with an 'evolutionary' theme, the point here is that Communism was a human mental construct imposed upon the organic reality of society and was largely incapable of evolving due to its rigidly imposed totalitarian structures. In contrast, Capitalism has evolved over hundreds of years and has emerged, unplanned, feeding off the baser instincts of human nature. **34** The much vaunted Indian government foodgrain buffer stocks, as well as fending off starvation in times of shortage, act to raise prices by limiting supply in normal times (I use this to show something of the cruel effects of market forces rather than to attack the buffer stock policy which helps reduce dependence on foreign aid and 'food aid imperialism' as suffered in the 1960s. **39** *bustees* shanties **40** S. Goonatilake (*Aborted Discovery: Science and Creativity in the Third World*, Zed, 1984) has described technology such as the Green Revolution as 'social genes' in that the social patterns existing in the society in which the technology was developed begin to manifest themselves in the recipient society. In this case the use of expensive fertilisers, new strains and pesticides has led to the increasing prosperity of the already better-off farmers and increasing landlessness (mirroring the pattern of rural America in which this technology developed). In regard to this work's 'Oneness/Otherness', implicit aspects of our being, notion, note that migrant individuals also act like 'genes', transplanting culture. **41** *ryot* tenant farmer or cultivator in India (generally meaning poor peasant). **43-46** The epic *Rāmāyaṇa* of Vālmīki is in Sanskrit, a language accessible only to a small elite. The Hindi vernacular of North India first appears historically in the *Rām Charit Mānasa of Tulsīdās(a)* (AD 1532-1623), a popular version of Vālmīki's epic. It has been called the 'Bible' of the North Indian peasantry in that it is often the only literature that they will be acquainted with. There are many other regional versions of the *Rāmāyaṇa.* **47** *Rāmarājya* (Rule of Rām), meaning either a past Golden Age or a future Utopia.

M.K. Gandhi's concept of *Rāmarājya* envisaged a Golden Age of village India which existed only in his imagination and, fortunately, not in Nehru's or in other Congress leaders (see line 99). **49** *Mahā Bhārat* means Great India here. **52** Glass ceilings — the subtly imposed barriers preventing immigrants from rising up to the more senior jobs. In Britain, the fact that Asians often do not go with work colleagues to the 'pubs' or other social gatherings to which they are unaccustomed is often used to prevent their progress. **53-56** 'By the rivers of Babylon, where we sat down, yeah and there we wept, as we remembered Zion'. The segment of the Indian diaspora in Britain, faced with numerous, usually subtle, forms of discrimination, naturally bears sentiments resembling those of early Zionism as reflected in my previous verse. As with the European Jews' obliviousness to the presence of a native Palestinian population, I fear that we Westernised Indians tend to look upon our dreams for a future India in terms only of the small Westernised elite already in a position to exploit the benefits of modernisation. **57** refers to the 'ethnic cleansing' of the Palestinians by the Zionists. **59** 'make bomb' — to make a lot of money; referring to those who have profited from the Green Revolution (the IRA make explosive devices from fertiliser nitrates). **62** *masala* spice(s); Bombay's thriving cinema industry is renowned for its escapist *'masala'* movies **77** *gram* village **85-88** There has been an ongoing debate in India over the distinction between *modernisation* and *development;* the two often being falsely equated. Ashis Nandy in his essay, *Science as a Reason of State,* argues that all Indian governments have unquestioningly prioritised the goal of modernisation and thus subverted democracy in favour of the elite which is in a position to exploit the jobs and other benefits which accrue from modernisation (in A. Nandy (ed.), *Science, Hegemony and Violence: A Requiem for Modernity,* vol 1, Oxford UP, 1988). The counterpoint of such a technocratic world-view would be the development of appropriate technologies which are accessible to everyone which has occurred to some extent in China (see also my notes on the parallel with Zionism above). The Sanskrit word *āryā* means noble; the Indian elite and the elite bureaucracy are largely drawn from the Aryan ethnic group. **93** *Shūdra* the fourth traditional caste (*varṇa)* drawn from the non-Aryan peoples which traditionally constituted the serf/cultivator caste between the *twiceborn* castes and the untouchables. Today this group consists of countless subcastes (*jātīs*) based on occupational status, some of which have attained status comparable to the traditional upper castes in some regions, hence a modern distinction between 'forward' and 'backward' castes. The so-called 'backward castes' (see below) are the numerous subcastes who hold a status position between the modern high status subcastes and the untouchables and tribal peoples. *Dalit* (oppressed), this term is now often used in preference to the derogatory *untouchable* and M.K. Gandhi's patronising *harijan* (children of God). It was in fact introduced by the late B.R. Ambedkar who led a movement amongst his own *Mahar* people of Maharashtra (the indigenous people from which the state actually gets its name, who held untouchable status having been brought into civil society to undertake menial labour) for mass conversion to Buddhism to try and escape their cruel humiliations in Hindu society. Brought into the Congress government (famous for defusing dissent by coopting rather than confronting) after Independence as Justice Minister, he introduced the positive discrimination system for the so-called Scheduled Castes (the *dalits* and the *ādivāsī* (original inhabitants — term preferred by the 'tribal' peoples of India) which involves a system of reserved political constituencies and quotas in state jobs and education. **94** *bhai* brother. The Indian National Congress, was from the start, dominated by *brāhmaṇas* (whose traditional educated status had allowed them to flourish as lawyers etc. under the British (see also XI(c) (69-80)) leading to charges that the Congress was not a National Congress but a Brahman Congress. The Southern Dravidian states, where caste distinctions between *brahmans* and the native population had in many regions been more extreme than in the North, were lukewarm towards the Congress both before and after Independence. **95** *'Swarāj* is my birthright and I will have it' (*swarāj* — self-rule): The famous slogan of the militant Hindu Nationalist leader from Maharashtra, B.G. Tilak. Tilak was himself drawn from the *Chitpavan* brahman community of Maharashtra which provided many of the Nationalist leaders including his moderate rival Gokhale. The *Chitpavan* brahmans had also provided the Maratha confederacy with its chief ministers *(peshwās)* two hundred years earlier; a rare example of brahmans holding supreme political power prior to independence. **96** *Hindūstan hamara hai* India belongs to me (Hindi) A famous slogan which I think stems from a song from a 1940s wartime musical which circumvented British censorship by sneaking this song into a theatre performance within the storyline. **97-100** *satyāgrahi* from *satyāgraha* ('holding firmly to the truth'), M.K. Gandhi's celebrated form of mass political action including passive resistance. Gandhi's simple appeal, rather like the traditional Indian holy man, was what finally brought the Indian masses out behind the elite Nationalists. *Khadī,* the homespun cloth worn by the Ghandians. *Ramarājya* (Rule of Ram), as previously mentioned, Gandhi's conception of an ideal society based on traditional village life. It should be noted that Gandhi did not do away with caste, an issue which led to much resistance to Ghandian ideas from Ambedkar. As noted above, the Congress leaders played along with Gandhi's simple visions for the purpose of mass mobilisation and then pursued a policy of modernisation. Indeed Gandhi's principle sponsor, the Calcutta businessman and industrialist G.D. Birla (like other leading Calcutta business families, the Birlas are Marwaris, originally from Rajasthan and Jains, hence presumably well-disposed to the concept of *ahiṃsā,* reformulated by Gandhi (see III(39) note)) won many industrial concessions from the Congress government. **101-104** I have used brahman *rājā* to refer to Nehru; the point being that rajas were traditionally drawn from the *kshatriya* ('warrior') caste, whilst the brahmans held the power spiritual (see also note on *Chitpavan* brahman *peshwās* above). Nehru's major land reform programme was the abolition of the universally hated *zamīndārs* (pronounced jomaidar), the owners of the huge estates. Undet the Mughals, the *zamīndārs* had simply the right to collect revenue from the cultivators retaining a proportion. With the English landed gentry probably in mind, Cornwallis, in his Permanent Settlement of the Bengal land revenue made them the landowners who had to pay a fixed due to the government (the actual settlements between the British and the landlords/tenants etc. varied between the provinces, Munro in Madras settled directly with the *ryots* and this practice was followed in Bombay). Nehru basically bought out the *zamīndārs* (*lakh* — one hundred thousand). The further land reforms involved the imposition of ceilings on landholdings, which were hardly ever seriously enforced and flagrantly violated (*lathi* stick). **105-108** *Garibi hatao* (drive out poverty), Indira Gandhi's celebrated 1971 campaign slogan as she broke from the conservative wing of the Congress. She tried to push through land reforms which, in the Hindi-speaking belt, were mainly of benefit to untouchables (*harijan*) resulting in a backlash from the so-called 'middle peasants' the 'backward castes' (see above) who felt threatened by the the advancement of those worse off than themselves. In the Hindi belt of North India, the anti-Indira campaign was based as much on an explicit platform of driving out the brahman-dominated government which was in league with the untouchables as on the resistance to the state of emergency. The overall anti-Indira campaign was led by the veteran Nationalist, J.P. Narayan. Nārāyan is one of Krishna's many names. Krishna killed Kaṃsa, the wicked king of his home city of Mathura. **109-112** 'backwards' — the Backward castes (see above note to line 93). The growing politicisation of the Backward castes has been the major underlying trend in Indian politics over the last twenty years (although now the rise of the BJP is overshadowing this). *Kisāns* means peasants; and Krishna was born of the Yadav clan of North India. The Yadav community is now classified as a Backward subcaste of Shūdras along with the Jat community of North-western India. These two communities are the two most prominent 'new rich', 'middle peasant', Backward castes who have attained a position of relative prosperity through their use of Green Revolution methods of agriculture (see above). This new prosperity has been coupled to political clout with political organisation developing towards a class based platform, away from the old divisive caste based politics where subcastes organised themselves for their own specific advancement. The most potent manifestation of this new force was the 1990 disturbances when the V.P. Singh government, relying on the Backward caste 'vote bank' tried to implement the Mandal Commission recommendations for extending state job/education quotas to the Backwards provoking a Forward caste backlash including the self-immolation by burning of high caste youths. **115-116** I ought to explain such a disdainful attitude which is perhaps unfair. It is perhaps the innate sense of the brahman who recognises the special role of his caste in preserving India's distinctive tradition and who feels that the backward castes, long discriminated against by the social aspects of that same tradition, clearly would not feel so strongly committed to the preservation of India's distinctive heritage and the vision of India's role in the world (see also the Introduction and the Postscript). It has something to do with the disdain felt by the traditional impecunious, educated classes towards the 'new rich' who have not acquired the 'high culture' along with a disdain towards the pettiness and materialism of the cultural imperialism associated with American mass culture (see also XII(89-96)). In fact, having said this, there is a strand of such thought in the ideology of the BJP although they would see the USA as the economic model. **117-120** Turning to the BJP (the *Bhāratīya Janata Party*), with its use of Rām (*Rāma*) as a figurehead which some have seen as a 'semitisation' of Hinduism in having a central figure as in Christianity and Islam instead of the decentralised panoply of deities and beliefs that comes under the generic term 'Hinduism'. *Hindutva* is the BJP buzzword meaning Hindu culture ('Hindudom') whilst Army of Shiva is the translation of the name of the paramilitary, semi-fascist *Shiv Sena* organisation, closely associated with the BJP and the Hindu Mahāsabhā etc. The 'semitisation' thesis sees the focus on Rām's birthplace Ayodhyā as the Hindu Jerusalem or Mecca. The verse was written in 1991 before the destruction of the *Babri Masjid* (Babur's Mosque) on the supposed site of Rām's birth at Ayodhyā. In 1990, BJP leader L.K. Advani toured India in a so-called *Rath Jatra* (chariot tour) stoking up the flames of communal hatred and was followed by thousands of *kar sevaks* (rather like 'crusaders' in this context) to Ayodhyā where they were held back by troops. It is worth noting that both the Chief Ministers of Uttar Pradesh (in which Ayodhyā falls; M.S. Yadav) and Bihar (L.P. Yadav) in

1990 were Yadavs and both took tough stands against the BJP. **121-124** *Hindu Rāshtra* (Hindu State/Nation) another BJP catchphrase. Although this may seem a rather provocative statement to some secularists, I see nothing wrong in stating my basic position, which I see as essential in winning back the claim to the true spirit of Hinduism from the BJP. As noted in Section XI(c) of this work, Indian Nationalism arose from the rejuvenation of Hindu society and a growing sense of 'Hindu identity' through the influence of Western ideas and historicism under British rule. Muslim thinkers always suspect that liberal, secular 'neo-Hindus' have an underlying position much in accord with the BJP although they will never openly admit it. This is to an extent, correct. The oldest mosque in Delhi was built with the stones from dozens of Hindu temples destroyed by Muslim invaders. Krishna's birthplace at Mathura has a Mughal Mosque on top of it, like Ayodhyā had. The ancient Hindu city of Prayāga, one of the sites of the Kumbh Melā, retains the Islamic name Allahabad. These facts do 'sting' the Indian Hindu who identifies Islam with the impositions of foreign invaders. The much-publicised case of Shah Banoh being coaxed by the *ulema* to lose her rights as a divorcee guaranteed under the Indian constitution, deferring to *Shariat* law impinges upon modern, liberal sensibilities in India as much as similar calls for self-imposed Islamic separatism in Britain arouse British resentment. None the less, as a 'neo-Hindu', I believe in secularism and as a non-theistic Hindu, all popular forms of religion, including most of 'Hinduism' along with the semitic religions are *bhaktimārga* (the popular path of loving devotion suitable for the less well-educated) to me. As the 19th century Bengali saint Rāmakrishna **(123)** preached, I can take all of these to be different paths to the same ultimate goal, which the mystic tries to apprehend directly. There is of course a thriving tradition of Islamic mystic scepticism (Sufism) in the subcontinent which has afforded some overlap between Islam and Hinduism (as of course was sought by the great Mughal Akbar). Line **122** refers to Bankim Chandra Chattopadhyay (see also VII(172) notes), the early Nationalist who in his novel *Ānandamaṭh(a)* had his heroes fighting foreign Muslim rulers in an earlier period which avoided any censorship problems. None the less, the whole thrust of Bankim's ideology was one of a rejuvenated Hinduism with little or no reference to

Islam (half of Bengal was Muslim). It is worth noting that Bengali Hindus still hold Sirāj-ud-Daula (see IX(99) as a hero in his role as a defender of India against the British takeover; the Muslim rulers at least committed themselves to being Indians whereas the British worked, it seemed, only for the interest of Britain. **125-128** *Sanātan(a) dharma* — Hinduism (the eternal *dharma:* see III(19) note, *dharma* is loosely used nowadays for 'religion'). The last two lines of this verse may be translated as 'Whether your name is Īśvara or Allah, let everyone give respect.' From Tagore's national hymn. Īśvara (Lord), is a name for the personal (*saguṇa*) *Brahman* (see XII(33-34) note). **134-136** *Āryāvarta* (see III(70) note) I am culturally a Bengali, although ethnically an Aryan, closely related to the brahmans of Bihar (deepest *Āryāvarta*). As in a number of India's peripheral regions, the traditional four *varṇa* system did not exist in Bengal. Initially, there were native Bengali peoples (classed as shūdras) and the brahmans (see III(70) note on 'import' of brahmans). For a number of reasons, including the fact that much of the native population of Bengal remained Buddhist long after Buddhism withered away in the rest of India (they later converted *en masse* to Islam, partly to escape caste restrictions, and now form the population of Bangladesh), there has been a strong nonconformist tradition in Bengal which nowadays manifests itself in the leftist politics which has long gone against the grain of mainstream India. I really am torn between my Bengali cultural inheritance and my ethnic bonds to mainstream India. I believe that I have some mental traits which are in accord with mainstream high caste (Aryan) India springing from my ethnic background; it is interesting to note some local Gujarati shopkeepers see me as 'one of us' and dispute that the likes of Tagore were actually Bengali although the Bengali *bhadralok* (polite folk: the educated class of Bengal drawn from brahmans and the educated castes of brahman/shūdra halfcaste origin, especially the *kāyastha*) see themselves as culturally distinct from mainstream India. **138** The idea of 'India' of course has its origins in empire. It is not fair to say that it was a British creation, the Mauryan Aryans had already united the subcontinent in the third century B.C. and the sprinkling of brahmans across the peripheral regions created a 'nervous system' (with their so-called brahmanical ideology giving a common core to India's diverse sects. This 'nervous system' later manifested itself in the brahman-dominated Indian National Congress (see above). **141** I am well aware of the heavy-handed tactics used by the Indian state in states with separatist movements. I must admit that my loyalty to the idea of 'India' as an integral whole overrides the sense of the injustice being done to those who do not identify so closely with India. I would argue that simply because the people of a particular region are not of the same faith, does not immediately entitle them to sovereign status. As with the Holy Land in Palestine, the Hindu is historically and sentimentally attached to parts of India which may now be populated mainly by other people of other faiths and which Hindus are legitimately entitled to consider as a part of their 'homeland' even though they may not live there. Although this sounds rather 'fascist', I simultaneously hold to the secular ideal of unity in diversity. **145-148** Refers to the huge and controversial project to construct a series of dams along the Narmada river in Gujarat and Madhya Pradesh, displacing, mainly tribal, residents of the valley in order to create power for 'modernisation'. Recently, the Indian Government has decided to 'go it alone' on the funding side rather than submit to unreasonable World Bank demands (see Postscript). **150** *Āryā Dharma* 'Noble' Truths): the four central tenets of Buddha's original teachings. **152** By *karma* here and in line 155, I am referring to the notion of transmigration up the social hierarchy justifying the social order putting the blame for misfortunes of birth on one's actions in previous lives. **153-156** *Borolok* ('Big people') — the rich. *Chotolok* ('Little people') — the poor. *Bhavan* Mansion. *Bustee* shanty dwelling. The role of the brahmans in the traditional political order tended to be that of legitimising the authority of kings in return for privileges (see also notes to lines 95 and 101). **158** J.K. Galbraith's famous phrase, 'public squalor, private greed' was used in regard to the 'affluent society' of post-war America. It is perhaps more apt in the land where Galbraith was the first US economic adviser. **159** The Middle Kingdom: China **160-161** The reference is to the 1989 massacre of student demonstrators in Tiananmen Square. The Chinese would no doubt argue that they have far more pressing concerns than the disaffection of the privileged urban elite. Also note the almost total neglect in the Western media of the shooting to death of about 2,000 student demonstrators in Kwang Ju, South Korea in May 1980. **163-164** Refers to the five million or so

Indian children under five who die each year from preventable causes (i.e. due to the poverty that the authoritarian Chinese communist regime has in a large measure eradicated, with infant mortality rates in China close to those in the developed countries). *Crore* Ten million. Moloch; the Canaanite god of Biblical times to whom parents sacrificed their children. **165** *yajña* sacrifice **173-176** In the classic 1951 Hindi cinema film *Mother India,* this line (almost always used in clips) is spoken by the poverty-stricken single mother when the lecherous village usurer offers food to her two hungry sons. (The Hindi film is not to be confused with the 1927 book *Mother India* by the American Katherine Mayo which focused on the status of Indian women, serving as an apology for British imperialism). **177-180** In the film, the younger son (the first to spit out the userer's food) grows up to be a bandit leader and kills the wicked usurer who has for so long swindled his family. However, when he tries to abduct the usurer's daughter, his own mother shoots him to death in the final scene of the film. As many have commented, in this most famous of Hindi films, the moral at the end is one of not taking one's grievances against social injustice too far, a sort of Hindu conservatism in relation to social 'progress'. Sociological historians have long noted the amazing success of dharmic ideology in preventing serious challenges to the Indian social order over such a long period of history. **181** Naxalites (see V(61-62) notes). **185-188** Refers to Subhas Chandra Bose or 'Netaji' (*Neta* Leader) (see Section XI(a)). Bose and Nehru were the two young stars of the Indian National Congress before the war and the contrast in their temperaments reflects that of the two brothers in *Mother India* with Bose the fiery rebel and extremist militant in contrast to the rather passive and deferential Nehru. In 1939, Bose was re-elected to the post of President of the Indian National Congress (an honour only attained by Gandhi's protege Nehru). Gandhi, displeased with the success of the disrespectful Bengali militant, conspired to have Bose removed from the post; an act that fuelled the resentment felt towards Gandhi by Bengalis. Bose died in a plane crash in Indo-China in 1946, but the myth lived on amongst many illiterates that the fiery, charismatic leader of the nation had not died but was going to return to save India. **192** 'Long years ago we made a tryst with destiny, and now the time comes when we shall redeem our pledge, not wholly or in full measure, but very substantially'. From Nehru's 'midnight hour' speech. **193-194** I must admit that, despite my cultural and emotional attachment to Bose over Nehru (see XI(a) for instance), India was fortunate to be led by the cool-headed, pragmatic Kashmiri brahman rather than the hot-headed Bengali *kāyastha*, who would, almost certainly have managed to alienate various factions and could well have led India to disintegration. The argument that a dose of authoritarian government from Bose might helped overcome resistance to social reforms is usually cited in Bose's favour. See lines 102-103 for Nehru's toothless land reforms. Nehru's 'global ramblings' refers to his tendency to dwell on vague matters of international solidarity when Bose concentrated on the practical problems at hand in India. There is of course much to be said in favour of Nehru's internationalism (see also III(95-96)). *Soma* the legendary intoxicating plant juice of the Vedas.

IX. SATANIC MILLS

10 The word homespun is pregnant with meaning in this context in that homespun cloth (*khadī*) came to represent the challenge to the colonial economic relationships between Britain and India in Gandhi's *khadī* campaigns (see also VIII (98)). The economic boycott had begun earlier, following the partition of Bengal in 1905, a campaign of purchasing only homemade (*swadeshī*) products had helped spread the message of economic exploitation under colonialism. **18** As Indian Ambassador to the UN from 1952 to 1960, Krishna Menon won himself many admirers with his outspoken attacks on colonialism and his championing of Non-Alignment during the period of greatest Cold War paranoia in the West. This of course did not make him popular with conservative Westerners. **20** Referring to George Kennan, who in 1947 was made the first director of the US State Department's Policy Planning Staff by George Marshall (famous for the vast economic reconstruction aid given to post-war Europe by the Americans which bears his name). In a once top secret memorandum, Kennan wrote '. . . we have about fifty per cent of the world's resources but only 6.3 per cent of its population. This disparity is particularly great as between ourselves and the peoples of Asia. In this situation, we cannot fail to be the object of envy and resentment. Our real task in the coming period is to devise a pattern of relationships which will permit us to maintain this position of disparity without positive detriment to our national security. . . . We should cease to talk about vague and — for the Far East — unreal objectives such as human rights, the raising of living standards, and democratization.' (Cited in R. Bonner, *Waltzing with a Dictator: The Marcoses and the Making of American Policy*, Random House, 1987; the American author states that Kennan's words give a 'far more honest description of American policy . . . throughout the third world, during the past four decades than all the rhetoric'.) **22-23** I think that this metaphor comes from A.M. Schlesinger, pointing out that the US, in its period of crisis in the 1930s turned to the New Deal style of government intervention which US foreign policy has tried to eliminate in other countries which have been facing economic crises (in some cases, of course, intervention simply exacerbated problems). Again, Cold War expediency allowed certain client states, such as Japan, to flout US dictates (see below). **25-26** As stated above, it was Cold War geopolitical strategy that helped countries like Japan, South Korea, Taiwan and Singapore to attain prosperity. The Japanese motor industry was near the point of collapse when the US demand for trucks for use in the Korean war provided it with a lifeline. Kennanite strategy was to keep Japan as a manufacturer of third rate manufactures (Tonka toy cars rather than todays Toyotas) which would not compete with the USA. Singapore's strategic location and fine harbour allowed it to boom as the supply base for US intervention in Vietnam. **27-28** Bhilai: In the 1950s, when India tried to develop heavy industry, the West pressed it to concentrate on its 'traditional' products (i.e. the raw materials of the plantation economy imposed upon India by British imperialism (as dealt with in this Section)). The West also objected to state sector operations at a time when Britain and other Western European countries had most of their heavy industry in the state sector. The USSR stepped in and built a steel mill at Bhilai, the first major Soviet aid project in India. This prompted the West to give 'aid' more in tune with India's real needs for Cold War purposes of keeping India out of the Soviet camp. (P.J.S. Duncan, *The Soviet Union and India*, Royal Institute of Economic Affairs/

Routledge, 1989). In contrast, Yawata, the first major Iron and Steel works in Japan was paid for by the tribute extorted from China after the Sino-Japanese War (1894-95) provoked by Japanese aggression in Korea and violation of treaties. Indeed, Japan followed the 'Western model' of development. Helping the West to suppress the Boxer Rebellion, the invasion of Manchuria, the rape of Nanking etc. were all in accord with the Western model of development by colonial expansion. **57-60** Stranger, tell the Lacedaemonians that we lie here, in obedience to their orders'. (Better known as, 'Go tell the Spartans, He who passeth by; That here, in obedience to their laws, we lie'.) The epitaph on the memorial at Thermopylae. **63-64** (See also V(45) note). **69-72** Prior to the British conquest, trade with Bengal was financed in a large measure by the ill-begotten gains of the slave trade in which the British played a prominent role (see also X(121-132)). Indeed, over one and a half millennia earlier, Pliny had complained about the drain on the Roman treasury caused by the import of luxuries from India. Bangla *desh* here is used to mean the 'country of Bengal'. In the Eighteenth Century, the huge province of Bengal, a satrapy of the Mughal empire, under the Muslim Nawab, consisted of modern West Bengal, Bangladesh, Bihar and Orissa. Orissa was later ceded to the Hindu Marathas following their invasions (1742-51). **73-80** At the time of the British Conquest, Bengal had perhaps the most successful textile industry in the world. The huge tribute paid by the Nawab to the Mughal emperor iṇ Delhi was made partly in bonds which the famous Jain banking family, based in the Nawab's capital Murshidabad, the Jagat Seths could dispose of in Delhi largely on the strength of the volume of Bengali textile exports to North India. Bengali textiles were also prized throughout Europe. The British were to impose a 78% duty on Indian textile imports into Britain in 1813 (the reciprocal tariff being 3½%). Breaking the fingers of the weavers was one of the methods employed by the British to destroy the Bengali textile industry which competed with their nascent factory-based textile industry. Cutting off of thumbs was a punishment for breaking production laws. Line **80** is based on, 'The misery hardly finds a parallel in the history of commerce. The bones of the cotton weavers are bleaching the plains of India.' (William Bentinck, Governor General of India, 1834). **81-88** The British adventurers returning with their plunder from India were called Nabobs (from *Nawāb*) due to the ostentatious display of their newfound wealth. The link between the capital inflow from the plunder of India and the birth of the Industrial Revolution has been highlighted by Indian historians. Between 1757 and 1815 the transfer of wealth from India to Britain was in the region of 500 to one thousand million pounds sterling (a phenomenal sum in those days). Of course, other factors were involved as well. The slave trade, with all of its associated inhuman atrocities, brought great wealth to Britain which also contributed to the financing of the early Industrial Revolution. Herein lies the 'bastard birth' of the world market system dominated by the West. **89-92** Of course, the story of Bengal as India's richest province, pauperised by the British is exaggerated to some extent as part of Nationalist mythology but the elements of the story of British rule given here are ones usually omitted from British accounts (see Postscript). As it was the fertile deltaland, Bengal proper was agriculturally very productive as well having its thriving textile industry. I have put in Taj Mahal for poetic reasons, although the direct financing of the Taj cannot be attributed to Bengal. I have used it to represent the vast tribute paid to the Mughals prior to the vast tribute extorted by the British. **93-96** Sirāj-ud-Daula, Nawāb of Bengal had ordered the European traders to stop fortifying their trading posts on his land as fortification 'touched the sceptre'. The French, the threat to the British as this was the time of the Seven Years War, had stopped but the British continued leading to Sirāj's capture of the British trading post Calcutta. This led to the so-called 'Black Hole' incident in which about forty British died largely due to Sirāj's neglect rather than any preconceived act of punishment as modern studies have shown. However, as ever in such cases, the British choose to remember the grossly exaggerated accounts of Holwell and the Black Hole remains in the popular imagination as an example of Asiatic barbarity that is subliminally used as a justification for imperialist aggression in that the revenge and a 'civilising influence' can then be cited rather than the actual profit motive underlying the superficial motives. **97-100** The Battle of Plassey (1757) was basically a cannonade between the British and the French guns which were on Sirāj's side. The British, in league with the fabulously wealthy Jain bankers, the Jagat Seths, had bribed Siraj's General Mir Jaffa who would not engage his troops in return for being made Nawāb. None the less, the French cannon had the British on the verge of defeat until a thunderstorm caused a cessation of hostilities. The British, unlike the French, had gun covers and were able to resume after the storm and thus plucked victory from the jaws of defeat. **101-108** Richard Becher, an English observer in Bengal wrote in 1769, 'since the accession of the Company to the *Dīwāni* (revenue collection rights) the condition of this country has been worse than it was before this fine country, which flourished under the most despotic and arbitrary Government is verging towards its Ruin'. (cited in J.Liddle and R.Joshi, *Daughters of Independence: Gender, Caste and Class in India,* Zed, 1986). Prophetic words indeed, in 1770, following the barbaric expropriation of Bengal's wealth by the British plunderers, the failure of the monsoon led to the greatest famine in Indian history. Up to ten million people, died. The East India Company (known as 'the Company') kept foodgrains locked in its magazines whilst the population starved. The unusual severity of this Great Famine may be attributed to the expropriation by the British, in previous cases of monsoon failure, the people would not have been so helpless as they would presumably have kept reserves for such crises. During the 19th Century, after the British Government had acceded to power in India, the creaming off of the *ryots'* net produce ('rent') under the influence of the new political economy's Rent Doctrine (zealously advocated by James Mill at India House), the Indian peasantry was largely kept at a subsistence level although the high minded idea (based on the inappropriate doctrine derived in an English context) had been to tax the peasantry lightly to help them out of poverty. Despite the shortages in the 1960s, India has not suffered a full-blown famine since the British left (the last being the Bengal famine of 1943; see below). Whilst on the subject of the economic relations resulting from Empire, it is also worth noting that the Indian economy remained stagnant for the last thirty years of British rule making a mockery of British claims of benevolent and efficient administration. I have emphasised the most negative attributes of British rule here as it is important to show just how the world market system and today's neocolonial economic order came into being; some more positive aspects are touched upon in Section XI(c). **109-116** In 1942-3, as the Japanese (with the Indian National

Army; see Section XI(a)) were approaching the Assam border, the commandeering of rice by the British authorities for military use and export and other policies (see Postscript) coupled with British suppression of the facts led to famine in Bengal with 3 million deaths. **117-120** This is a true story told to me by a relative of how a poor father spent what little he had (*paisa*, 'pennies') on a jackfruit (*kathal*) which he gave to his starving children and left them to die whilst they consumed it. It was the very poor, those who get by on little more than rice who were, as ever, the worst affected. **121-124** My father often mentioned this phase of the 1943 famine, showing the marked impression that such events left on the collective memory. The starving refugees begged not for rice, as was usual, but for *fanna*, the wastewater skimmed off from the ricepan, such was the severity of the rice shortage. Although the British have disputed the traditional Bengali figure of about three million dead, recent studies by the highly regarded Harvard professor, Amartya Sen on 'excess mortality' during the famine confirm the figure of three million. The causes of this British-made famine and British attitudes towards it are discussed in the Postscript.

X. *LEBENSRAUM*

1-4 *varṇadharma* — the caste system. *Varṇa*, the traditional 'caste' literally meant 'colour'; the light-skinned Aryans separating the twiceborn Aryan castes from the shūdras, the dark-skinned natives. See note to VIII(93) for the positive discrimination steps taken by independent India. More recently, a degree of autonomy has been granted to tribal regions in various parts of India. **9** Should anyone wonder why I make such a brief reference to the far greater genocide by Catholic Europeans south of the Rio Grande (117-120), the answer is that I am looking at the 'bastard birth' of the world market system and the original 'Spirit of Capitalism' within the context of the foisting of 'free market' economics on less-developed countries (see Postscript). **11** 'Thus God made way for his people, by removing the heathen'. (from the *Chronicles of the Pilgrim Fathers*). It was, of course, Old World diseases which wiped out most of the native North Americans in the early stages of European colonisation. **13-24** 'Brothers, I have listened to many talks from our Great Father. When he first came over the wide waters, he was but a little man . . . very little. His legs were cramped by sitting long in his big boat, and he begged for a little land to light his fire on. But when the white man had warmed himself before the Indians' fire and filled himself with their hominy, he became very large. With a step he bestrode the mountains, and his feet covered the plains and the valleys. His hand grasped the eastern and western sea, and his head rested on the moon. Then he became our Great Father. He loved his red children, and he said, "Get a little further, lest I tread on thee . . ." Brothers, I have listened to a great many talks from our Father. But they always began and ended in this — "Get a little further; you are too near me." (Speech by an Indian leader at a conference of the so-called 'Five Civilised Tribes' (see 60-72) on the 'Permanent' Indian Frontier proposed by President Jackson which was to force them out of their homes in the Southeastern part of N. America (some having moved South to flee European colonists' terror in their original homes in the Northeast) to 'reservations' West of the Mississippi (from which they were later driven out again). (From *Savagery and the American Indian,* Timewatch, BBC Television, 1991). **25-28** In 1637, English Puritan settlers burnt the Pequot fort by the Mystic river, slaughtering the Indians who escaped from the fire. In line 25, I am referring to the tendency amongst some liberal New Englanders in the nineteenth century to speak out against some of the atrocities being committed against the Indians in the 'Wild West'. Many of the tribes which were persecuted by Europeans in the 'Wild West' had been driven out of their homes in the East by the greed and savagery of the ancestors of these same liberals, the 1637 incident being the most famous atrocity. **29-32** In the 1760s, Britain promised a 'permanent frontier' along the Appalachians to prevent further encroachment onto Indian homelands by European settlers. The newly independent USA opened the frontier on the basis that any land appropriated would be Government acquisitions. This, of course, boiled down to annexation as European settlers encroached on Indian land, incidents of Indian violence concocted and Indian land forcibly annexed. The Indians were forced into signing paper treaties supposedly giving away their land for paltry sums. The 'Quill of Common Sense' is Thomas Paine, whose pamphlet 'Common Sense' helped inspire the American revolutionaries. A major motive behind the War of Independence (the sort of thing that wouldn't appear in Paine's high-minded treatises) was for the settlers to be given a free hand in regard to the Indians. Line 31 is a parody of the *Rights of Man* author's famous first line of *The American Crisis* paper, 'These are times that try mens' souls', which Washington read to the troops at Valley Forge and, according to legend, the inspirational message helped turn the tide of the conflict against the British. After Independence, George Washington brutally repressed the Iroquois for having sided with the British. **34** Although scalping was practised amongst certain Indian tribes (it also occurred in ancient Europe), the settlers used it as a means of confirming Indian 'kills'. The Reverend John Chivington (line 81) had Indian women and children scalped. **37-52** 'Our land is worth more than your money. It will live forever. It will not even perish by the flames of fire. As long as the sun shines and the waters flow, this land will be here to give life to men and animals. We cannot sell the lives of men and animals; therefore we cannot sell this land. It was put here for us by the Great Spirit and we cannot sell it because it does not belong to us. You can count your money and burn it within the nod of a buffalo's head, but only the Great Spirit can count the blades of grass of these plains. As a present to you we will give anything we have that you can take with you; but the land never. '(cited in T.C. McLuhan, *Touch the Earth: A Self-Portrait of Indian Existence,* Abacus, 1971). It should be noted that some of these speeches were rewritten by the translators and historians but the 'nobility' of the message remains in spite of this. **53-56** "This land was ours before we were the land's . . . ."; opening line of Robert Frost's poem *The Gift Outright* which was recited by the poet at J.F. Kennedy's presidential inauguration. I have noted the sense of Destiny felt by the Pilgrim Fathers (line 11). In the nineteenth century, as Russia expanded eastward into Siberia, and Britain was busy grabbing territory everywhere, the Americans developed the Doctrine of Manifest Destiny, that it was the divine mission of the USA to extend its borders from the Atlantic to the Pacific. (See XI(c)(53-56) for another example of imperialist expansionism leading to semi-religious self-justification). **57-60** 'The first man who, having enclosed a piece of land, bethought himself of saying, "this is mine", and found people simple enough to believe him, was the real founder of civil society'. (J.J. Rousseau, *The Social Contract,* who was, of course, sympathetic towards the 'noble savage'). **61-72** The Cherokees (one of the so-called Five Civilised Tribes) of the Southeast, (*c.* 1830) had adopted European methods of farming, housebuilding, government etc. Sequoya had invented the famous Cherokee alphabet. With gold strikes on Cherokee land in Georgia, settler agitation led to President Andrew Jackson's proposal to move the Five Tribes West of the Mississippi. Jackson, as an army General had led the infamous Seminole War campaign whilst seizing Florida from Spain; wiping out most of the native Seminole population (along with renegade slaves) in the act. The Cherokees pursued their case through the courts, but, despite the Chief Justice's ruling in their favour, Jackson's reply was, 'now let him enforce it', sending in the army to forcibly remove the five tribes. Over four thousand Cherokees died on what became known as the 'Trail of Tears'. **71-74** 'a war of extermination will continue to be waged between the two races until the Indian race becomes extinct', from California Governor Peter Burnett's annual message of 1851 (cited in N. Chomsky, *Deterring Democracy,* Verso, 1991). It would perhaps be too kind to the likes of Burnett, to point out that, at this time, a few years before Darwin published *On the Origin of Species,* such Spencerian notions of 'survival of the fittest' were commonly applied to human phenomena. I recall reading somewhere that Charles Darwin agreed with the sort of sentiment expressed by Burnett. **77-80** The Indian population of California was reduced from *c.* 260,000 in 1800 to *c.* 15,000 in 1900 mainly by white vigilantes who simply went out and exterminated the populations of Indian villages (*Savagery and the American Indian,* Timewatch, BBC Television, 1991). General (later President) Polk seized Texas, California and other parts of Northern Mexico using the pretext of maltreatment of white settlers to fulfil the 'Manifest Destiny'. **81-92** Sand Creek Massacre, 1864. Methodist Minister, Colonel John Chivington led this unprovoked pogrom against Black Kettle's Cheyenne settlement killing 180 Indians, mainly women and children. Black Kettle had signed a peace treaty with the USA and flew the Stars and Stripes to show that he was not 'hostile'. Chivington's men ignored the waving of white flags by the Cheyenne. (*Sav. & Am. Ind.*). **93-96** Sand Creek provoked a war in which the Plains

Indians led by the Sioux Chief Red Cloud defeated the US Army and forced the USA to sign a treaty recognizing the Sioux's territory. **97-104** Having failed militarily to exterminate the Indians, the US government then adopted this policy of wiping out the buffalo which constituted the central cog in the Plains Indians' entire way of life. **105** Hitler said that he based his idea of concentration camps on the American reservations for Indians. He also admired the British (before 1776) and their American successors for the way that they dealt with 'inferior races'. **110-116** In 1888 an Indian, Wovoka, had a vision that by performing the 'ghost dance' and certain rituals, the ground would roll up like a great carpet taking the white settlers away with it and restoring the dead Indians and the exterminated animals on which they depended. **115-116** In December 1890, 300 unarmed Sioux ghost dancers (including many women and children) were shot dead by US troops at Wounded Knee reservation. The ground was carpeted with thick snow at the time. **117-120** The figures given here for Central and South America (80m in *c.* 1500 A.D. down to 4m in *c.* 1650 A.D.) are 'current estimates' cited by Chomsky (*ibid.*). Someone gave me another set of figures which put the decline in the native population at about 60m in about one century! (As with other figures given, such as the Great Bengal Famine of 1770, I have used the figures for poetic effect although I am aware that they may not be wholly accurate). **135-136** In recent years, some recognition of the vast, involuntary contribution made by African slaves to the 'opening up' of North America has been granted largely due to the work and perseverence of Afro-American scholars. Much of the clearing of forests was carried out by gangs of slaves. **141-142** The entire aboriginal population of Tasmania was wiped out by various means, including organised hunting and the distribution of poisoned flour (see Postscript).

XI. INDO-EUROPE

XI(a) *Chol Dilli*

1-4 M.N. Roy (real name Narendranath Bhattacharya) went as emissary of the Bengal Revolutionaries to Berlin in 1915. He eventually went on to Moscow where he befriended Lenin and became a communist. Roy and Lenin disagreed over the Colonial Thesis (see also XI(c) (89-96)), Roy arguing that Moscow should only support communist organisations within the liberation movements whilst Lenin held that, as communist movements were not strong in such under-developed countries, the bourgeois democratic movements should be supported. Roy later came round to the latter position. He led the Indian Communists from the 1920s and abandoned Communism at Independence. At one point he had high hopes of converting the great leader of the Bengal Congress, C.R. Das (under whose tutelage Subhas Bose developed his political career) to communism but this did not occur. **6** *Neta* Leader. 'Netaji' Subhas Chandra Bose was *Rāshtrapati* (President) of the Indian National Congress, 1938 and 1939. Nehru had been the only re-elected President before Bose, 1937 and 1938 and the two were the young stars of the Congress. Gandhi had ousted the radical Bose after his re-election in 1939, an act for which Gandhi is still much reviled in Bengal (see also VIII(186-188)) Bose escaped from house arrest in Calcutta in January 1940 and made his way to Kabul. The Russians, fearing German attack and thus not wanting to offend the British, refused him aid but let him pass through to Berlin from where he broadcast a number of messages. In his one meeting with Hitler, Bose spoke out against Hitler's racist views. **9-12** In October 1942, Bose went by U-boat to German Mozambique and from there by Japanese submarine to Singapore (Lion City, *shingha pur*) where the so-called Indian National Army was formed from Indian PoWs etc. Their Indian tricolor bore a Springing Tiger in place of Ásoka's *chakra*. His famous rallying cry to the INA at Singapore was, *Chol Dilli, Lāl Qīla'* (Let's go to Delhi, the Red Fort) which was the British Army HQ. **21-24** As his nephew Mihir Bose notes in his book *The Lost Hero* (Quarto, 1982), as with the Irish heroes of the 1916 Dublin uprising, Bose's small band of men was to achieve moral success in the face of military defeat by inspiring revolutionary fervour into the nation by their self-sacrifice. Bose died in a plane crash, on his way to Japan in August 1945. **35** Nehru, who had not practised law for over twenty years wanted to defend the INA officers. **45-48** Herbert Morrisson led the British Parliamentary Commission to India in 1946 amidst the near-revolutionary situation created by

Indian anger at the INA show trial. The message to a bankrupt and war-weary Britain was that to hold on to India would require the dispatch of thousands of white troops, so, in its own way, the small INA adventure (which had rapidly blown up to legendary proportions in popular mythology) finally forced the British to realise that they could no longer hold on to India; the watershed marking the beginning of the end of the colonial world.

XI(b) *Old Indian Air*

4 *patrikas* papers/publications **5** *Hindutva* Hindu culture ('Hindudom') (see also VIII(118) **9-12** Wilberforce's Clapham Sect, which pressed for missionary entry into India based their Evangelism on a 'born again' experience which might have had Indian origins and, if so, would constitute a more direct example of *Hindutva* going abroad, taking on new manifestations and then having a dramatic impact on the course of Indian history. (Interestingly, the Anti-Slavery League still exists in Clapham, where one of its key concerns is child slavery and bonded labour in India). **13-16** William Jones' Asiatic Society of Bengal (aided by native *paṇḍits*) helped to piece together the disjointed fragments of India's history and translated many of her ancient works. *Áchārya* means 'the master', as in 'master of philosophy' or preceptor. Jones prepared the standard orthography for Sanskrit translation. The 'rediscovery' of Hindu India's glorious past (along with the realisation of the 'Aryan' link between the Indo-Aryans and the Europeans) was a major impetus behind the emerging Hindu Nationalism of the late 19th Century as it restored a sense of pride and self-respect to the long subject Hindus. (Just prior to the British, the Hindu Marāthās had been the dominant power in India, defeating the Mughals, but this Hindu military resurgence was not accompanied by great cultural achievements). **18** *dada* elder brother. Jones, in his famous address to the Society in which he pointed out the similarities, asserted that Sanskrit was more perfect and more exquisitely refined than either Greek or Latin. (See also note to V(79-88) on Hittite link). **21-24** Jones translated the ancient Indian poet Kalidasa's 'play' *Śakuntala* (see note to VI(11-12)) and called Kalidas the 'Shakespeare of India' which led to racist criticisms in Britain, in for instance the liberal *Edinburgh Review.* In private Jones wrote that, "I should have thought that our great dramatic poet had studied Kalidasa". (O.P. Kejariwal, *The Asiatic Society of Bengal and the Discovery of India's Past,* Oxford U.P., 1988). A.L. Basham, in his foreword to this book, notes how, contrary to Nationalist assertions, the Society's work was driven by scholarly interests although Warren Hastings had, officially, stated the need to learn about India's culture in order to consolidate imperial power. Note also that Bankim Chattopadhyay pointed out the underlying racism (nowadays called 'Eurocentrism') of much of the Orientalists' views on Indian history and achievements, making Jones' views even more enlightened considering the racialist climate. Nirad Chaudhuri (*Thy Hand Great Anarch,* Chatto & Windus, 1987) notes how Curzon decided not to recommend Tagore for an Oxford Doctorate in 1912. A year later Tagore (whom the Irishman Yeats had done much to help in Britain) won the Nobel Prize (the first non-European winner) and the British hastily conferred a knighthood upon him. (See also the quote about Ramanujan in the introduction.) **27** Refers to quote from Herman Hesse on Bhartrihari given in note to XVI(65-66). **29-36** "Indian air surrounds us, and original thoughts of kindred spirits. And oh, how thoroughly is the mind here washed clean of all early engrafted Jewish superstitions! . . . It has been the solace of my life, it will be the solace of my death. (Arthur Schopenhauer, *World as Will and Representation,* 1st Edn). The German intelligentsia went through a period known as 'Indomania' following the early translations of the ancient Sanskrit texts into German. Schopenhauer's ideas were strongly influenced by Indian thought, for instance, his 'principle of individuation' appearing to be very similar to Shankara's view of the *ātman's* sense of separateness from *Brahman.* **37-40** Cited by Bernal in *Black Athena* (see Section V). Humboldt also appears in IV(9-12). At the age of 12, I myself was profoundly influenced by a translation of the *Bhagavad Gītā,* in the commentary of which I found theological speculation of an altogether different order to the simplistic mythologies taught at my Christian schools under 'religious education'. The notion that everything in the universe was a manifestation of one underlying reality came to me from this reading and fuelled my metaphysical concern in relation to the 'oneness/otherness mystery'. **41-44** Based on an essay by

Peter Medawar (immunologist and popular science writer) in which he ridiculed German philosophy as deep tuba blasts bellowing forth from the Rhine (an attitude shared my many British, steeped in empiricism, towards continental European metaphysics). I noted then that whilst the likes of Rutherford worked out the boring details of atomic structure, the Germans were developing the metaphysically profound Quantum Theory (some of the metaphysical influences behind this work is noted below as it is of critical importance to the overall theme of this passage). Incidentally, Calcutta's S.N. Bose was the only non-European involved in the original development of Quantum Theory, his famous letter to Einstein leading to the Bose-Einstein statistics. *Rāga* in Indian classical music, a series of notes used to construct a melody (the *sa ri gha ma pa dha ni sa* — as in the film Close Encounters of the Third Kind where these notes are used to communicate with the aliens). *Tāla* rhythm in Indian classical music. **45** *Nirguṇa* without form/qualities. In Vedantic philosophy a distinction is made between *nirguṇa Brahman* and *saguṇa* (with form/qualities) *Brahman.* The latter is immanent in the empirical world whilst the former is the transcendental *Brahman* (the Ultimate Reality). This distinction into two levels of reality, is basically the way in which Vedanta tackles the problem of the relationship between empirical reality and Ultimate Reality which is similar to the relationship behind Kant's noumenon (things as they are in themselves)/phenomenon (things as they are apprehended) distinction. Kant is known to have read the translations of Indian works available in his time (before Indomania). Schopenhauer held Kant's 'appearance' to be identical to the Indian concept of *māyā.* **46** *Jagati* The 'collective movement'; in Vedic thought, the whole universe is a system of continual flux (*jagati*). (See also note to line II(79)). I had in mind, when I wrote this line, something I read by a couple of Marxian thinkers who described Marxists' hero Hegel as the man who introduced the concept of the universe as a dynamic process with hierarchical structuring. **47** Refers to Schopenhauer (the *Upaniṣads,* the scriptural basis of *Vedānta,* were the 'solace' of his life and death, as above). Schopenhauer deliberately timed his lectures to clash with Hegel's (but the latter's proved more popular, Karl Marx attended them of course). Schopenhauer held Hegel to be "a scribbler of rubbish and a corrupter of minds" whose philosophy was "confused, empty verbiage" (W. Halbfass, *India and Europe*). Schopenhauer outlived Hegel by thirty years, gaining access to Indian material not available to Hegel. The extremely Eurocentric Hegel had a low opinion of Indian thought which he studied extensively (Halbfass, *ibid.*) and probably would not have acknowledged any influence on his own thought. I do agree, however, with his criticism of the Indian philosophy (he at least accepted it as such, unlike some later Europeans) he encountered as just 'abstract unity' but had not found its way back to the concrete particularity of the world. **48** The concept of the Aryan Race seems to have its origins in Friedrich Schlegel, who was not anti-semitic and even married a Jew. His brother Wilhelm was the first Professor of Sanskrit at Bonn. He went through a phase of infatuation with India and asserted that India was the birthplace of all civilisation (*see* p. 222); his interest in linguistics led him to the view that there were two sorts of language, the 'noble' inflected ones (Indo-European) and the non-inflected languages. This paved the way for the Aryan/Semitic distinction. He held that clarity of thought and high philosophy were only possible with the inflected Indo-European languages. (Bernal, M., *Black Athena*). Schlegel was a leading figure in the German Romantic movement which looked upon Indian thought for inspiration in its critiques of the one-sided rationalist, materialist development of Enlightenment Europe. Of course, the likes of Adorno saw the traces of Voltaire and the cold reason of the Enlightenment in the clinical organisation of Hitler's 'Final Solution'. **49** Refers to Newton's famous comment that he was like a boy on a beach seeking out the smoothest pebbles. **51-52** Heisenberg, the founder of quantum mechanics, said that Indian philosophy had at least a subconscious influence on his thinking. On a visit to Calcutta, he discussed science and Indian thought with Tagore. He said that discovering that a whole culture subscribed to views resembling those which had shocked the European Mind came as a great help to him (Capra, F. *Uncommon Wisdom*, Flamingo, 1988). Heisenberg's colleague on Hitler's atom bomb project, physicist Carl von Weiszacker (brother of a recent German President) has a deep interest in Indian philosophy. **53-56** Schrödinger developed the famous wave function which replaced Heisenberg's 'matrix mechanics' and was inspired by Vedāntic ideas. At the end of his well-known little book *What is Life* (1944), he included an appendix relating to *Vedānta* of which he was an advocate. He left Nazi Austria for Dublin. **57-60** The notion of the purity of the German *Volk*, never conquered by the Romans thus linguistically and racially pure existed in Herder's thought, the racial nationalism increasing in the late 19th century. Halbfass (*India and Europe*) notes that speculative ideas about India in conjunction with the notion of the Aryan Race played a role in racial theory. In his infamous *Essai sur l'inégalité des races humaines* (1853-1855; German edition 1898-1901), Gobineau gives a paradigmatic role to the Aryan invasion of India and the development of the caste system. According to Gobineau, realising the danger of intermixture with the natives of India, the Aryan lawgivers implemented the caste system for self-preservation, to prevent degeneration. (Views similar to Gobineau's on the bastardization of liberal Britain seem to be held by many Japanese today, keen to prevent social degeneration through racial mixture, as they hold to be the case in the USA). In Vienna, Hitler was a regular reader of the Ariosophists' journal *Ostara* which in 1908 had two special issues on the code of Manu (*Manusmriti* — the ancient Indian law book) and race cultivation amongst the Indo-Aryans. *Áryāvarta* (Aryan Homeland) Indo-Aryan name for Eastern Gangetic plain where the great Aryan kingdoms sprang up early in the first millennium B.C. The founder of the Ariosophic movement, G. Lanz-Liebenfels was one of the early propagators of the swastika. (Numerous other influences were, of course, at play with the Nazis such as the contemporary Eugenics movement, popular in Britain and America; Henry Ford was a strong advocate).

XI(c). *A Nation Born through Synthesis*

1-16 These four verses are drawn from the famous *Science an Civilisation in China* J. Needham (ed.), Cambridge U.P., 1953. Th Western Christian Church founded in Rome constructed a Go as a Roman Governor who laid down laws; conceiving the 'God' as *supermundanus*, an agent beyond and separate fro Nature which established the laws by which Nature operates. 2 *Hindudharma* means here the thought underlying the Hindu wa of life. **29-32** The Bengali revolutionary who became a mysti philosopher and poet after seeking refuge in French Pondicherr Aurobindo Ghose ('Sri Aurobindo') who also helped develop th

India as Mother concept. In relation to the Indian mode of response to the challenge of the West, he noted that the true enemy of a thesis is not the antithesis but the synthesis. This is because the synthesis includes the thesis and thus does away with its *raison d'être*. He illustrated this with the withering away of Buddhism in India following Shankara's interpretation of the Vedānta ('Upaniṣadic exegesis') which incorporated elements of Buddhist thought. Shankara also went and defeated the Buddhist thinkers in disputations at the great Buddhist centre of learning, Nālandā (See also III(10)). **34** Alexander Duff led a vigorous campaign for proselytization in Bengal in the early 19th century. Duff saw the introduction of English education as the engine which would destroy Hinduism which he despised. **35-44** Features of Christianity were incorporated into Hindu thought by the likes of Rammohun Roy (the so-called first modern Indian) who stressed theistic, monotheistic and other tendencies in the Hindu spectrum which were in line with Christianity. He founded the small but influential *Brahmo Sabhā* (later *Brahmo Samāj*) in 1828 which mimicked certain aspects of Christian worship and abandoned idolatry, worshipping *Brahman* 'directly'. The later trend towards so-called Hindu Revivalism, although it reaffirmed popular forms of worship (*bhakti*), was none the less, in its liberal forms, deeply imbued with the idea of progress and humanism, drawn from the Christian tradition. Although there are a number of 'schools' of Vedānta (interpretation of the Upaniṣads (also known as the '*Vedānta*', meaning 'the end of the Vedas'), the Neo-Hindu emphasis has been on the *Advaita* (non-dualistic tradition of interpretation which lays emphasis on the Upaniṣadic declarations of identity between the Self, *ātman* and *Brahman*) where Shankara is the dominant figure. Vivekānanda interpreted the teachings of the Vedānta, that *Brahman* is present in everyone, to argue, on the basis that everyone has the same God in them, for egalitarianism. *Bhaktimārga* the 'path of loving devotion' usually involving devotional hymns etc. to a personal idol. In response to the missionary criticisms of idolatry, educated Hindus stressed the fact (known to many European visitors to India for centuries) the Hindu approach of providing different forms of worship appropriate for the educational status and inclinations of the worshipper. The idols were merely symbols which the human mind could grasp and identify with; behind all the cults and deities lay the one Ultimate Reality, *Brahman. Naiti* (*na iti* or *neti*) 'not thus'. The famous words of the *via negativa* found in the passages of the Upaniṣads, used by the teacher when a student tries to compare *Brahman* to various things. In the Vedāntic interpretations of the Upaniṣadic scriptures, these passages are used to stress that *Brahman* is beyond all words and mental categories. Given that *Brahman* cannot truly be conceived, it is not surprising that the *bhakti* cults with their colourful deities and ceremonies are far more popular than the arcane Vedāntic debate. **45-58** This passage is based on Ashis Nandy's, 'The Psychology of Colonialism' (in *The Intimate Enemy*) which itself draws on Morris, J. *Heavens Command: An Imperial Progress*, (1973, Faber). The idea of empire did not really take hold in Britain until the 1830s. Prior to this, most Britons in India lived like Indians, wore Indian dress, observed Indian customs and offered *pūjā* to Indian deities, with respect for the *brāhmaṇas*. Some married Indian women. Nandy notes that the first two Governer Generals, although famed for their rapaciousness, were also committed to all things Indian. Missionary activity was banned and Indian laws dominated the courts. Morris writes that the "superior tone of voice came not as it would later come, from an arrogant Right, but from a highly moralistic Left. The middle classes, newly enfranchised, were emerging into power: . . . who would prove . . . the most passionate imperialists of all." As I have noted elsewhere, the Evangelical Clapham Sect campaigned for missionary entry into India. Eric Stokes (*The English Utilitarians and India*) notes that the sect's connection with India was particularly intimate, Shore and Grant became Wilberforce's neighbours in Clapham after their return from India. T.B. MacAulay's father was a founder of the Sect. The Evangelicals believed that human character could be transformed by a direct assault on the mind. Wilberforce considered Hinduism to be a grand abomination. Charles Grant's famous treatise (1797) on the degraded nature of Indian society was a plea for evangelizing India; to effect a Reformation liberating the individual Indian's mind from the tyranny of brahmin priestcraft. Education was required to dispel the ignorance that maintained the superstitions and to pave the way for Christian truth. Grant proposed "the further civilisation of a people, who had very early made considerable progress" but who had stagnated and indeed become retrograde. The beneficiary of this civilising mission would be British commerce. Drawing on Grant's treatise, the Evangelicals launched a great campaign in 1813, the year of the Company's Charter renewal, with Wilberforce (a friend of the Pitts) leading the campaign in parliament. **59-60** Refers to Rammohun Roy's famous letter to William Pitt Amherst (Governor General 1823-28); showing that the introduction of Western ideas was not just a one way thing, as with Roy's campaigning for the abolition of *Satī*, Indians took the initiative to further their own society's progress. **63-64** Nirad Chaudhuri (*ibid.*) explains the moral message of *The Jungle Book*, Mowgli represents the white man who fraternises with the natives. The monkey people (*bandor lok*) represent the Bengalis aping the British. Nirad Chaudhuri wonders what Kipling, with his hatred of Bengalis, must have felt like when Tagore won the Nobel Prize for literature. **65-68** Based on Nandy, A. 'The Uncolonised Mind' in *The Intimate Enemy*. **69-72** The British admiration for the so-called 'martial' races of India seems to have grown out of the views of men like Munro, Governor of Madras (1820s), influenced by Romanticism who held a strong contempt for the legalism of the social transformation school of British opinion on India. They were perhaps a little too ahead of their time in criticising the introduction of 'inappropriate' and British customs onto Indian society. They were in favour of the personal '*ma-baap*' approach of the collector going out on horseback rather than abstract laws, of maintaining the old Indian states and customs and had the Romantics sympathy for the 'noble savage' type. Ainslee Embree (*Imagining India: Essays on Indian History*, Oxford U.P., 1989) notes that Elphinstone and Malcolm (both associated with Munro's approach) recognised the brahmans as the natural enemies of British power. Both had taken part in the Marāthā wars. The brahmans in Marāthā territories, unlike their Bengali counterparts, held considerable political and economic power. The contemptuous references to the Bengali babu began to appear in the late 19th century. Nandy (*ibid.*) discusses the psychological aspects of Kipling's concept of the fake sahib or 'babu' (see also VII(159-166). English-educated Bengali civil servants like Bankim Chattopadhyay were themselves rather self-deprecating in their writings, orthodox Hindus poured ridicule upon the babus. Bankim wisely left the heroic military action against the foreign rulers to his novels. Partha Chatterjee (*Nationalist Thought and the Colonial World,* United Nations U.P., 1986) quotes a reply Bankim gave to a public address by Rajnarayan Bose in 1874, in which Bose castigated the newly educated classes of Bengal for aping the English. Bankim noted that "one cannot learn except by imitation". Imitation of the English was natural and could be beneficial as the first step towards national regeneration. The English themselves imitated other cultures he noted. As the verse notes, the English-educated Bengalis, serving as the lower officials of the Raj, did the real damage to British power which no martial race heroics could have achieved. Posted across India, they spread the ideas of the likes of babu Bankim Chattopadhyay, ideas which gave birth to the Indian Nation. **72-76** The racial discrimination against the likes of Surendranath Banerjea (the first Indian admitted into the elite Indian Civil Service) and judge W.C. Bonerjee (see Postscript) played a significant role in turning progressive Hindus away from notions of British tutelage, towards a sense of pride in their own customs, beliefs and race which manifested itself in the so-called 'Hindu revivalism', nationalism and the early lobbying for Indian participation in government and future self-government. **77-80** Based on old Bengali adage. **81-84** Cited in Best, G. (ed.) *The Permanent Revolution: The French Revolution and its Legacy,* Fontana, 1988). Swami Vivekananda, foremost apostle of the '19th Century' to 19th Century Bengali saint Rāmakrishna, founder of the Rāmakrishna Mission and leading Neo-Hindu thinker who pressed for social reform through his reinterpretations of Hinduism. **85-88** Cited in Best, G. (*ibid.*). Soon after India's Independence, Malraux, as French Minister of Culture, offered Nehru an exhibition, either one on Norman sculpture or one on the Revolution. Nehru replied that in India, France <u>is</u> the Revolution. **93-96** The Tatar, Mir-said Sultan Galiev, a member of the Central Muslim Commissariat, first propounded this famous thesis in 1918. (See also notes to XI(a) (1-4)). It is interesting to note the Muslim link in this statement of the global anti-colonial struggle; with the collapse of Communism, there is a tendency in certain quarters to perceive Islam as the 'ideology' of the oppressed peoples of the world.

XII. NO SURE GROUND

48-52 I am actually referring here to Roland Joffe's film version of Dominique Lapierre's book about the slums of Calcutta, *City of Joy*, the filming of which was causing quite a stir in Calcutta at the time I wrote this work (see also Introduction). My point in the verse was to raise the question of the commodification of 'Third World problems' for the Western markets. We have recently seen such issues being taken up by pop musicians, comedians and the like whose normal activities, one could argue, tend to involve the promotion of the consumerism which helps to maintain the inequalities in global resource distribution. Despite the genuine goodwill and generosity displayed, these things always smack of peer pressure and appearing to be 'right on'. Of course, the very nature of the Western mass media encourages shallow 'sound bites' and the juxtaposition of fabulously wealthy, glamorous and, often, people not reknown for mature behaviour with issues of grave concern. Coming from Bengal, I was irritated by Joffe's comments on a British TV programme about the filming of *City of Joy* where he seemed to accuse the West Bengal government of being rather indifferent toward the plight of Calcutta's poor. I would refer him to Atul Kohli's *The State and Poverty in India* (Cambridge U.P., 1987) which shows that the WB government has been foremost amongst state governments in trying to tackle rural poverty; the state government acknowledging the fact that, historically, Calcutta (like other big cities) appropriated the rural surplus. Thus the government has concentrated on tackling the crisis at its roots. The real problem of the *bustees* lies not in Calcutta itself but in the poverty of the hinterland. The appalling poverty of Calcutta's hinterland is also partly a legacy of British Colonialism (see Section IX, *Satanic Mills*) and the neocolonial economic relationships of today which have their roots partly in this Colonial legacy. My concerns raised in the verse is that the tear-jerking, romanticised plight of a few semi-fictional characters may move some cinema-goers but avoids the broader issues about the context in which this poverty exists, which might entail raising issues which would not attract cinema-goers. There was concern in Calcutta, that Joffe, the man who made *The Mission*, was again showing a white Christian priest (described by a Bengali politician as the 'Tarzan figure') coming to show the natives the way (see also Section XI on the historical missionary legacy). None the less, I grant that there is a value in 'raising awareness' and Dominique Lapierre and his wife have done much charitable work in Calcutta using the royalties from his book and donations from those reading the book (including money raised by the inmates of a French prison). One of the points of *No Sure Ground* is to stress that there are no absolute rights and wrongs ('Oft good intentions bring ends vile' etc.). **75-76** LCD/HCF Lowest Common Denominator and Highest Common Factor **77-80** See Postcript **86** See Introduction **97-100** See Postscript **105-108** Spinoza earned a living by grinding glass to make optical lenses for telescopes and microscopes (rather like the young Einstein who worked for eight years in a patent office, including his most creative years). Spinoza died from the effects of glass dust inhalation. **113-116** Subhas Bose felt that, had he not been born into the freedom struggle, he would have liked to have spent more time on philosophy. Aurobindo Ghose gave up his revolutionary activities for philosophy and poetry when he found refuge from the British in French Pondicherry. His *Life Divine* was nominated for the Nobel Prize for literature by Pearl Buck and Gabriella Mistral; ironically the prize that year went to the Western mathematical logician, Bertrand Russell, who was hostile to mysticism rather than the Hindu mystic. **145** *māyā* illusion **164** *Shiva Nāṭarāja* (Shiva, the Lord of Dance); the well-known form of this deity, within a ring. The verse has nothing to do with the mythology or religious significance surrounding this icon.

XIII. THAT ONE

NB. The discussion here reflects my thought in 1991-93. My new work synthesizing Science and Mysticism is presented in the final essay.

XIII(a). *Tad Ekam*

18 *avidyā* ignorance of Reality/illusion **29-44** This passage is directly based on the famous hymn 10.129 of the *Rigveda, Nāsadīya sūkta*, the first three verses here, with some poetic licence, directly drawn from the beginning of the hymn; the fourth verse directly from the end (I have left out a passage which falls in between). The multivalency of Sanskrit terms precludes direct translation. I have drawn upon a number of translations and have been biased by my own favourite interpretations as well as constrained by the structure of my own verse, but I think it captures the 'spirit' of the original hymn which has been the subject of much metaphysical speculation. *Tapas* literally means 'burning' but has numerous other related meanings such as a 'creative ardour' and 'psychophysical energy' etc. **45** *Purush* (*Puruṣa*) I have used this term for the void in *Nāsadīya* primarily for reasons of poetic Convenience. The equivalent source of Creation has been called *'Brahman'* (i.e. Creation is but a part of this greater *Brahman*) or *Parabrahman* (the Supreme Brahman). **48** Self-limitation (*yajña* which primarily means sacrifice); as in lines 53-56. Shankara and his followers held that the transcendental Brahman did not really transmute (as a perfect being would have no need to change, concocting an unconvincing charade involving the notion of *māyā* (see also Section XIV) but the *Brahma pariṇāma* (Brahma modification) position is repeatedly stated in the *Brahma Sūtras*. **51** *yajña* self-limitation; as in the following verse. **57** *shristi* (literally 'throwing out') means Creation. **61** *kalpa* (literally 'imagining' or 'carving out'), the 'Day of Brahman' refers to one cycle of creation and dissolution. Brahman dissolves back into the void (*Puruṣa/Parabrahman*). Such creations are cyclic in the Vedic 'oscillating universe'. (See also II(65-68)). Each *kalpa* supposedly consists of thousands of *mahāyugas*, each 4.3 million years long. Note the interesting literal meaning of *kalpa*, 'imagining', related to ideas of Creation being like a dream or to ideas like Shankara's view of Creation as merely a sort of illusory 'superimposition'. **65-68** David Bohm (*Wholeness and the Implicate Order*, Routledge, 1980) notes that modern physics assumes a vast ocean of energy (which has no form, therefore it can't be measured and is thus, for all intents and purposes ignored; like a fish being oblivious of the ocean) — the matter in the universe being but a tiny part of this energy 'crystallized' into matter. **69-72** Cosmologists, when faced with the question as to what gives rise to the Big Bang, tend to give the unsatisfying answer 'nothing', or if pressed they admit that such questions are beyond the realm of empirical and scientific enquiry. Note that, nowadays, Space and Time are not conceived as existing independently of matter, they are created in the Big Bang and expansion of the Universe (the 'singularity's extension'). **73-76** Refers to a number of cosmological notions. Shifts — the Red Shifts in the radiation spectra of galaxies play a central role in the expanding universe view. Free lunch — refers to Alan Guth's inflationary universe model (or 'free lunch hypothesis') relating to the early period of cosmic expansion. Lines 75-76 refer to the notion of 'dark matter', matter which is not directly detected as it does not radiate but which may account for most of the mass of the universe. Such mass is required for the expansion to stop and perhaps for gravitational forces to bring about a collapse (Big Crunch). Recently there have been a spate of reported discoveries of 'dark matter' involving slow moving heavy particles etc. *Pralaya* — the dissolution of the cosmos at the end of the cycle (*kalpa*) and also the formless state into which the cosmos returns (as in II(84)).

XIII(b) *Tat tuam asi*

The scriptures known as the *Upaniṣads* (or the *Vedānta* — the 'end of the Vedas') get their name (*Upaniṣad*) from the Sanskrit words meaning to 'sit down near'. This refers to the students sitting down near the gurus in order to be instructed in ways of coming to 'know' *Brahman*. Some of the key ideas from the Upaniṣads are alluded to in this passage, hence I begin with the same line for each verse. **8** *naiti naiti* (*na iti* or *neti*) — 'not thus, not thus' (see also XI(c) (44)). **10** *AUM* (OM) the sacred symbol composed of three sounds (corresponding to a, u, m) which represent various important triads. *Brahman* is said to be speech and said to be *AUM*. See lines 21-24. *Śabdatattva* (the word/ sound principle). The actual OM symbol represents the three states of consciousness (waking, dream and deep sleep) and the transcendent ground-consciousness underlying all states. **19-20** *Tat tuam asi* is the famous identity thesis propounded in some of the *Upaniṣads* which, as line 19 indicates, states an identity between *ātman* (the Hindu Self) and *Brahman*. The exact nature of this identity is the subject of much metaphysical debate in Vedānta philosophy. **21-24** This is a personal interpretation of *AUM* (the *śabdatattva* or *śabdabrahman*). I am suggesting in the verse that the exhalatory 'drone', especially during the continuous incantational speech of a mantra, which is broken up into separate words is like the ground of speech and is thus a metaphor for *Brahman,* the Ground of all things. The *AUM* notion is of little importance in the dominant Vedāntic traditions although it does have prominence in the work of Bhartrihari (see also XVI(65)) who focused on language. **28** 'Words and mind go to Him, but reach Him not and return.' (*Taittirīya Upaniṣad*). **31** *mahāvākya* grand pronouncement **33-36** (See also XI(b) (45) notes). Shankara, the foremost philosopher of the dominant *Advaita* tradition of Vedāntic interpretation (*Advaita* means 'non-dual' and refers to this tradition's approach to the identity thesis of the *Upaniṣads, tat tuam asi*), stresses the two 'aspects' of *Brahman,* the transcendental *nirguṇabrahman* (without qualities/form) and the immanent *saguṇabrahman* (with qualities/form). This distinction is not spelt out with total clarity and seems to be in part a response to the theistic schools of *Vedānta* which hotly disputed the monist schools' (especially *Advaitavēdānta*'s) identification of *ātman* with *Brahman* as this cheapened the supreme transcendence of *Brahman;* who in the *Upaniṣads* is characterised more by His total Otherness than by the rare identity thesis with *ātman.* *Mokṣa,* 'liberation', the state of 'union' with *nirguṇabrahman* which is the ultimate goal of meditative practises. **37-40** Shankara stressed that it was not the ordinary egoistic Self which 'was one with' *Brahman* but the transcendent ground-Consciousness (*Chit*) underlying all individual conscious minds. I have thus used the Upaniṣadic notions of *Brahman* as the 'Be-er' which underlies all Being, and the 'Seer' which underlies all Seeing in the verse to emphasise this notion of the ground of Consciousness or Pure Consciousness. **41-44** *Mokṣa* (or *mukti,* is the state of 'enlightenment'), usually translated as 'liberation' (as its traditional interpretation involves 'freedom' from the bonds of *avidyā* (ignorance of Reality) which tie us to the world of everyday reality) is the central 'soteriological' goal of all six major Indian systems of philosophy, *darśanas,* not just of Vedānta. In the form of *nirvāṇa,* it also lies at the heart of Buddhist thought. *Mokṣa* is supposed to be the state attained after all mental activity has been extinguished. It is said to involve an experience devoid of the ego and of the 'world', a state of pure consciousness (*chit*) which, as the term 'enlightenment' indicates is an experience of being Light.

Lines 42-43 relate to the ethical rationale behind attaining *mokṣa*. Human suffering is caused by innate drives linked to the ego not being satisfied. Even when basic drives are satisfied, frustration results as further desires arise etc. The extreme logic involves ending suffering by eliminating the ego which leads to such false selfish desire based on the illusion of being a separate Self. *Bhoi* fear.

XIV. MIND GAMES

15 Idols of the Market. Francis Bacon's doctrine of the Four Idols (the constraints on human understanding) from *The Advancement of Learning* (*De Augmentis*). The Idols of the Market are the constraints placed on human understanding due to the use of words and names (i.e. Language). True understanding being constrained by the meanings associated with words and the way language operates in relation to thought etc. Bacon, of course, did not know the Indian approach of transcending Language and Thought through direct experience of underlying Reality. **17-24** The Analytical School, which dominates Anglo-American academic philosophy concentrates on the analysis of language. This idolization of Language has followed, in largely as a result of Wittgenstein's exhortations; Wittgenstein having been a sort of 'holy man' who gave away his wealth, had an overzealous obsession with seeking the truth (leading to intellectual 'tunnel vision'), could not tolerate criticism, and kept going off to live as a hermit. He also came out with some memorable *mahāvākyas* (grand pronouncements) although his actual writings are most confused. This only goes to show that even the best-educated Westerners can fall for the personality cult and misguided teachings of an oddball holy man, something the 'hard-headed' philosophers of the West mocked Indians for doing! Obsessed as it is with Language, the Analytical school seems to have developed a sort of dogma about Language being 'prior' to thought. They try to prove assertions such as that the necessary condition for the existence of thought was the presence of two people in communication. Anyone with an understanding of modern science, including studies relating to cognitive processes and the use of language etc. can see through the silliness of such futile debates. Recent suggestions by some psychologists that the mind manipulates 'mental models' in terms of 'semantics' have been shown to be tenuous; such semantic levels of operation would have to be based on some lower level of 'logic' which could be realised by the 'machinery' of the brain. As the verse notes, rudimentary visual reasoning would almost certainly have been in operation long before speech evolved. Studies in human cognitive function showing that, where possible, we use visual reasoning rather than more elaborate forms of reasoning. The rest of this Section emphasises the fundamental importance of vision in relation to our understanding of the world. None of us actually does our .thinking in the form of words. Language evolved as a means of communication to transmit thoughts through the linear channel of speech sounds; thought is not such a linear process. Lines 20-24 refer to the interesting argument that, once hominids stood up on their hind legs freeing the hands for tool use, visual and tactile senses needed coordination. Neural evolutionary studies show that evolution of such 'association areas' between different sensory modalities in the brain proliferate in those areas most closely associated with 'thinking'. Such cross-modal connections provide the basis for sense-independent generalisation (abstraction) of representations leading to conceptualisation and then to language as a means of communication. **30** I have in mind famous equations like Einstein's mass/energy equivalence as the *mahāvākyas* of modern science. **33-36** *Mahāvākya* (Grand Pronouncement). Newton forged minutes of the Royal Society's proceedings to 'prove' beyond doubt that it was he, and not Leibniz, who first invented the infinitesimal (differential) calculus, a cornerstone of modern physics. Newton was first but his first principles method was most cumbersome and the simplified system developed by Leibniz is the one that everyone uses. The action-at-a-distance of Newton's gravitational model caused metaphysical problems as to how a body had an effect on other bodies far removed from it. It was impossible to visualize; a critical component of our supposed 'understanding'. Einstein's model of a field (continuum), distorted by the presence of a body is much easier to 'picture' despite the far more sophisticated mathematics. Newton's famous reply to such metaphysical concerns is given in line 36 (an answer reminiscent of the Buddha who refused to be drawn into metaphysical debate).

37-40 *māyā* illusion (in the sense that the world as we perceive it is a sort of illusion although the emphasis on "illusion" is misleading because the notion of *māyā* originates in the notion of a divine, magical, creative power). **41-44** This verse is based on Jaques Derrida's notion of *S'entendre parler* (hearing/understanding oneself speak) which he has claimed as the basis of the notions of the origin of the world. In the "moment of speech", Voice seems to be the direct manifestation of Thought. The spoken words appear as an emanation in one realm from an altogether different realm, resulting, according to Derrida, in the idea of the worldly and the non-worldly. (Cited in Sturrock, J. (ed.) *Structuralism and Since,* Oxford U.P., 1979). There may be something in this notion especially in relation to notions involving the "Word" but this is clearly not the basis for the Vedāntic notion of the transcendental and the mundane which comes from yogic/meditative experiences. **45** *līlā* See II(73) notes. **50** *Niṣkāma karma* (non-desire action) 'disinterested action'. This phrase has different meanings in different contexts. It is most well-known as the doctrine of selfless action taught to Arjuna by Krishna in the *Bhagavad Gītā.* In the Vedāntic context, the phrase applies to the notion that *Brahman,* being perfect, has no intrinsic need to create the universe nor any goal to fulfil in regard to the development of the cosmos (Lott, E. *Vedantic Approaches to God,* MacMillan, 1980). Note the modern cosmological speculations about the universe being created as merely a random fluctuation in the underlying source of the universe(s); these modern notions also resemble Bohm's notion of the background energy ignored by physics/**54** Great Chain of Being. See Section II notes. **58** Anamorphosis: Evolution towards greater complexity. **69-76** *yajña* (literally "sacrifice", the self-limitation of *Purush* (*Puruṣa* or *parabrahman*) which results in a 'Creation' (of a universe). These verses allude to the notion, based on the so-called Anthropic Principle (which basically involves the argument that the universe is the way we find it, with all the seemingly amazing coincidences of fundamental constants and peculiar properties of critical phenomena, because, if these 'amazing coincidences' did not exist, we would not be around to observe them, as we could not have evolved; that this is just one of many universes existing in a 'multiverse' (which could involve all manner of combinations of randomly distributed, cyclic, parallel etc. creations. It has even been suggested that so-called Black Holes, which involve the mathematical notion of singularities, breed new 'universes'). In most of these universes, the fundamental constants are such that no complex structure, and eventually, intelligence, evolves. Only in a universe such as ours, where by chance the constants are in harmony, do intelligent beings like ourselves evolve to look back in wonder. **77-96** Alludes to the well known Many Worlds interpretation of the so-called Schrödinger's cat thought (*gedanken*) experiment (actually the problem of the 'collapse' of the wave function; see Postscript). The Many Worlds proposal was put forward by Hugh Everett III.

XV. THIS ONE

NB. The text below represents my thought from 1991-93. The later development of these ideas, including the direct identification of the physical correlate of *chit* (the Divine Light, Pure Consciousness) and the broader ramifications of this synthesis will be presented in the final essay. The text below thus represents the position I had reached before I began to look into the yogic sources of Vedānta. I had in 1993 come to associate *mokṣa* with a retreat of brain activity associated with the mind from the forebrain towards the brainstem, based on the evidence of the experience of the 'Light' in near-death patients, unwittingly stumbling over the answer I reached later on in one annotation to a book, and was going to present these ideas in my Postscript to the verse. Following the identification of the physical correlate in 1994, I have come to know the ideas of the so-called "Perennial Philosophy" which were not really known to me at the time of writing the text below.

6 *lathis* sticks **8** *hathi* elephant. The point here is that each physicalist (materialist) conjecture as to the nature of consciousness has an 'element of truth' in it (it describes some aspects of the reality). However, these conjectures (there is no coherent hypothesis) glorify one element, failing to see the whole picture. The reason why physicalism can only put forward such clearly insufficient conjectures is that physicalism cannot account for conscious awareness. **13-14** Science is grounded on the materialist picture of the universe which, although radically transformed over the last century by the new physics, remains a 'physicalist' ontology which holds that everything in the universe, including the existence of awareness, can be explained in terms of physical processes (spatio-temporal patterns of activity). More complex phenomena, e.g. living organisms, are higher level spatio-temporal patterns of activity built up of lower level processes such as atoms and molecules (which are now seen as dynamic processes, although usually very stable). This picture developed out of the initial mathematical description of moving bodies, such as cannonballs and planets, and remains inherently 'behaviouristic', i.e. it only describes spatio-temporal patterns of activity ('behaviour'). The fact is that awareness is not reducible to behaviour. Even if the physical activity inside the brain were described in its entirety, this would not show us how there is awareness associated with it. It is interesting to note that Newton and his Anglican supporters deliberately pushed a picture of 'matter' as intrinsically inert (motionless) in order to retain God in the cosmic picture as the Prime Mover imparting motion upon the inert matter and maintaining the harmony of regular universal laws of behaviour (Jacobs, M., *The Newtonians and the English Revolution 1689-1720*, Cornell U.P., 1976). Early on, the likes of Descartes, Spinoza (see XII(106)) and Leibniz (see XIV(34)) were pointing out that conscious awareness did not fit the emerging scientific, materialist picture (Descartes favouring Dualism, Spinoza and Leibniz putting forward different forms of Panpsychism). Newton, who had cautioned against framing hypotheses (see XIV(36)) in regard to the metaphysical meaning of the new 'experimental philosophy', saw his ideas being used by others to support all manner of metaphysical speculation. What seemed to cause Newton and his supporters most concern was the hylozoic/pantheistic metaphysical views, especially those of the freethinker John Toland, in which matter was a sufficient cause for action, perception and order. Hobbes' picture of 'matter in motion', where matter was intrinsically active, dynamic, was similarly 'atheistic' to the Newtonians; and such views were used to support radical political ideas (Hobbes' metaphysical materialism was seen as fuelling selfish, socio-economic materialism). In a draft version of the twenty-third query to his *Opticks*, written around 1705, Newton wrote:

> *Life and will are active principles by which we move our bodies and thence arise other laws of motion unknown to us. And since all matter duly formed is attended with signes of life and all things are framed with perfect art and wisdom and nature does nothing in vain; if there be an universal life and all space be the sensorium of a thinking being who by immediate presence perceives all things in it, as that which thinks in us, perceives their pictures in the brain; these laws of motion arising from life or will may be of universal extent.*
>
> (Cited in Jacobs, *ibid*.: my emphasis)

Although this was not published, it shows that Newton (whose studies of alchemy and unpublished mystical writings are well-known) at least entertained notions far removed from the picture associated largely with his name. Mary Hesse in her essay "Hermeticism and Historiography" (in Stuewer, R.H. (ed.), *Historical and Philosophical Perspectives of Science;* University of Minnesota Press, 1970) writes that Newton appreciated the symbolic nature of the ancient wisdom which he felt needed to be decoded. He seems to have believed in a version of the 'Great Chain of Being' with inert matter at one end of the spectrum, passing through immaterial, to quasi-spiritual forces at the other. He thought that the laws of God were to be found throughout the hierarchy and that these laws had to be found by patient experimentation rather than mystic communion of the mind and spirits. **15-16** Life is now interpreted as an 'emergent phenomenon' or an 'emergent process', a higher level pattern of behaviour of a complex system of interconnected components. The 'life' is imputed in the higher level, 'emergent' totality of the system rather than in the components of the system (although, in the case of multicellular organisms, most of the cells are living entities as well although not capable of independent maintenance of life processes). Thus we have two levels of 'life', the life of a cell and the life of a multicellular organism; the two are not exactly the same thing, but may be considered so for convenience. Both levels of life are emergent in relation to their components; the 'life' being attributed to the organised, constrained pattern of behaviour between the components as a whole. Atoms and molecules in a living system obey the normal physical laws of behaviour but the patterns of behaviour are constrained within the interconnected system so that 'organised' higher level behaviour *emerges*. Line 16 refers to the fact that this notion of emergence is now the basis of most physicalist conjectures as to what consciousness might be. **17-20** The point stressed in this verse is that consciousness (awareness) cannot be an emergent phenomenon (which, as noted above, is merely higher level patterns of behaviour in a complex system; terms like 'emergent property' serve rather to mystify this simple, whole-is-more-than-the-sum-of-its-parts notion). If life was created *de novo* in, say, a test tube (i.e. a living cell was constructed out of biomolecules), we would be able to determine that *life* had been created by detecting/measuring certain higher level patterns of activity (behaviour) which we identify with a living system. In contrast, if we suspected that consciousness had arisen *de novo* in an information processing system, we would not be able to determine this by measurements analogous to those which would determine the presence of life in the former case. Describing the emergent higher level behaviour patterns of the information processing system would not be sufficient to prove that awareness was present. There is a ludicrous view associated with the so-called Turing Test which holds that behaviour isomorphic to that of a human in regard to answering some questions is all that is required to prove the presence of consciousness. The more general points implicit in this verse are that physicalism (materialism) is inherently behaviourist, as I noted above. It only deals with the interpretation of spatio-temporal patterns of activity (behaviour) which can be monitored (measured) by instruments. It should be glaringly obvious to anyone with a basic capacity for ontological reasoning (a faculty conspicuous by its absence in many of today's ardently physicalist 'philosophers-of-mind') that if conscious awareness were an emergent phenomenon, the problem immediately arises as to how it differs ontologically from the countless other emergent phenomena occurring everywhere in Nature. Why should one particular emergent process have this amazing property of awareness whereas all the other emergent processes don't. If the interpretation of *mokṣa* given in this work [refers to 1993 interpretation not to current Postscript] is correct then this gives further support to the case against physicalism. If awareness exists when the field activity associated with conscious mentation has retreated from the cerebral forebrain down towards the brainstem, then this undermines physicalist conjectures which assume that awareness is created by the complex processes occurring in the cerebrum. The notion of *emergence,* like all other physicalist conjectures (except for the extreme 'eliminative materialism' which tries to deny that awareness actually exists ontologically!), is an attempt to disguise an appeal to magic; because in the physicalist world-picture which has become a sacred cow for many scientifically-minded rationalists, awareness can only appear by one means, magic. **21-24** The dominant epistemological approach underlying the scientific method gives credence only to that which can be measured with instruments (i.e. spatio-temporal patterns of activity). In fact, it also requires *regular* patterns of activity as the need to construct scientific laws and make predictive models is based on seeking out the repetitive patterns in nature. Conscious awareness, as it cannot be measured (or detected with an instrument), is either ignored (eliminative materialism) or tacitly 'brushed under the carpet' using mystifying terms such as emergence in order to disguise the fact that it is something that Science simply can't come to terms with. As David Bohm says in regard to the underlying ocean of energy which is ignored because it cannot be measured (see XIII(a) (65-70)) it's like a fish not being aware of the ocean. This metaphor is even more appropriate in regard to awareness as our awareness is the ground of our existence (see also XIII(a) (3-4); all of our experience, all of our 'world' is known to us only as contents of our awareness. I shall discuss below how the so-called 'physical world' (the external world as we interpret it; rather than the external reality) is, in the final analysis, part of our awareness. **25-28** 'The Book of the Universe is written in the language of triangles, circles and other geometrical objects; the language of mathematics'. Galileo Galilei. *Sat* Being; *Chit* Raw Awareness. By positing raw awareness as an irreducible attribute of the underlying reality, I am asserting a position of Panpsychism. In Western terms, *sat,* would be physical existence (perhaps 'energy') and saying that *sat* and *chit* go together is saying that the universe is psychophysical and not just physical. Awareness is not a magical property that arises late in the evolution of complex physical systems. Awareness is an intrinsic property of all reality, which also has spatio-temporal (physical) character. **29-30** As noted in Section XIII(b), *Brahman* is identifed in the Vedānta with *sat* and *chit*. *Riṣi* seer. **33-34** Spinoza held that God was the underlying 'substance' of all Nature and that this 'substance' had an infinite number of attributes of which two, the mental and the physical, could be apprehended by Man. Ignoring the other supposed attributes, his system thus involved an underlying reality with two attributes, the mental and the physical, which ran in parallel. Events in the two attributes were correlated on a one-to-one basis but did not have causal connections between them; the physical world could be wholly explained in terms of the laws governing the physical world. In regard to the relationship between awareness and the physical world, Spinoza's view resembles my own which drew inspiration from my knowledge of his parallelist view. However, I stress that the parallelism is a construction of our minds (see lines 53-56) and that the underlying reality is a more subtle psychophysical non-duality, as such parallelism if analysed can be shown to be untenable, except as an approximation to reality. I do not share Spinoza's hylozoism ('life' as a property of all matter) or his determinism. In my view, Spinoza did correctly picture the individuation of finite entities (his 'modes') which maintained their unity by maintaining a complex pattern of relationships amongst changing parts. My picture is one of individuation at every level of physical order, with the individual entity as a sort of self-organising process. The individual is thus not truly separate from the whole (*Brahman*) but is a system of organisation maintaining a dynamic autonomy (the system can exchange information with the external world). Spinoza could not answer the glaring question faced by such Panpsychist views: why does awareness only seem to be associated with some sort of brain activity in higher animals. Why does everything else seem to have just physical properties. How can we avoid an ontological dualism which would leave the question of why mental events are closely correlated with physical brain phenomena an unanswerable mystery. I would grant that my answer to these fundamental hurdles faced by Panpsychism could only have been formulated in the late twentieth century when a number of issues regarding the nature of mentation had been clarified, to some extent, by the advance of science. None the less, I am putting forward my Panpsychist interpretation at a time when Panpsychism is the least fashionable approach to the problem of awareness amongst rationalists, mostly indoctrinated by scientific physicalism, and keen to steer well clear of ideas strongly associated with mysticism. **45-48** *saṃsāra* (literally 'that which is constantly changing'), here means the ceaseless flux of phenomena (the 'physical' world). This Kekulean 'snake swallowing its tail' picture of the moment of inspiration is actually poetic licence. The vision of brain cells came with the notion of subjective autonomy for 'closed' systems (i.e. that each system, at every level of order, which maintained its spatio-temporal identity through self-organising processes constituted an autonomous sentient entity). The picture was that of a sort of whirlpool in the phenomenal flux, a temporary, discrete, self-organising process in which, as with Spinoza's modes, the individuality is inherent in the maintenance of organised relations (the process) and not the components of the process. In my system, at every level of physical order, each such whirlpool-like process is a subjective monad. Thus a sentient entity will itself contain subsystems·which are sentient entities in their own right and this is repeated right through all the levels of physical order. Each closed subsystem 'hides' its information content (its pattern of relations) from the higher level entity of which it is a component. Thus each sentient entity experiences events correlated only with the higher level physical processes (or higher level information) within itself as the lower level information (processes) tend to be contained within 'closed' sentient subsystems. By limiting the awareness of each entity, in this way, to the correlate higher level information in the physical realm, my picture reformulates the higher-level pattern (information) significance also found in the physicalist notion of emergence (see above). However, this emphasis on the higher-level information in my picture is based on a completely different metaphysics where lower-level information is also associated with awareness and there is nothing ontologically special about the higher-level information. As we shall see below, the 'meaningfulness' of our conscious awareness is directly related to the emergence of higher-level 'meaningful information'. **49-52** My 'whirlpools' may be called *fields,* a notion which is used here to emphasise wholeness, interconnectedness, unity (and a degree of ethereality) and which also conveys something of the notion that the individual exists in the maintenance of an organised pattern of relations rather than in the components as the term 'field' may be used to delimit such a spatial domain of organised activity. The field is the region of space in which the process maintaining a sense of individuality is occurring. Critical entities in cosmic evolution such as particles, atoms, molecules, living cells, and multicellular organisms may be interpreted as such 'fields' of activity. The field concept also ties in with notions of autonomy of 'closed' subsystems (I got the idea of the autonomy hierarchy from mathematical notions related to the mathematical notion of a 'field'). I identify such critical entities as some of the individuated sentient entities in my picture. Entities such as galaxies, stars, planets and numerous other less enduring self-organising 'fields' may also be sentient entities (see Postscript). The field notion also implies a degree of 'blurredness'; the individuated sentient entity is not a sharply distinct entity, but a whirlpool-like ephemeral process which temporarily appears to attain autonomy from the cosmic flux. **53-56** The physical and the 'subjective' (awareness) attributes of the underlying reality can only be pictured like two sides of the same coin (parallelism) with each physical event correlated on a one-to-one basis with each event of awareness in the subjective attribute. The underlying reality is taken to be a 'psychophysical non-duality' but we cannot grasp it as such. The parallelist picture, in which there is no causal connection between the attributes, breaks down if we consider how we can think about 'awareness' or write about it as in doing so, the very existence of our subjective experience is influencing physical events. My [1993] view is that we must explain the physical world in physical terms, accepting the limitations of this approach at the limits. The need for this false parallelism stems, at least partly, from the constraints of our mentation. We simply cannot conceive reality as it is in itself because mentation is constrained by its use of simplified representations (see II(93-94); see also lines 73-76 below on the nature of 'phenomena' and the so-called 'Physical World' which helps to mollify this situation as the 'Physical World' as such is a construction of our minds; there is a world external to our minds but its true character is not simply the physical picture our mind constructs. We cannot know the external reality as it is, we can only monitor some of its spatio-temporal characteristics by information transfer to us and the 'spatio-temporal', physical picture we construct necessitates a sharp distinction of the physical and the subjective resulting in the parallelism whereas the two are, in some mysterious way, more intimately related. **57-60** All the sentient entities in the cosmos (including our Selves) are assumed to have an awareness that exists only on a moment by moment basis in relation to the spatio-temporal flux with which it is correlated. The awareness changes in parallel with the physical flux and, at any one moment in time, the awareness reflects the physical state (the higher-level information pattern) at that same moment. In most sentient entities, which I call 'non-mindlike' entities, there is no awareness of Self or awareness of Time or indeed of anything 'meaningful'. This is because the organisation of the physical processes which constitute such sentient entities involves merely cyclical and random flux patterns and the subjective attribute merely reflects this 'vegetative' flux. However, our own 'meaningful' awareness (Consciousness) is, in essence, no different from the awareness of such non-mindlike systems. Our self-apprehension, time-apprehension and general meaningfulness of experiences arise as a correlate of the 'meaningfulness' of the physical organisation of 'mindlike' systems (see below). It is only this difference in physical organisation that distinguishes our consciousness from the awareness of non-mind-like systems; there is no ontological difference. **61** Anamorphotic evolution. Evolution towards greater complexity (I am not imputing teleology here (see XIV(57-68) and Postscript). **69-72** This verse deals with two points. First, I believe that the physical correlate of the conscious mind is a, self-organising, electromagnetic energy field associated with world-modelling simulation processes in the cerebrum ('World-Model Field'). The World-Model Field is assumed to have the property of subjective 'closure'; i.e. it constitutes an individuated, self-organising process which has a high degree of topological closure in the spatial attribute (i.e. it is a fairly discrete entity). The sheer 'messiness' of physical activity in the brain, in which so many different processes are occurring together poses a problem for any interpretation of consciousness. The model I have described above of a hierarchy of subjective autonomy 'tidies things up' to an extent in that the World-Model Field co-exists spatio-temporally with a number of physical processes but retains its subjective distinctness due to the closure of the lower level processes which form atoms, molecules and cells. I am aware that this is not a wholly satisfying picture; but at least, using it, we can put together a rather coherent, self-consistent interpretation of consciousness which is also open to future empirical testing. The closure of the atoms, molecules and cells leaves largely the higher level patterns of electromagnetic field activity, which have the emergent 'meaningful organisation' (see below) open to the World-Model Field's subjectivity (awareness content). This meaningfully organised awareness constitutes Consciousness as we know it. The second point is that of meaningful organisation itself. This arises because the events occurring within the World-Model Field are strictly controlled by brain functions in order to constitute a 'faithful' (in regard to predictability rather than reality) simulation of the external world on which the organism bases life and death judgements. Evolution has resulted in the selection of faithful world model processes as these give organisms possessing them huge selective advantages; hence it is meaningful organisation which results in the development of mindlike systems which has evolved rather than consciousness *per se*. Throughout this work I have stressed that 'meaning' exists in relation to the 'whole', that is, an entity has meaning only in terms of its relations to other entities which together constitute the system under consideration. The organism must maintain a strict ordering of events within the World-Model Field in order to predict future events by faithfully simulating the external world. This consistent nexus of relations is maintained through time, though it can gradually evolve due to cellular processes. The existence of memory systems which allow re-incorporation of past state information into the field, a self-representation frame, a time frame etc. which are vital components of such a world-modelling process give 'meaningfulness' (with reference to the organism and its 'world') to this 'mindlike' system. **73-76** The World-Model Field, as with all sentient entities, is only aware of events within itself which are not closed to it within sentient subsystems. *Phenomena* are events inside the field generated by events outside the brain (information being transmitted into the field via the senses and nervous system; i.e. information from the outside world becomes part of the field's internal information (spatio-temporal patterns of activity)). Thus the 'Physical World' is really our interpretation of such phenomena (occurring within our Selves; the field) in terms of an 'outside world' of physical events. This is not solipsism as I grant that there is an outside world but the noumenal reality of the world external to our Self cannot be apprehended, we can only know it through phenomenal representations generated inside our Selves through information transmission (perception). *Mokṣa* seems to be a sort of pure state of awareness (*chit*) devoid of world-modelling constructs, including Self and Time frames. *Mokṣa* could thus be interpreted as a sort of noumenal state (i.e. the field as it is in itself, being aware only of itself). [NB — the previous sentence was written in 1993 prior to my investigation of the yogic sources; the loss of individuation and the states of consciousness were not considered]. The noumenon/phenomenon distinction in this panpsychist system reduces to one of being the very thing itself and of representing other things within oneself; i.e. it is impossible to know something 'noumenally' unless you are that very thing. Everything that is not oneself must be known as phenomena). **77-84** The first verse here is stating that consciousness is basically raw awareness (*chit*) which is devoid of Self and Time apprehension. The sense of Personal Identity through Time (or Self-continuity, i.e. the sense that one remains the same Self throughout time; the continuity of which appears to conflict with my assertion that our experience is essentially a moment-by-moment one) is created by memory systems which create a 'Time frame' (in which the passage of time would be mapped onto a spatial dimension) which allows us, at any one moment, to be aware of our relative position in time in relation to past states etc. Past state information can also be re-incorporated to 're-create' past experiences to some extent. The existence of such memory systems and the Time frame can easily be explained in terms of their necessity in a world-modelling system. The second verse here stresses that in dreamless sleep we, that is the World-Model Fields, literally do not exist. Upon awakening, the World-Model Field is regenerated. Although, in a sense, it is a new entity, the new field draws upon the same life history information from the brain's memory and the same Self-reference frame is created in conjunction with a Time frame which is based on all the previous activations of the World-Model Field. Thus Personal Identity through Time is maintained despite the fact that we are a discontinuous series of activations, rather than one continuous process. **85-88** See Sections XIII and XIV for the parallel here with the cyclic universe. Although I am calling the field the 'Self' here, it should be clear that the field simply cannot exist without the the particular body and the particular brain in order to retain self-continuity through retention of life history information in the brain's memory. Thus although we, the conscious minds, are the fields, we are also inseparable from the particular body which generates us; we can only exist and retain self-continuity within one particular body. As line 87 states, our Potential Self remains in the memory systems. **89-92** It could be that dreams are the product of activation (or more likely 'de-inhibition') of a separate simulation process in which the 'minor' cerebral hemisphere plays the dominant role. It need not be that the normal World-Model Field of our waking state is localised to the major cerebral hemisphere and the dream state 'Sister Model' to the minor hemishere. It could be that the respective hemispheres play the key roles in generating the the respective simulation processes based on the differences in aspects of their modes of information processing. The minor hemisphere processes information in a more visual, non-linear and emotionally coloured manner than the dominant major hemisphere. A de-inhibition of the minor hemisphere's simulation activities caused by de-activation of the waking state World Model (clearly the two could not be allowed to operate simultaneously) would be likely to 'reflect' upon recently acquired information as it is likely that, during sleep, the brain is 'sorting out the grain from the chaff' of the day's (or recent) experiences held in intermediate term memories in order to lay down the long-term memory. Information with a strong emotional colouring is also likely to figure strongly due to the minor hemisphere's role in emotional processing and the very nature of emotional colouring which tends to accentuate things. Such information, of course, reflects the usual contents of dreams. No strict world-modelling is required during the sleeping state thus the Sister Model's modes of information processing which do not faithfully model the external world can be tolerated without detrimental effect to the organism. Once again, the existence of a separate series of Sister Model activations would still be consistent with self-continuity as both the World Model and the Sister Model fields are drawing upon the same life history information and same Self-reference frame. **97-100** The points above about the Potential Self and the identification with a particular life history laid down in a particular brain's memory clearly stress the fact that we, the Self (the conscious mind) are a product of the body's biological activity and not some sort of 'soul'. The World-Model Field may be rather ethereal but it is none the less a form of energy, a process, created by processes in the body and wholly dependent upon the body. The only difference from the other sentient entities in Nature being that the World-Model Field is meaningfully organised so that our awareness includes Self, Time and 'world' apprehension rather than a meaningless, disorganised flux. At the end of Section II, I stated that I foresaw manmade conscious forms. Although others have also predicted such developments, they have not done so upon the basis of a sound picture of what consciousness actually is and have thus often made wild predictions based on naïve misidentifications of consciousness with lesser properties. The emergent materialist views of many workers in Artificial Intelligence (AI) research involves them confusing what I call 'meaningful organisation' with 'awareness'. It is clear that meaningful organisation is a critical component of meaningful 'consciousness' (as distinct from non-mindlike awareness) but meaningful organisation can exist in systems which are not subjectively closed (sentient) entities and thus there is no consciousness even though there is meaningful organisation of information. (Of course, in the AI workers' pictures, the universe is physical and thus they fail to come to terms with 'awareness'). Meaningful information, in regard to the function of a system, resides in the higher-level information. For instance, the dots (the lower-level information) on a liquid crystal display are 'meaningless' whereas the higher-level information (the characters formed by the dots; words, numbers; symbols, pictures etc.) are 'meaningful' in regard to the function of the gadget with the display. It is on the basis of such reasoning that many people mistakenly postulate that consciousness is but some higher-level, emergent, information processing. My theory asserts that, in this psychophysical cosmos, a system has to be a closed, self-organising energy field (a rather vague but pragmatic notion) and the whole of this closed field must be meaningfully organised (with a Self-reference frame, a Time frame based on memory systems, world-modelling etc.) for the closed field, as an entity with 'individuality', to experience meaningful consciousness. In other words, we must have a subjectively closed system which is also mindlike (i.e. meaningfully organised). Whereas our current artefacts may possess some degree of meaningful organisation of their information processing activities, and may possess rudimentary frames, such properties are not localised within a subjectively closed field which imparts the 'individuality' that is also required. Therefore, even though some meaningfully organised information may be present within some of our artefacts, this information correlates with the subjective experience of some higher-level closed field, which, as a whole, is not meaningfully organised (mindlike). Given that the first level of subjective closure above our artefacts may belong to the planet, then it is clear that the meaningful information inside our computers, even if it were to become mindlike, would be irrelevant parts of the whole experience of the higher-level entity experiencing this information as part of its overall experience. This does not preclude the possibility of meaningfully organised closed fields arising, probably unexpectedly, in our artefacts; especially those based on bio-organic materials. If so, then we would have meaningful organisation of the whole of an individuated sentient entity, a mindlike subjective entity with consciousness.

XVI. THE WEB INTRICATE

65 'Like you, forerunner and brother, I too go through life zigzagging between natural ways and spirit, today a wise man, tomorrow a fool, today intimate with God, tomorrow intensely devoted to the flesh'. (Herman Hesse; referring to the ancient Indian philosopher Bhartrihari. Cited in A.L. Basham (ed.) *A Cultural History of India*, Oxford U.P., 1975). **90** Refers to Ernst Mach's principle (the first relativistic principle in modern physics) that the inertial properties of terrestial matter are determined by the total mass of the universe around each entity.

IN THIS AGE OF FALLING CURTAINS

Indian society has no history at all, at least no known history. What we call its history is but the history of its successive intruders who founded their empires on the passive basis of that unresisting and unchanging society. Karl Marx[1]

A nation which has no history has no future either
Bankim Chandra Chattopadhyay

THE HISTORICAL MESSAGE OF THE WORK

Western mythology and Indian reality

We have often been reminded that 'History', as it is known in Europe, came late to 'Hindu' India. Indeed, without the work of the British scholars of the Asiatic Society of Bengal, Indians would not be able to glory in 'the wonder that was India'. Asoka would have remained but a legendary character, little more real in the folk memory than Krishna or Rama.

> *in an age when every schoolchild in the fifth class knows of Samudragupta, the realization that there was a time when Samudragupta was not known at all!* O.P. Kejariwal[2]

Of course, the coming of Islamic rulers to Northern India, resulting in the widespread destruction and neglect of much of the non-Islamic Indian heritage, a point largely ignored by Orientalist historians and their followers, did not help. But even though in 1921, R.D. Banerjee and D. Sahani discovered the cities of Mohenjo-Daro and Harappa, leading to the discovery of the vast and ancient Harappan civilisation, the Orientalist myths did not give way. Nirad Chaudhuri[3] repeated the 19th Century Orientalist view that India has been merely the receptacle of historical movements introduced by invading races. He suggested that future research may show that the Harappan civilisation was *only* a cousin of Sumerian civilisation!

In fact, recent research has made fools of Orientalist Chaudhuri, archaeologists and historians. Numerous lines of research now show that the supposed Aryan invasion was a myth created by Orientalist projections of 19th Century European racial conquests onto ancient Indian history with no real evidence to support it, the date of 1500 BCE being but a figment of Max Muller's imagination. Recent archaeological evidence shows that the Harappan civilisation began around 6,000-7,000 BCE and ended around 1,900 BCE. Subhash Kak, following similar arguments made by B.G. Tilak in the 19th Century, has shown that the *Rig Veda* contains astronomical information dating back eight or nine thousand years. Kak has also shown that the Indus script is related distinctly to the old Brahmi form of Sanskrit. Thus the Harappans were in fact the Vedic Aryans! Even the word *Purusha* (Man) comes from roots meaning town-dweller and chariots were always the vehicles of ancient urban elites, not of nomads. Evidence shows that the legendary Vedic river Saraswati did exist, drying up around 1,900 BCE to form the Great Indian desert. Thus the Vedic Aryans migrated eastwards, living for a while in forest settlements (hence the *Āranyakas* or 'forest scriptures' follow the *Rig Veda*) before building a new civilisation along the Ganga and the Jamuna. The lengthy dynastic lists found in the *Purāṇas,* dismissed by Orientalists as exaggerated fantasies, thus reflect the vast antiquity of Indo-Aryan civilisation. Furthermore, evidence also indicates that Sumerian civilisation began as a colony of the Indian cradle of Civilisation.[4] Incidentally, the universal adoption of the Indian use of ten as the basis of our number system goes back to the Harappans.[5]

British historians constructed a picture of Indian society to fulfil their fantasies of being modern 'scientific' scholars, categorising civilisations in an evolutionary hierarchy, teleologically moving towards the supreme form, that of Western Europe. Nirad Chaudhuri, doubtless imbued with such a 19th Century evolutionism alongside the self-hatred inculcated by colonialist education, asserts, with Indian Nationalists' aspirations in mind, that no civilisation which has attained greatness in the past can rise to greatness again. A very odd view given the periodical 'flowerings' of the great continuous civilisations. Countless Western social 'scientists' and others wrote their influential works basing their 'theories' on the supposedly 'objective' histories of the colonial historians generating countless further myths which permeate modern Western thought.

> *a current Late Modern Western convention of identifying a parvenue and provincial Western Society's history with 'History' writ large, . . . the preposterous off-spring of a distorting egocentric illusion to which the children of a Western civilisation had succumbed like the children of all other known civilisations and known primitive societies.*
>
> from Arnold Toynbee's *A Study of History*[6]

Following the savage conflicts of 1914-18 and 1939-45, fuelled by various factors including the tribal nationalisms of the Europeans, the logic of colonialism etc. which led to the collapse of the Europeans' political stranglehold on the rest of the world, attitudes are changing although the myths which helped define European identity still hold a remarkable sway over the minds of the majority, just as did the myths of any other society at any time. In reaction to the wishing away of historical and human agency from Indians and the fantasizing about the essence of 'effete' Indian civilisation by the Orientalists, Ronald Inden has recently written the aptly named *Imagining India*[7] undermining the imaginary Orientalist construction of India as the civilisation whose history was determined by rigid castes, hermetically sealed villages, spiritualism and imagination running riot over Reason. Contrary to the Orientalist picture of India prior to the first Muslim incursions being in irreversible decline, Inden notes that the Arabs of the Eighth and Ninth Christian Centuries did not see India as a land of petty warring fiefdoms ripe for the plucking in the name of Allah but as a single complex political entity. The Rāshtrakūtas, then paramount amongst Indian rulers, were viewed by the Arabs as one of the four great imperial powers of the world. The idea of India as a unitary whole existed in the notion of the 'conquest of the quarters' to restore the unity that had been established by the Mauryan Empire. (This notion is found in a variant form in Shankara's philosophical 'conquest of the quarters' with the establishment of his missions in the 'four corners of India' as mentioned in the verse). Furthermore, contrary to the Orientalist myths linking 'Hinduism' to India's decline, temple Hinduism, at the close of the first Christian millennium, remained a powerful, triumphant religion.

Using recent research on the Chālyuka, Rāshtrakūta, Pratihāra and Pāla dynasties, Inden shows that Indian history was being recorded by Indians prior to the first Muslim invasions. The Indian polity did not consist of an aloof, repressive state and inward-looking villages riven by caste divisions. Similarly, contrary to Marx's picture of closed Indian villages:

> *the so-called "village system", which gave to each of these small unions their independent organisation and distinct life . . . . The boundaries of the villages have been but seldom altered . . . the inhabitants gave themselves no trouble about the breaking up and divisions of kingdoms, while the village remains entire, they care not to what power it is transferred, or to what sovereign it devolves, its internal economy remains unchanged.*
>
> Karl Marx[8]

Bengal's villages, prior to British conquest as discussed later in this work, were integrated into a complex web of trading relations, between themselves, with the rest of India and with the rest of the world. Inden challenges the Western myth that the notion of progressive historical development was conceived exclusively by Europeans, in contrast to backward-looking non-Europeans. The Indian rulers were striving, through their statecraft, to give "a better account of the world than had their predecessors". The Indian statesmen were anti-utopian, they did not view their polities as permanent states or as imperfect actualizations of an ideal state; they assumed oscillation between periods of order and disorder as the natural way of things. Nor did they seek the impossible utopian dream of eliminating all social evils for once and for all. They understood that the dark side of human nature had to be domesticated, and, due to the cyclical nature of things, this process of domestication had to be renewed after each period of social decay. In today's world where infantile Hegelian-Marxian notions and the rigid, dichotomous thinking of modern Europe in general have proven to be false constructions superimposed upon organic reality; where linear models of order are giving way to non-linear models of chaotic fluctuations underlying stable phenomena etc., the great civilisation of India, long chastised by Westerners for failing to adhere to Western conceptions of reality, a civilisation which has had the longest experience of trying to manage a chaotic social reality will have an important role to play in the future of a world where the ideological constructs and indeed the fundamental metaphysical orientation of modern Europe are seen to be superficial impositions masking the actual nature of things.

The modernisation and globalisation of Indian civilisation

As noted in Section XI, the attempted reconstruction of India's past by British scholars, aided by Indian *paṇḍits* was not a totally negative enterprise. Furthermore, it helped fuel the rise of (Hindu) Indian Nationalism. This nationalism arose, less from the need for historical retrospection, then from the forward looking vision of predominantly Bengali intellectuals who dreamt of the regeneration of Hindu civilisation in a form suited for the modern world. Foremost amongst such nationalistic writers, Bankim was well aware of the contemporary historical research, writing critiques of the racialistic European assumptions, a century before such critiques came into fashion in Western academia. Whilst acknowledging some of the valid criticisms of Indian civilisation, he refused to accept the 'essentialist' view of the Orientalists that Indian civilisation was immutable. Ashis Nandy has written about the 'burden of history' and the way 'third world' cultures attempt to come to terms with it.

> *Some cultures prefer to live with it and painfully excavate the anti-memories and integrate them as part of the present consciousness. Some cultures prefer to handle the same problem at the mytho-poetic level. Instead of excavating for the so-called real past, they excavate for other meanings of the present . . .*
>
> *What seems an ahistorical and even anti-historical attitude in many non-modern cultures is often actually an attempt on the part of these cultures to incorporate their historical experiences into their shared traditions as categories of thinking, rather than objective chronicles of the past.* Ashis Nandy[9]

In 1857, the feudal reaction to British rule failed, leaving the field free for the forces of modernity to work their way through the subcontinent. The Indian National dream was not merely the emulation of Europe, as the quote from Bankim in the Introduction indicates, the dream was to fuse Indian spirituality with European science to create the basis for a higher, universal civilisation transcending the civilisation of the modern West. In the following essay entitled *The Oneness/Otherness Mystery*, this dream shall begin to become actuality as I link together Mysticism and Science, reversing the Cartesian dichotomy at the heart of modern Western thought. It is hardly surprising then that I take objection to the likes of Francis Fukuyama, who following Hegel and the academic 'end of ideology' tradition, present Mickey Mouse utopias of 'main street America' as the universal world civilisation which shall follow the collapse of Communism, suggesting that 'History' is nearing its end. My people may have come late into the light of Western-style historicity but we have not lost touch with the eternal Light of spirituality, so deficient in the civilisation of the modern West. The West may have given us 'History' with a capital 'H' but we are not going to let the West take it away from us!

Communism may be dead, Western political parties converging in ideologies, and most of the world pursuing 'Western-style' economic restructuring. Science and technology may have integrated the world in an irreversible manner preventing independent trajectories of development, but this hardly amounts to the final triumph of Western civilisation precluding any alternative mode of development. Nor is it at all a simple matter of the West, having basically attained all that needs to be attained, remaining static with nowhere to go. The majority of the world's human population still live in relative poverty and, to them, the 'West' tends to mean maintenance of the *status quo* through its hegemony built largely upon the legacy of the recent colonial past and this is clearly an unacceptable state of affairs. We know that socio-economic developments are emergent, organic processes and that such processes tend to be cyclic in nature, rather like the traditional Hindu view of *yugas* ('ages'). As the great civilisations of China and India become fully modernised, the reverberations will be felt all over the world. Unlike Europe, they will not go around imposing their culture upon others but, as 'globalisation' is today's acceptable substitute for yesterday's unacceptable 'imperialism', the global presence of these rising great civilisations will inevitably result in major adjustments in the existing world order in order to accommodate them; adjustments far more fundamental if less violent than the integration of Germany and Japan into the big power league this century. Japan, for all its economic and technological prowess, remains largely an Asiatic satellite of Western civilisation; outdoing the West at its own game. With the increasing modernisation and globalisation of the two great continental civilisations of Asia; re-orientations are likely to occur which will fundamentally challenge some of the key ideological principles underlying the world order under Western hegemony. The collapse of the Soviet Union, far from removing the last alternative to mainstream Western 'dominion' of the world, has removed the major distortion factor skewing the underlying reality of the global state of affairs. With such unsustainable, artificial strictures removed, 'History', far from nearing its end, is free again to run its natural course.

Western universalist pretensions

One of the factors which led to the creation of this work was my being given a copy of the *New York Review of Books* by a friend early in 1991, around the time of the war over the princely state of Kuwait. As I was protesting against the double standards of the West, this daughter of a British diplomat and daughter-in-law of a British army Major, wanted me to read the script of a lecture given in New York by the Trinidadian writer of Indian descent, V.S. Naipaul, entitled 'Our Universal Civilisation'. Naipaul, considered by most Indians to be a panderer to Western Orientalist preconceptions (rather than the paṇḍit on India he purports to be) focused on the limitations of the world-views of peoples colonised by Islamic conquerors. Such Islamic nations tend to see the advent of Islam as a sort of 'Year Zero' for the history of their country (note the relevance of this to the 'lost history' of Hindu India). He noted the lack of interest shown by Pakistanis towards the Harappan civilisation of the Indus Valley and Western India. (It is interesting to note that the founding fathers of Pakistan objected to the use of the name 'India' (rather than the Sanskrit term *Bhārat*) by the Indian Union as this effectively appropriated for the Hindus all the historical heritage conjured up by the name 'India'). Naipaul contrasted such views with "the extraordinary attempt of this civilisation (the West) to accommodate the rest of the world and all the currents of that world's thought." Except at the superficial level of eating exotic foods, copying various musical styles etc., the accommodation that there has been, is hardly the result of any conscious effort to truly *accommodate* the rest of the world or even to assimilate its thought, rather it has largely been subtle modes of exploitation and a piecemeal absorption of Westernised 'Orientalist' knowledge serving 'comparative' academic exercises, a byproduct of European Colonialism that conquered the globe and ordered everything in a hierarchical manner, placing Europe *über alles.*

In a sense, this work is a response to Naipaul and others who make this sort of claim of Western universality, as if the rest of the world has become wholly subsumed into a global Western civilisation in which the only option remains to try to copy the West in every way. (I have more recently found that Naipaul, in his *India: A Wounded Civilisation*[10], for all his derogatory remarks about India, judging things from a naïve, purely Western perspective, simultaneously pays lip service to the well-understood need for Indians, not to merely copy the West but to develop ideas tailored to suit the Indian context. He then immediately concludes that Indians have failed to do this like they have failed, in his opinion, at everything else! His mode of criticism is itself hardly original, is he not himself copying the West.) Many Westerners arrogantly assume that the values that apply in their countries should apply equally across the world. Western thought is partly built upon a myth of European philosophical genius, a myth of intellectual purity which attempted to write out the vast and varied contributions made by other civilisations to the making of the modern world. Of course, such views are nowadays being 'deconstructed' in many respects. This work reflects the hostility of the ex-colonial world towards what it perceives to be the neocolonialist West, rejecting simplistic 'global village' notions based on the *status quo* of glaring global inequality subtly supported by the global 'lord of the manor'. It emphasises the contributions of other civilisations to the philosophical and technological development of the West and goes on to argue that the dominant Western metaphysical picture, although extremely successful technologically, is a limited one which will be surpassed with a view which resembles the commonplace tradition of Eastern mystical thought. Although such metaphysical issues may seem far removed from the mundane matters of history, all realms of human thought are ultimately grounded upon a metaphysical picture and a revolution in the metaphysical ground eventually permeates and influences all thought and subsequent action. Every field of human enquiry will have to re-interpret itself in order to harmonise itself with the new metaphysics; the fundamentals of which will be presented in this work.

Historical developmental relativism

In 1991, a time when President Bush was speaking of America leading the world in the 'next American Century', India and China proclaiming the dangers of a world dominated by one superpower as the USA steamrollered over the United Nations, the dissolution of the Soviet Union led to an ideological vacuum in regard to any serious alternative to the narrow mercantilism, and 'trickle-down' economics pushed by the 'Reaganite' Americans whose own 'New World' society's development has not suffered the same land and population pressures of the Old World through its violent appropriation of the North American continent, dispossessing the natives. The new Indian government, faced with a balance of payments crisis was introducing wholesale economic reforms (without the usual resistance from vested interests), my mind was in turmoil, faced with the seeming prospect of an upsurge in neo-colonialist manipulations of global affairs by a strident USA hailing the coming of a 'New World Order'. Now as President Clinton speaks of the coming 'American Pacific' Century and the USA turns away from Cold War trans-Atlantic priorities towards free trade with Latin America and increased trade with Asia, the capitalist industrial phenomenon seemingly spreading across Asia, prospects for peace in Palestine, and the limits of US will, if not US power, manifest in Bosnia and Somalia, my fears about a neo-colonialist upsurge have faded considerably. For instance, the reference in the verse to George Kennan's 1947 view of US strategy towards Asia (to suppress Asia's economic aspirations, ignoring the lip service paid to 'democracy' and 'human rights' etc. in order to maintain the USA's disproportionate control of half the world's resources) is largely out of date although Asia is still wary of possible US motives of attempting to control Asia's affairs. The Western moralising over the 'human rights' question has become one of the neo-colonial sticks used with double standards by the West; note the arm-twisting of democratic India over Kashmir whilst totalitarian China retains Most Favoured Nation trading status despite its far worse behaviour in Tibet and use of political prisoners for export manufacture. Tagore told an American audience in 1931 that the USA did not respond to the appeal of India to be free because Americans only responded to power. They had responded to Japan because, by copying Western-style nationalism and colonialism, Japan proved she could make herself as obnoxious as the West[11]; today little seems to have changed with 'realpolitik' making a mockery of Western rhetoric.

A theme relevant to such situations, which was prominent in my mind in 1991, is that of the relativism of socio-historical development. The post-war, supposedly 'post-modern', West finds it all too easy to berate the developing world for behaviour which resembles that of Western states not very long ago and of course nothing like as severe as what the West got up to during the height of colonial expansion. It seems as if it is now the West which has forgotten (or chosen to ignore) its own history. This question of socio-historical relativism was a key factor behind the writing of Sections IX and X of this work which look at the historical legacies of the nascent USA and the UK from the point of view of the people whose lands they colonised. I readily accept, however, that the raising of such issues by the West is generally not a bad thing in itself. From a short-term humanistic perspective it tends to be a very good thing in most cases, although such matters are not half as simplistic as the Western media tends to present them. I chastise the naïve, popular Western romanticisation of the plight of India's poor in *No Sure Ground.* In regard to the 1989 Tiananmen Square massacre I note that Western identification with bourgeois individualism fails to note the real interests of the vast majority of the Chinese population. Indeed, soon after the massacre, British government departments were involved in covert sales of electric shock torture equipment to the Chinese knowing that the Chinese would mass produce copies for use in their 'gulags'. In Eastern Asia, economic and social progress has come through authoritarian rule where Western-style democracy (remember the authoritarian regimes of the developing West) would probably not have succeeded. American economic help to China, raising the living conditions of 1.2 billion people, far outweighs the current 'human rights' issues within China itself (Tibet is another matter). The ideas of the European Enlightenment are simply not appropriate in many contexts, whatever idealistic Westerners like to think. Asia will forge ahead developing its own appropriate ideologies. For developing states trying to consolidate their socio-economic structures, the high-handed, and often hypocritical, moralising from the West is usually, quite justifiably, unwelcome imperialism. The recent decision of the Indian government to reject World Bank funding, with strings attached, for the controversial Narmada Valley project, mentioned in the verse, highlights this situation as does the concern of developing countries that Western pressure groups raising the 'Green card' on environmental matters is a threat to their developmental aspirations by those who have reached the 'promised land' paying no heed whatsoever to the environment.

> The global media gets the scent
> And poor men's plans for progress foils
> With pious cant their forebears scorned
> For poverty the Earth despoils (No Sure Ground)

For the wretched of the Earth, the hope lies in the fact that the historical process, being of an emergent, non-linear, organic nature is thus unpredictable and uncontrollable, thus those who lord it over the world now cannot guarantee through any form of imperialism that the disparities in wealth will be maintained for centuries to come (a point that should be noted especially by the European Union with its Fortress mentality; if disorder does befall large parts of the outside world, as some strategists predict, Europe will not be able to hold out the 'barbarians' for ever). As I note in Section XII, the outcomes of human efforts to control situations contingent upon such emergent processes often tend to backfire, or, at least, work out in a way completely unlike that planned. In the short-term, one can see how US efforts to stop countries like India developing space technology, supposedly to prevent the proliferation of missiles, will only lead to India developing her own systems. In the short-term, India's weather and remote-sensing satellite programmes will be delayed, along with development, but such neo-colonial policies will eventually lead to greater technological independence in this sector with unforeseen long-term consequences. President Clinton is most probably correct in asserting that the development of strong underlying trading relations with Asia will probably be of greater long-term significance than the development of political superstructures (as in Western Europe). In relation to the latter and our discussion of history, the fact that India did not develop along the Western European pattern of nation states in the past has been of some benefit in that highly developed nation states are a hindrance to the development of subcontinental unions as the European Union has already found. Whereas the Orientalists saw India as failing to ascend to the next stage of their universal historical scheme of things, India is bypassing such evolutionary paths altogether whilst Europe, with its highly developed nations, simply tries to constrain the irresistable tide of history.

The interchange of ideas

As I noted in the Introduction, it is the ideas manifest in social institutions and technologies, and distributed in the minds of men that can really shape such emergent processes, but even then, such distributed informational control cannot dictate the outcomes. The revolutionary influence of ideas (and inventions) borrowed from other civilisations is one of the lesser themes which appears in the verse. Karl Marx, in the 1853 article, *The Future Results of British Rule in India,* from which the quote at the head of this essay is taken, goes on to predict the 'revolutionary' implications of English education which was being introduced in Calcutta, the main theme of *A Nation Born Through Synthesis.* Jeremy Bentham had seen himself as the lawgiver of British India, hoping to transform Indian society through the introduction of progressive laws; replacing arbitrary despots with the Rule of Law[12]. James Mill noted how men's world-views are shaped by the laws governing their society; in todays global media information deluge, the greater global scenario shapes cognitive structures and this very work was the product of the effect of the changing world order upon my own cognitive structures, which like those of countless others were set into disarray by the collapse of the only concrete challenge to the Western economic system in the form of the Soviet Union. Friedrich Hayek, although he argues against notions of human solidarity, is correct to an extent in recognising the limitations of attempting to control the emergent socio-economic reality. His arguments for simply engaging in 'honest' negotiating in a 'free trade' environment, however, are as much, simplistic, idealistic nonsense as the exaggerated claims of human solidarity which he dismisses. Although the world may remain locked in competition for a long time yet, leading to collective benefit in some respects, there will inevitably be detrimental aspects as well, such as environmental deterioration where global solidarity is vital. A notion recurring throughout this work is that of *quiet violence,* the diffuse and often distant consequences of our actions such as the detrimental effects of Western overconsumption of vital resources on the developing world. The technological integration of commodity markets across the world, for instance, has greatly increased the capacity for speculators to inflict quiet violence in distant parts of the globe, on people the speculator will perhaps never encounter face-to-face and thus he will never really register the human consequences. Although, the diversity of interests between competing players does not lend itself to reaching any global consensus on such matters, some moral philosophers have pointed out that beneath the apparent relativity of perspectives, lies a universality in the basis of communication which allows us all to communicate with each other[13]. The global media, for all its faults, does open the channels of communication through which one day a better world may be built.

It was not only the Iron Curtain that fell in the 1990s. In 1993 and more so in 1994 whilst attempting to reconcile my own Panpsychist theory of consciousness (presented in Section XV) with my belief in a form of Brahmanism (also evident in the verse — based on intuition and supported by my rationally deduced and inchoate Panpsychism), in preparing my essay on the metaphysical content, the curtains of conceptualization, its false abstractions and relative truths fell away from before my eyes to let in the Light of Reality as it ultimately is. As explained in the essay on my metaphysics that follows, I synthesized Indian *yogic* philosophy and modern science at their most fundamental levels. This metaphysical synthesis establishes the grounds for a truly universal, global civilisation which will truly accommodate all the currents of the world's thought on an equal footing; all conceptual constructions having to bow before the whole Truth of the Absolute Reality.

TWO INTEGRATING THEMES

The individual as a microcosm

> But can I truly claim myself
> Free from nation, race and history
> Clan, class, sex, species, cosmos, fate
> This oneness/otherness mystery

This is the key quatrain which frames the entire verse work; the metaphysical dimensions of the work related to the use here of 'cosmos', 'fate' and partly also to 'species', in relation to the animal nature of my being, are discussed along with the rest of the metaphysical content of the work in the final essay. Although this mystical phrase has its deepest significance in the metaphysical realm in regard to the relation between the individual and the Absolute, the quatrain above is supposed to indicate the dichotomy of my being an individual, simultaneously part of, yet distinct from, my 'greater beings' (such as nation, species, the economic system, cosmos as well as temporal dimensions such as, 'history' and cosmic evolution) at all levels of existence. These greater beings frame my existence in both Space and Time and include such abstract entities as 'history' and the 'world market' which along with the other non-metaphysical greater beings constitute what I will call here the 'mundane' realm in contrast to the metaphysical. In the following essay on the metaphysical content of the verse and my more recent metaphysical work, which arose through the analysis of the contradictions and dualities in my own thought presented in the verse, I shall begin to use the word *mundane* in its more conventional, traditional sense as relating to the surface level of Reality as opposed to the deeper psychical and spiritual levels, associated with such terms as supernatural and transcendent.

The integration of the metaphysical and the 'mundane' dimensions of the verse work thus operates through this overarching framework of the Oneness/Otherness nature of our existence. Emergent entities such as my nation, race, caste, class, sex, species (in the sense of 'humanity' for the 'mundane' realm as against my 'animal being'), 'history', and the world market economic system are some of the greater 'mundane' beings of which I am at once both a part of and from which I exist apart from as an individual. These 'greater beings' permeate the mundane sections of the work, with one or two of them dominating each of these sections. Inclusion of nebulous entities such as 'history' and the world market system may appear rather odd. Their inclusion is not to be interpreted simply by saying that it is my 'mental being' (or my cognitive structures) that is being considered, although I have described the work as such in the Introduction as it had laid out the major contours of my mind before me. I note below the need for people to feel part of a greater 'cause', a progressive historical process. What follows resembles the traditional notion of the person being a *microcosm*, existing in an analogical relationship to the world, that is reflecting the outside world in some way, leading to related notions of 'resonating' in harmony, or in discord, with the world.

Although 'history' is an emergent process, not deducible from its constituents, this process none the less must emerge *partly* from the everyday actions of individuals. It is a two-way complementary relationship between myself and my 'history' as my very physical existence as an immigrant in Britain, as well as the character of my mind, is very much informed by the history of my people, as is my outlook for the future; history is a very important part of my 'being'. I also discuss below how the world market economic system gets its sustenance from inherent human motivations which have shaped the character of the institutions which go together to form this emergent reality arising *partly* out of individual transactions; I stress the word 'partly' here as this view of transactions between individuals forming the essential basis of the social order is closely tied historically to the materialist metaphysics which views the universe as the product of transactions between 'atoms'. The market system, reciprocally, shapes the character of individuals and institutions in the society in which I exist, so the world market system is also a very important part of my 'being'. My 'history' is closely linked to the notion of my *civilisation* which has been subsumed in this work as one of the components of my concept of *nation.* As discussed elsewhere, Tagore and many other Indians rejected nationalism as a post-medieval European cultural construct, based on tribalistic chauvinism, in favour of a patriotic view of India as a *civilisation,* open to the world. There are no fixed rules in poetry, one can abstract various higher-level manifestations of one's microcosmic being from the 'web intricate' of the cosmic being and various such intermediate beings are interpenetrating within and between sections, along with other themes, weaving the *sūtra* together into an integrated whole.

My original intention in writing the Introduction and this Postscript, in 1993, was to explain the integral nature, emergent themes and political content of the work. I have explained how the 'Oneness/Otherness Mystery' (both metaphysical and 'mundane') forms the overarching framework and that there exists an underlying theme of Indian Reassertion which emerged rather unconsciously. The latter is clearly apparent in both the metaphysical and the mundane Sections. This Reassertion is partly a response to the claims of the universality of Western civilisation as well as the manifestation of my inherent 'Indianness'. It is also a reassertion of the positive, often 'noble' values of the traditional world against the many shallow, shoddy, short-sighted values of the mercantilist 'world of *baniās*'. My rejection of the limited Materialist world picture in my interpretation of consciousness and my recent identification of *chit* (Pure Consciousness) with a scientifically known process constitutes an integral part of this Reassertion in rejecting the metaphysical schism at the heart of Western modernity undermining the greatest intellectual construction of the modern West, the Physicalist picture of the universe which, in one or other of its many forms, is held by countless modern Westerners and Westernised non-Europeans to constitute the Ultimate Reality. The mystical nature of the overarching philosophical framework in terms of 'bonds' (and the very word 'bond') to greater beings may also be seen as part of this 'Indianness' as is clear from the quote from A. Bharati in the introduction about the Hindu preference for holistic approaches to philosophy. The Indianness manifests itself also in my interweaving of the metaphysical and the 'mundane' in a way which is most uncommon in the modern West given its secular compartmentalization of the spiritual and the mundane. I intend to restore metaphysics to the study of 'the world as a whole'.

This very interweaving is important in regard to the Nationalistic aspect of the Reassertion in that the metaphysical world picture underpins the mundane social order. I discuss below the rejection of Sanskritic education in favour of English by Rammohun Roy as English represented the modern world whereas Sanskrit encapsulated an ancient world. In a sense my writing of a sort of *sūtra* in English is a product of the Indian Nationalist 'Synthesis'; and I clearly view the philosophical content of this work as part of this ongoing Synthesis. As population growth, industrialization, environmental degradation, the global media, the breakdown of the traditional social fabric etc. lead to more holistic views of the integral nature of the various aspects of our being, and as India begins to abandon the old nationalist, anti-colonial emphasis on economic self-reliance and begins to 'globalise', we may expect to see significant long-term changes in the mundane realm emanating from an Indianisation of the dominant global rationalist outlook, as, for instance, Arnold Toynbee had prophesized. Leaving aside the relativistic approach, used above in relation to Orientalist myths about Indian history, which legitimately emphasises the differences between the traditions of India and Europe, and taking a universalist perspective, it is clear that much of what may be conveniently labelled *Indian*, as opposed to *Western*, resolves itself into the differences between traditional and modern society. I have mentioned above the 'realism' underlying the traditional Indian picture of cyclical processes of social developments and decay, and the anti-utopian view of repeatedly domesticating the disagreeable manifestations of human nature. The traditional notion of *dharma*, in spite of all its negative connotations, holds some positive value for the future in its emphasis on social harmonization, finding a role for everyone within civil society. After all, the masses, as history (including contemporary Russia) shows, do tend to value peace and orderliness before freedom which involves risk and uncertainty. Such notions are of immediate concern given that contemporary Western socio-economic dogma is leading to the creation of so-called 'underclasses'. There is also a need to counter the alienating modern emphasis on production and wealth accumulation which 'dehumanises' the individual into a mechanistic component and skews behaviour patterns towards mere self-interested actions with an emphasis on sense gratification and monetary rewards at the expense of deeper fulfilment and the broader social consequences of one's actions. Such issues need to be re-examined in the light of the new metaphysical understanding of the individual's actual relationship to the Whole.

*The true **brahman** and the world of **baniās***

I now wish to turn to some of the themes that emerged in the mundane sections of the work. Many of the links between notions arising in different sections were noted in the Commentary in order to emphasise the interpenetrating nature of the work but such cross-referencing is not sufficient to explain more general or more subtle points, or the contexts from which the thoughts in each section arose. Let me begin with the ubiquitous reference to the world of *baniās*, the modern mercantilist world, as seen by this Indian who retains much of the Old World within his being. In regard to the interweaving of the metaphysical and the 'mundane', as I discuss below in relation to Science and Society, it was not superior logic on the part of the Renaissance men of the Scientific Revolution in Europe which allowed the new Science to progress towards hegemony. Rather it was the recognition by the new mercantilist classes of the economic value of the new 'natural philosophy' with its compasses, maps, sextants, guns etc. which allowed Science to overcome the resistance of the Catholic Church and herald in the modern world. The Cartesian split between Spirit (Mind) and Nature (Matter) underlying modern thought partly reflects the 'steering clear' of the realm of Spirit by early modern men of Science to avoid conflict in what was viewed as the domain of the Church. The realm of Spirit was recognised by the likes of Newton, who, along with his Anglican followers, attempted to maintain their lawgiver 'God' as the Prime Mover in the Newtonian system to counter the 'godless' 'matter in motion' of Hobbes which gave succour to rampant social materialism[14]. But the man who showed how the rise and fall of the tides was due to gravity could not hold back the tide of scientific despiritualization of Nature which continued into the early twentieth century in regard to the nature of living organisms. As the rise of the bourgeoisie was closely tied to the rise of Science, we may expect a respiritualization of Nature to lead gradually to a decline in the social prestige of mercantilist values.

The specious reas'ning of the *baniās*
Who whole world in their hands now hold
Economise with truth their salesmen
Utopia made of tinsel sold (Section I)

Not born or bred for world of *baniās*
Jñānamārga path I follow
Quaker to my cohorts, legion
In false idols *bhakti* wallow (Section III)

And in this wretched world of *baniās*
True brahman shows much abnegation
To debase his currency too proud
Yet bearing such humiliation (Section XII)

The bourgeois, mercantilist world of the modern capitalist world market is represented by the term *baniā,* the name of an Indian subcaste of traders or merchants. The term is often used in a pejorative sense in relation to the greedy, self-interest ascribed to *baniā* subculture which appears to care not for the greater good of the community. This term clearly parallels a widespread antipathy towards the middlemen. The word *negotiation* comes from the Latin *neg otium* (non-leisure), which was originally a term used with disdain by the leisured classes for the haggling merchants pursuing naked worldly motives. The world of traders is centred upon the objects traded and the transactions between traders and this reflects the materialist metaphysics of distinct 'atoms' and interactions between such objects. Hence the materialism of the new science and the materialism of the mercantilists of the European Renaissance complemented each other in their conceptual frameworks as well as in their technological collaborations.

The counterpoise in this work to the *baniā* type tends to be the true *brahman* as in the quatrain from Section XII above. The term would clearly be applicable to the sentiment expressed in a quatrain from Section IV which begins, 'This worldly soil in which weeds flourish' and emphasises my leaning towards a life of contemplation (*jñānamārga,* above, means the path of contemplation/gnosis). In *Bande Mātaram,* the political attitude expressed in the verse is a sort of paternalism which is related to the implicit brahmanical ethos of India's elite nationalism. As I note in the verse, the Indian National Congress in its early days was derided by some as being just the 'Brahman National Congress' due to the extremely high proportion of brahmans amongst its ranks. The world of *baniās* infiltrates deep into the domain of spirituality these days, especially in the USA with its television evangelists and Indian cult 'gurus' selling their packaged 'spirituality' to disaffected Westerners. Less brazen perhaps but equally market-driven are the Westernised Indian academics whose study of the ascetic traditions of Indian philosophy seems to serve only as a means of peddling exotica to the West in order to live in America rather than any serious effort to try to develop Indian thought to meet the changing needs of their country, given the serious problems associated with transplanting Western 'packages' into an alien context. Long gone are the days when Vivekānanda first took Vedānta to the Americans in the service of his down-trodden country, refusing the offer of a Chair at Harvard, whilst raising funds for his mission.

The world of *baniās* is not just the economic world of the 'free market' but also the cultural manifestations of it, especially the shoddier aspects of mass culture, 'Cola culture' as I refer to it occasionally. Although I tend to come across as a man of the Old World, this is not to say that I do not appreciate the positive aspects of the Modern World which, in general, far outweigh those of the traditional society and make today's world a far far better place to live in. My objection is to the polarization of categories underlying modern thought manifest in the attitude, prevalent amongst so many, that anything associated with traditional values is, of necessity, to be discarded as outdated and invalid. I am not averse to many elements of mass culture; my disdainful attitude towards it stems more from its seemingly detrimental influences on lowering standards, cheapening values, and somewhat undermining the very fabric of civil society in abandoning some positive aspects of traditional, elitist, society. The modern mind's infatuation with change has led to a neglect of the factors that provided social stability which had certain positive attributes alongside the oft berated negative ones. I have found that I have grown out of my childhood infatuations with some elements of mass culture but I fear that many people simply do not get the opportunity, or perhaps are inherently disinclined, to mature mentally as they grow older.

> I see the sons of unschooled fathers
> With whom as child I talked and jested
> Lost in worlds with short horizons
> In adolescent minds arrested (*Bonds of Kinship*)

I retain something of the Liberal view that we should attempt to 'uplift' the masses to a higher, more 'mature' psychological plane and cultural condition rather than leaving them literate but not truly 'educated'. Of course, a well educated mass market, if indeed this were attainable, may not appeal to the high priests of advertising dependent upon psychologically manipulating the expectations of the masses, using the crudest forms of materialism as a basis. The *baniā* mentality involves the retention to a high degree of childish cravings, interwoven with the Cult of Youth. The emphasis on rampant consumerism, material status symbols, short-sighted imprudence and superficiality reflects the value given to the sensorimotor and related planes of the psyche, 'lower planes' in the traditional order. The traditional Indian *brāhmaṇa* was literally supposed to be closer, 'psychologically' (spiritually), to the Absolute Reality (Brahman), i.e. was able to see the deeper nature of things.

Despite the worries expressed in Sections VIII and IX in relation to the effects of India's economic liberalisation; I never wished to oppose the economic reforms. As I originally noted in my commentary in 1991, India has no option but to follow this path. The old nationalist emphasis on self-reliance, born of the de-industrialization and plantationization of India by British colonialism (as discussed in *Satanic Mills*), has become a serious handicap in the new, highly integrated, global economic order. A *baniā* mentality has to be adopted to some degree at the national level, if only for a critical period in the modernisation and development of the nation. No man is really a true brahman just as no man is merely a *baniā*.

The political aspect of Section III (*Rashtra is My Word for Nation*) and the powerful sense of oneness with my nation has been elaborated in the introduction. Section IV (*Bonds of Kinship*) is an autobiographical piece, contrasting the utopian dream of a world where everyone could fulfil their 'potential' with the reality of constraints imposed by the circumstances of one's birth, the subversions of meritocratic progress and the mismatch between the true brahman, inclined towards a contemplative life, and the world of *baniās* which, with its emphasis on ends regardless of means (stemming partly from the modern world's split between Reason and Feeling), tends to reward the obsequious, narrow-minded, the greedy and similar sorts. Individuals pursuing self-advancement at all costs, regardless of their own unsuitability and the exclusion of more able people, and cliques which operate to exclude real talent from progressing are certainly not new to the modern world. Rather it is the lack of being 'true to oneself', the emphasis on shallow image over substance, the lack of concern for the subtle long-term damage to the sustainability of the enterprise etc. which repulse the plain-speaking 'true brahman' for whom such falseness, fawning and dismissal of the warnings of the 'inner voice' that are perceived as diametrically opposed to his rather old-fashioned self-image as being dignified, 'noble', self-respecting and being his 'own man'; virtues which seem to have largely disappeared from the world of *baniās*. As Bengali *bhadralok* society moved from traditional roles to the alienating modern world of *chakri* (salaried) work in the British bureaucracy, Bankim wrote of the incompetent, fawning Indians he encountered in the Subordinate Civil Service, kowtowing to the British, always eager to emphasise their marked inferiority to them (even if this meant deliberately mis-spelling words etc.) who rose rapidly through the ranks whilst the educated, competent and self-respecting Indians (the 'upright brahman' types in the contemporary debates in Bengali society) like Bankim were held down. It is also interesting to note in regard to this tradition/modernity issue Weber's point that the Protestant work ethic involved secularization of the ascetic virtues associated with monastic life, remodelling the virtues of ascetic contemplation into the virtue associated with the 'ascetic' devotion to labour.,

TWO TWO-LEGGED HUMAN RACES

Post-colonial changes in Western perceptions

Section V, *Two Two-legged Human Races,* introduces the major political theme of the work, Colonialism, by looking at the change in the relationship between the West and the rest of the world over the twentieth century beginning with that watershed in Indian Nationalist history, the Amritsar Massacre of 1919 (which was followed by a brutal Draconian imposition of martial law in Punjab including the notorious order from Dyer that Indians had to crawl on their bellies in one street). The second half of the first passage focuses on the major changes in Western attitudes that occurred during the decade of the 1960s, brought about by the conjuncture of a number of factors which are often the subject of today's fashionable discussions of so-called 'post-modernism'. The verse focuses on some of the major geopolitical issues behind the tumult in the Western Mind especially that of the West's youth benefitting from expansion of tertiary education, relative prosperity born of the pre-1974 cheap oil era, and a reaction against the traditional elitist structures of society. The influence of Marxism and Socialism cannot be neglected, especially in the case of France. I recall a middle-aged Briton, recounting on television the influence of the socialist movement amongst the British conscripts during the Second World War leading to the 1945 Labour Party landslide victory, telling of how his army socialist society had already 'freed India' in their minds during their wartime debates, a few years before the British Labour Party actually did the great deed. This, of course, came much to the chagrin of wartime premier Winston Churchill who saw British India as the linchpin of Britain's Great Power status and presumably held to the belief shared by the 1917 British Cabinet, led by his close friend David Lloyd George which granted reforms towards future Indian self-government, that it would take perhaps 500 years before India should be given self-government[15].

In regard to changes in Western perceptions and the hypermasculinity of colonial culture, manifest both at home and abroad, Churchill makes an excellent case study. He was a "man's man", stuck in the mentality of the Boer War period. One hundred thousand troops were lost during the 1914-18 war in the Dardanelles fiasco which Churchill had hoped would bring him great glory, faced with the stalemate in the trenches. (Ironically, the recent controversy about the British government's purchase of some of his papers using about $12 million of British National Lottery money, followed the announcement of the purchase on April 26th, ANZAC day (the acronym standing for the white British Commonwealth countries, Australia, New Zealand and Canada). The slaughter of Commonwealth troops at Gallipolli, thanks to Churchill's desire for glory, remains a poignant memory in ANZAC folklore, commemorated each year. Churchill unleashed the murderous 'Black and Tans' to suppress Irish rebellion, shooting Irish people indiscriminately from lorries and strengthening the cause of the freedom struggle. The British army used gas shells against the tribesmen of the Euphrates who rose up against British rule in 1920[16]. Churchill was Colonial Secretary from 1921 when the British Air Force was attacking Kurdish villages in a 10-year bombing campaign after the British had gone back on their word of granting autonomy to the Kurds. Churchill repeatedly pressed for the use of mustard gas against the Kurdish villages despite the warning from advisers that it would kill children and the sick, and that the Kurds had no antidote. The poison gas was not used for technical rather than humanitarian reasons[17]. Churchill also expressed his desire to bomb to death all the Hindus! Given the origins of this work in 1991, during the Kuwait War when the attacks of Saddam Hussein on the Kurds, were demonized by the West (which had armed him and supported him before), need to be placed in historical context. Back at home, Churchill propagandised against the basic rights of the brutally treated British miners during the 1926 General Strike. It is interesting to note that the British have put up a statue of him outside their Parliament building, along with Boudicca (the rather barbaric warrior queen who fought the civilising Romans), and Richard I, the anti-semite responsible for the burning of the Jews at York leading to the later forced expulsion of British Jewry, and whose own Plantagenet chronicler brags about the mass murders and barbaric atrocities committed by his Crusaders (the earlier Crusaders had practised cannibalism amongst other frenzied atrocities) against the highly civilised non-believers in Palestine[18].

Although the post-colonial changes in Western attitudes are welcome and have led to a much better global situation, the Section ends with a passage reminding us that the post-colonial reality remains a subtle 'neocolonial', imperialist order which manifests itself through the emergent politico-economic relationships between states and groups of states regardless of the well-intentioned moralising of liberals in the West.

> I ask why is it decent people
> Stop not such deeds done in their names
> Part powerless, emergent forces
> And part misled from real aims

Although the deeds in question were largely a product of Cold War paranoia and substantial progress has been made in many hotspots, including the two cases which the people of the developing world often perceived as the frontlines in the anti-colonial struggle, Palestine and Southern Africa, my point about the powerlessness of well-intentioned liberals in the West to feed their good intentions through the complex, emergent reality which distorts the outcomes remains valid in regard to the issues of 'Third World' development and neo-colonialism, and of environmental degradation (see discussion of *No Sure Ground* below).

International solidarity against colonialism

Whilst acknowledging the countless negative features of Soviet Communism, let us also remember that, in the anti-colonialist struggle, Soviet thoughts, if not hearts, and Soviet guns were in the right place although the same guns often fuelled internecine strife later on. International solidarity against the forces of oppression stirred the emotions in a way that little else can match. The story of the volunteers who fought for Spain (while the British government secretly aided the Fascists, alongside the open support of Hitler and Mussolini) in the International Brigades has brought tears to my eyes. An aura tingled on my scalp as I sang along with the largely white crowd at London's Wembley stadium upon the appearance of the recently released Nelson Mandela, "Walk on, Walk on, With hope in your heart, And you'll never walk alone, You'll never walk alone". Although idealists have often been misguided in supporting some causes, blind to the shoddier aspects of the actuality, it is vital that this idealistic sense of Internationalism, which was so strong in the 1960s, does not fade away with the rise of petty nationalisms and economic blocs. The Invisible Hand of the World Market can never capture the imagination of peoples around the world. We require a substitute personal god which inspires and arouses passions, as did the old Internationalism, promising the transformation of the world into a better place for everyone. The dream of a truly universal, global civilisation in the coming 'New Age' in which all sorts of aspirations, besides simply materialistic ones will be fulfilled with a holistic perspective on society and the environment can fulfil this role. The Internationalist aspect of Soviet ideology, although based on false premises (and Christian humanist utopianism), devoid of the Soviet legacy has widespread appeal and we must seek to rekindle the idealistic spirit of Internationalism that aims to 'unite the human race'.

Of course there was more truth in China's rejection of the Non-Aligned Movement on the basis of its (American and Russian) 'Two Imperialisms' thesis[19] than many in the NAM publicly acknowledged, but, despite Fidel Castro's efforts to push the Soviet Union as 'natural ally' line, Indira Gandhi maintained a more balanced role for the NAM. It was in a way the realisation of Mir-Said Sultan Galiev's 1918 thesis, mentioned in *A Nation Born Through Synthesis,* that the colonial subjects of all classes formed the international proletariat in the international 'class' struggle[20]. In this context Indians may look back with pride on the fact that the only two non-communist leaders honoured with statues in Moscow by the Soviet regime were Mohandas Gandhi and Indira Gandhi, due to their international stature in standing up to Western imperialism (Indira signed the Indo-Soviet mutual defence pact to prevent US intervention during the liberation of Bangladesh; see also the discussion of *No Sure Ground* below on the special Indo-Soviet relationship). The Mig fighter-planes and the AK47 automatic rifles churned out by the Soviet military-industrial complex shall hold a special place in history of liberation from Western colonialism. In the current euphoria over the peaceful enfranchisement of South Africa's blacks following the end of Cold War rivalries, let us not forget the heroic efforts of the Cubans against the white invaders in Angola which culminated in the decisive victory at Cuito-Cuanavale.

In fact I had brought these issues into the verse at the end of *Rāshtra is My Word for Nation* where I spoke of my inherent disposition towards the forces of anti-colonialism ("Still saw the world through eyes of ruled") and thus could not see myself as an "ersatz Westerner".

> While still not out of single figures
> Howzat! Such joy from heart would well
> As peasants poor from pockmarked paddies
> Sent Ravan's *vimāns* down to hell
>
> Evolves my mind upon small island
> Drifts not from species left behind
> Knew not Nehru, Nasser, Nkrumah
> But knew my heart was non-aligned

The first verse above refers to the shooting down of the B52 bombers inflicting mass murder on the Vietnamese people; the 'Rolling Thunder' in *Two Two-legged Human Races,* which led to the ongoing nightmare in Cambodia. Although the allusion to the evolutionary concept of Genetic Drift, where small isolated populations of a species (usually on small islands) lose traits through lack of transmission due to the random sample effect, is not entirely valid as my father's open enthusiasm for the Vietnamese cause did help transmit Indian anti-colonialism to me, my views grew more out of the subliminal racial identification with the oppressed non-white peoples ("I see my kin like archer Arjun") and the basic sympathy for the underdog. The sheer asymmetry of the power relations between the Western military machine and the wretched of the Earth dictated my orientation long before I could frame anything more than inchoate thoughts about the 'good' and the 'bad' in geopolitical relations.

Differing politico-historical perspectives in Asia and the West

Within the context of this essay's emphasis on 'history', it is worth recalling a view apparently quite entrenched amongst the Vietnamese leaders that Vietnam had a history of over two thousand years and was prepared to go on fighting for a thousand years if need be. In contrast, the US, the home of live-for-the-moment culture, would soon tire of its bloody and costly effort to contain the spread of Communism. As I have reiterated throughout this essay, 'good' often comes out of 'bad' intentions in history and the US interventions in Korea and Vietnam to contain Communism undermined its other imperialist ambitions by having to bolster the 'Cold War countries' of the Far East and Japan, which are are now aggressively competing with the US (see the George Kennan reference under *Satanic Mills* below). In regard to long-term historical outlooks, China and India, both with many thousand year old civilisations with occasional flowerings of greatness, have seen numerous upstarts, like Alexander, Gengis Khan and the British come and go. We may predict with some confidence that both will be flowering again after the great civilisation of Western Europe, that has dominated the world for the last few centuries, withers into the background of history.

The fact that the Vietnamese War of Independence from France, which continued against the Americans, resulted, with hindsight, in a rather Pyrrhic victory is irrelevant besides the global repercussions of this conflict in regard to changing attitudes. The vast global impact of this war stemmed from American hegemony, both military and in terms of dominating the global media. However, as I note in the verse, it was another War of Independence from the stubborn French colonialists, that had the initial effect in Europe.

> Fiery blast from Fanon, "Leave this Europe..."
> Resounded on Left bank of Seine
> The slaughterers-of-Setif's children
> Cried, "Algerie algerienne"

As Fanon was quick to point out in the quote alluded to above, this was the same France that trumpeted the Rights of Man across the world as it brutalised the native populations. France, of course, refused to leave Vietnam before Dien Bien Phu. It was perhaps Providence that put the French guns out of action at

Plassey and gave India to the British, less in thrall to the cult of tribal nationalism. The bombing of the ship belonging to the environmental pressure group Greenpeace, the testing of nuclear weapons, despite protests, in other people's parts of the world, and the rise of the *Front National* shows that French Nationalism retains this stubborn, tribal character. I recall an Arab recounting the joy he felt in 1947 when India finally cast off the mantle of the Raj; the Indian Freedom Struggle was the elder brother of all the great anti-colonial freedom struggles and India's freedom came as an inspiration to the enslaved peoples of Afro-Asia telling them that their day would also come, and come soon. The Indian National Congress had shown solidarity with the freedom-fighters in Ireland, Palestine and elsewhere before independence and extended this solidarity through the Non-Aligned Movement and other channels after independence. The change in the world order as decolonisation occurred was reflected in the changing composition and character of the United Nations although it remains to this day a Western imposition purporting to universality, as was seen in 1991 in regard to the Kuwait war when China's formal objections were ignored and is manifest in the permanent membership status in the Security Council with the power of veto remaining largely in line with the old colonial order. In 1948 the UN split between the white majority and the non-white minority in the vote which allowed Western colonialism to divide Palestine, with the US armtwisting its Latin American clients and Stalin betraying Soviet principles. Britain abstained, having been forced by President Truman to allow further unlimited Zionist settlement in order to secure the American Jewish vote; Truman threatened to withhold Marshall Aid, during the winter of 1947 when the seas around Britain froze, which could possibly have led to people starving in Britain. Colonialism ensured that the West would not have to pay for salving its own guilt conscience over its historical persecution of the Jews by opening its own doors to them; the Palestinian people were dispossessed instead. It was with good reason that, at her funeral, Yasser Arafat described Indira Gandhi as having been like an elder sister to him. Indira's father Jawaharlal Nehru, as President of the Indian National Congress in 1936 had led the Indian campaign of solidarity with the Palestinian Uprising against Zionist settler colonialism. In spite of the American initiative, based on US domestic politics in 1948, the Palestinians remember how it was the brutal suppression of the uprising by the British colonialists which neutered effective Palestinian resistance to their dispossession after the Second World War. Similarly, it was British colonial policy in South Africa which laid the foundations of the Apartheid system for which the Afrikaaners have taken nearly all the blame. The British employed a deliberate taxation strategy to force Africans off the land and into the mines; this paved the way for the barren wastelands (*c.* 13% of the total land) as Black "homelands" policy and the cruel migrant workers scenario under the Afrikaaners. It was the Indian National Congress which first raised the issue of Apartheid at an international forum at the United Nations Organisation in 1946[21].

International repercussions of internal 'class struggles'

The 1960s brought to world attention another 'freedom struggle' which, like Vietnam, grabbed the world's attention due to American hegemony. I have no intention of romanticising the 1960s as some magical decade as some tend to do although I have concentrated upon them, for good reason, in the verse. It should be noted that I was born in the middle of this decade ("And born was I amidst this thunder") and that the first verse of *Two Two-legged Human Races* ends with the words, "And History shaped new world around me/I live in this privileged time". Struggles for the civil rights of oppressed groups began long before the 1960s and continue to this day. The Suffragettes fought long and hard for the enfranchisement of women in Britain long before the so-called 'sexual revolution' of the 1960s, which, with hindsight, many women's campaigners do not consider to have been as significant or as beneficial as the euphoria at the time made it appear. Germaine Greer seems to be espousing some traditional values these days such as the extended family, which provides childcare, giving the mother a degree of freedom from childrearing chores. Ambedkar's struggle for the civil rights of his *Mahar* untouchable community in Maharashtra began with the conversion to Buddhism campaign before Independence and continued after Independence when Ambedkar, as Minister of Justice instituted the reserved parliamentary seats for the untouchables and tribals and positive discrimination for them in government employment and university admissions.

In regard to Mao Zedong's 'Great Proletarian Cultural Revolution', I like to tell the following anecdote to highlight the lack of relativity and historicity that still permeates the 'post-modern' West which sees its parochial views as universal visions. In 1989 the Sino-Belgian novelist Han Suyin was interviewed on television by a wishy-washy liberal British intellectual, Michael Ignatieff, about her life through tumultuous periods of China's history. Han Suyin stated that she looked somewhat favourably upon the Cultural Revolution as a democratizing process, in that, for the first time, the Chinese masses became involved in the political process. Ignatieff, a man of, I think, 'White Russian' ancestry, interjected with cries of, "How can you say that, how can you say that", as thousands of people had been killed. Han Suyin replied by saying, then how could President Mitterand a few months earlier have spoken so glowingly about the French Revolution. I note that the once great revolutionary leader Mao Zedong became a megalomaniac dictator after the Communist victory, losing his grip on reality and seeing himself as a modern Emperor. He revelled in the fact that an ancient Chinese empress had executed a few thousand or so 'intellectuals', playing on the Chinese masses' antipathy towards the better off classes and boasted of the vastly greater number of 'intellectuals' he had eliminated. Mao's one time personal physician, now exiled in the USA, has revealed secret films of Mao's dance parties during which he was supplied with pubescent young girls; the ex-physician states that, Mao, coming from a Chinese peasant background, had a very simple view of the world and the only entertainment known to poor Chinese peasants was sex. The Red Guards even practised cannibalism upon their victims. Up to 43 million Chinese died from the famines brought on by the maniacal fiasco known as the Great Leap Forward which highlighted the peasant turned Emperor's complete inability to understand the workings of the modern world. This was perhaps best highlighted by the lunatic attempt to turn China into a leading steel producing nation by melting down the people's iron and steel utensils in cottage kilns. History will clearly show his successor, Deng Xiao Ping, lacking the charisma of Mao, ruling from behind the scenes, to be the true Great Emperor of twentieth-century China.

But then Napoleon Bonaparte was a megalomaniac dictator responsible for great death and destruction across Europe. However, regardless of the Reign of Terror and countless other failings in practice over ideals, the French Revolution has had a profound influence on all ensuing political thought (note the references to its influence in India in *A Nation Born Through Synthesis).* Soviet Communism, in spite of the Terror, has forced the pace in political progress throughout this century, with the tremendous support it has given to the anti-colonial struggles and also, by its very existence, forcing liberal concessions from the ruling classes in the West to stave off revolution. It is in regard to the much smaller scale, mould-breaking, ideological influence around the world in the particular period I focused on, the 1960s, that, regardless of the appalling actuality of Mao's Reign of Terror, that I refer to his influence in the verse. A close look at any inspirational period in history will reveal the darker side of human nature lurking beneath the mythology. Mao had bloodied the nose of the Americans in Korea and he had three million Chinese 'volunteers' fighting in Vietnam. Today Mao's face still adorns the gravestones of Naxalite 'revolutionary' peasants continuing their 'class struggle' in the Gaya district of Bihar where once upon a time Buddha had attained enlightenment and challenged the social elite. But the middle class students in India's universities have abandoned Mao and most are now set on becoming 'yuppies'. Although many of their teachers, themselves the radical students of the sixties and seventies may look upon this situation with dismay; it will hopefully be this generation of would-be 'yuppies', who will serve the utilitarian cause in India far more than their mixed-up, middle class, self-styled 'vanguard of the proletariat' predecessors, by not being satisfied with the material and economic conditions prevalent in India today, lifting India towards economic take-off tomorrow.

THOU ART THE REASON & WE ARE TWO BRANCHES OF ONE RIVER

The male-female dyad and the 'feminine' Hindu Mind

Sections VI and VII may appear a little out of place amongst other sections in the verse work which appear to fall more easily into the metaphysical and 'mundane' realms. The entire work was written together, many sections in parallel in a period of frenzied 'outpouring', and conceived as a single grand philosophical poem. The overarching framework began to appear as the work took shape although there were numerous inspirational factors behind the sudden burst of activity which created the work. If one were to seek justification for *Thou Art the Reason* in terms of the overarching framework, it is as follows. Just as the hereditary relationships underly the 'greater beings' of kin and clan, so the relationship of love, in its various forms, results in dyads of which the individual (monad) becomes a part.

> This love, this need to share one's being
> Part born of lust yet lust transcends
> Gives purpose to two pointless monads
> When on the other each depends

And later in the section we have the bond at its most intense:

> Playfully coy, gasping in joy
> Clasping me yet my spirit freeing
> Sworn is this union, I behove you
> Thou art the reason for all being

Thou Art the Reason focuses on the romantic male-female relationship leading to the formation of the dyadic husband-wife relationship although there are of course many forms of loving relationships resulting in many looser dyads. The inclusion of the reference to betrothal in the verse resulted from the process of poetic construction rather than from any conscious ideological motive. In this age when the husband-wife relationship, especially in the West, is no longer as 'sacred' as it once was, partly due to far greater individual economic freedom but also due to factors linked to some of the pernicious influences berated in this work, it is important to remember that the institution of marriage, for all its faults, is an essential element in the fabric of civil society providing children with a stable environment in which to develop. There is increasing concern in Britain in regard to the growing number of single parent households resulting from high divorce rates. Of course women (and men) should be free to opt out of mismatches but the problem seems to be more one of the happy-go-lucky attitude of many people today, perhaps related in part to the 'throwaway culture' and 'inbuilt obsolescence' of modern consumerism, which leads to naïve, immature, imprudent, hyper-individualistic decision-making. So-called 'politically correct' people will of course stress that romantic love does not necessarily entail a male-female bond but this is a work about my relationships to my 'greater beings' and the very character of this work, with its emphasis on mysticism and traditional virtues, could be described as rather Romantic.

The use of the word 'sex' in the eleventh quatrain of Section I refers to my being a male of the species, my 'maleness' being a 'greater being' insofar as it 'bonds' me to male humans in general just as my being human 'bonds' me to the humanity in general. Section VII (*We are Two Branches of One River*), rather than looking directly at maleness, looks mainly at the male/female dimorphism with an emphasis on the historical status of women and my attitude towards women in general. The Female, being the Other to the Male, is critical in defining what it is to be male just as the Western concept of the Orient was constructed in order to define what it was to be the West. The parallel between women and the subjugated peoples of the colonies has taken precedence over any focus on maleness. The historical emphasis of the Indian Reassertion *vis-à-vis* Western Orientalism is prominent with my reference to the status of women in the ancient Babylonian Code of Hammurabi (probably the source of the Ten Commandments) showing the relativity of Progress set against Western preconceptions of steady evolutionism and of the West being the most progressive of all civilisations in all respects, especially in relation to the status of women, which it has used to chastise other civilisations. I have pointed out the male domination of my own civilisation as well with the reference to the classing of women with base-born serfs in the *Bhagavad Gītā*.

The reference to the Aryanisation of the female deities of Bengal is not only interesting in relation to *dharmic* metaphysical justifications of the mundane but also because the native female deity, Durgā, whose cult many Bengali brahmans were to adopt became the Mother in Bankim's hymn *Bande Mātaram* in his famous nationalistic novel *Ānandamaṭh* which went on, through the influence of Aurobindo (in his revolutionary phase) emphasising the Mother as the (female) *shakti* or energy of the Absolute, to become *Bhārat Mātā* Herself. The tantric tradition of Bengal, alluded to in the verse, gained great influence through the popularity of Ramakrishna *Paramahaṁsa's* teachings in the 19th century. Ramakrishna, for all his eclecticism, primarily worshipped the Absolute symbolized as the Great Mother of the Universe (Durgā/Kālī). It should be noted though that the Vaishnavite Cult of Krishna, associated in Bengal with the great medieval poet Chaitanya, is at least as popular. Krishna is himself a rather hermaphroditic character, and the female characteristics of the Absolute are represented in his divine consort Rādhā, together forming the Rādhā-Krishna dyadic whole. I have noted in the introduction that Indian Nationalism is not a petty tribal affiliation, although the Nation concept, stemming in part from Spinoza, has something of the God of the Israelites in it. Indian Nationalism, born of the reaction to hypermasculine British Rule has many feminine characteristics such as inclusiveness, cooperation and championing the oppressed of the world. Ashis Nandy, in his *The Psychology of Colonialism*[22], has noted how the nineteenth-century Bengali Christian poet, Michael Madhusudhan Datta, retold the story of Rāma's escapade into Sri Lanka in his *Meghnāvadh Kauvya,* championing the masculine ('Western') characteristics of the traditionally despised demon king, Rāvaṇa, as against the feminine ('Hindu') virtues embodied in the traditional heroes. In fact, Rāma's consort Sītā, taken with Rāma, also tends to form a gender-transcending Sītā-Rāma dyad. Ronald Inden views the Jungians (including Mircea Eliade and Joseph Campbell) as the New Romantics holding to outdated notions of mental and racial stratification. Jung was well acquainted with the work of G.F. Creuzer (1771-1858) who categorised the Indian as one of the 'archaic' civilisations which expressed their religious thought in mythopoetic and symbolic terms rather than in rational terms, holding the former to be valuable knowledge in relation to the divine. The Jungians have their own version of progress based on psychical factors which predominate in a particular culture.

> *Finally, India is the civilisation in which, since the unconscious of a man is a female entity known as the* ***anima****, the feminine predominates over the masculine. . . . This notion of a feminine Hindu mind has even been taken over by some Indian psychoanalysts. . . . India is . . . where the female layer of the human unconscious is most in evidence. . . .*
>
> Inden, R. *Imagining India*

The rights of women today is a major issue of growing importance, transforming the very character of the emergent realities of history which, in the past, were almost entirely shaped by men and masculine values. We may expect to see in the future the rise of values which are currently recessive within the dominant modern culture, associated with the growing influence of women which may harmonize somewhat with the Indian view of the world.

A large part of Section VIII (*Bande Mātaram*) focuses on the dichotomy between my elite nationalist views and their seeming irrelevance for the Indian masses and marginal groups, the Others who constitute the majority of the 'one' nation. In a somewhat similar sense, in regard to the Oneness/Otherness Mystery, the point of the opening passage of *We are Two Branches of One River* should not be lost:

Our forms unfold in common pattern
Choreographed to the same tune
Yet I prance Man and thou dance Woman
Like ray of sun and ray of moon

Thou art the ground of human being
Thou art the pattern of default
Would-be Man would be born 'Woman'
If impulse male came to a halt

Woman is at once both one with Man and the 'Other' and, although I am a male, I am also partly feminine in my being a human as indicated by the quatrain in Section I:

What if we would extol the Female
The woman that's within us all
Could we transcend this manly conflict
Would everyone then have a ball

> *Erikson doubts whether there has been another political leader who prided himself on being 'half man and half woman' . . . more motherly than women born to the job.*
>
> Nanda, B.R. *Gandhi and His Critics*[23]

Nanda adds that Gandhi came to regard women as the incarnation of *ahiṃsā* (non-violence). I myself boast of being mentally hermaphroditic, capable of utilising synthetically the full range of mental faculties which normal society splits into masculine and feminine.

Masculine 'imperialism' and historical progress

The final passage of *We are Two Branches of One River* touches upon the link between British colonialist expansion and the hypermasculine British culture of the colonial era. Although I attack Western colonialist imperialism, I admit that I too have a rather 'imperialistically-inclined' masculine mind in many respects although my rather open expression of my emotions and various other traits appear rather effeminate to the repressed British mind. Hypermasculine cultures have of course been associated with the self-justifying ideologies of various non-Western societies during periods of aggressive expansion; the *Pūrva Mīmāṁsā darśana* (one of the six great Indian systems of philosophy) reflects something of the character of Indo-Aryan imperialism with its emphasis on worldly duty, resembling the emphasis on duty found at the height of the British Empire. I have equated femininity in this work with cooperativity, caring and consensus-seeking, as opposed to the cruel, competitive, domineering attributes of masculinity. At the height of British Imperialism, British women played a significant role in the campaign to abolish slavery. A number of Irish or British women were associated with either the Indian Nationalist movement or its spiritual counterparts; foremost amongst them the Irish-born Theosophist, Annie Besant, who became a Congress *rāshtrapati* (the term for 'president' literally means 'Father of the Nation') and Margaret Noble (known as Sister Nivedita), the spiritual disciple of Swami Vivekānanda who after arriving in India became a vehement critic of the Raj and helped to arouse patriotic resistance to it amongst Indians. (The close link between Indian patriotism and spirituality are also seen in the lives of Vivekānanda, Aurobindo and others and also in the attempt by Gokhale to harness the ascetic tradition of self-sacrifice to the patriotic cause with his Servants of India Society). The selfless labours of Woman as Mother are acknowledged as 'noble', which in this work usually represents worthiness and selflessness although it also represents notions along the lines of Old World 'honour' set against the cheap values and herd mentality of the modern masses. Hearing a recent British radio programme in which female scientists highlighted the often forgotten contributions of women to scientific history[24], I could not help drawing the parallels with the glorification of past Indian scientific achievements and scientific role models found in Indian Nationalism (see the quote about Ramanujan in the introduction). In focusing on the empathy between myself as a subjugated Oriental with this subjugated half of humanity, and having associated masculinity with British colonialism, I have given a misleadingly negative picture of masculinity which I wish to redress.

Since writing the verse I have come to realise the negative effects of feminine influence upon social order which, as with other 'weaker' groups, can verge upon Stalinistic exclusion of natural ability and self-assertion, in favour of bland toil leading to a conspiracy of mediocrity (the British Feminist movement is currently facing criticism from American feminists over its close identification with 'Socialism'). Women, given positions of power, are equally capable of sexual discrimination. One has come to appreciate in the microcosmic manifestations of the assertive, restless, competitive attributes of masculinity, the driving forces of change, discovery and also heroic resistance to injustice although the heroic, plain-speaking 'noble savage' syndrome, as with the Amerindian 'noble savages' of Section X (*Lebensraum*) tends to lead to ultimate, if glorious, defeat. Nandy, in *The Psychology of Colonialism,* points out how the British much preferred the 'manly' martial races of India (Marāthās, Rājputs, Sikhs, Pathāns, Gurkhas and others who fought heroically but lost to the British) to the 'effeminate', intellectual Bengali 'babus' who did not put up a struggle. However, the pen was mightier than the sword and the 'effeminate' Bengali babus, the interface between the British rulers and the ruled Indians, bided their time and in amongst them were the 'upright brahman' types like Bankim who developed the ideological core of the new nationalism which allied to Gandhi's non-violent, turn-the-other-cheek, *satyāgraha* (which Nandy sees as a brilliant psychological strategy to which the liberal British didn't really know how to respond) were modern forms of resistance that served India infinitely better by taking what was good from the British whilst gradually forcing them out.

> The babu fought not like the martial
> Yet in the Lion's paw stuck thorn
> By spreading word to far-flung districts
> That a new *Bhārat* would be born

Ainslee Embree notes that the British in Western India did recognise the brahmans in the Marāthā territories (where the Chitpavan brahmans had assumed the power temporal, providing the Marāthās with their *Peshwā* (Chief Minister) and ministers) as the natural enemies of British rule whereas Bengali brahmans were not initially seen as a threat. Only in the late nineteenth century, as nationalist aspirations began to be voiced in Bengal, did the contemptuous references to the Bengali babu appear[25]. The babus were also ridiculed by the Bengalis themselves, including much self-deprecatory literature.

A lot could be said, of course, for the historical value of imperialism in spreading civilisation, modernity and progress although there is no acceptable justification for the brutal plunder and slaughter that often 'prepares the way'. In *Bande Mātaram*, I refer to the Indian Union as a 'shadow empire' and, of course, this is how it must be perceived by people like the Ahom (a branch of the Thais) of Assam where I was born, many of whom see my community as colonialists. The difference between British colonialism/imperialism and the Indian Union (or even the Mughal Empire) is that the British did not see themselves as part of the society, and their activities were primarily aimed at the betterment of far-off Britain at the expense of India. As I note in *A Nation Born Through Synthesis*, as the power structure in Britain changed so too did the attitude of the British ruling class to the imperial possessions:

Transformed into a race apart
Thought born to civilising mission
Translated possessions of plunder
Into a grand imperial vision

Today, imperialism has taken on new, less brutal forms, with the USA leading the way with economic neo-colonialism (although it should not be forgotten that this mode of imperialism followed the traditional mode of brutal territorial expansion as noted in *Lebensraum*, and fighting for overseas colonies such as the Philippines). The 'cultural imperialism' of American cinema and television, usually glamorising the American 'lifestyle' tends to promote the interests of American industry which caters for such a lifestyle's requirements, however detrimental this may be to other societies. I mentioned in the introduction the copying of the brutal American ghetto gang subculture by teenage boys in Britain who also pay ridiculous prices for the brand-name clothing associated with the subculture, sometimes committing crime to pay for such clothing. I also mentioned Margaret Thatcher's lobbying of East Asian countries for tobacco giant Philip Morris in the name of 'free trade'. The American emphasis on so-called 'free trade' reflects a belief that this is the 'American Way' and what is good for the USA must be good for the rest of the world or perhaps, at bottom, what's good for the USA is what the rest of the world must abide by. The Victorian British held similar views about the benefits of British imperialism. Clearly, there have been many positive contributions to the world at large resulting from the 'American Way'. Britain and France were taught who called the shots by the Americans after their cynical invasion of Egypt in 1956; the Americans took the Second World War rhetoric about national self-determination a lot more seriously than the old colonialists, having pressed the British for Indian independence and thus opening the closed market. I originally had a verse near the beginning of *Lebensraum*, which I omitted for continuity, acknowledging the great contributions to progress and prosperity brought to large parts of the world through the development and spread of American civilisation, even though the price paid was the savage slaughter and dispossession of the native Americans.

The natives numbers should incense us
Like Christ they died so we might live
In New World culture built on graves of
The tribes who of themselves did give

Of course it is even possible to interpret the USA's aggressive annexations of Mexican territories such as California and Texas along the lines of the original American self-justifications relating the 'squandering' of the developmental potential of these territories by the Mexicans. With the USA's population becoming increasingly Hispanic, especially in the territories grabbed from Mexico, and with the NAFTA Free Trade agreement, the 'Mexican' people (many now US citizens) are likely to benefit, historically, from American imperialism. A similar interpretation could be given to the situation in the Southern African subcontinent.

Although I sympathise with the demands emanating from certain circles, especially US feminists, for so-called 'political correctness' in order to combat psychological structures of discrimination against various oppressed groups, I wish to stress that, although parts of this work do appear to give uncritical support to such positions, this is not my intention. I am all too aware that such over-zealous 'PC' tends to defeat its own purpose through its stridency and often ludicrous demands. The Right will always seize upon the excesses and stigmatise the whole programme despite the general 'good sense' behind it. Although some aspects of this work are 'politically correct', much of it is clearly elitist and I have already declared my brahmanical, paternalist ('Whiggish') frame of mind in regard to certain aspects of politics, something which many on both the Left and the Right will think of as anachronistic. I believe that uncritical relativism, like Kundera's 'democratic Utopia' referred to in the introduction, is anarchic, degenerative nonsense, contrary to the best long-term interests of subjugated groups and a hindrance to 'real progress' which to me means something along the lines of building up the basic institutions which facilitate individuals' opportunities to develop along their own chosen path and includes a notion of 'uplifting' the subcultures of the masses through education rather than tolerating everything. This requires the imposition of constraints upon the chaotic tendencies of things left to themselves in order to harmonize the overall activity for the benefit of all, meaning the curtailment of certain so-called 'freedoms' which naïve liberals often take to be god-given rights. It is worth recalling a famous lesson from the history of technology about the spread of technology. Although the water mill was invented in about 100 BC, it took about 1500 years for it to gain widespread acceptance in Europe where it played a key role in the Agricultural Revolution which preceded the more glamorous developments. In the end, its widespread use boiled down to an authoritarian imposition of laws by feudal regimes, as has been the case with other inventions or innovations, which brought increased general prosperity and concomitant progressive developments, but met, quite justifiably, resistance from traditional societies[26]. Similarly, Marie Stopes was less interested in women's rights than in controlling the birth rate of the poor in her efforts to promote contraception. In *Bande Mātaram* I dismissed the Tiananmen Square protest of 1989 as the 'roaring mouse' of the privileged urban middle classes, not representing the long-term interests of the vast majority of the Chinese population. For all the hypocrisy spouted over human rights, all the double standards and ulterior motives, one must none the less acknowledge that, in maintaining China's Most Favoured Nation trading status, the USA is serving the global utilitarian cause on a grand scale. Let us not read total evil into the great injustices of the past even though the motives may have been reprehensible, at least by today's standards. Progress towards a better society for all is a slow, painful, roundabout and relative process which is always open to conflicting interpretations. As I stated above, the great thing about emergent systems is that 'good' is often the outcome of the worst intentions.

Returning to the link between masculine 'imperialism' and progress, I do not hold that the imposition of authority in a, 'parental' (to use a gender-neutral term) manner is necessarily unreasonable although some passages in the *sūtra* may question such authority. In the nineteenth century, many Indians publicly acknowledged that British Rule was a blessing in disguise giving India tutelage in modern procedures although economic considerations along with numerous other factors eventually outweighed this 'blessing'. In the final chapter of *Ānandamaṭh*, the novel which inspired India's revolutionaries, Bankim's hero realises that British rule is God's will, preparing the way for a restoration of Hindu rule. Section VIII (*Bande Mātaram*) belabours the contradictions inherent in my own elite nationalist sympathies although acknowledgement of the problematic nature of such views does not lead me to abandon them (see below). Of course, the values imposed on societies in the past such as the values espoused by the American 'founding fathers' have been the values of, in this case, white, male, middle class, property owners and cannot be wholly endorsed as progress leads to greater and greater enfranchisement and, hopefully, empowerment of once-excluded groups whose 'life-worlds' are determined by factors far removed from the self-justifying values of the 'founding fathers'.

However, we are witnessing the disruptive and often damaging consequences of certain aspects of liberal relativism allowed free reign (for which the British Right tends to blame the '1960s' and their pernicious influence). Although I have paid tribute to the decolonialisation of Western thought in the 1960s in Section V (*Two Two-legged Human Races*), I will go along to an extent with the Right-wing critique of the societal 'decline' although not pinpointing the root cause to the catch-all bogey term, 'the 1960s'. Civilisation does involve a degree of 'parentalism' and the imposition of value-judgements designed to preserve social stability, prosperity and cultural heritage and 'progessive' civilisations attempt to raise everyone, not only materially, but also 'spiritually'. The example set by Japan cannot be ignored even though Japan remains in the rather unusual position of having a very small ethnic minority population and tries to maintain racial 'purity' (even in relation to the racially near-identical Koreans; Japan also has its untouchables and indigenous people who are treated shoddily). The glorification of the Cult of the Youth and similar aspects of supposedly free expression tends to result in short-sighted behaviour patterns with damaging long-term societal consequences. Taking relativism to the point where criticism of deleterious aspects of subcultures becomes taboo leads, as stated above, not to a democratic 'Utopia', but to anarchic chaos and social decline. Of course the repressive structures of the past should be done away with to help unleash the untapped potential of those who were excluded but this should not go to the mindless extremes of rubbishing everything associated with the past simply because they were framed in an elitist context. Those who know whence they have come, know whither they are going.

> *The literatures of Greece and Rome provide the longest, the most complete and most nearly continuous record we have of what the strange creature* **Homo sapiens** *has been busy about in virtually every . . . activity. Hence the mind that has canvassed this record is much more than a disciplined mind, it is an experienced mind . . . Cicero told the unvarnished truth in saying that those who have no knowledge of what has gone before them must forever remain children.*
>
> Aldous Huxley[27]

Patriarchal institutions and the status of women

Feminists, quite justifiably, complain of an inherent misogyny in social norms and institutions resulting from historical male dominance and patriarchal imposition of authority. The verse refers to the suppression of an early women's rights group, whose name I have forgotten ('Minerva' perhaps) soon after the French Revolution by the same revolutionaries who had proclaimed the ideals of Liberty, Equality and Fraternity.

French men and women stormed the Bastille
Much of the Rights of Man was said
When sisters questioned *patrie*-archy
The brothers said, 'Off with their heads'

I note in the verse that, although one could impute a cold, calculating rationale for the asymmetric role of the husband and wife in regard to household work etc., it is not generally the case, that these unfair social norms are maintained by patriarchal collusion (despite the continued existence of misogynous judges, Masonic societies etc.), rather such misogynous structures tend to be maintained by systemic constraints which are resistant to radical changes in the *status quo.*

Few truly hold such views unseemly
But matters not what people say
For higher forces shape Society
Emergent systems act this way

The status of women in most societies has improved dramatically over the last couple of centuries as the Idea of Progress has worked its way into minds and institutions. Some of these improvements have been aided by technological developments, reducing the need for household chores etc. and also through the industrial system requiring a more skilled labour force, leading to mass education and other socio-economic developments. These economic, technological and other developmental factors are the progressive 'higher forces' in the emergent systems which no amount of supposed patriarchal conspiracy can resist. Nevertheless, the same emergent, holistic character of societies places constraints on the nature and pace of change, preventing radical dislocations of existing relationships due to the very interconnected, organic nature of the system. Many of the social 'Revolutions' in history tend to be 'Revolutions' in the minds of the historians who fail to see the underlying continuities with the past, the reinterpretations of traditions, and the slowness with which the initial transformations actually tend to gradually work their way through the system[28].

Keeping 'imperialism' and patriarchal misogyny in mind, it is worth recalling the case of India under the British. Indeed, the apologists for British imperialism cite the improvement in the status of Indian women as one of the benefits accruing to India from the Raj; this was the main thesis of Katherine Mayo's *Mother India*, 1927. This notorious best-selling book by an American travel writer deeply coloured Western perceptions of India and was damned by Gandhi as a drain inspector's report although he urged all Indians to read it. Tagore first encountered the book through the review in the *New Statesman* mentioned below and it infuriated him. Mayo had deliberately misquoted an article by Tagore in regard to traditional Indian society's attitudes towards women, omitting the words "said India" and thus making it appear that Tagore himself held such attitudes. One of Tagore's American admirers, Will Durant, educationalist and author of *The Story of Philosophy* and *The Story of Civilisation*, countered with his *The Case for India* which the British banned in Bengal[29]. The well-educated Durant was clearly better positioned to give a reasoned argument unlike Mayo's impressionistic diatribes (a tradition continued by the likes of V.S. Naipaul). Today's feminists, Joanna Liddle and Rama Joshi give a balanced view of Mayo's work recognising that Mayo conflates the issues of male dominance and imperialism.

> *Whatever Mayo's motivation—and the fact that her earlier book,* ***Isles of Fear****, made the case against granting independence to the Philippines cannot be ignored—the British seized on the book's attack on male dominance to argue against Indian self-rule . . . London's* ***New Statesman and Nation*** *ended its review 'Katherine Mayo makes the claim for* ***Swaraj*** *(self-rule) seem nonsense and the will to grant it almost a crime'.*
>
> J. Liddle and R. Joshi.[30]

Mayo, whilst conflating imperialism and male dominance, was obviously not bright enough to make the link between imperialism and and the attitudes of male dominance underlying colonialism with the natives seen as being feminine and hence to be subjugated. Mayo and *satī*-sensationalist types choose to ignore the fact that millions of women were burnt to death in Christian Europe on suspicion of having psychical abilities (see also the quote from Ambedkar in my discussion of *Satanic Mills* below).

I would not deny that traditional Hindu society involved numerous practices which are perceived as shocking to the modern mind although, as I note, many of the reforms came from Indian campaigning rather than being readily bestowed upon the natives by the British rulers. The changes in Hindu laws on *Satī* and child marriage were instigated by social reformers such as Rammohun Roy (known as the 'Father of Modern India' — a patriarch if ever there was one!) whose campaign against *Satī* stemmed from his application of the Western notion of individual freedom (and also from the traumatic experience of his sister-in-law's self-immolation[31]). I should add that *Satī* was a very rare phenomenon in India, being practised by the Rājput clans when abduction beckoned with military defeat and being adopted for the two centuries before abolition in Bengal although, for instance, a British university graduate I worked with appeared to think that it was the norm. Numerous, more widespread changes in the male-female relations were brought in through petitioning by Roy and other *bhadralok* such as the abolition of the polygamy of *Kulīn* brahmans with the lower subcaste *Srotriya* brahman females and the abolition of child marriages. Given the thorough self-examination, self-criticism and self-reform of Indian society during the 19th century, which continued despite the concomitant nationalist self-assertion in the 20th century and continues in a low key way today, it is all the more amazing that Western reviewers, who pose as intellectuals, heap praise upon that panderer to Western preconceptions, masquerading as an intellectual, who follows in the Mayo tradition of looking only in the drains, V.S. Naipaul.

> *But no Indian cares to take political self-examination that far. No Indian can take himself to the stage where he might perceive that the faults lie within the civilisation itself, that the failure and cruelties of India might implicate all Indians.*
>
> Naipaul, V.S. *India: A Wounded Civilisation*

It should also be recalled just how long and hard was the campaign of civil disobedience that led to the enfranchisement of women in the Empire's 'mother country'. Those so quick to condemn us seem strangely oblivious to parallel problems found everywhere else in the world; it seems that those, like Naipaul (now knighted by the British), who talk of universality in the West, do not apply the same standards universally. Having said this, reports of female infanticide and cynical exploitation of the dowry system are constantly coming out of my motherland and from amongst its diaspora. Nearly two centuries after Roy, a lot clearly remains to be achieved.

Negative and positive social manifestations of male tendencies

Although developmental changes are slowly mollifying the misogynous structures of societies, a major obstacle remains at lower levels of social interactions in the biological nature of the male of the species. As I state in the verse in Section VII (*We are Two Branches of One River*), 'within me the problem lies'. The problem is that despite all the changes in attitudinal norms and the socio-economic reality, no amount of indoctrination can fully eliminate the inherent bigotry of the male in relation to females, stemming from the very nature of the sexual dimorphism.

> But this it seems is natural process
> Inbuilt for seeking out our mates

But carried into social discourse
False concept now discriminates

The misogynous structures of social relations, as with the Capitalist World Market system, must ultimately draw its sustenance from inherent human motivations; the misogynous structures feeding off and reflecting the basic motivatory constitution of the human male to some extent. The nature of male motivations, stems somewhat from the evolutionary role of the male (in sexually dimorphic species) organism which increases the beneficial variation in the population through its generation of vast numbers of meiotic gametes.

I am your fugue composed by Nature
My countless seed my one true asset
The cutting edge of variation
The species' jewel I multifacet

Whereas the female produces a few eggs and, in mammals especially, invests very heavily in the early development of the offspring, the male, biologically, need only contribute some semen. The first verse of *Thou Art the Reason* points at the evolutionary logic behind the difference in behaviour between sexes in that the male is able to increase the proportion of its alleles in the population by fathering as many offspring as possible whilst the female, lumbered with gestation, is better off enhancing the chances of its potentially fewer offspring. Unfortunately, it does seem extremely difficult to prevent the innate tendencies manifesting themselves in the social realm in subtle ways if not in the old explicit forms. In the final section of the *sūtra,* I frequently use the term 'apemen' for humanity in order to stress that we are but 'glorified apes' and not distinct from Nature. The term 'apemen' is particularly apt in regard to the male of the species which quite readily reverts to baboon-like behaviour.

I state in the verse that there are probably inherent, *statistical,* differences in mental aptitudes between the sexes, and that we should be able to live comfortably with these differences by altering our values from associating prestige with predominantly male characteristics to equal acknowledgement of the sorts of contributions which are typically female. As stated above, I claim to be able to fuse harmoniously modes of mentation which are categorised by normal society as predominantly masculine or feminine traits. Given the synthesis of Eastern and modern Western metaphysics presented in the following essay, I would expect the eventual de-emphasis of the primacy given to modes of thought which the modern West perceives as 'masculine'. The Indian philosophical tradition has long grasped the limitations of logical analysis and emphasised experience, vision, intuition, insight and holistic thought. Of course logical analysis, discursive thinking, reductionism etc. have a vital role to play and cannot be replaced in certain contexts; rather it is the over-valuation of such modes of mentation especially in regard to social prestige and the concomitant 'isolation' of thinking from feeling, leading to cold, mechanical, calculative realpolitik, that marks the modern age that will be sent into retreat. Increased emphasis on such 'feminine'/Indian modes of mentation are necessary for both a fuller appreciation of Reality and for creative developments towards a more cooperative world order.

Having said this, I wish to state that certain aspects of male behaviour, often ridiculed by feminists, have often proven to be of great benefit to humanity, however infantile and distasteful they may appear to certain women. I like to illustrate this point with the case of Rosalind Franklin, which has been raised by feminists to exhibit the misogyny of men in overlooking the important contributions made by women to historically significant achievements.

Franklin was the X-ray crystallography specialist whose high quality data on DNA provided Watson and Crick with the accurate information they required in order to deduce the correct structure of DNA using their model-building approach to the problem. Without Franklin's data, it could well have been that Linus Pauling, who had originally developed the model-building approach to deduce the structure of proteins, would have got the glory that Watson and Crick craved in working out the structure of the hereditary material which was of great importance to biology. However, it was Franklin's project manager, Maurice Wilkins, who shared the Nobel Prize with Watson and Crick. Watson later wrote in a rather patronising manner about Franklin in his popular book about the discovery.

Franklin died in 1958 and the Nobel Prize for Biology was awarded to the three men in 1962. As Nobel Prizes are not awarded posthumously, the omission of Franklin was not really an issue. In contrast, Jocelyn Bell, who, by chance, discovered the first pulsar was still alive a few years later in 1974 when her project manager, Anthony Hewish, received the Nobel Prize for the discovery. In regard to male-female differences, it is interesting to note Franklin's negative attitude towards Watson and Crick, much to the annoyance of Wilkins, when they tried to persuade her, to reveal her unpublished data. She furiously dismissed them as 'little boys' whose only aim was to be the first at what they perceived to be a mere game whereas Science was supposed to be the careful, arduous accumulation of data from which inferences were to be drawn[32]. It was *not* about trying to grab the glory whilst doing the least possible work. Interestingly, in the radio programme in which contemporary women scientists championed their favourite historical female scientists, Jocelyn Bell lauded the drudgery approach of accumulating data in her chosen historical figure, Elizabeth Herschel. It was, of course, acknowledged that Society frowns upon assertive women but it was toil as a monastic virtue that was being praised. Another female scientist championed Marie Curie whose story of laborious toil is well-known. It was pointed out that her husband Pierre was the intellectual giant in the partnership. I noted in the introduction how the proposal of the Danger model, challenging an established fundamental hypothesis, by an ex-bunny girl turned immunologist has provoked strong hostility from Immunology's 'old guard'.

Although the view of scientists as unassuming, impartial collectors of data is often instilled into students, the fact is that often it *is* the 'little boys' dreaming of glory who are the driving force behind many of the great leaps forward in Science and many other fields of human endeavour where the drudge cannot see the wood for the trees. Einstein said that he was a 'late developer' (neotenically retaining his boyhood mental character) and Newton, for all his modest statements in writing, was ferociously competitive in regard to 'being first' as the verse in *Mind Games* about the dispute over primacy in the invention of the infinitesimal calculus indicates. The double helix was there for the taking and Pauling or someone else would have got it even if Watson and Crick had not existed. But in numerous other cases it has been the 'puerile' characteristics and ferocious competitiveness, so often derided by feminists, which have allowed great men to transcend the foreseeable horizons and dream up solutions to problems or see new vistas of concrete or abstract achievement and drive themselves towards the fulfilment of their ambition for 'immortal achievement' with all its glory. However, the apotheosis of DNA by materialist biology as the key to all the secrets of life is a negative consequence of an equally 'puerile' reductionist focus on abstractions.

> Were all men same, Man would be dead
> We live as variants on one theme
> Within the pale most born in blindness
> Few at the margins, men of dreams

BANDE MĀTARAM

Market forces and the Nation — the modern gods

Section VII (*Bande Mātaram*) opens with the 'Invisible Hand' passage, setting the global scene of economic liberalisation, before the verse turns to look at the effect of 'Invisible Hand' (the *baniā* world's apotheosis of emergent market forces as the solvent for all socio-economic ills) on my own nation. The greater beings of the world market economic system, the nation, class, caste, race and creed are interwoven in *Bande Mātaram* ('I bow to the Mother'; the old Indian Nationalist salute). Written, as was the whole of the verse work, in the tumultuous summer of 1991, as the Soviet Union disintegrated and the new Indian government embarked upon the road to economic liberalisation, my mind reflected the turmoil in the world scene, wary of the Western free market gurus and of the over-zealous apostates to the *baniā* mentality, ready to abandon everything tainted red by the Socialist past in order to make way for the brave new world of the free market. We have already seen the backlashes from the dispossessed in Russia and Poland whilst the Indian government has had to tone down its earlier pronouncements of will. As stated above in regard to technological innovations, I am well aware that, in the long run, the painful restructuring should help bring material benefits to the societies who are suffering now. My intention was never to oppose the economic liberalisation, but to raise doubts about the utility of an unmitigated free market system, especially in regard to hundreds of millions living at the subsistence level in India.

Plentiful crops painted Gangā's plain
Buffer stocks bulged in government keeps
Pushing up prices in the bazaar
Near half the nation went hungry to sleep

The first major passage of *Bande Mātaram* focuses on the dichotomy between my grandiose elite nationalism and the down-to-earth, parochial aspirations of India's masses.

Oh wretched *ryot*, Son of the Soil
Could we ever as true brothers pass
My Rām, 'high' Rām of Vālmīki
Your Rām, 'low' Rām of Tulsīdās

My Rām he speaks in noble Sanskrit
Your Rām he speaks in common tongue
Can we two dream same *Rāmarājya*
Could we one day sing the same song

In regard to the issues of nationalism and socialism, I should stress that I do not identify my *nation* simply with the *people*. The *nation* is a god-like, conceptual entity which transcends the *people* whilst simultaneously remaining immanent in and amongst the *people*. Above the *people*, the concept of the *civilisation* with a unique heritage and a unique perspective comes to the fore. India is not just the peoples of India writ large. India is a great civilisation, with a great heritage and tradition, which will never become but a satellite of Western civilisation. The rise to global economic power of the likes of India and China are far removed from the economic rise of, say, Brazil. Geographically, India is the antipode of the United States and, despite some similarities in political structure and ethnic diversity, India is the antipode of the hyper-materialism of the New World (my rebuttal of Richard

Rorty in the introduction reflected this cultural divide). Indian civilisation has subsumed all the ideological incursions into the subcontinent, Aryan, Islamic, Christian, American . . . and maintained a distinct sense of Indianness. Reformulating oneself in the face of Western global expansionism does not mean losing a deeper sense of Indianness; just as the 'brown Englishman' turns out to but one aspect of certain modern Indians, so modern Indianness will have many Western features. My attachment to my nation is attachment, not directly to the people, but to the civilisation. But, as stated in the introduction, the nation is also the Self writ large and to see the people of the nation (in a sense the *body* of the nation) sunken in destitution reflects most badly upon oneself. Thus a socialist element enters nationalism independent of broader humanistic motives. Humanity as the Self written even larger lapses too easily into contradictions in the current neocolonial world order where large sections of humanity are too easily perceived as the Other.

> *Despite occasional attempts to base Indian nationalism on unalloyed self-interest, 'pure nationalism' had never been able to mobilize even the Indian middle classes fully. Indian nationalism still vaguely reflected, in however distorted a form, what could be called the ultimate civilisational ambition of India: to be the cultural epitome of the world and to redefine or convert all passionate self-other debates into self-self debates.*
>
> Nandy, A., *The Illegitimacy of Nationalism*[33]

The Green Revolution and the rise of Backward castes

The first passage of *Bande Mātaram* touches upon the 'Green Revolution', Norman Borlaug's 'gift' to the developing world, which has brought both great benefits to the better-off farmers and, indeed, the nation (providing the buffer stocks for shortage periods which also help to protect against Western 'food aid' imperialism — even food for the starving comes with strings attached) and great socio-economic dislocations, generally hitting the landless the hardest. As the verse indicates, the Green Revolution was the agricultural manifestation of the god 'Invisible Hand', a god who tends to penalise the poor. Such, it seems, is the price of Progress. In the telescoped modernisation processes of today's newly industrialising societies, it may be that we are seeing industrial revolutions following hot on the heels of agricultural ones.

The Green Revolution's broader effects on the political order are alluded to in the second major passage of *Bande Mātaram*, in regard to the rise of the 'Backward' castes, in rural areas the 'middle peasant' subcastes, especially the Yadav and Jat communities of North India. Before the recent rise to prominence of the sectarian BJP, the major development in Indian politics had been the growing political power of the 'Backward' castes (mainly the old *Shūdra* castes, between the high ('Forward') castes and the 'Scheduled castes (untouchables) and tribes'. Taken together, the various Backward Castes form the largest of the three groupings above, lacking the privileges of the various high castes and the government job and educational reservations (and parliamentary reserved seats) of the Scheduled castes. The repercussions of their rise are being felt in India today as the last Congress government gave way to the Backwards' demands for similar job reservations for them, stealing the thunder from the leftist parties closely associated with the Backwards and hopefully getting a share of the Backward 'vote bank'. It was the attempt by V.P. Singh's Janata Dal government to implement a more comprehensive reservation system, as was recommended by the Mandal Commission, which led to its prompt downfall in 1990; with the high castes protesting that many Backwards, especially those best placed to take advantage of reservations, were not economically disadvantaged, indeed, after the Green Revolution it was their increasing economic power which led to their growing political organisation and power.

The politics of accommodation

At a more general level, the second major passage of *Bande Mātaram*, alludes to the political history of accommodation by the once brahman-dominated Congress faced with the the vertically and horizontally fractious conglomeration of communities which constitute the Indian Nation. I have not alluded in the verse to the co-option of Ambedkar and the Scheduled castes, which I have mentioned above, although in the first line of the first verse of this passage, the reference is to Backwards, Untouchables and Tribals:

Oh *Shūdra, Dalit, Ādivāsī*
'Twas always 'Brahman Congress' *bhai*
Swarāj my birthright, I will have it
Now *Hindūstān hamara hai*

As the following verse notes, it was M.K. Gandhi's great achievement to translate the elite nationalism of the early Congress into an idiom which would appeal to the masses and the diverse castes and communities, forging them together to face up to the British as one aspirant nation (although of course the Muslims eventually went their own way). As the Congress appealed to India's masses, Gandhi also instituted the All-India hierarchy of committees reaching down into each district, paralleling the structure of the British administration it was fighting for power. The verse alludes to the half-hearted land reform programmes of Nehru and the more vigorous efforts of his daughter, Indira Gandhi. The latter's land reform programme helped to precipitate the mobilization of the Backward 'middle peasants' in North India as they perceived that their interests were being threatened by a coalition of the brahman-dominated government above and the landless untouchables below[34].

V.S. Naipaul's *India: A Wounded Civilisation* was written during Indira Gandhi's (state of) Emergency; one distorted snapshot of subcontinental history being taken by this supposed 'intellectual' as the basis for a final indictment of a great civilisation with thousands of years' history. Whilst digging up all the dirt, Naipaul fails to mention any of the underlying tensions in the socio-economic situation; no mention is made of the fact that Indira Gandhi was trying to push through land reforms for the poorest Indians. The political mobilization in the face of Indira Gandhi's increasing authoritarianism helped develop the political organisation of the Backwards. Very recently the brahman-*dalit* alliance has broken in Uttar Pradesh as *dalit* assertiveness grows with new alliances being formed between *dalits* and the Backwards.

The rise of Hindu sectarianism which has overshadowed the rise of the Backwards is related to this process of accommodation as the 'shadow empire', as I refer to the Union, confronts the problem of separatism in the peripheries and Muslim fundamentalist tendencies within the cities of India's heartland. In the introduction I discussed my attitude towards the call for Hindu sectarian nationalism by the BJP, itself born partly of the need to transcend the petty divisions of region and caste. Political historians note that all Indian governments have to spend much of their time and energy holding together a fractious coalition of interests rather than concentrating on strategic development programmes[35]. Clearly, the Union needs a unifying vision, but this cannot be achieved by alienating the minorities. In the end, the best attraction that the Indian Union can offer those who have doubts about remaining in it is the prospect of economic prosperity, bringing with it broader opportunities in general, and foreign investment can only be frightened away by the prospect of communal strife and political instability. I reaffirm in the verse my allegiance to Hindu tolerance, restating Rāmakrishna's famous doctrine of the Unity of Faiths which becomes all the more pertinent now given my interpretation of the mystical union with the Light of Pure Consciousness, which, known as the Godhead, lies at the heart of all religious thought.

Secularism in India

The debate in India as to how to respond to the BJP challenge in attempting to redefine Indian Nationalism has focused in large measure on the concept of Secularism in the Indian 'communal' context. There is no denying that there is some truth in the BJP assertion that the Congress pandered to Muslim sectarian interests, in order to maintain the Muslim 'vote bank', at the expense of the greater national interest in maintaining a secular administration. Indian secularism entails neither the rationalist, anti-religious state nor the fairly clear separation of religious leaders from affairs of state as has been the case in Europe. This is not surprising given that so-called 'Hinduism' is not a Western religion with a 'church' which can be easily distanced from the state. Furthermore, the *sanātana dharma* involves the social order, and thus the basic activity of the modernising state impinges upon the 'Hindu' domain; the social reformers of 19th century 'Neo-Hinduism' tended to work within the overall 'Hindu' framework although at odds with the orthodoxy. Given the liberal, progressive nature of Neo-Hinduism, there has been little conflict prior to the rise of the BJP. The naïve hopes of Indian Marxists of creating a class struggle have floundered on the primacy of caste over any emerging class identification amongst the Indian masses[36] (although some signs are now emerging in the *dalit* alliance with the other Backward castes in Uttar Pradesh). Indian secularism has involved 'playing with fire' for political expediency as highlighted by Indira Gandhi's early manipulations of the Sikh fundamentalist Bindranwale in order to gain the upper hand against the liberal Sikh establishment in Punjab, leading to greater destabilisation in Punjab and, of course, her assassination. In the introduction, I have stressed the need to challenge the 'soap opera' appeal of the Hindu icons, manipulated by the BJP for sectarian mobilisation, with mass education affirming Rationalism and Science, as well as reaffirming secular Neo-Hinduism. The good thing about the god 'Invisible Hand' may prove to be its drawing power amongst those currently drawn to the BJP's sectarianism. As stated above, the promise of future prosperity is the greatest unifying factor and it is necessary to inculcate the message that sectarian strife is bad for attracting investment, bad for development, bad for Mother India. Increasing modernisation (and the new interpretations of religious experience as given in this work) should play their parts in undermining the sectarian manipulation of superstition on both the Hindu and Muslim side; the adherence of Muslims to feudal Bedouin values will only perpetuate their marginalised status as an underclass in an increasingly modern society underpinned by secular values and the Rule of Law. Rather than simply rubbish things like the BJP slogan, 'Say with pride, I am a Hindu', the positive elements of the BJP *raison d'être* must be extracted and reformulated to serve the common national goals. Indians do need to have a sense of pride in themselves, in the sense of self-confidence and self-belief that as Indians they can rise up out of poverty towards greatness. The slogan must be, 'Say with pride, I am an Indian'.

Ashis Nandy[37] notes that Gandhi rejected the modern West primarily because of its secular, scientific world-view. Nandy focuses on what Freud called 'isolation', the modern world's separation of thought from feelings (which culminated, as Adorno and others argued, in the bureaucratised genocide of the Nazi death camps). Gandhi knew that modern Western ideology held secular societies to be superior to non-secular ones. The constitution of the Republic of India of course declares it to be a 'secular' state. The 19th century Bengali 'Neo-Hindu' social reformers had reconciled modern Science with Brahmanism so that the modern Hindus did not have to become fully secularized even when they adopted the 'scientific frame of mind'. Note that, contrary to Western views of Hindu society being steeped in religion, Brahmanical Hinduism came to terms with Science (and modernity) before either Indian Christianity or Islam. Hinduism is of course more akin to paganism than to the semitic 'religion'. Nandy notes that as Gandhi was challenging the orthodox Brahmanical ideology, championing the lesser folk traditions and the rights of the masses, the scientific world-view, which to Gandhi seemed to endorse Brahmanism, was perceived as being allied to the old Hindu social order and thus this association lay partly behind Gandhi's anti-scientific viewpoint. Interestingly, Nandy notes, that Gandhi's orthodox brahman assassin, Nathuram Godse, accused Gandhi of threatening the newborn Indian nation with his anti-scientific, spiritualistic ideas relating to morality etc. which had no place in modern Realpolitik (based on the isolation of Reason from deeper feelings). My direct synthesis of Science and Brahmanism in fact supports the Gandhian view that Reason cannot be taken to stand alone, separated from experience and deeper feelings and supports some, but not all, of his spiritualistic assertions about the order of things which were once ridiculed by Westernised Indians.

Scientific modernisation, development and social justice

In regard to Science, Religion and modernisation, I am reminded of a few stories from the history of Science in regard to its social context. First, despite the scientific hagiography, idolizing the likes of Galileo and mocking the obscurantism of the Church, it is now recognised that the learned men of the Church put forward numerous sound arguments against some of the new scientific theories. As I have stated above, it was not superior rationality that won the day for Science, it was the new mercantilist establishment's recognition of the economic value of the technological offshoots of the new science, allowing for better navigation etc., that allowed Science to establish itself regardless of the resistance from the Church. One also recalls the worries of the Anglican church in late 17th century England that the Hobbesian materialist metaphysics of 'matter in motion' would only reinforce the materialism of the social world which was increasing with the new mercantilism. One of the reasons why Newton and his Anglican supporters maintained God in the universal system, as the Prime Mover which imparts motion upon inanimate matter and as the cause behind the harmonious maintenance of the universal Laws, was in the hope of constraining rampant social materialism which could prove harmful to the greater social good[38] (something which remains as relevant today as it was then). A century and a half later, Darwin held back from propounding his theory of evolution until power in Britain had shifted from the feudal, aristocratic Anglican conservatives (who vehemently opposed evolutionary notions partly because their social interpretations gave succour to emancipatory forces; evolutionism was associated with the French Revolutionaries) to his own Whig class, and industrial capitalism had established itself firmly enough to make the scientific world-view the undisputed metaphysical system underpinning society[39]. In all cases we see the forces of economic modernisation aligned with Science. The new Liberal political theories were themselves attempts to establish 'scientific government'. One of the reasons why Britain managed to industrialise was because the spirit of Science had percolated through society[40], helped in part by the Newtonians like Boyle who disseminated the new science, albeit with a particular moral emphasis. Scientific literacy is not only a counter-measure to sectarian obscurantism, *it is a prerequisite for a society seeking to enter the modern industrial world as a self-reliant technological power.*

Although not mentioned in the verse, the Dravidian South had long been wary of the Aryan-dominated Indian Union. The humiliations of caste had been the most cruel in the South, especially in Kerala. However, the South is now solidly integrated into the 'shadow empire' with Congress victorious across the South for the first time in 1991 (and the first Prime Minister from the South), whilst losing ground to the BJP in its Northern heartland. This is where the pseudo-imperialist elite nationalism (my 'shadow empire') really comes into its own as the Dravidian South has recognised that it is better off as part of the Union rather than going it alone in the modern world, as banana republics. The down-to-earth and parochial aspirations of the masses and the regionalists/separatists cannot provide for the emergent benefits which arise out of the Union, the synergies between the particular strengths of each region and the pooling of resources to fulfil our scientific, technological, social and cultural aspirations which must be geared to a national, political will which mobilises the fruits of the pooled resources to develop every region in the land and to raise everyone, eventually, out of abject poverty. Although we are currently faced with separatist movements on our borders, I think that any realistic long-term assessment of potential for modernisation even in the Indus Valley or the Gangetic Delta must involve the cooperation of the regional giant, the Republic of India. In this regard, Vincent Smith's famous phrase about Indian history, *Unity in Diversity*, remains an apt slogan for the *nation*.

Within the context of my elitist soul-searching, *Bande Mātaram* alludes to the great debate concerning the related but separate notions of *modernisation* and *development*, the latter entailing a comprehensive transformation of society bringing the benefits of modernisation to everyone and society, in turn, benefitting from this unleashed potential.

> As meek now speak through ballot boxes
> Who stops to question, who asks why
> Who makes the most from modernising
> Guardians Aryan speak Aryan Lie

As stated in the commentary, the inspiration behind this verse came from Nandy's essay *Science as a Reason of State*[41] which opened the first volume of a series of books looking critically at the links between Science/modernisation and social disparities and injustice in the Indian context. Although my elite nationalist attachment to Science and modernity remains strong, I am aware of the negative social consequences that can also arise from them. It is here that my Brahmanical paternalism is clearly manifest, a modern manifestation of the guardians of the *power spiritual* questioning the legitimacy of the *power temporal*, the rising power of the *'baniā'* mercantilist world; not too dissimilar to the concerns of the Newtonian High Anglicans cited above. For all the elitism, the acute sense of Aryan ethnicity, the glamorous appeal of the 'Space Age' etc., the concern for the plight of the masses is genuine, although partly born of the *nation as self writ large* considerations. The poverty and deprivation of the Indian masses cannot but have a lowering effect on one's self-esteem, thus simply for such selfish considerations, I would reiterate Indira Gandhi's old campaign slogan used in the verse, *garibi hatao!* This factor of lowering one's own self-esteem also has the reciprocal effect, subliminal though it may be, of colouring the perceptions of non-Indians towards Indians abroad, the state of the nation does affect one's identity however much some Indians try to deny it. It is partly in this respect that I chastise those members of the Indian diaspora who refuse to acknowledge their own 'Indianness' ("I laugh at all these ersatz Westerners"). The self-justifications given in terms of, "When in Rome, do as the Romans" etc. usually masks a deeper lack of self-esteem, for if India is the self-writ large, then one is associated with poverty and squalor. If one reads the likes of V.S. Naipaul, one discerns a subtext along the lines of, I'm not one of these damned good-for-nothing natives, not me master, I'm a Westerner like you. The *baniā* mentality, although vital in many respects, also includes 'trickle down' economics which simply will not suffice in the long run. As stated in the introduction, it is the very alienation of the Outsider, the 'ascetic priest', that allows him to break the bonds that tie him to his class interests — "his very misanthropy stems partly from a sense of deep frustration with the preoccupation of the vulgarians with their materialist 'pursuit of happiness', their consumerism and their wasteful consumption, when so many in the world are forced to live in such abject poverty".

> Who keeps in mind the higher motives
> Beyond approval from their peers
> And cares to shed the wasteful lifestyles
> Behind the crocodilian tears *(No Sure Ground)*

The rejection of Simplistic Christian Humanism

Of course Christian ethics, born of the self-justification of oppressed imperial subjects, preaches the cause of the dispossessed and, although Neo-Hinduism has adopted Christian Humanism,

I find the simplistic humanism, imbibed by many from the dominant ideological milieu of the global media, wholly insufficient to meet the actual challenges faced by humanity. As with my reference to *City of Joy*, I do not wish to ridicule or discourage such altruism, if that is what it is, only to state that reality is far more complex than the simple pictures we are often presented with and it doesn't always help to adhere too firmly to a belief which is, after all, just a grandiose idea. The philosopher has to question the very notion of *Humanism* and ask if there is any metaphysical justification to granting humanity such a privileged status, when it is equally possible to conceive humanity, from a global perspective, as being rather like a virus as in my allusion to James Lovelock's 'Gaia' view of the planet in the verse. As noted in the introduction, what I write does not always truly reflect my own attitudes as a person. In examining the philosophical content of this work, I have become aware of the separation of thought from feeling that exists within myself; my reasoning faculty, faced with what is to be done about mass poverty, moves towards scientific (Stalinistic perhaps) solutions, treating humans as mere abstractions. Faced with human suffering in person, I am usually filled with empathy and kindheartedness, far removed from my remote reasoning. I am now aware that these responses stem from the distinction between my egoistic self and the 'deeper Self'. In spite of the denial of Spirit in secular, modern Western thought, modern Western ethics remains rooted in a premodern, spiritual metaphysics which could not be justified by a purely logical, scientific-style analysis which tends to reduce people to abstractions. The Cartesian split between Spirit and Nature left humankind, endowed with Spirit, separate from Nature. This tended to justify humanism, in theory though not in practice, as well as having implications for animal rights. My metaphysics shows this separation of Spirit and Nature to be false; Nature too is Spirit. Such a shift obviously has implications for the future of humanistic thought with humans no longer set apart from Nature in the foundations of future ethical thought. The holistic implications of such a return to Spirit also has implications in regard to human suffering in relation to the damage that human overpopulation has on the rest of Nature which cannot be justified by any special status accorded to humans.

Those holding most firmly to such simplistic, humanist notions tend to be idealists with utopian dreams who fail to comprehend the complex processes at play in historical progress. In the colonial world, evangelical Christian Humanism did play a leading role in the abolition of slavery through the campaigning of non-governmental organisations (NGOs). I hold many of today's Western NGOs, which consciously make an effort to understand the perspective of the people they are trying to help, in respect but such charity is but a drop in the ocean and no sustainable development can rely upon charity. I have put the West's newfound governmental concern over human rights into historical perspective, showing how it can act against the long-term interests of developing nations. Just as good intentions, working through emergent processes, can bring 'bad' ends so, history shows us, Progress has emerged through rather 'bad' motivations. The British conquest of the India, the European conquest of the Americas, the USA's propping up of Japan etc., in order to contain Communism, have led to overall progressive developments although much blood was shed. We have become immune to the images of suffering constantly brought to our attention by the global media, and resigned to the impotency of the United Nations in stopping faraway internecine struggles when no Western interest is threatened. Faced with the natural disposition of our minds to repress such harsh realities, I can only hold firm to such positive aspirations as are associated with the grandiose aspirations of my elitist sense of nationhood and history, which I believe will eventually serve the utilitarian cause in my country and its neighbours; one-fifth or so of humankind.

In spite of the fact that the current world order leads one to be wary of any naïve 'global village' outlook as if everyone is happy and in spite of my doubts about simplistic humanism, as I have already suggested, Indian Nationalism has broader implications in that the East-West Synthesis lays the basis for a truly universal, global civilisation in which the heartless Realpolitik of mercantilist modernity will be mollified by a sense of spiritual unity between people, between humanity and Nature, and individual and collective motivations will need to be re-examined as perceptions of various relationships are transformed.

Learning lessons from China

We are currently witnessing the remarkable economic rise of

China which, from the Indian vantage point, is rather like the Athenians looking at the relative success of authoritarian Sparta. Numerous historical factors are working to China's advantage, such as the massive investment in China by the Chinese diaspora, who dominate the business sectors in non-Chinese South-East Asian countries, as well as from Taiwan and Hong Kong. The Indian diaspora must follow suit. The total accumulated foreign investment in China in 1996 was around US $50 billion. The Indian diaspora could easily match this figure to help India attain economic take-off as has already occurred in China. One cannot help but partly attribute India's relative sluggishness to the inertial mass of mass poverty. The final passage of *Bande Mātaram* contrasts India's elitist trickle down economics with China's recent 'Iron Rice Bowl' policies of confronting mass poverty head on and largely eliminating it at the expense of bourgeois aspirations, hence my reference to the 1989 Tiananmen Square massacre.

Some mourn but thousand angry young ones
The well-schooled mouse like lion roars
Half crore each year we feed to Moloch
Their feeble cries *Mātā* ignores

The following verses question the link between India's tolerance of mass, abject poverty and its population problems, questioning the appropriateness of democratic 'freedom' which must appear like an elitist sham to those whose lives are dictated by the need to meet the most basic requirements for survival. I have called for mass scientific literacy above, at a more basic level there is a need for mass literacy simply because the spread of literacy amongst the poorest females, as is well-known, helps reduce rampant population growth. The shameful fact is that there are more illiterates in India than in the rest of the world put together! It may be that the only means of mobilising India to overcome the enormous hurdles she faces is to create conditions in which a degree of 'benevolent authoritarianism' can be tolerated whilst maintaining democratic controls on any excesses. At the end of *Bande Mātaram* I refer to one of the great 'might have beens' in Indian history, Subhas Chandra Bose (see *Chol Dilli* discussion below), who, had he lived, might well have been

India's first Prime Minister. Bose favoured an authoritarian regime for independent India, for the first fifty years or so at least, in order to force through the necessary social reforms. As I note in the commentary to the verse, such an approach at independence would probably have led to India's disintegration. Indira Gandhi's attempts to impose authoritarian rule in the 1970s were a clear failure. Clearly a strong national consensus has to be formed where everyone clearly perceives the long-term benefits before India can take such a road. It is not impossible that, with increasing modernisation, the burgeoning urban middle classes across India will reach some sort of consensus on what has to be done. It is amongst the urban populations, alienated from the firm sense of 'rootedness' one finds in rural areas that regional identities dissolve and a sense of national identity grows. For all of China's successes, India is not China where ninety per cent of the population are Han Chinese, and the Confucian tradition fosters deference to authority. Any attempt at Chinese style authoritarianism would result in the break-up of the union. It is well-known that the 'Hindu' pace of change is slow and, as I have noted above, 'Hindu' ideology is anti-utopian, recognising that social evils cannot be fully eliminated but need to be accommodated as best as possible in each cyclical phase of social development and decay.

At least we have not attempted maniacal 'great leaps forward', killing over forty million in the ensuing famines, anti-intellectual purges wiping out many of the most skilled people, gulags, gross environmental neglect, invasion and systematic destruction of the unique cultures of neighbouring countries. Aldous Huxley[42] has chastised the tendency in Western philosophical thought (followed by the Chinese Communists), influenced by evolutionary theories, to view 'God' as emergent, evolving in Time rather than being eternal, beyond the temporal order (this will be discussed in the following essay). Hegelian and Marxian philosophies have substituted 'History' for the Divine, and are concerned with humanity as a succession of generations rather than with individuals at any given moment. Huxley stresses that all the evidence points to the fact that it is the individual 'soul' alone that can contact the Divine. Although I would agree with Huxley in regard to the false substitution of 'History', and the primacy of the individual's relationship to the

Absolute, which I myself stress in this work, I would temper Huxley's dismissal of the temporal order by referring to Rāmakrishna himself; Huxley was a member of the Rāmakrishna Mission. Rāmakrishna stressed that the eternal Ground and the temporal order emanating from that Ground could not be taken independently of each other, nor could the temporal order be dismissed in the manner of Shankara. Yes, the Kingdom of Heaven is within us but we have also been created within this temporal order, where suffering exists in individuals, although Rāmakrishna says that the Ground remains forever in bliss regardless of the suffering experienced in individuals. Rāmakrishna also says that one cannot realise the Absolute without participating in the dance of the relative[43]. The answer must lie in striking some sort of balance between seeking utilitarian progress between generations which provides material progress for all by sacrificing individual aspirations to some extent but also seeking to give the individual a degree of autonomy in which to seek his or her own 'fulfilment'.

Asian social values versus *the 'free market'*

In the West, we have seen the creation of the 'underclasses' as the parliamentary democratic process develops to cater for the needs of roughly the top two-thirds of the population, leaving the poorest stranded as the impetus of the old labour movements fizzles out. With overpopulated India, even if we were to follow the Western pattern, this would leave hundreds of millions of people effectively disenfranchised by this sort of marginalisation process. The Western attempts to create welfare systems are already showing signs of strain and degeneration, at least in their more comprehensive forms. The message is glaringly obvious, even without adding the growing concerns over the state of the global environment, we cannot just blindly follow the Western models of development.

Of course it is not easy to contemplate any drastic shifts away from Western-style patterns of socio-economic development given the convergences imposed by technological 'social gene'/ 'modes of production' effects, global economic integration, transnational open media etc. What one can say is that, perhaps, as the two great civilisations of Asia, both burdened with over a billion people, begin to emerge as major players on the world scene, there is likely to be a shift towards people-oriented Substantive Rationality in the organisation of socio-economic systems as against the current Western emphasis on ever-increasing Formal Rationality where increasing economic efficiency and statistical measures of output growth are the only desired ends. This distinction between Substantive and Formal Rationality is related to the discussion, above, of Gandhi's attitude towards secularism. Nandy[44] notes that Gandhi held that you could only separate politics from spirituality if you accepted Machiavellianism and heartless ('isolated') *realpolitik*, opting for a scientific instrumentalism which separates ends from means.

The traditional Chinese social virtues associated with Confucian concepts such as *jen* ('humanheartedness') and government for the good of the people (related to the famous 'Mandate of Heaven' notion) along with traditional Indian social perspectives related to the concept of *dharma* where everyone has a useful role to play within a stable social system will find reinterpretations blending the positive aspects of the tradition with the modern social reality. Such positive elements of tradition include a respect for the elderly and traditional self-help for the extended family and community which modern attempts at creating 'Welfare States' have failed to compensate for, even with far smaller populations blessed with relative prosperity. The productivity principle of the modern Western capitalist system which judges everything in terms of productivity in relation to the economic base, hence devaluing the elderly and numerous social and contemplative activities which do not register as part of the GNP, has to be challenged with *dharmic* notions of social harmony and other reinterpreted traditional values geared to the contemporary situation. Such patterns of development in these stirring giants could begin to tip the balance against the shortsighted, 'fast buck' mentality of the *baniā* world. The Chinese stress that theirs is a *Socialist* market economy and it seems as if China still remains the *People's* Republic despite its economic liberalisation. You cannot just throw away the Iron Rice Bowl without serious disruption to the social system.

As is clear in my restatement of the passage from the introduction above, I link the materialist 'pursuit of happiness' (or supposed happiness) with poverty. This was framed in the context of my reply to Rorty's critique of the 'ascetic priests'[45] (who sought after 'underlying realities') in that the seeking of underlying realities shows how the consumerist 'pursuit of happiness' in the rich world (which is linked to the emphasis on Formal Rationality where consumerism is vital for growth in economic indicators) curtails the utilitarian progress of developing countries through the polarizing nature of the market system which diverts resources to those who can pay more. At a national level it is also important to make the link between hedonistic, consumerist lifestyles, imprudence and the degeneration of the traditional social fabric. This leads to extra pressure upon already overloaded welfare systems which are further undermined by the weakening of economic prowess through the cultural and educational degradation of the workforce stemming, at least in part, from such lifestyles and attitudes linked to the consumerist mass market system. Environmental problems may act to force societies towards new lifestyles nearer the ideals of the 'true brahman' (i.e. towards the *via contemplativa*), simple in terms of material consumption but sophisticated in terms of the life of the mind. Of course there are already a number of somewhat utopian thinkers already espousing such ideas related to the old Romantic tradition which views industrialization and urbanisation as putting Man out of his natural context. Some seem to think that the clock can actually be turned back and we can undo much of what has occurred over the last couple of centuries and that the industrial capitalist vested interests will not resist any challenge to their power base. Such Western thinkers tend to take a rather blinkered view of the developing world, maintaining in their minds the disparities in technology and political power that exist today as if the developing world wants nothing more than a simple Ghandian village existence and I chastise such 'neo-colonialist' attitudes in *No Sure Ground*. Such movements in the West may succeed in helping to change attitudes and putting consumer pressure on the system but these are unlikely to drastically alter the socio-economic systems. The 'true brahman' lifestyle has always been the philosophers' Utopia which would probably never catch on with the majority whose 'lifes of the mind' would be barren. Perhaps technology will be able to provide them with less wasteful 'bread and circuses'.

Although the attempts to impose a Socialist political superstructure on the organic, industrial socio-economic reality have failed:

> Species born of mortal mind
> Immutable, at the mercy of Time
> Tigers on paper leapt not from page
> Though noble cause and words sublime

the need remains for a shift away from the emphasis on Formal Rationality (striving towards ever more efficient organisation and utilisation of resources regardless of the social consequences), which informs the spirit of Capitalism today as if modernisation and efficiency in themselves constitute progress and *development.* None the less the capitalist market system driven towards higher productivity will be the engine which provides the basic material needs which are the primary utilitarian ends in an instrumental, Substantively Rational, organisation of the system. I have already touched upon the inherent difficulties in trying to manage emergent processes in order to fix particular outcomes. Although there can be no confident planning out of the future, the system can be steered in general directions through both macro-level political constraints (especially as computer modelling of complex processes becomes more complex and gives better guidance) and, more sustainably, through distributed informational control as in the genetic control of multicellular organisms model. A multicellular organism develops, controlled by autonomously acting genetic information contained within each cell as well as higher level constraints on local processes. The new perspective on the world which the new metaphysical understanding will bring, acting in the minds of individuals will be the key to re-orienting the socio-economic reality. However, technological developments will also play a role. New microprocessor technologies are already beginning to have some impact on socio-economic organisation and the new biotechnologies will clearly play an increasing role which may influence our use of resources and environmental degradation. After the 1997 Earth Summit, President Clinton promised a $20 billion pump-priming of solar power to make it a commercially viable alternative to oil and coal as an energy source. I do not want to make a god of Technology, as many tend to do; indeed the editor of a contemporary international computer-network magazine, on a television programme about 'futurology', even talked of finding redemption through technology whilst standing in a dimly lit, supposedly 'high-tech' location full of huge air-conditioning ducts and other alienating features which looked more nightmarish than an inviting image of a brave new world. In such alienating environments, humanity has lost touch with Nature and concocts wild fantasies about what he thinks reality actually is and what the world should be like. Although we live in a world where the pace of technological change is accelerating, technology can only play a limited role in any attempt to salve our social wounds, many of which have been exacerbated by technological changes in the past. On this note we move on to discuss *Satanic Mills.*

SATANIC MILLS

The savage birth of the Capitalist world market

Satanic Mills (Section IX) opens with a return to the question of global economic liberalisation with which *Bande Mātaram* also opened. As stated above, I am less wary about this process now than I was at the time I wrote the verse in 1991. The reference to the views of George Kennan will obviously appear out-of-date but I would maintain that the statement of this extreme position of neocolonial, imperialist motives serves to illustrate the, less clear-cut but none the less remaining, underlying imperialistic economic motives masked by the humanistic, 'global village' rhetoric that emanates from the centres of power. The recent conclusion of the Uruguay round of GATT negotiations brought to the surface the neocolonial substratum of the world economic order, with the debate focusing on the needs of France and the USA, and the Euro-American requirements in general although much of the developing world had a lot more to complain about. The deal should however reduce the threat of 'Fortress Europe', putting up the ramparts to protect the relative economic position it has procured for itself, which has come about in large measure through centuries of colonial plundering of the rest of the world.

The ramparts are also being put up to try to prevent 'nonwhite' immigration into Europe, with some strategists talking in terms of holding the barbarians out beyond the gates of the new Roman Empire. Whatever gains may flow from Europe's economic retrenchment, the highly developed nation states of the European (Economic) Community, yesterday's children, cannot truly come together under one flag; even if they were to, Western Europe would remain, historically, a civilisation in relative decline, turning in on itself as more vigorous, more hungry competitors aggressively prepare to globalise.

As repeatedly stated above, while keeping these concerns in mind, we should remember that progress has often resulted from schemes which were ill-intentioned or designed to procure advantage for the powerful at the expense of the weak (see below on the 'Cold War countries' for instance). The question raised in the verse is whether or not the developing world should blindly follow the clearly false doctrine of unmitigated 'free trade' when those trying to impose this path on the rest of the world did not get to where they are today by actually practising what they preach.

But the main point of *Satanic Mills* and *Lebensraum* is to look at the birth of the capitalist world market system from the point of view of the victims of the strident USA and its British yes-man, partly as a lesson in historical developmental relativism following the Kuwait War in 1991. In regard to the latter, it is worth noting that the Indian princely states (seen as collaborators with the colonial rulers) which refused to join the Union were, in general, annexed by the new republic; the West had no neocolonial strategic resource manipulation interests in these princely states. *Satanic Mills* focuses on the economic aspects of the British conquest of Bengal, which led to British dominion over India and, to the integration of India into the colonial world market system, converting India into a plantation and captive market for Britain's new industrial economy which itself came into existence partly through such colonial crimes. Britain's trade deficits with its Western trading partners were largely made good by holding India as a captive dumping ground for its industrial produce. The international economic order of the world market berated in this work as 'neocolonialist' was created by the parasitic colonial conquest of the world by Europe.

This seemingly the least of evils
This selfish devil that we know
Presents himself as benign blessing
Though as a parasite did grow (Section I)

As Section X (*Lebensraum*) reminds us, we have repeatedly been shown the horrors of the Stalinist and Maoist terror on which the Communists tried to build their politico-economic system. Western presentations of history generally overlook the fact that the capitalist world market system was built on even more atrocious foundations, extermination of native populations (up to 80 million wiped out in Latin America alone), the brutal slave trade, manmade famines, deliberate deindustrialisation and plantationisation of native economies, prevention of modern industrialisation, and of course the brutal repression of the subject populations in order to maintain control. The British have succeeded, not altogether unfairly, in presenting a picture of benevolent paternalism in regard to the history of the Raj but this belies the barbarous behaviour they were capable of when their rule was challenged. Following the 1857 rebellion, numerous atrocities were meted out on Indian peoples in revenge, with wholesale slaughter of townsfolk and the murder of Indians just for being Indians in certain regions. Right up to the end, the fact that power ultimately rests on breaking heads rather than counting heads was never far from the surface of *Pax Britannica.*

'Read you true book of History'
Lamented voices faint
'Writ large across the world in blood
Which soul of Europe taints' (*Satanic Mills*)

The Ruin of Bengal and the Industrial Revolution

In Section V (*Two Two-legged Human Races*), I introduced the subject of European colonialism into this work, including a verse which alluded to the 'Fiery blast from Fanon'. It is worth repeating the actual words of Fanon here to emphasise the depth of feelings aroused in the subject peoples by the experience of European colonialism.

> *Let us waste no time in sterile litanies and nauseating mimicry. Leave this Europe where they are never done talking of Man, yet murder men wherever they find them, at every corner of every one of their own streets, in all the corners of the globe.*
>
> Fanon, F.[46]

A recent Booker Prize winning novel, Michael Odaantje's *Sacred Hunger*, focusing on the slave trade, stresses the contribution this vile trade made towards financing Britain's Industrial Revolution (the Booker McConnell Company, in fact, has its roots in the slave trade and the Caribbean sugar plantations). I note in the verse how silver earned from slave trading was used to buy produce from Bengal. I focus, however, on the link between the conquest and deindustrialisation of Bengal and the birth of the Industrial Revolution in Britain.

> *France was ahead of any other country in scientific achievements during the eighteenth century, yet the Industrial Revolution did not occur there. Instead it occurred in Great Britain, where there were richer resources of coal and iron, where foreign trade was greatly expanding, where capital could more easily be mobilised . . . . . where there were greater opportunities for applying scientific knowledge.*
>
> Musson, A.E. & Robinson, E.[47]

Of course there were numerous, interconnected factors at play in Britain in the prelude to the Industrial Revolution. Musson and Robinson, in their classic work, noted the close links between the men of knowledge and the practical men in Britain, and the widespread dissemination of scientific knowledge. Claude Alvares has noted how, prior to the Industrial Revolution in Europe, the textile industries were revolutionised by close study and imitation of the work of Asian craftsmen and that in the 1790s, Indian *wootz* steel was pronounced by several English experts as the best steel in the world at the time.[48] The claims that Science has a high degree of universality are valid, although numerous cultural factors inform the spirit of enquiry, framing of experiments and interpretation of the results. My point here, as with the Chinese inventions that revolutionised Medieval Europe is to stress that modern Science and Technology are not the pure blooded heirs of European civilisation as many Europeans seem to think, although numerous critical breakthroughs came in Europe. Regardless of the fact that the underlying conditions in Britain were predisposed for industrial transformation, the phenomenon might not have been capable of developing had it not been for the historical circumstances of colonial exploits bringing in vast quantities of ill-begotten wealth seeking investment opportunities and the deliberate destruction of the rival textile industry of Bengal.

The thriving trade of Bengal's textiles
Just like her cloth you tore asunder
Your nabob parvenus brought loot home
The Hindi word to rob and plunder

Too much loot for lives of luxury
So loot found work through speculation
Primed forge and clanking loom and engine
World's first industrial revolution

That same plunder and destruction of the economy of Bengal turned the failure of the 1769 monsoon into the most devastating famine in Indian history, the Great Bengal Famine of 1770, which killed up to ten million people. I have used this traditional figure for the death toll although it may be exaggerated, based on extrapolation from the death rate in the worst-hit areas. The traditional figure of three million for the 1943 artificial famine in Bengal has been supported by recent research on excess mortality in that year by the distinguished Bengali development economist and professor at Harvard, Amartya Sen[49]. The Great Irish Famine of 1845-48 may have been caused by the potato blight fungus but it would be a gross misjudgement to put the whole tragedy down to one fungus devastating one staple crop. Historical reality, like natural reality is never so simple as to be properly accounted for by reductionistic explanations. The colonial situation in Ireland played a key role in forcing the poor Catholics to depend upon the potato, the wealth of Ireland being maintained in the hands of Protestant settler landlords living in semi-isolation from the natives almost like the situation in more distant colonial possessions. The British government viewed the loss of up to a quarter of the Irish population as mere natural wastage amongst an inferior race. British soldiers convoyed dairy produce and eggs to the seaports for export during the famine in order to deter the Irish natives from interfering with the natural laws of the free market.[50] As I note in the verse, the East India Company kept grain locked away in its storehouses whilst the Indian peasantry, who had produced it, starved in their millions around them. Early in the 19th century, British trade in Chinese tea at Guangxiou (Canton) was heavily weighted in China's favour. In order to 'balance trade', the British brought in opium grown in India and wreaked havoc amongst the Chinese population. Messrs Jardine and Mathieson, founders of Hong Kong's largest company, were the biggest opium barons in Guangxiou, a situation reminiscent of the prominent role that the slave trade played in building the wealth of the English middle classes and seaports such as Bristol. When the Chinese emperor sent in a new governor to stamp out the opium dealing, the British navy intervened at Pearl River and seized Hong Kong. The Chinese view these acts of aggression by the British as paving the way for future aggression against China by the Western powers and their imitator Japan. This world as shop writ large mentality remains prominent in the Thatcherite wing of the British Conservative party. In the commentary to the verse, I quoted the famous words of Richard Becher[51], written a year before the 1770 Bengal famine, twelve years after Plassey.

> *It must give pain to an Englishman to have reason to think that since the accession of the Company to the* ***Dīwāni*** *the condition of the people of this country has been worse than it was before — and yet I am afraid the fact is undoubted — this fine country, which flourished under the most despotic and arbitrary government, is verging towards its ruin*

Ainslee Embree[52] argues that the tradition linking the Industrial Revolution and the economic ruin of Bengal has its roots in Becher's famous letter and he points out that Becher actually goes on to argue for British takeover of all India. Similarly, Dadabhai Naoroji's famous *Poverty and UnBritish Rule in India* (1871), in which he propounded his 'drain' thesis of the siphoning off of India's wealth by the imperial rulers, has served as the basis of later critiques of the economic legacy. Both the 'ruin of Bengal' and the 'drain' thesis have been criticised by British economic historians[53] as being far too simplistic, which indeed they are. None the less, there is far more than a germ of truth in both and the link between the textile industry of Bengal and the Industrial Revolution cannot be wished away even though the picture is complex. Karl Marx wrote in 1853[54]:

> *It was the British intruder who broke up the Indian hand looms and destroyed the spinning wheel. England began with driving the Indian cotton from the European market; it then introduced twist into Hindustan, and in the end inundated the very mother country of cotton with cottons.*

At the end of the article, Marx concluded[55]

> *Can mankind fulfil its destiny without a fundamental revolution in the social state of Asia? If not, whatever may have been the crimes of England, she was the unconscious tool of history in bringing about that revolution.*

Although traditional Nationalist claims are perhaps exaggerated, a sizeable appropriation of Bengal's wealth did occur during the period of Company rule. Again, in the late Nineteenth Century, two-fifths of Britain's huge trade deficits were met by India's trade surplus appropriated through 'home charges'. My verse purports to giving the natives' views and this I have done; the way I have presented things in the verse is the way most Indians tend to see it, even though, as is the case with any nation's folk memory, some of the claims may be somewhat exaggerated. That there was devastation of traditional Indian industries, that the land revenue system based on the 'Rent Doctrine' left the peasantry at a subsistence level, and that the British deliberately acted to prevent the development of modern industries in India to maintain the captive imperial market and colonial plantation relationship goes without question. To quote Ambedkar, the aforementioned leader of the untouchables, from his 1930 Presidential Address to the All-India Depressed Classes Congress:

> *I am afraid that the British choose to advertise our unfortunate conditions, not with the object of removing them, but only because such a course serves well as an excuse for retarding the political progress of India.*
>
> Dr B.R. Ambedkar[56]

The opening passage of *Satanic Mills* alludes to another example of industrial development going hand in hand with colonialist aggression and exploitation which was, after all, the Western model. Japan's first major iron and steel plant, Yawata (1897-1901), was built using the tribute extorted from China in the 1895 Shimonoseki treaty, following the 1894-95 Sino-Japanese war after the Japanese occupation of Korea. It should be recalled that Japanese participation in suppressing the Chinese Boxer Rebellion (1900), Manchuria, the Rape of Nanking etc. were part and parcel of following the Western colonialist model of economic development. At the end of Section X (*Lebensraum*), I restate in verse the well-known thesis that Hitler's conquest of Europe was perfectly logical in regard to the European attitude to the world, it was basically European colonialism, as practised all over the world, being brought home. What is less well-known is that Hitler said that he got the idea of the death camps from the US government's 'reservation camps' for the native Americans, forging another link between this final passage of *Lebensraum* with the main part of the Section, the carving out of European *lebensraum* in North America.

Economic development in the Cold War

In the 1950s when newly independent India tried to develop heavy industry, the West pressed it concentrate on its 'traditional' products,[57] i.e. the very plantation economy commodities that British colonial rule had forced India to limit itself to in order to serve the industrialised 'metropolitan centre'. Even during the Second World War, the British resisted pressure from the USA to build aircraft factories in India in order to help fight the Japanese in Asia. Despite the overwhelming logistical sense of this proposition, the British refused as they did not want to leave aircraft factories in an India that might soon become independent and which could then compete against Britain. In the 1950s, the West also objected to India's plan to develop heavy industry in the 'state sector',[58] whilst Britain had been nationalising its coal and steel industries! The Soviet Union stepped in and built a steel mill at Bhilai, the first major Soviet aid project in India. It was this that prompted the West to give 'aid' to India's industrialisation programme in order to help prevent India going wholly into the Soviet camp. Similar hindrances are being put in the way of our Space programme in the 1990s with blatantly false military arguments being used against us developing our own meteorological and remote sensing satellites and launch vehicles, vital for the prediction of natural disasters and the development of our natural resources.

Bhilai provides yet another example of the positive effects that emanated from the threat of Communism forcing progressive developments in the post-colonial, neocolonial world order. The allegiance of the "workers' state" with the colonial subjects, forming, in a sense, Galiev's 'world proletariat' fighting the colonial order proved to be immensely successful in wresting direct political control from the colonial powers. Fanon notes what the situation was before Soviet support for the liberation movements turned each local conflict into a global confrontation.

> *'Mr Krushchev brandishes his shoe at the United Nations, or thumps the table with it, there's not a single ex-native, nor any representative of an underdeveloped country who laughs. For what Mr Krushchev shows the colonized countries which are looking on is that he, the moujik, who moreover is the possessor of space-rockets, treats these miserable capitalists in the way that they deserve. . : . In 1945, the 45,000 dead at Sétif could pass unnoticed; in 1947, the 90,000 dead in Madagascar could be the subject of a single paragraph in the papers; . . ."*
>
> Fanon, F. *The Wretched of the Earth*

The first two lines of the verse from *Satanic Mills* above refers to the 'Cold War countries' like Singapore, Taiwan, and Hong Kong which benefitted hugely from US intervention in the civil wars in Korea and Vietnam in order to contain the spread of Communism. The doctrine of 'containing Communism' stems largely from a paper in the journal *Foreign Affairs* written by the same George Kennan who argued that the USA should attempt to maintain the gross global disparities in wealth, especially in regard to Asia. The man who appointed Kennan as the first Director of the US State Department's strategic policy-making unit, George Marshall, has given his name to the massive US aid programme to Western Europe aimed primarily at preventing the wartorn subcontinent from turning to Communism; thus Western Europe, like Japan has prospered as a result of Cold War geopolitical considerations. Indeed, the Japanese motor industry was on the verge of terminal decline when US orders for trucks for the Korean War threw it a lifeline. The irony is that the Kennanite US strategy for post-war Japan had been to maintain Japan as a third rate manufacturer of 'Tonka' type toy cars etc. rather than the manufacturer of Toyotas and Nissans which would compete with General Motors and Ford.

The Bengal Famine of 1942-3: A British-inflicted holocaust

Satanic Mills ends by switching from the largely man-made Great Bengal famine of 1770 to the British-made Bengal famine of 1943, marking the beginning and the end of the British Raj. Just as this book was going to press, at the time of the fiftieth anniversary of Indian Independence, Channel 4 Television (UK) showed a programme in its Secret History series entitled *The Forgotten Famine* (12th August 1997) which detailed the true causes of this "British-made famine" which killed three million Indians. Whilst certain British newspaper commentators are cynically suggesting that India's poor had been better off under British rule, this documentary showed how the British officials had suppressed the facts, both during and after the famine, caused by their own incompetence, mismanagement and disregard for the suffering of Indians. The neglect of Indian suffering, even when the streets of Calcutta were strewn with dead bodies, led to denials that there even was a famine by the incumbent British rulers in the first year of its existence. British officials, including a certain Amery (presumably Leopold Amery) attempted to suppress the so-called 'Nanavati Report' which investigated what had gone wrong but this damning report has survived, hidden away in the archives of the British Raj.

Most at fault was Bengal Governor Herbert who was described in the documentary as a mediocre politician who had been given the prestigious position as a political reward (the British so-called 'Honours system' of knighthoods continues to serve as a rather farcical system of political patronage). Herbert was incapable of understanding the complexity of the situation in the huge province for which he was responsible and ignored the advice of his civil servants that his policies would lead to famine. The main cause of the famine was the commandeering of the rice crop for military food supplies, feeding war-related factory workers and for export to other British colonies. Furthermore, the British confiscated or destroyed tens of thousands of small wooden boats belonging to villagers along the coast arguing that they might become useful to the Japanese. The wholesale expropriation of the rice crop resulted in there being no rice for the poor cultivators themselves. The boat denial further exacerbated the famine by preventing people in the worst-hit areas from trading with other regions. As tens of thousands of starving refugees poured into Calcutta, forcing citizens to walk over dead bodies in the streets, the British rulers censored any news coverage of the famine: Bengali publications like a little book of graphic sketches, entitled *Famine in Bengal,* depicting the gruesome scenes was seized and destroyed. Eventually, the British-owned *Statesman* newspaper broke the censorship rules and published pictures of the starving refugees. Official British reports lied about the true death tolls of around 40,000 per week and reported only, "1,000 per week, maybe more". No effort was made by the British rulers for famine relief or even changing their policies which were creating the famine.

Herbert's criminal neglect and suppression of the facts could have been overruled by Viceroy Linlithgow. (Linlithgow had brought India into Britain's war without consulting any Indian leaders. Similarly, after the war, the British hastily drew up the partition boundaries with scant consultation of Indians leading to the communal violence which is given such prominence by the British to imply subtly Indian barbarism. The partition deaths could have been prevented or at least reduced by consultation, a realistic time-scale and proper supervision rather than the cynical 'let them stew in their own broth' attitude which one British official has stated was prevalent amongst the British officials at the time). In 1942 and 1943, as famine raged in Bengal, Linlithgow refused to visit the province to assess the situation.

There were grain surpluses in the other parts of India which could have been used for famine relief but Linlithgow did nothing. In fact, nothing was done for a whole year until Linlithgow returned to Britain to take up a position as the chairman of the Midland Bank. He was replaced by Wavell who immediately went to Bengal and began famine relief operations. None the less, when rice was sent from other regions to Calcutta it was simply piled up in pyramids of sacks in the Botanical Gardens as a reserve for army supplies and not used to feed the starving. Indian protestors moved the dead bodies of famine victims to line the streets outside the Botanical Gardens.

Wavell discovered apathy, total disregard and cynical contempt for the plight of starving Indians amongst his political masters in London. Note that, simultaneously, half of Montgomery's 'Desert Rats' in North Africa were Indians fighting for Britain! Wavell was told to lie to the public by announcing the import of 150,000 tons of rice without mentioning that 450,000 tons were being exported from India. Some British politicians dismissed the famine which would kill three million people as a figment of the imagination of the officials in Bengal. The documentary noted that Churchill's private secretary had reported a comment from Churchill which may not have been directly related to the famine. Churchill stated that he thought that the 'Hindu race' had only escaped from extinction by overbreeding. He continued that, if (Arthur) 'Bomber' Harris could spare some bombers, he would bomb all the Hindus to death. (Note that Arthur Harris had been involved with Churchill in the RAF's bombing of the Kurds in the 1920s when Churchill had wanted to use chemical weapons against defenceless villagers). If the comment was in regard to the famine, the minor point to note would be that Churchill was too ignorant to know that most of the victims were Muslims in East Bengal. The more serious point was that, as the Nazis were inflicting a holocaust upon the Jews, Gypsies and others in Europe, the same British leaders who have demonised the Nazis and portrayed themselves as the saviours of humanity were displaying the same contemptuous attitude towards the death of three million Indians, a holocaust created by British racism.

Since the British left, India has not suffered from a full-fledged famine although there were shortages in the 1960s (which prompted the 'Green Revolution' strategy); another gain for the regions from participation in the union. For the thirty years leading up to Independence, British colonial mismanagement resulted in economic stagnation with no economic growth. For all the positive contributions of the coming of modernity to India (which I acknowledge in *A Nation Born Through Synthesis*), it should not be forgotten that these positive effects were largely side-effects of the savage politico-economic reality of colonial exploitation.

LEBENSRAUM

European savagery in the Americas and Australia

Having focused on a small part of Britain's historical misdemeanours, the spotlight of historical developmental relativity is then turned on the loudest, most self-righteous moralists of our time, the Americans, who in 1991, under a self-proclaimed Texan from New England, preached to us the rights and wrongs of disregarding United Nations resolutions, disregarding the fact that between 1970 and 1991, the USA had blocked 67 UN resolutions condemning aggression against neighbouring states by South Africa, Israel, Indonesia and any other of its client states. We have since heard of the extensive covert funding of Saddam Hussein's regime by the USA prior to the Kuwait War; Hussein had thought that he had been given the 'green light' for annexation of Northern Kuwait, just as Kissinger had given Suharto the 'green light' to annex East Timor. It was primarily in this context that I wrote *Lebensraum*, noting in my mind the picture in a newspaper of a military battalion from the oil-rich, desert state of Texas (once brutally seized from Mexico) marching through the oil-rich deserts of Arabia. Very recently American Airlines advertised Nashville, Tennessee on a London radio station by glorifying its son, Andrew Jackson, who appears in *Lebensraum*. Given the withdrawal of World Bank funding from the Narmada Valley project (the dam project probably partly inspired by the Tennessee Valley Authority), partly because of tribal resettlement concerns, it is worth remembering Jackson's brutal conquest of Florida with the forced resettlement of the Seminoles and his disregard for his own Chief Justice's rulings in driving the five 'Civilised Tribes' out of Georgia. In 1976 the British Labour government obeyed its American masters and expelled the inhabitants of the Indian Ocean island of Diego Garcia to allow the Americans to build a naval base. Back in the Eighteenth and Nineteenth centuries there had been treaties aimed at protecting the rights of the American natives from further encroachment on their homelands by the European settler-colonialist squatters but, then as now, the United States government disregarded treaties when treaties stood against the economic interests of the United States.

As lawless settlers rout the Redcoats
Appalachian Frontier westward rolls
Quill of Common Sense of what Man writes
These times that tryeth Red Mens' souls

Indeed one of the key motivations behind the American War of Independence was to get a free hand to deal with the Indians without being constrained by London's occasional expressions of guilt in regard to the shameless crimes of its settler subjects such as in imposing a limit to settlement on Indian territory along the Appalachians. George Washington made light of the Appalachian Frontier as no more than a temporary expedient to quiet the minds of the Indians. In 1779, Washington ordered the 'destruction and devastation' of Iroquois villages for having sided with the British in the War of Independence.[59] Such destruction and devastation of Indian villages was nothing new to the European settlers in New England although their descendants in the Nineteenth Century sometimes forgot that what was being done to the Indians 'out West' was much the same as their great grandfathers had meted out to the Indians, many of whom had been forced out West by such ethnic cleansing. Such barbarity continued, very often with government sanction, as the settlers headed West with most of the Indian population of California being systematically exterminated after the United States forced Mexico to give up this territory.

A few months before embarking upon this project, the BBC had broadcast an excellent programme in its outstanding *Timewatch* history series called *Savagery and the American Indian* and the main part of *Lebensraum* is largely based on the information from the up-to-date historical research provided by this programme although this only gave a brief outline of European savagery and greed in the creation of the United States of America. My title *Lebensraum* serves two purposes. I am aware of the fact that the meaning of Ratzel's *lebensraum* concept was distorted by the Nazis and I have played upon this more well-known meaning. First, it highlights the link between the brutal settler colonialism of the Europeans in the Americas and German colonialism in Europe in the 1930s and 40s, as is stressed in the final passage. But *Lebensraum* also indicates a link to the birth of the industrial world (as did *Satanic Mills*) in that Europe was able to relieve the pressure of its population explosion and modernisation of its agriculture by brutally expropriating the land of the native Americans and, to a lesser extent, of the native Australians.

The fact that the slaughter of native Australians gets only two lines in my verse stems from both the immediate influence upon me at the time of writing in 1991 along with my ignorance of Australian history. The two lines were based on a letter to a newspaper during the Australian bicentennial celebrations a few years ago. By chance I came across a chapter entitled *The End of the Tasmanians* in a book which I had bought but not read, which was the source cited by Nandy in regard to the development of the Victorian British idea of the civilising mission as mentioned in *A Nation Born Through Synthesis*, James Morris' *Heaven's Command*,[60] the first volume in his highly acclaimed trilogy on the rise and fall of the British Empire, *Pax Britannica*. The chapter begins with the words, "Empire was Race." It paints a very sad picture of the appalling brutality of the supposedly "civilising" British hunting down to the point of near-extermination the Tasmanian aboriginals, a people distinct from the natives of Australia, who had they survived, would have been of immense anthropological importance, living in splendid isolation at the farthest reaches of the world. We are taught in school about the hunting to extinction of the dodo, but the British carefully choose to forget the story of the Tasmanians as they seethe at the barbarity of foreigners who simply do not know how to behave in a civilised manner.

> *Sometimes the black people were hunted just for fun, on foot or on horseback. Sometimes they were raped in passing or abducted*

> *as mistresses, or as slaves. . . We hear of children kidnapped as pets or servants, of a woman chained up like an animal in a shepherd's hut; of men castrated to keep them off their own women. . . . the men shot, the women and children dragged. . . to have their brains dashed out. Bushrangers used to catch aborigines in man-traps, and use them as target practice.*
>
> James Morris *Heaven's Command*

Following some aboriginal resistance to their slaughter, the Europeans, as ever, came to perceive themselves as the victims and decided to solve the aboriginal problem for once and for all. The British government (*c.* 1830) decided that genocide would not go down well with public opinion and so decided to deport the few remaining Tasmanians to a small island 'reservation' totally unsuited to their way of life, where they were to be brought up as Christians. Displaced from their homes, the Tasmanians quickly died out. Even after death their bodies were dug up and their skulls and skeletons stolen for display. The story is, sadly, not unique. Entire island populations were exterminated by the Spaniards in the Antlantic, and I do not mean the wiping out of the native Caribbeans by disease here. Incredible brutality was used by plantation owners to terrorise the African slaves into submission in the Caribbean and in the Americas.

> I looked upon the frontispiece
> Of Wilson's controversial thesis
> Became one with those savage apes
> The fathers of our savage species (*And Born Was I*)

In *Lebensraum* as in *Satanic Mills,* I air the point of view of the victims of the birth of the capitalist world market system, using two verse passages closely based on speeches by native Americans. As with the brutally ravaged people of Vietnam, Hollywood's culturally-imperialistic 'movie' machine has churned out sentimental stories about the American aggressors almost as if the native Americans, as with the Vietnamese, had no right to fight for their homeland (we are usually asked to sympathise with the psychological traumas of a few Americans which evidently weighs heavier than the slaughter of countless 'gooks' or 'redskins': here we have the self-consciousness that modernity brings taken to its extremes). I implicitly acknowledge in the very first verse of *Lebensraum* that the seizure of land by more advanced peoples from hunter-gatherer tribes, as occurred in Ancient India and in modern South Africa is nothing new. Indeed the ancient Indian epics brazenly eulogise brutal treatment of natives by the conquering Aryans, although we should keep in mind that the ideology of the Aryans three thousand years ago paid no lip service to 'all men being created equal'; quite the opposite of course. In both Ancient India and in South Africa, as stated in the verse, the conquerors learnt to live in mutual coexistence with the conquered, albeit on terms of separate development. The 1981 Indian census put the total population of India's countless tribal groups at over 50 million. This coexistence has at least allowed the descendants of the natives to fight for their rights in these more progressive times. A large part of Southern Bihar was recently designated a semi-autonomous territory, called 'Jharkand' for its tribal inhabitants. The experience of the natives of America under the Conquistadors and the North American settlers was far nearer to extermination than to apartheid, even though Old World diseases took the heaviest toll and ever smaller bantustan-like wastelands were allotted to dispossessed 'Indians'. Even when native Americans, such as the 'Five Civilised Tribes' of Georgia, adopted modern ways of living they were brutally driven out to far-off, unknown territories to make way for more cotton plantations worked by African slaves.

US settler colonialist imperialism and Nazi parallels

It was not at all surprising that Jules Verne in his *From the Earth to the Moon* made his, century ahead of time, American astronauts think it a *casus belli* if Mexico refused to give them a mountain top from which to launch their mission to the moon.[61] Indeed the actual Moon launches involved the use of Cape Canaveral in the state of Florida, which was brutally seized from Spain (as later were the Philippines) by Andrew Jackson in his murderous Seminole Wars in which the Seminole natives were, like the Civilised Tribes of Georgia, expelled from their ancestral homes (some committed suicide rather than leave the sacred lands of their ancestors) to Oklahoma. As with Britain and

Russia in the Nineteenth century, the USA was aggressively expansionist, constantly seeking new countries to annex. Canada, Cuba and what remained of Mexico after Texas, California, Nevada and New Mexico had been seized were all targets at one time or another.

In an age when Muslim fundamentalists claim the Will of *Allah* to urge *Jihad* against invaders (once it used to be *Allah's* Will to conquer infidels of course), it is worth recalling the not too dissimilar claims to Providence and 'Manifest Destiny' which were repeatedly exhorted to justify American conquests. A related argument was that the Americanization of the conquered territories fulfilled God's wish to make full use of the lands which were wasted in the hands of Indians and Mexicans, leading to a sort of racial, Social Darwinism, before Spencer and Darwin (see the verse about the California Governor's speech) which was later applauded by Hitler. In regard to modern utilisation of natural resources, it is worth recalling that the offspring and other beneficiaries of these settlers, amongst others, now berate us for our 'inadequate' resettlement of the tribal natives of the Narmada Valley. Again, as I note in the verse, behind the Protestant Work ethic, log cabins and apple pie images of the selective folk memory of Thanksgiving etc., lies the hidden reality of how much of the 'opening up' of North America was actually achieved by the use of African slave chain gangs, whose forced contribution to the creation of the New Europe is one of the sorriest legacies of European colonialism.

The epithet I use towards the end of the main part of *Lebensraum*, in relation to the Sioux at Wounded Knee, 'two-legged beasts' is taken from a modern case of settler-colonialism, Zionism. Apparently, it is used by Zionist settlers to refer to the Palestinian natives. It was not without reason that I called Section V, *Two Two-legged Human Races.* The great Irish nationalist, Roger Casement, who came from a Protestant background, spent most of his life as a British diplomat. He shocked the world with his reports from the Belgian Congo and from South America detailing the barbaric treatment of native peoples by the European colonialists. He privately referred to the world's people as being divided between the 'hunters and the hunted' and decided to devote the rest of his life to the cause closest to his heart, the 'hunted whites', the Catholic natives of Ireland, for centuries the victims of oppression under English occupation (including the rampaging armies of Oliver Cromwell, idolised by many English as a hero of historical progress, who held the most reactionary views in regard to the Scots and especially the Irish; I have already mentioned the terrorism unleashed upon the Irish by Winston Churchill above). The famous 'forged diaries' homosexuality scandal was used by 'perfidious Albion' to stem the flow of poignant appeals from all over the world to commute his death sentence. The narrator of the television programme from which I have drawn this text, chose his favourite appeal, from an organisation for the advancement of Black Americans who wrote to the British King, quoting Shakespeare, "The quality of mercy is not strained. . .". But the British had to make an example of this 'traitor', this protestant, one of their own, who had received an Empire medal and a knighthood for his reports on the barbarity of foreign Europeans against natives (what if he had been around in Tasmania I wonder?). Casement had accepted the awards but never opened the medallion boxes, realising that his true purpose was served in pretending to play along with the British game. He wrote that in this world, there were two sorts of white men, the compromisers and the Irishmen, "thank God I am an Irishman".[62]

The final passage of *Lebensraum* makes the link with Hitler's colonial exploits in Europe. My *sūtra* is largely a work about ideas; ideas manifesting themselves in societies, cross-fertilising civilisations, cross-fertilising different realms of human activity (e.g. the references to Post-Fordism, cosmic *chakra*, technology as a social gene, Christian cosmos became clockwork etc.), ideas about the nature of our existence etc. Just as Voltaire was not responsible for totalitarianism (nor the legendary Manu for the Nazi's doctrine of 'racial purity'), I am not attributing responsibility for the Nazi atrocities which clearly evolved out of specific, chance historical trajectories. I have already noted how Hitler said that he got the idea of the death camps from the American reservation camps and how he admired the way the British, followed by the Americans, had dealt with the inferior native race in America. Hannah Arendt's study of Adolf Eichman prior to his execution shows him to have been a non-ideological bureaucrat who saw Hitler's 'Final Solution' merely as an organizational problem; Arendt recognised that such isolation of feelings made Eichman the ultimate product of the modern world.[63] Others have argued that Eichman was only trying to cover up his true güilt by presenting this bureaucratic image. In Britain in 1995 we have been deluged with VE day nostalgia, telling us how the world was supposedly saved from Nazi tyranny by the British forgetting the fact that the same British, who had secretly aided Franco alongside Hitler's Stukas, had helped to lay down the whole underlying colonialist frame of mind in relation to the world which Hitler, who admired the British Empire, had taken to heart. (It is not too different from the Saddam Hussein story where those who had been falling over themselves to arm him, both for sheer profit and to do down Iran, then bragged about ridding the world of his evil military might). I noted above how the British shipped aircraft to Asia, risking U-Boat attack, rather than build aircraft factories in India which might one day serve an independent India in escaping British imposed plantation economy servitude. Add such considerations and Hitler's brutal use of slave labour to the well-known thesis that the Nazi phenomenon was European colonialism brought home to Europe, the racialist and scientifically organised logic of modern Europe taken to its extreme conclusions, and it becomes clear that the Nazi phenomenon was an extreme expression of the underlying European culture developed over the previous four hundred years.

> Swallow your words you hypocrite Europe
> 'Freedom, self-determination'
> Faced with your own true alter-ego
> Slavery and extermination

How hypocritical it sounded to the people of the colonially occupied countries when the European countries called for reparations and compensation for the Nazi atrocities. The people who had looted the treasures of India, Egypt etc. wanted the return or compensation for the art treasure looted by the Nazis. But what was found to be most hypocritical was the Western allies' eulogies to their belief in 'Freedom' and national self-determination, usually couched in humanistic rhetoric. Those who had enslaved and lorded it over the rest of the world, parasitized the resources of the globe, exterminated (directly and indirectly) native peoples all across the world, profited hugely from the most inhumane slave trade etc., now cried, "Foul play!"

CHOL DILLI

British myths about the End of Empire

It is as a continuation of this theme of Western hypocrisy that the work switches from 1940s Europe to 1940s India in Section XI(a), *Chol Dilli.*

How loudly Churchill ranted, raved
Would fight on, Britain, to be free
Even Nehru dusted down his robes
It's right for you, why wrong for me

The second part of Section XI (*Indo-Europe*), XI(b) *Old Indian Air,* also takes the Nazi phenomenon as its starting point, after all, Hitler was a gift to the colonised world, bankrupting and chastening the French and British empires in attempting to build his own colonial empire in Europe.

Old emigre our ancient culture
Preceded Roy to Germany
Played part in shaping cataclysm
Reshaped the world, set *Bhārat* free

In the postwar world the British have sought vicarious imperial power in their supposed 'special relationship' with the USA. Recently the British establishment was taken aback by the US government's decision to allow *Sinn Fein* leader Gerry Adams to raise funds in the USA following the peace accord in Northern Ireland. Clearly the fact that President Clinton's mother was half Irish and half Cherokee has coloured his view of such matters. In the 1920s, Tagore found his own fundraising efforts in the USA, for Viśva-Bhārati University, thwarted by British diplomats in the USA, dissuading potential donors. Ironically, Tagore was, at the time, disowned by Indian nationalists because of his criticisms of copying European style nationalism.[64] The powerful influence exerted by the British over the Americans, which Tagore's entourage discovered, was drastically reduced during World War II when Roosevelt forced a bankrupt Britain to give up its stockholdings in the USA in return for 'Lend-Lease'. Following the war, with little attachment to the sentimental 'special relationship' so cherished by the British establishment, the US further helped dismantle the British Empire, backing pro-Western nationalists in order to open up the markets and clear the way for its own new style, far more progressive, imperialism.

India's freedom, which came far sooner than it otherwise would, thanks to the Second World War, was won for us by the struggles of countless Indians in the nationalist movement, and the roots of that movement go back further to Rammohun Roy, the so-called 'first modern Indian', and Section XI(c), *A Nation Born Through Synthesis,* looks at the influence of Europe in the creation of the Indian Nation. In a world accustomed to the myths surrounding the 'saintly' figure of Mohandas Gandhi and the diametrically opposed stigma quite rightly associated with Adolf Hitler, the man whom many Indians feel was their true leader during the Second World War period remains something of an unsung hero; Richard Attenborough's hagiographic film *Gandhi* failed to acknowledge his existence, stressing the 'alls well that ends well', Nehru, Gandhi, and Mountbatten, all good chums underneath interpretation.

Bengali bhadralok nationalism and Gandhian nationalism

More generally, the dispute between Bose and Gandhi reflects a deeper dichotomy in Indian Nationalism than the superficial distinction between the extreme and moderate wings of the Congress. This dichotomy is itself manifest in the very nature of this work to some extent. Subhas Chandra Bose, the Bengali *kāyastha,* was the scion of the Bengali *bhadralok,* the upper caste professional classes whose great intellectuals had formulated the basic principles of modern Indian culture and Indian Nationalism and who had led the Nationalist struggle for the first thirty or so years of its formal existence. The first great European war of 1914-18 led to relaxations of the British restrictions on indigenous industrial enterprise, fuelling the aspirations of the Indian mercantile classes, whose interests were placed firmly behind those of the most ardently racist and imperialist group, the British mercantile community which wanted India kept as a huge plantation. The tide turned against the British, despite their divide and rule policies, with the 1919 Amritsar Massacre and Gandhi's mobilisation of the illiterate masses with his traditional 'holy man' style reinterpretations of the elite nationalism of the *bhadralok.* Although Gandhi, born into a Gujrati *baniā* subcaste, held Rabindranath Tagore, the prodigy born into the most famous of Calcutta's *bhadralok* families, as a spiritual mentor (although Tagore held gross reservations over Gandhi's naïve utopianism), his main financial backer was the richest of Calcutta's businessmen, G.D. Birla, who was richly rewarded by Congress after Independence with the self-reliance policy's, import barriers protecting the Birla-owned Hindustan Motors' near monopoly of the Indian car market with the 1950s Morris Oxford design. Birla came from the Rajasthani Marwari mercantile community which dominates Calcutta's businesses; the great Eighteenth century bankers, the Jagat Seths (known as the 'Rothschilds of India'), who controlled the bullion trade and colluded with the British in the political intrigue before and after Plassey, were also Marwaris. Such power in the hands of a small migrant community has rather naturally led to an antipathy amongst the *bhadralok* professional community towards the Marwari *baniās* who were often out of step with mainstream Bengali opinion. Thus Gandhi was going against the great modernising spirit of the *bhadralok* Bengali's Nationalism with his backward-looking emphasis on the spinning wheel and his *Rāmarājya* of cottage industries, and playing on the old 'holy man' religious traditions with its superstitious elements which Bengali Neo-Hinduism had tried to eradicate.

Defending the actions of Subhas Bose

As *Chol Dilli* stresses, the picture presented in such British presentations of the end of the Raj, gloss over the hard-fought reality, focusing on communal violence during Partition than on the violence of the British authorities. *Chol Dilli* notes that, despite the military failure of the highly-exaggerated Indian National Army adventure, the Spirit of Freedom that Subhas

Chandra Bose's legendary force infused into the people of India, resulting in the INA trial disturbances of 1946 which rocked the Raj, made rapid British withdrawal inevitable. For all the heartfelt empathy of most educated Indians with the titanic, heroic struggle of the Soviet people against the Nazi invader, there really is no deep sense of contradiction in simultaneously applauding Subhas Bose, who sought help from Germany, after Stalin wisely refused to provoke the British. M.N. Roy, leader of the Indian Communists, who, as I note in the verse, had also sought help from Germany in 1915 as an emissary of the Bengal revolutionaries, led the campaign to help the British War effort, and rubbish Subhas Bose. The British shrewdly legalised the Communist Party in 1942 and released Roy after Hitler invaded the Soviet Union. Roy had earlier fallen out with the Congress over Congress' 'collaboration' with the British. Some Congress leaders who were friendly with British officials, like Nehru, perceived Hitler as a greater evil than the Raj, but, as I note in the verse, he brought out his old lawyer's robes to defend the INA officers against British double standards. Aurobindo Ghose, who around 1909 was branded by the British, 'the most dangerous man in India' for his subversive writings, deep in *samādhi* at Pondicherry, claimed that he knew that India's freedom was certain and willed victory for the British against the greater evil of Nazism.[65]

As with three million other Indians, my own father volunteered to serve in the Imperial forces. It was only after the war that Bose's escapades became known to the Indian public, and by then, the Soviet and Nazi issues were irrelevant to Indians, Bose had only done what he thought best for his nation, following the old dictum, 'my enemy's enemy is my friend'. There was a parallel between the Indians fighting for the Raj and the British working classes fighting for the 'Queen and Country' that had treated them largely as dirt. The hope was that their sacrifice would help to change things after the war; and let us remember that it was the British Socialists who bravely began the process of decolonialisation. Sultan Galiev's world proletariat thesis again had a ring of truth. Let us also remember that the British government, as official records have revealed, secretly did everything it could to support Nazi-backed Franco in the Spanish Civil War[66] and how, until Hitler actually encroached upon Anglo-

French interests, he was not perceived as such a bad thing. Recently we have been finding out how the Nazi genocide and war machine was propped up by 'neutral' Switzerland famed for the secrecy of its bankers. Gold looted from national banks and from death camp victims was readily converted into hard currencies by the Swiss who clearly knew that it was stolen gold. The Swiss also manufactured weapons for the Nazis in the later years of the war. One wonders how much wealth stolen by more recent dictators from various countries lies hidden in the banks of this little country whose institutions are held in such high esteem by the high priests of free trade. We also know now that the British played down the reports coming out of Nazi Europe about the extermination of Gypsies, Jews and others. This was not known to Indians (they did, however, know full well of Churchill's racism). Bose, in his one meeting with Hitler, spoke out against Hitler's racial policies.[67]

Similarly, Bose's association with the Imperial Japanese Army is anathema to many Westerners basing their views on war films like *Bridge on the River Kwai* and other clearly one-sided representations of the war in Asia. Of course the Japanese committed numerous atrocities which went largely unpunished because of Japan's strategic importance to the USA in the post-war Cold War context. However, there is an underlying racism in Western criticisms of Japanese atrocities, the question of compensation of British soldiers and the whole colonial situation. Given that the Japanese were simply trying to replace various, very alien, colonial rulers with their own, 'less alien' rule, following the pattern of development through colonial conquest set by Western countries, there is more than an element of truth in Japanese assertions that they perceived themselves as the freeing Asia from its exploitation by the white men. The respectful Japanese treatment of Subhaṡ Bose actually lends some credence to this view; Bose was determined not to be a mere puppet if India was 'liberated'. The clamour for Japanese apologies for the cruel treatment of white prisoners of war smacks of appalling racism. When have the Europeans, bar the German apologies to Israel, apologised for their colonial atrocities all over the world. One has to add to this the very different conception of individual rights held by the Japanese; they were not proclaiming the Rights of Man with one hand whilst murdering men, women and children all over the world. One must similarly consider the very different attitudes the Japanese hold of the relationship between the natural world and human needs rather than hysterically berate their whalers and fishermen. Today it is Japanese money that has helped to fuel the industrial development of Eastern Asia; the 'co-prosperity sphere' which the Japanese claimed they would create through conquest is coming about through peaceful means.

In fact, I refer to Bose earlier in the work, at the end of *Bande Mātaram*.

> His face adorns a million *pān* shops
> The angry son 'Mahātma' spurned
> Some dream that he'll return to save us
> Our *Nēta* Subhas who never returned

As with all heroes who die prematurely, we are saved from having them prove their human frailties. Had he lived, Bose would probably have swept to power, ahead of Nehru, on the tidal wave of adoration and enthusiasm for his INA adventure (even non-violent Gandhi became captivated by Bose's exploits, all the other nationalist leaders had fallen into slumber during the war). Whereas Nehru was known as the *paṇḍit,* Bose was known as *Netaji, Neta* meaning Leader. It would perhaps have been fitting if Bose, the scion of my own Bengali *bhadralok* 'intelligentsia', who provided so many of the fathers of the Nation and who laid its ideological foundations had taken the crown as the first leader of the new nation. But as I note in my commentary to *Bande Mātaram,* with hindsight and sober reflection, it was perhaps a lot better for the nation that the cool-headed, relatively half-hearted, Kashmiri brahman, Nehru rather than the uncompromising, fiery Bengali *kāyastha* (who styled himself partly on Mussolini and sought radical, authoritarian transformation of India) became the leader of the then extremely fragile, fractious, newborn nation.

As with the aforementioned Irish Nationalist leader, Roger Casement, who like Roy and Bose had travelled to Germany to seek support for his liberation struggle and who also travelled like Bose in a U-Boat, Subhas Chandra Bose shall remain above the fray of the corruption and broken promises of government, a noble martyr to the freedom struggle.

I have fought all my life for my country's freedom. Go and tell my countrymen to continue the fight for India's freedom. India will be free, and before long.

Netaji Subhas Chandra Bose on his deathbed, 1946[68]

OLD INDIAN AIR

Indomania and the second European Renaissance

Section XI (*Indo-Europe*) continues with the Nazi link from the end of *Lebensraum* in XI(b) *Old Indian Air*, looking at how elements of Indo-Aryan culture came to manifest themselves in the ideology, terminology and symbolism of Nazi Germany. In relation to the higher theme of this work, Section XI as a whole is entitled *Indo-Europe,* the main theme of the Section being the interplay of ideas between India and Europe. In a sense, the Section is inverted in that *Chol Dilli* can be viewed as a follow up to Section XI Part (c), *A Nation Born Through Synthesis,* in that *Chol Dilli* tells the story of the fruition of the nationalist aspirations that evolved through Western influence, as told in XI(c). This inter-civilisational exchange frames my intellectual being as was indicated in *The Reassertion of the Indian,* my mind being a microcosmic product of the encounter between the Indian and European 'Minds'. The historical encounter of the Indian Mind (in fact the Bengali *bhadralok* Mind) with the West is the theme of *A Nation Born Through Synthesis.*

As Orient does live in Europe
So too does Europe live in me
Transplanted into India's thinking
So much of West's philosophy

Old Indian Air stresses that the invigorating, cross-cultural exchange of ideas was not just one-way traffic as the British tend to present it (note also the transfer of techniques from Asia to Europe prior to the Industrial Revolution mentioned above). Whilst Rammohun Roy was petitioning against Sanskrit education for Indians as this would leave India trapped in the closed world of scholastic tradition, more and more of the ancient

Sanskrit texts were being translated and the influence of Indian thought on European philosophy grew in parallel. The study of the common ancestry of Indo-European languages played a key part in the development of the racial theories which permeated Nineteenth century western thought. Indeed, the German intelligentsia went through a phase of infatuation with Indian culture, known as 'Indomania'[69], as manifest in Wilhelm von Humboldt's comment about the *Bhagavad Gītā's* influence upon him, expressed in the verse as:

> Wilhelm von Humboldt who Berlin's
> Great university had founded
> Thanked God he was alive still when
> The *Gītā* in his land resounded

In more recent times, Carl von Weizsäcker, the physicist brother of a recent German president and a co-worker with Heisenberg (the Indian influence on whose revolutionary work is mentioned in the verse) on Hitler's atom bomb project, has been closely associated with Indian philosophy, even using the yogic notion of *prāṇa* in speculations regarding the metaphysical paradox raised by the Austrian advocate of the *Vedānta,* Erwin Schrödinger in his famous thought experiment involving a cat. Schrödinger reformulated Heisenberg's matrix mechanics in his wave function. He had studied *Advaita Vedānta* before becoming a physicist. His biographer notes that Schrödinger saw the unity and continuity of *Vedānta* reflected in the unity and continuity of wave mechanics. He saw the superimposed waves of probability amplitudes in his wave function to be entirely consistent with the Vedāntic concept of the All in One.[70] I am not claiming that quantum mechanics was inherent in Indian philosophy in the manner of some of the Hindu zealots who claim that ancient Indians already knew modern scientific ideas. I am simply stressing that ways of thinking about the world which, however ancient, were new to the European Mind of the time, were introduced into Europe with the Sanskrit translations showing the two-way exchange of ideas that is often lost in focusing on the Indo-British relationship alone (see below). Rabindranath Tagore, as Indian civilisation 'incarnate', drew huge audiences in Weimar Germany, thousands being locked out of his lectures. He also had a significant influence on numerous Western poets early in this century.[71]

In the case of the Chinese inventions which revolutionised Medieval Europe, it was the way Europeans thought about the world along with revolutionary European developments in analytical and experimental philosophy that allowed Europe to transcend the rudimentary technological applications developed by the Chinese. In the case of Indian Philosophy, as with the Renaissance, the rediscovery of ancient knowledge inspired new developments using Europe's own revolutionary tools for thought. The influence of Indian thought on the great German philosophers is fairly well-known though often underplayed. J.J. Clarke[134] states:

> *The interest in Indian ideas during the Romantic period was as pervasive as was the interest in China during the earlier epoch, and it was the extent of this interest that led the Orientalist Raymond Schwab to revive the idea of an 'Oriental Renaissance'. He believed that the introduction of Indian thought into Europe from the late eighteenth century onwards and its integration into the cultural and philosophical concerns of the period amounted to a cultural transformation of the same order as that of the Renaissance of fifteenth-century Italy, that 'the revival of an atmosphere in the nineteenth century brought about by the arrival of Sanskrit texts in Europe. . . produced an effect equal to that produced in the fifteenth century by the arrival of Greek manuscripts and Byzantine commentators after the fall of Constantinople'.*

The linking in the verse between *nirguṇa* and noumenon and the suggestion that Indian thought might have played on Hegel's mind is purely arbitrary (the actual relationship between such concepts from Eastern and Western philosophy will be elaborated in the following essay). I am reacting to Western hagiographies which present Western philosophers as having thought up great ideas from thin air, when similar notions from other civilisations were clearly known to them (hence the reference to Plato and Indian thought in Section V). I am, of course, reacting particularly to Hegel who had a very low opinion of Indian thought, holding Indian thought not to constitute 'real philosophy' like that produced by the 'hard' European intellect.[72] Halbfass says of Schopenhauer's attitude to Hegel:

> *He considered Hegel as having a "completely worthless, indeed, thoroughly pernicious mind", as being a "crude and disgusting charlatan," a "scribbler of rubbish and a corrupter of minds"; his philosophy was "confused, empty verbiage," a "philosophy of absolute nonsense".*
>
> Halbfass, W. *India and Europe*

Halbfass notes that Schopenhauer predicted that a new Renaissance would be inaugurated by the study of the Indian tradition, bringing about "a fundamental change and reorientation of our thought". I note in the commentary, Heisenberg's meeting with Tagore in Calcutta, which Heisenberg said came as a 'great help' to him in coming to terms with his own ideas in physics which had come as a shock to the Western Mind.[73] It was comforting to know that a whole civilisation subscribed to a view of the universe which resembled that of the new physics in certain ways.

Continuing Indian influences upon the West

Countless Westerners born with a natural tendency to experience altered states of consciousness and associated psychical activity have discovered the validity of Indian texts (Hindu and Buddhist), such as Patañjali's famous *Yoga Sūtras,* which have also aided research by Western investigators into paranormal phenomena. A former head of the department of Electrical Engineering at City University, London, has written of his beginning to see the larger picture of reality aided by Indian thought.

> *As I reached this glimmer of an understanding, I was fascinated to read a parallel explanation, amounting perhaps to much the same thing, by Professor J.H.M. Whiteman (a former professor of applied mathematics at the University of Cape Town and also a mystic). He states that everything is described in the classical Eastern (Hindu) literature.*
>
> A.J. Ellison[74]

Nobel laureate geneticist Barbara Mclintock[75] and Nobel laureate physicist Brian Josephson[76] have been led towards Indian thought through their own experiences of altered states of consciousness. Late in life, Nobel laureate neurobiologist, George Wald, received an insight into the fundamental nature of consciousness which had eluded him through scientific knowledge and enquiry. He soon found that his insight placed him in great company; alongside Eastern philosophy and great physicists such as Schrödinger, Eddington and Pauli[77].

> *Let me say that it is not only easier to say these things to physicists than to my fellow biologists, but easier to say them in India than in the West. For when I speak of mind pervading the universe, of mind as a creative principle perhaps primary to matter, any Hindu will acquiesce, will think, yes, of course, he is speaking of Brahman. The Judeo-Christian-Islamic God constructed a universe and just once. Brahman thinks a universe and does so in cycles, time without end.*
>
> George Wald[78]

Schopenhauer's New Renaissance has taken some time to gestate but in 1994, whilst examining the philosophical content of my *sūtra,* I finally made the first direct link between Science and Indian mysticism. The New Age is upon us.

Continuing with the theme of the asymmetric relationship between East and West, Western authors have taken the evolutionary ideas of the Bengali revolutionary turned mystic Aurobindo Ghose, to be but a revamping of Bergson's creative evolution. In fact, the historian of philosophy, A.O. Lovejoy, in his *The Great Chain of Being,* considered Bergson's thought to be largely a revamping of Schelling's thought.[79] Schelling, as Halbfass notes in his *India and Europe,* ranks before even Schopenhauer as the German philosopher most influenced by Indian thought. Thus we come full circle, as Indian thought likes to do, and find that Aurobindo was only identifying with new European elaborations of modes of thought that were characteristic of Indian metaphysics. Indians identify a lot with Spinoza's metaphysics (though not the determinism), because it resembles Indian metaphysical thought although Spinoza does not seem to have been directly influenced by Indian philosophy (Einstein proclaimed that his God was the God of Spinoza and held firm to Spinoza's determinism although he does not seem to have accepted Spinoza's panpsychism, as seen in his discussion with Tagore[80]). The influence of India on European Deism,[81] including the French Revolution's Cult of the Supreme Being, has been noted in the introduction. The Western Mind of the Enlightenment became over-infatuated with the skeletal constructs of logical reasoning which had helped drive Europe into modernity. Evolutionary theory and quantum physics drove home the organic interconnectedness of Reality, the latter also pointed to the transcendental realms of Reality; both aspects in keeping with Indian metaphysical thought.

As is implicit in the point above about Aurobindo, the influence of Indian thought on the European Mind is of direct relevance to my own thought; I have become familiar with my own Indian heritage largely by way of Western interpretations. My early Westernisation led to the development of subliminal barriers which prevented me from taking Indian thought (and traditional interpretations of Nature in general, e.g. medieval European alchemy) seriously; an attitude that is rudely manifest in many 'bloody-minded' Englishmen following the tradition exemplified by Dr Johnson's kicking of a rock to disprove Bishop Berkeley's Idealism, convinced of their own hard-nosed common sense, oblivious of their own ignorance.

> Ignorant of their own ignorance
> Yet in their own esteem so wise
> On premises false great mansions build
> Fed by their oracles with lies

The above verse applies equally to their geopolitical outlooks. Even the work of Indian scholars discussing Indian thought is, like Neo-Hinduism, strongly influenced by Western assumptions and expectations. Indeed, Sarvepalli Radhakrishnan, for a long time the foremost exponent of Indian thought in the West, has rightly been criticized by academics for distorting the 'true spirit' of Indian thought in order to appeal to the West[82]. I admit that I fall into this age-old trap, generally being able to come to terms with Indian philosophical concepts by first reinterpreting them into more familiar Western concepts (see the discussion of

Sanskrit versus English below). Although the advocates of comparative philosophy warn us of the 'incommensurability' problems associated with comparing ideas from vastly different conceptual frameworks,[83] there exists an underlying universality in human thought based on the common modes of representation which operate in all human brains. I am not interested in expounding the ancient 'spirit' of Indian thought but in determining the fundamental validity of its existential approach to philosophy and determining which components of Indian philosophy are truly universal and which need to be discarded or reinterpreted in the light of new knowledge and understanding. For national, political purposes, the question as to whether or not it is right to redefine traditional concepts is irrelevant if one holds to a notion of progress. Indian thought, like European thought is constantly evolving, reinterpreting old concepts over and over again until the original meaning has long been forgotten. Indian thought 1,000 years ago was hardly the same as Indian thought 3,000 years ago. European thought itself, as I have stressed in this work, is an amalgam of thought originating in various civilisations although Europeans have tended to mask the borrowed elements (an obvious but significant point is that Christianity is not of European origin). As the title of Section X part (c) indicates, such 'synthesis' was the key to the ideological programme of Indian Nationalism as developed by the Bengalis the key to the universal, global civilisation.

Of course, Indian thought has had a far wider influence than just Germany. Throughout the ages, Indian ideas have travelled West (and *vice versa*) through the Persian Empire, Alexandrian Empire, the Arabs and other Eurasian media, just as Europe first encountered Chinese technology such as gunpowder, through the Mongol Empire. The visit of Swami Vivekānanda, the most famous disciple of Rāmakrishna *Paramahaṁsa,* to the 1893 Parliament of Religions in Chicago (and his following lecture tour) brought the *Vedānta* to the Americans. The Bengali *kāyastha* became a *cause celebre* in American high society, especially amongst the so-called 'Boston brahmans'. He was treated with the respect that probably no other non-Westerner had previously received in Western learned circles, even being offered a chair at Harvard. The Indian influence upon the American Transcendentalist poets is well known; I quote the third verse of Emerson's *Brahma* which played a 'mystical' role in my coming to terms with Reality, at the head of the Preface. T.S. Eliot, who studied Sanskrit and Indian Philosophy at Harvard, was clearly influenced by such learning and also it seems by the visit of Tagore to Harvard, at the invitation of one of Eliot's teachers, J.H. Woods, Professor of Indian Philosophy.[85] That scion of two distinguished English families, the Huxleys and the Arnolds, Aldous (brother of Julian who developed the action potential model of nerve impulse propagation) became a member of the Rāmākrishna Mission in California under Swami Prabhavānanda,[86] writing the influential *The Perennial Philosophy*. Also in the late 1940s, in the Rāmākrishna Mission in New York, Swami Nikhilānanda and Margaret Wilson (daughter of Woodrow) translated the Bengali *Kathamrita* into the famous *The Gospel of Sri Ramakrishna*, which Joseph Campbell helped to edit.[87] This early Vedantic influence upon the West proliferated during the 1960s as Western youth began to loosen the shackles of colonialist cultural chauvinism.

> *When the late sixties came, I welcomed them as an eruption of India into a stagnant and soul-dead West.*
>
> Andrew Harvey[88]

The philistinism of the English establishment

Indian spiritual thought and Tagore's and Ghandi's ideas have influenced civil rights, environmental, educational and countercultural movements in the West. Britain itself, England in particular, stands out for its lack of acquaintance with Indian thought, partly due to the racialist attitude fostered by imperial rule towards the colonial subjects and their innate capacities, associated with the likes of Kipling (see XI(c)).

> *"Colebrooke", said Max Muller, was "the greatest Oriental scholar that England has ever produced", and added that had he lived in Germany, "we should. . . have seen his statue in his native place, his name written in letters of gold on the walls of the academies; we should have heard of Colebrooke jubilees and Colebrooke scholarships. (But) in England . . . not one word."*
>
> O.P. Kejariwal[89]

Andrew Harvey, who at the age of twenty-one, became the youngest fellow of All Souls College, Oxford in 1973 found that amidst the dominant Positivist, Empiricist culture at Oxford, the very idea of Religion was looked upon as ridiculous, something for foreigners, not for the English. The English establishment tends to take a similar view of the metaphysical thought of continental Europeans; the ridiculing of German philosophy by Peter Medawar, as great tuba blasts bellowing forth from the Rhine, inspiring my verse in *Old Indian Air.* I have often encountered this deep-rooted philistinism amongst many of the English who seem to think that metaphysical enquiry is a psychopathological condition best cured by taking a walk in the outdoors or playing football. Some English people have mocked me for openly discussing the theology-related metaphysical matters discussed in the following essay. One work colleague, unable to understand a conversation between myself and another, could only manage the pathetic put-down, "this is what we go to church for", as if the ritual gathering she undertook for the sake of convention was the same as sincerely discussing the relationship between the individual and the Absolute out of a genuine desire to understand. In the television programme, *The Making of a Modern Mystic,* Harvey, who taught English, told of how W.H. Auden told him that he envied T.S. Eliot because Eliot had spirituality. For a young arrogant fellow at Oxford to learn that everything that he had ever learnt was wrong was very difficult, says Harvey. Obviously the English attitude towards intellectuals, partly manifest by the likes of Kipling in regard to the Bengali babus (see XI(c)), is very different from that of the Germans or the French. I do not myself mention Colebrooke in the verse, paying tribute to the better-known William Jones, a lesser scholar as Muller notes, but the founder of the Asiatic Society of Bengal and its driving force in the early years (Jones also prepared the standard orthography for Sanskrit translation). It should, however, be noted that the translation and interpretation work usually involved liaison with native pandits. Bankim, as I previously mentioned, wrote perceptive critiques of much of the Orientalist scholarship, pointing out the underlying racialist assumptions (a century before today's similar critiques). Kejariwal notes that, contrary to the Nationalist assertion fuelled by Warren Hastings' statement that knowledge of the culture and customs of India would help consolidate Imperial rule, most of the members of the Asiatic Society were driven by intellectual curiosity and usually showed a genuine sympathy for the civilisation they were studying. The British authorities showed little interest in sponsoring the Society. I note in the verse how Jones' own view of Kālidāsa met with racialist disapproval in Britain.[90] As I stated at the beginning of this essay, the Society's work had profound implications for the future of India, instilling a deep sense of cultural pride in the face of constant British condescension and ridicule (the racial linkage between the Indo-Aryans and the Europeans through the similarities between Sanskrit and Latin/Greek also played a role in building Indian self-confidence). Moreover, it fuelled the growing sense of Indian destiny, the descendants of the people who had created this great civilisation could not languish for ever in the degenerate condition that they found themselves in, they would reclaim the mantle of that great heritage. As founder and inspiration behind the Society, I pay homage in the verse to Jones, the 'midwife to the Indian Nation'.

A NATION BORN THROUGH SYNTHESIS

> *The great event of the meeting of the East and the West has been desecrated by the spirit of contempt on the one side and a corresponding hatred on the other.* Rabindranath Tagore[91]

The sword and the pen of resurgent Hinduism

A Nation Born Through Synthesis opens with a short diversion to another example of the revolutionary impact of the transplantation of ideas/inventions from one civilisation into another; the inventions of Chinese origin that transformed Western Europe, ushering in the new age of modernity. Although not as important as printing, the compass etc., the windmill was another invention of Chinese origin and it played a role in Europe's Agricultural Revolution. They also helped Western Europe to conquer most of the world and thus bring her revolutionary ideas to countries still firmly rooted in tradition. At the time of Plassey (1757), India was locked in endless war between rival powers fighting over the remnants of the old Mughal empire. Foremost were the Marāthās, the warrior-peasant *Shūdras* from Maharashtra, whose clans had united into something approaching nationhood under their legendary leader turned king, Shivājī, the scourge of the Mughals. Later, under their *Chitpavan* brahman Chief Ministers (*peshwās*), the Marāthā armies effectively destroyed Mughal power, although they decided to prop up a Mughal figurehead in Delhi, and established a confederacy of their five main branches. In the 1740s repeated invasions of Bengal by two separate Marāthā armies weakened the Mughal *Nawāb,* forcing him to concede to them the territory of Orissa, which, along with Bihar, was ruled by the *Nawāb* of Bengal. In spite of their glorified status in Indian Nationalist folklore, as the resurgent sword of Hindu power after the failure of most of the Rājput kingdoms to stand up to Muslim incursions, the Marāthā raids into Bengal only alienated them from the Bengali Hindus, due to their sheer brutality in extorting tribute on pain of death. A century later when the dispossessed feudal landlords and chiefs, both Muslim and Hindu, tried to restore their power in the 1857 revolt, Bengalis working for the British flocked to the British cantonments for shelter; true they were 'collaborators', but by this time the humble Bengali clerk also had something new in his mind; western-style education and the beginnings of a modern outlook.

The Marāthā chieftains schemed against each other, though uniting haphazardly against British incursions and maintained rather backward administrations based on tribute from feudatories. The Marāthās, like the Mughals before them, did try to modernise their military machines, obtaining cannon etc., but without learning scientific principles. (Sultan Tipu of Mysore set up ordnance factories but these could not be maintained in a society that was not imbued with the scientific frame of mind in an economy lacking a modern infrastructure).

Although a strong nationalist movement was later to emerge in the *Peshwā's* capital of Poona, linked chiefly to the rather reactionary Bal Ganghadur Tilak, the modern Indian nation was conceived at the very heart of British power in India, in Calcutta. The pen really did prove mightier than the sword as modern Indian culture was forged in the predominantly literary activity of the 19th century so-called Bengali Renaissance.

> *a nation's rise or fall depends on its great men. . .The main reason for the special distinction we find in Bengal is that many great men were born there during the last century.*
>
> M.K. Gandhi (1905)[92]

Origins of the Bengali Renaissance

Tradition has it that Bengali culture was in a degenerate state in the Eighteenth century, the elements of truth in this assertion being grossly exaggerated by the influence of James Mill and his like who held that Indian civilisation was totally debased and stagnant. Bengal's economy was thriving due to to its massive export trade to much of the world, which was paid for in silver; the bullion trade was controlled by the aforementioned Marwari banking family, the Jagat Seths who conspired with the British to remove the *Nawāb*. The *ryots* (cultivators) remained miserably poor in this extremely fertile delta land, their surplus produce creamed off by Muslim and Hindu gentry. Historical research shows that, although the native *shakti* cult of the goddess Durgā (Kālī) and the Vaishnavite cult of Krishna (brought to Bengal by the great *bhakti* poet Chaitanya) were predominant amongst Hindus, numerous centres of Sanskritic scholarship were thriving in Eighteenth century Bengal. William Jones spent sometime at the 'brahmin university' at Nadia[93] which specialised in the *nyāya* system of logic. Again, contrary to the myth that the educated Bengali elite were a product of imperial administration (although the Whigs had planned to create an English-educated middle class to act as intermediaries in disseminating Western knowledge amongst the Indians), historical research[94] shows the existence of a highly educated Bengali elite (mainly brahmans and the literate *Shūdra* subcastes, prominent in Bengal, the *kāyasthas* and the *baidyas* who now form the modern Bengali *bhadralok* 'intelligentsia'). Most of the brahmans had become associated with the native Durgā cult, which they incorporated into 'mainstream Hinduism'. The caste system in Bengal was less severe than in other parts of India, partly because of the Buddhist legacy amongst the natives (avoiding caste) and the later mass conversions to egalitarian Islam. Buddhism itself had arisen as a reaction to the brahmanical domination of Indo-Aryan society; it was open to all castes and to women, and used regional languages rather than the brahmans' Sanskrit for its dissemination. These new Muslims were cut off from mainstream Islam, unlike the foreign ruling class, and this added to the liberal climate of thought, pre-existing in Bengal.[95]

> I too am torn 'tween state and union
> To *Āryāvarta* bond by caste
> But mind of Bengal nonconformist
> Shaped by non-Aryan *Shūdra* past *(Bande Mātaram)*

The Bengali brahman, Rammohun Roy is known as the 'first modern Indian', being one of the first Indians to adopt progressive Western ideas. Along with various social reform campaigns (I mentioned his anti-*Satī* campaign above), he started the Christianisation of Hindu ethics and introduced a form of Hindu monotheism modelled on Christianity and Islam. He founded the *Brahmo Sabhā* (later known as the *Brahmo Samāj*) in 1828, devoid of idols and brahman priests, and emphasising the *nirguṇa Brahman* of the *Vedānta* (as against the *saguṇa bhakti* idolatry) which was to have a tremendous influence on Bengali culture. Later in 19th century Bengal, there occurred a 'revival' of more traditional and conservative forms of Hinduism, partly as a reaction to overt racism by the British administration[96] (see below). None the less, the so-called 'revival', associated chiefly with Rāmākrishna and Vivekānanda, involved reinterpretations of the tradition with forward-looking motives closely implicated to the emerging Hindu nationalism, a prerequisite for which was a sense of self-respect. The West has its own form of *bhakti*, Christianity itself with its cult of personality of the man Jesus Christ. I note in the verse, Aurobindo's linkage of the new Synthesis, of Western ideas to Hinduism, to Shankaracharya's rather Buddhistic interpretation of *Advaita Vedānta* over a thousand years earlier, which had coincided with the steep decline[97] and, later, the virtual extinction of Buddhism from India. Aurobindo's nationalistic point was that the synthesis, rather than the antithesis would defeat the (British) 'thesis' as the synthesis, in including the thesis, did away with the latter's *raison d'être*.

We follow great Shankaracharya's
Upaniṣadic exegesis
Reclaiming *Bhārat* from the Buddha
By conflict not but by Synthesis

Of course, the synthetic, assimilative tradition is as old as Hinduism. I cited the mistaken view of the supposed Aryan assimilation of yogic practices from the mythical 'Harappans' in the verse as well as the actual assimilation of Bengali Tantric *shakti cults.* The *Bhagavad Gītā* was itself an attempt to forge a synthesis of the various divergent strands of Hindu thought prevalent some two thousand years ago, especially *Bhakti* and *Vedānta.* A number of religious reform movements were formed in various other parts of India during the 19th century, both Hindu and Muslim. Foremost amongst them the *Ārya Samāj.* The Bengali *Brahmo Samāj* had an influence all over India with branches formed in the South.[98] Bengali thought spread all over the country with the English-educated babus filling the lower reaches of the Raj administration. The teachings of Rāmakrishna and Vivekānanda remain closely associated with elite Indian Nationalism, with the Congress government of the early 1990s calling for a return to the liberal tradition of Vivekānanda in the wake of the BJP's sectarian rabble rousing.

The introduction of English education

It was the introduction of English education that truly opened up the world of the modern West to the Bengali *bhadralok.* It should be noted that English language education was introduced by the *bhadralok* themselves with the founding in 1817 of Hindu College in Calcutta where the first generation of English-educated Indians (indeed the first Western-educated Asians) were taught. (Similarly, contrary to Raj apologists' myths about the great scientific boons the British brought to India, it should be noted that the first Indian city to have electric lighting was Bangalore in the Indian-run princely state of Mysore, now India's 'silicon chip city'). I note in the verse that, as the idea of the uplifting, civilising mission took hold of the mind of the British rulers as Liberalism became prominent,[99] Rammohun Roy petitioned the then Governor General, William Pitt Amherst, arguing the case for the use of the English rather than the Sanskrit medium.

They would 'uplift' us, 'educate' us
Colleges they would establish
Wrote Rammohan Roy to Lord Amherst
Teach not Sanskrit, teach us English

R.K. Dasgupta has discussed the background to this historic letter in his essay 'Rammohun Roy and the New Learning'.[100] The first pronouncement on the need for Western learning in India came in Charles Grant's famous *Observations on the State of Society among the Asiatic Subjects of Great Britain* (drafted 1792, first printed by Parliament in 1813). Grant was closely associated with Wilberforce's Evangelical 'Clapham Sect' which I have referred to elsewhere in this work. Grant argued that the best remedy for the 'disorders' of Hindu society was the 'communication of our light and knowledge' (this was a restatement of the Liberal principle that the ills of society are the result of ignorance). He argued for this communication to be made through the English language and, as did Wilberforce, he envisaged a future Christian India.

In 1823 the General Committee of Public Instruction was appointed in Calcutta (including the famous Asiatic Society Sanskritist H.H. Wilson as General Secretary). The Committee's first major policy statement envisaged a union of European and Hindu learning which would promote improved cultivation of science and literature. The Committee rejected a purely Western education system as this would antagonise the Hindus. Around the same time, the Government proposed the founding of a Sanskrit College. Rammohun felt that this 'balanced diet' would be a useless compromise believing that such 'union' would only perpetuate Hindu learning leaving the Hindu Mind bonded to a lifeless tradition. In opposing Sanskrit, Roy opposed the premodern world mentality and scholastic education encapsulated in Sanskrit. In the 1940s and 1950s, Fellows of Calcutta University learning Indian Philosophy would seek instruction in the *darśanas* (systems) from traditional pandits in order to try to recapture something of the original spirit of Sanskritic learning;[101] the *darśanas* appearing most alien in the modern setting.

Rammohun's letter to Amherst (dated 11th December 1823) anticipated Macaulay's more famous *Minute on Education* of 1835 and, imbued with the Baconian Enlightenment notion of the advancement of learning, appealed for Europeans to instruct Indians in mathematics and natural sciences.

> *we already offered up thanks to Providence for inspiring the most generous and enlightened nation of the West with the glorious ambition of planting in Asia the arts and sciences of Modern Europe.* (Cited in R.K. Dasgupta)

In regard to Sanskrit, Rammohun wrote:

> *The Sanskrit language, so difficult that almost a lifetime is necessary for its acquisition, is well known to have been for ages a lamentable check to the diffusion of knowledge, and the learning concealed under this impervious veil is far from sufficient to reward the labour of acquiring it.* (R.K. Dasgupta)

Rammohun went on to reject the 'world-' and 'life-negating' doctrines of the *Vedānta.* The Sanskrit system of education would keep India in darkness, he asserted. It should be noted that his views, of course, did not go down at all well with the Hindu orthodoxy.

The government maintained its official policy of trying to please the native communities by encouraging Sanskritic and Islamic studies and introducing Western education with extreme caution. The proposed Sanskrit College was founded in 1824. In the 1850s, the great Bengali thinker and social reformer Īśwar Chandra Vidyāsāgar, then Principal of Sanskrit College, wrote to Ballantyne, Principal of the Sanskrit College in Benares, that they were obliged to continue teaching the *darśanas,* even though they were, beyond doubt, false sytems of philosophy. He argued that these 'false' systems of philosophy should be opposed by teaching 'sound philosophy' in the English course. The appearance in Calcutta, during the Bengali Renaissance, of the god-intoxicated saint Rāmakrishna seems, with hindsight, an act of Divine Providence as many have suggested. Rāmakrishna was to encounter most of the great figures of 19th century Bengal, maintaining the appeal of the ancient wisdom at the very time it was being rejected by so many under the influence of modern education. Vidyāsāgar conversed with Rāmakrishna and the latter respected his sincerity, but Vidyāsāgar (literally 'ocean of learning') for all his learning, failed to grasp the wisdom of the existential knowledge of the Absolute.[102] Rāmakrishna also had a famous encounter with Bankim, Bengal's leading spiritual figure chastising Bengal's leading temporal thinker for his frivolous reply to the question, "What is our ultimate responsibility?"[103] (See also the quote from A. Bharati in *The Reassertion of the Indian* about trying to teach Western analytical thought to students at Benares Hindu University). I have noted how modern science ('natural philosophy') limited itself to the analysis of particular problem domains rather than taking the traditional metaphysical approach of trying to understand 'the world as a whole'. As with medieval Europe, traditional India's best minds were squandered on theological nitpicking over the writings of ancient scholars; in a review of V.S. Naipaul's recent book on India (in which he has second thoughts about his previous negative assessments of Indian civilisation), the reviewer mentioned how Naipaul found a preponderance of brahmans in India's scientific community, transferring their great tradition of learning from the Sanskrit scriptures to the new natural philosophy. An example, I would say, of the ascetic contemplation of tradition being remodelled into ascetic 'experimentation', given the cloistered world of scientific laboratories.

Macaulay's famous *Minute on Education*, presented to the Liberal Governor General William Bentinck in 1835, seems to have been written with prior knowledge of Rammohun's letter. Although much has been made of Macaulay's outrageous remark that that 'a single shelf in a good European library is worth the whole native literature of India and Arabia', Macaulay also held that modern English literature was more valuable than that of classical Europe. In his address to Parliament of 1833 Macaulay stated, 'Are we to keep the people of India ignorant to keep them submissive' and looked forward to the day when, imbued with European knowledge, the Indian people would demand European institutions and self-government.[104]

> *Whether such a day will come I know not. But never will I attempt to avert or retard it. Whenever it comes it will be the proudest day in English history.*

For all my criticisms of British colonialism and insularity, their lack of the metaphysical bent as found in continental Europeans etc., I do recognise the genius of the British, although I would add that the English often take the credit for the genius of great Scots (Newton himself claimed ancestry from the Scottish aristocracy, Maxwell, Napier, Bell, Baird *et al.*), who, along with the Welsh and the Irish in general, seem to have a natural empathy with the plight of the colonised peoples and with traditional philosophical views. I have mentioned in the introduction, that James Morris in his history of the British Empire, noted that, amongst the predominantly racist empire builders, there were a few honourable exceptions, especially Irishmen, Scotsmen and Welshmen whose views were tempered by the history of their own people at the hands of the English.[105] Across, the modern West, including South Africa and the USA, the 'white' Jews have been at the vanguard of the anti-racialist struggle, remembering their own history of tremendous suffering over many centuries at the hands of the European Christians. India's first encounter with modern Europeans included the shameful burning of Malabar Jews by the Portuguese Christians in Goa. In spite of all the wrongdoings of British colonialism which have framed Indian Nationalist thought, I recognise that there is a deep-rooted liberal tradition amongst the British which genuinely holds a progressive, internationalist view, many of these Britons have also empathised with the Indian Nationalist view. As individuals, I have found the British, in general, to be extremely decent people and the British at home have frowned upon the rabid excesses of some other Europeans in regard to ethnic minorities. Indeed, I myself sometimes feel very antagonistic towards the immigrants in London, usually dark-skinned, who behave in a most uncivilised manner, or seek only to scrounge state hand-outs, or live as if they are still living in feudal villages and I can easily understand the antipathy felt by many Britons towards them. The day shall come when India shall fulfil that tryst with destiny that began with the rainstorm at Plassey and Indian thought and Indian science shall lead the world. I hope that when this time comes, that both British and Indians will look with pride at the coming together of Eastern and Western traditions into the universal global civilisation through our shared history.

The use of English in independent India

At the end of *A Nation Born Through Synthesis,* I refer to the current concern amongst many in India regarding the use of the 'alien' English medium, the 'foreign tongue within our heads'; some seeing it almost like a lingering foreign rule within our minds. Dasgupta[106] says of this movement to eradicate English:

> *At a time when the colonial power does not exist, we have identified English as a residue of that power and we are determined to expel it.*

He states that this stand against English is essentially a stand against any form of elitism. The fear amongst the exponents of this anti-elitism being that the English medium education will create a small intellectual elite cut off from the masses. He notes that Sanskrit itself was the language of a tiny brahman elite who created most of India's great philosophy and literature so dear to those who berate the elitist nature of English. He notes that the Romans prized the learning of Greek and that Bacon and Newton wrote in Latin after Shakespeare's English had appeared. I would add that, as English is the language of Science, the new computer technology and the language of the global media, Indians cannot afford not to have access to English if India is to become a scientific superpower and if India is to get its message across, effectively, to the world. In this sense English is a great asset to India as India prepares to globalise. The Chinese talk of Chinese ideas becoming increasingly important in the world but one must question the ability of the Chinese to communicate their views to other societies through the global media dominated by Americanised English. Just as the West is obliged to use Indian numerals (which it mistakenly calls 'Arabic'), the Indian decimal system and the Babylonian duodecimal system for historical reasons, so the rest of the world, not only India, has to use Americanised English.

Of course Indians have to develop 'appropriate' philosophies and institutions for the Indian setting, reframing new developments to fit the Indian context based on the Indian tradition, rather than rely upon unsuitable transplants from other countries which evolved for reasons unrelated to India's immediate needs.

I have mentioned the 'social gene' effects of the transplantation of 'green revolution' technology in the verse. In his *India: A Wounded Civilisation*, V.S. Naipaul castigates Indians for copying other civilisations without developing indigenous alternatives. Naipaul seems to forget the massive scale copying of other civilisations by the Japanese and the Chinese (or, as I note in this work, the origins of many modern European developments in non-European civilisations). Naipaul accuses Indians of intellectual parasitism, talks of India's creative incapacity, its intellectual depletion etc. As I have already stated, such rantings and ravings by this pseudo-intellectual are applauded by his European *'bwanas'*. It doesn't take an ounce of intelligence to note the glaring problems faced by India; it takes intellectual ability to recognise that, in spite of all the problems, there has been slow but steady progress in India since Independence given a most difficult situation. Fifty years after its wholehearted approval of Katherine Mayo's *Mother India*, London's left-wing *New Statesman* did not seem to have grown out of its colonialist ignorance, calling Naipaul's views "obvious". For instance, in regard to appropriate/-intermediate technology, Naipaul posed as the fount of all wisdom, rubbishing the efforts of India's scientific establishment (this was prior to his more recent book mentioned above). In regard to efforts to improve the efficiency of bullock carts, Naipaul asks why they can't provide engines rather than using animal power! No mention is made of developments in solar power or crop improvements by Indians. One is reminded of the British ambassador to Meiji Japan's contemptuous attitude towards Japan's technological potential mentioned elsewhere in this essay.

Framing our thoughts in an Indian context does not mean having to think or communicate in Hindi or an Indian language. As I stated in regard to *Bande Mātaram*, my *nation* is not just the *people;* it is also the *civilisation.* If Indian civilisation is to flower again as a great civilisation then it must have languages which facilitate scientific enquiry and clarity of thought in relation to the complex realities of the modern world. There is an echo of Friedrich Schlegel's argument about the superiority of inflected languages which facilitate philosophical enquiry here. I believe that there is an element of truth in Schlegel's view. Thought relating to the modern world, ubiquitously informed by science, high technology and Western institutions is articulated with far greater felicity in the language of Shakespeare than in the language of Tulsīdās. The ultra-nationalistic Japanese have had problems with their own pictograph-based language in relation to the modern world and they do not shirk from using English when it suits their purpose. The fact that I shall use English for the presentation of my metaphysical thought in the following essay does not mean that my work is not a continuation of the Indian tradition; it is the reformulation of traditional Indian thought by a modern Indian, using the only language he can use, given his upbringing. Better to use English than attempt to think and communicate in modern terms and have to keep translating back and forth. High culture has always been elite culture and, just as Britain's scientists and thinkers do not speak in Cockney English, Indians must not be restricted to the restricted language of the marketplace.

Bankim and the regeneration of Indian culture

Returning to Calcutta in the 19th century and the birth of the so-called 'Bengali Renaissance'; at first, many young English-educated Indians became intoxicated with everything Western (note the parallel with the German Indomania) and followed the likes of James Mill in deriding everything Indian as useless or outdated. The fact that many of the British in India developed a deep sense of contempt for the intellectual, English-educated Bengalis, whom they derided as weak and effeminate was not simply because the 'public' school educated Britisher identified with the robust, uncomplicated 'martial' races. The 'martial' races were also very conservative peoples, who, along with their open hostility to British rule, were also hostile to the new ideas the British brought with them whereas the Bengalis' enthusiasm for Western thought led them towards the progressive political thought which the British realised, as indicated in the quote from Macaulay above, posed the real long-term threat to their power.

Partha Chatterjee, in his *Nationalist Thought and the Colonial World*,[107] notes that Bankim, although he accepted some of the Orientalist characterizations of 'Orientals', did not accept that this character was *immutable*. Bankim invoked a National Will for the total regeneration of national culture leading to a transformation of this culturally determined 'oriental' character. Rajnarayan Bose (the grandfather of Aurobindo Ghose) had ridiculed the English-educated Bengalis for aping the English. Replying to Bose and similar satirical commentaries, Bankim noted:

> *One cannot learn except by imitation. Just as children learn to speak by imitating the speech of adults,. . . Thus it is reasonable and rational that Bengalis should imitate the English. . . Such imitation is natural and its consequences can be most beneficial. There are many who are angry at our imitating English habits in food and dress; what would they say of the English imitating the French in their food and dress? Are the English any less imitative than Bengalis?*
>
> Bankim Chandra Chattopadhyay. Cited in: Chatterjee, P. *Nationalist Thought and the Colonial World*

But, as Chatterjee notes, Bankim knew that imitation was but the first step in learning, the first step in transforming the backward culture. Bankim was unhappy with pure imitation even if this did not entail losing the distinctive national character. Later in his life, Bankim was to find a solution to this problem of one-sided adoption of the alien culture. Culture did not only consist of the material aspects of life, emphasised by the Europeans, it also consisted of the spiritual aspects of life where Eastern culture was superior to that of the European Enlightenment. Chatterjee elaborates on Bankim's actual notions on Indian spirituality revolving around his concept of *Anusilan* (system of culture). For Bankim, the modern Western conception of culture was incomplete, focusing only on knowledge of the world and excluding knowledge of the self and knowledge of God. Bankim's *Anusilan* was based on his notion of *bhakti* as the union of knowledge/gnosis with duty, which meant action without expectation of reward (related to the *Bhagavad Gītā's* famous doctrine of *niṣkāma karma;* disinterested action). Thus, as the quote in the introduction indicates, Bankim saw the fusion of European science and technology with Indian spirituality and self-control leading to a better world where science and technology would be put to better use.

In the same article from which I have taken the quote at the head of this essay, Marx spoke of England's 'double mission' of destruction and regeneration in India:

> *From the Indian natives, reluctantly and sparingly educated at Calcutta, under English superintendence, a fresh class is springing up, endowed with the requirements for government and imbued with European science. . . At all events, we may safely expect to see, at a more or less remote period, the regeneration of that great and interesting country,. . .*
>
> Karl Marx, *The Future Results of British Rule in India* (1853)[108]

Racial discrimination and the rise of Nationalism

In the 1790s, Governor General Cornwallis, who stated that every native of India is corrupt, dismissed all Indian high officials and all posts paying over £500 a year were reserved for the Company's civil service which was, of course, exclusively European. To be fair to Cornwallis, his Lockean ideological aims were to replace the arbitrary despostism, as he perceived it, with the Rule of Law.[109] It was Cornwallis who had engineered the Permanent Settlement in Bengal where the *zamīndārs,* who had held rights of revenue collection under the Mughals, became the landowners and payed a fixed due to the Government. Although this *zamīndāri* settlement was grossly unfair to the *ryots* (Madras and Bombay 'settled' their land revenues directly with the *ryots;*[110] and Nehru's *Zamīndāri* Abolition (VIII(102) met with great popular approval although this and later land reforms were largely just tinkering with the land problem[111]) the institution of private property was perceived by Cornwallis as a key step in European-style bourgeois development. British Law has many positive features and is an integral component of Western-style modernisation in India, but, as with the Permanent Settlement, it benefitted the rich at the expense of the poor. In 1826, the Calcutta *bhadralok* (literally 'polite folk' but based on the 19th century English gentry), sent a petition to the House of Commons protesting at their exclusion from senior official positions. In 1858 came the proclamation promising impartial admission on a non-racial basis. However, when Surendranath Banerjea eventually became the first Indian to join the elite ranks of the Indian Civil Service (ICS), he was dismissed soon afterwards for a minor lapse for which no British official would ever have been dismissed (we hear similar stories in Britain today involving women in male-dominated professions as well as non-whites even involving liberal institutions like the Commonwealth Institute). I mentioned above how Bankim wrote of the fawning, uneducated Indians in the Subordinate Civil Service, ever keen to display their inferior status to their British masters, who rose up rapidly through the hierarchy. W.C. Bonnerjee (this surname is another anglicisation of the Sanskritic Bandhopadhyay usually spelt 'Banerjee'; my maternal clan) who was rated by Chief Justice Garth as "second to none" in ability, was excluded from the office of Standing Counsel by the same Garth on the grounds of his race.[112] I note in the verse how the coming to power in Britain of the social reform minded Whigs, paradoxically increased racial exclusivity as the new sense of civilising mission also brought with it the 'race apart' *pukka saheb* keeping up appearances. Indeed the European Clubs of Calcutta only opened their doors to non-Europeans in 1946.

In 1876 Banerjea founded the Indian Association of Calcutta (an Indian League already existed). In 1883, he founded the Indian National Conference, which merged in 1886 with the Indian National Congress, founded the previous year in Bombay. W.C. Bonerjee became the first *rāshtrapati* (president) of the Congress. In later years, the likes of Aurobindo Ghose and Subhas Chandra Bose would, after being expensively prepared by their fathers for the much-prized careers in the 'heaven-born' service and sent to England to take the ICS exams (as the British later tried to dissuade Indians by limiting the entrance exams to England), would desist from 'collaboration' and choose instead the impecunious path of the freedom struggle.

At first we welcomed Western Progress
Fine talk of fairness, equal rights
But blocked was progress up the ladder
On new horizons set our sights

Subhash Bose's political mentor C.R. Das, the great leader of the Bengal Congress and an INC *rāshtrapati*, had been Calcutta's most successful lawyer before giving up his practice for the freedom struggle and dying in debt.[113] Although in 1857, the Bengali babus had taken refuge in the British cantonments, their grandchildren were to lead the extreme wing of India's freedom struggle. The 'Old School' Congress leaders like Surendranath Banerjea and numerous lawyers educated in London, knew the history of only one European country, Britain. They would learn of the gradual enfranchisement of the British people, then still far from complete, over hundreds of years and read only the likes of James Mill's *On Liberty*. They saw Indian self-rule coming through a long process of gradual legal reforms.[114] The next generation of nationalists were aware of the histories of France and Russia and the rapid transformation of Japan. Such gradualism was not for them. A senior British official, who had twice escaped assassination at the hands of Bengali revolutionaries, said of the revolutionaries that he had hanged that "they were the cream of Bengal's youth".[115] It is the brightest and best who feel most keenly the indignity of their people's subjugation. Narendranath Bhattacharya (better known by his false name of M.N. Roy), the emissary of the Bengal revolutionaries to the Kaiser in 1915 was reknowned for his intellectual brilliance; his dispute with Lenin over Lenin's Colonial Thesis in 1920 being quite famous in Marxist historiography (although Roy later came to accept Lenin's view that the communist movements in undeveloped colonial countries should aid the bourgeois nationalist liberation movements).[116] The famous story from the 1908 Alipur Bomb Trial tells of how the Judge, C.P. Beachcroft, who acquitted Aurobindo and most of the defendants (although Aurobindo's brother and another were sentenced to death), had been a contemporary of Aurobindo's at Cambridge, coming second to Aurobindo at Greek in the final examination. C.R. Das, before his Congressman days, as Calcutta's leading lawyer defended Aurobindo with an eloquent speech saying that this poet of patriotism stood, not only before the bar of the court, but before the bar of the High Court of History.[117]

In his *The Illegitimacy of Nationalism: Rabindranath Tagore and the Politics of Self*,[118] Ashis Nandy discusses how Tagore criticised the narrow, single-mindedness of the revolutionaries. Tagore himself was associated with Brahmabandhab Upadhyay (real name Bharanicharan Bandhopadhyay) whose daily newspaper *Sandhya* was supportive of violent resistance to British rule. As Nandy notes, Upadhyay perhaps reflected some of Tagore's own inner conflicts. My own intellect has matured to a condition where I can appreciate Tagore's critique of the revolutionaries, relating to the dehumanisation of their personalities as they became 'robotic' slaves to their cause and also reflecting Tagore's view (later developed by Gandhi) that India had to hold firm to a higher truth than petty, tribal European-style nationalism. However, my 'heart', remains with the revolutionaries even though they stood no real chance of success and sometimes lost sight of the bigger picture. No single approach in the freedom struggle can be taken to have been the correct approach. Although the Tagore/Ghandi style approach was, to a large measure correct, the British had to be shown that if they did not respond to passive resistance, even the 'effeminate' Bengalis, stung by the criticism of the British and of well-wishers like the Japanese Kakuzo Okakura,[119] were prepared to fight and die for their country's freedom. I have noted in the commentary to *No Sure Ground* how Aurobindo Ghose turned from revolutionary leader to mystic philosopher/poet, nominated for the Nobel Prize, and how Subhas Bose had said that, had his life not been taken up by the freedom struggle, he would have liked to have spent more time studying philosophy.[120] Indeed, the deep thinker whose mind reaches beyond itself and becomes possessed by the collective afflictions of his people and seeks a creative solution to his or her people's problems, has already come closer to the spiritual depths of our beings.

> Those born in freedom struggle, between
> Bullets and jails no time to pause
> Their life stories are simply written
> The meaning of their life their cause

> *They might be small in number, but in the fragmented society of India it is the educated community alone which shows the union of learning with feeling. And it is this educated community which is in a position to express the heart-felt pain of the Indian people and to spread awareness of it by various means.*
>
> Rabindranath Tagore (1894)[121]

Of course, as the British were quick to note, Indian society was itself riven by caste exclusivity (many a Bengali *bhadralok* from the non-Aryan or Aryan/*Shūdra* halfcaste *kāyastha* subcaste, which produced Vivekānanda and Subhas Bose, would experience discrimination in the Hindu temples etc. of more conservative North India). Tagore himself, whilst chastising the reactionaries in his writings, had instituted separate dining for brahmans at his cultural centre at Śāntiniketan. With hindsight, one can see the positive influences that British racialism had upon the Indian Mind in its attempt to overcome this contradiction. In 1946, the Indian National Congress first raised the issue of apartheid in South Africa at the United Nations Organisation; after Independence, with Ambedkar as Minister of Justice, it instituted positive discrimination for the 'Scheduled Castes and Tribes' in the new 'truly Indian' Civil Service.

The influence of France and Soviet Russia

It was not only the racism of the British administration that fuelled the growth of Indian Nationalism. As mentioned at the beginning of this essay, the rediscovery of Hindu India's glorious past (masked as much by the disregard of Muslim invaders as by a lack of historicity on the part of the Hindus) and the ethnic links between the speakers of the Indo-European languages emboldened the educated Hindus. Many Western-educated Indians, including many Nationalists, still saw the historical incursion of the British into India as an act of Providence but, whilst acknowledging this, the main lesson that was to be learned from British tutelage was that of modern self-government, allowing Indians to control their own destiny. Coupled to the negative motivations aroused by the racism of the British were the positive motivations inherent in Western political thought, especially those emanating from the French Revolution. France, whose cannon had blazed for the *Nawāb* against Clive's at Plassey (during the Seven Years War), but which were incapacitated by an act of God (Providence perhaps—see *Satanic Mills*), exerted a powerful hold on the Western-educated Indians' mind (as the versified quote from Nehru indicates), just as *la grande nation* had inspired the *patriotes* in other European countries.[122] Bengal, whose language is known as the 'French' of India due to its pronunciation, has also been the heartland of modern Indian radical thought.[123] The Marxian emphasis on economic determinants in the development of the bourgeois capitalist world system could not go unnoticed by Indian nationalists. The non-Bengali Dadabhai Naoroji's *Poverty and UnBritish Rule in India* (1871) propounding the 'drain thesis' was the seminal work fuelling the economic arguments for self-rule (see my discussion of *Satanic Mills* above). Bengal led the way in the practice of economic nationalism with the *swadeshī* (home-made) campaign following the partition of Bengal in 1905.

M. N. Roy (real name, Narendranath Bhattacharya), the Bengali revolutionary who befriended Lenin, brought Communism home with him. As the verse notes, Lenin's critique of colonialism endeared him to most Indian Nationalists and Soviet Russia became the new bastion of Progress. I have mentioned above Lenin's dispute with Roy in 1920 over the Colonial Thesis in which Lenin argued that fledging communist movements in backward colonial countries, like the one Roy was to form in India in December 1926, should support the mainstream 'bourgeois' liberation movements like the Indian National Congress. (In later times Stalin would take a similar attitude towards the Chinese (non-proletarian peasant) communists, prior to the communist takeover, urging them to back the Kuomintang). Of course, prior to Gandhi, the Congress (often derided as the Brahman National Congress) was the bastion of India's elite classes, hardly the industrial proletariat. But as I note in the verse, the famous thesis first pronounced by the Muslim Tatar, Mir Said Sultan Galiev, redefined 'class struggle' at the global level to incorporate the struggle of the exploited, colonised peoples into the revolutionary struggle of the workers of the world. During the 1930s, Nehru, like other future leaders of developing nations, witnessed the phenomenal industrial development of the Soviet Union under Stalin, as the West stagnated in the capitalist depression. Although Communism never caught on beyond Kerala and Bengal (M.N. Roy himself abandoned Communism at independence), Socialism, along with Secularism, became enshrined in the constitution of independent India which, none the less, remains in essence a statement of (European) Enlightenment Liberalism. Following the Soviet rapprochement with capitalist India in the 1950s resulting in the building of a steel mill at Bhilai,[124] a special relationship developed between elite nationalist, capitalist, caste-ridden, spiritualistic India and the 'classless', atheist, communist superpower. This special relationship was spelt out by Mikhael Gorbachev and Rajiv Gandhi in the joint declaration of 1986, known as the 'Delhi Declaration', of which Gorbachev wrote:

The global interest in the document is natural. . . an entirely new philosophical-political approach to interstate relations. . . the recognition of the priority of human values. . . the unique nature of Soviet-Indian relations. . . the deep respect and liking our nations have for each other.

M. Gorbachev[125]

NO SURE GROUND

The globalisation of the Capitalist industrial phenomenon

Although the Soviet Union is no more and both Russia and India are venturing into the new world of free market economics, I believe that the spirit of Gorbachev's 'philosophical-political approach' should not be considered totally effete in the 'New World Order'. The free market 'shock therapy' in Russia is already provoking a backlash with the growth of some fascist elements leading some observers to make comparisons with Weimar Germany's destabilising influence, as Russia remains a nuclear superpower. Gorbachev's plans for the Soviet Union involved trying to retain some of the positive aspects of the old Soviet Union and to maintain some sort of alternative system to the naked market capitalism advocated by the West. I have said much the same in regard to India's economic liberalisation programme at the end of my discussion of *Bande Mātaram.* Although there is no real alternative to the 'world of *baniās*' at present, there remains a need to seek new principles of Substantive Rationality faced with the increasing tendency of technology and the short-term financial profit motive to steer social systems towards economic organisation based on principles of Formal Rationality, where the efficient running of the 'machine' has priority over human needs and the higher aspirations of civilisation. Furthermore, the 'free market' ideology, devoid of higher visionary, progressive objectives, appears vacuous, failing to cater for the 'spiritual' needs of the people, who, despite the fact that most seem to want no more than what Juvenal referred to as 'bread and circuses', do have a need to feel that they are part of a greater, noble historical process (an aspect of my so-called 'Oneness/Otherness Mystery').

Recently, a few years after the Soviet Union's collapse, there has been much talk about the New World 'Disorder' manifest in the internecine conflicts, chaos and anarchy which is erupting in various regions and left to fester unresolved due to the lack of superpower intervention and the lack of any motivating ideology behind many of the warring factions, such as in Somalia. The growing influence of organised crime, warlords, banditry, the rise of ethnic conflict and violence by shanty dwellers in huge cities does constitute a serious cause for concern. As stated above, people need to feel that they are part of a greater, 'noble' historical process which an 'uplifting' ideological movement provides and is notably lacking in the current emphasis on free market solutions. However, much of the pessimism seems inspired by the proliferation of the new mathematics of Chaos in the study of various complex systems including socio-economic processes. With the Free Market and Technology as their gods, some materialist thinkers have taken a notion of Chaos to be their ultimate reality. This pessimism also reflects an underlying Eurocentrism especially when there is talk of the new post-Cold War order becoming one of the prosperous North as the new Roman Empire holding at bay the barbarian hordes from the poverty-stricken South. The element of realism in this view reflects the sad truth that all the fancy talk of a global village is largely wishful marketing rhetoric hiding the dirty reality beyond the confines of the luxury hotels. But such Eurocentric pessimists cannot imagine that, with the ideas of the modern West running out of steam, the drive towards a New World Order restoring hope with the sense of an uplifting mission, faced with the vacuity of free market demagogy, might come from the newly industrialising countries of Asia. It is worth keeping in mind the positive attributes of the free market system, which encourages investment in, and development of, less-developed regions where higher growth rates should lead to greater profits. There is also something at least to be said for the old adages which stressed the mutuality of free trade and peace between nations, if not within them.

Although structural constraints evidently exist which result in convergence towards Western-style, liberal democratic, market-oriented systems, environmental and logistical considerations indicate that, with current strategic technologies at least, 'more of the same', may not be a feasible option. I may chastise the Western environmentalists who argue along similar lines, in Section XII (*No Sure Ground*) but this is because, at present, there is no alternative for developing countries but to go along with the 'devil we know', regardless of the potential environmental consequences. We are not going to be put off from industrialising by the sensitivities of some privileged, sentimental Westerners. The recent 'Earth Summit' in Rio de Janeiro was a step in the right direction but involved a lot of talk and few deeds. The developing world has no power while it remains agrarian and poor, it has to go for industrial growth not only to alleviate poverty, but also to strengthen its hand in future negotiations on the world order. Western charity, although well-intentioned and often vital in emergencies, for longer-term purposes only masks the underlying problems. At bottom, as Tagore told the Americans in 1931, those who have only temporal power only understand temporal power.

> No brainchild bold the world bazaar
> Its creepy growth as grows a mould
> On rot it feeds, organic, civil
> Now whole world has in hyphal hold

As this verse from *Bande Mātaram* indicates, the capitalist economic system has been so successful (in terms of its spread) because it is based on the socio-psychological realities determining human motivation and economic behaviour. The capitalist system, although closely associated with the colonialistic globalisation of Europe, is not a bold 'brainchild', like Communism, forced onto the organic, socio-economic reality, it is, to a very large extent, the emergent manifestation of the microcosmic transactions of our everyday lives determined by human nature. Factors like technology may determine the exact nature and degree of integration of the transactions, and social institutions can constrain the worst excesses of our selfish motivations, but the system as a whole draws its strength from the inherent motivational nature of humans ('On rot it feeds').

The Communist anthem 'The Internationale' may have stirred the heart with the words, 'the Internationale unites the human race' but international Communism left the world divided like never before. Environmentalists and moral philosophers point out to us that increasing global integration of activities has created new sets of common concerns and that it is in everybody's broader self-interest to act in order to alleviate these potentially catastrophic problems. I take a seemingly cynical view of such arguments in the first passage of *No Sure Ground,* emphasising the neocolonial aspect of such arguments and the inherent difficulties in trying to turn individual actions into the desired emergent results, but in the final verse I clearly state that I agree that such problems need to be addressed. It should be clear from my comments about the capitalist system drawing its strength from inherent human motivations and from the allusions to the historical origins of the world market system in this work that such an incredibly complex phenomenon as the global economic system is not going to be radically transformed overnight. As with other complex global phenomena such as the global climate, the particular phases of growth, spread and degeneration, are likely to have extremely long cycles (although sudden shocks may occur). In the case of the global economic system, we are seeing things speed up as the longest phase was clearly going to be the original development in Western Europe which relied on numerous historical accidents, whereas now, technology and institutions can be copied or transplanted wholesale to a certain extent and processes such as scientific creativity, technological research and development, and socio-economic transformation have been so thoroughly analysed. When the British Ambassador in *Meiji* Japan was asked if the Japanese could send a delegation to Britain to study British society, he dismissively replied, let them go, it will take them three hundred years to get to where we are now.[126] A couple of years ago ex-Chancellor of Germany, Helmut Schmidt was reminding his audience, at a meeting on Europe, just how poor the vast majority of the population of China actually was in relation to Europe. Indeed, China has largely hidden from the outside world the desperate poverty of up to 350 million Chinese, mainly in Western China where United Nations relief programmes are in operation, while economic boom occurs in the East. But one should note that China is the size of the whole of Europe and we only need to look at Albania, Romania and the likes to find subcontinental disparities in wealth. It is worth remembering the evolutionary principle noted by Toynbee that the same factors which made an empire great, in a changing world, are likely to lead to its decline. I would add the following words from a 1960s American Civil Rights anthem: "And the slow one now will later be fast; For the times they are a changin."

Despite the fancy speculation of so-called futurologists, we are still very much in the industrial world; the advanced industrial states are not in some post-industrial world that is in some way essentially removed from the socio-economic processes that emerged with the capitalist industrial world.[127] Of course there never has been, nor will there ever be, homogeneity, but it is becoming apparent that the global capitalist industrial phenomenon does have something of a levelling tendency within it. Japan seems to be playing a role in Asia somewhat akin to Britain's historical rôle in Europe in regard to industrial development (both are islands with 'tributary' cultures, offshoots of their respective continental civilisations from which they remained autonomous).[128] Historical circumstances will obviously fine-tune the actualities brought about by such underlying processes. Simultaneously however, the 'polarizing market forces' which I berate in *No Sure Ground* remain in operation at global, national and local levels diverting resources to the rich and raising prices. Of course a major point in the Neocolonialism argument is that the West deliberately attempts to prevent the global capitalist phenomenon from running its unhindered course in order to maintain the disparity in global resource distribution.

This point of view has to be tempered somewhat as we witness the USA's contribution to the rapid economic rise of China and Latin America's seeming recovery from the debt crisis. The fact that enormous social problems remain in such countries has to be judged against the history of the West, which as recently as the 1930s was suffering from mass unemployment with environmental disasters in the American Mid-West. Of course the USA has its own long term economic interests at heart in both cases but all good deals involve reciprocal 'exploitation'. The Australian global media tycoon, Rupert Murdoch, berated for his lowest common denominator mass market output, has struck a deal with the once insular Indian government by offering India the strategic telecommunications technology she desires in exchange for a stake in her huge potential market.

Although some aspects the influence of men like Murdoch are questionable (he is despised by the left-wing media establishment in Britain for his newspaper empire's support of the Conservatives), the anti-establishment approach of such 'market men' whose allegiance to the market system outweighs national allegiances does help to break down the neo-colonialistic stranglehold of the established powers over the spread of strategic technology. The globalisation of the media, including the new global computer 'internet' system, has been compared to the revolutionary impact of the introduction of the printing press in regard to broadening horizons; clearly the notion of the 'global village' is not total nonsense. None the less, geopolitical power games are never far from the surface and the USA's help to China, partly born of the need to ensure that Japan does not monopolise the huge China market, will increase China's leverage with its neighbours. The USA is likely to see the bolstering of India as a counterweight to China (as well as a buffer to radical Islam) to be in its own interest. Thus geopolitical chess-playing, as with the 'Cold War countries' mentioned in *Satanic Mills* is likely to help foster development.

As I mentioned in *No Sure Ground*, there may be some hope emanating from advances in science and technology (such as cheap, clean limitless energy sources) but, even if useful technological advances occurred, given the economic/political contexts in which they emerged, would they actually make things better or would they be made to serve some particular economic or political interest at the expense of the majority. I have already mentioned the famous case of the water mill which was forced upon ordinary people by feudal powers as being a case of long-term progress despite negative consequences in the immediate and intermediate term. This example does not necessarily hold good in all cases. The reason why I used the term 'technofix' in the verse was to highlight the narrow-minded approach of looking for technological solutions to systemic problems which require more basic but often politically sensitive changes. As mentioned above, there is a tendency to deify 'Technology'. In regard to new technologies, the sheer cost of nuclear fusion research may prove to be something of a bonus in the future as it is forcing governments to collaborate in order to share the cost, so, if something practical comes out of it, it will not be monopolised by one power at the expense of the rest of the world. It is also possible that newly industrialising countries might be able to benefit from more from new technologies, 'leapfrogging' over older, 'heavy' and 'dirty' technologies and not having to make expensive transitions from earlier generation technologies. The imminent development of commercially viable solar power will come as a godsend to India.

Mass market society and cultural degeneration

No Sure Ground continues with a passage in which the 'true brahman' castigates the cultural manifestations of the 'wretched world of *baniās*'. Idealistic notions, though necessary to motivate people towards attaining higher things, have to face the soul-destroying reality of the large body of humanity which seems generally satisfied with the mindlessness of mass culture and could never contemplate a more contemplative life. The highest levels of analytical thought they seem to attain is to regurgitate mass media discussions of tactical failures by the national sports teams; for those with no hope of glory in their lives can only seek the vicarious glory of such gladiatorial circuses. Their contemplation does not seem to rise beyond the two-a-penny novels churned out these days by every fool who attains notoriety be it as a politician, a broadcaster or a comedian, with plots full of murders, sex, violence and all manner of imaginable perversions and whose authors often, pretentiously, claim some 'profound' underlying message as justification. As I stress in *The Web Intricate*, the true brahman sees himself as the 'would-be human', faced with the behaviour of the mass of humanity, dictated by animal instincts.

And in this world of monkey business
The would-be human at a loss
What monkeys hold as gold and silver
The would-be human sees as dross

The fickle fashions, childish zoetropes
Like glass beads captivate the apes
Apes not the apes the would-be human
But from their world he can't escape

Here again we have the double-edged sword of Progress, on one side bringing greater freedom of expression and acknowledgement for once-suppressed 'subaltern' culture, but this very 'liberation', taken towards extremes, bringing with it much infantility which has a detrimental effect on the general character of society.

Like it or not, civilisation has been based on a degree of authoritarianism, suppressing many of the natural tendencies of the human animal, both as individuals and as the mob, in order to bring about orderliness and stability. The above-mentioned rise of banditry, organised crime, inter-clan bloodletting and aimless destructiveness in the so-called 'New World Disorder' highlights the fact that humans are not born civilised; civilisation has to be imposed. Popular democracy with its appeal to head counts tends to care little about intrinsic values and broader implications when all that counts for attaining power is the counting of heads, regardless of how 'empty' they may be. Factors such as the over-zealous rejection of all aspects of traditions built on elitism, the Cult of the Youth (which includes, amongst other things, an element of childish craving used to fuel hyper-materialism, infantile 'rebellion' against minor authority, and lack of respect for parents and teachers), the tyranny of mass production, mass media and mass marketing, the glorification of image over substance, new technologies utilised for trivial gimmicks, the breakdown of stable families and traditional childrearing, and poor standards of education have all exacerbated the pernicious effects of mass culture. I make no bones about my basic attitude of disdain towards the general egregiousness and infantility of it all although I accept that it has positive aspects (not least the decolonialisation of Western thought as noted in *Two Two-legged Human Races* which was partly a manifestation of cultural liberalisation). I should also reiterate here the fact that the general empathy of the Western working classes for the cause of peoples around the world oppressed by the Western ruling classes which has helped the causes of decolonialisation and multicultural tolerance in post-colonial Western society. The working classes in the 'metropolitan centre' of the colonial world were themselves exploited and maltreated; I have mentioned Churchill's contempt for the plight of the British miners in 1926 and how the so-called "workers' state" championed the cause of decolonisation. I have stressed that my conception of the good of my nation has as much to do with elite concerns about higher achievements of the *civilisation* as with the well-being of the *people.* As I stated in the introduction, one should be aware of the mood-dependence and deliberately provocative nature of some aspects of my thought and work, especially the misanthropic and elitist passages. I have based my misanthropic elitism largely on the evolutionary principle of *variation* as stated in the following verse from *No Sure Ground.*

To small avail I fear their nurture
Though clearly hides some grain this chaff
We are all seeds of variation
Most good for feed, for fodder, raff

Hereditary myths, elitism and consumerism

Of course many will argue that I over-emphasise *nature* in the nature versus nurture debate. Perhaps I do, but this is partly a reaction to the downplaying of nature (to almost taboo status) in liberal debate over the last few decades. Indeed the rather Marxian orientated scientist authors of a book entitled *Not in Our Genes,*[129] note that the "post-1968 New Left in Britain and the United States has shown a tendency to see human nature as almost infinitely plastic, to deny biology and acknowledging only social construction". In fact I largely agree with the complementary approach of these authors, my main point of contention being their naive materialist metaphysics. It is worth recalling here my view on gender-based differences in mental capacities expressed in verse in Section VII.

Prophecy self-fulfilling beckons
When the schoolteacher then forgets
These differences but norms, statistics
Not essences by nature set

Although I see myself as having acquired part of my 'brahmanical' mental disposition through heredity, my equally hereditary *brāhmaṇa* brothers are most certainly not my 'true brahmans'; variation has seen to that. The principle of variation is also implicit in the following verse from *No Sure Ground* which is clearly anti-hereditarian:

> The noblemen born of nobodies
> Like grinder of the glass for lenses
> Shine forth in the polished reflection
> Which shortlived surface filth soon cleanses

My snobbery is intellectual snobbery; this outsider's 'true brethren' are, as I state six verses on from the one above, "Beyond the bonds of blood and nation". Despite my emphasis on variation over heredity, I disagree somewhat with those who pose questions like, how many Einsteins were lost picking cotton in the Deep South,[130] or, how many Ramanujans lie hidden amongst the poverty-stricken masses of India.[131] Of course a few geniuses are likely to be found amongst any large number of people according to a simple model of genetic variation but, in the above two hypothetical cases involving mathematical genius, I would answer that the actual answer is likely to be few if any at all. Closer examination of the 'nobodies' into whose families the great minds are born usually reveals at least a tradition of learning and a degree of heredity in producing them; the variation in question tends to be fortuitous combinations of already manifest traits amongst the offspring of the intelligent, rather than random variation in the population at large. Our heredity is a temporal 'greater being' helping form the warp and the woof of our existence and the final passage of *Bonds of Kinship* stresses hereditary influences upon me. I am well aware of the fact that, especially in the past, education was only available to a privileged elite. I see myself as a philosopher born into a hereditary caste which was supposed to produce 'philosopher-priests', and my very surname is a hereditary title conferred upon a brahman of great learning acquired by one of my ancestors.

The verse cited above refers to Spinoza, the Sephardic Jew whose anonymously published *Tractatus Theologico-Politicus* undermined the French Church which provided the metaphysical sustenance for the *ancien régime*.[132] However, the *philosophes,* who continued this assault on the Catholic Church, and are remembered as the creators of the Enlightenment and ideological precursors of the Revolution that smashed the aristocracy, were largely from the French nobility itself. Of course many intelligent people are trapped by the circumstances of birth into underprivileged groups and it is in any nation's interest to try to make full use of its human resources. The traditional restrictions of caste may have had some utility in the organisation of civil society thousands of years ago but are of little or no value in the modern world. Caste restrictions on occupations would, as Weber noted, have hindered bourgeois developments in India even if other factors had been favourable. I do believe in attempting to provide meritocratic opportunities for all, one Einstein is worth more than all the royalty and privileged hangers-on, the mediocre brandishing their parents' famous surnames etc. who fill the glossy magazines which captivate the crowd. But even if we could achieve a true meritocracy, the result, as Michael Young noted[133] would probably be that those at the top and those at the bottom would gravitate towards even more rigid classes, and greater social polarization as each would believe, if it was a meritocratic system, that they deserved to be where they were in the hierarchy. We have to shift from the rigid conceptual structures favoured by the Western Enlightenment to the more fluid mental structures which recognise the world as a constantly changing (*'saṃsāric'*) process.

> No system stands upon these pebbles
> No plodding logic stands the heat
> To stand upright we must be nimble
> With no sure ground beneath our feet

The classless society is an idealistic notion which tends to mask the underlying social structures highlighting the success stories of a privileged few from the underprivileged groups whilst the rest still languish in relative poverty. Part of the success in maintaining the stability of open government systems like the British and the post-Independence Indian 'politics of accommodation' has been through the embourgeoisement or co-option of aspirant sections of disaffected groups, 'creaming' off the talent. Many of the middle class 'trendy' Left in the West, who live very comfortably and seek all the advantages for their children, live very uncomfortably with their public pronouncements, just as the puritanical Victorian moralisers did a century ago. I am reminded of the song called *Working Class Hero* by John Lennon which includes the lines: 'You think you're so clever and classless and free; But you're still f...ing peasants as I far as I can see'.

I feel submerged in tides of progress
This cultural diktat of the proles
These great great grandchildren of peasants
Transmigrate not their peasant souls

This verse, at first sight, may seem to indicate a straightforward hereditarian view of class but this would be far too simple an interpretation. The verse laments the failure of the urban masses of modern society to develop a more elevated culture in keeping with their increased level of education rather than the urbanised, modernised, multiculturalised, consumerised forms of degenerate, mindless culture which one would pejoratively label 'peasant' culture in keeping with the lack of education in traditional peasant societies. This is perhaps most unfair to traditional peasant societies where opportunities for uplifting themselves did not exist and I myself am very fond of traditional folk music etc. from many societies which might be labelled 'peasant societies'. This verse was meant as a deliberately provocative attack on the lower forms of Western popular culture and 'lifestyle', and the 'inverted snobbery' of its loudmouthed exponents who spew out drivel demeaning anyone who does not conform to their lowest common denominator herd mentality. It is not difficult to see in the imprudent, vulgar, loutish behaviour of the urban masses the modern manifestation of 'low culture' found in all ages amongst those whose minds have not been deeply impressed with the stamp of civilisation (one aspect of the 'order old' remaining beneath the 'sleek veneer of Progress'. In the introduction, I compared today's 'rave' gatherings with the drug-crazed frenzies of tribal peoples. In *Rashtra is My Word for Nation*, I draw the parallel between the popular idol-worshipping form of Hinduism (*bhakti*) with the popular culture of the modern West.

Not born or bred for world of *baniās*
Jñānamārga, path I follow
Quaker to my cohorts, legion
In false idols bhakti wallow

Although both involve the worship of cult figures by poorly educated or uneducated people (Christianity, the Cult of Christ, began this way, appealing to the simple masses), it is perhaps unfair to *bhakti* in that, at least within the perspective of the better educated, *bhakti* is the worship of *Brahman* in a symbolic form which the uneducated mind can easily come to terms with. In contrast, much of popular Western culture is imbued with the hidden hand of mass marketing or is almost totally vacuous, cult of youth nonsense. The idolization of actors, the extreme case of the glorification of the media, reflects the emphasis on image over substance, medium over message, mathematical symbols over Spirit. Today's Western culture, at a more sophisticated level tends to take the the latest fashionable ideas from popularised science, such as Chaos theory as the Ultimate Reality (Science itself idolizes image over substance; symbols over Spirit) and 'High Technology' and Sex as gods. Of course, entertainment or sport, does not need some spiritual or 'uplifting' *raison d'être* to justify it, but when the masses know nothing more than 'circuses' then it is rather disturbing, both from the point of view of individual development (*bildung,* see Section IV), especially given the West's self-proclaimed championing of the individual, and also from the collective perspective, as the underdevelopment of their minds does not bode well in regard to long-term socio-economic consequences.

Many of the West's 'less civilised' folk, will rant and rave about the greedy 'rich' people who vote for the conservative political parties without considering the fact that many of today's 'rich' people, the middle classes whom the 'squatter types' perceive as 'rich,' were the prudent poor who sacrificed in the past in order to build for the future. When I talk of the New Age, I am aware of the negative associations this sometimes elicits. I cringe at the thought that the British media uses the term 'New Age travellers' for some gypsy-style counter-cultural drop-outs who periodically hit the headlines by causing a nuisance, usually by trespassing, in rural areas. As I have stated above, it is the very imprudent lifestyle of hyper-individualistic hedonism that places extra burdens on the welfare systems, transmits countless problems to future generations and, through degradation of the cultural/educational standards, weakens the economic prowess of the society and its ability to sustain the welfare system. One looks at the degenerates racing around dangerously in high performance motor cars, proud of their possession of such lurid vehicles. How little such morons know of what it takes to produce a society capable of successfully producing the various technological gadgets which they so cherish. A society full of such degenerates would be as able to build motor cars as the Mughals were able to build cannon; unless they were simply used as cheap labour for some foreign corporation's assembly plant. I saw a television programme contrasting a recent American advertisement broadcast at Thanksgiving with one produced during the McCarthy era. I think that the intention was for the viewers to cringe at the moralising tone of the 1950s broadcast whilst finding the recent broadcast mildly amusing. The recent advertisement had a black American family dressed like the Pilgrim Fathers, wildly dancing and singing in rap style as they prepared for Thanksgiving dinner in order to advertise some gimmicky basketball shoes. In contrast, the 1950s broadcast, sponsored by some association, showed a couple of children, unhappy that they were not having the full traditional Thanksgiving dinner that year being given a sermon by their working class father as to why they should be thankful (after all it was Thanksgiving) for all the material benefits that their society had provided for them. This year, the family's finances were strained and the father could not afford a proper Thanksgiving celebration. For all the wrongdoings of the McCarthy witch-hunt in the USA (including the blacklisting of David Bohm for his refusal to testify against Oppenheimer), I for one much preferred the 1950s moralising broadcast to the trashy basketball shoes advertisement. We hear of street crime committed by gangs who seek to acquire the brand name status symbols of hyper-materialism such as the same gimmicky basketball shoes mentioned above, including murder for a pair of such shoes!

This image-over-substance culture of rampant materialism is, of course, inculcated by the advertising industry presenting its infantile, lurid images of how successful people are supposed to behave. The same image-over-substance culture leads to the perception that working in something as shallow as advertising is glamorous and confers high status. Presumably, those devoid of real talents in some truly creative art can find satisfaction in the role of medium whereas a truly gifted person can only find satisfaction in the role of creator. As the verse in *No Sure Ground* indicates, the so-called 'pursuit of happiness' tends to be a *conditioned*, socially acceptable state of being which has at least as much to do with the herd mentality and the need for acceptance as it has with actual satisfaction. Higher aspirations or those not fitting the consumerist, cult of youth lifestyle tend to be frowned on or derided and thus avoided by those who are not secure in themselves, which accounts for the vast majority. As I note in the verse, even conscience has become a marketable commodity, with charity often becoming more a matter of socially acceptable image rather than serious concern.

> Now conscience sold within a package
> And fashion dictates what to buy
> Exotic flavours, Third World problems
> Packaged outrage, *City of Joy*

No doubt, the raising of serious issues is to be applauded even if the motives and actual understanding of broader issues by the counter-culture brigades, advertisers and others is questionable.

Many 'successful' people are so indoctrinated into the shallow culture of consumerism, with its ostentatious displays of wealth and constant search for superficial novelty, that they set an appalling example as to how to behave. A few may be saved by the call from within known as the mid-life crisis but many are so deeply implicated in this deluded world of poseurs, with its live-for-the-moment, sense gratification values, that they spiral ever deeper into the abyss of corruption to maintain their social prestige through wealth or they turn to drugs to achieve new 'kicks', or they seek some other unsustainable means of maintaining the impetus of material 'fulfillment', the 'pursuit of happiness'.

It is often the children of the middle classes (in Britain given a free university education) who come out of college trapped in the underdeveloped mind associated with student culture with its largely infantile rejection of the 'bourgeois' values of their parents and grandparents which actually helped to build the very institutions giving the children of the middle classes free tertiary education at the expense of the entire nation. Of course, the state has to play an 'enabling' role providing opportunities open to everyone. In today's debates about 'society' and the rights of everyone within the society it is worth remembering that civil society was imposed upon the masses by the more intelligent, prudent and, according to most legends, mystically inspired members of the populations at the birth of civilisation. Humans are not born with an inherent disposition towards civilised behaviour. The modern middle classes have created social institutions in their own image, reflecting their values; although everyone should have equality of access to progress through these institutions and negative features of these institutions' traditions should be eliminated, society can only maintain its stability and prosperity by building upon the positive values inherent within the tradition. The tyranny of the infantile masses leads only to chaos and decline.

American cultural imperialism and India's strategies interests

It is not without good reason that I state in *Bande Mātaram:*

> Progress I greet with reservations
> New power for those long kept down
> But fear their dreams to me a nightmare
> Culture Cola on which I frown

American 'cultural imperialism' threatens to plant the virus of American decadence, born of relative prosperity, New World rootlessness, hyper-materialism, colonial settler gun-toting, the vengeful bitterness of ex-slaves and other such factors into an India which, to rise out of poverty, requires a sense of mission and destiny in order to encourage a degree of sacrifice amongst its citizens to serve the higher cause, the well-being of the Nation. As I stated above, the *Nation* is not to be simply identified with the *people* but also includes the *civilisation.* The wellbeing of the Nation is not a simple utilitarian identification with the material condition of the people although this is the most important component, especially as the Nation is partly the Self-writ-large and the state of the Nation reflects upon one's own self-esteem. Of course the improvement of the material wellbeing of the people must involve the mass production and consumption of consumer goods and this is intimately linked to economic growth and development. There is a Chinese proverb that an *intelligent* people learn from their mistakes whereas a *wise* people learn from other peoples' mistakes. The over-individualistic, live-for-the-moment, image conscious, consumerist, fickle, immature youth-like pursuits of supposed happiness of Western popular culture are wholly inappropriate for a society plagued by mass poverty, overpopulation, tremendous inequalities and countless other burdens. It is neither clever, nor sophisticated to ape the lowest common denominator culture of the West, this is the culture associated with societal decline. Just as we would not accept the dumping of toxic waste in our land, we must guard against such pernicious influences. Of course, with the growth of satellite television controlled by foreign media magnates etc. this will be a difficult task. As modernisation progresses, mass pressure will continue to create more lucrative markets for the purveyors of pernicious, puerile pop culture which will inevitably appeal to the majority like the cheap idolatry of old. No one has ever lost money *underestimating* the intelligence of the public said a man involved with the *National Enquirer*, a US magazine full of modern fairy stories. Market pressure will lead to high technology being squandered on low ends and medical research efforts wasted on the diseases of the rich whilst the masses continue to die from preventable diseases. Like it or not, the way forward to national 'greatness' involves a degree of civilising authoritarianism in order to build for the future rather than live for the moment and die in misery, unable to cope with the burdens of old age, cursing offspring with economic, psychological and educational deficiencies so as to perpetuate the blight on society. The *Nation* is also a substitute for a personal god and as such demands sacrifices.

The good of the Nation cannot be served by succumbing to fashionable Western views of society, politics, Humanism, Nature etc. thrust upon us by the Western media. A successful, sustainable system must be grounded on Realism, not wishful thinking. The long-term good of the people, will almost certainly require short-term curtailments of certain liberties which simply cannot be taken for granted as if they were God-given rights. The liberal West's tendency to romanticise the plight of our poverty-stricken underclasses as simple victims of an elitist system, absolving them of any responsibility, must not deter us from using sticks as well as carrots to deal with problems of overpopulation. Given the need for scientific and technical knowledge, managerial and business skills to succeed in the modern world we have to accept a degree of elitism in our educational system to ensure we have skilled people. We have to accept that, given the current socio-economic situation, those born into privileged groups are going to be much better placed to pursue the activities which can bring a much improved level of prosperity to the entire nation in the long run, allowing for more equal systems of enablement and opportunity in the future. Just as a reliance on trickle down economics would be bad for the nation, so too is the Maoist-Naxalite anti-elitism of the poorly educated masses; a little learning is a dangerous thing. A civilisation aspiring to greatness must impose an 'uplifting' set of values upon the masses. It is the duty of those born into privilege or blessed with talents to gear their own 'good' as much as possible with that of the nation, and it is the duty of the state to facilitate this.

Culturally, Indians must aspire to creating the highest standard of work in every field, from engineering to entertainment, and not be satisfied with cheap, shoddy, imitative produce. Imitation can be for the good, as Bankim noted, but we must also be wary of the negative consequences flowing from the transplantation of artefacts (including cultural artefacts) which have evolved in alien societies for alien purposes (the 'social gene' effects). Of course in some economic activities the market encourages excellence but where the market threatens the best interests of the nation, the state should not hesitate to intervene. A frame of mind that does not aspire to appreciating sophisticated culture which requires a degree of discipline and effort in order to actually appreciate and enjoy it is not a frame of mind that aspires to world-leading excellence in the technological and economic realms. Let us remember the popular expression of the Neo-Hindu Synthesis of East and West which lies at the heart of Indian Nationalist ideology; to take the best from both civilisations and to discard the rubbish.

Prelude to the metaphysical essay

I began this work with the following quotation from Eusebius relating to the encounter between India and Europe:

> *Aristoxenus the musician tells the following story about the Indians. One of the men met Socrates at Athens, and asked him what was the scope of his philosophy. "An inquiry into human phenomena," replied Socrates. At this the Indian burst out laughing. "How can we grasp human phenomena," he exclaimed, "when we are ignorant of the Divine ?".*

No Sure Ground ends with an invitation to look beyond your conventional views, your convictions in this or that theory or system and dance upon the red hot 'pebbles' of Reality, the 'bubbling broth of contradictions', where logic is of little use, upon which the intellect cannot stand for more than a momentary, insightful glimpse. The verse then leaves human affairs and looks at metaphysical questions. These metaphysical questions and the ramifications that have arisen from them in my own thought whilst writing these essays shall be the subject-matter of the following essay. As the Indian told Socrates, we cannot consider human affairs in isolation, we must seek the bigger, deeper picture. We have seen how a naïve, false materialist metaphysics of historical progress like Marxism can captivate the minds of millions of well-educated people. All human social thought is grounded upon a metaphysical base. When I chose the quotation from Eusebius in early 1993, my intention was to show that the cross-fertilisation of Indian and European thought had been going on even in ancient times. I had only the vaguest notion of what was meant by the Divine, and I was not totally happy with linking Indian thought in general to such words. Now, as I have made the connection between Science and Mysticism by identifying the physical correlate of the Divine Light, I have begun to appreciate the nature of the Divine as has long been known to all societies in one or another form of the so-called Perennial Philosophy. It was as if the quotation was chosen for me in order for me to fulfil this project. For those who wonder what Indian civilisation with its ancient hymns and aphorisms has to offer which can stand alongside the great achievements of modern science, the answer will become clear. Where the limited abstract models developed by modern science break down into paradoxes, silence and outright denial of evidence by scientists, we begin to obtain glimpses of the bigger, deeper picture beyond the limited focus of materialism. This greater picture allows us to begin to resolve the confusing paradoxes that Science has conjured up through its relative approaches. This greater picture is basically the core truth behind the various attempts to come to terms with it in various yogic traditions. As Indian civilisation flowers again after over a thousand years in the doldrums, it is the modernisation of the yogic knowledge of the bigger, deeper picture of Reality that stands as the great metaphysical task before us. All that I can hope to do is sketch the overall outlines of this bigger, deeper picture, showing why indeed it is the way forward in our understanding of Reality where Science has failed. To those steeped in the world-view of modernity with a firm belief in the universality of Science and a distrust of anything to do with mysticism, and especially those with a subliminal racial contempt for Eastern thought, what follows in the next essay will come as a shock. Eleven years after I had, as an eighteen-year-old boy, abandoned materialism for my own inchoate panpsychism (ignorant of the relationships to the Perennial Philosophy), the realization that dawned upon me when everything 'fell into place' still came as a tremendous shock. I will not make things more tolerable by writing in the manner expected of a Western philosopher or scientist by avoiding the subjective factors and mystical influences surrounding the development of my ideas. These are all relevant to the 'whole picture' I am presenting. This is not to say that I will not give logical arguments and empirical and scientific evidence supporting my work where appropriate. To those accustomed to the plodding logic of Western philosophy, I ask you to dance, and I ask you to suspend your judgements until you have considered all that I have to say.

REFERENCES

1. Marx, K. (1853) *The Future Results of British Rule in India.*
2. Kejariwal, O.P. (1988) *The Asiatic Society of Bengal and the Discovery of India's Past: 1784-1838.* Oxford U.P.

3. Chaudhuri, N.C. (1987) *The Autobiography of an Unknown Indian*. The Hogarth Press. (Originally published in 1951).
4. Feuerstein, G., Kak, S. and Frawley, D. (1995) *In Search of the Cradle of Civilization: New Light on Ancient India*. Quest Books.
5. Joseph, G.G. (1991) *The Crest of the Peacock: Non-European Roots of Mathe matics*. Penguin.
6. Cited in Young, R. (1990) *White Mythologies: Writing History and the West*. Routledge.
7. Inden, R. (1990) *Imagining India*. Blackwell.
8. Marx, K. (1853) *The British Rule in India*. Reprinted in Feuer, L.S. (1969) *Marx and Engels: Basic Writings on Politics and Philosophy*. Fontana.
9. Nandy, A. (1992) *Traditions, Tyrannies and Utopias*. Oxford U.P.
10. Naipaul, V.S. (1979) *India: A Wounded Civilisation*. Penguin.
11. Dutta, K. and Robinson, A. (1995) *Rabindranath Tagore: The Myriad-Minded Man*. Bloomsbury.
12. Stokes, E. (1959) *The English Utilitarians and India*. Oxford U.P.
13. Apel, K.-O. (1991) A Planetary Macroethics for Humankind: The Need, the Apparent Difficulty, and the Eventual Possibility. In Deutsch, E. (Ed.) *Culture and Modernity: East-West Philosophic Perspectives*. University of Hawaii Press.
14. Jacobs, M.C. (1976) *The Newtonians and the English Revolution 1689-1720*. Cornell U.P.
15. Nanda, B.R. (1985) *Gandhi and his Critics*. Oxford U.P.
16. Omisi, D. Baghdad and the British Bombers. *The Guardian*. (London) 19th January 1991. Based on Omisi's *Air Power and Colonial Control: The Royal Air Force 1919-1939*. Manchester U.P.
17. *ibid*.
18. *Gengis Khan*. Channel 4 Television. 1990.
19. Singham, A.W. and Hune, S. (1986) *Non-Alignment in an Age of Alignments*. Zed Books.
20. Hosking, G. (1985) *A History of the Soviet Union*. Fontana.
21. Singham and Hune (1986) *ibid*.
22. Nandy, A. (1983) *The Intimate Enemy: Loss and Recovery of Self Under Colonialism*. Oxford U.P.
23. Nanda, B.R. (1985) *ibid*.
24. *Women's Hour Special*. BBC Radio 4. December 1993.
25. Embree, A. (1989) *Imagining India: Essays on Indian History*. Oxford U.P.
26. Bhattacharya, S. and Redondi, P. (Eds) (1990) *Techniques to Technology: A French Historiography of Technology*. Orient Longman.
27. Huxley, A. (1956) Knowledge and Understanding. *Vedanta and the West*. Reprinted in Bridgeman, J.H. (1992) *Huxley and God: Essays*. Harper Collins.
28. Kumar, K. (1978) *Prophecy and Progress: The Sociology of Industrial and Post-Industrial Society*. Allen Lane.
29. Dutta and Robinson (1995) *ibid*.
30. Liddle, J. and Joshi, R. (1986) *Daughters of Independence: Gender, Caste and Class in India*. Zed and Kali for Women.
31. Barua, B. P. (Ed.) (1988) *Raja Rammohun Roy and the New Learning: (Raja Rammohun Roy Memorial Lectures)* Sangam/Orient Longman.
32. *The Double Helix*. BBC Television. *c*.1993.
33. Nandy, A. (1994) *The Illegitimacy of Nationalism: Rabindranath Tagore and the Politics of the Self*. Oxford U.P.

34. Frankel, F.R. and Rao, M.S.A. (Eds) (1989) *Dominance and State Power in Modern India: Decline of a Social Order*. Volume 1. Oxford U.P.
35. Brass, P.R. (1990) *The New Cambridge History of India. IV.1. The Politics of India Since Independence.* Cambridge U.P.
36. Frankel and Rao (1989) *ibid.*
37. Nandy, A. (1992) *ibid.*
38. Jacobs, M.C. (1976) *ibid.*
39. Desmond, A. and Moore, J. (1991) *Darwin*. Michael Joseph.
40. Musson, A.E. and Robinson, E. (1969) *Science and Technology in the Industrial Revolution*. Curtis Brown.
41. Nandy, A. (1988) Introduction: Science as a Reason of State. In Nandy, A. (Ed.) *Science, Hegemony and Violence: A Requiem for Modernity*. The United Nations University and Oxford U.P.
42. Huxley, A. (1960) Some Reflections on Time. *Vedanta and the West*. Reprinted in Bridgeman, J.H. (1992) Huxley and God: Essays. Harper Collins.
43. Hixon, L. (1992) *Great Swan: Meetings with Ramakrishna*. Shambhala.
44. Nandy, (1992) *T.T.&U.*
45. Rorty, R.L. (1991) Philosophers, Novelists and Intercultural Comparisons: Heidegger, Kundera and Dickens. In Deutsch, E. (Ed.) *Culture and Modernity*.
46. Fanon, F. (1967) *The Wretched of the Earth*. Penguin.
47. Musson and Robinson (1969) ibid.
48. Alvares, C. (1979) *Homo faber:* Technology and Culture in India, China and the West 1500-1792. Allied Publishers.
49. Sen, A. (1990) How is India Doing? In Chaudhury, R.A., Gamkhar, S. and Ghose, A. (Eds) *The Indian Economy and its Performance Since Independence.* Oxford U.P.
50. Morris, J. (1973) *Heaven's Command: An Imperial Progress*. Faber and Faber.
51. Richard Becher (1769) Cited in Embree, A. (1989)ibid. and Liddle and Joshi (1986)ibid.
52. Embree, A. (1989) *ibid.*
53. Charlesworth, N. (1982) *British Rule and the Indian Economy 1800-1914.* MacMillan.
54. Marx, K. (1853). *The British Rule in India*. Reprinted in Feuer, L.S. (1969) *Marx and Engels: Basic Writings on Politics and Philosophy*. Fontana.
55. Marx, K. (1853) *ibid.*
56. Cited in Liddle and Joshi (1986).
57. Duncan, P.J.S. (1989) *The Soviet Union and India*. Royal Institute of International Affairs and Routledge.
58. *ibid.*
59. Kiernan, V.G. (1978) *America: The New Imperialism. From White Settlement to World Hegemony*. Zed.
60. Morris, J. (1973) *ibid.*
61. Kiernan, V.G. (1978) *ibid.*
62. *Timewatch*. BBC Television. 29th October 1992.
63. Cited in Nandy, A. (1992) *T.T.&U.*
64. Dutta and Robinson (1995) *ibid.*
65. Heehs, P. (1989) *Sri Aurobindo: A Brief Biography*. Oxford U.P.
66. *Timewatch*. BBC Television. 1991.
67. Bose, M. (1982) *The Lost Hero: A Biography of Subhas Bose*. Quartet.
68. *ibid.*

69. Bernal, M. (1987) *Black Athena: The Afro-Asiatic Roots of Classical Civilization.* Free Association Books.
70. Moore, W. (1989) *Schrödinger: Life and Thought.* Cambridge U.P. cited in Kak, S.C. (1997) *Indian J. History of Science* 32 (2): 105-120.
71. Dutta and Robinson (1995) *ibid.*
72. Halbfass, W. (1988) *India and Europe.* Indian Edition. (1990) Motilal Banarsidass.
73. Weber, R. (1981) The *Tao of Physics* Revisited: A Conversation with Fritjof Capra. Article reprinted in Wilber, K. (Ed.) (1982) *The Holographic Paradigm and Other Paradoxes.* Shambhala. Also a full interview between Capra and Heisenberg in Capra, F. (1988) *Uncommon Wisdom: Conversations with Remarkable People.* Century Hutchison.
74. Ellison, A.J. (1987) Western Science and Religious Experience. In Singh, T.D. (Ed.) *Synthesis of Science and Religion: Critical Essays and Dialogues.* The Bhaktivedanta Institute.
75. Weber, R. (1986) *Dialogues with Scientists and Sages: The Search for Unity.* Routledge and Kegan Paul.
76. Josephson, B.D. (1987) Science and Religion: How to Make the Synthesis? In Singh, T.D. (Ed.) In Singh, T.D. (Ed.) *Synthesis of Science and Religion.*
77. Wald, G. (1987) The Cosmology of Life and Mind. In Singh, T.D. (Ed.) *Synthesis of Science and Religion.*
78. Wald, G. *ibid.*
79. Barrow, J.D. and Tipler, F.J. (1986) *The Anthropic Cosmological Principle.* Oxford U.P.
80. Dutta and Robinson (1995) *ibid.*
81. Halbfass, W. (1988) *ibid.*
82. Parthasarathi, G. and Chattopadhyay, D.P. (Eds) (1989) *Radhakrishnan: Centenary Volume.* Oxford U.P.
83. Deutsch, E. (1991) (ed.) *Culture and Modernity: East-West Philosophic Perspectives.* University of Hawaii Press.
84. Raychaudhuri, T. (1988) *Europe Reconsidered: Perceptions of the West in 19th Century Bengal.* Oxford U.P.
85. Dutta and Robinson (1995) *ibid.*
86. Bridgeman, J.H. (1992) *Huxley and God: Essays.* Harper Collins.
87. Hixon, L. (1992) *ibid.*
88. Harvey, A. (1991) *Hidden Journey: A Spiritual Awakening.*
89. Kejariwal, O.P. (1988) *ibid.*
90. *ibid.*
91. Cited in Dutta and Robinson (1985) *ibid.*
92. Cited in Kripalini, K. (1988) Rammohun Roy and Mahatma Gandhi. In Barua, B.P. (Ed.) *Raja Rammohun Roy and the New Learning.*
93. Marshall, P.J. (1987) *The New Cambridge History of India. II.2. Bengal: The British Bridgehead. Eastern India 1740-1828.* Cambridge U.P.
94. *ibid.*
95. *ibid.*
96. Sen, A.P. (1993) *Hindu Revivalism in Bengal:* 1872-1905. Oxford U.P.
97. Isayeva, N. (1993) *Shankara and Indian Philosophy.* State University of New York Press.
98. Jones, K.W. (1989) *The New Cambridge History of India. III.1. Socio-Religious Reform Movements in British India.* Cambridge U.P.
99. Nandy, A. (1983) *ibid.* based on Morris, J. (1973) *ibid.*

100. Dasgupta, R.K. (1988) Rammohun Roy and the New Learning. In Barua, B.P. (Ed) *Raja Rammohun Roy and the New Learning.*
101. Mohanty, J.N. (1993) *Essays on Indian Philosophy: Traditional and Modern.* Oxford U.P.
102. Hixon, L. (1992) *ibid.*
103. *ibid.*
104. Cited in Stokes, E. (1959) *ibid.*
105. Morris, J. (1979) *ibid.*
106. Dasgupta, R.K. (1988) *ibid.*
107. Chatterjee, P. (1986) *Nationalist Thought and the Colonial World: A Derivative Discourse.* United Nations University and Zed.
108. Cited in Halbfass, W. (1988) *ibid.*
109. Stokes, E. (1959) *ibid.*
110. *ibid.*
111. Kohli, A. (1987) *The State and Poverty in India: The Politics of Reform.* Cambridge U.P.
112. Ray, R.K. *Social Conflict and Political Unrest in Bengal: 1875-1927.* Oxford U.P.
113. *ibid.*
114. Heehs, P, (1993) *The Bomb in Bengal: The Rise of Revolutionary Terrorism in India 1900-1910.* Oxford U.P.
115. *Tales of the Raj.* BBC Television. *c.*1982.
116. Nossiter, T.J. (1988). *Marxist State Governments in India: Politics, Economy and Society.* Pinter.
117. 'Navajata' (1972) *Sri Aurobindo.* National Book Trust of India.
118. Nandy, A. (1994) *ibid.*
119. Heehs, P. (1993) *ibid.*
120. Bose, M. (1982) *ibid.*
121. Cited in Ray, R.K. (1983) *ibid.*
122. Best, G. (Ed.) (1988) *The Permanent Revolution: The French Revolution and its Legacy.* Fontana.
123. Ray, R. (1988) *The Naxalites and their Ideology.* Oxford U.P.
124. Duncan, P.J.S. (1989) *ibid.*
125. Gorbachev, M.S. (1987) *Perestroika: New Thinking for Our Country and the World.* William Collins.
126. Cited in a dramatised documentary based on the diaries of a British diplomat living in Meiji Japan. *Timewatch.* BBC Television. c.1992.
127. Kumar, K. (1978) *ibid.*
128. Amin, S. (1989) *Eurocentrism.* Zed.
129. Rose, S., Lewontin, R.C. and Kamin, L.J. (1984) *Not in Our Genes: Biology, Ideology and Human Nature.* Pantheon.
130. Gould, S.J. (c.1985) *The Mismeasure of Man.* Penguin.
131. Kanigel, R. (1991) *The Man Who Knew Infinity: A Life of the Genius Ramanujan.* Scribners.
132. O'Brien, C.C. (1988) Nationalism and the French Revolution. In Best, G. (Ed.) *The Permanent Revolution.*
133. Young, M. (1961) *The Rise of the Meritocracy.* Penguin.
134. Clarke, J.J. (1994) *Jung and Eastern Thought: A dialogue with the Orient.* Routledge.

THE ONENESS/OTHERNESS MYSTERY

One has the feeling that the thinkers of the East knew it all, and if we could only translate their answers into our language we would have the answers to all our questions.

John A. Wheeler

PART ONE
My Path to the Light

MY METAPHYSICAL THOUGHT UP TO 1994

It has been one and a half years since I finished the rest of this work. Things have changed quite a lot since then. I have begun to discover the metaphysical validity of the Perennial Philosophy about which I had been unsure as it was not clear to me how phenomenological experiences could yield such profound metaphysical revelations. The year 1996 has been a traumatic year in which my mother, who had only recently taken early retirement after a lifetime of self-sacrificing struggle, has been diagnosed with Parkinson's Disease thus spoiling her retirement and seriously affecting my work. The sense of fulfilment after years of struggle which I felt in late 1994 and 1995 has been severely eroded, sapping my self-confidence, my hope in some transcendent sense of justice and affecting my ability to absorb myself in the philosophical questions posed by this work. Perhaps there is some transcendental meaningfulness behind the fact that crisis struck just as I was ready to start this essay, forcing my mind to realise the importance of the mundane activities which I usually ignored, and also the importance of love, belief, prayer and the possibility of healing.

My journey towards the completion of this work begins perhaps at age twelve in 1977 when I read a translation of the *Bhagavad Gītā* and encountered the notion of God as the underlying ground of all things although at that time I only grasped it in a simple pantheistic sense that all was God. It came to me as a profoundly inspirational insight at the time even though I could hardly contemplate the full significance. With time this notion was pushed deep into the background of my thought, almost forgotten, as I began to acquire knowledge from Science and Western philosophy.

My teenage encounters with metaphysics

I recall two incidents from my fifth form at secondary school (age sixteen) which indicate that such concerns were still occupying me as I began to specialize in Science. Both occurred just before I was about to take my first public examinations when thoughts of the future were prominent in my mind. A teacher of French stopped the class during one lesson and asked me what I wanted to do when I grew up. I answered him with some vague talk about propounding the Vedānta. In fact I had very little idea as to what was meant by the word Vedānta; I had only picked it up from a little book about Swami Vivekānanda which my mother had brought back from India a few months earlier. For reasons unknown to my normal self, the very word "Vedānta", especially with the nationalistic connotations given to it by Vivekānanda, had captivated me and I felt a powerful resonance with it even though I had little idea what it referred to. At about the same time, the school headmaster, who taught Religious Education (RE) supervised my class in the absence of our teacher. He had taught my class in the second year (age 12-13) and had considered me to be the star pupil in RE. Both this headmaster and the other RE teacher had made pronouncements to my class, back in the second year (when we started RE lessons) to the effect that I was 'spiritually' more advanced than my classmates, nearly all of whom were Europeans (including a high proportion of Jews). Now, whilst supervising my class in the fifth year, he opened his enquiry into how our thoughts had advanced since he last taught us by asking me what I now thought in regard to religious matters. I spoke about what I had picked up from books like the *Gītā* and Vivekānanda's speeches, restating ideas I had imbibed about God as 'spiritual energy' which was somehow present in every man. My words elicited a very favourable response from the headmaster who spoke about how he too was still learning about these matters and how one never stopped learning. However, my words provoked a sarcastic response from an English boy with a very stereotypical English middle class character, who, although very friendly towards me generally, thought that such talk of 'spiritual energy' was outright nonsense, a fanciful idea with no evidence to support it. (Indeed, in 1994 when I tried to explain my work to a work colleague, a physics graduate who was something of a pariah due to his staunch support for the Tory party and British nationalistic views (who collected militaria and supposedly sang along to "Land of Hope and Glory" at the end of Tory party conferences on television), by mentioning books like *The Tao of Physics,* this young man replied along the lines that physics was correct and Eastern mysticism was a load of rubbish.)

I should also mention that at age 15-16 years we were taught basic Newtonian physics. I could never come to terms with this system of thought. Notions of a world constituted of billiard balls bouncing off each other simply did not make sense to my intuitions and I never managed to master Newtonian physics as I simply could not picture reality in this way. Another factor was that I was not as good at mathematics as some of the boys, a few of whom went on to get Firsts in maths at Cambridge. Being in the top sets in maths and sciences with these boys, I noticed that outstanding academic achievement in maths and physics seemed to require one to use up so much 'brain-space' for the symbol manipulations that these boys could not develop other mental faculties. Most of them seemed to lack creative imagination as evident in their minds going blank when asked to think up a storyline in English lessons. I recall one expressing surprise that the scientific knowledge that we were being taught was only old theories which had since been superceded. I was well aware of this having received my philosophical education at home where my father had bought the *Encyclopaedia Britannica* when I was eleven, months before he died. Unlike the house, for which my mother had to pay off the uninsured mortgage for a further twenty-one and a half years, the Britannica Company allowed the offspring to keep the books without further repayments if the purchaser died. Thanks to their generosity, I was to encounter the thoughts of Western philosophers from an early age.

My panpsychist theory of 1983

Around April 1983, at the age of eighteen, shortly before I took my final school examinations and put forward my panpsychist theory of consciousness (July 1983), I had been broadening my mind through reading books on general philosophical matters whilst the other boys concentrated on getting good examination grades. I wrote an essay which won its section of a schools' literary competition. It was called *Something to Believe in* and I put the following quotation at its head from the hymn, "When a knight won his spurs":

> *And let me set free with the sword of my youth*
> *From the Castle of Darkness, the power of the Truth*

The opening paragraphs mentioned my "tempestuous marriage of instinctive passion and conditioned reason" sending me "careering through the worlds of subjective and objective knowledge resulting in virtual schizophrenia". It went on to describe my eclectic approach drawn from "Newton's pebbles and the pearls of philosophical insight", never wearing like Patroclus, the seemingly impenetrable armour of any great hero but, taking Alexander Pope's advice, making use of every friend or foe for, "A little learning is a dang'rous thing". I wrote of my early childhood paganism and contemplating the worrying possibility of reincarnation when, as a child, I was unhappy with my lot in life. I wrote that, " I felt special, there was a Jungian synchronicity in my life" and that I came to see my suffering as a "preparation for the tough world which lay ahead of me". The essay continued:

> *At the age of twelve, mainly because it seemed a trendy thing to do, I started to read the 'Bhagavad Gita'. All was one, all was God, it exclaimed; matter was just an illusory temporal manifestation of His energy. This unitary revelation struck a harmonious*

> *chord in my mind, its simple beauty still enchants the homunculi. Meanwhile, my ego had become suspicious and worried over my Lord's failure to deliver and matters related to free will. This eventually culminated in my metamorphosis; I dumped Him as a creation of my mind.*
>
> *Stepping out into the objective world of Science, I adopted biology after reading about how an inanimate virus comes to life. [In fact, I had read this at around age ten.] Here, I thought, was the key to a true understanding of life and, after initial hesitation, I deposed myself from my spiritual throne. I understood how I could be a product of blind cosmic evolution, my body a gene vehicle, my mind an abstract aspect of brain activity. However, I could not accept the blind faith of many a physicist in meaningless fundamental disorder. Surely there had to be a reason for the existence of the cosmos in the first place? On this issue my instinct and logic were accordant. And, if there was this ultimate reason, then it followed that everything in the cosmos had a meaning. I was aware that natural selection had designed my brain to distil order from apparent chaos in order to systematize the world but I found no conclusive evidence for a repudiation of my ultimate meaning in life.*
>
> *I had drifted into the ethereal world of metaphysics which convinced me that I was really a panentheist and not the pantheist I thought I was. I would meditate on the relationship between the conscious mind and the cosmos. The latter seemed to be an unconscious extension of the material human body; perhaps there was a sort of mind pervading the cosmos. Perhaps I was really a panpsychist. I found that most of my ideas had been entertained by the great metaphysicists* [sic] *of the past. My ego assumed that this was because great minds think alike but upon sober reflection realized that all human minds, fundamentally, think alike. The human brain fixed the parameters of human understanding. Metaphysics came to a full-stop in Spinoza's circular reasoning of the 'elementary substance' being a cause unto itself.*
>
> *'The point is to change the world', said Marx, words that sent an aura tingling to my scalp. I had little appetite left for the Buddhistic vegetation of philosophy . . .*

I was soon to 'eat my words'. Although I had been sympathetic to panpsychism in the essay quoted above (I had not been aware of this until I re-read this essay in 1995) and argued that metaphysics was futile, a few months later on July 1st 1983, I began to write entries in a hardbound notebook which I entitled "Certain Philosophical Questions". I had just read Christian mystic Teilhard de Chardin's *The Phenomenon of Man*, a book supposedly inspired by Bergson's creative evolution view. Teilhard wrote that he was fond of Spinoza's view in which mind and matter were, respectively, like the 'inner' and 'outer' attributes of reality. In my first entry in my new notebook on July 1st 1983, I jotted down that I thought that this view was "mystical nonsense". Perhaps Teilhard's Christian anthropocentrism had tended to colour my view of Spinoza through the association in Teilhard's book. A few days later a strange compulsion drove me to the local library to pick up a book, *The Self and Its Brain* by the confused dualists Karl Popper (who also rubbished Spinoza and mysticism for no good reason) and Nobel laureate neurobiologist John Eccles. Suddenly I found myself totally absorbed in the problem of consciousness. On July 9th 1983, I came to the conclusion that it was impossible to construct a physicalist (materialist) model of consciousness as Materialism was fundamentally a false picture of Reality and that the only viable approach to the problem of consciousness lay in Spinoza's basic approach. This realization came by trying to pursue the ramifications of every sort of materialist approach to the problem through in my mind and finding that all of them missed the point. All of them just described patterns of spatio-temporal behaviour with no reference to any awareness. No amount of increasing complexity of spatio-temporal patterns could bring about awareness. No amount of self-reference, emergence etc. could explain the basic issue of how awareness was present if awareness was not a fundamental property of Reality to start with. A critical issue which the materialists ignored was that their supposed 'explanations' for the supposedly unique human consciousness could not be limited to information processing in the human brain. If arguments about emergence etc. were valid then why should consciousness not be present in all emergent processes; the universe was full of them. The materialists simply could not explain what was so special about human brain processes giving them this amazing property of awareness. Those who held to the uniqueness of the human or animal brain process view had only one option, dualism, which only created countless problems without really resolving anything as there was no explanation as to why this dualist realm should come to be associated with only certain brain processes. The only way forward was panpsychism.

However, although it became clear that the only viable approach was panpsychism, it seemed as if this was about all that could be said in this regard. Faced with the questions as to why there was a plurality of individually conscious entities rather than just one universal consciousness and why only certain brain processes seemed to be conscious, I gave up trying to come to terms with such seemingly intractable issues telling myself that these were beyond the capacity of the human mind to comprehend. Having given up exhausted, I went about my normal life for a few days. Then on July 12th 1983 as I sat and watched television, my mind somewhat sedated with antihistamines for my hayfever, I suddenly became aware that entering my mind was a vision of what seemed to me intuitively to be a living neuron. Coupled to this vision was the powerful intuition that this living cell was in itself a sentient entity and that if I developed such ideas, I would arrive at the answer to my earlier seemingly impossible questions. Following this brief experience I was driven by a strong compulsion to look again at a book I had read a few months previously, Jean Piaget's *Structuralism.* With hindsight I recalled that I had been mysteriously drawn to this book when I first read it in the sense that my being seemed to split into two parts as I read the brief description on the back cover. My normal self was interested and intrigued whereas my deeper Self was telling me very strongly that this book was going to be very important for me. However, when I read the book I found it very heavy going, partly due to it being a translation, and I really was not very clear as to what exactly Piaget was getting at. But on July 12th, my deeper Self was insistent that the answer I was looking for was in that book and the book seemed to open where the seeming answer was given. It was early on in the book where Piaget discussed the concept of a 'structure' as an autonomous subunit; a concept derived from mathematical Group theory. The autonomy of the structure was related to the concept of 'closure'. My intuition leapt into action and at once told me how to put together this notion with my vision of the cell and thus came my picture of the nested hierarchy of topologically closed fields within fields with each closed field constituting an individuated sentient entity. *Structuralism* also brought to my attention Gestalt Field theory, which had long gone out of fashion in Anglo-American psychology. I knew that this was a very imperfect picture, just a model which seemed to work, but none the less it seemed fairly self-consistent and capable of providing a viable approach to the understanding of consciousness in a monistic universe. The basic approach which I developed has been given in the poetry and the commentary so I will not repeat it here.

My very immature paper entitled "The Hypothesis of Structural Subjectivity" was sent out to anyone I could think of, not knowing anything about academic philosophy and normal procedures. Very soon afterwards, in August 1983, I received a letter from J.J. Williamson, DSc., President of 'The Society of Metaphysicians' in Hastings, who wrote that "works of this sort are very important indeed if formal science is to extend its frontiers beyond limited frames of reference". Williamson asked to publish it and I readily agreed. Williamson had not realised that it was written by a schoolboy and he asked in his correspondences how parapsychology fitted into the picture. At the time, I was still deeply entrenched in my scientific, rationalist phase, naïvely seeing my work as an extension of Science and holding parapsychology to be irrational nonsense. Even though I knew next to nothing about parapsychology, I replied that, given the problems of information transfer etc., I could not see how parapsychology could exist.

I also received a very positive response from the then editor of *Mind* (the leading academic philosophy journal), D.W. Hamlyn, who was "amazed" that an eighteen-year-old boy had written the paper and he urged me to seek scientific evidence for my vision. Karl Popper replied that I tried to tackle far too many things at once; a specialist's attitude, I wonder what he would have said of this work! His acolyte, Brian Magee, a historian who appeared on television hosting a programme called *Men of Ideas* and who also happened to be my local Member of Parliament, was not interested at all. Thomas Nagel passed on my paper to a friend of his at London University, Arnold Zuboff, who commented that, although the work was immature, the boy showed much promise and may go on to do things. Trying to publicise my views at the meetings of the Aristotelian Society, I was befriended by M.F.H. Roe, a retired professor of Chinese Philosophy who had studied neurology as a young man at Cambridge under Warren McCulloch. He was excited by my mentioning 'fields' as Gestalt Field theory had been all the rage in his Cambridge days. It turned out that he was a friend of David Bohm, which got me excited as I had by this time bought Bohm's *Wholeness and the Implicate Order* and the book of articles by various writers entitled *The Holographic Paradigm* which discussed the ideas of neurologist Karl Pribram and physicist David Bohm in relation to mystical knowledge. I had just turned nineteen and knew nothing about mysticism and the two books, although most intriguing didn't make much sense to me. I picked up the term Perennial Philosophy from the latter but did not know what this was actually referring to although I wrote in my revised paper that I liked the idea from the Perennial Philosophy that the universe created forms to look back through them upon its own creative evolution. Although I could not really understand what these books were discussing at the time, they none the less left in my mind the feeling of reassurance that there were famous scientists who were prepared to question the basic assumptions of Science. I knew that my use of the term 'field' was vague and I was reassured to find theoretical physicist Bohm pointing out that nobody really knew what a field was; scientists used the concept pragmatically to get mathematical results and were not interested in the deeper question as to what a field actually was. In fact, even before I wrote my paper I had sent Bohm a brief letter attempting to explain my view in a few words but I received no reply from the first person I had tried to contact. M.F.H. Roe told me that he was very ill at the time.

After the initial burst of enthusiasm in autumn 1983, things quietened down and life had other priorities as I had also started at university and at the end of 1983 went on my first trip to India and was disturbed by my encounter with Calcutta. I had taken a copy of Fritjof Capra's popular book *The Tao of Physics* on this trip but gave it away as a present to an unemployed Calcutta physics graduate. (When I did get around to reading this book in 1990, I found it more intriguing than informative as no clear indication was given as to what mysticism was and thus one could not understand the significance of the parallels between the vague generalizations drawn from physics and mysticism). Although I continued to think about the problem of consciousness, I was not to find the time to concentrate upon the problem again until after I graduated. Although I had graduated with outstanding distinction, as stated in the introduction, I was not cut out for scientific research and I found myself not knowing what to do, not having any job in mind that I really wanted to do.

The 1987 paper on consciousness

It took me almost three years to settle down in steady permanent employment. Given that my mother earned a pittance doing a strenuous job, whilst paying off the mortgage and bringing up four sons after the death of my good-for-nothing father, life was even more depressing as I had dreamed of getting a good job to pay off our debts. The years 1987 and 1988 were particularly bleak and at times in 1988 my will to live reached its lowest ebb and I was finding it hard to lift myself out of the bed to face the world each morning to play the humiliating game of life. An invisible web of interconnected circumstances, partly psychological, seemed to pin me down (the "web intricate" of my verse). Yet at this time when I felt that I was being totally crushed by the world, from the depths of my being arose the urge to reinforce and preserve the greatest achievement of my brief existence. At this point of total despair, when thoughts of doing away with myself sometimes crossed my mind, it was as if my deeper Self was surging forth, driving me on to create, to leave my message to the world and make my existence meaningful. At that time it seemed to me as if my message would be like the plaque on the Voyager satellite, a message that would have to wait an eternity to be discovered and deciphered, to be lifted from the vast, cold indifferent void of the cosmos. Yet something inside drove me on to keep working on the problem of consciousness through the darkest days of that period even though it seemed like the most insane pursuit when my priority should have been to find myself a suitable job and start earning some money.

This effort resulted in a far more mature work entitled *A Panpsychist Interpretation of Consciousness.* The presentation of my ideas in the commentary and the verse is largely based upon this revision of my initial ideas which I attempted to publish in some Western journals but found that there was no place for the outsider in the closed world of Anglo-American academic philosophy. One journal sent a brief set of comments from a reviewer which stated that, although the work was well written, it used "folk psychology". I didn't know at the time that this was the term introduced by the eliminative materialist Richard Rorty who would have us think that subjective experiences do not really exist! Although deeply frustating at the time, with hindsight it was better not to have ever associated one's name with such publications. I did in fact try an Indian journal whose address I found listed somewhere and they were far more positive. They replied that I had given dualism a cursory dismissal, and were I to re-examine this point and resubmit the paper they would reconsider it. At the time I knew nothing about the vast cultural difference between India and the West in regard to the understanding of consciousness such that the word "panpsychism" would not conjure up such negative connotations amongst many Indians. Instead, after having spent a long time writing the paper and feeling too proud to re-examine dualism, which I considered to be so totally untenable that it wasn't worth serious consideration (a view I still hold), I never took up the offer.

The encounter with Indian philosophy

Another factor was that by then I had started steady work at long last and my motivation was drifting away from what seemed a futile pursuit. Indeed I was not to return directly to the problem of consciousness until late in 1993 when I wrote the first version of this essay which resulted in a couple of significant developments leading directly to my current position. In the meantime I had, in my search for my roots, developed the knowledge of Indian history and the rudimentary acquaintance with Indian philosophy which was presented in the verse. I tried to comment upon my notion, developed in ignorance of mysticism, of an underlying "psychophysical non-duality" (which could only be grasped in a limited way with our parallelist conceptual constructions of the 'psychical' and the 'physical') with my vague notion of *Brahman* drawn from my rudimentary knowledge of *Vedānta*. The Vedāntic claims of a transcendental *nirguṇa brahman* caused me serious concern at the time as Shankara's dominant interpretation seemed to imply a dualistic co-existence of an immutable, non-subtantial realm alongside the substantial existence of the material world in a most problematic manner. To say that it was inconceivable would be to miss the point that it was meant to be inconceivable to the thinking mind although it could be realised in experience. I knew that other Vedāntic schools disputed Shankara's immutability doctrine as the *Brahma sūtras* themselves repeatedly asserted *brahmapariṇāma*, or the transformation of Brahman, which Shankara reinterpreted in his exegesis to suit his own views[1]. Attempting to elaborate on the possible nature of this underlying "psychophysical non-duality", it just came to me that what my notion of the mind as a self-organising electromagnetic field process actually implied was that the scientific principle *energy* and my "Raw Awareness" (my vague notion of the essence of consciousness which I had come to equate with the Vedāntic *chit* or "pure consciousness") were two attributes of the same underlying reality which I began to call *Brahman*.

Mokṣa and Near-Death Experiences: An intuitive leap

Attempting to make some sort of comment about the Vedāntic concept of *mokṣa*, in relation to my own views on consciousness, I found myself at a total loss. I could not imagine what a 'higher state' of consciousness could be in terms of brain functions. The term "higher" seemed to imply a more ramified, complicated process involving new developments on top of existing processes. Whilst contemplating this problem, there appeared on the television a preview for a religious programme about Near-Death Experiences (NDEs). I had seen one programme on NDEs some years previously in which patients talked about floating above the body etc. but had thought nothing more of them. Yet upon watching this preview it suddenly came to me in a flash that this light or 'God' or whatever these patients claimed to have experienced had to be related to the *mokṣa* experience of unity with *Brahman*. In fact, although not indicated on the preview, the actual programme that night discussed the same issue, that the NDE experience of the Light was related to yogic enlightenment. But this was not the only intuition that came to me. The NDE link immediately provided me with another intuition. This was that the NDE must involve a retreat of the physical correlate of mental activity (which I viewed as a self-organising field) away from the outermost neocortical areas which most scientists think are associated with consciousness, towards the brainstem (the knob-like structure at the top of the spinal cord lying at the centre of the brain surrounded by subcortical structures which in turn are surrounded by the cerebral cortex). I recalled that I had read in a book in 1987 that brain death was technically defined as the cessation of the activity of the reticular activating system located in the brainstem. The yogic path towards enlightenment, I reasoned, must involve a similar retreat of mental activity towards the brainstem. 'Higher' states of consciousness were not more ramified, more complicated processes but were in fact less ramified, simpler underlying processes. (Although I knew that *chit* was supposed to be the ground of consciousness, the talk of 'higher states' etc. had left me confused). Most scientists would probably hold that consciousness is a product of specialized activity in the cerebral cortex and view the subcortical regions surrounding the brainstem as devoid of any conscious activity. It began to cross my mind that if one could somehow monitor the brain activity changes during NDEs one could show that consciousness was not limited to the cerebral cortex. Of course, my real intention was to argue that consciousness, in the sense of some sort of generalised awareness rather than the meaningful world-modelling we normally experience, was omnipresent. Although I had no evidence to back up my retreat to the brainstem intuition, I had great confidence in the essential validity of my views and believed that, as Reality was ultimately one, the scientific and mystical perspectives had to be different perspectives upon the one Reality.

Having made these speculative assertions, I completed my first attempt at writing this essay in late 1993, equivocating over my inchoate 'mystical' interpretations of my own existence in the verse, seemingly in the hands of fate. My discussion paralleled the equivocating verse of *The Web Intricate*, 'blowing hot and cold', and ended upon a sceptical note born partly of the need to impress upon scientifically-minded people that I was not stupid, stating that I was well aware of the fact that what I privately held to be 'meaningful coincidences' might also be interpreted as 'chance'. A short while after I wrote this first draft, I began to experience a recurring rhyme rising up unintentionally into my mind, spinning in my head and refusing to go away like the recurring dreams that some people experience. It was a verse I already knew from Ralph Waldo Emerson's poem *Brahma:*

> They reckon ill who leave me out
> When me they fly, I am the wings
> I am the doubter and the doubt
> And I the hymn the brahmin sings

It gradually dawned upon me as to why I was experiencing this recurring rhyme. I was repressing my true beliefs (not being "true to my Self") in writing equivocally about my synchronicity experiences and other experiences linked to my sense of 'guidance', fate and destiny. Upon realising this and deciding that I would change the ending of my essay so that I "came out" wholeheartedly in support of the mystical view, the recurring rhyme ceased. I rewrote the discussion of *The Web Intricate* stressing that the scientific concept of chance was only the imposition of mathematical constructions based on probability theory upon the spontaneous "bubbling broth" of reality resulting in an artificial construction of "statistical normality" which people confused for the real order of things.

The intuitive communication with my deeper Self in coming to understand the meaning of the recurring rhyme included another component which, in my innocence, I told other people about. Basically, the message was that I had to come out with my true beliefs as the work I was writing would be of great significance. Although I would have liked to have thought this, even in 1993 I could tell deep down that the essay I had written was not very good. I was not confident of my assertions and I had little background knowledge in regard to the issues I was tackling. In spite of my speculative linkage of energy and pure consciousness, I still had little time for the claims of yogis about their amazing experiences such as oneness with the cosmos. That my deeper Self was telling me that the work I was writing would be of great significance seemed at the time to be typical of the exaggerated, bombastic nature of any such encounters with the deeper realms of our being as Jung claimed.

Learning the meaning of Spirit

Early in 1994, I had lunch with an old schoolfriend. As I tried to explain to him what I was writing about, he pointed out that what I was calling "psychophysical stuff" was what was called, in the West, *Spirit*. Now the word "spirit" had come to evoke negative connotations in my mind due to my scientific indoctrination. I had not thought of *Brahman* as *Spirit* prior to this, tending to see the latter as an irrational conception associated with religious superstitions. My uncertainty over such matters is reflected in the fact that in 1992 I had bought Swami Prabhavānanda's book *The Spiritual Heritage of India*, summarizing the various systems of Indian thought, and never paused to think why the Indian philosophies were called the "spiritual heritage". Due to my preconceived bias that yoga was some futile exercise best left to unthinking Buddhists and the like, I had skipped over the chapter on yoga in this book. I had mentally distanced Vedāntic thought from its yogic sources due, partly, to my Western indoctrination resulting in my valuing words and thought over experience and also due to my lack of acquaintance with any yogic practitioners. One problem was that I could not understand how some sort of breath control could possibly give remarkable insights into the true nature of things but I had never seriously paid any attention to yoga to understand what it was supposed to be about.

A few months later, whilst commenting on a television programme about the famous chemist Linus Pauling spending the latter part of his life promoting the benefits of Vitamin C, I stated that it reminded me of Newton's "spiritual bollocks" (the latter word is slang for 'testicles'), referring to Newton's profuse mystical writings which he held to be more valuable than his scientific work. It was pointed out to me that I myself had recently been talking a lot about "spirituality" and wasn't this also "spiritual bollocks". Embarrassed, I retorted that Newton's writings involved Biblical stories of the Israelites as the chosen people etc. (which I had read somewhere) and thus were a "load of bollocks" whereas my writings on mysticism were based on the rational knowledge of the Vedānta. As with my assertion in 1983 that Spinoza's views were "mystical nonsense", soon after this incident of automatically rubbishing spiritual views, I was soon to become engrossed in spiritual knowledge. It seems to me as if when my normal self, indoctrinated into such a hostile stance towards mysticism and spirituality, made such strong assertions, it seemed to trigger some response from my deeper Self to teach me what a fool I was in taking such a closed-minded attitude.

Spirit had seemed to imply something insubstantial, beyond all human enquiry like the Vedāntic *nirguṇa brahman* with which I had so much difficulty. My reference to the Great Spirit in my verse section entitled *Lebensraum* was not intended to imply any link with the Vedāntic notions found later in the verse. There was some deep intuitive resonance with the Great Spirit idea which I couldn't explain, perhaps partly derived from my view that this naturalistic conception amongst this group of so-called savages, persecuted and derided by the European settlers, was vastly superior, in my opinion, to the ridiculous personality cult of Christianity. Once my old schoolfriend had put the word "spirit" into my mind in relation to my own work, subconscious processes were brought into play as I toyed with the relationships between "psychophysical nonduality", *Brahman,* and Spirit. With hindsight, it is clear that the notion of underlying unity which had so appealed to my intuitions when I was twelve must have continued to operate subconsciously in my belief in there being but one Reality, one actual World rather than incommensurable dualities. I mentioned in the introduction how the belief in the underlying unity of all phenomena inspired the work of Faraday who first put forward the notion of a field of force and tried to show the unity of electromagnetism and gravity back in the 19th Century.

THE DEVELOPMENTS OF 1994

In the spring of 1994, I found myself embroiled in a crisis situation and my sense of disillusion with the ways of the world plumbed to even lower depths of disbelief combined with anger and frustration that fate seemed to have trapped me in such an intolerable situation from which there seemed to be no short-term way out. After a nervous breakdown in early 1993 brought on by similar concerns, I had decided to focus my energies on my writing which I hoped would lead to life changes. I do not normally read horoscopes but, on the day of my nervous break-down, I had read the horoscope in a newspaper[2] which stated:

> *Provided you can accept that certain plans are no longer viable, what remains stands every chance of eventual success. So commit yourself only to what is essential and remind yourself constantly that limited expectations yield only limited results.*

I had noticed during the nervous breakdown that I seemed to be aware of deeper connections between events, not normally perceived, which most people would immediately dismiss as the delusions of a madman. This was perhaps my first lengthy experience of an altered state of consciousness. Following the crisis in early 1994, I concentrated with even more zeal upon rewriting *In this Age of Falling Curtains.* Whilst doing this, I began to realise that a positive transformation of human society required a shift away from Western-style materialism towards a more Eastern style introspective culture, which curbed egoistic excesses. This was something that many people had been asserting but I had not taken such ideas very seriously before. This led to a growing sympathy for the approach of the Indian tradition marking a complete turnaround from my youthful days when, steeped in Western materialistic individualism, I would have laughed at any such self-abnegating approach as primitive non-sense. Meditation, of which I still knew next to nothing, was beginning to acquire positive value in my scheme of things through the possibilities I began to see that it might hold for transforming human behaviour though introspection and control of our rampant drives. As stated in the introduction, the deeper I pushed into the underlying structure of my thought, the more I began to discover the resonances with the Indian tradition, my underlying 'Indianness'.

Learning from Jung and Synchronicities

In the summer of 1994, I read in full for the first time a book I had bought in 1983 containing selected extracts from the writings of Jung[3]. I had initially only intended to read the section on the concept of synchronicity in order to reconsider what I had written in my 1993 attempt at this final essay. However, I decided to read all of the book and was struck by some of its contents such as the Gnostic notion of the *pleroma*, the plenum/void from which the universe arises, which was clearly equivalent to the plenum/void of *Nāsadīya Sūkta.* In an extract from Jung's *On the Psychology of the Unconscious,* I read of how the idea of the Conservation of Energy came to Robert Mayer in a sort of mystical realization on his first visit to the tropics. Jung related Mayer's insight to the primitive 'dynamistic' religions with their universal magical power or energy called, for instance, *mana* (by the Melanesians). The historian of philosophy A.O. Lovejoy had called such primitive ideas of a primal power "primitive energetics". Jung argued that this same essential notion, this 'archetype', of the conservation of the magical power manifests itself throughout history in metaphysical and theological notions. Thus the idea of the Conservation of Energy was but a modern reinterpretation of this perennial insight.

In the summer of 1994 a Bengali song that I had known since childhood kept spinning in my head. The words translate into something like, "Like a hibiscus at the feet of the Mother, Awake and flower my mind". A hibiscus plant in our house that had stubbornly refused to flower in 1993, flowered in 1994. At work, a female colleague would offer to make me a cup of tea asking me, "Sutapas, is it your time?" I would jokingly reply in a deep voice, "My time has not yet come". One day, I decided to take an alternative route as I left work for home and came across a huge billboard poster announcing the visit of an American faith healer, Morris Cerullo, to London later that year. The slogan read, "YOUR TIME HAS COME". Deep down inside I felt that it was a message to me although at that time I was in dire straits not knowing what to do with my life, seeming to have no way to break free from the various traps fate seemed to have set for me. Although my normal self could see no way out, my deeper Self seemed to acknowledge the message of the billboard poster linking it to my joking replies to my colleague which were none the less based upon my serious, deep belief that one day the time would come when people would start taking notice of my ideas. The very next day I caught the end of a television programme about the Shoemaker-Levy comet which was crashing into Jupiter at that time. At the very end of the programme, an astronomer was asked if he felt that the comet signified anything. The astronomer replied that it portended a New Age of Enlightenment.

In July 1994, plagued by the feeling of being trapped by the invisible web of connections that framed my being, I had a very strong impulse to learn more about the problematic relationship between the transcendental and the immanent, *nirguṇa* and *saguṇa*, aspects of *Brahman*. This was partly due to the fact that my deep frustation with my life situation made me inquisitive as to what it was all about, why did I exist. I picked up a couple of books on Shankara's thought as he was supposed to be the greatest of the ancient Hindu thinkers. Randomly opening one of the two books, entitled *Māyā in Śaṅkara*,[4] I suddenly noticed my name, Sutapas, on the page. It should be noted that I have never come across anyone else, real or fictional, called Sutapas. The Sutapas in the book was a sage in a Hindu myth who sought to know from the god Vishnu the 'secret of Creation'. Vishnu told him that he could not tell him the answer but, if Sutapas really did want to know the answer, he would have to throw himself into the ocean. I interpreted the meaning of this myth as that the secret could not be stated in words but could be realised by attaining enlightenment. At the time I really did not understand how enlightenment could actually tell you about the creation of the universe but the idea of a Sutapas deeply concerned with the meaning of existence was particularly pertinent to my state of mind at that time. I told people that I was experiencing these meaningful coincidences even though it seemed to raise questions about my sanity.

Learning the significance of the Light

Around this time I picked up the book *Hidden Journey* by Andrew Harvey[5] as I had seen half of a programme about Harvey on television entitled *The Making of a Modern Mystic.* Although the book was largely just a popular story about Harvey's search for spiritual awakening leading to the Aurobindo Āshram in Pondicherry and an Indian girl with strange psychic powers, what was significant for me was Harvey's repeated reference to the "Light". Until then I had not actually equated enlightenment with actual *light* as Vedānta spoke of *Saccidānanda* and the Buddhists spoke vaguely about things like the 'void' and 'nothingness' as far as I knew at that time. The reader will note that I make no mention of the Light in my verse work or in the commentary. Even though I had made the link between *mokṣa* and NDEs, I had only thought about it in terms of a retreat of the mind towards the brainstem. I knew that there was some sort of light in NDEs but I hadn't really thought much about it at the time. Reading Harvey's book, I was reminded of the fact that Halbfass had mentioned the Jesuits applauding the 'natural light' of Brahmanism which I had taken to be just a metaphor.

Intrigued by Harvey's mystical experiences and his references to the great Western mystics such as Meister Eckhart, I ordered a book entitled *Mysticism and the Religious Traditions*[6] which I saw listed on the back of another book in the same series. After picking up this book a couple of weeks later, I crossed London's Charing Cross Road on my way to Oxford Street when a book gleaming in the window of another bookshop on the other side of the road caught my eye and something within me drew me back down the road a little to take a closer look. Emblazoned on the front in huge gold lettering was the title *Embraced by the Light*[7]. It was a popular account of an American woman's near-death experience. As my only knowledge of NDEs was from a couple of television programmes, I decided to purchase the book even though it was written for the popular market in order to find out what these people claimed to experience.

The next day, which happened to be my thirtieth birthday, I interrupted my reading of *Mysticism and the Religious Traditions* to have a quick look at *Embraced by the Light*. I began to read the foreword by a Melvin Morse, M.D. who was something of an expert on NDEs. Morse pointed out that the author was actually talking about NDEs and not about what happens to you after death as she claimed. To my great surprise Morse also mentioned that a specific brain area had been identified which, "allows us to have the experience". Morse was not at all clear on this point, not stating which brain area, which experience(s) or citing any sources for this claim. Having confidently put forward my retreat towards the brainstem hypothesis, I was bewildered by Morse's statement. Could my intuition have been completely wrong. I was shaken but took hope in the fact that Morse was so vague. Perhaps he was only talking about part of the NDE experiences (I only had a vague idea of what happened in NDEs at that time, knowing only of an out-of-body experience and some sort of tumbling towards a light) and my brainstem hypothesis would still hold good. I had to find out more. It was late evening on my thirtieth birthday after a crisis earlier in the year leaving me feeling very depressed about reaching this age with nothing concrete to show for all of my efforts, all of my sacrifices over the years. My career, domestic, social and psychological situations had conspired to trap me in a most unhappy state of affairs from which there seemed no escape except through my writing. Although my overall panpsychist view was not threatened, the possible loss of my brainstem hypothesis would weaken the overall coherence of the ideas I was putting forward. That evening it seemed as if fate was playing yet another cruel trick upon me, rubbing salt into my wounds.

As I had taken the next day as a holiday, I decided to go down to Foyles, the huge bookshop in Charing Cross road to see if I could find out more about Morse's NDE-related brain area. I rely on my own purchases for my research and Foyles, claiming to be the world's largest bookshop, did not return unsold books and thus one could find many older books amongst the latest publications. It didn't take long to locate a book by Morse. It was a small paperback entitled *Closer to the Light*[8] aimed at the popular market, full of stories told by various NDE patients along with some discussion. I took the opportunity to look around Foyle's philosophy and psychology department and picked up a number of other titles. One was entitled *Gathering the Light: A Psychology of Meditation*[9]. Before returning to these two titles, I will discuss what I learned from *Mysticism and Religious Traditions* which I completed before reading Morse's book in full as a quick glance through Morse's book allowed me to find what I was looking for and allay the fears that had driven me to seek it out.

Divine Light, Nothingness and Saccidānanda

Most of the authors in *Mysticism and Religious Traditions* (edited by Steven Katz) were rather hostile to Perennial Philosophy type views, focusing on the variety of mystical experiences, the supposed impossibility of separating out a pure mysticism from cultural tradition, the conservative affirmation of the traditional orthodoxy by most mystics (reiterating the dogmas indoctrinated into them) and the social meanings of yoga. The subtext of the book seemed to be, don't get carried away by the perennialist 'hype', we are the scholarly experts, we know best. In 1995 I was to read a book entitled *The Problem of Pure Consciousness: Mysticism and Philosophy*[10] in which another group of academics provided a set of rejoinders to an earlier anti-perennialist book on mysticism also edited by Katz, showing, amongst other things, the lack of any serious argument by Katz in his assertions that there were no universal core mystical experiences. I shall discuss the general philosophical points about mediated and unmediated experiences later in this essay; the actual academic exercises taken seriously by such anti-perennialist religious scholars are not worth serious discussion, seeming to be little more than anti-perennialist prejudices provoked by the perceived threat it poses to their favoured religions and a total reliance upon simplistic and outdated Kantian epistemology (as discussed in Section 2(a)).

In one of these essays, which set out to challenge the assumption that mysticism can be treated separately from the contexts of culture, history and tradition, I found the views of Tsung-mi, a 9th Century Chinese patriarch of two different schools of Buddhism. Tsung-mi distinguished the Buddhist *via negativa*, traced back to the great Indian philosopher Nāgārjuna, which emphasised the doctrine of emptiness from the Buddhist *via positiva* which stressed the omnipresence of the Buddha nature:

> *Now if there were not such substantial realities as insight what could be revealed as the Buddha-nature, what could be said 'neither to be born nor to perish' and so forth? One must recognise that understanding in the very perception of what is presently at hand is precisely the Buddha-nature of the mind . . . .*
>
> *Men of these days all regard negative discourse as profound and expressive discourse as shallow . . . . This is all due to their mistaking purely negative discourse for profundity and to their failure to aspire after an intimate personal realization of the substance of the truth.* Tsung-mi (780-841)[11]

This helped clear up the confusion in my mind over the difference between the Buddhist "void" or "nothingness" and the Vedāntic *saccidānanda.* Those who followed Nāgārjuna's "emptiness lineage" ended up describing the substantial reality in such negative terms such as "emptiness" and "void". In the final chapter of *Mysticism and Religious Traditions,* J.E. Smith[12] stated the following:

> *The Buddhists tell us that 'emptiness' is not to be understood on a relative plane as absence or extinction, but only on the basis of pure experience which is the mind reflecting itself and no other content. This is what is called* ***sunyata*** *. . .*

Smith went on to briefly discuss St Bonaventure's thoroughly rational treatise *The Mind's Road to God* which speaks of the *uncreated light,* the significance of numbers and that the universe and the mind are both mirrors of the divine.

> *Being as the condition for all beings, and light as the condition for all that is seen, become the final objects of contemplation, at the end of the process the mind passes beyond itself.*
>
> St Bonaventure[13]

I realised that the Light, the "uncreated light" or the "eternal light" of Bonaventure was the *chit* of the Vedānta; Being and Light were equivalent to *sat* and *chit.* These ideas were now established in my mind (I was later to find confirmations of the Light equals *chit* equation in both Vedānta and monistic Kashmiri Shaivism).

Scientific perplexity over the Light

I read Morse's book and found that the brain area associated with NDEs was the Sylvian fissure of the right hemisphere. However, this was only associated with the basic out-of-body experience (OBE) where it seems as if one is hovering above one's own body. The famous Canadian neurosurgeon Wilder Penfield had found that electrical stimulation of this area induced OBEs and this association had also been rediscovered more recently by some Chilean neurologists. Morse touched upon various scientific attempts to explain NDEs, most of which were just crude attempts to debunk anything that went against the modern scientific world-picture with reductionistic nonsense about chemicals, oxygen depletion etc. which do not actually account for the actual experiences although some of these physiological factors may be correlated with the experiences. Of course oxygen depletion would be associated with NDEs but oxygen depletion, in itself, is nothing more than one small part of the complex processes correlated with the experiences and hardly comes near to a sufficient explanation as to why NDEs occur although it is touted like some magical formula explaining everything by a number of scientists. The sort of argument put forward by many scientists was exemplified by some comments addressed to the Dalai Lama by a Harvard professor of neurobiology in one of the other books I had picked up at Foyles.

> *I am a cellular scientist and a notorious radical materialist. I have a question that may be shared by other scientists or neuroscientists, as to whether one should invoke a non-material mind in order to understand brain science, or increase our understanding of human behavior . . . the particular nerve cells upon which cocaine is known to act are neither clear nor formless; they are amazingly intricate in shape and they occur in collections of nerve cells whose form is wonderfully intricate. They are not clear, they contain a pigment...though no one knows whether it is related in any way to these phenomena [referring to euphoria].*
>
> David D. Potter[14]

The argument as to how you can experience a "clear light" when nerve cells are not clear is in many ways a rather puerile one ignoring nearly all the metaphysical issues involved. If our experience was limited by the structure of nerve cells and their pigmentation we would certainly not be able to experience the everyday world of forms and colours which we none the less do. However, although Potter's reply highlighted the inability of scientists to come to terms with the limitations of their own metaphysical presuppositions, this question as to why the structures of the physical brain do not appear in our conscious experience is one that needs to be addressed within the context of my own views. My original model of a nested hierarchy of fields with the notion of 'subjective' closure attempted to account for this sort of question although it remains problematic and needs re-examination.

Not surprisingly, as Morse noted, the NDE Associations formed by people across the USA who have had NDEs resent such crude attempts by materialists to try and wish away their spiritual experiences with such pseudo-explanations. Morse had found that the scientific establishment discouraged anyone from investigating NDEs (although things have changed a little recently and grants have been provided for a major study). Morse himself, to his credit, remained open-minded, accepting the testimony of patients in regard to paranormal phenomena and noting the fact that such death-related experiences have been known since time immemorial all over the world. The Egyptian Pharaohs had to undergo an initiation ceremony involving suffocation for a period of time in a sarcophagus which would have induced such experiences. Morse referred to Jung, the *Tibetan Book of the Dead* and related texts from around the world. He also suggested studying brainwave patterns in NDE patients and comparing them to those found in meditation.

Of the Light itself, Morse stated:

> *The Light is the one element of the near-death experience that brain researchers can't even come close to explaining. The testimony of children is clear on this point. The Light is the key element of the NDE.*
> *How can we scientifically explain this light after death? I do not know of any biochemical or psychological explanation for why we would experience a bright light as the final stage of bodily death.*

He continues:

> *And then — there's light? Where does this light come from? The brain has nearly stopped functioning . . . Then why the Light?*

Faced with this mystery, Morse mentions beliefs that this light represents some sort of rebirth. This view seems to be encouraged by the experience of 'tunnelling' that is experienced by most NDE patients prior to encountering the light which leads one to imagine some sort of journey across some boundary between this world and the next (in fact it is Western NDE patients who tend to experience passing through a tunnel whereas people from other cultures tend to have other equivalent experiences such as walking down a road or passing over a body of water[15]). Morse attempted to eliminate cultural bias by concentrating on the testimony of very young children, who spoke in simplistic language about Jesus etc. but he also cited the testimony of a 14-year-old boy who stated:

> *As I reached the source of the Light, I could see in. I cannot begin to describe in human terms the feelings I had over what I saw. It was a giant infinite world of calm, and love, and energy, and beauty. It was as though human life was unimportant compared to this. And yet it urged the importance of life at the same time it solicited death as a means to a different and better life. It was all being, all beauty, all meaning for all existence. It was the energy of the universe forever in one place.*

Here in this rather sophisticated testimony from a fourteen-year-old (it may have been given years after the actual experience at age 14) the parallel with the Vedānta and other mystical traditions was glaring with the Light being experienced as all being and all the energy of the universe. (The boy's references to 'all meaning for all existence' etc. also ties in with notions of the Light as the Ground of all Being containing the potentiality for all possible forms of existence). I was satisfied from these remarkable parallels between the more sophisticated NDE testimonies and the Vedānta that my association of *mokṣa* with NDEs was totally justified, at least in regard to the final stages of the NDEs where the Light appeared. Morse's Sylvian fissure information and his bafflement with the Light restored my own confidence in my retreat to the brainstem hypothesis.

The puzzle of coherent alpha rhythm

Perusing a book on Synchronicity[16] which I had bought along with Morse's book, I discovered that the brainwave patterns of yogis, supposedly in the state of enlightenment, had been measured. The pattern was a unique one, so-called coherent alpha rhythm all over the scalp. The source for this information was a article by Orme-Johnson published in a journal entitled *Electroencephalography and Clinical Neurophysiology*[17]. Some months later I rediscovered an article I had cut out of a 1991 issue of *New Scientist* and kept for possible future reference entitled *Is Meditation Good for You* by Susan Blackmore[18]. I have seen Blackmore on a number of television programmes attempting to debunk claims of paranormal activity. I also read about her in a book about supernatural phenomena also picked up that day at Foyles. In the past Dr Blackmore had been associated with psychical research but was now an arch-sceptic. Her zealous anti-paranormal stance seemed to indicate a subconscious desire to regain respectability with the scientific establishment after her earlier flirtations with the paranormal. In the *New Scientist* article Blackmore discussed the history of EEG measurements of meditators. She then went on to discuss Orme-Johnson's work, especially a study claiming to show paranormal influences by groups of meditators, pointing out that much of the research into EEG patterns during meditation is carried out by members of the Transcendental Meditation (TM) organisation and published in their own publications where it is not subject to peer review. *Electroencephalography and Clinical Neurophysiology* certainly does not sound like a TM publication to me. (West notes the deficiencies in all the scientific studies of meditation which, due to ignorance, misconceptions, limitations of suitable subjects and time etc. simply cannot do justice to meditation[19]. Taylor notes that when the US Army commissioned a study of meditation, they completely misunderstood and distorted the issues making vague generalizations, relying on one outdated review of meditation studies, one irrepresentative practitioner and concluding along the lines that *mantrayāna* (chanting) was equivalent to the counting sheep cure for insomnia[20]). Blackmore continued with a statement, "A strong motivation to 'prove' the efficacy of TM could bias the findings". Whilst this is a valid concern, Blackmore fails to register her own interests and biases or even contemplate the possibility that her own presuppositions may be wrong. For instance, she dogmatically appeals to the 'laws of physics' as an argument against paranormal phenomena as if such laws are sacrosanct and indisputable. Reading her sarcastic comment that increased EEG coherence is also associated with epileptic seizure, coma and death was 'music to my ears' as this again confirmed my linkage with the process of dying. The *prāṇāyāma* or breath control of the yogi is known to result in minimal oxygen consumption. The comatose state of yogis deep in *samādhi* ('absorption') appeared a number of times in my readings of 1994 and I was later to read that it was not possible to detect a heartbeat in Rāmakrishna when he was deep in *samādhi*.

Returning to the actual development of my thought, let me recap that I had discovered the coherent alpha rhythm (all over the scalp) information perusing a book on Synchronicity. I registered this in an open-minded manner, having no motivation to rubbish such studies, and it lay at the back of my mind. I recall telling someone at work about this information and that it meant nothing to me. I had already purchased a scientific review book on event-related brain potentials but I had not got around to reading it (although with hindsight this would not have helped understand the coherence information).

Zen meditation and alchemy

Odajnyk's book, *Gathering the Light*, began its back cover promotional material with the sentence, "What exactly happens in meditation?". It went on to claim that it was the first book to apply the insights of Jungian psychology to the process of meditation. It claimed that it would give a ground-breaking explanation of Zen meditation based on the notion of a 'meditation complex', a psychological explanation of the mystical union of opposites and a psychological definition of 'self-realization'. Unlike the earlier book I had read on Jung, Odajnyk gave a number of insights which to me, at that time, were most revealing. He pointed out, for instance, that the Chinese text *The Secret of the Golden Flower*, which Wilhelm had translated and for which Jung had written a famous foreword, was a meditation manual. Odajnyk referred to Jung's visits to India and focused on Jung's studies of alchemy. Alchemy, a most mysterious term for the modern mind, was really supposed to be a form of meditation resulting in the *mysterium coniunctionis* or the mystical union. Western alchemists had projected the final stages of the alchemical/meditative process onto the external world resulting in the ideas of transmutation of metals to gold associated with mysterious terms like 'chymical wedding'. *The Secret of the Golden Flower,* on the other hand, immediately identifed the 'gold' as a simile for the Light. Thus the philosopher's stone and its transmutation into the philosopher's gold really represented the mind/soul and its union with the Light. In Storr's book I had read that Jung had spent about a decade discovering that the seemingly nonsensical medieval alchemical texts, full of what appeared to be medieval rubbish relating various groups of symbols which had no obvious logical basis, made sense when the relations were understood as symbolic representations of psychological processes. Odajnyk noted that later post-medieval Western alchemists like Gerard Dorn and Paracelsus (upon whom the Faust legend is based[21]) had begun to realise the psychical nature of the alchemical process..

Jung sought to find Western parallels to Eastern spiritual practises and parallel Western terminology. Jungian literature is thus full of references to the *unus mundus* representing the unitary ground of the universe with which the 'soul' unites in alchemy/meditation. He claimed that the West had never developed anything comparable to yoga because of the Western fear of the contents of the personal unconscious, the inner fantasies that surge to the surface as soon as one begins to 'let go' of normal egoistic control. Odajnyk praised the "remarkable accomplishment of Buddha" in that, although enlightenment was nothing new or unique, he was the first person known to history to describe Self-realization in primarily psychological and non-religious terms. And he did this *two and a half thousand years ago* when most of humanity was still very deeply involved with primitive deities and supernatural forces.

> *There is no eternal soul or God to speak of: at the core of everything is only eternal Consciousness, the Enlightened Mind.*
>
> V.W. Odajnyk, *Gathering the Light*

Odajnyk also quoted the first lines of the *Tibetan Book of the Dead:*

> *O nobly born . . . listen. Now thou art experiencing the Radiance of the Clear Light of Pure Reality . . . is the very consciousness, the All-good Buddha.*

The *moment of death,* he noted, is supposed to provide a supreme opportunity for realizing one's true nature.

On Saturday 10th September 1994, I was awoken from my slumber by the doorbell ringing. It was about 8 a.m. and I heard someone downstairs answering the doorbell and paying the milkman. This was most unusual as the milkman normally delivered the milk early in the morning and then came back at about 11 a.m. or later to collect the money. I was thus unexpectedly awoken early for a Saturday and, not fully awake, looked up above me to see four beams of light on the white ceiling of my room. The beams, a purely natural phenomenon, entered my room through a small gap at the top of the region of overlap of the two curtains. The window was at the end of the room nearest my feet so the beams entered and spread out above my head. The beams kept shifting across my ceiling and diffracting into various colours of the rainbow. I had never, in the 18 months I had had those curtains, noticed such light beams on my ceiling before. Indeed, in early 1993, when the room had been refurbished, I recall that I had the very strong sense of my deeper Self looking through me with approval in anticipation of the work it wanted me to do in this room, which should be pursued whatever happened on the career front. That Saturday morning, only half-awake, I was mesmerized by these seemingly animate, shimmering beams of light silently swaying and diffracting above my head. I felt a numinous presence in their ectoplasmic transformations and later, looking back upon the experience, the thought that arose from my deeper Self was, "howsoever you shall conceive me, in that form shall I appear". Mesmerized by the light, I began to contemplate all the knowledge that I had been acquiring over the previous two weeks, like Bonaventure's final meditative state of Being and Light paralleling the Vedāntic *saccidānanda,* the mystery of NDEs and the insightful ideas I was beginning to acquire from Odajnyk. Looking at those light beams, it was crystallizing in my mind that the central element of mysticism was the Divine or Uncreated Light. The Pure Consciousness was this Divine Light. I kept recalling Bonaventure's statement that both the universe and the mind, the external and internal worlds, were mirrors of the divine. It was dawning upon me, gazing at the diffracting colours in the light beams, that if Pure Consciousness was Divine Light, then *colours* were not just part of the human or animal visual experience but universal experiences of consciousness with nothing essentially to do with vision. It seemed to me at that time that I was beginning to understand intuitively why the visual mode of perception was so different from other sensory modes and that this was related to it being the higher energy processes dominating our perceptual modelling of the world and thus visual consciousness was differentiated into colours as colours were the primary gradations of the Light of Pure Consciousness. It seemed as if the other sensory modes were operating 'below' the energetic level of the visual mode and cast ghostly shadows of touch, smell, taste and sounds into the field of consciousness dominated by the visual patterning. None the less, these other senses and all the other thoughts and feelings were still differentiations of Pure Consciousness. Unusual experiences such as synesthesia indicated the underlying inter-relatedness of all the sensory modes with non-visual sensations or thoughts experienced as colours etc. It was becoming clear to me how this one unitary Light of Consciousness could become the multitudinous forms of experience.

Thoughts also crossed my mind about how I had completely failed to consider the possibility of ever knowing what sort of experience individuated entities far-removed from human minds might be having in this panpsychic cosmos. My interpretation of *phenomena* had been that they were events (experiences) within ours 'selves' (the world-model fields) generated by external events transmitted by information flow via the senses. In essence, my position was a restatement of the Indian view that *knowing* is *being* and thus everything we ever experience (know) is a part of our self (our 'being'). It followed from such reasoning that we could not really know how things other than the physical correlate of our 'selves' were in *themselves,* i.e. what it felt like to be something other than my postulated 'world-model field'. My earlier draft of this essay in 1993 had tried to discuss the broader implications of my inchoate panpsychist ideas with only the most rudimentary acquaintance with knowledge of mysticism. My panpsychism had been based largely on abstract reasoning superimposed upon insights based upon the primary insight that nothing existed without awareness; i.e. I intuitively understood that all existence had to be sentient existence, and I had realized that the so-called "physical world" was but the description of patterns of behaviour exhibited by phenomena and not a description of Reality as it actually is. Thus, having held that we could never know what the subjectivities of other entities were like in themselves and not having imagined that there were other states of consciousness (apart from dreams) it was coming as a shock to me to discover that mystics experienced altered states of consciousness and claimed experiences of oneness with other things. I had of course heard of "higher planes" of consciousness but had not encountered, prior to reading Odajnyk's book, any serious description of such a "higher plane" which tried to relate such experiences to knowledge I could begin to come to terms with thus I had never been able to develop in my mind even an inkling of what was being referred to in such talk of "higher planes" if indeed such states actually existed at all. From my modern, evolutionary perspective, a "higher plane" implied some more highly developed form of world-modelling, i.e. some process more complex than the processes correlated with our normal consciousness. If such processes existed, what possible evolutionary function could they serve to maintain whatever the brain structures that underlay them and why could we not easily attain these states. An even greater shock was that mystics claimed that it was possible to transcend what I had called 'subjective closure' (individuation) and become one with a "universal consciousness". In fact, my panpsychist model had been largely consistent with such mystical notions but I had never before pressed deeper to contemplate the full ramifications of such lines of reasoning, never having experienced such states myself. Such mystical views had seemed totally preposterous to my modern, scientifically indoctrinated mind. Having had such thoughts cross my mind in the presence of the beams of light above me which seemed to be mysteriously illuminating my mind through their sheer presence, I fell asleep again before waking up fully some time later.

Later that Saturday, I continued reading Odajnyk's book and discovered that Zen meditation involved dissolution of the so-called ego complex and formation of a so-called 'meditation complex' into which the ego first has to merge before further progress occurs. The ego attempts to monitor and unify all psychic contents that enter its field of awareness. More interestingly for my purposes, the ego was described as a *"closed energy field that strives to maintain its integrity and resists penetration"*.

Odajnyk defined the term *complex,* following Jung, as a "feeling-toned cluster of psychic energy". The Jungian 'complex' has its own personality and volition. It struck me reading this discussion of the Zen meditation process that these closed energy fields described as complexes, each with its own personality, was much the same as I had pictured my self-organizing field processes which constituted individuated sentient entities, or like the dissipative structures, self-organizing processes generated by flows of energy under certain conditions, in the the new far-from equilibrium thermodynamics of open systems developed by Nobel laureate Ilya Prigogine.

The Light as experienced in the slow paths

The Zen path to enlightenment is a quick path not involving the step-by-step progress of more conventional yogic paths which I was soon to discover. Further, Odajnyk's use of Jung's arcane terminology (based as we shall see on Jung's misunderstandings of yoga and lack of acquaintance or acceptance of the deepest, spiritual realms) made things most confusing. None the less, I was getting very excited; the mind was being described, on the basis of introspective knowledge of altered states, as a closed energy field constituted of the clear light of consciousness. I could sense that things were stirring in my subconscious; I had to find out more about what happened in yoga. Where should I look? I had the idea in my head that the sort of information I was looking for could probably only be found in American journals or studies published in America which may not be available in the UK. I thought that there may be numerous such studies. How would I, with no qualifications or academic position get access to such knowledge which might involve searching through journals.

None the less I decided to go and look in a bookshop to see if I could find anything more. I went to the largest bookstore near to my place of work, part of a large chain. I did not realise at that time that another bookshop nearby, which I had thought was full of only Marxist and radical tracts was also one of London's largest New Age stockists and would have been a far better place to look. In the mainstream bookshop I looked around the psychology section finding nothing of relevance. After about half an hour I gave up and turned to go when my peripheral vision was somehow guided to a green book spine with the Shambhala logo (Shambhala had published *Gathering the Light*) bearing the name *Transformations of Consciousness.* It was edited by Wilber, Engler and Brown[22] and I recognized it as one of the books I had marked in the Bibliography given in the afore-mentioned Harvard MindScience Symposium book as a book I would like to get hold of if possible. I had not noticed it before as it had been misplaced out of correct alphabetical order. Quickly perusing the contents and back cover promotional material I saw that this attempt to synthesize psychology/psychiatry with spiritual knowledge of deeper states of consciousness was the sort of thing I was looking for.

The key chapter in this book turned out to be Harvard psychologist Daniel Brown's detailed study of the stages of meditation compared across three authoritative yogic traditions, the Tibetan (Mahāyāna) *Mahāmudrā,* the 'Hindu' *Yogasūtras* and the Theravāda *Vipassanā,* describing the similarities and differences across the traditions[23]. Within days of seeking more information on what happens in yoga, I had been guided to what I later discovered was the best available description of what happens in the slow yogic paths leading to enlightenment. The detailed information available in this study will be discussed later, suffice to say that it described meditation as the deconstruction of the perceptual process, "stopping the mind" as one yogic tradition called the earlier steps, and experiencing the subtle flow of the light hidden beneath our gross perceptual constructs. Amidst the wealth of amazing information I found in Brown's study, most of which I could not assimilate at one reading, one key point stuck in my mind. The light flow underlying our gross mental content was described by the Hindu *Yoga Sūtra* tradition as a *tanmātra* (literally, "coordinates of that previous gross content") or a continuously vibrating energy field in a state of continuous wave propagation. The Buddhists, focusing on discontinuities, described the light as coming in pulses or movements. I realised that these were just differences of attitude, the Hindu focusing on the underlying continuity, the Buddhist focusing on the wave peaks and thus experiencing the light as pulses. Such differences in focus lead to differences in metaphysics with the Hindu *ekatattva* (the one (continuous) principle) and the Buddhist *kṣanika* (momentariness) devoid of a ground. Clearly the Hindu focus, not limiting itself to merely the wave peaks, was inclusive of more of Reality. The very origins of the Buddhist focus on discontinuous aspects could have been a result of attempts to challenge the Hindu *dharma* by challenging its metaphysical base.

All of this fascinating knowledge could not be easily digested by my mind. I had vague mental pictures of the subtle pulses of light flowing through the field of attention, free of gross cognitions. I imagined the gross cognitions bouncing back into attention if the yogi failed to maintain his concentration. Brown had mentioned how the ordinary self-reference frame drops away as the flow of light becomes clearer with practice and what remains is a sense of self-agency, awareness of directing attention, exerting oneself and rejecting or developing the subtle flow into gross cognitions. Eventually, as the yogi lets go of all activities that interfere with the flow of the light, even this sense of self-agency drops away. After exploration of intriguing realms, beyond the time and space constructions of perception, where reality operates through acausal interactions in an undivided wholeness and the subtle karmic activity underlying the gross activity of the ordinary phenomenal world, awareness turns in on itself as the last remaining artificial activity (i.e. that which is not the spontaneous activity of the primordial state) is brought to cessation. The yogi realizes that pure awareness exists as a continuous backdrop to all activities and, if lucky, attains 'Basis Enlightenment' in which all events, content and activity drop away leaving a vast awareness in which the observer becomes one with the observed. This Basis Enlightenment is the one step in the process for which all three authoritative yogic traditions in Brown's study gave identical descriptions. Brown went on to discuss further developments which the yogi could undertake where again the traditions differed. Brown claimed that his study showed, contrary to the perennialist view of various paths leading to the same goal, that the various paths were essentially the same and the goals were different. I disagreed, as the key stage was clearly the dissolution of a separate identity in Basis Enlightenment which was the same across traditions.

Eureka

All of this information had been pouring into my head over a period of eight or nine days since my thirtieth birthday. I could sense that things were crystallizing to some extent in my subconscious depths. The answer, I felt, was coming to me. Speaking to a friend at work, who herself had psychical experiences, I began to realize slowly that such phenomena could not be explained by simple information transmission models but that one had to understand our normal spacetime as a sort of barrier between normal realms and transcendent realms where such limitations of space and time were not relevant. On September 14th 1994 as I went out from my workplace to buy my lunch, the basic answer suddenly came to me; the pulsing waves of light were the pulses of activating energy from the reticular activation system, flowing through all of the brain structures. The coherent alpha rhythm measured all over the scalp reflected the fact that, as the self-organising process (or dissipative structure) that was the field of attention finally dissipated, the only major activity that remained in the brain, devoid of mental activity, was the flow of these activating waves from the brainstem passing through to the scalp without interference.

Here at last was the direct linkage of Science and Mysticism, the physical and the psychical. Energy and the Divine Light of Pure Consciousness, the stuff of the universe in Science and the stuff of Reality in Mysticism were two attributes of the one Reality. Although this answer came to me on September 14th 1994, I later noticed something that I had written in late 1993 at the time I prepared the first draft of this essay. After re-reading parts of *The Holographic Paradigm*, I had written the following on the final page:

> *Although my attitude towards the mystical has transformed dramatically in the last 10 years, I am now of the inclination that moksa (or nirvana) far from being a higher state of consciousness, let alone mystical union, is in fact a rudimentary state of awareness, the primary brainwaves from which the conscious mind takes form — akin to near-death experience. What conclusions to draw from this I have yet to decide.*

In September 1994, I remained largely sceptical at first in regard to the awesome metaphysical and cosmological claims made by many mystics in regard to the experience of enlightenment. How could the dissolution of the mind processes into the activating flow of psychophysical energy amount to an understanding of the secrets of Creation.

In the days following 14th September, I experienced something akin to a mild nervous breakdown. I told people that my cognitive structures were reorganising, interfering with normal mental processes. I had experienced a nervous breakdown in 1993 faced with a reality which so contradicted my largely innocent view of worldly affairs. This breakdown had led to a drastic reappraisal of my worldly situation and my approach to the problems I faced had been permanently transformed as I focused single-mindedly upon my writing. The 1994 experience was far more pleasant, slowing my memory recall and other functions a little. I was again 'waking up' to a new understanding, this time of the metaphysical problems I had been grappling with which had perplexed me for years. It was dawning upon me that the so-called Perennial Philosophy, towards which I had remained largely sceptical was not as preposterous as it appeared at first sight although it made profound metaphysical, cosmological claims on the basis of phenomenological knowledge. I was intuiting that there was far more to it than met the eye, indeed, I sensed that it was, in its various forms, stating fundamental truths which were only now beginning to make sense to me. How ignorant and arrogant I had been to dismiss many of the claims of mystics in the past, confident that my scientific knowledge was vastly superior to this 'primitive nonsense' which I had falsely perceived as being irrational. How foolish I felt I was not to have seen these things before, how totally and utterly naïve and stupid I had been in the past. I had been transfigured.

There also came a sense of fulfilment as mentioned in the introduction to this work. All my life, it had seemed as if things were terribly wrong in some deep sense. Whatever little things I was trying to do to try to pull out of the mess life had created for me was just tinkering with the problems, failing to address the underlying sense of dissatisfaction with my lot. Life seemed to have forced me into a rather hermit-like isolation which I had not wanted but seemed unable to do anything about. Something deep within me was driving me to pursue this seemingly forlorn ambition of tackling deep metaphysical problems which did not bring me any material benefit although I was still suffering from the legacy of the relative poverty I had been brought up in and, in spite of outstanding qualifications and natural ability, I had not been able to make any progress in my formal career, remaining a lowly clerk.

> Cast out by modern *varṇadharma*
> Cast out as too true to his caste
> This brahman true born of pariahs
> Misfit, misplaced and so miscast

Suddenly it seemed as if these ordeals which I had had to face up to all of my life were meant to be, for they were leading me away from wasting my life pursuing normal ambitions and leading me towards my true vocation. All the status symbols of normal worldly achievement which I thought that I would have been happy with when in my darkest hours they seemed impossible to attain, given the hidden forces conspiring against me, now seemed trivial and ordinary, devoid of any deep satisfaction, of any real sense of fulfilment. Early in 1994 I had again been in deep crisis, seeing no real way out of my entrapment. The deep depression that ensued seemed to have triggered something in the deeper realms of my being because now, in September, only a few months later I had made a breakthrough which, although attained at remarkable speed with lots of intuition and very little background information, opened up the way for me to start finding my real role in the world.

PART TWO
The Emerging Picture

Don't listen to those voices/That say it can't be done
...Imagine... If all of them had given up too soon
...Yes, they were always taking chances/Looking for the answers
That took the whole world to higher ground
"Keep a Dream in Your Pocket", Bruce Woodley (The Seekers)

It is now over two years since the events following my thirtieth birthday. In these two years I have completed the other parts of this work and have tried to find out as much as I can about mystical experience and its relationship to scientific knowledge. In 1994 my power's of intuition had leapt well ahead of my clearly articulated reasoning and my mind was dancing nimbly upon a few stones which I had found protuding from the waters of my ignorance. It seemed as if I had been guided towards the critical breakthrough that laid the basis for a future synthesis of Science and Mysticism whilst remaining largely ignorant of mysticism and the so-called Perennial Philosophy. This had, in some ways, been most fortuitous as it meant that I had not been conditioned by the gurus of the Western 'New Age' counterculture into thinking that such a linkage, let alone a future synthesis, was impossible.

> *The same reason we have never and never will find the "missing link" between animal and man is the same reason we find so few links or parallels between the levels in the Great Chain: each higher level, to the extent it transcends its predecessors — it is "emergent", "creative", "novel", transcendent".*
>
> Ken Wilber[24]

We shall see that, following Wilber's terminology, it is in fact the 'lower levels' which are the emergent levels, emerging out of the transcendent planes. We shall see that Wilber's, previously mentioned, tacit New Dualism between the material and the spiritual planes is invalid as we find that 'transcendence' basically involves a broadening of perception of the One Reality from the limited mental constructs of the material plane to the spiritual unity underlying the seeming multiplicity at the material level. When mystics talk of the "material plane", they do not actually mean matter in the sense of atoms and subatomic particles but our gross perceptions of the "material world" including everyday forms such as trees, animals, clouds etc.

> *For to the supramentalised seeing the material world and space and material objects cease to be material in the sense in which we know, on the strength of the sole evidence of our limited physical organs and of the physical consciousness that looks through them, receive as our gross perception and understand as our conception of matter. It and they are seen as spirit itself in a form of itself and a conscious extension.* Sri Aurobindo[25]

When has anyone ever perceived a neutrino, an electron, a quantum field or the space-time continuum of Relativity in the gross perceptions of the material plane. We shall explore later how such concepts from physics reflect the processes operating in the 'depths of our being' (the higher planes) which are projected onto the external world. I like to point out in regard to Wilber's assertions that, at around the same time as I found the link between the physical and the spiritual, the missing link between humans and animals, *Australopithecus ramidus,* was discovered in Africa.

> *Leading biofeedback researchers do not typically claim that alpha frequencies are reliable indices of mystical experience. Kamiya, for example, has steadfastly maintained that the well-being associated with increased alpha activity should not be equated with satori or other religious states.* Michael Murphy[26]

Murphy, who spent a year in the Aurobindo Āshram and co-founded the Esalen Institute (the leading American meditation research centre) goes on to state that comparisons between *satori* and the experiences of biofeedback subjects (controlling alpha waves) were facile. I would not dispute that the profound experience of enlightenment is not the same as the low level experiences of biofeedback subjects even though both involve increased alpha rhythm activity as measured on the EEG. It is of course necessary to counter the simplistic notions peddled by the likes of an American actress, probably best known for taking all of her clothes off, who was recently courting publicity saying that she was going to India to seek spiritual enlightenment and that she hoped to attain enlightenment in a month or so. Odajnyk noted the enormous hurdles that a Westerner faces in overcoming enculturation in regard to 'letting go' of one's individuality making serious depth meditation less attainable to Westerners. Brown noted the severe preliminary indoctrination practised by all of the authoritative yogic traditions in order to rid the mind of the prospective yogi of all worldly attachments. I suspect that the 'superstar' actress, steeped in the live-for-the-moment, convenience package, 'me society' culture touted across the world by Hollywood (along with glorifying violence and degenerate behaviour) failed to pass these prerequisites, let alone attain enlightenment in a month. In response to Murphy, I would state that such seemingly facile comparisons which seem, at first sight, to totally demean the significance of spiritual experiences can lead to much deeper understandings actually affirming the extraordinary significance of such experiences in regard to our understanding of reality. Indeed it is the purpose of this essay to do just that.

2(a). A FEW HISTORICAL WESTERN MISCONCEPTIONS

Some historical considerations concerning the relationship between Science and Mysticism and modern Western philosophy and mysticism have been mentioned in other essays and will be mentioned in later sections of this essay. I will bring together here a few points of interest which should help to elucidate the modern mind's misunderstanding of mysticism, clearing some of the prominent misconceptions which have clouded our understanding.

The Christian myth of Creation ex nihilo *and Spirit/Nature dualism*

As mentioned elsewhere in this work, Indian ideas and itinerant yogis ('gymnosophists') had reached the West long before the Christian era, especially in the wake of Alexander's incursion into the Indus valley and also of Ásoka's conversion to Buddhism and his dispatching of missionaries to foreign lands.

Plotinus, the father of Neoplatonism, who attempted to reach India in order to learn more, shared the same teacher in Alexandria, the mysterious Ammonius Saccas (Latinized *Shakya*?), as Origen, the first great Christian thinker[27]. Tarnas[27] notes the profound influence of Plotinus' philosophy on Augustine's thought including the Platonic undertones in Augustine's paradigmatic statement, "the true philosopher is a lover of God". Coward[28] states that the Christian gnostic Origen, who fascinated Jung, was much influenced by Eastern thought.

Segal[29] points out that Jung, working prior to the Nag Hammadi discovery, found it impossible to connect Gnosticism or Neoplatonism to modern thought until he began to understand alchemy. Jung saw alchemy as the form in which Gnosticism had continued to flourish into the Middle Ages even though Gnosticism had been branded as heresy very early on in the history of Christianity. He notes that Jung misinterpreted Gnosticism presumably because he saw it as akin to alchemy. Jung, reading Gnosticism through alchemy, reversed its world-rejecting ethos. As with his readings of Eastern philosophy, Jung confused metaphysical statements about divinity and matter to mean the same as his psychological terms 'unconscious' and 'ego' etc. In terms reminiscent of the Indian doctrines, Gnostic orthodoxy held that *ignorance* held humans tied to the material world whilst *knowledge* freed them from it. Gnostic myths taught total identification with the divine godhead, depicted in part as an impersonal principle which automatically creates the material world without willing it. The godhead, or *pleroma,* is undifferentiated, without distinctions and is at once nothingness and fullness; just like the void in *Nāsadīya Sūkta*. In many Gnostic myths, matter emerges out of the divinity although it does not lie latent in divinity; why matter emerges in spite of the omniscience and omnipotence of the divinity remains a paradox[29] (note the Vedāntic *niṣkāma karma* doctrine's attempted resolution).

Matt, in an essay discussing the origins of the Jewish mystical concept of *ayin* (nothingness)[30], looks at its origins in the disputes between Gnosticism and early Christianity over the source of the material world. Matt notes that no Hellenistic thinker had asserted Creation from nothing until the rise of Christianity. The Gnostic concept of God is one of total otherness and ineffability, with the likes of Basilides (the 2nd century Alexandrian supposedly channeled clairvoyantly by Jung in his *Seven Sermons for the Dead*[29]) trying to outdo his predecessors in negative theology favouring the term "nonbeing". The Christian concept of Creation *ex nihilo* arose in the 2nd Century as a response to the prevailing Hellenistic conception of *hyle,* eternal, amorphous, formless matter which, for the Christians, compromised the sovereignty of God. Immediately we see in the use of the term sovereignty the anthropomorphic projection of the human king onto the divine. The Christians also wanted to refute the Gnostics' views which often involved powers apart from God which were responsible for Creation. Thus Augustine asserts that Heaven and Earth were made from nothing by God, not made of God. Thus the Christians created a totally transcendent creator god set apart from the Creation, produced miraculously out of nothing whatsoever. Matt notes that Creation *ex nihilo* also collided with Plotinus' theory of the eternal emanation from the One, the Divine Light into which the mystic's sense of a separate self dissolves. The mystic who is 'oned' with the objectless vision of the Light transcends 'being' as, for Plotinus, the One is higher than 'being'. Although certain Christian thinkers tried to resolve the contradiction between Creation *ex nihilo* and Neoplatonic emanation and a Neoplatonized conception of Creation *ex nihilo* was developed, such pantheistic notions were condemned by the Pope in 1225.

From this Christian concept of a supermundane creator god, a Roman Governor writ large with sovereignty over his creation, laying down the laws, stems much of the future Western split between Spirit and Nature. The fathers of modern science explicitly referred to the Laws of Nature as God's laws and they still retain their transcendent status, independent of the material universe[31]. Recent feminist critiques of Science point out that positing supposed Laws of Nature reflects social dominance relationships projected onto Nature and similar projections of linear, hierarchical causal models taken from society are found in the simplistic flow diagrams of molecular biology with the "executive DNA", sitting in its nucleus, acting as a sort of 'master molecule'.[32] Goodwin[33] shows how the popularized form of Neo-Darwinism expounded by Richard Dawkins in terms of "selfish genes", which none the less allows for humans to escape their inherently selfish nature reflects vulgar forms of Christian fundamentalist beliefs. Numerous other examples could be described showing how scientific metaphors subconsciously reflect Christian mythology and superstition or even older mythology such as Darwin's Natural Selection reflecting the Great Mother who is immensely fertile and devours her offspring[31].

Laughlin[34] notes that the Western mind-body dualism is prescientific in origin with both Hebraic and post-Socratic Greek roots. He points out that the West's traditional bifurcation of metaphysics into epistemology and ontology reflects this dualism. Even Husserl's phenomenology, he states, is conditioned by the dualism that informs Western philosophy, science and theology. Heisenberg[35] pointed out that Einstein's inability to come to terms with Quantum Theory, which with Bohr and Heisenberg's "Copenhagen interpretation" began to blur the sharp distinction between subject and object, stemmed from the mind/body dualism that permeated Western culture. In more recent times, the 'Cartesian dualist truce' as Goswami[36] calls the compromise between Western science and spirituality has been resurrected by 'transpersonal psychologist' Ken Wilber as I have noted above.

Mystical influences on early science

At the birth of modern science, mystical influences played a significant role. Sufi and Kabbalist ideas from Spain, along with alchemy, lay behind the development of Renaissance nature philosophy which viewed all of reality as a single coordinated domain which could be known through spiritual transformation resulting in gnosis, direct perception, the union of the knower and the known[37]. Galileo dismissed the contents of our perceptions, the senses, as mere names, "secondary qualities" derived from the real "primary qualities" described by mathematics[31]. Interestingly though, Galileo also held that we are condemned to think in time, in a step by step fashion, whereas divine insight is timeless, grasping the truth without temporal discourse[38]. He also held that Kepler's view of the moon affecting the tides was 'paranormal', childish nonsense[39]. Francis Bacon was suspicious of the active, imaginative mind, asserting that the disciplined mind was the surer way to truth[37]. None the less, Bacon also stated that perceptions and conceptions bear reference to Man and not to the universe with the human mind projecting its own qualities onto objects[40]. The deep interest in alchemical knowledge shown by the likes of Newton is well-known. Grof points out that biographer John Maynard Keynes stated that Newton is better viewed as 'the last of the great magicians' rather than the first great scientist[41]. Equally well-known are the probable occultist interests, frowned upon by the Church, influencing the setting up of the Royal Society partly to disguise the real nature of the investigations.

Kant's a priori *dismissal of mysticism*

Kant correctly saw that human experience was not atomistic, as Hume had held, but permeated by *a priori* structures but his understanding of these structures was narrow and simplistic, reflecting his complete belief in Newtonian physics[27]. Perovich[42] notes that Kant was unremittingly hostile towards the claims of mystics to have experienced the divine in this life. He denied that mystical experience was possible because it would require cognitive faculties which we do not possess. Thus he insisted that mystical illuminations were only pretended. None the less, as Perovich goes on to show, many philosophical scholars of mysticism have been attracted to Kant's epistemological scheme even though no provision can be made for mysticism within his epistemology. The aforementioned Steven Katz bases his arguments against the existence of universal core mystical experiences as asserted by perennialists on the unqualified assertion that all experiences are mediated through the organizing structures of the mind. This assumption leading to the the assertion that unmediated mystical experiences (or direct perceptions) are impossible, knowingly or unknowingly follows Kant with his distinction between *phenomena* and *noumena*. We shall see that Kant's rudimentary realization of *a priori* structures in cognition and assertion that we cannot go beyond phenomenal constructions of Reality are transcended by yogic realizations of the deepest planes of existence. Eckhart scholar Robert Forman has edited a volume of essays[10] collectively showing the invalidity of Kant's and similar arguments against universal mystical experience such as Brentano's assumption that every mental event is 'intentional' in that it includes an object. This assumption of 'intentionality', which has had such a strong influence on Western academic philosophy in recent years, holds that there cannot possibly be any experience devoid of objective contents as is claimed in the mystical experience of the distinctionless void of pure consciousness. Woodhouse[43] notes that writers as diverse as Hume, James, Skinner, Bergson, Sartre, Strawson and Fodor are united in their opposition to some form of the idea of pure consciousness which has few friends in mainstream (Western) philosophy and science. Rothberg[44] states that many writers, such as Gadamer and Derrida, following Heidegger, "have denied the very possibility of ever transcending the particulars of one's linguistic tradition to reach some reality independent of language and tradition". A.J. Ayer, in his *Language, Truth and Logic*, even went so far as to claim that there are no subjective statements.

Freud and the uterine myth

Tarnas[27] states that, just as Kant was limited by his Newtonian presuppositions, so Freud's understanding of the mind was limited by his Darwinian presuppositions. Grof[41] notes that Freud was deeply influenced by his teacher Ernst Brueck who founded a scientific movement based on the view that all organisms were systems of atoms governed by strict laws. Grof goes on to show how many of Freud's ideas are in fact projections of Newtonian mechanics onto the workings of the mind. Also, in keeping with Newtonian-Cartesian science, the Freudian analyst is conceived as an impartial observer who does not interfere in the observations. These are very mild critiques of Freud's views related to the influence of Western philosophy and science upon his understanding of the mind. The reader is no doubt aware of numerous other critiques of Freudian psychology for various reasons and of Freud's dismissal of various ideas of colleagues which were later to bear much fruit. None the less, often nonsensical Freudian thought seems still to exert a captivating hold over large sections of the Western intelligentsia. Indich[45] notes that *Advaita Vedānta* postulated wish-fulfilment as one of various causes of dreams over a millennium before Freud who claimed that wish-fulfilment was a universal characteristic of all dreams! In regard to the difference between Freud and Jung on the question of the *libido*, it will become quite clear from the rest of this essay that Jung was correct in asserting a general psychological energy in contrast to Freud's unscientific notion of a 'sexual energy'.

In regard to mysticism, Freud is associated with the general tendency amongst psychologists to view the mystical claims of experiencing union with the universe or with God as a regression to the womb. Deikman[46] states that most psychological or psycho-analytical 'explanations' have been general statements emphasising a regression to the early infant-mother symbiotic relationship. These range from the extreme view of Alexander who held that Buddhist training led to an intra-uterine narcissism, "the pure narcissism of the sperm", to the view of Freud that the "oceanic feeling" was a memory of a relatively undifferentiated infantile ego state. Deikman himself took a much more sophisticated approach with his notion of the "deautomatization" of perception through the reinvestment of attention to processes which had become automatic and holding open the possibilty that the mystical perception of unity does correctly evaluate the world as it really is. Still we find the likes of Tarnas, who spent ten years at the Esalen Institute and who lauds Grof's LSD-based work (which, as we shall see, goes way beyond his focus on uterine experience and supports grand mystical claims), associating the reconciliation of the individual and the universal, the primordial unity etc. in terms of the mother-child symbiosis and womb experiences[27].

Jung's reduction of the spiritual to the psychic

Clarke[47] notes that Carl Jung saw no possibility or even desirability in synthesizing Eastern and Western world-views, rather, his aim was to understand common themes. Jung noted that Science had proved an invaluable tool but, by claiming that its mode of understanding is the only kind that there is, it obscured our insight. What the West needed was a "broader, more profound, and higher understanding" and for this reason it had to take seriously the philosophical approach of the East. In regard to the view that Science provides the only valid mode of understanding, it is interesting to retell the following anecdote.

> *Harvard physicist Sheldon Glashow recently proposed as part of a "creed" or "article of faith" shared by practising scientists (Glashow,*

1989) — that our sensory organs are sufficiently refined to discriminate such a unique, true theory from alternative candidates, and that science is a process that will lead, at some finite point, to a view that decisively and finally rules out all alternatives.

L.H. Nelson[32]

Volumes have been written about the validity or invalidity of Jung's assertions in regard to mystical knowledge and one has to admit that, for all its deficiencies, Jungian psychology has played an invaluable role in bringing mystical thought to the attention of the general public. As Clarke and other Jung scholars note, many of today's New Age followers of Jung would be rather surprised to discover some of Jung's actual views in regard to Eastern thought.

Coward[28] notes that the lack of distinction between philosophy and psychology in Eastern thought (an issue I will discuss in the section entitled *The Interface of Mind and Cosmos*) posed problems for Jung who held that this caused Eastern intuition to over-reach itself. This, for Jung, was most evident in the claim that the ego could be transcended and identity with some universal consciousness attained which Jung held had no foundation in human experience. Jung saw the Indian as "pre-Kantian" and Eastern yogic philosophy was nothing more than scholastic descriptions of psychic processes with no necessary connection to empirical facts and a curious detachment from the world of concrete particulars. None the less, Coward points out the profound influence that Indian thought had on the development of Jung's ideas. Jung himself in his major work, *The Psychology of the Unconscious*, admitted that Indian notions of *karma* were essential to the deeper understanding that led to the development of his notion of archetypes[28]. Chinese notions, derived from Jung's study of the *I Ching* which led to the concept of synchronicity, were also to help change his "archetypes" from simple *a priori* structures to more profound "psychoids" providing a link between the psychical and the physical[27]. Coward notes that although Jung credited *karma* theory with helping to elucidate the nature of archetypes, Jung's systematizer Jacobi and other Jungian scholars have omitted references to Eastern sources. Jacobi instead points to Plato, Bergson, Augustine and Gestalt psychology as sources for Jung's archetype notion. In this regard I note that Rupert Sheldrake points only to Western sources for his "morphic resonance" views which he went on to link to Jung's notions of archetypes and the collective unconscious[48,31]. His first book, *A New*

Science of Life mentions his work as a scientist in Hyderabad and states that the book was completed during a stay at a Christian āshram in South India. It was his visit to India in 1968 which undermined his materialist assumptions[49]. Such 'resonance of form' notions are to be found in the *Yoga sūtra* tradition's theory of the *ākāśa*[50,51] and are, as we shall see, clearly related to karmic notions. Returning to Jung, Clarke[47] notes that the likes of Wilber, Watts and Ajaya have asserted that Jung failed to draw the appropriate lessons from his Eastern explorations. Wilber asserts that Jung makes no distinction between a *lower* collective unconscious and a *higher* collective unconscious, resembling Satprem's criticism that the notion of a "collective unconscious" lumps together all the deeper planes into one great magician's hat[52]. In essence, as Clarke notes, Jung was reducing the spiritual to the psychic and thus failing to grasp the full significance of Eastern philosophy.

Wolf[53] tells of how Wolfgang Pauli (considered by many of the founders of the new physics to be the cleverest amongst them), who collaborated with Jung on the book *Synchronicity: An Acausal Connecting Principle*, became convinced that a new conception of Reality had to include matter and spirit as complementary aspects of one world. Perhaps because of such views, as Wolf notes, Pauli has until recently been largely ignored by historians of the new physics. In discussing the 17th Century dispute between Kepler and the alchemist Robert Fludd, who took Kepler to task over his quantitative view of the world, Pauli stated that he identified with both Kepler and Fludd. Pauli attempted to create a neutral language to unify the concepts of physics, psychology and parapsychology; he was reputed to have had psychokinetic influences on sensitive physical instruments. Given the limitations of Jung's approach, it is not surprising that Pauli did not get very far along this route, speculating that imaginary numbers may have a role to play.

Bohm, Pribram and the Holographic/Holonomic Metaphor

Much more progress was made by David Bohm who, in his later work, showed the clear influence of Indian philosophy acquired partly through his friendship with Jiddu Krishnamurti. (Bohm had worked under Oppenheimer who, when the first atom bomb was tested was reminded of the passage in the *Bhagavad Gītā* in which Krishna reveals to Arjuna his universal form). Bohm, had originally reformulated Schrödinger's equation with his Causal Interpretation in 1951, positing a 'quantum potential' and allowing a degree of mental picturing of what was actually occurring during the collapse of the quantum wave function which causes so many paradoxes using the conventional Schrödinger form of the equation. Bohm later went on to develop the notion of an underlying, holistic "implicate order", a transcendent realm from which the spatio-temporal world of phenomena (the "explicate order") was "unfolded" and "enfolded" back into the implicate order in a sort of projection like process helping to take account of some of the peculiar features of Quantum Theory such as non-locality where remote events influence each other even though no physically meaningful signal could pass between them due to speed of light restrictions[54]. These notions were gradually refined and will be referred to later in this essay. Griffin[55] refers to the variations in some of Bohm's views as his 'Thomistic' and 'Vedāntist' moods. Bohm's oft-repeated analogy of a moving particle as being like a projected sequence of flashing lights, giving the illusion of a moving separate entity, closely resembles the Buddhist yogic experience at the so-called "interface of mind and cosmos". The Buddhist yogi, focusing on discontinuous features, discerns the process by which phenomena come into and go out of existence as like very intense light which flashes at high frequency[23].

Brown[23] in his study of the authoritative yogic traditions noted certain resemblences to Pribram's holonomic theory of perception which I shall refer to later. Pribram is no stranger to mystical views having been a friend of the Zen exponent Alan Watts and being described as having become a radical defender of spiritual experi-ence in the late 1970s[56]. Grof[41] notes that the modern holonomi approach (associated primarily with the ideas of Pribram and Bohm) has its historical predecessors in ancient Indian and Chines spiritual philosophies and in the monadology of Leibniz. I would add that the emphasis in the writings of Aurobindo and his follow-ers on vibratory frequencies must clearly have had some influenc on the development of these ideas. Talbot, in his popular expositio of the holographic (or holonomic) metaphor[15], points out that quit a number of Śrī Aurobindo's assertions are indistinguishable from many of Bohm's and Pribram's conclusions, stressing Aurobindo' emphasis on the underlying wholeness appearing to become frag-mented as we descend to lower vibrational levels of consciousnes which closely resembles Bohm's basic viewpoint although Bohm was rather coy on the question of consciousness. Clarke[47] notes that Chinese influences, especially Confucianism, had a profound influence on the formation of the ideas of the European Enlightenment and that Leibniz was amongst a long list of Enlightenment thinkers professing an interest in Eastern Philosophy.

In regard to Eastern precedents of the 'holonomic metaphor' or 'holographic metaphor', writers almost always cite the *Avatamsaka Sūtra* :

> *In the heaven of Indra there is said to be a network of pearls so arranged that if you look at one you see all the others reflected in it. In the same way, each object in the world is not merely itself but involves every other object, and in fact is every other object.*

The relationship to Leibniz's monadology is obvious. Note also the relationship to Mach's principle which I referred to in the final section of the verse and which we shall encounter again later in a reformulation of Quantum Theory by Schommers which results in holonomic-like relationships between a normal space-time and the underlying reality from which space and time as we know it are generated.

Grof[41] states that in holographic imagery, an entirely undifferentiated field of light that, by specific patterns of interference, creates the illusion of separate objects. "The demonstration of how the seemingly irreconcilable difference between the part and the whole can be transcended", says Grof, is probably the single most important contribution of the holographic model to the theory of modern consciousness research". Pribram[58] notes that with the holographic metaphor, one sees parallels with the Indian notion of *māyā*, or the illusory nature of phenomenal reality; a point which is, as we shall see, discussed more fully by Kaplan.

The holonomic metaphor is of enormous value in helping us to understand a number of issues relating to perception and mystical phenomena. However, both Pribram and Bohm along with other proponents of this approach fail to address the fundamental metaphysical questions relating to consciousness. Pribram is clearly aware of the problems posed by consciousness and the question of panpsychism and he says that he does not attempt to explain all manifestations of consciousness in brain terms but he does not commit himself to any particular ontological position[58]. Rosen[59] has criticized Bohm for failing to address the question of mind, or the "undifferentiable", ending up with an endless sequence of abstractions in his infinite levels of deeper and deeper "implicate orders". Bohm, in later writings, did seem to be more open in expressing panpsychist sympathies but he never really addresses the basic metaphysical problems, writing more about meanings etc. The creation of seemingly separate objects in holographic imagery helps us to understand perceptual representations but does not tell us what is perceiving this world of seeming separateness. It does not really address the question of why we experience ourselves as seemingly separate individuals and why this sense of separateness can be dissolved in mystical union. The holographic metaphor does not directly address the questions such as whether Reality is panpsychic and what is the relationship of consciousness to the physical world. Willis Harman has stated[60] that, although the holographic theories appear to make more plausible the space-time transcending psychic and mystical phenomena, they still interpret the primary datum, consciousness, in terms of something ultimately quantifiable. Harman looks forward to a new science in which consciousness is more nearly cause than effect stating that the holographic theories remain part of the old science which attempts to explain away consciousness rather than understand it.

2(b). BRAIN DEACTIVATION, COHERENT ALPHA RHYTHM DEATH

I shall proceed with a consideration of coherent alpha rhythm which I mentioned in Part 1 as an important clue in my identification of the physical correlate of the Divine Light. Such EEG patterns also constitute the nearest thing to some sort of 'scientific measurement' which so many people indoctrinated into the modern scientific frame of mind demand before thay take any interpretation seriously. The vast majority of my arguments will proceed regardless of scientific measurements or direct evidence as this is clearly not available, especially in regard to consciousness which has almost completely eluded the naïve approach of measuring instruments. Indeed, we have seen a striking example of technological limitations framing the thought of scientists with the predominant use of microelectrodes, which monitor impulses, leading to the infatuation with impulses and electronic circuitry analogies for the mind. I will however use knowledge from authoritative yogic traditions whose empirical evidence has been acquired and repeatedly demonstrated to initiates over thousands of years and remains available to anyone willing to undertake the requisite procedures to elicit the phenomena.

EEG coherence, meditation and brain death

The likes of Murphy, as stated above, and numerous others have pointed out that the same EEG recordings may be produced by the different processes in the brain and that EEGs can only detect the most gross levels of activity in the brain with little discrimination. There are controversies amongst neuropsychological researchers as to the validity of some the assertions made from the study of event-related potentials (ERPs) using the EEG, especially in regard to the generating structures in the brain.

> *Unfortunately, experimental methods have often been based on the EEG/ERP folklore (which may involve implicit assumptions about sources) rather than scientific principles. The most glaring errors seem to originate from a misunderstanding of the reference electrode in scalp recordings.* P.L. Nunez[61]

The choice of reference electrode, rather than the source in the brain, affects the magnitudes of the isopotential lines (lines of equal magnitude potential drawn on the scalp). Nunez goes on to state:

> *It has become axiomatic that there exists no unique source distribution for any given scalp potential distribution.*

In discussing the Laplacean method, which emphasises local sources, Nunez defines coherence of spontaneous EEG as a correlation coefficient expressed as a function of frequency. EEG coherence is independent of amplitude and thus not affected by variations in skull resistance. In regard to my later discussions, it is worth noting that Nunez goes on to speculate about global standing waves in the brain with frequencies in the range of spontaneous EEG with ERPs involving interaction of such global resonant phenomena with local circuit effects. Fenwick[62] tells us, again, that any EEG picture will have multiple causation:

> *The alpha rhythm, for example, is found in the relaxed waking state, but also in deepest coma just prior to death.*

He notes that EEG coherence analysis has become very popular with meditation researchers, some of whom claim that coherence implies long range ordering of brain activity leading to creativity and holistic growth. Fenwick states:

> *Coherence is the frequency correlation coefficient, and represents the degree to which the frequency profile of two areas of the head are similar. There is nothing magical about coherence, and it is not possible to argue from coherence values to underlying brain states or brain functioning.*

He points out that high coherence is found during epileptic seizure, delta coma, schizophrenia and even during death. What can be argued, says Fenwick, is that higher coherence involves synchronization and spreading out of spindling within thalamic structures, causing an increasing similarity of spectral profile in different cortical areas. In regard to the generation of EEG activity in general, he notes that the synchronous activity in the cortex arises from the thalamus which in turn is controlled by the reticular activating system (RAS). Mavromatis[63] notes that the RAS appears to be the only system that can be demonstrated to be involved at each or all levels of neural activity. Fenwick mentions a study showing high alpha and beta coherence being associated with breath suspension in meditation. Alpha coherence in particular increases with meditation practice. He also cites a study by Earle suggesting that there is a reduction in cortical activity or diminished cortical participation in the generation of mental phenomena during advanced stages of meditation. This contradicts the widely held view that meditation involves right hemisphere activation, which may indeed be the case in the earlier stages of meditation[62].

Now let us recall that brain death is defined as the cessation of activity of the reticular activating system which also acts as the underlying control system for all EEG activity. EEG coherence increases in meditation which involves decreasing the breath and deactivating the cortex. Coherent alpha rhythm is found in deepest coma just prior to death as well as in enlightened yogis. I suggest that the evidence is consistent with my interpretation as, in death, the brain structures are depleted by oxygen depletion until one reaches a point where, just prior to death, all brain centres have been deactivated throughout the brain leaving only the residual activity of the RAS corresponding to the detection of coherent alpha rhythm all over the scalp due the activating waves passing through the brain unhindered by interference from activity in local networks.

The mystical union has always been associated with dying as is clear from the importance given to the moment of death as a special opportunity for attaining liberation as in the *Tibetan Book of the Dead*. In the Indian Buddhist tradition, the attainment of *nirvāna* is defined as "the non-occurrence of mind and mental concomitants". Cessation *(nirvāna)* is distinguished from death in that, although mental activity has ceased, vitality and heat are still present (i.e. heartbeat, basic metabolic functions)[64]. Sānkhya philosophy (the theoretical *darśana* associated with the *Yoga sūtra* tradition) holds that eternal and absolute *kaivalyam* (liberation) is not attained until death[65]. The link between enlightenment and death is also found in the debate in the *Advaita Vedānta* tradition over the status of the so-called *jīvanmukta* (one liberated in life) as to whether liberation can actually be attained in life or if it is only truly attained at death. Thus it is clear from both the bodily condition of mystics experiencing enlightenment and the similarities in the EEG patterns between advanced stages of meditation and NDEs that enlightenment closely resembles states close to the point of death. Furthermore, given the testimony of countless NDE patients that they too have experienced mystical states similar to those attained through meditation, we may confidently conclude that brain activity in the enlightened yogi is similar to the brain activity of someone on the verge of death.

Some materialist pseudo-explanations

Benson[66] states that medicine can partly explain the physical processes causing the NDE subject to "see light" and experience joy and peace stating that depletion of oxygen causes brain cells to register tunnels of light and that the pleasurable sensations are due to endorphin release. Benson, who has played a leading role in the scientific study of meditation, continues that nevertheless NDE subjects remain convinced that these experiences are religious. As I noted in relation to Morse's book above, the attempt to reduce NDEs to oxygen depletion explains nothing. As stated above, tunnels of light are not universally experienced but a culturally limited phenomenon and a simplistic statement of oxygen depletion explains nothing about the cultural variations and the visions of crossing a road etc. The attempt to dismiss mystical rapture and ecstasy as merely the equivalent of some pleasurable sensations induced by endorphin release or the euphoria induced by cocaine, as in the case of radical materialist Potter above, smacks yet again of the naïve confidence tricks attempted by materialists to pass off their dogmatic, simplistic, reductionistic speculations as sufficient explanations as to why people claim that such experiences are so profound and often life-transforming when the same endorphins etc. are involved in the most mundane pleasurable experiences and do not leave people transfigured. The materialist relies upon the assumption that millions of NDE subjects, for no good reason, are making wildly exaggerated claims about their experiences which can be nothing more than the few little mechanisms known to the materialist, the idols of the materialist's faith.

For instance, in his recent book *The Astonishing Hypothesis: The Scientific Search for the Soul,* Francis Crick[67], begins his preface, "This book is about the mystery of consciousness — how to explain it in scientific terms". Although Crick points out that, whereas some philosophers are under the delusion that they have already solved the mystery, and that he is only proposing a particular research strategy, he opens the first chapter with a statement of what the "astonishing hypothesis" he is putting forward is:

> *The Astonishing Hypothesis is that "You," your joys and your sorrows, your memories and your ambitions, your sense of personal identity and free will, are in fact no more than the behavior of a vast assembly of nerve cells and their associated molecules. As Lewis Carroll's Alice might have phrased it: "You're nothing but a pack of neurons."*

As is typical of most scientists, once Crick moves away from discussing technical details, his arguments in regard to spirituality etc. are little more than naïve clichés. For instance, Crick refers to religious cosmologies where the distances and time scales of modern scientific cosmology were unimaginable stating that certain Eastern religions, such as Hinduism, were exceptions as they inflated times and distances for the "sheer joy of it". There is a tendency amongst Western scientists to project the ridiculous myths and superstitions of Western religions onto Eastern mysticism as well and thus to believe that no evidence is given by any spiritual tradition in support of its views. He grants that there may be some aspects of consciousness such as qualia that science will not be able to explain but, as with the limitations of quantum mechanics, we will learn to live with these. The aim of Science, Crick tells us, is to explain *all* aspects of the behavior of our brains, including those of mystics. I found it most amusing that at the end of the main part of his book, Crick, who was a British 'boffin' during the 1939-45 war, urges every human vision research laboratory to stick up a poster on its walls with the words "CONSCIOUSNESS NOW" along with the shadow of the huge outline letters spelling now. The term *qualia* is employed by Western academic philosophers to denote the qualitative content of experiences, which is at the heart of the mind/body problem and thus Crick has, correctly, largely abandoned the hope that Science can say anything about the mind/body problem or the mystery of consciousness. And yet Crick's "astonishing hypothesis" is that qualia such as "joys and sorrows" are nothing more than the *behaviour* of nerve cells and molecules. Science's aim *is* to explain the *behaviour* of our brains. What is truly astonishing about such blunt views is that no attempt is made to say why it is that the behaviour of neurons in the human brain should be any different ontologically from the behaviour of other systems and why this does not logically entail panpsychism. Ironically, in asserting that we should learn to live with the paradoxical aspects of quantum mechanics and other such difficult problems, Crick is himself adopting the dogmatic, safe, secure received cosmology approach for which he chastises religions and going against the whole spirit of scientific enquiry. Clearly, the boys in human vision research, inspired by Crick's poster, may find out quite a lot of interesting things about the *behaviour* of human brains but when it comes to understanding the real issues relating to the mystery of consciousness which Crick states that he wishes to address, it is clear that the poster that they should be putting up is one saying "CONSCIOUSNESS NEVER".

Subcortical and brainstem involvement in Mysticism

I wish to stress that, although I am correlating deep mystical experiences to brain activity similar to NDEs, I am not attempting to deny their profound significance. The study by Earle cited by Fenwick also indicates that meditation involves deactivation of the cerebral cortex as would also be expected to occur in the process of dying. Neurologist Pribram, discussing the mystical experiences beyond the world of appearances where paranormal phenomena, synchronicities etc. occur states, "such a shift might be mediated by the brain's connection between the frontal lobe and the older limbic region, the tie between the cortex and the deep brain structures. This region is a major regulator of attention"[68].

Lancaster[69], attempting to link Jewish mysticism to cognitive science, refers to consciousness as "Being". Whether or not Being exists in a stone or in a computer are unanswerable questions he claims. He feels sure that we will not find Being in particular brain processes as it is a different order of reality. Lancaster states that Taub has noted that meditation is accompanied by a suppression of electrical activity in the cerebral cortex. Taub argues that the primitive brainstem, and in particular the reticular formation, are central to our experience of Self. Lancaster also states that physiological data including the brainstem events associated with sleep and dreaming seem to support the view that entering trance involves a descent from cortical to brainstem regions. Comparing hypnotism to mystical states, Lancaster speculates that the 'letting go' aspect of both involves a 'descent' to the brainstem region and a consequent loosening of the bonds of self.

Mavromatis[63] points out that decrease in cortical activity, contrary to the belief of many neurobiologists that consciousness resides in the cortex, does not necessarily mean decrease in awareness. The fact that the slow alpha-theta EEG rhythms are produced in meditation and some psi (parapsychological) states implies that thalamic activity has been induced which damps down the cortex. The (subcortical) medial thalamus can drive the cortex into synchronized slow rhythms such as alpha and theta EEG rhythms. Sleeping, dreaming and hypnagogia are also associated with deactivation of the cerebral cortex. Mavromatis cites the famous neurologist Penfield who argued that the system essential to consciousness is to be found in the subcortical structures, not in the cortex. Mavromatis notes that:

> *clinically defined death is generally referred to as 'brainstem death', thus again pointing a strong finger at the importance of this part of the brain in the function of consciousness. Paradoxically enough, even though death is thought of as the moment of ultimate and irreversible cessation of consciousness, there are numerous reports of 'death' and near-death experiences in which consciousness appears to intensify rather than diminish or cease.*

Further support for the progressive deactivation of the brain interpretation of the mystical path towards enlightenment comes from the views of Swami Satyānanda Sarasvatī[70] on the nature of the so-called *chakras,* the supposed energy centres running along the spine which are progressively opened during various forms of yoga. Sarasvatī considers the *chakras* to actually be layers and layers of potential functions in the brain which normally lie dormant. Ken Wilber notes that most of the great mystics, including Krishnamurti, Śrī Ramaṇa Maharshi and Shankara, do not consider the *chakras* positioned along the spine to be real. Śrī Ramaṇa Maharshi considered them to be merely mental pictures for beginners. The fact that certain ganglionic centres in the spine seem to be associated with various states of consciousness may be due to mental projection of the activity of the brain onto these regions which are perhaps connected to the brain centres actually correlated with the state of consciousness[71]. Measurement of increased electrical activity at the traditional *chakra* sites, as has been reported by some scientists (as we shall see), does not mean that this activity is directly correlated with the mystical experiences of the opening of the *chakras;* i.e. the actual physical correlate of the mind in mystical states is in deep brain centres although there may be associated activity elsewhere.

Krishnaswamy Iyer[72] stresses the correspondence between mystical states and waking, dreaming and sleeping (there is also the fourth state *turīya* beyond these three) as found in the *Māṇḍūkya Upaniṣad* and its associated *Vedāntic* lineage. This classical linkage of the mystical states to dreaming and sleeping (the yogi, unlike the normal person, remains lucid during these states) ties in with Mavromatis' linkage between hypnagogia, dreaming, meditative visions, parapsychological states etc. which he associates with subcortical activity becoming prominent as cortical activity diminishes, rather than with right hemisphere activity as is often assumed (I myself had previously linked dreaming to right hemisphere activity as is clear from the verse). Thus the classical linkage of mystical states to various states of arousal is consistent with the model of brain deactivation starting with the cerebral cortex leading to various mystical states (if lucidity is maintained) and ending with deactivation even of the subcortical structures, leaving only the residual activity of the reticular activating system as occurs at the verge of death. In Section 2(d) I shall present remarkable support for my reticular activating system interpretation of the Light of Pure Consciousness from the *Kauṣītakī Upaniṣad's* description of the processes of death and entering dreamless sleep but before this we must consider the nature of the mind.

2(c). THE MIND AS A SELF-ORGANISING PROCESS

In 1983, mystically inspired by a vision and a compulsion leading me to Structuralism's nested hierarchy of autonomous structures, I was given the insight that the psychophysical stuff of the universe individuates into autonomous sentient beings by means of forming whirlpool-like 'closed' fields existing in a nested hierarchy at various levels of order. Self-organising processes such as particles, atoms, molecules, cells, organisms, galaxies and various other not so easily discernible self-organising 'fields' corresponded to individuated sentient beings with the property of 'subjective closure', a sense of being a separate, autonomous individual entity.

I was not aware at the time that similar notions had been put forward by others such as Whitehead, who also used the term *aggregate* for non-individuated collectives. The popular writer Arthur Koestler[73] had suggested the term *holon* for such autonomous, self-governing entities although he, like many others, applied the term to social organizations such as family, tribe, clan, nation etc. as well as cells, organisms etc. I would not consider such social organizations or notions such as ecosystems to be actual individuated entities. The subjective sense of closure, in my view, reflects an actual, substantial closure that is discernible in terms of physical processes. As stated in Part One, my initial panpsychist picture was adopted from what I knew of Spinoza's view from popular accounts of it. At the time I knew nothing about his views on individuation. I heard on a television programme in 1987 that he had a notion of individuated *modes* which in a sense remained part of the whole[74] which resembled my view. His actual views are not very easy to decipher; Edgar[75] states that Spinoza "insisted that what there is is not divisible *and* that there is individuation of modes". The modes are individuated by motion. Edgar's difficulties with such plenum views, as with Spinoza himself it appears, seem to stem from his application of Newtonian style mathematical reasoning to such issues in terms of rotation and boundaries of spheres etc. David Bohm was fond of using the model of the vortex for explaining the emergence of autonomous stable entities out of the individuated 'holomovement', just as I had initially done and as I have done in the verse. Various mystical sources refer to the consciousness of atoms, molecules, cells, organisms and other such self-organising wholes. I shall focus upon my notion of the mind, the field of attention, as a self-organising process or, to use the term arising from the work of Prigogine on the thermodynamics of open systems far from equilibrium, "dissipative structures". I mentioned above that Odajnyk described the ego as a closed energy field which integrated the activity of the complexes. The Zen meditation complex, into which the ego merges, is, as Odajnyk notes, related to Jung's notion of a complex, a psychological entity with its own personality and volition. I shall discuss below the striking evidence for the existence of such complexes found in Multiple Personality Disorders. First I shall look at some evidence from neuroscience.

Dissipative structures and the brain

Aharon Katchalsky, a physical chemist, studied the dynamic patterns of brain function trying to determine the relationship between the brain's rhythms and oscillations and the integration of the separate activities. Conditions in the brain seemed ideal for dissipative structure formation. Organizing a meeting of cognitive scientists at Massachussetts Institute of Technology in

1972, he introduced Prigogine's ideas to neuroscience, asserting that dissipative structures might represent the transition between brain patterns and mind as in the sudden transitions in perception studied by Gestalt psychology[76]. Katchalsky died two weeks later in a terrorist attack by the Japanese Red Army Faction at Tel Aviv (Yafo) airport. The possible role of self-organising processes resembling dissipative structures in neurobiology, general biology and other natural and socio-economic systems has received attention from a number of authors and has been generalised by Jantsch to all levels of the universe in a popular exposition of such ideas[77]. Karl Pribram[78] states:

> *In the holonomic brain theory the principle of least action leads to minimizing the amount of information, defined as an ensemble of minima of least entropy. Such minima, defined by isovalent contours representing junctional polarizations (polarons) of equal value, can compose a temporarily stable holoscape far from equilibrium. In short the holoscape is a dissipative structure, composed of ensembles of uncertainty minima.*

Pribram[78] points out that such stabilities far from equilibrium operate as *attractors* towards which the process tends. He even uses the metaphor of vortices developing in turbulent systems. Physicists David Bohm and David Peat also use the metaphor of whirlpools and vortices in describing the nature of dissipative structures[79]. Briggs and Peat[80] again use the metaphor of vortices in describing *limit cycles* which are simpler cyclical processes found in various systems, including neural networks, which can lead to dissipative structure formation. Pribram[78] originally thought of stabilities in neural processes in terms of equilibrium but later realised that Prigogine's far-from equilibrium stabilities (dissipative structures), when perturbed, could develop into novel states whereas perturbations of equilibrium states led only to a return to equilibrium. The restabilization of the dissipative structure is unpredictable. Pribram notes the interesting fact that leading neural network researcher Hopfield, in his study of the development of stabilities in neural networks used the same Liapunov functions which Prigogine had used to model dissipative structures. Pribram's point in noting this is presumably that the requirement for the same mathematical functions indicates that similar, or isomorphic, processes are operating in the two cases.

Freeman's studies of the rabbit brain's olfactory bulb have shown the existence of limit-cycle behaviour (which may lead to self-organizing processes) in the extracellular fields associated with the EEG measurements[77]. Recall that Nunez speculates that the fields associated with the EEG and ERPs may be global standing waves involved in integration of local functions[61]. The key feature of the rabbit olfactory bulb's activity is spatio-temporal patterns of activity which do not depend upon the detailed functioning of individual neurons[81]. As Lansner and Liljenstrom state, "Self-organization of patterns appears at the collective level of a large number of neurons".[81] Haken has developed "synergetics", an interdisciplinary field dealing with spontaneous formation of spatial, temporal or functional structures by self-organization in order to study visual pattern recognition[82].

Auto-reverberation and lucidity

Laughlin, McManus and d'Aquili[83], who like myself found inspiration in the writings of Piaget on Structuralism (interestingly Pribram also lists Piaget's *Structuralism* in his reference list) call their approach 'biogenetic structuralism' and recently have attempted to develop a 'neurophenomenology of human consciousness' drawing upon the vast fund of information about consciousness available from various "windows" including a number of scientific fields, psychology, anthropology and also, to a limited extent, Buddhist Abhidharma philosophy which they state is the most sophisticated analytical description of consciousness of which they are aware. They note that most scientists when faced with the vast complexity involved in understanding consciousness take refuge in specialization. Although their approach is more broad-minded, accepting that transcendental aspects of consciousness exist, the actual attempts at interpretation tend to be limited to talk of neural networks and where yogic knowledge is utilized, the emphasis is on the experience of dots (analogous they say to the Hindu notion of *bindu*) of which, the authors claim, the entire world of experience is constructed although no such dots were mentioned in Brown's study of authoritative yogic traditions. They suggest that these dot-like units of experience could correspond to the activity of the cortical columns, the basic units of the cerebral cortex composed of thousands of neurons. They state that structure as process is an activity with formal properties. In regard to the 'empirical ego' (our normal self) they say that it is appropriate to talk of a process that fluctuates within a range of functioning. The ego is "a compound structure, constituting itself moment-to-moment from an enormous number of re-entraining networks". This is essentially the same as in my World Model Field interpretation of 1983 which I saw as a self-organising process delimited by an energetic threshold, having no fixed location but transforming as the patterns of activity changed throughout the brain as a result of information processing functions.

Interestingly, the whirlpool metaphor is also found in the *Yoga Sūtra* tradition. In the *Yogabhāṣya, citta* (the 'mindstuff') whose *vritti* (fluctuations) constitute mentation, is described as fluid-like, like a stream. The cause of the 'hardening' of the *citta* into stable configurations is the tendency of water to eddy and form whirlpools due to obstructions or dispositions (*saṃskāra*) in the water created by upstream obstructions[84]. Aurobindo also speaks of the soul manifested in vital Nature being momentarily imprisoned in that little whirling vortex of life and the swirling, eddying constructs of the sense mind[25]. Taimni[85], commenting on the *Yoga sūtras* describes how the transition between planes of consciousness is experienced as a 'cloud'. This critical phase between two planes of consciousness, says Taimni, is like the critical state between the liquid and gaseous states of matter. The yogi must wait 'in the cloud' until his mind automatically emerges into the next plane. Taimni describes such experiences of *Asaṃprajñāta Samādhi* as hovering between two vehicles. The 'vehicles' represent stable states of consciousness thus the cloud experience of *Asaṃprajñāta Samādhi* suggests an unstable, intermediate state between two stable self-organising states. Taimni also describes the difficulty the yogi has in attaining enlightenment as the emergence of *pratyayas* (contents) throws him back again and again into the world of appearances or illusion, back into the vehicles which he has transcended. This is suggestive of a spontaneous tendency to reconstitute a self-organizing process due to the very constitution of brain processes which requires a supreme effort of will on the part of the yogi to overcome.

I shall argue that the ability of the advanced yogi to remain lucid in states resembling dreaming and deep sleep involves the capacity to maintain self-organising stable processes at different energy levels, activating different brain centres through lengthy practice. This presumably also involves a degree of neural reorganisation to facilitate the maintenance of such stable states. I would add that such neuronal reorganisation is likely to follow as a consequence of the redirection of energetic processes through the power of the will. I am speaking metaphysically here in terms of a degree of freedom available to the individuated 'mind', and in terms of so-called *downward causation*, both of which I shall discuss later. This development of lucidity by the yogi is related to Laughlin *et al.*'s[83] discussion of will and reverberation:

> *"willful consciousness" means that conscious network is significantly auto-reverberative — it remains entrained with a particular array of models, more or less independent of external factors. When we carry out a disciplined program to "strengthen our will" . . . what we are doing, in part at least, is increasing the auto-reverberative capacity of our conscious network.*

The term auto-reverberation, entailing a self-sustaining activity in the neural networks of the brain independent of activity generated by sensory input, corresponds to some extent to my maintenance of a self-organising stable process. Thus by effort of will the yogi develops the capacity to maintain a self-organising process in brain centres which normally do not sustain such activity, resulting in lucidity in regard to deeper brain processes and the ability to exert some degree of volitional control over such processes assuming that the individuated, self-organising process (corresponding to the Jungian term 'complex') is endowed with volitional capacities. The yogi clearly remains both lucid and retains the exercise of will in the deeper states allowing the progressive elimination of all the subtle contents of the mind which have a very strong tendency to spring back into the formation of gross cognitions. In Zen meditation, the ego complex (the normal mind; described by Odajnyk as a closed energy field), against all its natural tendencies, wills itself into merger with the meditation complex (another such energy field created by repetition of the word "Mu") which maintains its own intentionality (volition) in order to attain *satori*.[9]

Individuated complexes and Multiple Personality Disorders

The existence of a number of complexes within the psyche each with the capacity of displaying personality and intentionality appears, as stated above, in Jungian thought. Aurobindo speaks of every part of us having its own complex individuality, the representative ego, of a mass of pre-existent personalities which supply the material and motives behind our surface existence, and of the multitude of subordinate personalities created by the past history of the central person's manifestation or by expressions of it in the inner (deeper) planes which support its present play[25]. Satprem also speaks of the "fragments each with its individual personality and a very distinct centre". These various anarchic centres are brought to order by the sovereign power of the mind which snaps up all the movements of our being and covers them with a coating of thought.[52] This ordering of the anarchic centres is reminiscent of the integrating role of the ego complex as described by Odajnyk in regard to Zen meditation Taimni refers to the creation of 'artificial minds' by the yogi in the *Yoga Sūtras* with the one (natural) mind as the director of the many artificial minds[85]. This clearly seems to be a reference to the same phenomenon of psychical complexes.

These autonomous centres, which under normal circumstances are integrated by the functioning of the ego complex, may come to the fore and take over the body in situations where the normal personality dissociates. This is especially the case in Multiple Personality Disorders (MPDs) where, in extreme cases over a hundred subpersonalities may exist. I should note here that, although MPD is widely known in the USA, it has been largely ignored by British psychiatrists for a number of reasons One British psychologist who has written a book on it calls it a "transatlantic hoax", a phenomenon induced by doctors[86]. Although MPD has been associated with misuse of hypnosis, false child abuse claims etc., the fact remains that it was recognised by early psychologists like Janet prior to the rise of Freudian psychoanalysis which, whilst copying some of Janet's original wor could not come to terms with MPD. Regardless of narrow-minded scepticism, it is difficult to challenge the fact that similar phenomena are reported by diverse sources.

Putnam[87] states that MPD tends to develop in children subjected to severe trauma arising from physical and sexual abuse especially in cases where isolation and sensory deprivation are also invoved in the abuse. MPD cases tend to be highly hypnotizeable, a trait linked to the dissociative potential of the individual. Dissociation ranges from simple cases of daydreaming, through a continuum of more complex experiences ending up with MPD as the most extreme form. Children have a propensity to enter into dissociative states especially when faced with a variety of different situations but, as they grow older and longer attention spans are required, a more unified sense of self across various situational contexts develops. In MPD cases dissociation becomes adaptive due to sustained trauma as the memories of the traumatic experiences are compartmentalized within one or more of the subpersonalities separated off from the others. Sustained trauma reinforces the process of dissociation preventing natural healing of the dissociative states.

With the development of MPD, a variety of subpersonalities may take control of the body leaving the normal 'host' personality (which is not the normal unified personality) experiencing frightening blackout periods, often regaining control of the body in unfamiliar circumstances unaware of how it got itself into this situation (in some cases the subpersonality storing the traumatic memories of sexual abuse, aggrieved by its unfair burden, may take over playing the role of a seducer and then leave the host to return and find herself seemingly being 'raped')[87]. Remarkable changes in bodily function may be associated with the appearance of these alter personalities with even changes in eye colour sometimes reported indicating the powerful influences exerted by the mind over the body[15,88]. There also tends to be found in most, if not all, cases an enigmatic personality called by therapists the Internal Self Helper (or Inner Self Helper (ISH)) which plays the role of a guide, helper, and healer to the whole personality system, speaking rather cryptically like the traditional 'Inner Voice'. Most interestingly, the ISH claims to have always been, to be unborn and uncreated, claiming to remain when the body dies and other personalities disintegrate[89].

From the perspective of the mind as a self-organising process, let us consider the following evidence about the relationships between so-called 'alters' (subpersonalities). Certain groups of personalities are to be found in 'layers' with one overtly recognizable personality masking several covertly active ones. In many cases the layered alters all relate to a specific trauma or life issue[87]. This phenomenon of complexes forming around specific life issues or powerful emotions is also found in the LSD psychotherapy of Stanislaw Grof. Grof refers to these constellations as COEX systems, recognising their similarity to Jung's 'complexes'.[41] Putnam notes that there may also be family groups of alters based on the same traumatic experiences which are *co-conscious* of each other though not of other groups. Co-consciousness implies a degree of overlap between the identities of the alters; some permeability in the dissociative barriers. Alter personalities branch off from the original core personality with each branch itself branching further with the development of the MPD case with the creation of more alters likely if the dissociative trauma is experienced earlier in life. The currently active alters represent the most recent branches of the 'family tree'.[87] Such branching and layering of alters is very suggestive of neural structuring with layers of past personalities lying submerged beneath currently active ones indicating a possible correlation with the layers of neurons in brain tissues.

Therapy involves preliminary fusion of closely related, co-conscious alters. Eventually, after weeks or months of therapy, a more pervasive and thorough psychic restructuring known as integration may occur restoring the original whole personality. Interestingly, such healing seems to require the use of trance, rituals and ceremonies with images of blending together of light or the flowing together of water.[87] Although Putnam states that virtually nothing is known about these processes beyond phenomenological observations and subjective reports, the facts above, taken in conjunction with my previous discussion of dissipative structures, the Zen ego complex, the yogic metaphor of the flowing stream of *citta* (mindstuff) etc. are highly suggestive of self-organising processes operating in separate localities failing to integrate into higher level unified processes. The processes of fusion and integration coupled to the imagery of light and water are especially indicative of energy flows coupled to long-term neuronal reorganization resulting in the breakdown of dissociative barriers (again involving 'downward causation' from the higher level energetic field processes down to the cellular processes underlying their generation).

The existence of MPD clearly poses a serious challenge to attempts to account for mind in terms of conventional scientific notions (Putnam notes that some therapists still have to keep their MPD cases secret from their disbelieving colleagues) whereas it fits in rather comfortably with the view I am presenting here in which an individuated sentient being corresponds to a self-organising process regardless of whether or not this process involves all the features we associate with a normal human personality. It is interesting to note Whitehead's view that every true individual has a unity of experiences in which a vast myriad of influences are synthesized. Electrons, atoms, molecules, cells and organisms constitute individuals and compound individuals (higher level individuals). Sticks, stones and tables are *aggregates* of individuals lacking a sense of unity and unified movement. For Whitehead, 'mind' refers to what an actual entity is in itself, whereas 'matter' refers to what it is for others[90]. I had no knowledge of Whitehead's ideas when I put forward my model of closed 'structures' and 'aggregates' back in 1983. In 1988 I even used the Kantian terminology to describe the psychical attribute as 'noumenal' and the physical attribute as 'phenomenal' which corresponds to Whitehead's 'what an entity is in itself and what it is for others' although this use of Kantian terminology was anathema to the referee who considered my work "folk psychology" as Kant himself had not used these terms in this way!

Theoretical (mathematical) biologist Brian Goodwin, discussing the nature of organisms, asserts that the organisms' fields constitute a regulative whole defined by a logical property of closure. He stresses that *closure* and *autonomy* do not mean independence; the organism is a 'dissipative structure' in Prigogine's phrase[33]. Biophysicist Mae-Wan Ho states that an organism is a dissipative structure in the sense that it is maintained in a steady state by a flow of energy and chemicals[91]. Interestingly, Briggs and Peat note that spiral galaxies are formed by the same autocatalytic types of processes that produce simple chemical dissipative structures[80]. Friedman, discussing the pictures of the

3-dimensional world as an emergent process arising from the projection and introjection of energy from a transcendental order as in the ideas of David Bohm, states that, if this is so, the material realm can be viewed as a dissipative structure, with a self-organizing principle. He speaks of a creative element at work in Nature's self-organization[39]. I will discuss in a later section the relationship between yogic phenomenology, which has inspired picture's like Bohm's, and cosmology. The point to note here is that such cosmologies are derived from yogic phenomenology where the world of space, time and (normal) causality are seen to be projected from the subtle flow of the Light beyond space and time as we know it. Thus by stating that the material realm in David Bohm's picture can be interpreted as a dissipative structure, Friedman is, in effect, stating that the process of phenomenal world-creation in the mind can be viewed as a dissipative structure. The creative element at work in Nature's self-organization must be identified, in physical terms, as the flow of energy which maintains such organization.

2(d). ENERGY AND CONSCIOUSNESS

> *True energy is the energy of consciousness.* P.D. Ouspensky

> *The energetic activity considered in physics is the emotional intensity entertained in life.* A.N. Whitehead

At the end of his book comparing the views of David Bohm, the Perennial Philosophy and Seth (a personality supposedly clair-voyantly channeled by novelist Jane Roberts whom I would interpret as her own inner voice/*ātman*/inner self helper), Friedman notes that the velocity of light relates matter and energy in Einstein's $e = mc^2$ and that the *Tibetan Book of the Dead* states that the Light is the only Reality. He states that Bohm saw his 'holomovement' (the total Reality including Bohm's explicate and implicate orders) as an ocean of light energy[39]. Although Bohm, in his later work, hinted at panpsychism with statements along the lines of consciousness and matter being indistinguish-able at subtler levels of order, he was rarely, if ever, explicit on this point. Steven Rosen[59] says of Bohm:

> *Rather than facing the problem of undifferentiability head on — in classical Cartesian language, facing the problem of mind — this problem is put off interminably by an endless series of abstractions upon the differentiable or physical.*

Rosen acknowledges that Bohm, in his 'Vedantist' moods recognised that mathematical abstractions such as 'implicate orders' do not approach undifferentiable, ultimate reality or the 'infinite totality'. It is clear that Bohm found the issue of consciousness very problematical and focused on the physical aspects of Reality, stressing energy rather than consciousness. It is interesting to note that Einstein, who like Bohm was influenced by Spinoza stating that his God was the God of Spinoza, did not actually accept the panpsychism that followed from Spinoza's 'substance' endowed with the attribute of thought and hence a self-conscious God. Heisenberg saw Einstein's inability to come to terms with the problems of Quantum Theory involving the observer's role in determining what was observed as stemming from the subject/object duality permeating Western culture sharply delimiting observer and observed[35]. In fact, Einstein's inability to shake off his belief in Spinoza's determinism also hindered his understanding of the Quantum Theory which indicated an underlying spontaneity. At the very end of his aforementioned book[39], Friedman says:

> *reality at its most fundamental level is consciousness. As Seth says, "All energy contains consciousness". If we accept that simple statement, it would indeed change our world. What we call matter is a gestalt of consciousness, and consciousness is light. So: All is light, and light is consciousness, and that is All that Is.*

Origins and nature of the concepts of energy

I have mentioned how Robert Mayer came to postulate the principle of the Conservation of Energy without knowing much about physics and how this idea, as A.O. Lovejoy noted, represents a modern version of similar ideas found in many societies of a power or energy underlying the transformations of the phenomenal world such as the Melanesian *mana*, the Chinese *chi* (*qi*) or the Indian *prāṇa*. Native American Vine Deloria states that if you substitute the word 'energy' for 'spirit' in some of the passages of recorded Sioux knowledge then you have something very similar to the modern notion of matter and energy. Spirit or energy was the primary mode of existence for the Teton Sioux[92]. Heisenberg[35] notes that if we replace Heraclitus' word 'fire' by 'energy' we can almost restate the modern picture:

> *Energy is in fact the substance from which all elementary particles, all atoms and therefore all things are made, and energy is that which moves. Energy is a substance, since its total amount does not change . . . Energy may be called the fundamental cause for all change in the world.*

Heisenberg compares the concept of *energy* to Aristotle's *potentia* which becomes 'actualized' by means of form. Stapp[93] points out that the intuitive idea of the wave function of the quantum theory as representing 'tendencies' or 'potentia' for actual events was first made explicit by Bohm in 1951 and later endorsed by Heisenberg. Matt[30] notes that the Jewish mystical concept of *ayin* (nothingness), like the Platonic primordial, formless matter *hyle*, is capable of assuming any form. Transformation is only possible through *ayin* which embraces all potentiality. In the Hindu Tantric tradition, the stuff of all existence is energy, the primordial energy known as *mahāshakti*.[94] Long[95] states that the basal universal energy (*tejas, tapas, shakti*) in Hinduism creates, supports and (according to some schools) constitutes all living things. This universal energy is conceived to be something on the order of an electrical current or a bundle of forces fluctuating within an electromagnetic field. Ho[91] states that *qi* in Chinese Taoist thought is "the undifferentiated primal energy pervading the universe which is the substrate for realizing the multiplicity of things". She points out the similarity to Whitehead's underlying, eternal "energy of realization".

Saul-Paul Sirag notes that the concept of 'energy' did not exist in Newtonian physics; 'energy' was used in a personal context, the feeling of being able to move freely, the feeling of vitality[96]. Newtonian physics involved concepts such as *work* and *force*, which I noted in the Introduction was projected onto Nature from our experience of volition. It is also very interesting to note that Newton stated that the ultimate mechanism of change in the universe was the mystery of how mind controlled matter[97]. Sirag points out that 'energy as freedom and vitality' was championed by the Romantics like Blake who objected to the determinism of Newtonian physics. The concept of energy in physics arose in relation to the study of heat (another subjective feeling projected onto the operations of Nature). Joule made the concept of energy respectable by showing an exact correspondence between heat energy and mechanical energy. Sirag says that the notion of a *field* developed in relation to the notion of energy. Now all the forces are understood in terms of 'energy' fields. Physical properties such as mass, charge and spin are forms of energy[96].

Taylor and Taylor state that energy constitutes both the material and the efficient causes for Science, which does not seek Aristotle's two other causes (formal and final). Natural science is content to accept energy as a given which requires no ontological explanation[98]. Indeed, in a recent television programme about physics and religion, a physicist working with the huge particle accelerator at Fermilab in the USA rambled on about the creation of the universe out of 'nothing' apparently oblivious that he was contradicting himself in that he also talked about a pre-existent energy for which he offered no explanation. I have referred to Bohm's views regarding the underlying ocean of energy which Science assumes but then ignores for practical model-building purposes; Friedman describes the mathematical trick called "renormalization" whereby the infinite energies associated with the fields surrounding particles are removed and points out that J.A. Wheeler has also calculated that empty space (vacuum) may contain unimaginably vast amounts of energy[39]. Griffin states that Herbert Spencer saw the principle of the Conservation of Energy as the most fundamental law of physics which, as being the basis of Science, cannot be explained by Science. Spencer, like most 19th century positivists believed that the mysterious link binding cause and effect which had eluded Hume had been discovered in energy as the substrate for all transformations[55].

The information given above should give a clear indication as to the status of *energy* as the ground-stuff of natural science. As I stated in the Introduction, the argument put forward by Bernstein that if you hitch your mysticism to today's physics theories it will be lost when the theory is replaced, does not hold in regard to my correlation of Pure Consciousness with energy. Physical theories describe the transformations of the forms of energy and the theories change in regard to such descriptions of the transformations, not in regard to the ontological status of energy itself which, as we have seen, Science says nothing about. It is appropriate here to mention the ridiculous notion of so-called "Theories of Everything" often touted in popular scientific writing, sometimes by quite eminent scientists. Clearly any such theory, describing only transformations, says nothing about the psychical attribute of Reality and realms beyond Space and Time are usually ignored or given short shrift. The nonsensical status of such modern mythology is best contemplated by trying to picture these mathematical formalisms and trying to imagine whatever they represent becoming every conceivable aspect of Reality. It soon becomes clear that such abstractions are no more than mental constructions, skeletal features of the fullness of actuality, describing only some regular, stable features. On the contrary, in the mystical union, the yogi realises oneness with a reality of conscious energy which by direct intuition reveals its status as the Ground of all Being which has the potential to become every imaginable psychophysical form.

Energy and matter in mysticism and altered states of consciousness

Keeping in mind that the scientific concepts of force and energy arose as projections of our subjective feelings of volition, freedom and vitality, let us now consider the notion of energy in mysticism and related areas especially in regard to its close association with consciousness. In the introduction I quoted Rāmakrishna's assertion that *Brahman* (the pure consciousness) and *Shakti* (the divine energy) were not two but were like the snake and its smoothly flowing motion. In monistic Kashmiri Shaivism, Ultimate Reality is Consciousness, Pure Universal Consciousness which is called *mahāprakāśa* (the Great Light) and is uncreated. All other divine attributes are attributes of Consciousness. However, in monistic Kashmiri Shaivism, Consciousness is not a passive witness (*sākṣin*) as is the case in the dualistic *Sānkhya* philosophy (associated with the *Yoga Sūtras*) and in the supposedly non-dualistic *Advaita Vedānta* but is full of the conscious activity (*citikriyā*) through which it generates the universe.

This activity, resulting in the manifestation of the universe, is vibration (*spanda*). *Māyā* in Kashmiri Shaivism is the power of the Absolute to appear in diverse forms and not an illusion as it is in *Advaita Vedānta*. Matter and the entire universe are absolutely real as congealed or contracted Consciousness. Consequently, no object is totally insentient, even stones bear a trace of Consciousness[99,100].

Satprem, a follower of Aurobindo, also states that matter is the final precipitate, the ultimate product of the densification of consciousness. Aurobindo spoke of *consciousness-force* as consciousness *is* a force. Satprem states that the ancient Indian tradition never spoke of consciousness *chit* without adjoining it to the term *agni* (heat, energy, flame); *chit-agni* or *chit-tapas* (consciousness heat or consciousness energy). All the forces are conscious and the Universal Force is a Universal Consciousness. Referring to Einstein's $e = mc^2$, Satprem points out that matter is condensed energy; this energy in practice is discovered to be consciousness and thus matter too is a form of consciousness[52]. Aurobindo states that the force of the Divine is the one energy that alone exists[25]. Both Aurobindo and Satprem quote the *Muṇḍaka Upaniṣad:*

> *By energism of consciousness (tapas) Brahman is massed; from that matter is born.*

The Prāṇa/Ātman relationship

Jordens, in comparing Jung's concept of libido (the general psychic energy rather than Freud's sexual energy) with the concept of *prāṇa,* focuses on the *Kauṣītakī Upaniṣad* in order to catch the *prāṇa* doctrine at a stage of development where it is vigorously presented but before it is caught up in the complex mythology and symbolism of later developments[101]. "As long as *prāṇa* resides in the body, so there is life", states the Upaniṣad, hence the often used term 'life energy'. The Upaniṣad also states that *prāṇa* is *prajñā* which Jordens says means consciousness in general. The *prajñāmātrāh,* the elements of consciousness, are fixed on *prāṇa* and dependent upon it. *Prajñā* is reabsorbed in the *prāṇa* in deep sleep and in death. Jordens states that the close observation of the gradual retreat into deep sleep and the process of dying suggest that phenomenal experience and empiric consciousness emerge from the vital force of *prāṇa*. Jordens notes that in both the *Kauṣītakī Upaniṣad* and Jung's thought, (phenomenal) consciousness wells up from a more original and basic life force (it should be noted that Jung's "consciousness" is ego consciousness). The *Upaniṣad* also states that, "this *prāṇa* is indeed *prajñātman*, asserting that the *ātman* is both the vital force (*prāṇa*) and consciousness (*prajñā*) which are two aspects of the same reality. Thus *prāṇa* the energy without which the body cannot remain alive and into which the phenomenal consciousness dissolves in deep sleep and death (highly suggestive of the brainwaves from the reticular activating system whose cessation entails death) is identified with *ātman*, the 'superconsciousness' realized in deep sleep and trance which is one with *Brahman*. Chennakesavan[102] notes that in the *Brihadāraṇyaka Upaniṣad* it is specifically stated that the *Prāṇa* or life-principle is the immortal *Ātman*. She also mentions that the same identification is found, as we have seen, in the *Kauṣītakī Upaniṣad*. Again in monistic Kashmiri Shaivism[99] we are told that Pure Universal Consciousness transforms itself into the vital breath (equivalent to *prāṇa*). Aurobindo asserts that Supramental Consciousness is not only a Knowledge, a Bliss, Love and Oneness, it is also a Will, Power and Force which are the native substance of the Life-Energy. Our whole mind-consciousness, he says, is shot through with threads and currents of *prāṇa* which has both physical and psychical aspects[25]. Panda[100] notes that Gaudapada asserted that the world of appearance is due to the vibration of *citta* or *prāṇa*. Thus we see that the concept of *prāṇa*, the energy without which the body cannot sustain life and which is an aspect of the Pure Consciousness, is perfectly compatible with my identification of the Pure Consciousness with the activating brainwaves from the reticular activating system which is the energy that flows through the brain activating the brain centres and upon whose cessation, death occurs. The description of the dissolution of normal consciousness into the *prāṇa* in dreamless sleep and death described by the *Kauṣītakī Upaniṣad* again fits my interpretation of the mind as a self-organizing process in the energy fields dissipating as the frequency of activating waves of energy slows in dreamless sleep.

The link between consciousness and energy is also to be found in more recent texts relating to the nature of the psyche. Mavromatis[63], speaking of hypnagogia and related experiences, states that the altered realities may be thought of in current scientific terms as fields of energy of varying types and intensity. All these realities interpenetrate each other, existing in one space with their ultimate nature as "sheer Energy". This underlying energy, says Mavromatis, is not so much physical as psychical. In relation to LSD-induced experiences, Grof[41] (who notes that the drug appears to act simply as a catalyst for activating potential brain states) states that an important characteristic of psychedelic experience is transcendence of the sharp distinction between matter, energy and consciousness. What appears as solid material stuff can disintegrate into patterns of energy, vibrations, or a play of consciousness. Those who considered matter to be the basis of existence with mind as a product of matter are led by their LSD-induced experience of altered states to realise that, ultimately, consciousness is the only reality.

Thus repeatedly we see the association of consciousness with energy in the mystical traditions and also in modern experiences of altered states of consciousness. We have seen that the scientific concept of energy is itself derived from projections of subjective feelings associated with freedom and vitality which in turn may be associated with flows of energy in the body associated with the term *prāṇa,* which tends to be used more generally for bodily energy rather than in the restricted sense described above. *Prāṇa* also appears as the macrocosmic universal energy tying in with the modern scientific concept of the universal energy which is the same energy that flows in our bodies. The authoritative yogic traditions speak in terms which translate into energy fields and Zen meditation, according to Odajnyk, involves experiencing the mind as a closed energy field which merges with another such field, the meditation complex. The identification of *prāṇa* with the *ātman,* the descriptions of the pulsating, vibrating consciousness in Kashmiri Shaivism and Gaudapada's interpretation of the phenomenal world being the result of *cittaspandita* (the vibrations of the mindstuff) all point towards the correlation of mental experiences with the energetic pulsations in the field activity of the brain. More generally, given the status of energy as the ontologically unexplained groundstuff of physical phenomena in Science which tends to ignore the unimaginably vast amounts of energy implied to exist in empty space by its own theories, the correlation of consciousness and energy indicates that Reality is indeed panpsychic and suggests further that the universe may indeed actualize from an 'ocean' of consciousness energy. We see in the origins of such scientific concepts, the projection of subjective qualities or feelings onto Nature, showing that Science itself is based on the same sort of animistic projections for which modern philosophers poke fun at premodern societies. However, Science abstracts from the psychophysical reality of our experience but the spatio-temporal, physical attributes for projection onto Nature which is then conceived as devoid of psychical attributes. This in effect results in a "despiritualization" by abstraction of spatio-temporal and regular features of the world of experience taking this artificial world of abstractions to be the actual, substantial Reality. These metaphysical facts are incredibly simple to grasp and yet seem beyond the capacity of countless supposedly great thinkers of the modern world, whom history will no doubt judge to be far lesser minds than the hagiographers of the modern world present them to be. It is clear that the scientific concept of energy plays the role played by spirit in traditional metaphysics as the Ground of all Being except that the modern split between mind and matter leaves it shorn of its true psychophysical nature as the energy of consciousness.

2(e). THE INTERFACE OF MIND AND COSMOS (PHENOMENOLOGY AND ONTOLOGY)

Not surprisingly, many people who encounter yogic philosophy can come to terms with it as phenomenology, the description of conscious experience, and in regard to matters parapsychological etc. but are wary of the assertions of cosmic significance which sit, seemingly uncomfortably, alongside the descriptions of how the phenomenal world of experience is constructed. Kaplan, for instance, stresses that the Advaitic notion of *māyā* should not be considered merely as ontological and epistemological statements but needs to be considered in its phenomenological aspect in the light of the Advaitic theory of perception[103]. Chapple, commenting on such debates in regard to *Sānkhya-Yoga* states that cosmological explanations are simply irrelevant to the Sānkhyan thrust[65].

Monistic Kashmiri Shaivism, on the other hand, asserts that the manifestation of the universe is equivalent to the emergence of thought in Universal Consciousness[99]. Carl Jung, like Kaplan, preferred to leave to one side the broader metaphysical assertions and focus on the psychological, claiming, as we have seen, that in failing to distinguish between philosophy and psychology Eastern intuition had over-reached itself. I too was at first inclined towards this position finding it very difficult to see how such phenomenological knowledge of the perceptual processes could reveal the secrets of Creation. Thus in 1994 when I had the synchronicitous encounter with the Hindu myth concerning the character Sutapas in the book *Māyā in Śaṅkara*, I was a bit perplexed as to what my thought on the nature of consciousness had to do with the secret of Creation. Although I had myself juxtaposed the creation hymn *Nāsadīya Sūkta* and related ideas involving *Brahman* as the source of the universe with the Upaniṣadic teachings of *Brahman* as the ground of consciousness within us in the verse, how these two sets of ideas about *Brahman* were linked together and how this knowledge of Creation was arrived at did not particularly bother me at the time of writing as I did not understand how any of this philosophy was derived.

In Daniel Brown's study of the three authoritative yogic traditions[23], in addition to describing the deconstruction of perception in the main path to enlightenment, he also describes so-called 'insight meditation' in which, after attaining proficiency in progressing along the deconstructive path, the yogi reverses the perceptual deconstruction processes slowly to see how the mind creates the world. A stage is attained in which the yogi refines his or her awareness of the flow of the light to the temporal structure of ordinary perception. The yogi is then able to discern the very process by which phenomena are manifested. The yogic traditions assert that since the same laws governing the manifestation of mental phenomena operate in the wider cosmos, the yogi has reached "the interface of mind and cosmos".

Microcosm/macrocosm, analogy and projection

Bohm and Peat[79], in discussing the origin of the notion of Reason in the concept of ratio, discuss the question as to why the universe should be intelligible to us at all. The ultimate relationship between human intelligence and the intelligibility of the universe, they state, can be understood through the traditional notion that each person is a *microcosm* standing in analogy to the the whole cosmos. Thus through intelligent perception of *ratio*, a person can produce analogies to whatever exists in the universe. They state:

> *For if this person is an analogy to all this, then looking outward and looking inward will be two sides of one cycle of activity in which any aspect of the totality can in principle be revealed.*

In the Western tradition, similar ideas of the person as a microcosm have been associated with the phrase, "As above, so below". As with the Vedāntic doctrine of the *Ātman-Brahman*, Plotinus held that the centre of the soul coincided with the centre of the All[104]. It follows that if the *Ātman* is one with *Brahman*, the Ground of All Being, then in realising one's deeper, true Self one is realising what it is to be that which manifests the entire universe. In using the term *realising* here, I am equating *knowledge* with *being*. All knowledge reflects states of our being, the information of the mind, hence all knowledge is in fact realization or knowledge through being one with that which is known in the sense that that which is known is usually a representation rather than the actuality. Those who find the notion of mystical realization unacceptable should consider that our everyday experiences are no less realizations but, as we are so familiar with them, we take these miracles for granted. It is during meditative exercises which result in so-called *deutomatization* of perception, using Deikman's[46] term, in which each perception of commonplace forms appears as if it is being perceived for the first time that one begins to really appreciate this fact that our everday perception is just as much a mysterious realization as the realizations that come to us in flashes of intuition or in other mystical states of mind. As Aurobindo often states, our everyday mental faculties are but limited expressions of the higher powers of the spiritual reality experienced in the higher planes which he called Overmind and Supermind.

I have pointed out that basic scientific concepts such as force, energy, heat, etc. are derived from animistic projections of subjective experiences. Thus again we are encountering analogical relations between microcosm and macrocosm, although the relationships are subtle. As I say in the verse, though in a somewhat different context, "We look far out into our mind". E.A. Burtt in his classic *The Metaphysical Foundations of Modern Physical Science* stated that the "whole vast realm which science reveals finds its rational order and meaning in the knowing activity of the human mind."[105] Jahn and Dunne[40] state:

> *It is also essential to our approach that the common concepts of established physical theories, such as mass, momentum, and energy; electric charge and magnetic field; frequency and wavelength; the quantum and the wave function; and even distance and time, be regarded as no more than useful information-organizing categories that consciousness has developed for ordering the chaos of stimuli bombarding it . . .*

In support of their stance they quote Francis Bacon, who stated that all the perceptions of our senses and mind bear reference to man and not to the universe, Heisenberg, who stated that the same organizing forces shaping nature have also shaped our minds, and Planck, who pointed out that all our ideas of the outer world are ultimately only reflections of our perceptions. They correctly note that such arguments need not be restricted to scientific concepts, *analogies* from any field of human knowledge reveal the organizational properties of the human mind[40]. In this regard, it is interesting to note that Karl Pribram, following Denis Gabor (the Nobel laureate inventor of holography) has been using the mathematical formalisms of Quantum Theory to model the processes involved in perception in his Holonomic Quantum Field Neurodynamics[78] which I have referred to above in regard to the mind as a dissipative structure. Remember that Heisenberg[106] himself stated that whilst thinking up quantum mechanics he was subconsciously influenced by Indian philosophy revealing again the subtle hidden relationships between scientific theories and the processes of perception. Various authors, including Penrose[107], have played upon the idea that quantum coherent states, in which a collection of particles behave as a unified whole, are somehow maintained at the macroscopic level in the functioning of the brain in a manner resembling the macroscopic coherence in superconductivity. We will again encounter this concept of coherence in regard to mind-body interactions. I will later discuss the problematical question of realms beyond our normal experience of space and time especially in regard to paranormal phenomena. As stated above, the yogi, on the path to enlightenment must deconstruct the time-space matrix of perception, whereby (s)he experiences the unitary realm which underlies this. It becomes clear that the notions like Einstein's in which gravity is pictured as the curvature of a space-time continuum is itself partly a projection of such deep perceptual organization. I have mentioned that Laughlin, McManus and d'Aquili[83] state that atomistic theories were probably projections of the dots (or *bindu*) which they assert make up the field of perception. We must keep in mind though that human perception has evolved to model (or re-*present*) the gross features of the external world which are of survival value to the human and thus such projections of perceptual organization can lead to reasonable, abstract, predictive models of the external world as achieved by Science (which is now learning the limitations of such simple mechanistic models through developments such as Chaos theory), just as the mind itself attempts to predict the outcomes of events through its own imaginative faculties.

Realms of potentialities, actualization and transcendental causation

Nobel laureate physicist Brian Josephson thinks that Fritjof Capra was being pessimistic in asserting that science and mysticism were unlikely to be connected. Josephson[108] applauds the efforts of Bohm and sees mathematics as the key. The ordinary reality of the senses corresponds, he says, to classical physics, the subtler planes ("astral, celestial") to the physical reality described by Quantum Theory and finally the transcendental experience, he asserts, corresponds to Bohm's implicate order. Josephson says that ordinary scientific instruments are of no use in explaining the deeper planes as they are designed to function in the material realm. Scientists of the future, he says, should re-explore the deeper realms already well-known to mystics and perhaps attempt to describe these realms mathematically. He points out that the subtler planes of mystical experience relate to fantasy or possibility which is reminiscent of the possibility or potentiality aspects of Quantum Theory. He holds that there is an actual identity behind this parallelism. I would be more cautious here in directly equating the two, but Josephson is clearly pointing to a fascinating parallel here between the flux of possibilities associated with dreams, fantasies and deeper realms of consciousness, where reality does not seem to have become set into a fixed pattern and the uncertain, unpredictable deeper realms beyond the measurements of Quantum Theory which seems to involve tendencies, or *potentia*, as Bohm and Heisenberg noted. Keeping in mind Gabor's and Pribram's work using the mathematical formalisms of Quantum Theory for modelling perception-related processes in the brain, it seems clear that Quantum Theory with its actualizations of measurable events from a realm of uncertainty which is *nonlocal*, transcending normal spatial relations, reflects the projection of similar actualization processes in the brain whereby fixed states are resolved from a flux of possibilities.

Friedman[39] states that Heisenberg developed the idea that the world beneath the realm of phenomena contains all possible events in potential form. In *potentia*, particles have no real existence, only tendencies to exist. Numerous writers have tried to relate the transcendental aspects of our mind with the aspects of Quantum Theory that transcend our conceptualizations. Physicist Amit Goswami has incorporated Heisenberg's use of the notion of *potentia* in his attempts to show that the material world is a construction of our consciousness. Goswami asserts that it is the intentionality (volition) of our conscious minds being held responsible for the so-called collapse of the quantum wave function which results in the actualization of one variant from a set of possibilities (according to this interpretation of the so-called superposition of states in the wave function)[109]. From a more empirical perspective, Jahn and Dunne, reporting on their experiments at the Princeton Engineering Anomalies Laboratory which prove beyond doubt the existence of psychokinetic influences (in spite of the displays of the psychological defence mechanism of denial by the bewildered sceptics), state that, although such psychokinetic deviations from chance distributions are clearly demonstrated, when the results from various subjects are recombined in a balanced way, the total distribution again resembles the chance distribution. This suggests that what may be happening is that subjects are able to select from the grand chance distribution of potentially available outcomes those subsets suiting their purposes without affecting the overall distribution. They comment that what we denote as chance behaviour, rather than deriving from mechanistic behaviour and deterministic laws, may actually be a subsumption of a broader distribution of potentialities reflective of all possible resonances and intentions of consciousness with respect to the system in question[40] (i.e. chance reflects our ignorance of the actual processes at work on the system which are the subtle influences being exerted by mental intentions).

Similar ideas are expressed by physicist Thompson[110] who bases his views on Vedic views (from the *Bhagavad Gītā* and *Brahma Saṃhitā*) that *Paramātma* (the Supreme Self, superconsciousness or Supreme Being, usually called *Brahman*) creates the illusion that the material world operates independently by imposing certain regular laws on its behaviour, creating a field of activity for limited conscious selves (*jīvātmas*). If the laws were strictly deterministic then the *jīvātmas* would be mere epiphenomena riding helplessly upon these material processes but the Vedic literature asserts, says Thompson, that the laws are actually non-deterministic allowing the *jīvātmas* to manifest free will. The *Paramātma* provides a subtle link between the free will of the limited, individuated *jīvātmas* and the material realm (the latter is itself an emanation of the Supreme and not an independent substance). The free will of the individual is constrained by the laws of nature, resulting in a high degree of determinism although the laws are not fully deterministic. The limited influence that the *jīvātma* can have on the material realm is further constrained by the conflicting wishes of other individual beings. A balance is struck between these conflicting sets of desires by the *Paramātma* which operates like a sort of medium harmonizing the conflicting forces. Indeed, Thompson goes on to state that this picture helps us to understand the results of Jahn and Dunne's psychokinesis experiments in which, although goal-directed behaviour influenced by individual wills may occur, overall the situation generally accords with the laws of physics.

In fact Jahn and Dunne[40] themselves go on to state that very large databases are required to extract the consciousness-related anomalies as the effects are so tiny and continue:

> *In interactions with physical atomic domains, the consciousness margins of reality may become comparable in scale with the basic processes themselves, and thereby acquire much greater relative importance. In fact, they may just be the basic processes in toto, and all atomic reality may be established by these mechanisms alone.*

In support of this view, resembling karmic doctrines, they cite Schrödinger and Eddington with the former emphasising that mind and matter are made of the same stuff, sense perceptions, imagination etc. arranged in different orders with conscious minds in general controlling the motion of atoms.

Clearly, the attempt to link the actualization of events in the physical realm from a realm of seeming possibilities to the manifestation of the phenomenal world in the mind from deeper levels associated with coexisting multiple possibilities does support the yogic claim that the same laws govern the manifestation of phenomena in the external world as in the mind. Such ideas have been developed by Bohm who not only used metaphors of flashing sequences of lights for his unfoldment/enfoldment of phenomena from his underlying 'implicate order' paralleling the actual experience of certain Buddhist traditions, but also used models inspired by scientific knowledge of perception[54], as well as yogic knowledge, to help elucidate the relationship between the physical world of space and time to the deeper levels of Reality of which the material world is in fact a perceptual abstraction as will become more clear as we proceed if it is not already apparent from previous discussions of the physical world as our interpretation of phenomena, scientific concepts as abstractions of regular, spatio-temporal attributes of Reality and the material plane as being the plane of gross perceptions. Finkelstein states that, for Bohm, Science is a mode of perception before it is a mode of obtaining knowledge of the laws of nature; something Finkelstein himself, influenced by Bohm, has come to understand[111]. I would note here that both perception and Science, as I have stated above, utilise models constructed from limited information abstracted from Reality to predict future states of systems under consideration. The data studied by Science is a selection of the available data filtered through philosophical presuppositions, technological constraints, theoretical constructs and a variety of, individual and collective, subjective judgements which determine what Science should focus upon and how even this limited data is interpreted. The term *darśana*, traditionally used for the major systems of Indian philosophy, is appropriate in this context as it implies a particular "way of looking", which is not the only way. Similar ideas may be found in works such as *Science as Cognitive Process*[112] (which I have not read but is mentioned by one of its authors, Laughlin, in other articles[113]) which explores the neurocognitive foundations of Science. Laughlin points out that, contrary to the classical view of Hume, causation is demonstrably an *a priori* attribute of perception (as of course are space and time as was lately rediscovered by the modern West through Kant). Abstract patterns of causal relations encountered in perception may be projected upon experience, a process which Whitehead referred to as "extensive abstraction". Laughlin notes that in some yogic traditions, the adept is given a set of exercises specifically designed to develop awareness of causation. Scientific models of causation are found to be abstractions from a transcendental level of causation which is concordant with our subjective experience of causation[34]. The yogic realisation of the true nature of causation in the unitary transcendental realm beyond the time/space matrix of perception is also mentioned in Brown's aforementioned study of the three authoritative yogic traditions. In this regard, Willis Harman states that the Western concept of scientific causality is easily included in the Indian cosmology as a special case. The reverse, however, is not true[114].

Mythology, ignorance, prophets, icons and scripture in modern science

Returning to the question posed at the beginning of this section regarding how it is possible to make grand ontological/cosmological assertions from the phenomenal knowledge gained through yogic practice, we see that the issue becomes less problematical once we appreciate that all knowledge consists of realizations, that the ground of our own existence is the ground of the universe, and that the scientific cosmology is itself a product of a limited mode of perception involving subtle projections abstracted from internal realizations onto the external world which certainly is not known as it actually is through such scientific abstractions of limited features of the psychophysical reality of our experience. Thus, for instance, Jung's claims that Eastern intuition over-reached itself in making such metaphysical and cosmological claims and his assertion that the 'Indian Mind' was "pre-Kantian" are seen to be narrow-minded views based on a naïve Eurocentric model of the progress of human knowledge believing that European rediscoveries of facts such as the *a priori* nature of our mental categories of space and time, represent major breakthroughs in human understanding never attained by non-Europeans. Kant's simple insights come nowhere near the remarkable insight and understanding attained by yogis since time immemorial of the perceptual construction and deconstruction of our time-space (and causality) categories of perception. I have already mentioned W.V.O. Quine's surprise that de Morgan's law was already known to ancient Indians and that *Advaita Vedānta* had a far superior understanding of the causes of dreams, including wish-fulfilment, than that vastly over-rated Western icon, Sigmund Freud, whom Western pseudo-intellectuals and many intellectuals hold in such esteem clearly demonstrating the powerful hold of simple myths over the Western Mind.

If we consider the issue of the vacuum energy assumed but ignored by Science, as emphasised by Bohm, the problems Science faces in regard to the origin of the universe, the very status of the scientific concept of 'energy' and the supposed 'laws of nature', numerous other issues such as parapsychological facts, and of course the very question of consciousness and its multifarious implications in so many questions relating to our existence where Science remains silent or denies relevant issues as pre-modern myths, we see that Western scientific cosmology itself remains very much a mythology in spite of the vast arrays of empirical data it marshalls in support of its latest models. Here we encounter issues related to *frames of reference* where the person indoctrinated into the scientific frame of reference is often so closed-minded and dogmatic that he does not even acknowledge the broader issues, let alone understand their relevance in revealing the limitations of the scientific cosmology, preferring to show a contemptuous disdain for those who do consider these issues to be important and brazenly displaying his ignorance of his own ignorance. One only has read or listen to a few British newspapers or radio broadcasts to find pillars of the scientific establishment rubbishing anything that they do not really understand or cannot comprehend. It often seems is as if they think that inflections of an upper middle class English patriarchal accent is sufficient reason to dismiss all things they do not believe in. This, like some of the fundamental aspects of Western science, reflects a hangover from Semitic religious traditions renowned for their dogmatism and inability to see the viewpoint of others (overlayed with more recent Eurocentric, colonialistic hangovers). Ironically, this dogmatic, tribalistic approach of the Semitic religions is sometimes unwittingly used in support of the uniqueness of the Greeks myth which some still espouse whilst dismissing claims of scientific approaches in Eastern traditions. Similarly, the status of influential scientific and often pseudo-scientific psychological thinkers often has far more to do with their role as modern prophets endowed with some superhuman capacity to receive divine revelation, a capacity which must not be questioned for the modern West does not understand that the sources of such insight can be attained by anyone given practice and thus remains in line with the Western religious traditions in following the distortions of influential prophets rather than seeking universal knowledge.

For instance, as I was editing this passage, the BBC broadcast a programme about the role of the two Hungarians John von Neumann and Edward Teller in the development of the atomic and hydrogen bombs. The 'legendary' von Neumann (who thought up some of the mathematics used in quantum mechanics, the programmable computer, the theory of games, hypothetical self-replicating machines etc.) was almost deified as the "cleverest man in the world". The television programme told us that it took a von Neumann to see the possibility of this, or the possibility of that. However, for all of his undoubted achievements, it should be remembered that von Neumann also wrote a highly influential book entitled *The Mathematical Foundations of Quantum Mechanics* (1932) in which he provided mathematical arguments supposedly proving that the established results of quantum mechanics could never be re-derived with the help of hidden parameters. Most physicists took this as God's Word until in 1951 David Bohm re-derived quantum mechanics in his Causal Interpretation, which gave the same theoretical predictions, but based on a more apprehensible picture giving a physical interpretation to the wave function. None the less, the von Neumann approach of focusing on the mathematics rather than what the mathematics means still holds sway over most physicists. It should be clear that cleverness and mathematical prowess do not equate to a god-like understanding of Reality or some sort of divine communion not available to others. Grof notes how LSD subjects well versed in mathematics and physics can experience in altered states of consciousness ordinarily unimaginable mathematical concepts involving extra dimensions or different sorts of space and time relations some of which are utilised by physics[41]. The best-selling status of Stephen Hawking's *A Brief History of Time* reflects far more the naïve projections by laymen of supernatural powers onto the wheelchair-bound, motor neurone disease sufferer Stephen Hawking (whose computer-aided voice adds even more mystique to his remarkable personality) than any remarkable insights into the true nature of things presented in this run-of-the-mill popular exposition book. Hawking, whom I have seen on television espousing his belief in a grand mathematical theory which will explain everything that exists, characterises all attempts to interrelate Science and Mysticism as "pure rubbish".[115] As stated before, such beliefs in 'theories of everything' go completely against any serious contemplation of how the entities postulated by such abstract theories could become all that exists or can be imagined to exist. There is also a logical contradiction involved in how an abstraction which necessarily omits much of Reality could explain everything. Such beliefs involving some part of Reality to be the explanation of the Whole Reality, like the captivation of many little minds with hypothetical particles that are the key to all mysteries, resemble the captivation of many traditional Westerners and indeed the Eastern masses with the personality cults and trivial paraphernalia, conceived as profound, associated with historical and legendary figures imagined to be God incarnate.

Furthermore, the arcane scripture of high mathematics resembles the scripture of old, filling with awe even those who are themselves quite well-educated as this appears to be something for the initiates, the chosen few who may commune with this divine knowledge through this mysterious language of the gods. For instance, John Maynard-Smith, one of the world's leading evolutionary biologists discussed his 'wonders' of Science on a recent television programme. Being a mathematical biologist, developing simple mathematical models of animal competition etc. using von Neumann's theory of games, he spoke of the reverence in which he held theoretical physicists who managed to work with such complex, arcane mathematics. A most revealing point was his story about the mathematical explanation as to why a certain type of toy spinning top, very popular a few decades ago, turned upside down whilst spinning. Maynard-Smith claimed that, although he could follow the mathematical argument about the forces operating on the spinning top, he simply could not express this mathematical explanation in words, implying the almost magical status of mathematics to reach beyond our everyday language. I suspect that had David Bohm been asked to explain this phenomenon, he would not have shown such a lack of imagination or a lack of the poetic gift of capturing something of one's powerful feelings or intuitions in the limited forms of verbal expression. In the verse I have compared the great mathematical equations like Einstein's mass-energy equivalence equation as modern *mahāvākyas*, grand pronouncements. To point out the deficiencies in Einstein's understanding of Reality, as is evident in his inability to comprehend the psychical attributes of Reality and its fundamental indeterminism etc. still provokes strong reactions from those who are captivated by his status as a cultural icon. A similar status is given to Charles Darwin, whose Moses-like patriarchal features help consolidate his status amongst those for whom god-like personalities are not to be questioned but whose views are held as the final, authoritative statements. It is interesting to note, in regard to evolutionary theory, that, as with the magical status of exotic subatomic particles, we have a similar situation today with genes or DNA, where many a scientific thinker naïvely projects onto these components of organisms the answer to all the miracles of living systems. It is also fascinating to note that in the Hindu myth of the *avatārs*, the divine incarnations of Vishnu (representing the Divine Spirit moving from form to form), we have what clearly seems to be a mythological representation of the fact of our emergence as humans from simpler forms as mystically perceived by the seers in ancient times[116].

Now if we, for instance, consider the principle of the Conservation of Energy (which came to the non-physicist Robert Mayer in a sort of mystical intuition) we find that it is a clear metaphysical statement stating that *energy* is neither *created* nor destroyed. As with the transcendental laws of nature, supposedly independent of the Creation, which the founding fathers of modern science asserted were God's laws (remember that Newton kept matter inanimate so God could remain as the Prime Mover and upholding the laws), looking at the ontological status of energy, we have in this *uncreated energy* a divine principle as the Ground of all Being. Recall that the Divine Light, the Pure Consciousness, from whose attributes of volition, freedom and 'vitality' the scientific concept of energy is abstracted, is also known as the *Uncreated Light*, as the Creation arises out of the creative, uncreated principle. No wonder today's scientists, if they are aware of these matters, tend to keep quiet about these 'embarrassing' facts.

Broadening perception and shifting frames of reference

Thus the external world as known to us through Science and the scientific cosmology are themselves problematical issues as Science is not concerned with questioning the deficiencies in its own epistemology. Epistemological examination of the limiting cognitive modes utilised by Science, its abstraction of regular, spatio-temporal features, its animistic projection of perceptual categories, subjective and human qualities onto Nature, its denial of facts that do not fit its idealized models etc. taken along with more general epistemological considerations about knowledge as consisting of realizations, the mystical sources of scientific intuition, the instrumentality of cognitive projections onto Nature due to microcosm reflecting macrocosm and the knowledge of how the microcosm is itself generated through yogic introspection, reveal to us that there is far more to the proposition that yogic phenomenology can reveal to the yogi the secrets of Creation than at first meets the eye. As an example of how technological constraints shape the scientific world-view, it is interesting to note that new scans of vast clusters of galaxies, currently being reported, in which the frequencies monitored are altered, reveal that intergalactic space is full of gas which may make up the so-called "missing matter" or "dark matter" required by the various theories. Hence, limiting telescopic monitoring to normal ranges gave us the pictures of galaxy clusters spread out in empty space whereas this change in technological "perception" reveals a more complex, fuller picture of outer space. We shall see that deeper states of consciousness may also be interpreted as a broadening of perception revealing more of reality beyond the limited constructs of our mundane existence, the phenomena, the surface forms which our biological evolution has selected as vital for survival purposes. Thus the yogi broadens his or her perception beyond the realm of phenomena and sees how the realm of phenomena is generated and, at a certain stage of this progression, intuitively realises that this process applies not only for the manifestation of the phenomena of our mind but also for the manifestation of the whole of Creation. If we are to accept that the same Consiousness-Energy manifesting our mental constructions is responsible for the manifestation of the universe, then it is not so difficult to contemplate the possibility that similar processes are operating in microcosm and macrocosm and that these processes can be realised within us. When we consider that the evidence from paranormal phenomena and from experimental tests of Quantum Theory indicate that the world of spatio-temporal events is a product of a deeper unitary realm transcending our ordinary space, time and causality categories, then we begin to appreciate even more that the external world may be operating according to principles also at work in our mind.

But when we think of Creation these days, the image that comes to mind is whatever our imaginations can make of the notion of the Big Bang, the dominant scientific model. Interestingly, Lemaitre, who put forward the "primeval atom" or Big Bang hypothesis, was not only a scientist but also an ordained priest. Clearly such images of an incredible primeval explosion does not seem compatible with the yogic description of the world as a product of the energetic vibrations of the Pure Consciousness (see also Section 2(n)). I am not suggesting that the creation of our mental world is of such an 'explosive' nature. Here we have to address the problem of the frames of reference within which our mind operates when we try to imagine the Big Bang and when we try to contemplate the yogic picture. We have to come to terms with how the mystic can gain access to remarkable knowledge of various aspects of the universe in deeper states of consciousness, seemingly defying everything we normally think of as possible. The same realizations can be attained using LSD. We have to come to terms with the limitations of scientific models and the realms of existence which Science ignores because it cannot measure such subtle activities or make any meaningful physical interpretation. We have to come to terms with notions that by transcending the limitations of ordinary space and time the yogi gains access to the generative matrix of the spatio-temporal realm wherein each part involves every other part. We have to come to terms with notions such as that by losing one's individual identity in the Ground of all Being one in a sense gains access to remarkable realizations, for *knowledge* is *being*, although such remarkable insights cannot be translated into the limited constructions of our everyday thought and language which operate on the plane of ordinary space and time. As Vishnu told the sage Sutapas in the Hindu myth, the secret of Creation cannot be told but, if you really want to know, you have to throw yourself into the ocean.

2(f). ON THE EMERGENCE OF TIME AND SPACE

LSD experiences and dimensionality

The psychedelic states induced by LSD, says Grof, have a multidimensional and multilevel quality with the ordinary experiences of 3-dimensional space, time and normal causal relationships appearing to be teased out of a continuum of infinite possibilities. Psychedelic experiences transcend Space and Time disregarding the normal gradations between various levels of spatio-temporal order. The subject may identify with all manner of objects on all scales of order, sometimes simultaneously, from atoms to galaxies (or so it is claimed). Time may slow down, accelerate, flow backwards or cease to exist. It can appear to flow in a circular manner, circular and linear manner combined, or along a spiral path. Similar distortions can occur with the experience of Space. Space can be seen as a projection, an arbitrary construct of the mind with no objective existence. The LSD subject may transcend Time and experience the mystical 'Everpresent Now' in which Past, Present and Future coexist. As stated above, LSD subjects trained in mathematics and physics report experiencing insights into concepts which are not visualizable in the ordinary state of consciousness. Multidimensional spaces, non-Euclidian geometry, curved space and time, mass-energy equivalence and other difficult concepts may be experienced and understood in a new way[41] (note that such experience of insights confirms that knowledge is *being* or *realization*). In fact, the LSD subject is much like the Square in Edwin Abbot's classic *Flatland* which lives in a two-dimensional world and is given an insight into the third dimension which he had earlier thought to be a foolish and unimaginable notion and which leads to his imprisonment on grounds of insanity. Most people obviously have great difficulty contemplating realms with different orders of Space and Time. I think that dimensionality can best be understood in terms of *degrees of freedom* or the number of different sorts of basic relations that can be established. Friedman[39] states:

> *Three-dimensional space proved inadequate in quantum theory, since a quantum system must have enough dimensions to handle all independent possibilities. . . . As the number of possibilities goes up or the number of electrons goes up, the number of dimensions increases. In some problems, . . . the physicist uses the infinite-dimensional Hilbert space for calculations.*

Citing mathematician Rucker, who states that dimensionality really reflects the organization of information with certain sorts of arrangements most conveniently thought of in spatial terms, Friedman states that, "An increase in dimensions means an increase in information".[39] Note that organization or arrangement of information again links us with the operations or categories of perception and that, as we shall see, deeper states of consciousness may be thought of as broadening perception beyond the limited normal constructions which are convenient for our everyday activities as animals. Also note that once again we are seeing that deeper levels of Reality, as represented by quantum mechanics, are associated with possibilities which become more and more restricted as we move up to our normal macroscopic level of order. As I realised when I was eighteen years old, our difficulties with the concepts of quantum physics arises from our projection of modes of representation which have evolved to serve us in the macroscopic world of stones and waves on water onto a deeper level of Reality where such macroscopic behavioural patterns are not appropriate.

The time/space matrix of perception

In Brown's study of the three authoritative yogic traditions, the yogi reaches the interface of mind and cosmos when (s)he has refined awareness of the flow of the light to its very limit, to the temporal structure of ordinary perception. Observing the manifestation of phenomena, the yogi becomes aware of the very temporal/spatial structure of the flow of the light and begins to examine the subtle causal and spatial relationships within which ordinary perception occurs. When this ordinary 'time/space matrix of perception' is transcended, the yogi becomes aware of another order in which all the potentialities and interconnectedness of the universe becomes perceptible. In this extraordinary realm of undivided interconnectedness, interactions are seen to operate no longer by causal laws but by relativity to everything else[23]. As I mentioned in the previous section, Kant's realization that Time and Space are *a priori* categories of perception, not derived from our experience of phenomena, pales into insignificance besides the direct yogic realizations of these organizational features of perception and the realization of realms beyond space and time which Kant could not imagine and dismissed as false pretensions. In 1983 when I first put forward my inchoate picture of the mind, I used the notion of time frames based on memory reverberations and self-reference frames based on gross representations of the body. At the time even such limited views seemed far-reaching from my Western-educated viewpoint. I have of course used in the verse the Indian ideas of Space and Time as secondary features which arise with the Creation, having had an intuitive feel for what this actually meant as expressed in the verse:

In *Purush*, Time and Space, no meaning
Devoid of form there is *no thing*
Space, Time and differentiation
Into existence *yajña* brings

However, at the time of writing the verse these were only vague intuitions of these categories as products of differentiation and the processes of Nature to which I had not given much thought. My earlier encounters with space-time transcendence in physics theories had not made much impact as these were such abstract notions which left one wondering how much they were just the product of the imagination of physicists. It was in encountering Brown's article in September 1994 that these issues slowly began to crystallize in my mind, in spite of the resistance of habitual patterns of thought steeped in our everyday experience of time and space. The crystallization occurred especially in relation to the yogic knowledge of paranormal activity occurring when the time/space matrix had been transcended, giving me an intuition as to how these paranormal phenomena could co-exist with our everyday world. We shall see later that this knowledge ties in with the view of Western psychics describing the so-called "clairvoyant reality" in which the world exists as a unitary whole. On encountering Brown's article for the first time, thoughts also rushed through my mind about how Einstein's notion of a space-time continuum whose curvature represented the basic physical force of gravity seemed very much a projection of this time/space matrix of perception. Since then, having investigated these issues more carefully, I have begun to understand a little more about Time and Space.

Cosmic and microcosmic space-time emergence in Quantum Theory and Holonomic Models

Hiley and Peat describe how Bohm wanted to abandon the traditional notion of separate particles and fields in order to incorporate the holistic properties of Reality indicated by Quantum Theory. Inspiration in such matters came from the study of perception where the eye is found to detect not what actually exists outside but only those features which remain invariant for sufficient time to be perceived. Similarly, the vacuum state of Quantum Field Theory, which seems to be far from empty due to the fluctuations of virtual particles, could be pictured as being full of activity occurring at such high frequency that it cannot be perceived (i.e. it is physically meaningless). What our physics deals with are the quasi-stable, semi-autonomous features of this underlying wholeness[117]. Hiley and Peat state[117]:

> *One important feature concerning the holomovement is that it is not described in space-time but from it space-time is to be abstracted. Thus we no longer start with an* ***a priori*** *space-time manifold in order to discuss physics; rather we construct space-time from the underlying process.*

Bohm's notions of the implicate and explicate order have also been influenced by the work of Stapp showing how a space-time order could emerge as a relatively independent and autonomous context of low frequency waves out of a vastly greater background activity corresponding to the vacuum state[118]. Wheeler has put forward a similar idea that ordinary space and time emerge as a limiting case from a "pre-space", a "quantum foam" bubbling with an enormous amount of virtual activity. Wheeler, like Bohm, has treated the quantum vacuum as being full of vast energy which is physically meaningless[118,39]. Bohm says that his attitude is that the mathematics of the Quantum Theory deals primarily with the structure of this pre-space and with how the space-time order emerges from it rather than with the movement of particles. Interestingly Bohm states that if it were possible for consciousness to go into this very deep level of pre-space or beyond, then all "nows" would be one and the same[118]. Thus Bohm saw Quantum Theory pointing to a picture of matter as a relatively stable and autonomous pattern of activity emerging from a vastly greater ocean of energy which is beyond conventional notions of space, time and causality. Just as the eye can only detect the relatively stable, invariant features of the external world, so physics deals only with this emergent material order arising from the seething plenum which it falsely considers to be empty space.

Similarly Finkelstein, who, as noted above, had come to understand Bohm's view of Science as a mode of perception, views space-time as a statistical construct from a deeper quantum structure in which process is fundamental[119]. In regard to Quantum Theory and space-time structure, Mae-Wan Ho discusses the fascinating work of Schommers who has reformulated quantum mechanics showing how Time and Space are dependent upon real processes. Schommers, takes account of Mach's principle which considers any changes in positions of masses to be relative to all other masses in the universe rather than any spatial coordinates. Neither Relativity Theory nor Quantum Theory have incorporated Mach's principle. Schommers' reformulation, taking Mach's principle into account, shows that real processes are projected to "space-time space" from a fundamental space involving momentum and energy interactions which is a more authentic representation of Reality. The two spaces are equivalent and related by Fourier transformations. In more simple terms, space-time structures are generated by interactions of matter, or *processes*. Schommers' scheme results in the generation of different internal time structures for different systems relative to an external reference time structure[91]. This demonstration that Space and Time can be considered as products of processes is closely related to Prigogine's notion of "internal time" generated by dissipative processes[120]. Such concepts of a system's *internal time* is of great value to us in coming to terms with mystical experiences where time appears to speed up or slow down relative to external clock time such as the case described in Brown's study where the yogi, during insight meditation, conducts a search of every "moment" of the flow of the light to see if it matches the category of insight under consideration in the particular yogic exercise. Brown relates these exercises to Western psychological knowledge derived from tachistoscopic presentation of visual displays to subjects at very fast rates which reveals that subliminal, preconscious processes register such rapidly presented information. Brown also relates this to models of visual perception such as Pribram's in which information is converted into a temporal structure of frequencies[23]. The yogi in such exercises seems to be maintaining lucidity in the preconscious processes underlying our normal field of attention.

Furthermore, the Fourier transformation, which links Schommers' space-time order to the more fundamental process order, is also a central element of Pribram's holonomic theory of perception. In the holonomic theory, the space-time order is related to a spectral order of frequencies in which the brain processes information by means of processes constituting a Fourier transformation of the information. The original patterns can be reconstituted by performing the inverse transform. Pribram says that the inclusion of space-time coordinates in the holonomic theory incorporates the operation of structural constraints in processing. Structural (space-time) constraints operate not only as initial conditions (as in Gabor's holographic theory) but also as ongoing operations constraining the dendritic microprocesses[78]. Although this may seem very arcane to the layman, what Pribram's comments seem to suggest is that a space-time order emerges in brain processes as a limiting case of the underlying spectral, frequency analysis operations. Thus we have a scientific model interpreting perception in terms of frequencies, suggestive of Aurobindo's assertions (which as noted above have influenced the holonomic metaphor) that the planes of consciousness operated at different frequencies. Furthermore, this model involves a space-time order emerging due to constraints in the processing system which is most suggestive of the time/space matrix of perception actually realized by yogis. Schommers' reformulation of quantum mechanics using Mach's principle again relates to yogic knowledge in that the yogic experience of the realm transcending the time/space matrix of perception involves interactions which operate by relativity to everything else rather than by mundane causal laws indicating that incorporation of Mach's principle really does take us closer to the actual nature of things. Finally we are told that in Schommers' scheme real processes are *projected* to 'space-time space' from a more fundamental space of momentum and energy interactions. The term *projection* relates us again to yogic knowledge in which the realm of phenomena appears to be "projected" from a deeper realm and to the views of Bohm who suggests that each moment of time is a *projection* from the total implicate order. Bohm's use of the term *projection* is essentially the same as his aforementioned *unfoldment* and *enfoldment* sequence generating the phenomena of the 'explicate order' out of the deeper 'implicate order' which closely resembles yogic experience. Bohm notes the happy coincidence that mathematical projection operations are just what are required in order to incorporate such notions into Quantum Theory[118].

Energetic vibrations, phase-locking and Time as the process of Creation

In popular discussions of Pribram's models of perceptual and memory processes, it is often stated that Reality constitutes a so-called Frequency Domain, a realm of energetic vibrations in which our usual conceptions of space and time are meaningless and only appear by virtue of the constructive activity of our brains. This notion of a Frequency Domain clearly parallels the Indian mystical view of the universe as being manifested from the formless void of Consciousness through the energetic vibrations of Consciousness (corresponding respectively to Being and Becoming). I am rather sceptical of such views in which the external world is supposed to be devoid of any level of order resembling the space-time constructions of our perception of it as sometimes seems to be suggested. We must keep in mind the biological role of our normal perception in modelling the key features of the environment and also the notions such as Bohm's in which a space-time order emerges as a relatively stable component of a vastly larger and far more complex multidimensional reality and thus exists in so much as it is a perceptual abstraction of a geater reality which corresponds to the so-called Frequency Domain in the holonomic/holographic metaphor. Keep in mind also that the time/space matrix of perception itself emerges out of a broader and deeper system of energetic vibrations or frequencies so microcosm does indeed seem to mirror the macrocosm. The temporal order of Becoming arises out of the eternal order of Being. The fact that the yogi experiences the flow of the Light as waves or pulses which correlates well with our physical concepts and the fact that information like that presented in the *Kauṣītakī Upaniṣad* in regard to *prāṇa*, dreamless sleep and death correlate so well with physical concepts, as I have shown above, indicates that the space-time categories utilised by our perceptual processes which are reflected in our concepts and language do reflect gross features of Reality. Thus we may conclude that the external reality does have a spatio-temporal aspect, which corresponds reasonably with the spatio-temporal aspects of our perception, allowing us to develop our physical concepts, which, as we have seen, involve projections of the internal reality onto the external world.

Penrose has shown that the properties of 3-D space can emerge out of the cooperative interactions of elementary quantum entities called spinors in a pure mathematical domain devoid of space. When large networks of such spinors are joined together, they establish spatial relations between each other[121]. Briggs and Peat suggest that time may also emerge by means of similar interactions locking together quantum systems. Interestingly, they note that collective properties may emerge through individual oscillators becoming 'phase-locked' and resonating together. Collective oscillations form limit cycles which are more stable than individual oscillations[80]. I have noted above that limit cycles can lead to chaos and to self-organization. Phase-locking of neurons results in the synchronized activity detected by the EEG. Bohm asserts that time in a material frame is generated by the phase-locking of matter within that frame, i.e. it arises from the collective interactions of matter. Time is a measure of the amount of process within the system[115]. Briggs and Peat note that, although quantum objects may be described as combinations of all possible states, when considered collectively, stabilities and definite properties emerge and the collective cannot be described by linear combinations of different states. Thus macroscopic phenomena emerge as relatively stable process structures through the collective behaviour of microscopic phenomena which operate in a world of possibilities[80].

In monistic Kashmiri Shaivism, the cosmic process consists of a cyclic series of creations and destructions, brought about by the pulsations of the Absolute Consciousness beyond the realm of Time and Space. The change manifested by this cyclical process is the basis of Time[99]. Friedman, discussing the ideas of Bohm, Seth and the Perennial Philosophy, notes that all three see Time as an abstraction of the process of creation of the 3-dimensional world. At the universal level, Time is created by the succession of projections which manifest as matter which is constituted of a succession of projections of energy. The frequency of these projections is too fast to be perceived or detected by our instruments but what we perceive as stable matter is actually the persistence of a common form through this series of extremely rapid projections[39]. This again ties in with the notion of Time as process, the process here being the actualization of spatio-temporal phenomena (Becoming) from the transcendental realm.

Rosen[59] states:

> *As I see it, the problem of time is inextricably linked with that of the higher-order differentiation. I propose that the mystery of process or becoming, from which the familiar idea of time is abstracted, is the mystery of how the undifferentiable becomes differentiated. Time, I suggest, entails a differentiating of that*

which is undifferentiable. In more common parlance we may speak of an actualizing, a bringing into extensive continuity, of the purely potential or unextended.

I have collated above a number of lines of evidence showing how the 3-dimensional space-time order of our normal perceptions which we interpret in terms of the physical world is in fact a relatively stable order emerging out of the activity of a deeper realm of Reality which transcends our normal perceptions. Once again we see the *interface of mind and cosmos* in that the crystallization of a time/space matrix appears to occur in both the mind (microcosm) and the cosmos at large (macrocosm). Time is abstracted from the process of Becoming, the rapid succession of actualizations constituting both mental phenomena and matter. Three-dimensional space is also abstracted from a deeper level of Reality as a higher-level, emergent property that arises from collective interrelations between fundamental processes.

We see that both physics and the holonomic theory of perceptual processes have discarded the absolute status of 3-dimensional space and time. Routinely the hypotheses put forward by physicists involve hyperspaces of greater than three dimensions. An interesting point to note about Bohm's and Pribram's models is that both see the realm beyond Space and Time in terms of energetic vibrations of various frequencies which ties in closely with traditional yogic views of the Divine Energy as the pulsating, vibrating movements of the Universal Consciousness and with Aurobindo's more recent descriptions of the different planes of consciousness existing at different frequencies. This is not altogether surprising given that both Bohm and Pribram have been influenced by such views although it should be noted that their models have been aimed at resolving mysteries within Science rather than rehashing mystical views. The incorporation of Mach's principle, which parallels the yogic experience of a holistic, relativistic causal order underlying apparent space-time causality, into quantum mechanics by Schommers shows how Space and Time are *projected* from processes which are more realistically described in terms of energy and momentum interactions. Schommers, Prigogine and Bohm have all argued in favour of *process time* whereby a physical system generates its own *internal time* frame based on the basic progression of the process. As stated above, such considerations from scientific thought should be kept in mind when considering yogic experiences of altered rates of time flow. Experimental tests of Quantum Theory has already shown us that *nonlocal* connections exists between particles which defy our attempts to conceptualise them in terms of normal space-time interactions, pointing to a deeper, transcendental order of interconnectedness in which our normal view of causality becomes rather meaningless. I recall reading that Niels Bohr, in his famous discussions with Einstein over these paradoxical aspects of Quantum Theory, pointed out that such nonlocal connections indicated that our concepts of particles, atoms etc. were the constructions of our mind masking a unitary Reality. Normal space-time causality is woven into the very structure of our languages making discussion of such issues fraught with seeming contradictions. But, as yogis and LSD subjects well-versed in mathematics and physics testify, it is possible to realise in altered states of consciousness that normal space-time and causality are just abstractions from a realm of infinite possibilities.

2(g). SELF-LUMINOUS, SELF-LIMITING, ACTIVE/PASSIVE UNIVERSAL CONSCIOUSNESS

Self-luminosity

In *Advaita Vedānta* (Pure) Consciousness illumines everything, including itself; it has the property of self-luminosity *(svaprakāśatva).* Self-luminous, transcendental Consciousness is neither an object nor a subject and is known solely by means of itself[45]. In monistic Kashmiri Shaivism, the term *vimarśa* denotes the power of Consciousness to perceive itself, feel, reflect on and examine the events occurring within it. "This ability to reflect on itself is inherent in the very nature of the light of consciousness", says Dyczkowski, and is its most specific characteristic. The self-revealing nature of the light of consciousness determines its status as the Ultimate Reality; it alone reveals everything and needs no other for its revelation[99]. Logical arguments are clearly incapable of conveying the fact of this self-luminosity which is a concept derived from existential realization or, using Aurobindo's phrase, "knowledge by identity".

All knowledge is in fact knowledge by identity, Aurobindo asserted, restating the traditional wisdom that *knowledge* is *being* as I have stressed above with the term *realization*. This identity is with the object of consciousness which is in itself a construction of the mind. In the *supramental knowledge* as Aurobindo called the deeper intuitions attained in yoga (equivalent to such terms as *pratibhā* in the *Yoga Sūtra* tradition), the subject/object duality is transcended and the subject becomes one with the object. In such supramental knowledge, says Aurobindo, one sees, not only the physical object, but the vibration of energy, the light and force of spiritual substance of which it is a mode. The ordinary sense data are seen to be the outermost indications of the object[25]. Satprem, a follower of Aurobindo, states that once the *chakras* are opened, the yogi see the pure vibration in each thing rather than the external signs[52]. We shall look further into such matters later, here the point being that our normal perceptions are merely gross abstractions of surface features from the flux of information available to us. In "higher" states of consciousness perception shifts to the deeper processes generating our normal gross perceptions which we conceive as the material world. As we go deeper and deeper into consciousness we begin to realise that all phenomena are ultimately generated by the energetic vibrations emanating from the Light of Consciousness projecting the manifest phenomenal world. At the deepest level, when the phenomenal world-generating activity (the *cittavritti*, the wavelike fluctuations of the mindstuff) are held in abeyance, the realization is not one of objects but pure self-luminous consciousness. Thus this realization of the self-luminosity of the Pure Consciousness is, in essence, no different from our everyday knowledge of events in the material plane. Both are instances of *knowledge as being*. The yogic progress into ever-deeper realizations relates to the concept of *sublation* which is the Vedāntic criterion of truth. The phenomena on the lower planes are 'sublated', cancelled or contradicted, by the deeper processes which are realized to be generating them. The less capable the content of consciousness is of being sublated, the more real it is. Through this process one arrives at that which is non-sublatable, which is thus Ultimate Reality[45].

The Unmoved Mover

Much confusion exists due to the seemingly contradictory descriptions of this Ultimate Reality which is said to be unchanging, passive Being and yet is also the source of the ever-changing, active Becoming. Clearly, my identification of the physical correlate of the Light of Pure Consciousness with the brainwaves of the RAS suggests a highly active, fluctuating essence. This paradox of the active yet passive nature of the Universal Consciousness is apparent in Shankara's problematical *māyāvāda* (Doctrine of Illusion) in *Advaita Vedānta* which attempts to maintain that *nirguṇa Brahman* remains unchanged, untransformed by the world creating process of *Māyā*. This paradox is noted by the yogic traditions and some have attempted to account for this apparent contradiction although some, like Iyer, simply state that the contradiction exists only in the intellect[72] (which cannot transcend these seemingly opposite categories of thought). In monistic Kashmiri Shaivism, as described by Dyczkowski, the Pure Consciousness is not a 'passive witness' (*sākṣin*) but full of conscious activity. Being and Becoming are the inner and outer faces of Universal Consciousness. The inner face (*antarmukha*) is the pure subject, devoid of all objective content, existing beyond Time and Space. The outer face represents the continuous flux of the manifest world of objects. *Māyā* is not viewed as an illusion but as the power of the Absolute to appear in diverse forms through a process of projection, a pulsating movement outwards and then inwards again resembling the pulsations held to be responsible for the creation of Time (as discussed above) or Bohm's unfolding and enfolding. Although full of vibration (*spanda*) the Absolute, from another perspective appears motionless. Kashmiri Shaivism attempts to explain this in terms of subtle movements which, though not really moving (in the sense of motion between two points), manifests as motion[99]. Panda states that the *prakāśa* (Light of Consciousness) aspect of *Paramaśiva* (Absolute Consciousness) does not change at all, it appears as if it were changing. *Paramaśiva* pulsates without reference to Space and Time, *spanda* has no space-time distinctions which are only mental constructions. A pulsation is not a motion in the sense of a change of position but it is a movement, like a throbbing[100]. Again we see that such notions are similar to Bohm's oft-used metaphor of a flashing sequence of lights creating the illusion of a moving object.

Satprem also attempts to account for this paradox in terms of inner and outer perspectives. Seen from within it appears immobile, seen from without it appears as movement[52]. The Mother (of the Aurobindo Āshram) spoke of how difficult it was to explain, a Movement so complete, total and constant that to any perception it gives the feeling of a perfect immobility[52]. The Mother's description is reminiscent of the description of the Void in *Nāsadīya Sūkta* which is described using phrases like, no waves and no ripples but still a flow. Bohm calls his Totality of all levels of Being the "Holomovement".

Thus we see that, contrary to the *Advaita Vedānta* view of a static, passive and undifferentiated *nirguṇa Brahman* (which Aurobindo criticises), we have a paradoxical experience of static Being and dynamic Becoming coexisting in a mysterious manner. Aurobindo in his Integral Yoga, combining the approaches of various yogic traditions, describes the various approaches to the Ultimate Realization which result in the separation of the passive, silent witness (*Puruṣa*) and the active, dynamic mass of forces (*Prakriti*); the experience of the void; the experience of *Brahman* and the *Māyā* world; and the experience of *Īśvara* (the Lord) and *Shakti* (the Divine Energy). If one persists one realises that *Prakriti* arises out of *Puruṣa;* that the Void is full of content; that the *Māyā* world is also *Brahman*. The Divine Truth and the Manifest Creation, as Aurobindo calls them, are two poles of one Being connected, he says, by two simultaneous currents of energy. In the Ultimate Realization all personality, mind and life consciousness disappear in infinite, Absolute Consciousness which is realised as the sole truth. Nevertheless, Aurobindo asserts, even our greatest spiritual experience is but a diminished reflection, a faint shadow of the Absolute[25].

Mind moments and undivided wholeness

The authoritative yogic traditions described by Brown all assert that beyond the time/space matrix of perception there is an experience of undivided wholeness wherein parts only exist in relation to other parts, where every subtle activity moves into every other subtle activity, and where one relative mind-moment contains the information of the entire universe[23]. Grof states that LSD experiences suggest that each of us contains the information about the entire universe or all of existence, has potential experiential access to all its parts and, in a sense, *is* the whole[41]. Such experiences tie in with the notion of a "holographic" or "holonomic" Reality in which the whole is represented in every part. This point is illustrated by Bohm's analogy of placing a telescope anywhere in space and receiving information from all other parts of the universe converging upon the lense at whatever point you wish to place it[123]. Such analogies help us to begin to comprehend how it is possible for the yogi or the LSD subject to attain such seemingly fantastic realizations.

It is conceivable that each relative mind moment corresponds to an activating pulse of energy from the RAS (which can operate at various frequencies determining the state of arousal) flowing through the brain. Remember that the Buddhists focus on these pulses of the Light as discontinuous moments leading to their doctrine of momentariness (*kṣanikạ*). Laughlin states that there is substantial evidence for a temporal mechanism based upon a minute perceptual unit within which temporal discriminations cannot be made. Stimuli of different durations that appear to be phase-locked to cortical rhythms and presented within such a unit (epoch) will be perceived as simultaneous. Laughlin asserts that the duration of such an epoch seems to be around one-tenth of a second corresponding to the wavelength of the EEG alpha rhythm (which has a frequency of about 10 cycles per second)[34]. Mae-Wan Ho refers to a 40 Hertz (40 cycles per second) rhythm that is coherent over the entire brain which she says may define the duration of primary perception (if so this would be one-fortieth of a second). Ho's point is that coherent processes (extrapolating from quantum coherence at the subatomic level) result in integration of activity in biological systems. Processes coherent with the 40 Hertz waves will not generate any 'process time' relative to the wave[91]; i.e. all processes coherent with the duration defined by the wave will appear as simultaneous. This is equivalent to Laughlin's temporal phase-locking. We have in these observations, especially in the alpha rhythm correlation, some support for my suggestion that a moment in the stream of consciousness corresponds to an activating wave-pulse from the RAS, which can of course generate numerous frequencies. The situation is obviously more complex as, for instance, changes in subjective experiences of time flow as in the high-speed search tasks of the yogi in Insight Meditation as described by Brown, which may be related to preconscious processes, need to be considered. As stated above, such changes in subjective time may be related to the *internal time* generated by processes and would probably be related to the field activity in the particular brain structures which may be undertaking information processing at different rates. Yogic lucidity in centres of preconscious activity where processes are operating rapidly may lead to a subjective slowing of time relative to an external frame in that a much greater number of fluctuations would be occurring in the field of attention in a given number of seconds and, if reference is made to the normal time frame, time appears to slow down in that more operations are executed. Most people experience subjective distortions of time in periods of great danger when time seems to slow down where again the mind may retreat to preconscious processes to give the person more chance of reacting quickly as the information processing is operating much faster than in the normal state. However, returning to the yogic experience of relative mind moments beyond the time/space matrix of perception, this is likely to correspond with deactivation of most brain centres. It seems plausible to suggest that a relative mind moment may correspond to an activating wave of energy which, as stated above, may underly basic moments in the stream of consciousness in all states. In this regard it is informative to note that the yogic traditions assert that disruptions in the flow of the Light manifest as gross content[23]. Whether or not the mind moment is a pulse of activating energy or a cycle of some local process overlaid on the basic activating waves, it none the less seems to be the case that the mind moment corresponds to a pulse of energy. So what the advanced yogi experiences as being an inseparable part of the whole universe, reflecting the whole universe and, through its interconnectedness, containing the information of the entire universe, seems to be correlated with what appears in our limited mode of perception as a pulse of energy.

In this regard it is interesting to note the comments of Seth, the personality channeled by Jane Roberts which I would interpret as her own deeper Self or inner voice. The Seth personality states that pure energy has such pattern-forming propensities that it always appears as its manifestations, or that it "becomes its camouflages". Energy, says Seth, is undivided, in reality there are no parts although there may appear to be so from our plane.

Each (seeming) portion of energy holds the potentiality to become all forms of matter[39,124]. Seth's views are concordant, not only with the holonomic metaphor in which each part is in some sense a mirror of the whole, but also with the view found in both *Advaita Vedānta* and monistic Kashmiri Shaivism of the *ghatākāśa*, the space limited by enclosure within a jar which, when the jar is broken, becomes one with the infinite space (*ākāśa*). This relationship describes the relationship between the phenomenal world of *avidyā/māyā*, the world of the individual consciousness, and the Absolute Reality which remains undivided.

Self-limitation and Māyā

In *Advaita*, individual consciousness is said to arise from the mutual superimposition (*adhyāsa*) of Pure Consciousness and *avidyā* (Nescience, Ignorance) resulting in the identification of the self with the *upādhi* (limiting adjuncts) of body, sense and mind. This *self-limitation* of Absolute Consciousness results in an "objective attitude" resulting in the production of the mind (*antaḥkaraṇa;* internal organ)[45]. Panda says that each created entity, living or non-living, acts as a limiting adjunct (*upādhi*). These *upādhi* are empirically true but false from the perspective of Reality; they are *adhyāsa* (superimpositions) resulting from the (world-creating) activity of *avidyā/māyā*. Upon enlightenment, *avidyā* is held in abeyance and the individual self (*jīva*), devoid of limiting conditions (*upādhi*) is realised to be identical with *Brahman*[100]. Monistic Kashmiri Shaivism similarly refers to such self-limitation (*saṃkoca*) whereby the Universal Consciousness (*Śiva*) imposes countless limiting conditions (*upādhi*) upon Himself through which He becomes manifest in limited forms. Simultaneously, at a deeper level of being, *Śiva* continues to exist as the undifferentiated unity of Pure Consciousness. Unlike *Sānkhya*, which maintains that Pure Consciousness remains always formless, Kashmiri Shaivism asserts that the Light is both formless and omniform simultaneously. Whilst *Advaita* sees the diversity of forms as mere 'appearances', Kashmiri Shaivism grants more 'reality' to the forms whilst maintaining the ultimate formless unity of the Light which is free of limitations[99]. Interestingly, we find similar ideas in the philosophy of Pythagoras, who seems to have been influenced by Eastern thought. Sheldrake states[31]:

> *According to Pythagorean cosmology, there were two primordial first principles,* ***peras*** *and* ***apeiron****, which can roughly be translated as Limit and the Unlimited. These primary opposites produced the One through the imposition of limits on the Unlimited. But some of the Unlimited remained outside the cosmos as a void, which the One breathed in to fill up the space between things.*

The reader should recall that the term *yajña* was used in the verse for such self-limitation on the cosmic scale resulting in the Creation.

These limiting conditions are said to be the product of the mutual superimposition (*adhyāsa*) of pure, Absolute Consciousness with *avidyā* (nescience) or the worldly stuff. In *Advaita* the mind consists only of its functions which are merely modes or modifications of consciousness resulting from this mutual superimposition, creating the matrix of individual experience. Kaplan, discussing the various meanings of *māyā* which are often confused, notes that *māyā* (the cosmic generalization of *avidyā*) is the limitation of that which is without limitation. He relates *māyā* to *mātrā* (measure) and states:

> ***Māyā*** *understood in terms of* ***mātrā*** *superimposes categories of quantification such as space and time on the* ***amātro 'nantamātrśca. Māyā*** *is the traversing of the non-objectifiable with structures and limits which appear to make it into objects.*

Māyā is the power (*shakti*) that creates the appearance of duality, the power by which the measureless becomes measured. Kaplan relates this *māyā* power to Gauḍapāda's *vijñānaspanditam*, the movement/vibration of the mind which creates the appearance of duality. Through such power, the indescribable (*anirvacanīya*) world of *māyā* is created. In *Advaita* this *māyā* world is said to be neither *sat* nor *asat*. *Sat* is defined by Gaudapada as that which exists at the beginning and at the end. Kaplan interprets "neither *sat* nor *asat*" to mean that the perceptual world is neither ultimately real, not the being of things, but nor is it just the creation of the individual mind. As such it is indescribable. Kaplan says that he received an insight into the meaning of *māyā* when he saw holographic images. The projected holographic image looks real but there is nothing substantial there; we experience something 'out there' but there is no thing out there where the image is projected. Such holographic projection gives an insight into the paradoxical nature of *māyā*[103].

Now this power of *māyā* is equivalent to the *avidyā* with which the pure consciousness undergoes mutual superimposition (*adhyāsa*) with the imposition of limiting conditions resulting in the individualised consciousness and the world of duality. Spatio-temporal relationships are established by such superimposition. This process of superimposition, which is suspended in deep sleep[45], is very suggestive of superimpositions and interference between the activating brainwaves from the RAS and the brainwave activity resulting from sensory information processing (which could easily be interpreted as the Nescience, the 'worldly stuff' which creates the illusory world of phenomena). It is illuminating to reiterate here Grof's statement that holography involves an undifferentiated field of light that, by specific patterns of interference, creates the illusion of separate objects[41], which may parallel to some extent the perceptual world-construction processes in the brain. It is also interesting to note here that Pribram refers to a suggestion by O'Keefe involving theta waves which have *superimposed* upon them amplitude and phase relations representing sensory information[78]. *Avidyā/māyā,* the worldly stuff of Nescience for the world-renouncing yogi would most likely correspond to such sensory information and its activated memory representations, which, in the waking brain criss-cross the waves of activating energy from the RAS. The limiting *upādhi* would probably correspond to the limits of the self-organizing field of dissipative activity, the vortex which superficially appears to be an individualised entity but which, when considered more deeply, can be understood to be but an autonomous region in the undivided continuum of energy. At the superficial level of existence at which we ourselves exist, this individuality appears totally real and we maintain a sense of otherness from all that which is not the content of our present experience.

Panda[100] discusses at some length the generation of multiplicity as described by monistic Kashmiri Shaivism focusing on the *Pratyabhijñā* (Doctrine of Recognition) in which the individual self (*jīva*) re-cognizes itself as the Supreme Reality (*Śiva*), the Absolute Consciousness. As with a number of other mystical traditions, *Pratyabhijñā* holds that the *jīva* forgets its true nature through identification with the psychophysical processes of phenomenal world-creation and the goal is to re-cognize its true nature. The Absolute in its active, energetic *vimarśa* aspect (as opposed to the *prakāśa*, or light aspect) is a spiritual energy that has the potentiality to take on any form; the Absolute is like an undifferentiated mass containing the potentiality to become the entire universe in all of its multiplicity. The term *ābhāsa* refers to its appearances in limited forms. The *ābhāsa* are compared to waves in the sea of Universal Consciousness and are thus real (unlike Shankara's illusory *Māyā* which the Kashmiri Shaivites correctly dismiss as dualistic); the wave activity manifests as various forms which dissolve back into the underlying sea which effectively remains unchanged. Panda describes these *ābhāsa* as projections of the ideation of the Absolute creating the universe within the Absolute although it appears external to the limited subjects which are also created. Panda describes the *tattvas* (which I will translate as principles) of universal experience, the subtle ideational principles operating without limitation of the universal experience, beginning with the first vibration of the Absolute Will, which result in a still ideational universe which has not fully 'crystallized'. The operation of these *tattvas* are associated with a subject/object distinction appearing between the Absolute Consciousness and the manifest world primarily associated with the energetic *Śakti Tattva*. Panda states that the term *ābhāsa* only applies when the subject/object distinction occurs after the first two *tattvas*.

Panda then goes on to list the five *tattvas* of limited individual experience, produced by *Māyā*, whose manifestation does veil the real nature of the Absolute. In *Pratyabhijñā, Māyā* is the power of the Absolute which brings about multiplicity and the sense of separation, not the illusory universe-creating *Māyā* of Shankara. *Māyā* brings about distinctness and differentiation from the Universal Consciousness by veiling it with five limiting principles or coverings (*kañcukas*). These coverings limit the "universal authorship, omniscience, total satisfaction (creating desire), eternity (creating temporality) and freedom/pervasiveness (creating limited causality and spatiality) of the Universal

Consciousness. Further principles operate to bring about our ordinary experience of the world[100]. This limiting of the universal powers of the Absolute ties in with the assertions of the likes of Aurobindo that our everyday powers of volition, knowing, perception etc. are limited forms of the supreme powers of the Universal Consciousness. Although *Pratyabhijñā* differs somewhat from *Advaita Vedānta,* both are attempting to interpret the same processes by which the pure, Universal Consciousness becomes the individual subject. The *tattvas* of limited individual experience in *Pratyabhijñā* are *ābhāsa* (appearances in limited form) which are described as wavelike projections from the underlying sea of Universal Consciousness. We have seen that the mutual superimposition (*adhyāsa*) of the Pure Consciousness and the Nescience (*avidyā*) in *Advaita* could be interpreted as wavelike interference processes operating in the brain. In describing the same processes, taking a different interpretive perspective, the Kashmiri Shaivite yogi abstracts somewhat differently from the same reality and gives different labels which give us another angle on the same processes at work. In the *Māyā-tattvas* we see the limitations creating the time, space and causality matrix of ordinary perception, presumably by some wavelike processes laying down a basic matrix upon which are overlaid further patterns of energetic activity which together bring about the world of everyday experience. Although *Pratyabhijñā* asserts that by subjecting Itself to these limits the Absolute becomes the individual, we may confidently argue that other lines of evidence, such as Zen meditation and Multiple Personalities, require us to postulate further that to become truly individual we need some sort of vortex-like closure of self-organising activity. Indeed, individuality remains on the path to enlightenment even when the time-space matrix disappears although, of course, 'omniscience' and absolute, desireless bliss are not experienced until individuality itself disappears.

Thus the *Pratyabhijñā tattvas* seem to be describing processes accompanying individuation such as limitations of the powers of Universal Consciousness and the generation of the time/space matrix which normally lays the basis for individual experience. I have mentioned in Section 2(c) Taimni's remarks that the yogi initially has difficulty in attaining enlightenment as the emergence of *pratyayas* (contents) throws him back into the vehicles that he has transcended which is suggestive of a spontaneous tendency to generate self-organising processes corresponding to the 'vehicles' of the various planes of consciousness. I have also mentioned how the idea of self-organising dissipative structures developed by Prigogine has been speculatively extended to all manner of systems at all levels of order by various thinkers who see such self-organization as the general rule throughout the cosmos rather than as an exception. Thus the yogic traditions are each capturing something of the actual Reality from their various interpretive perspectives and meditative focuses giving us some insight into how the undivided oneness of the self-luminous, Universal Consciousness becomes individuated. This involves the wavelike activity of the energetic vibrations creating the matrix of space-time causality in which normal individual experience occurs. *Pratyabhijñā* asserts that certain principles operate in Universal Consciousness, resulting in the bipolarity between Universal Consciousness and the crystallizing manifest universe within it, prior to the operation of *Māyā* which brings about the subject/object duality and the sense of separateness. *Advaita Vedānta* relates the creation of subject/object duality to the vibrations of the mindstuff which the *Pratyabhijñā Māyā* is probably also describing. Somehow the activity within the field of individual consciousness appears as separate from the underlying consciousness. The various processes bringing about individuation tend to be subsumed in *Advaita* under the term *upādhi* which are not clearly explained although it is perhaps impossible to clearly convey in words the yogic experience of these processes. *Pratyabhijñā* tells us that the *ābhāsa* are like waves projected by the underlying sea of consciousness. I have argued that self-organizing fields of activity are the correlates of individual sentient beings, as seems to be supported by Zen experience and other lines of argument. The various positions are not mutually exclusive, rather they are considering the same reality from different perspectives. As I have stated above, all the seemingly individuated process structures which we normally consider to exist as independent entities are in fact autonomous fields of activity in an underlying continuum of energetic activity. Somehow such closure of fields of activity creates the sense of separateness we experience from the rest of the universe. As the yogi deactivates the time-space matrix of perception, this sense of separateness diminishes as the underlying unitary order is experienced by the still individuated consciousness retaining its limited volition. Upon enlightenment, individuality disappears and one attains oneness with one's true nature (*svarūpa*) with a virtually indescribable experience of the underlying self-luminous Universal Consciousness, realization of its potential to manifest the entire universe and its myriad forms, and sometimes the realization of the paradoxical bipolarity between the passive sentience attribute of this non-sublatable Ultimate Reality, the Unmoved Mover, and the energetic activity within it which manifests the universe.

2(h). THE WORLD-CREATING VIBRATIONS

> *Every activity in the universe, as well as every perception, notion, sensation or emotion in the microcosm, ebbs and flows as part of the universal rhythm of the One Reality.*
>
> M.S.G. Dyczkowski, *The Doctrine of Vibration*[99]

Matter as energetic vibrations in physics

N.C. Panda, in his book *The Vibrating Universe*[100], looks at the important notion of *vibration* in monistic Kashmiri Shaivism with its Doctrine of Vibration, in *Vedānta,* where less emphasis is given to it, and in modern scientific theories with their waves, fields and the recent concept of superstrings. Superstring theories attempt to unify the diverse particles and forces of current mainstream physics by treating them as expressions of vibrations of underlying hypothetical, multidimensional mathematical entities called superstrings. He notes that in the yogic view it is the waves, ripples and surfs of the underlying, tranquil Pure Consciousness which constitute *saṃsāra,* the phenomenal universe. Panda also points out that Shankara's teacher Gaudapada held that the world-appearance is due to the vibration of *prāṇa* or *citta* (the 'life energy' and the mindstuff, which we have seen are two attributes of the same psychophysical Reality). He quotes Isaac Newton in regard to, "a most subtle spirit which pervades and lies hid in all gross bodies", which underlies the forces acting upon particles and, through whose vibrations, all sensations are excited and willful movements of animal bodies occur.

Pribram states that processing of all sensations can be understood as amplitude modulations of frequency oscillations[78]. Prince Louis de Broglie, one of the founders of Quantum Theory, using a line of reasoning derived from Planck's fundamental relation between energy and frequency, implying wave motion, clarified the wave nature of matter[39]. Indeed, de Broglie's original work so shocked his peers that his paper had to be sent to Einstein who finally confirmed that it was to be taken seriously. David Bohm's 1951 Causal Interpretation of Quantum Theory followed on from earlier suggestions by de Broglie. Panda quotes Schrödinger, the advocate of *Advaita Vedānta* who formulated the wave function at the heart of quantum mechanics, who, in response to the question as to why a *wave* function is utilised, asserted that a particle is actually a group of waves[100]. Biophysicist Mae-Wan Ho says that Quantum Theory reveals that even atoms are thought to be composed of vibrations[91]. Jantsch, commenting in regard to the broader implications of Prigogine's work on dissipative structures, states that in the new picture of becoming, structure is an incidental product of process, no more solid than a standing wave pattern[77]. Physicist Nick Herbert says that Quantum Theory treats objects as "vibratory possibilities", oscillating opportunities for something real to happen[125], which is reminiscent of Bohm's *tendencies* and Heisenberg's *potentia*. Bohm pictures the quantum vacuum as a plenum, oscillating at unimaginably high frequencies (beyond physical interpretation) with matter a relatively autonomous, superficial pattern of lower frequency energy oscillations[118,54].

The wave-like fluctuations of the mindstuff

Satprem says of the superconscient gradations (the 'higher planes') that what comes closest to the universal Truth is not forms, which are always limited to a tradition, but luminous vibrations full of joy, love, knowledge and other higher qualities of consciousness. The planes of consciousness, he says, are composed of different frequencies. He also states that the inner force which supports our being is vibrating. It is everywhere, in all things[52]. Grof states that in LSD-induced experiences, solid and tangible material stuff can disintegrate into patterns of energy, a cosmic dance of vibrations, or a play of consciousness[41]. Theosophist

Madame Blavatsky also saw the universe as composed of vibrations[126]. Jane Roberts' channeled personality, Seth, states that all matter consists of high frequency pulsations too fast for us to detect[39]. Robert Monroe, author of books on out-of-body experiences which he himself has frequently experienced, asserts that our true form, once we drop all "disguises" is a vibrational pattern of many interacting and resonating frequencies[127], a view which corresponds with those of Aurobindo who pointed out that the so-called Beings of Light were revealed to be such vibrating patterns of energy if one maintained one's focus upon them[128]. Swedenborg described his mystical experiences of the creation of earthly forms in the heavenly realm in terms of energy flows paralleling yogic and holographic metaphor notions of wavelike processes generating phenomena. The material version was just a frozen version of the thought-built heavenly reality[15], a view that corresponds well with (Kashmiri Shaivite) *Pratyabhijñā's tattvas* of universal experience as divine ideations as mentioned in the previous section.

In classical yogic tradition we mainly encounter vibrations such as the pulsating activity (*spanda*) of the Kashmiri Shaivite Doctrine of Vibration or more subtly as the *vritti,* the wavelike fluctuations of the *citta* (mindstuff) in the *Yoga Sūtra* tradition. Panda notes that in the *Vedāntic* tradition we have Gaudapada's *cittaspandita,* the vibrations of the consciousness or mindstuff brought about by the deluding effect of *māyā* (note that this is not Shankara's notion of *māyā*). It is this vibration that creates the duality of subject and object. Without this vibration, the *citta* is free of objects. Panda also notes that vibration is implied in the notion of *Śabdabrahman* (the *AUM* which I mentioned in my verse) and that *Vedạnta* holds *Māyāśakti* (the power of *Māyā*) to be vibrating whilst *Brahman* is unmoving (*niḥspanda*)[100]. Brown[23] states that in the *Yoga Sūtra* tradition, as the yogi focuses on the flow of the light which constitutes the substratum of perception, it begins to manifest as a continuously vibrating energy field called *tanmātra* (a name incorporating *mātrā*, measure, referring to this field as a background matrix for the gross cognitions). The *Yoga Sūtra* tradition repeatedly refers to the wave patterns in the mindstuff. The manifestation of phenomena at the so-called 'interface of mind and cosmos' is experienced by the yogi taking the *Yoga Sūtra* perspective as peaks and troughs of waves rather than the discrete flashes of light 'seen' from the Buddhist focus on discontinuity. The Sanskrit term *vritti*, generally translated as 'fluctuations' or as a 'continuous transformation' is also used for 'gross activity', 'changing manifestations' or simply 'change'. Brown translates the term *cittavritti* as the 'continuous change of the mindstuff'. Such changes or fluctuations associated with the generation of phenomena correspond to the wavelike activity or vibrating energy field.

Advaita Vedānta distinguishes pure, universal consciousness (*cit, sākṣi caitanya*) from the phenomenal (or 'modified') consciousness (*citta, vritti caitanya*)[45]. *Sākṣin* means the passive witness as is also found in the *puruṣa* of the *Yoga Sūtras*. The term *vritti* associated with phenomena thus refers to activity. The Pure Consciousness remains as the underlying, unifying ground of all phenomenal states, like the *tanmātra* background matrix of light in the *Yoga Sūtras*. Chapple notes that, in the *Yoga Sūtras, citta* refers to the impure consciousness wherein the contents of experience take form. The term *cetana* in *Sānkhya* refers to the purified consciousness. *Citta* takes colouration with the arising *vritti*, waves that pervade the *citta* in the form of perceptions, thoughts and emotions. Perceptions of objects are ripples (*vritti*) in the field of objectivity (*citta*). The *cittavritti* constitute the world-generating process that must be held in abeyance in order to purify consciousness[65]. Kaplan states that in the *Advaita* theory of perception, the object as it is known is a *vritti* of the *antaḥkaraṇa* (mind, 'inner organ' with which we think, feel, remember). Kaplan interprets the term *vritti* to mean 'transformation' in the sense that the mind "turns about the object taking its form" (the mind assumes the trans-*formation* of the object). Perception of an object entails such transformation (*vritti*) of the mind into the form of the object[103]. Coward notes that a thought or *cittavritti* for *Yoga* is a shaping of the mindstuff or *citta*[28].

Aurobindo refers to the stilling of the waves of consciousness, its manifold activities, *cittavritti*, from the turbid *rajasic* mode (*guṇa*) to the quiet, luminous *sattvic* mode. Our emotions are the waves of reaction and response which arise from the *cittavritti*, says Aurobindo[28]. Potter notes that the *kleśas*, the erroneous awareness associated with emotions are fluctuations (*vritti*) of the *citta*[84]. Aurobindo repeatedly refers to vibrations in regard to intuition, psychic powers etc. and also the so-called Beings of

Light which resolve themselves into luminous vibrations[25,128]. Thus we see that the term *vritti* refers to *wavelike* fluctuations or vibrations in the mindstuff, the consciousness energy, through which the world of phenomenal experience, thoughts and emotions are generated. *Vritti* thus corresponds to Gauḍapāda's *cittaspandita* the vibrations of the mindstuff which create the world of subject-object duality. The mind transforms itself into the perceived phenomena by means of *vritti.* As we have already noted, at the so-called 'interface of mind and cosmos', the yogi realises that the laws governing the manifestation of mental phenomena are operable in the wider universe.

Contemplating the reality underlying scientific abstractions

In monistic Kashmiri Shaivism, as described by Dyczkowski, the outer reality of Becoming is a wave of activity emerging from the inner reality of Being, the Universal Consciousness. This movement from Being to Becoming is, in essence, an act of perception in which awareness moves from the inner unity to the diversity of outer forms. This activity consists of *spanda* (pulsations, vibrations) which are subtle movements rather than motions in Space or Time. The cosmic process consists of a series of such pulsations which create and destroy the manifestations and thus generate Time. The creative activity, although itself beyond Time and Space, is the basis of all spatio-temporal manifestations. Reality contemplated from the highest level of consciousness is experienced as a single, unchanging whole. Yet, from a lower level of experience, this same Reality appears to change in Space and Time[99]. Panda notes that such pulsation generating the mental constructions of Space and Time leads to the phrase, "the immovable moves" (The reader should now be familiar with the notion of Space and Time as mental abstractions from the greater Reality and the paradox of simultaneous passivity and activity). The self-luminous (*prakāśā,* Light) aspect of the Absolute does not change at all. Through the pulsating activity manifesting the phenomenal world, the Absolute becomes the perceiver and the perceived as each cycle of manifestation rises and falls away. This duality actually disappears in the dissolution phase of the cycle of creative Becoming. Everything in the universe is created by the *spandana,* the vibrations of the Absloute Consciousness[100].

We have seen the central role of wavelike activity, pulsations or vibrations in the yogic cosmology. I have asserted that the Buddhist focus on discontinuous pulses is an abstraction from the underlying continuum. The Buddhist Doctrine of *Kṣanika* (Momentariness) which arises from this limited focus is fraught with problems due to its denial of an underlying substratum which persists through the moments as, for instance, in regard to the Buddhist views of *Karma* where continuity is an essential factor. Clearly, it is easier to grasp the relevance of this vibratory picture to perceptual world-creation in the mind than its relevance on the cosmic scale as we have already begun to discuss in Section 2(e). We have seen that Science involves limited modes of perception, technological limitations, animistic projections of the internal reality onto the external world, numerous hidden subjective assumptions and other distorting factors which result in the naïve believer in the scientific cosmology taking these limited abstractions from the greater Reality to be Reality itself and thus denying the existence of numerous aspects of Reality which cannot be understood in terms of these abstractions. We have also seen that attempts to understand what Quantum Theory really means in regard to the true nature of the world and new theories such as the Superstring models and various hyperspace models have already begun to parallel the yogic picture in viewing the spatio-temporal order of conventional physics as arising from a deeper realm of broader causal possibilities with the two former cases also involving notions of the spatio-temporal order being the product of vibratory activity.

As stated in Section 2(e), once one has disposed of immature misconceptions that the abstractions of the scientific world-picture constitute the actual, substantial Reality, it becomes easier to accept the validity of the yogic picture which does allow for all aspects of Reality to be incorporated into the picture although it accepts that Reality can only be truly known as it is through existential realization. As I noted in regard to Ken Wilber's argument against the synthesis of Science and Mysticism, the everyday world, the material plane, consists of our gross perceptions and other gross cognitions. Using the modes of information reception available to our technological artefacts we detect patterns of activity at levels of order not perceived by our senses which we try to make sense of in terms of discrete particles or continuous wave phenomena. Such scientific concepts, as we have seen, involve projections from our everyday world of stones and water waves as well as animistic projections from our internal reality of perceptual world construction resulting from insights which arise from the depths of our being. As the mind is created of the same consciousness energy which manifests the universe at large and the microcosm of the mind generates a spatio-temporal matrix in order to model the gross features of the external world, there appears to be much truth in the yogic intuition that the same processes operate to generate phenomena in both microcosm and macrocosm. Through yogic deconstruction of the processes of microcosmic world-creation, insights are gained into the processes at work in the macrocosm. As knowledge is in fact *realization* through *being*, the yogi can attain realizations about these underlying processes by effectively becoming one with these processes within himself. Furthermore, due to the transcendence of normal time and space distinctions at deeper levels of being where it becomes apparent that a relativistic, holistic mode of causality underlies the seeming spatio-temporal causality of the everyday world, the yogi has access to knowledge far beyond the limits of our normal realm of experience limited by spatio-temporal constraints. Of course these realizations need to be interpreted in our limited frame of reference in everyday terms which do not do them justice but we see that there is general agreement that the everyday world of phenomena emerges from an underlying realm of energetic vibrations arising within the plenum of Universal Consciousness.

As I mentioned in the introduction, Eddington, who played a key role in establishing Einstein's theory of General Relativity, noted in his *The Nature of the Physical World* that what we actually detect in our scientific instruments are not atoms or particles as such but "schedules of pointer readings", i.e. masses of data, readings, even tracks in cloud chambers perhaps. He pointed out that such indicators do not point out the intrinsic nature of these entities. Eddington also showed that if we investigate what is meant by scientific terms such as *potential* or *matter* or *mass* or *momentum* etc. we find that the definitions are all interrelated, i.e. one quantifiable scientific concept is defined in terms of other quantifiable scientific concepts each of which is itself defined by the others so that we are constantly passed on from one concept to another without ever understanding what these concepts really mean. Eddington describes this network as being like "the house that Jack built", implying a superficial facade, empty on the inside. The scientific concepts are a system of interrelated symbols[129]. In more general terms Eddington is restating the point that scientific concepts are just abstractions of some measurable aspects of Reality. I would add that we do manage to break the endless cycle of interrelated symbols that Science presents us with when we look at the historical origins of such notions as projections and understand that these concepts reflect our perceptual modes of operation as much as they reflect the external reality. Also, we have seen that with the most fundamental concept, *energy,* we are presented with a metaphysical principle which states that energy is *uncreated.* Of course, Einstein did equate energy to the concepts of *mass* and the *velocity of light* so it can be woven into these networks of quantifiable indicator symbols. We have seen that changes in *mass* can be interpreted in a holistic way using Mach's principle which, if incorporated into quantum mechanics as Schommers has done, leads to our conventional notions of Space and Time becoming interpreted as abstractions from underlying processes involving energy and momentum. We are told that when matter and anti-matter meet, they annihilate each other producing vast amounts of energy and that virtual particle/anti-particle pairs are constantly being created in seemingly empty space. It does not take much insight to understand that the particle is itself an abstraction from process, a relatively stable form maintained by underlying energetic processes which may transform into other relatively stable forms of energy. The universe is not created out of a multiplicity of particles, the multiplicity of particles arise from an underlying substratum of energy. Thus the intuitive picture that Science itself gives us is that matter is secondary to the primary reality *energy;* matter is a sort of crystallization of the underlying energy postulated by Science.

We have seen that the scientific concept of energy is itself an abstraction from our psychophysical experience of having energy in the sense of freedom and vitality. The earlier Newtonian notion of *force* was similarly a projection from volition. Thus the scientific concept of energy is in fact an abstraction from the psychophysical consciousness-energy considered by mysticism. I noted in the introduction that Eddington himself understood that Reality was in fact like Consciousness. We have also seen that yogic philosophy asserts that matter is a congealed or crystallized form of consciousness which, as Aurobindo tells us, must be considered as consciousness-energy or consciousness-force. The yogic philosophy also tells us that at deeper levels of the macrocosmic world-creation process the situation remains somewhat in flux as in *Pratyabhijñā's tattvas* of universal experience. The phenomenal world is not fixed by deterministic laws but actualizes from creative, vibratory processes of the uncreated Ground of Consciousness; a view which ties in with the interpretations of Quantum Theory which view the spatio-temporal order as being generated from a deeper realm of energetic vibrations which constitute possibilities for actualizing particular phenomenal patterns. We have seen that Space and Time may arise through collective interactions or phase-locking of quantum elements resulting in macroscopic stabilities and regularities even though at a microscopic level the situation remains a bubbling broth of unstable fluctuations. Bohm has pointed out that there may be activity at levels of order so far removed in terms of scale and frequency from the relatively invariant features abstracted by our instruments that such activity is physically meaningless. Such considerations help us to contemplate what actually lies beneath the facade-like interlocking network of physical symbols presented to us by Science through its abstraction of measurable, quantifiable behavioural patterns. Given that yogic traditions (which have direct experience of the deeper processes), interpretations of the symbolic constructions of Science by a number of renowned scientists, and some recent attempts to unify scientific models seem to be in agreement, we may interpret such parallels as indicating that, from their various perspectives, all of these approaches are seeing aspects of the actual nature of the phenomenal world which is manifested from an underlying realm of energetic vibrations.

I mentioned in Part One of this essay my difficulties at school in coming to terms with the Newtonian physics taught to us at secondary school as it did not make sense intuitively. How could billiard balls attract and repel one another to form molecules and other conglomerates of matter, let alone form living systems. Anyone with an ounce of insight can see the insurmountable problems faced by this mechanistic picture which simply cannot be translated into the actual processes of the natural world. However, when one considers the world of phenomena at all levels of being produced by the superimposition of complex patterns of energetic vibrations in a plenum, with stable, complex forms emerging at various levels of order (which we superficially abstract and take to be separate entities), with Space and Time themselves arising from such emergent relations, this makes intuitive sense as deep down within us, the depths of our being recognizes that this is a parsimonious, workable representation of itself. After all, as we shall see, the source of our insights, our true creativity, lies in the depths of our being which transcends the distinctions of Time and Space and is, in a sense, one with all that exists.

The vibratory Creation and the Big Bang hypothesis

As I stated in Section 2(e), the dominant scientific model of the creation of the universe, the Big Bang hypothesis, does not seem concordant with the picture being presented here of the material realm as the continuously emerging product of a deeper realm of subtle vibratory activity in the plenum of Pure Consciousness. Indeed, such notions of continuous emergence appear, at first, to be more in tune with steady-state hypotheses like the now discredited model proposed by Bondi, Gold and Hoyle rather than the Big Bang hypothesis which has a fair amount of evidence supporting it. It should be noted however, as I have indicated in the verse, that the Vedic cosmology of the *kalpa* (the cosmic cycle, literally "the imagining"), is clearly concordant with the most popular speculative notions in regard to the future of the universe which hold that it will eventually return into a singularity (often crudely called "the Big Crunch"). As previously stated, the seeming incompatibility of the vibratory model and the Big Bang hypothesis arise from the different frames of reference within which the mind is operating when we contemplate the two. We should keep in mind, as many commentators have stated in regard to this issue, that the Big Bang cosmology is itself a modern myth, an attempt to convey some essential existential truth using the limited analogical modes available to us which hardly do justice to the actuality. Scientific cosmologists often remind us that it is impossible to picture notions like the Big Bang and what existed prior to it, if indeed the latter question has any meaning whatsoever as the laws of physics seem to break down close to the initial singularity, even though they are generally treated by most scientists as transcendent laws (existing independently of the Creation). We are told by scientists that Space and Time do not exist prior to the creation of matter, that in some way they are byproducts of matter and thus we cannot imagine what is truly meant by the remarkable expansion of the universe in which the vast space between the galactic clusters arises out of the expansion of the spaceless, infinitesimal singularity. As I stated in the introduction, our logic breaks down into paradoxes when faced with ultimate questions. But we have seen that seemingly unimaginable notions such as curved space, space-time emergence etc. can be realised in altered states of consciousness. In LSD-induced experiences subjects even claim to experience simultaneously oneness with entities such as atoms and galaxies even though the two exist at opposite poles of our conventional notions of spatio-temporal order[41]. Such claims are deeply reminiscent of the famous, seemingly paradoxical, Upaniṣadic assertions that *Brahman* is smaller than the smallest yet greater than the greatest. Francis Crick may assert that the Hindus simply exaggerated distances and time scales for the sheer joy of it but it seems that the *riṣis* were actually trying to convey their amazing realizations of the sheer unimaginable scale of the cosmos. Thus when we contemplate the notion of the Big Bang, what we do is to project our everyday notions of explosions, noise etc. onto an event which simply cannot be imagined within the limited frame of reference of our mundane plane of conscious existence.

As we have seen, Bohm stressed the point that physics assumes a vast ocean of energy which it cannot deal with practically and thus magics it away using mathematical simplification procedures. Physics thus limits itself to considering the relatively small excitation, constituting our material universe, in this background plenum. Although the background energy plenum is initially assumed, it is largely meaningless from the perspective of physical model-making, and can be ignored for practical purposes. Bohm saw the Big Bang as a ripple in this vast background void, a sudden wave pulse. Indeed, there are mainstream hypotheses which view the Big Bang as involving some sort of initial quantum fluctuation introducing inhomogeneity, breaking symmetries etc., which becomes amplified into the inhomogeneity we see in the universe at large. Such notions of an initial quantum fluctuation are suggestive of an initial wave or vibration (psychophysically a sort of ideational wave) that distorted the distinctionless void and created further vibratory activity which began to manifest the universe. Such notions correspond to the Upaniṣadic notion of the *Śabdabrahman* (the *AUM*), the initial vibration, or *Pratyabhijñā's Śiva tattva,* the first creative movement of the Absolute, the first vibration of the Absolute's Will[100].

When *Brahman* was reborn of *Purush*
New *AUM* in newborn heavens rang
Twins Space and Time reborn through *yajña*
And born was I in this Big Bang

Of course, from the yogic perspective, the source of the universe is not a problem; it is the same Ground of all Being that can be realized to be the Ground of one's Self, the Pure Consciousness of enlightenment. The realizations that occur in losing one's individuality in this Ground Consciousness reveal it to be the source of the universe. As we have seen, such mystical realizations are, in essence, no different to the limited realizations each one of us has in our everyday waking experience, which have become so familiar to us that the sense of wonder at their magical quality is lost unless one practices yogic exercises which deautomatize perception. Once one comes to terms with the problems of frames of reference and the limits of our normal imagination in regard to the cosmic Creation, it is easier to understand how the yogic vibratory model is compatible with the Big Bang hypothesis. The problems Science has in explaining in lay terms the the expansion of the infinitesimal singularity into the vast expanses of the known universe whilst maintaining that it does not expand into a pre-existent space indicates that Science is operating within a limited frame of reference. Viewed from a deeper frame of reference it is possible to conceive such expansion as an expansion of the relatively stable spatio-temporal realm of activity out of the background plenum, the Void which is void of physical meaning. Pythagoras' view that the One breathed in the Void to fill up the space between things seems most appropriate here and was probably based on yogic knowledge. Thus from the limited scientific frame of reference, this background Void is not considered, it is meaningless. Thus we can have an expanding Big Bang universe in which the matter is itself the emergent product of activity spreading within the Void. We have seen that such vibratory activity is said to have no reference to Space and Time although the spatio-temporal order manifests from this underlying subtle activity. Thus the material realm is being constantly manifested or actualized at a deep level by the vibrations or pulsations in the Void although the higher level, macroscopic stable forms of the material world remain as if concrete, even though the elementary activity producing them is one of constant flux, constant pulsation or vibration. Indeed, such maintenance of a stable macroscopic order in spite of a seething world of vibratory activity at the subatomic level is exactly the picture that Science itself presents us with. It is this continuous manifestation which is the Becoming, the process underlying Time.

2(i). THE PLANES OF CONSCIOUSNESS AND YOGIC SLEEP

The Light as the all-pervading Ground

It should be clear from the preceding discussions that the so-called *planes of consciousness* are not separate realms existing independently of one another but, rather, are levels of order abstracted from the One Reality through alterations in perceptual focus. Thus the supernatural and transcendental realms do not exist separately from our world, they co-exist with our world beyond the limits of our normal mode of perception. The Upaniṣadic assertions that *Brahman* is the Seer of Seeing and the Be-er of Being, reflect the fact that the Pure Universal Consciousness, as the *sākṣin* (witness) of phenomena persists throughout the various levels of manifestation as the background field within which all orders co-exist. This assertion that the Pure Consciousness is ever-present through all of our states of consciousness although it is not apparent as it is veiled by *māyā/avidyā* is again indicative of the RAS whose activating brainwaves are always flowing through the living brain submerged by the superimposed activity of various brain centres constituting the perceptual world-creation of *avidyā/māyā*. As the brain is gradually deactivated, the world-creating *avidyā/māyā* is held in abeyance leaving the Universal Light of Pure Consciousness to shine forth. In fact the very activity of the *avidyā/māyā,* all the mental activity, is itself born of the same universal Light, as I have discussed above, such microcosmic principles reflect macrocosmic world-creating principles where all processes are occurring as energetic vibrations in the plenum of the Universal Light of Pure Consciousness. Thus the Light is omnipresent as the underlying Ground of all Being in microcosm and macrocosm.

Satprem, the follower of Aurobindo, says that the "inner force" becomes diluted and gives the sensation of being a small muffled background vibration in our ordinary life. When one has discovered it, he says, it is *the same thing* everywhere, in all beings, in all things, allowing direct communication as if there were no wall between[52]. This is a modern restatement of the classical *ghatākāśa/ākāśa* metaphor in which the space in the jar, representing the *upādhi* (limiting adjunct) is not really separate from the infinite space outside the jar. This force, says, Satprem, is behind each centre of consciousness, behind all of our thinking, willing, desires and suffering. This force which links our various ways of being from waking to sleep to death is the Consciousness[52]. Again, the mystical view expressed here of a force linking together our states of being; waking, sleeping etc. is suggestive of the RAS brainwaves which, through alterations in their frequency determine our various states of arousal. Satprem adds that the various levels of being are like knots of force, each with its particular vibratory quality or special frequency. Each plane has its own wavelength and its own luminous intensity. The luminosity becomes more intense as one ascends the planes, time becomes faster and covering a wider range (in the future or past) until one emerges into the still Light in which all pre-exists. Thus, says Satprem, the Transcendent is not elsewhere outside the world, it is everywhere, at once totally inside and totally outside[52].

Monistic Kashmiri Shaivism distinguishes between *Prakāśa* (Light), the unchanging ontological ground and witness aspect of Absolute Consciousness and the 'reflective awareness' (*vimarśa*) which this Light has of its own nature. Consciousness has the ability to reflect, to bend back, on itself allowing it to know itself and what appears within it. This *vimarśa* aspect is linked to the power of Creation, the flux of Becoming[99]. As Dyczkowski states[99]:

> *By contemplating its own nature, consciousness assumes the forms of all the planes of existence from the subtlest to the most gross. The power of reflection is thus the inherent creative freedom of the light of consciousness to either turn in on itself introspectively and be free of its outer forms, or move out of itself to view its outer manifestations.*

The *prakāśa* aspect is always undivided at all levels of being whereas the *vimarśa* aspect, the activity of self-reflection creating the forms on the various planes, is not. Panda notes that *vimarśa* is the *Śakti* (power) and equivalent to *Spanda* (vibrations)[100]. Dyczkowski states that the *vimarśa* is the inner activity of the *spanda* principle, which is the inspired wonder of consciousness from which the powers of will, knowledge and action flow out[99]. Thus *vimarśa* seems to represent the psychical aspect of the vibrational activity manifesting the world of forms.

Friedman quotes the near-death experiences of a Stefan von Jankovich for whom God came to represent an inexhaustible and timeless source of primal energy, radiating and absorbing energy and constantly pulsating. Jankovich discovered that the different 'worlds' (planes) co-existed, differentiated by their frequencies[39]. Similarly, Wilber cites a Lama Govinda who describes the levels as mutually penetrating forms of energy, from the all-pervading luminous consciousness down to the densest form of "materialized consciousness".[130] Grof states that in LSD experiences any number of interpenetrating universes can be seen to co-exist. The space-time world appears to be arbitrarily teased out of a complex continuum of infinite possibilities[41]. The so-called 'higher planes' include the 'lower planes' with the all-pervading Ground containing all possible worlds. Tying this in with the distinction of planes through frequencies, the deeper levels of Reality would thus consist of higher frequency vibrations with larger scale, lower frequency vibrations emerging from the superposition of these smaller wavelengths. This ties in with Bohm's view in which the quantum vacuum oscillates so fast that it is beyond physical interpretation. This also ties in with models of perception involving 'tuning in' to certain wavelengths. The macroscopic world of gross perceptions would correspond to patterns of activity emitting vibrations of lower frequency than more microscopic realms. The more microscopic realms of order would include the macroscopic realms as high-level patterns which could be abstracted from them whereas the reverse would not hold true. Thus the mystical experience of the higher realms of increasing frequency and inclusiveness is compatible with the physical picture in which higher-level patterns of order emerge at the macroscopic levels of order arranged in a nested hierarchy. This is not to say that a plane of consciousness corresponds directly to a level of physical order, only that the two pictures are not contradictory.

The development of lucidity

The states of consciousness have been linked to the states of waking, dreaming and deep sleep in the *Māṇḍūkya Upaniṣad*, an approach followed by Iyer in his *Vedānta or the Science of Reality*[72]. Indich notes that the hierarchy of 5 sheaths which obscure or cover the self in the *Taittirīya Upaniṣad* correspond to the wake, dream and sleep states of the *Māṇḍūkya*. The purest and most subtle sheath (*ānandamayakośa*) corresponds to the *Māṇḍūkya's* deep sleep and is called the "causal body".[45] Aurobindo says that the dream state corresponds to the subtler life-plane and mind-plane whereas the sleep state is a consciousness corresponding to supramental gnosis which is not experienced because the causal body has not been developed. The yogi develops the ability to remain awake at the supramental level, i.e. develops lucidity (*suṣupti* — perfect deep sleep) corresponding to the development of the causal body[25]. Similarly, when Aurobindo talks of the yogic dream state in which the mind is in clear possession of itself and able to use its will, he is referring to the maintenance of lucidity. Satprem[52] says that, in the early stages of yogic development, the consciousness is not truly individualised at sleep or 'death' but with yogic development one attains conscious sleep and a "death which lives" (I would consider this to mean lucid deep sleep). He also mentions that a bridge to sleep may be attained with care when awaking, i.e. hypnapompia. Satprem also says[52]:

> *Try to develop your inner individuality says the Mother, and you will be able to enter these very regions in full consciousness, and to have the joy of communion with the highest regions without losing consciousness . . .*

Dyczkowski[131] directly links Yogic Sleep (*yoganidrā*) to lucid dreaming. The yogi observes the point of transition between waking and sleep (as in hypnagogia). Similarly, the references to deep sleep, which often causes confusion as we normally do not have any experiences during deep sleep, actually refer to lucid deep sleep. Dyczkowski states[131]:

> *the ascent occurs when we fall asleep. The difference between the average man and the yogi is that the latter is conscious of this process and experiences it as one of a movement through a graded series of divine energies located at their corresponding levels in the universe of manifestation.*

As indicated in Section 2(c), I would interpret the development of lucidity in terms of the maintenance of a stable self-organising process at levels of brain activity where such stability normally does not occur. We have come across above, in relation to the concept of *vimarśa* (reflective awareness), the inherent creative freedom of the light of consciousness to turn in on itself introspectively. The yogi applies this free will, with which the individual is endowed, to focus attention on the processes of mentation itself and, through sufficient practice, develops what Laughlin, McManus and d'Aquili have called 'autoreverberation' in underlying processes which are normally subconscious, resulting in the transition of the stable state to a different level of brain function. Laughlin *et al.*[83] state that when we carry out a disciplined programme to "strengthen our will", we are, in part at least, increasing the autoreverberative capacity of various networks. I have mentioned in Section 2(c) Taimni's descriptions of such changes in state, or 'vehicles', as being like physical phase transitions. Yogic development of lucidity in different brain centres would presumably involve some subtle structural changes in the neural networks, through the downward causation effects of turning attention inwards, which would facilitate the maintenance of stable lucid states in these networks. Presumably, in the so-called ascent to lucid dreaming and lucid deep sleep, dissipative structure activity is stabilised at lower energy levels, with the lowest energy stable process corresponding to bare individuality which the yogis call the "causal body" (or the *jīva*). It should be clear that I am denying the validity of any doctrine which asserts the persistence of individuality (or a *jīva*) through normal (non-lucid) deep sleep or death and thus confirming the Buddhist doctrine of *anatta* (*anātman*) which sees individuality as a transitory phenomenon. We are told that yogic masters have developed the capacity to pass from the normal state of waking consciousness to the unindividuated oneness with the Light, without delaying in the intermediate states. Again, underlying such capacities would presumably be subtle changes in neuronal organization facilitating such remarkable shifts in the state of consciousness requiring years of sustained practice and world-renunciation to attain although we find some natural born psychic types who seem to be able to attain similar feats without training.

Increasing freedom and creativity in dream-like states

Indich notes that the *Māṇḍūkya Upaniṣad* asserts that the (lucid) dreaming subject is freer than the waking one, dreams being broader in possibility than waking consciousness. Dream consciousness is purer and more homogeneous than waking consciousness and dream content more subtle and unified. In (lucid) deep sleep there is even greater freedom; the consciousness is free of body and mind (meaning it is not associated with the lower mental and bodily planes of activity). The consciousness is also more pure than in dream consciousness being a homogeneous unified mass of consciousness. However, this is still not freedom or *turīya* (the 'fourth state'), corresponding to enlightenment. *Advaita Vedānta* holds deep sleep to involve the cessation of mutual superimposition (*adhyāsa*) of *cit* and *avidyā* (which I have interpreted above as the activating RAS brainwaves and the brainwave activity resulting from normal mentation, sensory processing etc.). The limiting conditions (*upādhi*) of space, time, causality etc. are held in abeyance, and the experience is one of a dense mass of unified consciousness (*cidghana* or *prajñānaghana*).

Advaita negatively identifies (lucid) deep sleep with *savikalpa samādhi* (the *bhakti* experience of a personal god; indeed the *Māṇḍūkya Upaniṣad* identifies deep sleep with *Īśvara,* the Lord, or *saguṇa Brahman*) due to the absence of suffering and dualistic awareness in both although the two are not exactly the same. *Advaita,* of course, holds *nirvikalpa samādhi,* corresponding to the *Māṇḍūkya's turīya* to be the highest realization in which individuality is lost in the impersonal, distinctionless absolute of *nirguṇa Brahman*[45].

Thus we see that yogic progress involves the development of lucidity which I have interpreted as the development of the capacity to maintain a stable, self-organising process at lower energy levels in deeper brain structures or simply in other brain centres not normally associated with normal mentation depending on the yogic path. I have noted in Section 2(b) some evidence indicating that dreaming and related fantasy-like activity may be associated with activity in subcortical structures rather than right hemisphere activity. The basic planes of consciousness or the various sheaths covering the Self of pure, Universal Consciousness correspond primarily to the various levels of arousal (deep sleep, dream sleep, wakefulness) which are lucidly experienced by the yogi. This of course raises the question as to what happens in normal dream sleep in which we do not have a normal sense of self. We only tend to remember these experiences, normally, if we are disturbed and partly or fully awoken indicating that a degree of lucidity is normally required in order to register our dreaming activity which does not seem to operate using normal bodily reference frames. Dreams seem to operate spontaneously without our volition guiding their progress which may reflect emotionally charged memory activity operating without self-organisation into an individuated, volitional entity. The lack of guided progress and the often reported abrupt changes from one dream sequence to another with no obvious connection may reflect activity in neural networks which are spontaneously operating with some sort of sequential entrainment process based on competition for energy resources, usually associated with emotional intensity. We can associate the lack of normal world-modelling rules to deactivation of layers of superimposing activity which generate such causal relations through imposing limitations (*upādhi*) upon the spontaneous activity of consciousness. The yogis tell us that even greater freedom is attained in deeper levels where even more layers of limiting superimpositions have been held in abeyance allowing for activity well beyond the bounds of our usual experience. Clearly, the lack of normal causal rule-following in dream activity, whatever its physical correlates, lies behind its important role in creativity especially in hypnagogic states. The same processes seem to be involved in a wide range of visual activity associated with fantasies, madness, certain paranormal phenomena and creative visions. Thus we all have limited access to deeper levels of consciousness when we become aware of our dream activity. As stated previously, *Advaita* had recognised the role of wish-fulfilment in dreams, centuries before Freud's well-known thesis, although *Advaita*, unlike Freud, did not limit itself to this one sole explanation for dreams[45]. Jung's view of dreams as compensatory activity by parts of the psyche normally repressed clearly has some truth in it as well. It is not my purpose here to consider such theories.

Clearly there is not one single explanation for the variety of dream phenomena although the neurological basis of the activity may be similar in all cases, probably involving subcortical structures and thus perhaps explaining the greater degrees of freedom as presumably the strict world-modelling limitations are superimposed upon mental phenomena by the normal activity of cortical structures. I have noted in Section 2(e) Josephson's view that the possibility or potentiality aspects of Quantum Theory are reminiscent of the subtler planes of mystical experience which relate to fantasy or possibility. In regard to our previous discussions of microcosm reflecting macrocosm, it is obvious that the space-time order in the external world does not arise in a brain-like matrix imposing limitations upon the free activity of the consciousness-energy. Clearly the brain has evolved to model certain gross features of the external world and thus creates its own space-time order during normal functioning to simulate external space-time causality. The space-time causality in the external world is taken to emerge from more spontaneous levels of order through the operation of collective constraining relations like the phase-locking etc. previously mentioned. Thus both microcosm and macrocosm involve the operation of constraints upon the spontaneous activity at deeper levels which hold the potential for a wider range of possibilities than the limited law-like behaviour operating in the emergent space-time order. Microcosmically, this is related to our creative ability as discussed in the next section.

Shifts in perceptual focus and the subject/object distinction

Although I have focused on the *Māṇḍūkya Upaniṣad's* categorization of the four states of consciousness, the reader is most probably aware that other traditions give varying numbers of planes or sheaths. Numerous commentators have shown that these different classifications describe the same basic levels with the basic planes described above being subdivided into further levels presumably reflecting functional differences in the brain. Aurobindo's system, being formulated in modern times, has the advantage that he relates his yogic insights to modern knowledge of the mind. His basic order involves, the Material, Vital, Mental and Supramental planes which are further subdivided in regard to various psychological functions etc. which bears some relationship to modern biological and psychological knowledge[132]. Clearly the actual divisions given by each tradition depend upon the particular distinctions between levels which the yogi wishes to abstract from the overall activity. As I stated at the beginning of this section, the planes are abstracted levels of order reflecting the focus of perception. The microcosmic and macrocosmic planes seem to be related through the operation of perceptual filters in the normal functioning of the brain. Our normal waking consciousness is the product of a world-modelling process which has selected only key features of the information available both through the senses and through other non-sensory means of information reception. This results in the representation of the gross spatio-temporal features of the external world, primarily the surfaces of stable macroscopic processes. In the deeper microcosmic planes of consciousness such as those associated with the broad heading of lucid deep sleep in which normal world-modelling processes, including the time/space matrix and normal self/other distinction matrices based on the body surface have been held in suspension, the content of the lucid yogi's consciousness will reflect a much broader mode of perception which has access to far more of the information actually impinging upon the microcosm and perhaps identification with the content of the individuated field of consciousness. Shifts in perceptual focus at such deeper levels will involve perception of the deeper and more all-encompassing levels of the macrocosmic order than the superficial level of order abstracted through normal sensory perception in the waking state. We have seen above that Aurobindo says that development of the causal body (lucid deep sleep) corresponds to the attainment of supramental gnosis.

Identification with the content of consciousness means the disappearance of the subject/object duality. Consideration of the microcosmic planes of consciousness gives us some indication as to how the subject/object distinction may arise. It seems as if in our normal consciousness we experience the objective, lawful external world whilst remaining aware of our self as an imaginative and conceptual presence somehow co-existing with the objective, "material" world. It would thus seem that in normal consciousness the mind, although primarily active in the material plane of sense perceptions is also operating in a more limited way in the deeper imaginative plane and perhaps also in conceptual planes which would thus account for the subjective part of our experience as against the objective component of the sense perceptions projected or superimposed above these deeper levels. Indeed Taimni[85] states in regard to the philosophy of the *Yoga Sūtras:*

> *the manifest Universe is an emanation of an Ultimate Reality and its different planes, visible and invisible, may be considered to be formed by a sort of progressive condensation or involution of consciousness. At each stage . . . a subjective-objective relationship is established between the more condensed and less condensed aspects of consciousness, the less condensed assuming the subjective and the more condensed the objective role.*

He adds that the Ultimate Reality is the only purely subjective principle with each limited plane being objective to the higher planes and subjective to the lower ones.

2(j). CREATIVITY, LAWFULNESS, FREEDOM AND INSIGHT

The Christian myth of the Laws of Nature

Descartes recognized the paradox of the law-like behaviour of the Creation and the creative freedom of God and 'Man' (humanity) and thus posited a complete split between God and 'His' Creation[133]. Of course, the split between God and Nature had been established long before Descartes in the Christian tradition with the doctrine of Creation *ex nihilo* which, as we have seen in Section 2(a), was posited by the Christians in opposition to the Gnostics' view of the *pleroma* and the Neoplatonic emanation in which the Creation arises out of the primordial matter or out of the Divine. Creation *ex nihilo* provided a defence for the belief in one free and transcendent creator, a sovereign with miraculous powers who moulded the universe out of literally nothing[30]. The doctrine is strongly associated with Augustine and thus the Roman Church which we have seen also superimposed onto their projection of a Divine personality, the characteristics of a Roman Governor or a Sovereign who lays down the laws. This view of a personal god laying down the laws for his miraculously created, insentient Nature, along with the projection of the new mechanical clock technology onto Nature, subconsciously influenced the development of natural science in Renaissance Europe. Such developments were also influenced by the Platonic view that geometry and divinity were intrinsically associated and Aristotle's emphasis on logic and empiricism over mystical intuitions[27]. We have seen that Newton tried to keep God in the system by viewing matter as inanimate with God as the Prime Mover and sustaining the Laws. Sheldrake notes that both Platonic philosophy and mechanistic physics were conceived in the context of a static universe. Eternal Forms or Laws seemed appropriate in an eternal universe but were inevitably thrown into question by the idea of evolution. In the 17th century, the fathers of modern Science were explicit in their view that the Laws of Nature were framed by God but as God has been dropped by Science, Sheldrake asks, what makes and sustains the Laws[31]. Goodwin, following Yates, points out that Renaissance nature philosophy was strongly influenced by gnostical notions in which Mind and Nature were interwoven. However, political developments in Europe led to the persecution of such mystically inspired Renaissance magi and the rise of Descartes' scientific method with the Parisian monk and mathematician Mersenne, with whom Descartes studied, playing a key role in influencing leading figures of the new science with its split between the realms of Mind and Nature[37].

Heisenberg noted that the unexpected success of simple mathematical laws in physics bolstered the belief that Science was tapping into an external reality existing independently of our minds. However, Heisenberg pointed out, Quantum Theory also used simple mathematical laws but did not require that the world it described existed independently[35]. With the rise of the new field of Chaos, our orderly universe has begun to appear as an island in the middle of a sea of chaos[80]. It is becoming ever more clear that the so-called Laws are little more than mental constructions, abstractions derived from the observation of the regularities of Nature, which need not be immutable. We have seen that in the infinitesimal realms of the singularity at the origin of the universe in the Big Bang cosmology, it is often claimed that the laws no longer hold and thus physical statements become meaningless. This tells us something about the limited frame of reference within which Science is operating, closely tied to the notion of these laws. There are models involving Chaos in which the laws emerge as stable general patterns of behaviour from chaotic behaviour in early phases of cosmic expansion, paralleling mystical notions of law-like behaviour as habits. None the less, numerous scientists and fellow believers still appeal to the Laws of Physics as eternal, immutable, transcendental laws somehow existing independently of the material universe almost as if they were ideas in the mind of God. Claims made in favour of the existence of paranormal phenomena are often sneeringly dismissed by commentators appealing to the supposedly inviolate Laws of Physics in the manner of traditional clergy referring disputes to the higher authority of the prophets who laid down the scriptures through their unique power of communion with the Divine.

Transcendental creativity and emergent habits

In contrast, the yogic traditions have held creativity to be a fundamental attribute of the Divine Reality that manifests the material world. In the *Vedāntic* tradition, the universe is created through *līlā*, the spontaneous, purposeless play of the Absolute Consciousness or the spontaneous creativity of the Divine Ground. As Bohm says of his (transcendent) implicate order, creativity is fundamental and what really requires explanation are processes that are not creative[134]. According to monistic Kashmiri Shaivism, the material world is a product of *spanda,* the pulsating vibrations of Absolute Consciousness. The pulsations consist of two phases with, first, the coagulation of consciousness descending into matter and then its return to more subtle forms. As consciousness descends, it manifestations become increasingly subject to the power of natural law (*niyati*). Conversely, as consciousness ascends again it becomes less conditioned and more free[99]. Panda refers to *niyati* in the monistic Kashmiri Shaivist *Pratyabhijñā* philosophy as one of the five coverings of *Māyā* bringing about the limited individual experience as has been discussed in Section 2(g). *Niyati* is the *tattva* (principle) of limited individual experience which reduces the freedom and pervasiveness of the Universal bringing about limitation in regard to causality and space. Panda also notes that *Advaita Vedānta* holds that order (*rita*) operates amidst the prevalent chaos (*anrita*) of the universe and that the two are coupled in the proper functioning of the world[100]. According to *Advaita,* the greater creativity of the dream state is due to consciousness becoming more detached from its gross content[45]. I have argued in the previous section that this is because the gross content is the normal superimposed world-modelling activity which represents the spatio-temporal behaviour of the environment thus following law-like space-time causality relations. Wilber says that for a child to manipulate objects it must first begin to differentiate itself from its physical environment. The individual must ascend to a higher plane of consciousness in order to manipulate a lower one[130]. Interpreted according to my scheme this suggests a broadening of consciousness into a deeper level whilst remaining aware of the material plane in order to influence the material plane. This differentiation of self from the objects to be manipulated again indicates that the subject/object distinction may be based on such straddling of planes with the objective content remaining in the lower plane whilst the mind is also integrating a deeper level, giving imaginative scope for manipulating the objective world.

Aurobindo says that mind and life are far too subtle and complex to allow precise calculations from cause to effect. He says, "Life and mind are a constant flux of possibles intervening between spirit and matter." Remember that his planes include the vital and the mental between the material and the supramental. The stream of actualities is selected from the mass of forceful possibles, he asserts. Our mental nature at first appears to be just automatic machinery but with deeper realization it is found to depend upon the sanction of the *purusha* which can cease all the active mentality (a passive mentality continues in this case). This sanctioning control, in the ego sense, gives a sense of free will. However, the *purusha* as ego can only sanction the mental processes, it can only choose between certain well-defined possibilities, it cannot radically alter the dynamics of mental processes. To actively control mental nature it is necessary to ascend to a higher plane in which an active identity is maintained with the controlling spirit (rather than entering a trance of identity with it)[25]. The maintenance of active identity again seems to indicate the development of lucidity at a deep level of mind with the controlling spirit or the *ātman* equivalent to the RAS brainwaves.

> *the happenings of vital and still more of mental nature escape to a very great degree the means of inference and calculation from assured law that apply in the field of physical knowledge: it can apply there only to a limited range of regularised happenings . . .*
>
> Sri Aurobindo[25]

The apparent law-like behaviour of the material order is held by Aurobindo, Whitehead and others to be Nature's development of *habits* (stable patterns of behaviour emerging from repetition) rather than *laws* obeyed by Nature. Reality is fundamentally creative but patterns of behaviour can develop into habits and appear to be fixed. This mystical view is, as we have seen, gaining support with the development of Chaotic Dynamics in which stable patterns of order, once taken to be the only sort of order in physics, are now understood as stabilities emerging from an underlying order which is unpredictable. Bohm viewed the formative fields underlying the manifestation of particles as evolving rather than eternal. Talbot cites the fascinating views of Jahn and Dunne who suggest that some of the new particles discovered by physicists may actually be changing their properties depending on the expectations of particle physics community as to how these hypothetical particles should behave. They cite the case of the neutrino which was originally conceived by

Pauli as a massless particle. Originally neutrinos were found to be massless but as theoretical physics developed it became necessary to postulate that neutrinos may possess some mass after all and some laboratories began reporting that they had detected neutrinos with mass whereas other laboratories did not find this to be the case. The idea is that well-established entities which are abundant in Nature, such as electrons, do not exhibit any variation although they might have done so early in the history of the universe. However, exotic particles which are only created in unusual conditions like particle accelerators may not have stabilised into such fixed patterns of behaviour[15].

At first sight such ideas will no doubt appear preposterous to many people as is the case with ideas such as Rupert Sheldrake's *morphic resonance* which is based on similar mystical views of Nature having habits rather than obeying laws. Sheldrake's "morphogenetic fields" are conceived as existing beyond normal space and time and in some manner maintain the memory of forms that have been manifested. Such reverberations make it more likely that the same sorts of forms will be manifested again. Various commentators have pointed out that Sheldrake's view is a modern reformulation of the ancient yogic theory of the *ākāśa*[50,51]. Sheldrake, who wrote his first book *A New Science of Life* in a Christian āshram in India, has linked his "morphic resonance" to Jung's notion of the *collective unconscious* which, as Coward[28] points out, was deeply influenced by Indian notions relating to *karma* which I will discuss in a later section. If one can understand that the material world is a manifestation from a transcendental realm, then such notions do not seem as shocking as they do when one is confined to a naïve materialist frame of reference. Sheldrake is largely correct in pointing out the inadequacies of many scientific attempts at explaining the emergence of forms and behaviours especially when so many scientific thinkers bandy about terms like "genetic programs" as if such metaphors, which careful analysis of the facts of molecular, cellular and developmental biology show to be simplistic in the extreme if not ridiculous. However, given that Goodwin[33,135] has shown how certain, simple biological forms can be understood as the unfolding of the forces generated within the developing embryo, interpreted as spatio-temporal (not transcendental) *morphogenetic fields* with the genes only influencing the parameters of this unfolding process rather than acting as a determining "program", the usefulness of the notion of morphic resonance for the issue of biological morphogenesis has to be questioned. It is interesting to note that, as Goodwin points out, Dreisch introduced the field concept into embryology and went on to postulate that the organizing capacities of organisms arose from a realm beyond matter, space and time which he called *entelechy*[33]. Notions of morphic resonance, or reverberations existing at a transcendental level of order may have a role to play in instincts and learning as Sheldrake also suggests. Aurobindo points out that most of our thoughts actually come to us from outside of ourselves, indicating the presence of syncretic reverberations as in Jung's "collective unconscious". Such notions of transcendental reverberations may also be of use in regard to mind/body interactions and especially in regard to paranormal phenomena where time/space transcendence are often a distinguishing feature.

Mechanistic, holistic and transcendentalist perspectives on free will and life

At the level of the individual, the materialist, mechanistic picture fails to come to terms with the limited freedom of the individual personality and with the capacity of individuals to be creative both in terms of insight or in developing new patterns of behaviour. The materialist approach to these questions tends to involve postulating a number of chance variations which are available from which one is selected usually on the basis of some underlying, hidden constraints upon the system. The mechanistic approach is clearly incompatible with any real freedom of choice and it also adopts a limited view of causality which has been called "upward causation" in which the elements of a system determine the overall behaviour of the system with the higher levels of order being mere epiphenomena floating upon the component mechanistic causes. Recently there has been much fuss made over the issue of so-called "downward causation" in which the system as a whole influences the behaviour of its components and thus a two-way causal nexus, upwards and downwards, is constantly at work. From the limited frame of reference of materialist Science, this is often presented as a rather radical departure from conventional wisdom when it is really just stating the obvious in attempting to correct yet another distortion caused by Science's abstraction of limited aspects of Reality which are then taken to be the whole of Reality. Indeed, the Nobel laureate neurologist famous for his so-called 'split-brain' research, Roger Sperry, who was closely associated with the holistically-inclined view of emergent materialism and downward causation touts this approach as more than a mere shift in the frame of reference from the flawed reductionism of the Behaviourists. Sperry claims that it is the key to understanding consciousness and that it constitutes a new cosmology that makes possible the derivation of transcendent moral guidelines! He even states that "there is growing reason to suspect that the secret trick for generating consciousness could turn out to be some relatively simple form of network processing or programming, something that computer-cognitive science may already be close to discovering." Sperry asserts that because Science tests its "truths" against "outside reality", Science is lifted beyond culture, tradition, metaphysics etc. and is grounded directly in the interactions of reality itself. Sperry mentions that he sees his view as monistic and "mentalist" and that he takes objection with Bunge's naming of this view as "emergent *materialism*" and his classification of Sperry as a dualist. Sperry, believing that consciousness is but an emergent phenomenon, talks of "subjective emergents".[136]

Sperry's views are interesting because they clearly articulate a view which is shared by quite a large number of scientists and materialist thinkers openly displaying incredibly naïve epistemological arguments. A little shift towards holism is all that is required, they believe, for Science to resolve those discrepancies which the naive subjectivists keep pointing out. Although Sperry's claims for the emergent materialist paradigm as a new cosmology and as a means of coming to terms with consciousness are preposterous, in regard to the questions of freedom and creativity, we can see that the shift to emergent downward causation is a move in the right direction. I myself naturally assumed such downward causation at the age of eighteen when I saw the states of the World-Model Field holistically influencing the activity pattern of the neurons within it. We have seen earlier in this work that the emergent materialist view, although it makes the ridiculous claim to be able to account for subjectivity and transcendent values, relies upon a confidence trick to magically insert consciousness into parts of a materialist world picture which has excluded consciousness at its very roots and is inherently behaviourist even though Sperry and others may pay lip service to chastising the reductionism of the so-called Behaviourists. Bunge was clearly correct in labelling Sperry a dualist, albeit a tacit one. Thus the only consistent emergentist picture is of an insentient material collectivity holistically influencing the lower level processes without any real feelings of choice or freedom because there cannot be any feelings within the monistic emergent materialist picture. The monistic emergentist picture, properly understood, remains one of 'blind', insentient patterns of spatio-temporal activity and whether or not the causal chains operate 'bottom-upwards' or 'top-downwards' is irrelevant as there is no conscious entity there making any choices or seeking any insight or creative solution.

Of course, Sperry's emergent materialism is not the only holistic movement within Science. The Gestalt psychologists are perhaps precursors of the current emergent materialist movement with their "the whole is greater than the sum of its parts" philosophy. There has been a longstanding Organismic philosophical movement in Biology challenging the narrow reductionistic focus which has been imposed on Biology by the historical development of Science from the idealised description of planetary and projectile motions and the energetics of steam engines etc. which bear little relationship to the actuality of organismic functioning. Of course elegant biochemical and molecular biological pathways can be determined and this knowledge used for amazing technological manipulations of organisms but the linear, deterministic representations abstracted from the actual processes seem to fix in the mind of many biologists a picture resembling these symbolic pathways and a resulting mechanistic view of the organism. Indeed the original models of planetary motion are themselves now known to be mere idealizations based on naïve assumptions of God-given harmony abstracted from a larger picture represented better by Chaotic Dynamics. Similar developments are occurring in Biology where notions of complexity and living systems existing at the "edge of chaos" are challenging the older myths of simple deterministic rules allowing prediction of future states of the system. However, simultaneously we have the widespread use of the computer metaphor in the cognitive sciences although it has been somewhat mitigated by a resurgence of interest in systems mimicking neural networks. I recently read a classic of organismic philosophy in Biology, entitled *The Organism* by Kurt Goldstein[137], first published in 1933, which has been reprinted once again. The jacket was covered in praise of this highly influential work from some scientific thinkers but the book turned out to be a great disappointment to me because Goldstein seemed to repeat just one insight, about scientific experiments treating the part in isolation from the organism as a whole and thus misunderstanding the true functional role of the part, over and over again. Although a valuable insight it did not require four hundred pages of repeated elaboration. As with Sperry and his emergent materialists believing their minor correctives to the scientific approach to be radical departures, such organismic philosophy is really much like a Trotskyist splinter group, split off from the mainstream Stalinists. Both fail to see the real delusions of the overall materialist picture.

Sperry[136] wonders whether neural networks need to be living in order to generate 'consciousness', his supposed "subjective emergents". John Searle, an academic philosopher whose name seems synonymous with his oft-repeated "Chinese box" argument against the claims of reductionist Artificial Intelligence researchers that a computer's central processing unit could have meaningful cognitions (another 'Stalinist' *versus* 'Trotskyist' argument between materialists), seems to be an emergent materialist. Searle asserts that he thinks that there is something special about living systems which allows for conscious experiences which thus precludes the possibility of their existence in computer systems[138]. Searle's position is clearly inconsistent with monistic materialism and is another form of tacit dualism faced with the problem of consciousness. As life is also viewed as an emergent phenomenon, it may not be surprising that emergent materialists link it to consciousness which they hold to be the same. However, it is interesting as Searle is intuiting that there is something different about living systems although he does not seem to say what this difference may be. Any attempt to intuit what an organism is like in actuality will reveal that the mechanistic picture adopted from the old physics and so cherished by mainstream biologists simply cannot capture the amazing complexity and subtle interrelatedness of just the known aspects of organisms let alone the subtle energetic processes which elude conventional scientific probing. Intuitive contemplation of the nature of the organism reveals that far from being a rigid mechanism an organism appears to exist in a flux of possibilities, a collective of sentient wholes. Indeed our everyday notions of what it is to be *alive* or *living* are related to the notion of *energy* which as we have seen meant the feeling of *vitality* and *freedom*. It is not surprising that mystics and NDE subjects speak in terms of the *Living* Light, the *Living* God, of the universal *Life*, or the universe being full of *Life* for they are talking of the *Prāṇa*, the *Life* Energy which is the Consciousness Energy of *Brahman*. Recall that Heisenberg identified *energy* as the modern equivalent of Aristotle's *potentia*. Prigogine's new thermodynamics of open systems (rather than the artificial test tube world of closed systems of the old thermodynamics which Science falsely superimposed upon organisms) has revealed secrets of self-organization hidden in energy flow systems[139,77]. The energetic aspects of living systems largely ignored in conventional scientific abstractions of the stable material components (like DNA), are what really make a living system alive, full of energy or vitality, and full of possibilities. Returning to Sperry's and Searle's dilemma over the question of living systems and consciousness, we can see that, from their limited materialist frame of reference, they are intuiting certain aspects of the nature of minds which don't seem to fit the mechanistic materialist picture and projecting these discrepancies onto 'life' rather than face the real challenge of panpsychism. The aspects they seem to be intuiting are the field-like aspects of the mind and the self-organizational aspects both of which can be accommodated within a living system whereas the latter does not seem compatible with the rigid silicon-based mechanisms of computers.

When one understands the perennialist panpsychist picture being presented here one begins to appreciate the difficulties involved with the various shifts in frames of reference. Naïve, simplistic notions of an *outside reality* independent of our perceptual world-construction processes and naïve conceptions of physical causality operating amongst independent parts are undermined by consideration of perceptual processes and the yogic knowledge of deeper realms where true causality is found to be relativistic and truly holistic in a sense transcending the simplistic holism of the emergent materialist. Indeed, it is this transcendental holism which gives us the word "holy". When we discuss physical models of brain function involving neural networks, neurotransmitters, field potentials, brainwaves etc. we are dealing with abstractions we have plucked out from the whole Reality and ignoring the true holistic, relativistic interconnectedness of all elements of the overall activity. To give primacy to sets of such abstractions such as the firing of neurons and the activity of neurotransmitters and assume that these are operating independently of the total context and determining the overall pattern of behaviour is simplistic in the extreme although this *reductionism* is the approach of mainstream Science and quite correctly challenged, although in a very limited way, by the emergent materialists. From the subjective point of view we experience a flux of limited possibilities from which we are capable of making a selection rather than automatic behavioural processes. This subjective experience clearly indicates a unitary, holistic physical correlate which I have interpreted as a self-organising field process maintaining an autonomous existence within the greater Reality.

As we have seen, the experience of a limited degree of choice has been associated by a number of thinkers with the flux of possibilities which seems to exist beyond the level of space-time as indicated by quantum mechanics. I have mentioned above that a number of thinkers have suggested that quantum coherence and quantum superpositions of states may be maintained at macroscopic levels of order in the brain and correlated with our subjective experience of existing as a unitary field of consciousness exhibiting a selection from a number of possibilities. Of course, given the projected nature of scientific conceptions, the ideas of Quantum Theory are themselves subtle reflections of our internal mental reality so we are again caught up in complex intermingling frames of reference. The objections of most scientists and scientific thinkers to the yogic view that freedom is an inexplicable capacity inherent in the Light of Consciousness, the Divine Ground, reflects their inability to see beyond their extremely limited frame of reference with its idealised models of abstractions into which everything must fit or else it must be denied. Aurobindo, as we have seen, supports the above view of a limited degree of freedom to select from a flux of possibilities and the general yogic view seems to be that the inherent freedom and creativity of the uncreated Ground of all Being, *Brahman* or Spirit, is subjected to progressive limitation by the imposition of limiting adjuncts or limiting principles such as *niyati* as it 'descends' into the material plane. We have seen that *Vedānta* associates increasing freedom with deeper states corresponding to dreams and lucid deep sleep. Our thoughts are clearly not limited to the strict rule-following sequences of our normal perceptions and this may be due to them operating at deeper planes beyond the limitations of spatial relations imposed by the time/space matrix of perception thus they have a greater degree of freedom to operate independently of the world-modelling rules of normal perception. Thus the individuated consciousness that is our normal mind retains a tiny part of the creative freedom of the Ground as it operates within the complex web of constraints that constitute the material world that emerges with microcosmic Space and Time.

Human creativity, intuition and gnosis

We have seen that, in some way, each part of the cosmos appears to have access to the whole and that in LSD-induced altered states of consciousness, it is possible to visualize concepts which are unimaginable in the normal state including numerous mathematical concepts involving dimensionalities of Space and Time which are far removed from our everyday world. Aurobindo states that all human imaginations correspond to some reality or real possibility[25], which is an extension of the fact that all knowledge comes from *realizations.* I noted in the introduction that the mathematical genius Ramanujan, who some mathematicians consider a "magician" given the difficulty in seeing with hindsight how he made such bizarre connections, stated that he received these insights in rather psychedelic visions whilst meditating. The great mathematician Gauss described how an enigma was solved as a sudden flash of light and said that he was unable to determine how the connection had been made between that which he previously knew and that insight which made his success possible[140]. Taimni[85], commenting on meditative absorption (*samādhi*) in the *Yoga Sūtras* states:

> *A great musician is able to create his best productions when he loses himself completely in his work. An inventor solves his greatest problems when he is not conscious of solving any problems. . . . It is the disappearance of self-consciousness which somehow opens the door to a new world which they cannot enter normally.*

Taimni adds that the apparent disappearance of self-awareness means dissolution of the subject-object relationship. Mavromatis notes that the likes of inventor Thomas Edison and artist Salvador Dali used techniques which allowed them to enter hypnagogic states rather like lucid dreaming in order to get their creative ideas[63]. Einstein's emphasis on visualizing ideas also relates to the greater freedom to explore possibilities found in dreams. EEG studies of Einstein in a creative mode revealed increased alpha rhythm indicating a relaxation of normal mentation and increased receptivity to deeper levels of activity. Recently Kary Mullis, who won the Nobel Prize for inventing the Polymerase Chain Reaction which is of importance in recombinant DNA technology, claimed that this discovery was made possible by his use of LSD to stimulate his creativity and similar LSD use has been reported amongst the pioneers of the computer software companies which were based in California's "Silicon Valley".[141]

Coward notes that most Hindu and Buddhist schools of thought distinguish between ordinary perception and supernormal perception or intuition (*pratibhā* in the *Yoga Sūtras*) which results from the removal of the normal ego and distorting *saṃskāras* (memory traces or dispositions) resulting in noumenal knowledge of the object of contemplation as it is in itself. Ordinary knowledge through the senses is limited in time and space and distorted through the attachment to the direct perception of word labels and meanings. *Pratibhā* gives an illumination transcending ordinary categories of space, time and causality and free of word constructions. The object may be any finite aspect of Reality. Coward refers to Vyāsa's commentary on the *Yoga Sūtras* which refers to purging the habitual patterns of word usage and inferential thinking leaving only the *sattva* (calm or crystalline) aspect of consciousness free of the *rajasic* (turbulent) distortions. (*Rajas* and *sattva* are two of the three *guṇas* or intermingled modes of consciousness. The transition from the *rajasic* to the *sattvic* mode is another way of describing the stilling of the *cittavritti,* the wave-like fluctuations constructing our normal perceptions.) The technical yogic term for such direct perception is *nirvitarka-samādhi* indicating absorption (*samādhi*) without distorting thoughts. The yogi advances to more advanced *samādhi* upon the object to reveal its inner essence. In *savicārasamādhi* the flow of consciousness identifies completely with the object, losing the sense of a separate ego, such that the yogi becomes "one with" the object. This experience remains limited in space and time although both the outer gross form and the inner nature of the object are perceived. In the final state of absorption, *nirvicārasamādhi,* space and time is transcended and the yogi experiences the object in its past states, present moment and possibilities for the future. The yogi has truly become one with the object. The subject/object duality is overcome in the two latter *samādhis,* with total identification with the object and this leaves "only the steady transformation of the pure *sattva* consciousness into the form of the object".[28]

Aurobindo[25] speaks of *vijñāna* (or "gnosis"), the Divine knowledge one with the Divine Will. Intellectuals mistake *vijñāna* to be synonymous with *buddhi* which they equate with the power of Reason. Equally false is the view of those mystics who identify *vijñāna* with Absolute Consciousness free from all ideation or else packed into one concentrated essence, the *caitanyaghana* (also *cidghana;* dense luminous consciousness) of the *Upaniṣads.* Aurobindo asserts that *vijñāna* is not only this *caitanyaghana* but simultaneously an infinite knowledge of the myriad play of the Infinite containing all supramental ideation which, unlike mental reasoning, is self-luminous, rendering identities rather than translations of sense impressions. There is, he says, a higher *buddhi,* an intuitive mind, which by its intuitions, inspirations, vision and luminous insight can proceed swiftly using visual concepts bypassing the plodding steps of the logical mind which follows and verifies these intuitive leaps. This is true or authentic *intuition.* But such intuition is not *vijñāna,* rather such inspirations, revelations etc. are but flashes of the higher planes finding their way opportunely into the lower mind.

Vijñāna, Aurobindo continues, does not need to seek the truth, it has in itself the direct perception, the immediate vision. Whereas the sense mind gets knowledge by a veiled contact (distorted by *saṃskāras;* memory traces), *vijñāna* is a knowledge by identity, free from doubt, self-evident and self-existent. *Vijñāna* gives not only the the thing but all the reality within it and, through the Divine memory, gives access to past, present and future. *Vijñāna* does not treat things as separate but shows things only in their relation to the infinite oneness. It is an oceanic and ethereal sense in which all particulars are waves or drops, a concentration of the whole ocean, inseparable from the ocean. The supramental sense is founded as a feeling of all in each and each in all (this is Aurobindo's version of the 'holonomic' Reality as with the pearls in the Heaven of Indra). The dense, luminous consciousness (*caitanyaghana, cidghana*) of *vijñāna* contains all the immutable principles of the Divine. *Vijñāna* loosens out this concentrated knowledge. The mental being rising up into this higher plane has to transform its movements into the movements of the *vijñāna* plane. The thing seen is not seen as an object, but as part of one's Universal Self. Thought is only a limited means of manifesting what is hidden in this greater self-existent knowledge of the *cidghana*. Supramental knowledge (*vijñāna* or "gnosis") involves a penetrating and enveloping luminous contact of the spiritual consciousness with its object. It is not an intellectual abstraction; it presents the idea as a luminous substance of being (I think that Aurobindo is describing what Coward described as the pure *sattva* consciousness transforming itself in the form of the object here). It sees, says Aurobindo, not only the physical aspect of the object but the vibration of energy, the light and force of spiritual substance of which it is made. The material world ceases to be material as we conceive it through our gross perceptions and is seen to be a form of Spirit. All objects are held in and by the consciousness in a spiritual space, all substance is a conscious substance, and the whole is unity[25].

We have already encountered the dense, luminous consciousness (*caitanyaghana*) of Aurobindo's *vijñāna* (which closely resembles the *pratibhā* of the *Yoga Sūtras*) as the *cidghana* (or *prajñānaghana*) of Vedāntic (lucid) deep sleep and, indeed, Aurobindo states that the (deep) sleep state corresponds to the supramental plane proper to gnosis. Gnosis is beyond our normal experience, he adds, because the Causal Body, or envelope of gnosis, is not developed[25]. Indich notes that in *Advaita Vedānta,* the most subtle and pure sheath covering the Self, the *ānandamayakośa*, is linked to deep sleep and is called the Causal Body as the basic *avidyā* (nescience) causing the other sheaths of *avidyā* is confronted here. The thick mass of unified consciousness experienced in (lucid) deep sleep is said by *Advaita* to be the coalesced content of waking and dream experience[45] rather than the immutable principles of the Divine which Aurobindo states are loosened out from it. We have already noted that *Advaita* negatively identifies (lucid) deep sleep with *savikalpa samādhi* or the *Bhakti* experience of intimacy with one's chosen personal god. The Causal Body here seems to correspond directly with the basic *jīva*, the individual self which creates the notions of duality and causality. Gauḍapāda had stated that the *jīva* is constructed first, prior to all internal and external things; it is the root construction of all phenomena[103]. Kaplan points out that this is so because the *avidyā/māyā* is always the illusion of an individual and it is the *jīva* which always appears with physical adjuncts which feels itself as a knower distinct from the world known. The *jīva* is the prototype of objectivity, the self known objectively as "me". The *jīva* accompanies and ensures all knowledge of the world as object which reinforces its sense of itself as an object[103]. Iyer says that we can never know the intrinsic nature of things through our objective knowledge as such dualistic knowledge requires us to stand in opposition to it as an object[72].

Talbot notes that during NDEs, in the presence of the Light, people may find that they have direct access to *all* knowledge. You can think of any question whatsoever, even about things of which you have no background knowledge, and the Light gives instantaneous realizations answering the question in a way in which you understand intuitively. Others report experiences of suddenly gaining an 'omniscience' after their 'life review' experiences although this knowledge cannot be retained. Such visions of 'omniscience' involve non-linear apprehension of total scenarios bursting instantaneously into one's awareness[15]. Such explosions of total scenarios bursting into one's awareness are also experienced by a psychic when receiving information psychically.

In regard to the *jīva* as the basis of individuality and the root construction of all the phenomena, recall Taimni's description of the difficulty in attaining enlightenment for the first time, with the yogi being thrown back into the vehicles and thus the phenomenal world of *avidyā/māyā*. This seems to be describing the spontaneous reconstitution of the *jīva* or the Causal Body, the most subtle of all the vehicles. The difference between *Advaita's* interpretation of the *cidghana* and that given by Aurobindo may not be as great as it appears at first sight. The coalesced content of waking and dream experiences, as *Advaita* describes it, seems like a way of saying that it contains the potentiality of all the phenomena of the lower planes, corresponding to the dreaming and waking states. Aurobindo's immutable Divine principles may be the same basic potential forms out of which all the forms of the manifest world are constructed. Thus both may be describing what Western mystics have sometimes called *archetypes.* Odajnyk discusses Wilber's critique of Jung's use of the term citing Wilber who states that the mystics' *archetypes* are the first subtle forms that appear as the world manifests, all other patterns of manifestation being based upon these *archetypes.*[9] Such notions are often associated with terms like Divine Ideas or God's Ideas of the World etc. and thus correspond with Western-educated Aurobindo's use of *immutable Divine principles* although he also describes the *cidghana* using Eastern terminology as the "seed state" of the Divine Consciousness.

Thus we have seen that insights are associated with deeper levels of the mind as associated with lucid deep sleep. The normal world-modelling of the waking mind and the imaginative fantasies of the dreaming mind need to be deactivated in order to reach this deep level of insight. Of course, as Aurobindo notes, flashes of the higher planes may find their way opportunely into the lower mind in intuitions. Kautz, using terminology reminiscent of Aurobindo's, states that the "superconscious" does not communicate in language or even in pictures although the intuitive message may be clothed in such sense forms and it may be screened through a rational filter as it comes through the subconscious mind[142]. Such descriptions of the distortions superimposed upon the intuitive flashes by normal mental processes, as also described by Aurobindo, hint at the filtering effect of normal perception which abstracts certain patterns from the true Reality, tending to seek out those aspects of Reality which fit into its pre-existent structures of space-time causality and rationality. When the lower planes are held in abeyance in the yogic *pratibhā*, or Aurobindo's *vijñāna,* true insight is experienced without such mental distortions. Coward refers to Vyāsa's description of the calming of the consciousness into the *sattvic* mode, free of the *rajasic* (turbulent) distortions of word usage and inferential thinking in the early stages of progress towards supernormal perception. As I have stated above, this transition from turbulence to calmness is equivalent to the stilling of the *cittavritti*, the wave-like fluctuations of the mind, which are superimposed upon the Pure Consciousness. Coward states that in *savicārasamādhi* the sense of a separate ego disappears and the yogi becomes one with the object and that the only difference in the transition to *nirvicārasamādhi* is the transcendence of space and time. In regard to loss of ego sense, Coward interpret's Vyāsa to mean that one is so absorbed in the object that there is "no room left" for a separate self-awareness. The identification with the object in these two latter states involves knowledge (by identitity) of the object's inner essence or microcosm whereas the earlier *nirvitarkasamādhi* was only of the outer form of the object[28]. This becoming one with an object, in spite of the loss of self-awareness, still involves an individuated consciousness corresponding presumably to the Causal Body. Aurobindo gives a clearer description in saying that, in *vijñāna*, the thing is seen as part of one's Universal Self where all objects are held in by the consciousness in a spiritual space in a unitary whole. In regard to the inner esence of the object, Aurobindo says that one identifies not only with the physical aspect but the vibrations of energy of which it is made. I have already stated that such identifications with any finite aspect of Reality are also claimed in LSD-induced experiences where subjects claim to become one with all manner of objects at all levels of order.

Knowledge by identity and divine realizations

We see that the deeper realizations involve a loss of the subject/object duality. Of course, one can become totally absorbed in one's 'world' in the ordinary material plane and temporarily lose the sense of separation. Coward interprets this identification as arising from there being, in some sense, no room left for a separate awareness of oneself. We have seen that the subject/object duality appears to arise from the straddling of planes with the lower planes constituting the objective content of higher planes. It is possible then that at such a high plane, there is no straddling of planes as the individuated consciousness is a bare individuality (the *jīva* or Causal Body) with its content the deeper, unfiltered flux beyond the constructions of space-time with all sense of a subtle body and conceptual mind, which would separate out into the subjective self, having been left behind in the lower planes which Aurobindo calls Vital and Mental.

The transition from *savicāra* to *nirvicāra samādhi* in the *Yoga Sūtras* is of course the deactivation of the time/space matrix of perception. We are told that when this occurs the object is known, not only in its present moment, but also in its past, and its future possibilities. Presumably this refers to a filtering process which occurs in perception which screens out the past reverberations of the entities perceived which co-exists with the information about the present. Careful consideration of the external world as described by materialist Science indicates that the information impinging upon us must include complex information representing the past state of objects as well as the present as this information doesn't just disappear in the way a naïve Realist would imagine. Perception creates the simplified, convenient world of our normal experience which moves through space-time with very little trace of the past. This would tie in with the clairvoyant reception of past information which is also associated with such deeper states of consciousness and a sense of a unitary Reality underlying the space-time constructions of normal perception. Again, as with the parapsychological experiences of premonitions in which possible future scenarios are imagined, the yogi seems to be describing the ability to "play forward" to possible future states of the object which are in the making although not yet actualised.

The knowledge by identity of the microcosmic "inner essences" of objects again indicates access to the wider domain of available information which perceptual screens normally filter out in order to construct our simplified convenient world. Normally we experience the gross forms of objects, their stable outer shells which are sufficient for our purposes of detecting the movement of objects in our environment. Presumably, as is reported by psychics who claim X-ray like perception of internal patterns of activity in people's bodies or other structures, the information flux impinging upon us contains such information from within the outer surfaces of external objects. We have already seen that, in reality, physical processes seem to be the emergent manifestations of the energetic vibrations of the Pure, Universal Consçiousness and this leads us away from a naïve picture of discrete billiard-ball like atoms and molecules to a more realistic picture of complex layers of vibrations, corresponding to such distinct levels as atoms and molecules as well as higher level energetic processes within complex systems of molecules, whose combined resonances are intermingled in the 'holographic' flux of frequency information constantly impinging upon us. As human minds, our own sense of ourselves seems to be correlated with the energetic fluctuations in the brain which coordinate the general activity throughout the body. Of course, this is not the same as being the body itself which I would assert constitutes a separate individuated field whose sentience is devoid of the meaningful organization of the mind. The gross experiences of any individuated entity will presumably be correlated with the major energetic pulsations, fluctuations etc. operating within it as a whole and these processes will leave memory traces in the environment. Thus when the yogi or the LSD subject claims to become one with the object and know it as if from within, I presume that the microcosmic inner essence is some sort of resonance with the memory traces left by that entity which recreates something of what that entity itself experienced. Such traces may be very recently produced as in the cases of psychic 'inner vision' and telepathy which can operate in the so-called 'present' like our normal perception. This becoming one with resembles the cases of spirit possession or supposed 'reincarnation' which I shall interpret later in terms of memory traces. What I am not asserting is that the yogi knows the detailed physical structure of the entity as it is in itself, rather only the gross experiences of being that entity when becoming 'one with' that entity. This does not exclude the possibility that, in principle, very subtle information revealing the complex patterns of physical activity at every level of order within the entity in question is available and that the yogi may have access to such information.

In regard to the question of the *cidghana* and its concentrated, archetypal knowledge, we seem to be dealing with a similar situation in that the concentrated essence of all phenomena could be interpreted in terms of the holographic metaphor of each part of Reality being suffused with the Whole and Aurobindo's loosening out of this "supramental knowledge" may refer to some sort of filtering out from this holographic mass of information some distinct information. The archetypal aspects of this "seed state" of the Divine Consciousness which serves as the basis for the great insights into general aspects of Reality lead us back into the sort of arguments presented in *The Interface of Mind and Cosmos* where it was discussed how it was possible to gain information about the nature of the universe by introspection. We saw that the Ground of the Self is the Ground of all Being and that knowledge is *being*, attained through *realizations*, becoming 'one with' or knowledge by identity as Aurobindo calls it. We also saw that microcosm reflects macrocosm in generating an emergent spatio-temporal order of manifest phenomena from a deeper transcendental realm which is not limited by normal space-time causality and which seems to be in a state of flux, or possibilities, from which the emergent, spatio-temporal order actualises certain possibilities. We saw that scientific concepts which have proven quite successful in producing models of the spatio-temporal behaviour of the physical realm have partly been projections from the internal, microcosmic reality onto our constructions of the external world. The fact that such projections can lead to predictive models of regular behaviour patterns of the external world indicate again the interrelationships between the microcosmic and macrocosmic order. We have also considered notions related to the 'holographic/holonomic' metaphor in which Reality at its deeper levels, underlying the emergent space-time order involves interpenetration of complex vibratory patterns of activity such that each part, in some sense, contains the Whole. This ties in with the yogic experience of a relativistic, transcendentally holistic realm of causality underlying the space-time order. Such considerations reveal to us that we have within ourselves access to the Ground of all Being which manifests the entire universe, to the basic archetypal principles involved in the manifestation of phenomena through realization of our deeper being and access to apparently any finite aspect of Reality through resonant realizations of other created entities. Once again we have to shake off our indoctrinations which have deluded us into mistaking scientific abstractions of entities and limited aspects of true causality to be Reality as it is in itself. Although I have tried to rationalise mystical realizations such as deep, profound insights and identification with alien realms of being, actual Reality always transcends our limited conceptualizations of it. The fact remains that human minds throughout history have received, by one means or another, insights, intuitions and visions which have lifted us out of struggle for existence in the jungle and created the remarkable world we live in today. It is perhaps most ironic that some of the great scientists who received such mystical insights in order to attain their achievements and many of their lesser followers, who have not experienced them, vehemently deny the existence of the spiritual realm which has provided us with these breakthroughs. This largely stems from the ignorance and denial of the spiritual implicit in the Modern world-view but also its emphasis on individualism and the exaggerated position granted to the human when faced with the mystery of such insight when a position of humility would be appropriate. As the verse from Emerson's *Brahma,* quoted at the head of the Preface, aptly states:

> They reckon ill who leave me out
> When me they fly, I am the wings

2(k). ON PARANORMAL PHENOMENA

The siddhis (supernormal powers) and space-time transcendence

In Brown's study of the authoritative yogic traditions, he describes how the yogi develops refined awareness of the flow of the light to a state in which it is possible to give up a specific focus and, instead, develop an awareness pervading the universe (called *nirvicārasamādhi* by the *Yoga Sūtra* tradition; which we also encountered in the previous section). The yogi is now ready to practise "insight meditation", gaining insight into the construction of normal worldly experience. This state corresponds to the deconstruction of ordinary perception and our ordinary sense of self. The psychic powers become available after, having gained knowledge in insight meditation, the yogi removes the subtlest (karmic) biasing factors and has deconstructed the time/space matrix which forms the basis of ordinary perception. Brown notes that this ties in with Western research on psychic abilities which shows that this peaks during transitional states of consciousness corresponding to the dissolution of habitual structures in yoga. With the dissolution of the time/space matrix of perception the mind switches from operating according to ordinary laws to the extraordinary laws of universal interconnectedness[23].

Taimni, in regard to the *Yoga Sūtras,* says that the *siddhis* are not really viewed as 'occult powers' but as 'accomplishments' in superphysical realms. The connection between the stages of self-realization and the powers inherent in them are so close that it is difficult to distinguish between the two. Patañjali (the legendary author of the *Yoga Sūtras*) only takes a few well-known *siddhis* and hints at the principles underlying their operations. Taimni states that the best way to get an insight into the operation of the *siddhis* is to consider knowledge and power as two aspects of the same reality. If one has knowledge of the inner workings of phenomena, one also has the power to manipulate these phenomena. Changes in matter are brought about by going to the source of all properties and manipulating them from there. All natural phenomena, he says, manifest from an unmanifest state and all properties of matter exist in a potential form in a substratum. As physical forces are based upon mental forces, physical phenomena can be manipulated without use of physical aids. The *siddhis* mentioned in the *Vibhūti Pāda* of the *Yoga Sūtras* include telepathy, omens, clairvoyance, possession of a disciple's body, passage through space (presumably referring to so-called Distance-Viewing) and knowledge of Past and Future[85].

In regard to Hindu, Buddhist and Taoist yoga, Murphy mentions the *anudrishti siddhi* which allows the yogi to apprehend small, hidden or remote objects including bodily structures. The *antaradrishti siddhi* provides a sort of X-ray vision of our bodies. It is equivalent to the *animan siddhi* of the *Yoga Sūtras,* through which it is possible, claims Haridas Chaudhuri, to perceive our body's cells, molecules and atomic patterns (similar claims are made by Western psychics). Murphy also notes that the theosophists Besant and Leadbeater studied the known elements, provided to them by Sir William Crookes, using the *animan siddhi.* In 1908 they claimed that some elements, including Neon, had more than one form. This was five years before Soddy put forward the concept of isotopic forms of elements. Murphy suggests that other physical phenomena may have been anticipated[26]. Such occult powers have been claimed by shamans and psychics in all human societies and anthropologists report widespread belief in such powers in many tribal societies today. Numerous anthropologists also claim to have witnessed paranormal phenomena in such societies although many such cases are kept quiet upon return to the West for fear of ridicule[41]. Taimni clearly links such phenomena to deeper states of consciousness and to manipulation of a deeper level of order from which physical phenomena become manifest. Grof states that such *siddhis* may result from the modification of the phenomenal world through influencing its generative matrix[41]. It should be noted that the *Yoga Sūtra* metaphysics is not idealistic. Objects are held to exist externally independent of the mind. Thus modification of the phenomenal world does not refer merely to perceptual constructions.

Although, at first sight, paranormal phenomena related to extrasensory perception (ESP) seem to be explicable on the basis of some sort of radio model within a conventional scientific framework, it was discovered early on in scientific studies by Vasiliev that telepathy was not inhibited by isolating subjects in a Faraday Cage. Jahn and Dunne[40] state:

> *Many efforts to invoke existing representations of electromagnetic theory, statistical thermodynamics, geophysical mechanics, hyperspace properties, and other approaches have been made, but none has proven adequate to encompass all of the credible data. In particular most are inconsistent with the lack of attenuation of the observed effects with distance, and all founder completely on the atemporal evidence. Clearly a more fundamental approach is required, one that explicitly acknowledges an active role for consciousness in the establishment of physical reality.*

I would point out here that, although paranormal phenomena involve realms transcending normal categories of Space and Time, this does not necessarily mean that the detectable physical phenomena are not in some way implicated (as we find with Hunt's work on human energy fields discussed below). As should be clear from my discussion of Space and Time emergence in Section 2(f), the physical world of space-time and normal space-time causality is one way of ordering the information abstracted from a Reality which has numerous other aspects. The space-time order emerges through a constant manifestation process from deeper levels of Reality and our minds have evolved to represent this level of space-time order from the greater Reality in which it exists. Taimni says that the 'higher' (deeper) planes which are associated with the *siddhis* have more dimensions of Space and Time[85]. We have seen that these planes are co-existent with the physical order which only appears to exist by itself due to the focus of our normal perception which abstracts only certain features from Reality, filtering out other information which is not convenient for our everyday purposes.

Aurobindo on psychical development and the subtle ether

Telepathy and precognition have been associated with dreams since time immemorial. We have seen that dreaming is related with the intermediate planes in the hierarchies abstracted by various mystical traditions. Normal causal relations need not be followed in our dreams and many such telepathic and precognitive experiences appear to us as dream-like visions. Aurobindo[25] links the dream state to ESP from the *cidākāśa* (subtle ether) and describes lucid dreaming and distance-viewing. He associates psychical awakening with the development of the *prāṇa kośa,* the vital sheath enveloping the physical, which is sensitive to the universal *Prāṇa* giving a sense of oneness with all things in the universe. This direct sensation and perception of the subtler forces are often included without distinction, says Aurobindo, under the heading of psychical phenomena. In this regard he mentions establishing a direct communication between minds without the aid of the physical organs which impose limitations. There is an inferior form of psychical awakening, he asserts, associated with clairvoyants, psychics, seekers of *siddhis* etc. where the desires and illusions of the mind lead to distortions and depravities. The true spiritual seeker must pass quickly through this realm and cleanse his mind of the distorting factors, allowing the pure psychical experience to pass into the representing mind. The complete power can only be attained with the opening of the Supermind (i.e. development of the Causal Body allowing *vijñāna*).

> *The power to see does not come from the eye, the power to hear does not come from the ear . . . but it is the spirit of man that sees through the eye, hears with the ear . . .* Paracelsus[143]

All the physical senses, say Aurobindo, have their corresponding powers in the psychical being. The physical senses are, in fact, only a projection of these powers into a limited realm of operation amongst gross phenomena[25]. Murphy notes that in Hindu and Buddhist yoga, perception of extraordinary events or entities are held to be products of the *indriyas* which are attributes of the 'subtle body' and correspond to the 'spiritual senses' in the Western mystical traditions. He also notes that the mystical traditions all differ in describing the structure of this so-called subtle body[26]. Aurobindo's *prāṇa kośa* or vital sheath would correspond with this level often called the subtle body and indeed Aurobindo says that the psychical consciousness is the subtle or dream self of Indian psychology. Aurobindo says that the psychical sight receives images formed in the subtle matter of the psychical ether, the *cittākāśa,* which contains impresses of whatever is, was or will be in the physical universe. The *cittākāśa* (or *cidākāśa*) is the subtle ether heavily curtained from the physical sense by the grosser ether of the material world. All sensible entities in all planes create reconstituting vibrations, images of themselves retained by the *cidākāśa.* The phenomena of clairvoyance, clairaudience etc. are only the exceptional admittance into the waking consciousness of the memory images of the *cittākāśa,* allowing knowledge of the Past, Present and Future. The Future is already accomplished on higher planes. Although these images may be seen in various states such as *samādhi* or in normal wakefulness, the real agent is always the psychical sight and the psychical being (the *prāṇa kośa*) must be awake (i.e. lucidity must be attained in the Vital Plane). This allows seeing at any physical distance as well as access to the Past and Future[25].

In addition, says Aurobindo, the psychical vision receives images and forms created by constant activity of consciousness in other humans which may or may not convey truths. These images may come from non-humans as well. The psychical consciousness reveals the ongoing interaction between the planes of consciousness, the hidden influences operating subtly upon us at deeper levels. Aurobindo also mentions the possibility of a "more direct, concretely sensible, almost material, sometimes actively material communication" and the possibility of temporary physical materialisations of powers and forces from other planes. He says that one becomes aware of the ongoing interaction between the activities of minds through the general mind atmosphere around us. With the development of the supermind (Causal Body and *vijñāna*) which universalizes individual consciousness, the psychical experiences are realized to be a part of a great spiritual realm and the distorting factors of the lower mind are cleansed so that the psychical communications are put into proper perspective. This supramental transformation results in a knowledge by identity, an experience of all in the unity of the cosmic consciousness[25].

Aurobindo says that the higher psychical knowledge reveals that the world is full of many systems of correspondences, which, although often misused can convey real supraphysical knowledge if the intuitive mind is properly developed. If the spiritual levels are developed and the interference of the imagination of the constructing mind is removed, it is possible to accurately receive information from the Past and the Future. This information is said to be contained in an eternal time consciousness. The psychical consciousness can also access the "etheric writing", the *ākāśa lipi,* that records all the events of the Past, transcribes the Present, and writes the Future. Again, intuitive faculties have to be developed to prevent distortion by the mental constructions of the lower mind which tries to select a definitive truth from the mass of actuals and possibles. The intuitive mind works on the complex of forces at play to intuit the future outcome by a sort of projection. It can only see what will occur if these forces operate undisturbed and its visions lose their predictive power if sudden disturbances occur in the play of forces. More accurate predictions may be made by development of the mind of luminous inspiration which sees the worlds larger possibilities and understands the stream of actuality as a selections from these possibilities. But passage of such information to the lower planes will still result in distortions[25].

In this regard it is worth noting Griffin's comment that most so-called precognitions of disasters can be accounted for through unconscious clairvoyant knowledge of present structural defects plus unconscious inference of the probable outcome. This results in a dreamlike vision. Other precognitions can be accounted for by unconscious telepathic knowledge coupled to inference[55]. In the 19th century, physicist Oliver Lodge, a member of the Society for Psychical Reasearch (UK) attempted to relate clairvoyancy to the physical ether of empty space which was still a feature of conventional physics at that time[40]. Jahn and Dunne note that the issue of the ether remains incompletely resolved[40]. Notions of empty space as being like an ether have reappeared in Bohm's work. Contrary to popular belief, Einstein's work did not disprove the existence of some sort of ether. Rather, it did without the existing notion of the ether. Vigier notes that in 1924 Einstein himself published a paper on a possible hidden 'ether' underlying gravitational forces as part of his attempted grand unification of the physical forces[144]. Of course such notions of an 'ether' in physics do not necessarily correpsond to yogic notions of the *ākāśa* (space). Aurobindo's description of the subtle ether as being hidden from the physical sense by the gross ether of the material universe does tie in with our understanding of the physical realm as an emergent stable order arising from subtler realms whose activity lies beyond the ranges of our normal senses and our instruments, thus being in effect meaningless in physical terms. We have seen that the physical world is abstracted from the gross levels of order out of the vastly more complex Reality. Thus in Physics, where the question of the ether remains speculative, and in yogic philosophy the notion of an ether involves a more subtle order underlying the gross order of physical phenomena.

The subtle ether and the notion of resonance

The notion of a so-called Akashic Record is widely known today in regard to parapsychological interpretations of ESP-type phenomena. Aurobindo's description of the *cidākāśa* as a storehouse of reconstituting vibrations from all realms resembles karmic notions and those of the Collective Unconscious put forward by Jung and Sheldrake's Morphic Resonance. Satprem criticises the so-called Collective Unconscious notion as it mixes up pell mell all the degrees of being as if it were an enormous magician's hat[52]. Coward has noted how Jung's notions of archetypes and the Collective Unconscious were influenced by yogic notions such as *saṃskāra* (memory traces) and *prakriti* ('primordial Nature')[28]. I have noted above how Sheldrake has linked his notions to the Collective Unconscious notion of Jung whilst others have viewed Sheldrake's Morphic Resonance as a reworking of the yogic theory of the *ākāśa*. *Yoga Sūtra* IV.9 states[85] :

> *There is a relation of cause and effect even though separated by class, locality and time because memory and impressions are the same in form.*

Aurobindo's descriptions of the ongoing interaction between the activities of minds through the general mind atmosphere around us is suggestive of such 'resonance' and notions of a Collective Unconscious. Goswami cites some interesting studies by neurophysiologist Grinberg-Zylberbaum in which two subjects interact until they attain a feeling of "direct communication". Then, after entering separate Faraday cages, one subject is shown a flickering light signal inducing an EEG potential. Interestingly, as long as a feeling of 'direct communication' is maintained, a similar potential can be measured in the other subject who has no sensory access to the flickering lights. Physicist Goswami relates such *transfer potentials* to quantum non-locality as demonstrated in the now well-known experiments by Aspect *et al.* relating to the so-called Einstein Podolsky Rosen (EPR) paradox[109] (see below). If confirmed, such transfer potentials would clearly constitute evidence for some sort of 'resonance' between minds defying conventional modes of information transfer.

The notion of *resonance* repeatedly appears in the literature relating to paranormal phenomena. In 1960 Marshall suggested that the physical principle of resonance in which two systems of similar form tend to become more alike may be involved in telepathy and precognition[145]. Jahn and Dunne note that for successful psychokinetic manipulation of the machinery in their experiments, the subject needs to attain a sense of 'resonance' with the device, a sense of flow or harmony with it. One experimental subject reports:

> *a state of immersion in the process which leads to a loss of awareness of myself and immediate surroundings, similar to the experience of being absorbed in a game, book . . .*

When in resonance with the device, the subject feels he has a "marginal influence" upon it[40]. Such a description clearly reminds one of the loss of self said to occur in yogic *samādhi* resulting in a sense of 'oneness' with the object and which is related to the supernormal powers or *siddhis*. Jahn and Dunne attempt to incorporate the notion of resonance in their theoretical models by associating it with the superposition of the quantum wave patterns of the subject and the machine[40].

In regard to resonance models in physics, Becker says that, as resonance theory is based on frequency and not on power, it permits effects from vanishingly small fields[21]. Mae Wan Ho, discussing resonant energy transfer in molecules, notes that chemical bonds vibrating at the same frequencies will resonate with one another and that this energy of vibration can be transferred through large distances, theoretically infinite, and theoretically at the speed of light[91]. I am not suggesting that such resonant energy transfer provides the mechanism for ESP phenomena but that the notion of resonance in general, which is associated with vibrations (or frequencies) seems to be indicative of the sort of phenomena we are encountering in ESP. Interestingly, Becker also notes that studies using ultrasensitive SQUID magnetometers show that we, and other living creatures, are surrounded by magnetic fields extending out into space and that the magnetic fields emanating out of the body from the brain reflect what is happening in the brain[21].

Human body fields and psychic phenomena

Using Space Age telemetry equipment capable of detecting frequencies up to 20,000 Hz (cycles per second), Hunt has discovered electromagnetic fields emanating from the human body at various frequencies above the normal range of 0-250 Hz associated with brain, heart and muscle frequencies[146]. Using a modified electromyogram Hunt has detected field frequencies as high as 200,000 Hz[15]. The higher frequency field activity is smaller in amplitude than the commonly measured brain, heart and muscle fields and Hunt suggests that scientists previously ignored this activity thinking it to be an artefact of their instruments. Her field recordings correlated well with the reports of psychic aura readers in regard to changes in colours and dynamics of auric fields suggesting that these are the physical correlates of the auras perceived by psychics. Hunt states that such field recordings increased in intensity at the bodily positions of the *chakras*, the psychic energy centres associated with the rising *Kuṇḍalinī* energy in various forms of yoga. (Remember that I have interpreted the actual experience of *chakras* with brain centres which may be connected with activity in such body centres). Hunt also reports that the body's energy field appeared to respond to stimuli prior to changes in the brainwaves, again supporting certain traditional assertions about auric interactions with the world. She asserts that higher vibrational states of the energy field are associated with experience shifting from the physical world and ego states to transcendental realms and insight. Psychics practising clairvoyant 'channeling' displayed vibrational frequencies in the low to middle ranges. Hunt distinguishes those in trance from those channeling; the former show small ranges of higher frequencies than channeling mediums which do not extend into the normal 'material' realm. Trance mediums do not remember their predictions. On the other hand, the 'mystics' showed a range of frequencies from the lowest 'material' frequencies through the psychical and trance frequencies right up to, and presumably beyond, the 200 KHz range of the telemetry equipment[146].

Hunt's studies are, needless to say, fascinating although the question of how one is to interpret such information remains extremely perplexing. The fact that the field measurements correlate with auras and *chakras* is not very problematic, indicating that psychical perception involves reduction in the normal filtering of sensory perception taking into account more of the available information. The role of such fields in, for instance, ESP phenomena and mind-body interactions is far more troublesome when one considers all the characteristics of such phenomena. I stated above, in regard to Jahn and Dunnes' assertion that a fundamental shift in our conception of the role of consciousness in relation to physical reality was required, that this did not necessarily mean that detectable physical systems were not involved, rather it might be the case that there are modes of interaction available to identifiable physical processes which elude our limited understanding. The variations in frequencies associated with altered states of consciousness is especially intriguing. This data immediately brings to mind Satprem's description of the different planes of consciousness existing at different frequencies with increasing frequencies in higher planes[52]. It also brings to mind the holonomic metaphor with its notions of the Frequency Domain whose information is converted by Fourier transforms into the spatio-temporal patterns of perception. The data is also very suggestive of the yogic ideas of the material realm of gross perceptions being constituted of slower vibrations masking the more subtle vibrations of the higher planes.

Hunt is rather loose and uncritical in her discussion and is inclined towards notions of the 'mind' existing outside of the brain, calling the bodily fields the "mind-field". That the fields around the body should reflect mental states is intriguing although not altogether surprising considering the interpenetrating nature of such activity. It almost seems as if extrasensory perception in altered states involves the body acting as some sort of antenna, resonating at higher frequencies. It could be that such body field effects are a result of focusing the mind onto higher frequencies resulting in some sort of phase-locked resonance in bodily structures which normally resonate at such frequencies being amplified in order to allow such perceptual information transfer.

Quantum non-locality and actualization of phenomena — evidence for a transcendental realm

As we have seen, the whole question of the 'mechanism' of extrasensory perception and related phenomena remains extremely controversial with explanations based upon extensions of conventional scientific paradigms failing to account for all the characteristics. Murphy highlights the ingrained resistance of certain sections of the scientific community towards such phenomena quoting Helmholtz who believed that transmission of thought independently of the recognized channels of sensation was impossible and no amount of testimony or evidence would make him believe it. He also cites a G.R. Price who wrote in a 1955 article in *Science* that no amount of scientific experiments giving results overwhelmingly against the odds would make him accept ESP[26]. I have mentioned previously the psychological 'denial' response which is exhibited by narrow-minded materialists when evidence challenges their 'safe and secure' world-picture. Persinger, who is associated with studies and hypotheses linking the Earth's geomagnetic field to certain ESP phenomena, points out that ESP percipients tend to be in mental states with predominant EEG alpha rhythm[147]. This and other factors led to much speculation about extra-low frequency electromagnetic waves as carriers of ESP information as these were of the same frequency range as the EEG alpha rhythm. However, as we have seen, shielding percipients in Faraday cages, which block out electromagnetic radiation, does not affect ESP performance and the violation of normal space and time relations cannot be accounted for in such hypotheses. From the point of view of my overall discussion, the predominance of alpha rhythm is interesting as it again shows us that ESP activity is associated with quieting normal mental activity presumably allowing greater access to attention of information which would usually be swamped by the normal mental processes.

As I have stated above, it could be that the conventional sorts of physical phenomena seemingly implicated in ESP activity are involved in modes of information transfer which transcend our normal spatio-temporal causality categories. Numerous authors have linked ESP with the notion of non-locality in Quantum Theory as Goswami has done in regard to transfer potentials. The aforementioned Einstein Podolsky Rosen paradox put forward in 1935 had been intended to show the invalidity of quantum mechanics but it could not be tested until J.S. Bell presented his famous inequalities in 1966 inspired by David Bohm's 1952 thought-provoking reformulations of quantum mechanics[148]. It was only in 1982 that these questions could be put to unequivocal experimental test and Aspect and co-workers showed that, contrary to Einstein's intentions, the predictions of quantum mechanics were confirmed by the experimental results. The conceptually disturbing aspects of quantum mechanics which most in the physics community had repressed whilst concentrating on the mundane mainstream work now had to be seriously contemplated. Put very simply, what is implied by such *non-locality* is that underlying our everyday world of phenomena is a transcendent quantum realm where our conventional notions of space, time and causality do not hold true. Correlations exist between the states of particles which have previously interacted which cannot be accounted for by means of normal physical modes of information transfer as signals would have to travel faster than the speed of light, thus violating an axiom of Einstein's Relativity theories. Although we tend to associate such mysterious behaviour with the realm of subatomic phenomena far removed from our everyday experience, in principle, all of our everyday phenomena are emerging from these deeper realms of being as we have discussed in earlier sections. Such non-local correlations have been related to the notion of quantum coherence, closely associated with notions of 'wholeness' in which the elements of a quantum system appear to behave as a unitary being as is manifest macroscopically in phenomena such as superconductivity[91]. I have noted that a number of thinkers have suggested that macroscopic quantum coherence may be present in the brain and associated with mental phenomena. Clearly such notions of a deeper quantum level of order underlying the spatio-temporal order in which strange connections remain between once-connected entities and a sort of underlying wholeness are deeply concordant with the mystical view and the existence of ESP-type phenomena, especially in the light of the fact that yogic knowledge associates such psychic phenomena with subtle vibratory activity normally masked by the gross vibratory activity of the physical world.

Quantum mechanics, Heisenberg's creation of which was influenced by Indian philosophy, also gave us a new understanding of matter which lends itself far more readily to the phenomena of psychokinesis and and even perhaps to the claimed materializations which have been part of the psychical repertoire as reported in nearly all societies throughout history. The concrete atoms of the old Physics dissolved into the mysterious actualizations of physical events from an indeterminate realm beyond our space-time order and beyond our ordinary imagination. We have seen that a number of physicists have interpreted quantum mechanics to imply a realm of possibilities from which actual events materialise associated with notions like the coherent superposition of states of the wave function. The Uncertainty Principle again indicates that entities in the quantum realm are not the fixed concrete entities which we encounter in the macroscopic world but that the physical entities we monitor with our instruments are abstracted from a reality which is far more blurred than the sharply defined categories within which we try to force it. Numerous physicists have speculated about the role of the observer or the possible role of a vaguely defined 'consciousness' in regard to the paradox raised by Schrödinger in regard to the so-called collapse of the wave function which is directly related to these questions of actualizing one particular state from a coherent superposition of states which seems to imply a realm where different pre-physical possibilities co-exist. Heisenberg's colleague Carl von Weiszäcker apparently attempted to come to terms with this paradox by invoking the Indian notion of *prāṇa*. The framing of attempts to resolve this paradox are often misleading and the term *consciousness* usually misused, often, as stated in my Preface, indicative of thinkers whose orientation to Reality is very confused presenting their confusion as profound mystery. The lack of clear resolution of such paradoxes need not concern us for such paradoxes are inevitable in a theory which, as Harman states, started with classical assumptions and then transcended itself[89]. What is of interest is that, where conventional materialist conceptualizations break down, the issues seem to make more sense when a new perspective is taken based on the Perennial Philosophy. We have also seen that Pribram has used the mathematical formalisms of quantum mechanics in order to model the processes of perception. This again indicates the subtle links between the supposedly concrete entities considered by Physics and the construction of our microcosmic phenomenal world by our perceptual process. It is no wonder then that so many attempts to come to terms with paranormal phenomena from a scientific perspective have invoked notions from Quantum Theory.

Academic Parapsychology : The failings of mimicking physical science

Murphy notes, in regard to the problems faced by academic parapsychology, that rare animals and rare minerals are not found in the laboratory, they are discovered in the field[26]. Western 'parapsychology' research began with the efforts of the likes of the British Society for Psychical Research (SPR) founded in 1882 which included a number of prominent physicists and other distinguished figures. J.J. Thomson, who discovered the electron, was a vice-president. Besides attempting scientific experimentation with famous psychics, the Society also collected numerous testimonies of spontaneous psychical experiences enabling the determination of common patterns underlying the diverse reports. Part of the motive behind the founding of the SPR was to challenge the materialism of contemporary Science. Modern Anglo-American parapsychology research sees its roots in the work of J.B. and L.E. Rhine at Duke University from the 1930s. The Rhines came to Duke University with the distinguished psychologist William McDougall, a staunch dualist, hoping to gather evidence against Behaviourism[149].

J.B. Rhine argued that materialism was refuted by psychic phenomena. Rhine tended to argue that, as psychic experiences are not attenuated by distance, they cannot be accounted for by 'physical energy' and that we must postulate a 'psychic energy' which is not limited by Space or Time. Rhine also noted that one would have no justification for any morality if materialism was to be taken to its logical conclusions with humans devoid of any freedom from the operation of physical laws[150]. I have noted in the Introduction how we continue to adhere to moral values based on a spiritual metaphysics which is largely rejected in regard to other aspects of life. Given McDougall's wish to 'legitimize' parapsychology research, the Rhines' research used ordinary student volunteers rather than noted psychics, simple quantifiable tests and statistical analyses of the data[149]. This approach is largely reminiscent of that of academic psychology which craves for 'scientific status' by devising simple tests producing data for statistical analysis from which numerous graphs can be plotted to present the appearance of 'hard' scientific research taking the physical sciences as their model.

Such approaches resemble the attempts of the so-called 'social scientists' to fit the cultural data of non-European societies into Eurocentric models. Given the pre-eminence of physical science as the supposed arbiter of the Truth in modern Western society, students of living systems, of the mind, and of society have felt it necessary to attempt to emulate, as far as possible, the methods which have given physical science its spectacular successes in order to gain respectability for their own disciplines. Although the emphases on reason, statistical rigour, supposed impartiality etc. have proven most useful, in certain respects, in the development of these fields, this mimicry has also resulted in seriously hampering the quest for knowledge through its narrow focus on the quantifiable aspects of phenomena which often exclude the issues of real interest. In the case of paranormal phenomena, one is immediately faced with the problem that statistics is largely the product of analysing the patterns of normal events which occur in sufficiently large numbers. Numerous criticisms of academic parapsychology have been put forward in regard to its focus on modest, boring tasks that can be performed under controlled laboratory conditions producing quantifiable results.

Thomson[151] notes that subtle subconscious interactions can occur between experimenters and subjects with the experimenter sometimes attempting to control the subjects' states of mind and the subjects sometimes resisting. Scientists have difficulty coming to terms with experimental settings in which the mental acts of all concerned need to be considered. Jahn and Dunne state that parapsychology has demonstrated the inherent difficulties in eliciting psychic phenomena in laboratory conditions. It has found that subtle psychological factors such as subconscious attitudes and relationships between particpants and experimenters can influence the outcome. Replication thus proves difficult and there is also a decline effect where initially good results fall back to chance distributions. The situation is further complicated by the fact that sometimes significant results occur opposite to those expected or the subject's predictions show 'displacement', correlating with targets or intentions adjacent to those chosen by the experimenter. The *a priori* dismissal of parapsychology by much of the scientific establishment has led to much introspective, over-cautious approaches with all the subconscious undertones associated with such exclusion affecting the whole field. Denied publication in academic journals and excluded from professional societies, the Rhines had to start their own journal and society[40]. Jahn and Dunne[40] state:

> *On the negative side, this forced insularity has produced a degree of intellectual inbreeding that has limited the range of conceptualization, implementation and interpretation brought to bear on the research issues and has perpetuated some less than productive protocols and techniques.*

They also note that the heritage of earlier psychical research and the psychological approach has focused on the search for 'gifted subjects' which has led to distortions based on personal factors and aroused much suspicion in regard to the integrity of these 'gifted subjects' and hence the experimenters. Jahn and Dunne point out parapsychology's reliance on methods which involve insensitive instruments and slow data acquisition rates. The data obtained has tended to be too gross in scale or too clouded with random noise to permit meaningful analysis. It has been the more recent involvement of some natural scientists and engineers, bringing in a new range of techniques and theoretical approaches, who have helped to shift the focus from *who* to *how*. Simultaneously, interest in the paranormal has been growing amongst scholars and researchers in other disciplines leading to a far more open atmosphere and masses of phenomena but no clear framework within which to set all this data[40].

Kautz, looking at the decline in parapsychology research after some promising signs of growth in the early 1980s, lists the reasons that have been offered. These include fear of the phenomena by the experimenters themselves who limit themselves to tiny, safe, boring experiments; the ego is threatened by anything beyond itself; the use of statistical methods to study one-off (one time) events; and that scientists are not ready to make the fundamental paradigm shifts required. Kautz places the roots of the problem in subconscious fear of confronting facts that challenge accepted notions which manifest as distrust, inappropriate beliefs and closed minds. Such subconscious fears result in collective attitudes and approaches which restrict the entire research community[152].

Kautz notes that, although there have been innumerable reports proving the existence of psychic phenomena, the parapsychologists tend to repeat the same small experiments with new variations as if the existence of 'psi' still needs proving. He states that, unlike the scientific ideal of a detached observer, it is important to gain personal experience of psychical phenomena in order to gain understanding. The most successful researchers have such personal experience. Rather than collecting statistical data through setting mundane tasks, he states that the intuitive faculties should be utilised for solving actual human problems, like finding items people have actually lost, which provides some motivation and interest. Intuition, he says, works best, when there is a good human reason why the information is needed. Such activity cannot be willed or produced on demand and the models developed should not be so reductionistic. Parapsychology should aim for overall comprehension of the holistic aspects of the phenomena rather than simply seek mechanisms[152]. Thomson notes that psychical and ordinary mentation seem to follow the same laws and it is wrong to make a sharp distinction between paranormal and normal mentation. Paranormal activity is associated with both normal and altered states[151]. Murphy states that there is a large body of evidence indicating that ESP operates in everyday life in ways which we don't always recognise[26]. I totally agree that this is so. Targ says that a "state of grace", a harmonious agreement between all involved in the experimental set-up and a sense of faith that what is being done makes sense is required[153]. Indeed, Targ describes successful psychic experimentation in almost religious terms, like the rituals of old.

Clairvoyant reality and the mystery of 'normal' reality

The majority of phenomena studied in parapsychology are associated with reception of information by means other than the normal senses. Apart from the obvious cases of telepathy, clairvoyance and precognition, phenomena such as out-of-body experiences, distance viewing, apparitions and spirit possession (or supposed reincarnation), as we shall see, may also be interpreted in this way. Paranormal phenomena which cannot be interpreted in terms of some form of ESP include psychokinesis, spiritual healing and the less frequent claims of materializations. I shall discuss spirit possession in the section on *karma* and spiritual healing will be discussed in regard to mind/body interactions. Spiritual healing does have a paranormal aspect but it also seems to involve physical processes which Science has largely ignored related to my discussion of *life, energy* and downward causation in Section 2(j).

LeShan reported the 'clairvoyant reality' experienced by the medium Eileen Garrett whilst displaying psychic ability. The world experienced by the clairvoyant in action is characterised by a fundamental unity of all things, the illusory nature of Time, and the superior apprehension of information by non-sensory means[150]. Garrett stated that at clairvoyant levels, Time is undivided and whole, one often perceives the object or event in its past, present and/or future phases in abruptly swift successions[15]. LeShan holds sensory reality and clairvoyant reality to be equally valid perceptions of reality which includes both and that exclusive modes of operation are available in sensory reality and clairvoyant reality[150]. It is clear that the 'clairvoyant reality' described by Garrett is the same reality as experienced by the yogis in the deeper *samādhis* or *vijñāna* (supermental perception) as Aurobindo called such insightful states in which all things appear to be part of a unitary Reality, past and future states become apparent, and, of course, *siddhis* such as clairvoyancy become available. Kautz, as mentioned above, proposes a 'superconscious mind' in which 'direct knowledge' accessed by 'intuition' may be omnipresent, which he relates to notions such as the Akashic Records, God's Book of Remembrance, or Jung's Collective Unconscious[142]. Such omnipresent 'direct knowledge' is again suggestive of the holonomic metaphor with its Frequency Domain and the yogic notions of a relativistic realm of unity composed of the interpenetrating energetic vibrations in the Pure Consciousness, in which each part has, in some sense, an access to the Whole.

Taking such considerations on board, the term *paranormal* becomes something of a misnomer, as the phenomena under consideration only appear anomalous from the perspective of the normally experienced material plane although this does not mean that they are not always operating as part of the normal operations of Reality underlying the material plane. The deeper, 'higher' planes contain all the 'lower', more superficial planes within them as well as going beyond the lower planes to include more of Reality. Thus it is the material plane which is the least representative of the whole of Reality and, from the perspective of Reality, is an anomalous phase in which the freedom of operation present in the deeper planes has become extremely restricted in our seemingly 'normal' lawlike behaviour. As I have stated above, and is apparent in the quote from Paracelsus, our normal ('physical') senses are only the projections of spiritual powers into the limited realm of operation of gross phenomena.

Such powers of the spirit become ever more restricted as they descend down the planes with their ever-increasing limiting principles coming into operation. Thomson states, "It is difficult to think of a single feature of normal mentation that is not shared by psi".[151] I have also pointed out above that all knowledge is gained by means of *realizations* although the realizations of our everyday consciousness are so familiar to us that we rarely question their rather magical character which, in truth, defies any materialist scientific attempt to account for them. Only when perceptual processes have been 'deautomatized' by meditative techniques and each normal perception is experienced as if for the first time does the magical nature of ordinary perception strike us. Indeed all the capacities we regularly display such as thought, voluntary movements of the body, freedom of choice etc. are, in the final analysis, mysterious powers which we take for granted and which cannot be explained away in simple scientific descriptions of the behaviour of physical abstractions. Those imbued with a Newtonian, mechanistic, frame of mind tend not to realise that Newton himself was aware of such problems as is apparent in his statement that the ultimate mechanism of change in the universe was the mystery of mind controlling matter. The scientific demonstration of nervous impulses and of EEG 'readiness potentials' prior to volitional acts may provide us with some physical correlates but they do not provide us with explanations as to how we possess such powers. Simple evolutionary arguments about mind serving the purpose of the organism cannot account for why mystics are able to renounce the world and the basic biological drives and bring themselves, through the exercise of their will, to the verge of death. Thus before we ridicule claims of *siddhis* or psychic powers as being impossible, because they do not fit our preconceived notions or limited frames of reference, we should ask whether or not we can truly explain the everyday psychical powers of perception, thought and volition. Careful consideration will reveal that beyond our convenient scientific myths we do not really possess any explanation for why these capacities should exist other than that they are limited expressions of the powers inherent in *Brahman*.

The myth of psychical energy in relation to space-time transcendence

Edge[150] notes that parapsychology is imbued with a dualistic attitude which holds mind to be separate from matter as is implicit in phrases like 'mind over matter'. I have noted above that J.B. Rhine thought that 'physical energy' could not account for the space and time transcending character of certain paranormal phenomena, postulating that this implied that a 'psychical energy' was responsible. I am asserting that such arguments miss the point that there is, in actuality, no such thing as physical energy for, as we have seen, the scientific concept of energy is itself an abstraction projected from subjective experiences indicative of psychophysical rather than merely physical energy. Much fuss is sometimes made about the so-called *prāṇa* being some sort of separate psychical energy or even a fifth force. As we have seen, such speculation is unwarranted because the *prāṇa*, clearly articulated in the *Kauṣītakī Upaniṣad* as the energy into which the normal consciousness dissolves in dreamless sleep and at death, can be identified with the RAS brainwaves. Following on from this, the more general meanings of *prāṇa* as a bodily energy and as a universal energy may be correlated with the universal scientific *energy* which in its various forms constitutes, brainwaves, bodily energy, the entire universe and beyond (if we consider arguments such as Bohm's about the ignored energy). We have seen that the aura and the *chakras* seem to be correlated with electromagnetic fields associated with the human body. The way to make sense of Rhine's distinction between his supposed 'physical' and 'psychical' energy would be along the lines of distinguishing between gross and subtle activity. The former would correspond to the emergent patterns of activity operating within the constraints of a space-time causality matrix. The latter would correspond to more subtle activity generating the emergent physical patterns, which in itself is not constrained by the space-time causality order. Thus there is no need to postulate a separate sort of energy, but there is a need to distinguish between modes of activity within the same psychophysical energy, between the physical modes and the space-time transcending modes. This again brings us back to notions such as non-locality in quantum mechanics and the deeper planes beyond the time/space matrix of perception known to the authoritative yogic traditions where space-time causality is transcended and a deeper holistic order is revealed where the conventional space and time relationships break down.

The transcendence of space-time causality in paranormal phenomena has been interpreted by physicist Rauscher as indicative of the existence of multidimensional hyperspace. Rauscher's own models involve positing hypothetical, faster-than-light, 'tachyon' signals and complex mathematical transformations. The gist of this notion appears to be that events separated in normal space and time may have 'local' connections in the complex space-time. In regard to the nature of perception, Rauscher links her ideas to the holographic metaphor in which information from frequencies and amplitudes is converted into normal space and time information by Fourier transforms[154]. As Edwin Abbott pointed out in his story *Flatland,* space and time in realms with more dimensions have different meanings. Great visions of lower-dimensional space-times may become immediately visible at higher dimensions. In a similar manner, one may experience other 'miracles' in realms of higher dimensionality.

The involvement of the ātman

Frederick Myers held that psychical phenomena were associated with what he called the *subliminal self* which seems to correspond quite well with the Vedāntic *ātman* in that it is a broader, more comprehensive consciousness co-existing in a largely potential state alongside our normal waking consciousness[150]. I have noted in regard to Multiple Personality Disorders, the existence of an *Inner Self Helper,* claiming to be unborn and uncreated, which lends support to the existence of such a deeper Self. I again would identify this deeper Self with the RAS brainwaves pointing out in this regard the *Kauṣītakī Upaniṣad's* identification of the *prāṇa* with the *ātman.* I have noted above that consciousness energy in itself would appear to be unindividuated and has, in some sense, access to the whole Reality whereas the normal mind is the product of the self-limiting activity of this consciousness energy, closing itself off from the whole and dominated by the gross activity of *avidyā/māyā,* the processes of perceptual world construction. Notions similar to that of Myers' subliminal self abound in regard to paranormal powers such as spiritual healing and also in regard to the firewalking capacity. In the Christian tradition it is held that the Holy Ghost takes possession of the person's faculties allowing firewalking, healing etc. Indeed Weil has speculated that the 'gut-level belief' that is required for such phenomena as healing and firewalking is linked to the brainstem[151]. I have discussed above how the personal deity concept arises from the *bhakti* experience of loving embrace by the personal god which *Advaita Vedānta* equates with *savikalpa samādhi*. As we have seen, this corresponds with lucid deep sleep in which a rudimentary mind, devoid of content, is permeated by the Divine Light of Pure Consciousness. Thus notions such as those of a subliminal self, personal deity or a Holy Ghost possessing the individual during paranormal activity again seem to point towards the RAS brainwaves which become more prominent to the denuded mind. This is not to say that the RAS is the only activity associated with such phenomena. It seems as if the auric fields detected by Hunt are more directly involved in healing. None the less, the basic experiential component of such processes is identified by the practitioners themselves as a sense of possession by the deeper Self or the Spirit.

Jahn and Dunne on psychokinesis

Robert Jahn, a professor of Aerospace Sciences at Princeton, and Brenda Dunne, manager of the Princeton Engineering Anomalies Research laboratory have reported on their important work establishing the influence of human consciousness upon physical devices. Using sophisticated methodologies involving computerized data acquisition, vast quantities of data have been accumulated showing quite conclusively that individuals can influence the outcome of random physical processes[40]. They state[40]:

> *the extraction of consciousness-related anomalies . . . requires very large databases because the marginal effects are proportionately so tiny. In interactions with physical atomic domains, the consciousness margins of reality may become comparable in scale with the basic processes themselves and thereby acquire much greater relative importance. In fact, they may just be the basic processes in toto, and all atomic reality may be established by these mechanisms alone.*

Although individuals can skew the expected chance distributions in the directions desired, when the data for all the individuals are recombined in a balanced mixture, the total distribution reconstructs the chance Gaussian distribution. As we have seen in a previous section, this suggests that a chance distribution of outcomes exists in potential form with individuals able to bring about anomalous results without altering the overall distribution.

The Princeton Engineering Anomalies Laboratory receives funding from sources such as the McDonnel Foundation associated with the aircraft manufacturers McDonnel Douglas. Such funding indicates that the problem of so-called 'gremlins' which wreak havoc with meticulously calibrated equipment is related to such psychokinetic influences operating subconsciously. Jahn and Dunne note that more recent technology tends to depend upon electronic information processing systems with very sensitive signal levels. Periods of intense emotional stress or of high intellectual demand seem to be correlated with mental influences upon the functioning of the machinery. As stated previously, a sense of resonance with the machine is critical for successful psychokinetic effects in experimental subjects. The psychokinetic effect appears to operate at the systemic level of information in the device rather than interfering with any particular component. Individual subjects tend to show consistent patterns of deviations from expected values, which Jahn and Dunne call *operator signatures*[40].

I have previously quoted Jahn and Dunne in regard to the failure of electromagnetic theory, geophysical mechanics, hyperspace properties etc. to account for the space-time transcending features of psychical phenomena. They recognise the merits of the hyperspace view, the holographic metaphor and the quantum mechanics related approaches in extending the scope of our theorizing but point out that all suffer from a serious lack of empirical data and the inability to incorporate subjective properties. I would add that all of these approaches fail to actually tackle the basic question of why there is any subjective experience at all although they may provide insights into space-time transcendence in paranormal phenomena. Jahn and Dunne recognise the need for a more fundamental approach recognising the role of consciousness in the establishment of physical reality.

However, their own approach fails to address the question of how consciousness (as subjectivity) relates to the physical world in spite of statements such as, "the process of consciousness interacting with its physical environment".[40] They explicitly state:

> *Thus, in our consciousness metaphor, any functioning entity capable of generating, receiving, or utilizing information can qualify as a consciousness.*

thus seeming to imply that consciousness is nothing more than information processing. Furthermore they also state:

> *It is a major hypothesis of the model that reality, encompassing all aspects of experience, expression and behavior, is constituted only at the interface between consciousness and its environment . . . the sole currency of any reality is information . . .*

They state that, if consciousness were to allow itself the same wave/particle duality that it has conceded to numerous physical processes, the wave-like properties could help account for most of the phenomena which seem anomalous from a particulate approach. Most importantly, the information and energy carried by waves may be diffused over broad regions of space and time. Jahn and Dunne rely heavily on notions from quantum mechanics. They stress that concepts utilized in any physical theory are creations of consciousness and hence may reflect the fundamental propensities of consciousness when ordering acquired information. Common physical concepts such as mass, momentum, energy, electrical charge, and magnetic field, frequency and wavelength, and distance and time are viewed as information-organizing categories that consciousness utilizes in its interaction with its environment (i.e. physical concepts are projections of the internal reality). They suggest ways of measuring the parameters of consciousness equivalent to physical parameters. Hypothetical notions such as 'consciousness distance', 'consciousness time', 'consciousness mass' 'consciousness charge' etc. are considered. It soon becomes clear that Jahn and Dunne are stretching this point of physical concepts as projections of consciousness too far when they start making consciousness equivalent analogies with physical notions such as covalent bonds, organic molecules, RNA and DNA! Thus Jahn and Dunne, although having moved in the right direction in certain respects, fail to seriously confront the problem of consciousness as is clear from their assertions that *information* is the Ultimate Reality and that consciousness is information processing. Although recognising the projected nature of physical concepts, they then take the consciousness equivalents of physical concepts analogies well beyond their scope indicating that they have not managed to transcend notions of the primacy of the physical order or confront the problems of the differences between the microcosm and the macrocosm in regard to their emergent structures.

Walker on quantum uncertainties and psychic phenomena

Physicist Evan Harris Walker, in his *Quantum Theory of Psi Phenomena*[156] also notes the failure of electromagnetic theory in accounting for paranormal phenomena. Walker states that his theory identifies consciousness with a quantum mechanical interaction involving; at any moment, about 0.2 per cent of the neuronal synapses (junctions between brain cells) which are engaged in firing! Walker argues that the Copenhagen interpretation of Quantum Theory (associated primarily with Bohr and also with Heisenberg) involves the conscious observer whose will biases the probabilities in the net of measurement. The Copenhagen interpretation, although vigorously challenged by alternative interpretations, has been viewed by many to provide some sort of interface between "consciousness" (taken to mean numerous, usually vague, properties) and the 'physical world'. In general, such thinkers seem to be playing around rather loosely with statements involving the quantum mechanical wave function's superposition of possible states 'collapsing' into a specific state only when it is observed which is then interpreted as some interjection of consciousness to produce the collapse of the wave function. Broadening the discussion from the rather simplistic abstract discussions of the physicists into a more metaphysical context, it seems that what the physicists are trying to come to terms with is the emergence into perception of particular phenomena from the indeterminate reality beyond which we have seen appears to involve a realm of possibilities. In his conclusions Walker actually states that, rather than Psi phenomena being understood in terms of Quantum Theory, Quantum Theory and much other science must look to an understanding of Psi phenomena for their further development. Here Walker is on the right track although the proper contextualizing of Quantum Theory involves, amongst other things, considering more than just paranormal phenomena but all the epistemological considerations relating to perception, including those that I have touched upon. Note that when such physicists use phrases such as 'quantum level', 'quantum reality' (as opposed to the macroscopic/classical level of Reality) or similar terms prefixed by *quantum* they tend to be referring to a deeper level of Reality, where normal space-time relations are not valid and which appears to be a realm of possibilities from which certain states are actualised. It is quite clear that just as the scientific principle of the Conservation of Energy is a modern restatement of the notion of the Ground of all Being, such uses of quantum levels or quantum reality are modern reformulations of some sort of transcendental order. The issues relating to the Copenhagen interpretation and the wave/particle dichotomy are, more generally, the issues of the transcendental and the mundane levels of perception. It is extremely naïve to consider Quantum Theory, or any abstract physical model, as some irrefutable standard framework against which everything else has to be considered. For instance, physicist Saul-Paul Sirag[157], in discussing mathematical structures called reflection spaces, used in attempts to unify physical forces, suggests that reflection space E_7 is universal mind (both 'consciousness' and the 'unconscious'), C[OD] is universal body, since it includes space-time, and C^7, which intersects both is universal consciousness! The criticism levelled by Rosen against Bohm in regard to describing the formless in terms of mathematical abstractions is even more appropriate here.

In spite of the weaknesses in Walker's metaphysical assumptions, Walker has produced some interesting results in his mathematical analysis of Forwald's 1950s experiments on the psychokinetic deflection off-centre of metallic cubes released down an inclined plane onto a table. Walker's model was based on the assumption that the initial quantum uncertainties in position and angular orientation of the cubes were amplified with each bounce as they fell down the inclined plane. This refers to the inability to determine simultaneously both of certain pairs of variables, primarily position and momentum, in a particle or any object, although this uncertainty becomes negligible at macroscopic scales and can usually be ignored. These exceedingly small uncertaïnties could be determined and were shown to increase exponentially so that, after a few bounces, these uncertainties reached macroscopic proportions. Forwald's experimental results matched Walker's predictions for deviations off-centre for cubes made of different materials and design[158]. Walker asserts that what is significant is that no new hypotheses have been utilised, only the Copenhagen interpretation of quantum mechanics has been used in a literal way. The question as to how this interaction between the observer and the physical system occurs has been postponed[156].

Rush states that there is reason to believe that Forwald's unique results reflected his expectations rather than physical dependencies but, if Forwald's results are valid, Walker's work is remarkable. Tumbling dice would involve similar minute quantum effects at each bounce. Rush says that Walker's theory does not require the subject to have any analytical knowledge of the situation, rather the subject's will bring's about a correlation between the imagined and actual outcomes of the quantum process. Walker's theory has been criticised for involving so-called *backward causation* as the subject's effort is effective only upon observing the outcome of the earlier quantum event. Walker responds with the counter-argument that Quantum Theory, as experiments show,. deals with *correlations of events* rather than classical causality[145]. We have seen that in experimental tests of the Einstein, Podolsky, Rosen paradox, the existence of *non-local correlations* have been verified which cannot be accounted for in terms of space-time causality.

Walker attempts to account for ESP in a manner similar to his view of psychokinesis, in that the mental process of formulating an ESP prediction becomes the random process whose outcome is brought into correlation by the subject's will with the imagined outcome (hence the parallel with the Copenhagen interpretation and the collapse of the quantum wave function's superposition of possibilities into a particular outcome). Psychokinesis, according to Walker's model, can only occur in indeterminate situations based on underlying quantum uncertainties. As quantum relations are non-local in space and time, such correlations result in precognition and distance viewing[145]. We see here an interesting similarity to Aurobindo's assertion that precognition involves imaginative construction from the current play of forces given no unforeseen disturbances. Walker's postponed question of the interaction between the observer and the physical system begins to resolve itself into the power of the mind to imagine possible outcomes which harmonise with the actual play of indeterminate forces constituting the phenomenon. Such ideas harmonise with the reports of subjects in Jahn and Dunne's psychokinetic experiments where a sense of resonance is attained with the machine. It is as if, at a deeper level, the individual and the machine system become one and the individual's will can guide the outcome of the systemic process. This sense of oneness with the object reminds one of the loss of self-consciousness in yogic *samādhi* which can be associated with paranormal phenomena. Such imagination of desired outcomes also ties in with the almost universal role of creative visualization in the attainment of 'metanormal' human capacities as noted by Murphy[26].

Imagination, resonance of form and physical manifestations

Of course such notions raise more questions than they resolve as to how an individual's imagination can bring about a significant correlation in the outside world, in the sense that the same anomalous phenomenon is observed by all observers. The reader may recall Thompson's speculations involving the many individual *jīvātmans* and the Supreme *Paramātman* or Superconsciousness which produced the individuals and gave them a limited degree of free will to influence the lawlike behaviour of Nature. The *Paramātman* acted as the harmonising medium through which the often conflicting individual wills operated upon Nature[110]. Notions of *resonance of form* spring to mind whereby intensive imagination of the desired outcome may produce deep, subtle resonances influencing the actual play of forces manifesting the world. Indeed the occult literature does suggest such relationships between intensely imagined *thought forms* and physical manifestations. Hunt states[146]:

> *Thought and mind have been said to precede the existence of matter, to continue through matter, and to exist at the termination of matter albeit in new forms . . . thought and mind do not disintegrate because they are not subject to physical laws. Matter is the denser of the vibrations, mind the finer of them.*

Hunt continues that, thoughts, especially when amplified by emotion, leave an imprint on matter. Previous thought forms, she asserts, may remain as fields in certain places affecting people who resonate with them. Similar ideas have been expressed by Tibetan Buddhists with their notion of *tulpas* and by psychics in regard to interactions of the aura with the body.

We have seen that attempts to account for the transcendence of space-time causality in paranormal phenomena have invoked notions of a transcendent Reality underlying our everyday space-time order. The models proposed by speculative scientists such as the hyperspace, the holographic metaphor's Frequency Domain and the realm of quantum non-locality are all relative approaches to this transcendent order abstracted from particular perspectives for particular purposes. This transcendent order, the underlying unitary Reality beneath the manifest order of seeming separateness, may be directly experienced through the practice of advanced yoga or, in the case of psychics, through the attainment of clairvoyant trance. Even during our normal wakeful states, when we are busy getting on with our mundane activities, some contact with such deeper levels of Reality is maintained although the subtle influences arising from these depths of our being are swamped by the normal processes of mentation. By holding the normal processes in abeyance the yogi is able to focus on the subtle level. However, in all of us, some of these subtle influences may spontaneously become amplified and reach the levels of gross perception although the very process of amplification will introduce distortions. This resembles certain dreams in which minor bodily disturbances result in surreal fantasies based upon the disturbances. Psychic intuitions may be central to significant worldly decisions such as one billionaire's hunch to sell his stake in the London Stock Exchange prior to the large crash in 1987. This information, which is beyond the constraints of our normal space-time relations, seems to exist all around us in Space, and is variously called the *ākāśa lipi, cittākāśa* or the Akashic Record. The LSD psychotherapy research conducted by Grof[41] and others seems to indicate that this information is accessed on the basis of similarity of form in relation to the receiving mind. When one has passed through the levels of personal memory and the perinatal experiences, one enters the so-called transpersonal realms of the mind. Initially, the information received is likely to relate to one's mother and near relatives. This then broadens out to clan, nation, race, species, genera etc. as one's experience deepens until one is able to attain oneness with the universe as a whole, or lose oneself in the Void. The experience of identification with various modes and forms of being may be composite experiences drawn from the collective experience of numerous individuals. Such composite, 'archetypal' experiences tie in well with the holographic metaphor as composite images may be formed by interference patterns acting in a holographic manner. Thus it seems that access to such transcendental knowledge occurs through some sort of 'tuning in' with similarity of form being the primary determinant although all sorts of diverse beings may eventually be realised. Grof notes that strong emotional charges may invoke resonance with memories from various sources of similar emotional quality[41].

This deeper order of subtle vibrations is probably not just a passive state of reverberances but also is or, at least, is closely associated with the generative matrix from which the spatio-temporal order manifests. Notions such as *karma* (to be discussed later), *ākāśa*, Sheldrake's morphogenetic fields and related ideas seem to be hinting at the influence of past manifestations upon the generation of new phenomena as is implicit in the Buddhist karmic doctrine of Dependent Co-origination. Bohm also saw resonance of form operating within his 'implicate order', the deeper realm manifesting the 'explicate order'. In the implicate order, unrestricted by normal space-time relations, resonance of form would stabilize manifestations of particular forms in the spatio-temporal explicate order[39]. Such ideas resonate in form with the yogic experience of acausal connections in the undivided wholeness beyond the time/space matrix of perception. In psychokinesis, the mind is somehow able to become one with the object, presumably through some sort of resonance occurring in this deeper, holistic, non-local order and is thus able to exercise a limited influence in regard to the manifestation of the target object. Presumably such influences can be developed in conjunction with yogic practice in order to develop lucidity in the appropriate states and thus allow one's volitional power to act in a controlled manner at the transcendental level. Through this transcendental order, all phenomena are interwoven in a relativistic manner. Clearly it is extremely difficult to come to terms with such activity given that our language is imbued with spatio-temporal categories. Although we cannot truly explain the paranormal, we are at least able to appreciate that normal, mundane experience is a limited perception of Reality which at deeper levels operates in a manner far removed from our every-day notions of causality. We again need to think in terms of different frames of reference which cannot easily be correlated. When we 'step back' from the changing flux of concepts and percepts which fill our attention we are struck by the fact that we are a mysterious field of everchanging experiences which displays magical properties of awareness and volition which no amount of scientific sophistry can come close to really explaining. Thus, as I have stated above, it is misleading to think of our everyday experience as if it needs no explanation and to view only paranormal phenomena as being mysterious because of their rarity. We do not really understand either the normal or the paranormal. However, when we understand that the phenomenal world is not made up simply of solid atoms and molecules constantly bumping into each other but is a constant manifestation from a deeper transcendental realm which unites all things through the depths of our beings, we can begin to appreciate not only that paranormal phenomena can occur but that there is nothing particularly mysterious about the existence of such phenomena unless we have shut ourselves off in an artificial manner from our true selves.

2(l). ON MIND-BODY INTERACTIONS

The Cartesian split in medicine and the rediscovery of pranic healing

In recent years much interest has been shown by the Western public in the phenomenon of spiritual healing. The willingness of Western medical practitioners to accept the role of mental factors in health and disease has been growing with publishers extending the mass marketing 'hype' of novels and cookbooks etc. to the latest offerings from the big name 'New Age' medical gurus, often claiming personal credit for traditional, collective wisdom in typical Western style. This follows the widespread rejection of such factors over much of this century. Locke and Colligan note that Hippocrates suggested that there were natural as well as divine causes for disease and that he believed that whatever happened in the mind affects the body. They also point out that Descartes' philosophy had two major effects on modern attitudes to health. Descartes' reductionist method led to the medical theory of specific aetiology, which held that every disease is caused by an identifiable micro-organism, and thus led to the magic bullet approach of seeking new drugs to kill the disease agents which dominated mid-twentieth century Western medicine. In addition, his splitting of mind and body led to the view that the body was a mechanical system independent of the mind and the neglect of the healing powers of the mind[159]. Traditionally it has been known that if such healing powers are to effect some sort of successful outcome then a degree of faith or belief is required. Psychologist David McClelland states that the key to self-healing may turn out to be existential or religious, "A kind of personal disengagement combined with a kind of faith in something beyond the self".[160] Indeed, the major religious icon of the Western tradition, Jesus Christ, was himself a healer of some repute (if we are to believe that some Biblical statements are factual), who told these whom he had healed that it was their faith that had made them whole again. Although there is some tantalizing evidence linking such interactions to known physical forces, it is not clear if such approaches can prove sufficient to explain the various phenomena involved. A parapsychological component is also implicated given that healing may occur at a distance or that prayer may influence the well-being of others. It has been suggested that the gut-level belief required for such extraordinary abilities, including firewalking, involves brainstem centres and that the power that humans tend to project onto placebos or gods is actually an innate power involving the breakdown of barriers between the cortex and deep brain centres controlling psychosomatic events[155]. Such physiological activity would perhaps be correlated with the traditional reports of allowing the power of the deeper Self, universal Self, Holy Ghost, *ch'i*, *prāṇa* . . . to act in place of the normal, limited self.

Herbert Benson, who worries that religious people will accuse him of "reducing God to neurons", is well-known for having determined the existence of the so-called Relaxation Response, a common physiological response induced by a variety of practises such as Transcendental Meditation and prayer. It is basically elicited by sitting comfortably and repeating a 'mantra' to oneself and refusing to let normal thoughts take over the mind. Elicitation of the Relaxation Response results in slower brainwaves detected by the EEG, as is also found with meditation. Benson notes that such rhythms often correlate with pleasurable feelings. Benson notes that twenty-five per cent of people eliciting the Relaxation Response (more frequently females) also feel more spiritual when it is elicited. A spiritual experience associated with the response is also associated with greater medical benefit gained from practising it. The spiritual experience is described as having two components: First, the presence of an energy, force, power or 'God' which was beyond themselves and, secondly, this presence felt close to them[66]. Note that this ties in with McClelland's suggestion in regard to the key to self-healing mentioned above.

From the perspective I have developed in this essay, it is clear that the Relaxation Response based on Transcendental Meditation, aims at stopping normal mentation through focus upon the mantra. Benson focuses on the physiological responses elicited by it which counteract the so-called 'fight-flight' responses associated with stressful situations. The reader will recognise that the Cartesian split in modern medicine results in the Western medical establishment demanding physiological proof of the effectiveness of a technique in terms of measurable correlates, usually ignoring other components of an individual's well-being associated with mental states which cannot be so easily quantified. The meditators' description of an energy beyond themselves which felt close to them and felt inherently sacred clearly describes the awareness of the presence of the underlying *prāṇa* attribute of the Pure Consciousness. Benson points out that this energy or force has been called *ch'i, mana, prāṇa* etc. in various cultures and that it is held that healers can direct and restore these healing forces. Using standard scientific methods, Benson has tried to isolate and measure this energy without success. He notes that a Chinese researcher at Sun Yat Sen University reported that *Chi Gong* elicited physiological changes like those evoked by the Relaxation Response[66].

Reductionist myths and the mysterious 'Life force'

Robert Becker, an orthopaedic surgeon who has specialised in the biologically regenerative role of electromagnetism asserts that, as we do not know all that there is to know about electricity and magnetism, it would be foolhardy to start assuming other forces about which we know nothing. This would be reintroducing mysticism. Becker prefers to think in terms of unexpected variations in known forces or perhaps new physical forces[21]. Here again we have a debate very similar to that found in regard to ESP-type phenomena and Rhine's postulation of a psychical energy separate from the normal physical energy. In regard to psychosomatic phenomena, Wilhelm Reich postulated the existence of a primordial, cosmic energy different from electromagnetic energy which he called *orgone.* One of *orgone's* main properties was pulsation and *orgone* differentiated into mechanical energy, inorganic mass and living matter[41]. Reich, obsessed with the orgasm, veered towards the lunatic fringe of one concept cult therapies. Becker's argument in regard to unexpected variations in known forces resembles my assertion that known physical phenomena may be involved in modes of interaction beyond those we are currently familiar with although I do not think that Becker is keen on accepting the possibility of space-time causality transcending interactions where the known electromagnetic modes clearly do not suffice. Indeed Schrödinger in his book *What is Life,* mentioned in my verse and which influenced the post-war influx of physicists into the Life Sciences, contemplated new physical forces or new manifestations of known forces in order to account for living phenomena. Indeed, Schrödinger's views helped to fuel my sense of adventure just before I started my degree course in Molecular Biology but in the main historical textbook, historian of Biology, Gunter Stent[161], stated that the rise of Molecular Biology has shown that living phenomena could be accounted for in terms of the making and breaking of hydrogen bonds. I would argue that all that Molecular Biology accounts for are the limited phenomena upon which it focuses missing out many of the key features of living systems. So many of today's scientific thinkers and popular materialists naïvely assert that the knowledge of the replication of DNA and related processes has given us the key to understanding Life itself. The DNA-based metaphor of 'life' resonates strongly with the computer metaphor with much talk of *information* and self-replicating computer 'viruses' being perceived by some as being living creatures. This highlights the naïve misconception so widespread in the modern materialist community holding the abstracted characteristic of information replication to be Life itself. I pointed out in Section 2(j) that what we intuively know as Life is closely correlated with what we call *energy,* the scientific conception of which was derived by abstraction from the subjective feelings of freedom and *vitality.* The reductionist focus on key molecules results in absurd projections upon these molecules of almost intelligent or anthropomorphic characteristics in regard to popular evolutionary discussions of 'selfish genes' and the like. Clearly, such molecules in themselves are nothing particularly special. Rather it is the organization of the organismic system as a whole which gives us the magic of Life. The field properties of energy seem to provide the key to understanding this integrated, organised behaviour amongst the atomic and molecular components. Becker has long maintained that conventional biological paradigms, based on knowledge of solution chemistry, fails to come to terms with many of the characteristic phenomena associated with living systems although he asserts that the key to understanding all of the unexplained mysteries of the life sciences is to be found in electromagnetic phenomena[162]. We shall see that as quantum mechanics begins to filter through into biological thinking, unexpected new physical phenomena are being contemplated which could account for some of the fascinating mysteries of living organisms. Prigogine's work on self-organization or dissipative structure formation is clearly of fundamental importance in understanding the basic processes of Life itself.

Fields and 'downward causation' in the Placebo effect and hands-on healing

Benson has renamed the so-called 'Placebo effect', 'Remembered Wellness' and says that most of the mind-body interaction phenomena can be interpreted in terms of such placebo-like effects. He cites a J.S. Levin who states that the mere belief that religion or God is health-enhancing may elicit a healing response in the same way that the placebo effect works with drugs or medical procedures. This does not of course explain how this placebo effect in itself has its effect. Benson attempts to account for such effects in terms of 'top-down' thoughts or what I have referred to in Section 2(j) as Downward Causation. Generating positive images, thoughts etc. results in activating neural patterns associated with healthy functioning of biological systems which have lapsed into unhealthy modes of activity through downward causation. The higher level images or thoughts bring about the same brain activity that generated them in healthy situations in the past, tending to restore the healthy pattern in the body. Therefore, Benson calls this Remembered Wellness and describes it as an "emotionally charged memory". Vivid memories, says Benson, trigger powerful top-down events. For instance, we may salivate in response to a memory of some delicious food. He notes the importance of emotions in assigning priorites to our decision-making functions. Thus the strength of the emotional charge associated with such memories is important in bringing about the desired effect[66].

Some sort of downward causation is implicated in Valerie Hunt's studies of electromagnetic fields and the healing phenomenon. I have mentioned in Section 2(k) that Hunt has used highly sensitive telemetry equipment to detect electromagnetic energy fields (above 500 Hz) correlated with the psychically perceived aura and *cḥakras* and also with altered states of consciousness. Hunt states that Robert Becker's studies and her own provide the most extensive evidence that healing occurs through changes in the electromagnetic field. From hundreds of electromagnetic recordings of hands-on healing sessions, Hunt found that the healer's and healee's fields start off distinctly different in amplitude, frequency spectra and patterning. The healer's field has a wider range of frequencies and often displays a unique pattern of frequencies when healing. Healers may shift their fields to affect different illnesses. Hunt found that healers specializing in different forms of healing, such as in pain relief or in tissue regeneration, displayed specific frequency ranges in their fields correlated with psychically perceived auric colours when they were healing. Sometimes the healer's and healee's fields do not resonate but, if they do, a transaction occurs and the healee's field changes towards a healthy pattern often identical with that of the healer. If this occurs, the healer stops the session[146].

Hunt[146] states that, "things are controlled not only from below upward, by atomic and molecular action, the micro-source of fields, but also from above downward from mental, emotional properties or fields". Hunt notes that the field is believed to radiate from cells, molecules, atoms and particles with the density of the tissue helping to determine the frequency and pattern of energy released. She states that dense fields are more likely to absorb more from other fields and that the complex body field responds more readily to elaborate fields than to simple ones. Field transactions, she suggests, are based on resonance with similar fields and 'repulsion' from fields with unlike characteristics. She points out that it has been suggested that biological membranes serve as the interface between fields and tissues, referring to notions like the 'edge of chaos' where normal order and chaotic fluctuations meet, a notion which has recently been applied to various biological issues.

Hunt clearly associates the healing process with organismic self-regulation, stating that the best description of healing involves activation of the body's energies towards dynamic equilibrium. In regard to tissue regeneration, she asserts that the field provides the template for regrowth. She notes that electromedical researchers believe that each disease or disorder has its own characteristic field pattern which disturbs the body's normal field pattern. Healing involves a restoration of the body's field to its normal healthy pattern. Hunt asserts that it should soon be shown that all tissue changes are preceded by field disturbances and potential health problems may be detected in the field prior to manifestation in the tissues[146]. This also ties in with assertions by numerous thinkers that many disorders have 'psychosomatic' origins and become 'physicalized'. For instance, Locke and Colligan refer to the role of depression in making people disease prone and to 'somatization', the tendency to let emotional conflicts work themselves out through their bodies[159]. Of course, not all field disturbances would be caused by emotional states but a depressed mental state may weaken the field's resistance to disruptions introduced by other factors.

Conventional and paranormal processes in pranic healing

Hunt also discusses the more complex aspects of the healing phenomenon such as tissue regeneration and immunological reactions. Interestingly, she states that studies by the likes of Singukin, in plants, and Becker, in humans, show that the electromagnetic field around a site of injury becomes dominantly magnetic as do the hands of a spiritual healer when healing. She suggests that the energy field is responsible for activating neuropeptides in distant body sites almost as soon as such neuropeptides are activated in the brain (the activation occurs too fast to be accounted for by nerve impulse transmission). She also suggests that neuropeptides are locally released through the laying-on of hands. Hunt notes the view of Norman Cousins that the 'Belief System' may act as the activator of the healing system. Meditation and imagery may stabilize the field but, unless the field is permanently changed to remove disruptions, the disorder persists or takes another form. Hunt states that it is calling upon God, or the power of Love, that releases the healing powers within[146].

Healers themselves, according to Hunt, enter an altered state in which they, "communicate with divine vibrations, experience lovingness and sense the healee's vibrations". She chastises the view expressed by some healers that they are merely 'channels', stating that the healer is more than just a mechanical circuit but the divine energies manifest[146]. None the less, I have found that the (British) National Federation of Spiritual Healers describes the role of the healer as tuning into and channeling the natural energy forces that constantly occur around us. The healer is said to, "scan and balance the patient's own energy centres to gently correct where necessary". The healee's body is said to be very receptive to this supportive energy and uses it to heal, restore or uplift whatever is needed at the time[163]. Hunt states that some healers feel heat or cold in the areas of pain indicating inflammation or lack of circulation. Other healers can see forms, shapes, colours, breaks and blocks in the energy flows of the field etc. Over time these signs are associated with various disorders. The best healer, says Hunt, does not attempt to heal, that belongs to the healee. Rather, by presenting a strong, radiant field, the healee's field is encouraged to restore its healthy state[146].

Benson, who tends to follow the Cartesian approach of appealing to chemical and neuronal factors and who views acupuncture as a manifestation of the placebo effect, has studied a spiritual healer with interesting results. Apparently his studies with, British ex-Olympic skier and spiritual healer, Lady Raeburn showed that salt-damaged corn kernels sprouted faster and cut flatworms regenerated themselves faster if she held her hands over them. However, Benson is rather wary of his results as he did not get a chance to replicate them[66]. Similar results have often been reported by other researchers. Significant results have repeatedly been obtained in some laboratory experiments[26,164]. Grad found that the famous healer Oskar Estebany had an influence similar to that later shown by Raeburn on salt-damaged seedlings[164]. Green found that healers produced bursts of electromagnetic energy when they focus their efforts[146]. Murphy has reviewed the studies looking into the paranormal aspects of spiritual healing where such effects upon bacteria, plants and animals in the parapsychology laboratory are viewed as manifestations of psychokinesis. Even in techniques such as Therapeutic Touch, a hands-on technique developed for nurses by Dolores Krieger, a paranormal component can be demonstrated. Some have argued that healing is a transpersonal, paranormal process which is made less effective by personal contact but it seems more likely that both normal and paranormal processes occur simultaneously in the healer-healee relationship. Murphy notes that Braude and Schlitz have shown that, using visualization techniques and biofeedback from their target subjects, one person can influence another person's skin activity at a distance. Murphy states that spiritual healing suggests that, "consciousness and living matter have a profound resonance with, and formative influence upon, each other". Indeed, Murphy cites the work of Stekel which suggests that various psychological disorders could be related to paranormal phenomena[26].

Becker limits his discussion of the healing phenomenon to more mundane electromagnetic effects. He has spent most of his working life studying the role of direct current (DC) electromagnetic fields in the regeneration of limbs in amphibians and in human tissue regeneration. He had found that extremely small electrical currents (measured in billionths of amperes), at the right strengths, could cause the dedifferentiation of frog red blood cells which then developed into bone cells. These minute electrical signals were produced from structures called neuroepidermal junctions which are also involved in limb regeneration in salamanders. He has undertaken research showing that acupuncture points and meridians can, to some extent, be shown to exist using electrical tests and he links the effects of acupuncture to his postulated DC control system regulating bodily structures. Becker argues that the changing values of current and voltage in such DC fields carry simple morphogenetic information in some sort of coordinate system which could trigger much larger information stores in the nuclei of cells (such ideas are reminiscent of Bohm's notion of the information carrying Quantum Potential which the quantum wave function may symbolically represent). Becker suggests that the body DC system uses an analog data transmission and control system, tying in with similar DC analog systems in the brain for which he cites some evidence. Indeed, in the 1930s several neurophysiologists had shown that DC voltages in the brain controlled the activity of neurons. Becker has found that during true hypnosis (as opposed to simulated hypnosis), the DC potential from the front to the back of the head drops sharply to a level resembling very deep sleep. General anaesthesia also produced such a drop in the brain DC current which then produced similar declines in DC potentials in the rest of the body. He has shown that local anaesthesia induced by hypnotic suggestion shows similar declines in local DC potentials to those induced by local anaesthetics. Becker states:

> *Since the primitive analog system controls growth and healing, it is possible that under certain circumstances, conscious thought can cause healing.*

He chastises the proponents of various alternative therapies who claim that theirs is the true energy medicine. As previously stated, Becker is against reintroducing 'mysticism' into energy medicine[21]. I would endorse such criticism of therapy 'cults'.

Becker[21] sees the link between the 'conscious mind' and the DC system as basic to what he calls minimal energy techniques (hypnosis and visualization) where no external energy is applied. His basic premise is that whenever someone develops a profound belief in the efficacy of *any* treatment, a state resembling self-hypnosis results giving access to the DC control systems. Locke and Colligan[159] also note that most hypnotists consider visualization techniques to be equivalent to auto-hypnosis. They cite some evidence suggesting that the frontal lobes are involved in hypnotic trance although this does not seem to fit in with Becker's results showing similarity to deep sleep (note again the link between deep sleep and trance). Becker's assertions in regard to the DC analog system's role in healing are supported by research into the role of embryonic control systems in controlling cancer growth and related processes suggesting that similar control systems may be reactivated in healing through self-hypnosis or visualization. It seems to me that the very analog nature of the DC control system may provide a clue as to why imagery is so important in such self-healing in that the process may involve some sort of resonance between mental images, or the waveforms underlying them, and analog information in the bodily DC fields.

In regard to spiritual healing, Becker says that it remains very little understood. He notes that it cannot simply be dismissed as a placebo because healers can also heal animals (I would add that the same applies to homoeopathy). He speculates that the healer may use his or her own electrical control system to produce external fields which interact with those of the patient restoring the balance in the patient's fields so that the body returns to normal[21]. We have seen from Hunt's work that such a process seems to occur although the external fields are always present and do not need to be specially generated although they may require some 'tuning'. Noting the experience of a Polish healer who affected the DC stage lighting at a demonstration in a theatre, Becker states that this lends supports to the view that electromagnetic energy is directly involved in healing. He also cites some Chinese studies of *Chi Gong* healing which suggest that electromagnetic fields may have some subtle effects through processes such as nuclear magnetic resonance with biochemicals in the body. Becker also mentions resonance processes such as cyclotron resonance in regard to explanations as to how low strength electromagnetic radiation can have damaging biological effects. He notes that, since resonance theory is based on frequency and not on power, vanishingly small fields may have biological effects. Indeed Becker suggests that electromagnetic resonance may help to explain both ESP and the ability of healers to diagnose and treat patients. He speculates that the field given off by the healer's hand induces electromagnetic resonance of some body component and the healer senses in his or her mind the energy released as the excited components return to the rest state in much the same manner as a magnetic imaging device. The detection of pathology by the healer would involve changes in the electronic states of target ions or particles caused by the disease. The therapeutic effects of healers, Becker suggests, may perhaps be explained by their influencing specific ions in the diseased region as well as through some resonant action between the healer's external fields and the patient's DC control system[21].

Both Hunt and Becker have shown that healing is linked to energy fields which may be involved in organizing cells and tissues in the body, perhaps linked to developmental processes. Controversy has raged over such issues in conventional biology throughout this century with the reductionist, positivistic mainstream hurling accusations of vitalism and mysticism at those who have recognized the need for holistic and transcendentalist approaches to the understanding of living systems. Echoes of this are found in Becker's assertion that positing unknown energies leads back to mysticism although I would agree with Becker on this point taking 'mysticism' here to mean the naïve, relativistic approaches of the various alternative treatment 'gurus' claiming unique status for their approaches which are all some sort of variation on some more general, underlying process. Clearly it is in the interest of such 'gurus' to preserve the mystique associated with their techniques in order to sell their packages and their personalities. Hunt, who is herself psychically gifted and very open to mysticism, apparently feels that there is more to the human energy field she has detected than its electromagnetic aspects[165]. When Hunt proposes "undiscovered energy", I would again suggest, as I did in regard to Rhine's speculation, that what in fact is meant by such speculations are not new types of energy but modes of interaction associated with these fields which are not known to us and which may involve space-time transcendence. Electromagnetic activity is a mode of energetic activity which can co-exist with other modes or forms of the same energy. As Hunt has discovered that the electromagnetic field activity is correlated with the phenomena and states of consciousness closely associated with paranormal activity, we may speculate that such field activity is involved in such processes although they may be but part of a more comprehensive picture yet to be discovered and they may be involved in modes of interaction with other processes which are beyond our conventional physical models. Bohm points out that we don't really know what any *field* is in itself, we only describe behaviour patterns associated with it which makes us feel that it is no longer mysterious[166]. This remark would of course be equally valid for most scientific concepts which we take for granted without really knowing what these concepts actually represent. Talbot notes that Hunt, along with physicist and spiritual healer Barbara Brennan and others tend to favour the holographic metaphor in regard to understanding the paranormal aspects of the aura and healing. Brennan asserts that the aura and healing forces emerge from frequencies arising from the space-time transcending Frequency Domain. They are non-local, potentially simultaneous and everywhere, only appearing to be localised through the process of perception abstracting them from the transcendental Frequency Domain[15].

Psychosomatic processes and body-organizing fields

Brennan also notes that the layers seen by some psychics in the aura, often given names such as astral body, emotional body, etheric body, mental body etc. are also products of perceptual abstraction and different psychics discern different layers depending largely on their previous knowledge of various teachings[167]. We have seen that yogis similarly perceive mental processes according to the selective focuses indoctrinated in them by their respective traditions although all are describing various aspects of the same actual processes. Hunt states that the aura layers seen by many people are actually visual perceptual organizations of information. Describing astral, physical, etheric and spiritual bodies as layers in the auric field is a misnomer, Hunt says, stemming from the metaphorical use of mystical 'bodies' by theosophist Madame Blavatsky which has been taken literally by some[146]. Similarly, Murphy states that all the mystical traditions differ in describing the structure of the so-called *subtle body*[26]. However, there is some agreement that there is an *etheric body* which may be described as a layer of the aura or as distinct from the aura. The etheric body is said to be about the same size as the physical body and is involved in guiding and shaping the growth of the physical body[15]. We have seen that spiritual healing and perhaps other mind-body interactions seem to involve some sort of downward causation from the bodily field to cellular and biochemical processes. If so, then this 'etheric body' is the prime candidate for such a role.

In regard to mind-body interactions in general, it is interesting to note that psychics describe the interpenetration of mental and bodily fields, with claims that a person's life history can be read from the aura and other similar claims. Hunt[165] notes that all of the body's electrical systems are distributed globally throughout the body and are thus, in a sense, 'holographic' (or 'holonomic'). For instance, the EEG recordings measuring brainwave activity can also be measured, though less easily from electrodes attached to the toe. Such notions of interpenetrating energy fields ties in with Ho's notions relating to coherent fields and organization of body processes discussed below. Hunt's work, showing that the aura responds to stimuli prior to brainwave activity, also ties in with Ho's suggestions regarding the sensitivity of organisms to environmental fields. However, I would of course disgree with Hunt's assertions that the mind is not in the brain but in the bodily energy field. Clearly, transfer of information and other interactions may occur between field activity in the brain and other field activity throughout the body. I do not doubt that, to some extent, memories and emotions reverberate in our bodily tissues and fields (as is clear from certain psychosomatic therapies and LSD psychotherapy) and that intuitive and extrasensory perception may be linked to the bodily fields which may be acting as extrasensory information receptors. I have previously noted that the so-called *chakras* at the sites along the spine are not the actual sites of higher states of our minds but these sites may be associated through some sort of connection with the attainment of deeper states of mind. Thus I hold that the actual mind is limited to self-organising field activity in the brain although the mind may have numerous subtle resonances with other bodily fields as well as with environmental fields. Hunt's point about measuring the EEG brainwaves at the toes indicates interpenetrating information throughout the body structures. I have interpreted the yogic *causal body* as the basic self-organising, 'closed' individuality formation in the brain corresponding to lucid deep sleep although psychics may use such terms as 'causal body' for a perceived layer of the aura. I would suggest that such auric interpretations are misunderstandings of the higher yogic knowledge. Furthermore, vast amounts of scientific evidence points to the localization of the mind in the brain and this correlation cannot easily be dismissed. The vague, confused, and often contradictory, descriptions of the auric layers, and the descriptions of subtle bodies and *chakra* energy centres associated with altered states can easily be interpreted as projections of the mind just as in our normal state of consciousness the mind projects itself onto the physical body when in fact the actuality involves representations of bodily features in the brain. Indeed, the drug ketamine can induce states of consciousness in which the physical body disappears from consciousness.

In regard to the question of fields organizing the body, I have mentioned in Section 2(j) that biochemist Rupert Sheldrake has proposed that biological forms take shape through the influence of space-time transcending 'morphogenetic fields'. I have also mentioned that this is related to the yogic notion of the *ākāśa* and to Jung's notion of the Collective Unconscious. Such notions will be discussed below in the section on *karma*. I have also mentioned that theoretical (mathematical) biologist Brian Goodwin, who has given much thought to the philosophical deficiencies of orthodox science, uses the same term 'morphogenetic field' in relation his mathematical models of biological pattern formation which involve clearly defined physical processes[135]. Furthermore, I have mentioned that, in tracing the origin of the field concept in Biology, Goodwin refers to Driesch's notion of *entelechy*, a domain beyond matter, space and time from which organisms derive their self-organizing capacities[33]. Goodwin says his ideas are resonant with those of Goethe whose *archetype* was a set of possible forms united under transformation, or the common generative principles underlying the various manifestations of a form. Goethe's archetype, unlike Driesch's entelechy, did not involve a transcendental realm. Referring to the work of Kauffman and others who have used computer simulations of complex biological systems which show the emergence of elaborately organised patterns of behaviour amongst groups of interlinked elements, Goodwin states that such results "point to biology as a domain of emergent order in space and time that arises from organizational principles of an essentially simple kind". Such simulations of complex systems involve notions of the *edge of chaos* in which attractors (stable states towards which a system is drawn) for living systems exist between normal order and unpredictable, chaotic behaviour allowing the living system a degree of flexibility through access to chaotic fluctuations.[135] Such abstract mathematical notions seem to be reaching towards the point I have made above in regard to Life involving a certain amount of freedom from normal lawful behaviour due to the play of energy which is associated with freedom and vitality.

Using mathematical models run on computer simulations of the forces acting on the cytoplasm of the green alga *Acetabularia,* Goodwin has shown that combinations of positive and negative feedback processes involving the concentration of calcium, which affects the mechanical properties of the cytoplasm, generate the unusual whorl-like cap structure found in *Acetabularia.* The point that Goodwin stresses is that, according to Neo-Darwinism, this whorl-like structure should be an unlikely possibility arrived at through aeons of chance mutations. Goodwin's model shows, on the contrary, that the form seems to be a natural consequence of the physical forces acting within the developing alga. The genes only define the parameters of the forces acting the developmental field in morphogenesis. The organism appears to be spontaneously expressing its intrinsic order or play of forces. Goodwin shows that such models help explain seemingly paradoxical evolutionary issues not satisfactorily explained by Neo-Darwinism, with its reductionist focus on gene mutations, such as convergent evolution and why some salamanders have not radiated out into significantly different forms over the past one hundred million years, as it is the developmental, morphogenetic fields and the chaotic attractors (stable states) associated with stable forms which are responsible for the form and resist the parameter changes brought about by gene mutations[33,135].

The misunderstanding of vitalistic and transcendendalist notions

Goodwin[33] views organisms as fields, "domains of relational order", with the distinctive property of *closure* entailing that an organismic field tends to complete itself if the whole is disrupted in some way. Closure and autonomy do not entail independence, the organism remains an open system, a 'dissipative structure' exchanging matter and energy, a self-sustaining unified field of activity. He is keen to stress the organised structure and the self-sustaining play of forces as opposed to the dualistic notions of matter being animated by a 'life force'. He speaks of 'immanent causation', as opposed to 'transeunt causation' (where cause and effect can be distinguished), drawing upon Faraday's conception of fields and forces to describe the organism as "distributed causality that closes on itself in space and expresses its nature through an ordered sequence of states that also closes in time, expressing a lifestyle". Goodwin recognises the "deep relationship between organisms and minds" highlighted by the above descriptions referring to the work of Piaget on Structuralism. Clearly such notions are relevant to the development of the self/other distinction which Goodwin relates to the question of subjectivity but he does not seem to have a clear idea as to what is meant by consciousness.

Goodwin's work, like Becker's, is significant because it shows that, before we start postulating space-time transcending factors in order to account for certain biological phenomena, we must consider more simple explanations involving known spatio-temporal processes which have largely been ignored by reductionistic science which has focused on molecular interactions and solution chemistry. Both are open-minded scientists who have gone beyond the extremely limited emergent materialism associated with the likes of Sperry and dabbled in the shallow waters of the more esoteric approaches without taking the plunge into the transcendental depths of Being and Becoming. As we have seen in other areas of debate, Reality transcends the opposites of relative knowledge abstracted by minds and includes elements of all approaches. Goodwin clearly shows the influence of Piaget with his recognition of concepts such as *closure* and the fascinating parallels between biological organization and cognitive organization[33] which relates to Gestalt psychology and organismic philosophy. Piaget has also influenced the 'Biogenetic Structuralists' such as Laughlin, whose work I have referred to, who focus on neural networks rather than the field aspects of cognitive organization. Goodwin's realization of the similarity between organisms and minds, especially taking into account his emphasis on organisms as closed, self-organising fields exchanging energy with the environment like 'dissipative structures', clearly relates to my views in regard to the nature of the mind but they also indicate possible resonance-like interactions between mental and bodily fields which may be involved in mind-body interactions.

Although Goodwin has shown much sympathy for the mystical views of the Renaissance magi who, prior to the rise of Cartesian Science, viewed Mind and Nature as a single co-ordinated domain[37], he does not seem to fully appreciate what such notions actually entail in regard to questions such as panpsychism and transcendentalism. In regard to the transcendentalist notions of Driesch and Sheldrake, Goodwin is correct to be sceptical as both Driesch and Sheldrake have failed to show how such transcendentalist notions can be practically applied to aid our understanding of biological organization, morphogenesis and related questions. As with numerous Western thinkers dabbling with transcendentalist notions, Driesch and Sheldrake are cut off from the living yogic tradition which has the long-established means of accessing transcendental realms and thus vastly greater knowledge in regard to matters such as mind-body interactions including those with transcendental influences. A closer examination of Goodwin's own work, taken within the context of this essay, shows how the old 'life force' and transcendentalist notions which Goodwin rejects remain hidden beyond his limited frame of reference. Goodwin has shown how the alga *Acetabularia* develops its characteristic form by spontaneously expressing its intrinsic order, the self-sustaining play of forces described by Goodwin's equations in abstract mathematical terms and simulated on a computer. But in the actual organism, existing in panpsychic Reality, such spontaneous expression of intrinsic forces (referred to in the plural) is in fact the free expression of (the singular) energy in the form of various forces, constrained by the spatio-temporal organisation of the organismic system so that it acts to recreate the characteristic *Acetabularia* form. This very energy, associated in ourselves with *freedom* and *vitality* is the source of the old vitalistic notion of the *life force* (or *prāṇa*) animating matter which, in a sense, is exactly what this energy, manifesting as the various forces, is doing. Similarly, if we consider this energy in itself, devoid of the limiting adjuncts imposed upon it by the organismic constraints which result in the manifestation of spatio-temporally limited forces, we will find that it is, in itself, free of these space-time relations, capable of modes of interactions beyond spatio-temporal limitations, and thus can be considered a transcendental principle. We have already seen that Prigogine's mathematical abstractions of self-organising 'dissipative structure' formation, which Goodwin himself links to what an *organism* actually is, indicate that the creative principle in Nature which brings about such self-organisation and seeming individuation is the flow of energy. Thus rather than talk of *entelechy* and/or a mysterious vitalistic life force, what we should really be considering is how the spatio-temporal process we call the *organism* emerges from the underlying activity of this, essentially transcendental, creative principle which brings about self-organization, integration and animates the material components of the living system which, in this two-way organismic process, constrain the spontaneous freedom of this principle.

The organism as a coherent, emergent space-time structure

A biophysicist who has been associated with Goodwin, Mae-Wan Ho, goes beyond Goodwin's Piagetian approach and refers to the philosophies of Whitehead and Bergson as well as to the perennialist wisdom. Ho is amenable to notions of a transcendental domain from which space-time orders emerge, referring to the work of Schommers who has reformulated quantum mechanics by incorporating Mach's principle, showing how Space and Time emerge from real processes. Ho states that an organism's internal space-time structure arises out of its own activities, being the organisation of these activities. Ho points out that, as well as being a spatio-temporally organised process, the organism is like a 'dissipative structure'.[91]

Ho is inclined towards the view of the world as energetic vibrations, noting that Quantum Theory reveals that matter itself is composed of vibrations. She discusses the inadequacies of conventional thermodynamic formulations of entropy, developed for bulk phases, in regard to the highly organised space-time structures which are organisms. More specifically she looks at the notion of *coherence* arising in Quantum Theory and the question of biological organisation. She refers to the ideas put forward by physicist Herbert Frölich that phenomena resembling the collective modes of activity found in superconducting materials may be operating in biological systems. Metabolic energy may actually be stored as collective modes of electromechanical and electromagnetic vibrations called *coherent excitations.* These collective modes may be bands of frequencies with varying spatial extents, with the frequencies coupled together so communication occurs between these modes or coherent excitations. Such modes would be involved in long-range order and in efficient energy transfer. Ho links such activity to the sensitivity of organisms to external electromagnetic fields from which they may detect faint signals below the level of thermal noise. The organism must be able to amplify such faint signals pointing to intrinsic electromagnetic fields organising the living system which exhibit a high degree of coherence reacting to the external fields. Ho cites evidence from her own work on fruitfly development which is disrupted by brief exposure to weak magnetic fields[91]. I have noted the similarities between these ideas and those of Hunt above.

Ho points out that the concept of *coherence* refers to *wholeness* although, in a coherent state, local freedom goes hand in hand with global cohesion just as we find in living systems. In order to achieve coherence, the collective modes need not all occupy one frequency, rather the various modes have to be coupled together so that energy propagates between them. Thus there can be domains of local autonomy within a globally coherent organismic field. Decoupling of local modes from the whole may be related to developments such as malignancies. Ho also refers to research showing coherence in biological rhythms, muscle contraction and brainwave activity. She also cites evidence for a system of communication that sends emergency messages simultaneously to all organs faster than could be sent by nerve impulse transmission[91].

Ho views the organism as a coherent space-time structure; the individual is a field of coherent activity. Within coherence time there is no space separation and, within coherence volume, no time separation so that all parts of a coherent field operate as a unified whole. Ho links this notion of coherence to quantum non-locality, the subjective experience of time and extrasensory perception[91]. Clearly, these actions of collective modes of excitations organising body structures and coupling together different structures accord well with our knowledge of biological organisation. Ho's ideas tie in with Becker's on electromagnetic fields in development and control of body systems. The coupling of local collective modes also allows us to consider possible processes underlying mind-body interactions with the suspicion that such theoretical considerations of collective modes of vibrations will one day converge with the empirical data of Hunt and others on the human energy field. Indeed, Ho herself is willing to consider amplification mechanisms for receipt of information involving some sort of resonance rather than conventional energy transfer. She is also willing to speculate that the transcendence of normal space-time relations in coherent systems may have some relation to extrasensory perception[91]. Such ideas remain highly speculative of course but they do show that, as Quantum Theory begins to encroach upon traditional biology, parallels again begin to arise between scientific speculations and mystical knowledge. The reader may recall the comment by Nobel laureate neurobiologist George Wald, whom I quoted in the previous essay, that it was easier to explain views such as mind as a creative principle, primary to matter and pervading the universe, to physicists than to biologists. This is not surprising given that Physics, at its limits, encroaches upon metaphysics and the developments that have occurred through the need to interpret the meaning of Quantum Theory. Biologists generally tend not to have much of an advanced knowledge of physics and may remain rooted to secondary school physics which does not go far beyond the developments of the 19th century. An interesting parallel is seen with the approaches of Freud and Jung in regard to Psychology. Jung remained keenly interested in the New Physics which was being created around him, even collaborating with one of its greatest pioneers, Wolfgang Pauli who realised that Physics was flawed in leaving out Spirit. Meanwhile Freud remain trapped in the old Newtonian world-view, with his psychological mechanisms, as Grof has noted[41], being little more than projections of Newtonian principles onto the mind. Just as the influx of physicists into Biology in the post-war period, partly inspired by Schrödinger, led to the developments of Molecular Biology, we can hope to see future creative developments in Biology as new ideas from metaphysically more open-minded Physics filters down.

Psychoneuroimmunology and visualization in mind-body interactions

More conventional interpretations of mind-body interactions have been developed including the new field of psychoneuroimmunology. The original research showing the effect of Pavlovian conditioning on the immune response was undertaken in the Soviet Union back in the 1920s. More recent work in the USA by Robert Ader showed that rats taught to associate saccharin-flavoured water with nausea, due to the presence of the chemical cyclophosphamide, also had their immune responses suppressed by the cyclophosphamide. However, immunosuppression was also found in conditioned rats given saccharin-flavoured water even when the cyclophosphamide had been removed. The interpretation of this result has involved the discovery of neuropeptide receptors on the lymphocytes of the immune system allowing modulation of the immune response through the release of neuropeptides into the bloodstream by nerve endings. Furthermore, hormones released by the hypothalamus in response to stress are known to release chemicals, from the adrenal glands and the pituitary, which directly affect the immune system. Apparently such findings have come as something of a shock to orthodox immunologists who took it for granted that the immune system operated independently as lymphocytes could operate effectively in test tubes[159]. Obviously, these orthodox immunologists had not been reading *The Organism* by Kurt Goldstein, which as I mentioned above, repeatedly warns against conclusions drawn from studies of parts of organisms studied in isolation from the whole organism.

Clearly, the discovery of chemical linkages between the brain and the immune system responsive to psychological factors tells us something important about mind-body interactions. However, it seems as if some researchers are prepared to go no further beyond known mechanisms in order to account for such interactions when a lot more is clearly involved than just the effect of hormones and neuropeptides on the immune system. How it is that mental states actually effect the release of chemicals is a question which is not seriously addressed by psychoneuroimmunology which ignores the initial downward causation processes through which the mind influences biochemistry and cell biology. Remarkable evidence is available from the study of Multiple Personality Disorders showing that the control of the body by different alter personalities can result in marked physiological changes. Cases of different allergic sensitivities could be interpreted using psychoneuroimmunological mechanisms but these cannot explain why different personalities may respond differently to different drugs, exhibit different scars, cysts and even tumours which appear and disappear depending upon which alter is in control of the body[15,88]. Bruises, birthmarks and skin colour changes are some of the physiological changes that may occur during the reliving of birth experiences in LSD psychotherapy[41]. The creation of stigmata in certain individuals seems to occur through constant application of visualization or self-hypnosis. Murphy notes that almost all instances of extraordinary bodily development or development of extraordinary capacities involves disciplined self-observation and visualization of desired capacities[26]. Such evidence seems to indicate the existence of organizing fields throughout the body which are in some way coupled to the mental field and open to modulation by the generation of appropriate mental imagery. It has been suggested that, as in psychokinesis, such transformations may involve influences at a transcendental level acting upon the generative matrix of the physical body's manifestation[15]. It seems as if the extraordinary control over physiological processes exhibited by certain yogis involves, once again, attainment of deep *samādhi* as is involved in the *siddhis,* along with symbolic visualization of the desired effects[168]. The yogis with their disciplined mastery of mind-body interactions are the ideal subjects for study and are already being investigated by certain open-minded biomedical researchers[169]. The now well-known Biofeedback techniques were developed following studies by Alyce and Elmer Green of the displays of mind over body by Swami Rāma. We should keep in mind possibilities involving influence of the transcendental generative matrix of the body whilst simultaneously considering more accessible interpretations such as some sort of resonance between the physical correlates of mental images and some sort of analog information in organising fields, along with downward causation processes whereby the states of these fields influence the growth and development of the cells and tissues of the body.

2(m). ON NOTIONS RELATING TO *KARMA*

> *The question, "Will I survive death" cannot be satisfactorily answered except as a subset of the larger question, "Who and what am I?"* Charles Tart

Origins of the classical Karma and Rebirth doctrines

Questions relating to the notion of *karma* and the possibility of reincarnation have long been shrouded in confusion as is evident in the difficulties faced by the Buddhist tradition which simultaneously held to the Doctrine of *Anatta* (no permanent self) and also to various doctrines pertaining to supposed rebirth. McDermott[170] notes that the Buddha chose to remain silent on this apparently contradictory state of affairs so as not to confuse the uneducated. Creel[171] states that it is widely agreed that *karma* is the basic fact whereas the doctrine of rebirth is derivative. Students of the Indian tradition are familiar with the assertion that the Doctrine of *Karma* was adopted by the Aryans from the Rājanyas of the Eastern Indian Vrātya country[172]. Halbfass points out that the theory and mythology of transmigration and *karma* is not found in the most ancient Vedic scriptures, remaining controversial and tentative in the *Upaniṣads,* the last of the Vedas. However, the classical Indian tradition, steeped in the Doctrine of *Karma,* projected the doctrine back into even the oldest Vedic texts. Halbfass notes that, as the tradition developed, religious schemes were increasingly superimposed upon empirical observations, with the *Mīmāṃsā darśana* carrying the heritage of the 'pre-karmic' past into the classical era where *karma* and *saṃsāra* (the cycle of rebirth) had become key doctrines[173]. The reader will recall that I use the term *saṃsāra* (literally "without cease") in the verse to mean the (ceaseless flux of the) phenomenal world which was its older, and I would argue its correct, meaning. Obeyesekere stresses the key role of ethicization of philosophy in the development of the *karma*/rebirth doctrine. Buddhism and Jainism concerned themselves with converting laypeople and thus with questions of the social world and morality. The Doctrine of Rebirth thus developed as a response to the questions of morality in the social world rather than as interpretations of empirical facts[174]. Long notes that the vocabulary of merits and demerits associated with good and evil deeds were adapted from the world of trade and commerce as though deeds were so many items on a financial ledger[95]. Such projection and superimposition of new doctrines onto the old are commonplace in all traditions and the superimposition of Christian doctrines over the older Pagan traditions being well-known. It is also interesting to note that Jesus Christ's teachings were partly a response to the miserable economic conditions of indebtedness prevalent in Galilee in his time, so one again finds particular economic conditions projected onto spirituality in Christianity.

Just a cursory glance at the history of the rebirth notion in the Indian tradition shows its rather tenuous status and current attempts to revive it, albeit bereft of the nonsensical ledger of merits and demerits, are fraught with seemingly insurmountable problems. It will be obvious from my interpretation of the nature of the mind as a brain process and of personal identity being based upon the life-history memories stored in the brain that I do not agree with notions of personal transmigration. However, like the Buddhists with their Doctrine of *Anatta,* it is necessary to explain why certain empirical facts seem to suggest the possibility that a person has transmigrated. Once we consider the actual nature of *karma* as described in the yogic texts and combine it with our notions of personal identity, transcendental planes of being, holographic/holonomic metaphors and mind-body interactions, it will become clear that the evidence suggestive of transmigration of personalities and supposed 'rebirth' may be reinterpreted in a manner consistent with the overall scheme of things presented in this essay.

Eradication of habitual memory traces (saṃskāra) in Patañjali Yoga

Coward describes *karma* as the 'filters' resulting from past personal and cultural patterns of behaviour through which our present experience is constructed. This is related to the notion of the mind as a reducing valve, filtering out the vast majority of stimuli impinging upon us. The purpose of Patañjali Yoga (i.e. the *Yoga Sūtras*) is to decondition the karmic filters that cover discriminate awareness. Coward notes that such deconditioning of habitual patterns of perception resembles the 'deautomatization' of perception notion put forward by Deikman in his attempt to explain meditation in psychological terms. *Karma* theory suggests, says Coward, that our instincts, predispositions and innate tendencies toward particular kinds of categorizations are derived from repeated karmic patterns[175].

The reader may also recall that Coward's description of the supernormal yogic perception (*pratibhā*) involved removal of the filtering or distorting *saṃskāra* (memory traces) allowing a direct transcendental illumination of the object in itself, devoid of mental constructions. Coward states that *saṃskāra* are the result of habitual repetition of a common thought or behaviour pattern until it becomes deeply rooted in the psyche. Or, using Patañjali's terms, such repetitive *cittavritti* leave behind a *saṃskāra* (memory trace) which is constantly ready to sprout and recreate the *cittavritti* from which it resulted, until a deeply rooted *vāsanā* (karmic pattern) is established. Meditation purges our 'unconscious' of these memory traces by bringing them into conscious awareness. The memories that arise come, not only from this life, but also from apparent past lives. A perfected yogi thus brings all of his 'unconscious' into his present knowledge. The removal of such distorting *saṃskāra* from this and past lives allows true knowledge of reality[28].

Potter, discussing Patañjali's view of *karma,* states that an act (*karman*), performed with purposive intent and passion (emotion), creates a karmic residue (*karmāśaya*) which is accompanied by dispositional tendencies (*saṃskāra*) of more than one sort. These include traces (*vāsanā*) which can reproduce memories of the originating act or *vāsanā* which produce afflictions (*kleśa,* which I would interpret as emotions). Patañjali Yoga goes on to give elaborate descriptions of the different sorts of karmic residues which are reactivated either in this lifetime or in another lifetime and the transmigration of the *citta* (mindstuff), containing the unactivated karmic residues, at death to a new body where it apparently determines three things, the kind of body (*jāti*, species), the length of life (*āyus*) under normal circumstances and the affective tone of its experiences (*bhoga*). The *Yoga* tradition denies any intermediate state between death and rebirth (as also did Theravāda Buddhism) whereas *Advaita Vedānta* develops fanciful notions of a transmigrating subtle body controlled by the *jīva* (individual self) which leaves the body through one of its apertures and travels to the sun or the moon[84].

Brown, in his study of the three authoritative (Hindu and

Buddhist) yogic traditions, states that *saṃskāra* are propensities, or subtle biasing factors, built into the very structure of perception at its most fundamental level which result in the habitual distortion of reality. Through insight meditation, the yogi eradicates these *saṃskāra* resulting in a significant transformation in the stream of consciousness, attaining so-called seedless *samādhi*. After the cessation of the gross content of perception, the mindstuff continues to transform due to the activity of *saṃskāra*. Yogic practice allows momentary cessation of the wave patterns and the *saṃskāra* are eradicated although these moments of cessation leave their own impressions which affect subsequent experiences[23]. Thus *saṃskāra* appear to be the subtle impressions left by the *cittavritti* (wave-like fluctuations of the mindstuff) which act as the predisposing factors underlying gross perceptions through their seed-like tendency to recreate the *cittavritti* from which they were produced.

Karma as avidyā/māyā and transmigration as dependent co-origination

Halbfass notes that, for Shankara, the whole world owes its very existence to karmic attachment and superimposition (*adhyāsa*). *Avidyā* (Nescience, Ignorance) is the root cause of our karmic involvement and, along with the *māyā*, is co-extensive with *karma*. Halbfass states that Shankara's universalization of *karma* so that it is co-extensive with the realm of *avidyā/māyā* in fact devalues *karma* in that *karma* is part of the cosmic illusion and thus, from an absolute point of view, there is no transmigration[173]. Potter states that, in *Advaita*, the *ātman-brahman* is never really bound nor really acts but only appears to do so due to the superimposition of *avidyā*. Realization of this true Self through attainment of *mokṣa* (liberation) ends the karmic process[84].

As I have stated above, McDermott has noted that the Buddhist Doctrine of *Anatta*, and also the Doctrine of *Anicca* (impermanence), do not sit comfortably with the Doctrine of Rebirth. This results in the Buddha's teaching that the being experiencing the fruits of past-life deeds is neither the same nor different from the past-life being who performed those deeds. The Buddha taught the Doctrine of Dependent Co-origination in which the transmigrant is not a permanent entity of any sort but a locus of points in a changing causal stream[170]. Matthews[176] states that what was reborn was an evolving consciousness (*viññana sotam*) whose quality had been conditioned by *karma*. McDermott notes that Nāgasena, the great Indian Buddhist philosopher, stresses this view that there is no transmigrant in the strict sense. Rather deeds (*kamma*) continue to exist through their potential to modify the continuity of life; the potential of the act (*kamma*) remains like a shadow and may actualise itself in the future. This notion resembles the later development by the Buddhist Vaibhāṣikas of the concept of latent *karma*, which is a latent potential impressed upon the psychophysical stream by an ethically significant act, which continues to reproduce itself imperceptibly and may produce results at some later moment in time[170]. Similar notions were developed by other schools in which a potential remains after an act, lying dormant like a seed. In Patañjali Yoga, *saṃskāra* are viewed as seeds (*bīja*) constantly ready to sprout[28]. In Theravāda Buddhism, *kamma* is identified with *cetana*, an intentional impulse, i.e. ịt is not only the will but also the impulse to carry through the will into action. Such intentional impulses or *kamma* are never lost; they cannot be wiped out unless their result is first experienced in this life or another[170].

Events at the moment of death

Theravāda Buddhism strongly denied the existence of an intermediate (between-life) being although some later schools of Buddhism disputed this. However, as with later Buddhism, Theravāda held that events at the moment of death were of particular significance and that one's final thoughts could affect the karmic ledger accrued during the course of one's life. *Nibbāna* (*nirvāna*) was the ultimate goal, the cessation of *kamma*, freeing one from the cycle of rebirth[170]. Schmithausen[177] notes that it may be significant that, throughout later Buddhist texts, one finds passages implying that it is one's resolve at the moment of death that determines where and how one is reborn. This brings us to the well-known *Tibetan Book of the Dead* which describes a number of steps during the process of dying where one can attain liberation from the cycle of rebirth.

Sogyal Rinpoche states that the Buddhist teachings aim to let the deep Mind, or Buddha Mind, shine through by removing the cloudy, confused thinking mind which covers it. This realization of the underlying Buddha Mind comes very clearly at the moment of death although some people may become unconscious and lose the opportunities to gain liberation[178]. First comes the 'basic clear light experience', when the light shines through. If the dying person can 'let go', leave behind all attachment to the world and 'direct the mind into its inherent luminosity', then complete and perfect liberation is attained. If this basic clear light experience is missed, the dying person begins to relive the strongest life experiences, (a near-death flashback of memories in my opinion). In effect nescience sets in again[179]. It is this return to nescience which creates rebirth, which Rinpoche says is simply a continuation of our habits and tendencies (i.e. *karma*). Apparently this 'waking up' involves feeling like you are being blown about by a wind to all the places you have been in life[178]. Stablein notes that the movement of the (karmic) wind entails knowledge of specialized yogic techniques. The so-called *bardo* state is an imagined state of wandering that dooms one to rebirth. Stablein says that it is misleading to say that *karma* moves, transforms or stands still although this is the popular view of rebirth. The 'wanderer' is battling with the forces of his own *karma* attempting to attain liberation, thrust up and down by karmic power[179]. Rinpoche notes that all the experiences are but mental projections and that the *Tibetan Book of the Dead* itself states that the wanderer should cultivate the thought that all this is the manifestation of the mind. He also states that, in this 'wandering' stage, the dying person becomes clairvoyant. The various visions that the dying person sees, says Rinpoche, are in fact displays of energies of the true mind (the deep Mind) and if the dying person realizes this and does not recoil from them, liberation can be attained at this stage[178]. Stablein points out that the Tantric Buddhism of Tibet and Nepal has a formalized conception of an in-between being not found in other parts of South Asia but, for all the colourful imagery of the *bardo* state, the various steps in the *Tibetan Book of the Dead* remain structurally related to the general Buddhist Dependent Origination process[179].

Insights from Rajneesh on Karma and Ribirth

Some insight into the nature of *karma*, given in modern terms, is found in the work of Bhagwan Shree Rajneesh, as discussed by Gussner[180]. The reader should note that Rajneesh, prior to founding the Transcendental Meditation movement was a university professor of philosophy and was well versed in the yogic texts. Recall that Coward described how *saṃskāras* were removed from the 'unconscious' by bringing memories into conscious awareness. Rajneesh accepts the traditional distinction of the three levels of *karma* as found in the *Yoga Sūtras* (or Patañjali Yoga) and in *Advaita Vedānta. Sañcita Karma* is the total *karma* from all of the past lives. *Prārabdha karma* is that portion of the total worked out in this life. The *Kriyāman karma* is the portion of the *prārabdha karma* worked out on a day-to-day basis. Rajneesh interprets these three levels as being equivalent to what he calls the *unconscious, subconscious* and *conscious* domains of the mind. The Rajneesh follower is supposed to become 'mindful' of the conscious level and gradually extend this state of alert mindfulness (which Rajneesh calls 'awareness') to the deeper mental processes generating normal conscious mental activity. Rajneesh asserts that what is done in 'unawareness' (or identification with surface activity without being alert to the deeper processes) becomes a *karma* and leaves a trace (*saṃskāra*). Thus every thought or intention occurring in a state of identification with the mental fluctuation (*vritti*) leaves *saṃskāra* but activity occurring when consciousness withdraws into its own nature as a witness does not[180]. This corresponds with traditional views of *karma* being generated by identification with the ego.

Rajneesh says that whatever one does in a state of identification generates a sort of reverberation, it persists in a potential manner. The act creates a 'channel' into which the energy from the First Principle runs readily into. This channel automatically deepens itself, absorbing energy from one's Being and eventually becomes a habit. In the end such habits take over and live through you although the ego continues to fool itself that it is in control. Gussner, in summarizing Rajneesh's view, states that if a channel is made it has to be completed. Situations will be encountered which activate the channel. Escape from entrapment in habitual patterns involves reliving the root cause of the habitual pattern in the light of awareness in *pratiprasava* which heals the wound or eliminates the pattern. *Pratiprasava* appears to be equivalent to abreaction, an intense reliving of the original impressions which are allowed to rise up into consciousness through relaxation and focusing. Reliving the experience without judgement is required to allow the light of consciousness to heal the wound. Gussner notes that this *pratiprasava* process resembles the reliving of traumas and other emotionally charged experiences in Primal Scream and similar forms of alternative therapy, and Rajneesh himself notes the similarity to Primal Scream therapy[180]. I would add that abreaction is common in LSD psychotherapy and also in therapy for Multiple Personality Disorders. Rajneesh asserts that karmic impressions disappear without trace if re-experienced with sufficient intensity, completing an incomplete unit of experience. This parallels the findings of Grof's LSD psychotherapy where reliving (usually traumatic) childhood, perinatal or past-life memories seems to complete, incomplete gestalts and alleviates the psychological or psychosomatic problems associated with it[41].

Gussner notes that, although Rajneesh accepts some aspects of traditional *karma* theory, he rejects the popular usage of *karma* in regard to social relations, chastising social *karma* theory as an invention of priests to maintain the *status quo*. Rajneesh also rejects determination of type of birth and length of life. He does, however, accept that *karma* determines the type of experiences one has. Gussner comments that Rajneesh tends to agree with those who hold *karma* to involve a person's reactions to what happens to them rather than what actually happens to them. The results of acts are the 'wounds' left in the mind rather than some future retributive event[180]. Hunt[146] also chastises the traditional views of *karma* and rebirth on various grounds. One interesting point she makes is that the doctrine of reincarnation professes tight cause and effect relationships between 'lifehoods' and the 'soul'. Cause and effect laws, Hunt points out, relate to the time-space aspects of the physical world which is not the world of 'lifehoods' and 'souls'.

In regard to Rebirth, Gussner notes that Rajneesh adopts a Buddhistic stance of transmigration without transmigrants. Although Rajneesh seems to take seriously some of the fantasies associated with the so-called *bardo* experience such as different types of soul and their likelihoods of finding suitable wombs etc., much of what Rajneesh actually says about supposed interlife states is of interest in the context of my discussion. Rajneesh compares such 'interlife experiences' to dreams but the dream-like transformations occur in a disembodied state. As in dreams, there is no normal sense of time passing. The dead, says Rajneesh, exist right amongst us, like air waves or radio waves and the like which can co-exist if they do not interfere with each other. It is meaningless to talk of movement as space and time depend on the presence of a body but spirit possession can occur in living people, especially those in great fear or those in deep prayer who become possessed by tortured, miserable souls and by higher souls respectively. The dead cannot communicate unless they possess living bodies. No personal development occurs in the interlife state although some may occur in the semi-deceased state which Tibetans call the *bardo* state[180].

Rajneesh's views are of particular interest, first of all because he identifies the dissipation of karmic forces with the abreactive reliving of deeply repressed memories as is also found in primal scream, LSD and Gestalt therapies. Why karmic traces should only form when identification with the ego occurs is not clear but it seems as if the yogic testimony on this point reflects some difference in processing of memory related to the involvement of attention whereby memory traces are only created if attentional processing occurs. This ties in with the Buddhist view of *kamma* as *cetana* or intentional impulse in which volition plays a key role. Clearly, Rajneesh's description of channels feeding off the energy of the First Principle or Being are suggestive of reverberating neural patterns drawing energy from the RAS brainwaves. Perhaps the non-karmic activity involves fixed instinctual repertoires which do not reverberate as no learning process is involved. Why the intense reliving of deeply repressed experiences should eliminate the traces of such traumatic experiences is not clear. Rajneesh speaks of completing incomplete units of experience, like Grof's talk of incomplete psychological gestalts. Given that *saṃskāra* are said to be like seeds (*bīja*) constantly ready to sprout, it seems as if the reliving experience may dissipate some sort of tension that has built up. Clearly there is some relationship here to Deikman's deautomatization concept whereby the focusing (or 'reinvestment') of attention on learned behavioural patterns seems to decondition these fixed patterns. Rajneesh says that the light of awareness or light of consciousness is the force which heals the wounds of karmic impressions. Coupled with the need for completion, this may imply that the investment of attention involves an additional supply of energy releasing some sort of tensions associated with the neuro-anatomic correlates of karmic residues, perhaps involving an energetic threshold.

Insight from LSD psychotherapy on Karma and the mythology of Rebirth

Rajneesh's comments on rebirth are also of interest as, although he uses the word 'souls', his comments make it clear that he is not referring to transmigrants. His use of the metaphor of airwaves or radio waves and his assertion that spirit possession involves a resonance with the mental state of the possessed person are also of great interest as such information ties in with knowledge gained from LSD research and parapsychological studies relating to such 'reincarnation-like' phenomena. Grof's LSD psychotherapy provides us with much useful informations in regard to issues relating to *karma* which become apparent at transpersonal levels of mind (i.e. when one has reached beyond one's own personal memories). Indeed Grof refers to the futility of suicide realised in transpersonal experiences which reveal the impossibility of escaping one's karmic patterns or the cycles of death and rebirth[41]. However, Grof does not elaborate on the workings of *karma* although he has mentioned that he personally believes that what survives death is an immaterial organizing principle which organises the body and also conscious contents[181]. In this regard it is interesting to note Hunt's view that, whereas memories from our present life are stored in the brain, past-life information is stored in the auric energy field. She even argues that, because acupuncture can result in the release of past-life memories, this again points to the auric energy field as their store[146]. Interestingly, the leading scientific journal *Nature,* closely aligned with the views of the British scientific establishment which is still steeped in positivism and reductionism, has just published a survey showing that, of 1,000 randomly chosen scientists from the USA, about 40 per cent believe in a personal god and an immortal soul. Indeed, the far less radical views expressed by Sheldrake in his book *A New Science of Life* provoked the response from *Nature* that it was "the best candidate for burning there has been for many years".

Grof's LSD psychotherapy reveals that we have access, not only to our memories from early childhood but also to memories from our existence in the womb and our birth experiences which seem to underly myths from various cultures and religious mythologies about rebirth after death. The baby passing through the birth canal, deprived of oxygen, apparently has a near-death experience and, upon escaping the constricting channel and beginning to breathe for the first time, has a feeling, which when relived as an adult, is like being reborn after (virtually) dying. Reliving this 'death-rebirth' experience often involves resonances with culturally indoctrinated images such as those relating to the supposed 'resurrection' of Jesus Christ. Indeed, Grof's work on such perinatal experiences should help to rid us, in the long term, of the childish myths of being born again after death and myths related to the experience of blissful life in the womb espoused by some religious traditions which are based on such shallow encounters with the 'unconscious'. Beyond perinatal experiences we have access to memories of a transpersonal nature, i.e. memories from other people, creatures and non-living entities. These memories may be of individual beings or they may be what seems to be syncretic fusions of the memories of countless individuals sharing the same sorts of experiences, usually linked on the basis of the emotional character of the experience. Of critical importance here is the fact that access to these memories seems to be determined by resonance of form in that such collective memories are experienced when one is reliving experiences with a similar emotional character to those of the collective experiences from the past. Grof notes that scenes from different historical contexts can occur simultaneously and appear to be connected by their experiential characteristics[41]. Recall that Rajneesh claimed that spirit possession occurs mainly in people experiencing traumatic fears or deep prayer and the possession is by spirits of the same character as the recipient's state. Karmic myths relating to choice of foetus and similar factors are all suggestive of an underlying principle of resonance of form of memories onto which are projected fancy mythologies involving rebirth of transmigrants.

The principle of resonance of form also seems to apply to the non-syncretic memories from other individuals in that it seems as if subjects are initially capable of reliving transpersonal memories from family members, relatives and ancestors. This then progressively broadens out to clan, race, species etc. and on to ever more far-removed types of beings[15,41]. Karmic folklore about the same protagonists or problems being encountered life after life (indeed Jung made related claims after spirit possession experiences supposedly by the Gnostic Basilides from ancient Alexandria[29]) seems to me to be nothing more than fanciful projections superimposed upon the resonance with experiences of similar form, either individual or collective, from the past. I myself, whilst deep in contemplation writing this work, have felt possessed by the spirits of philosophers past hunched over their texts in their monasteries, resembling the rather reclusive existence that my destiny has forced me to live in order to complete this work. Whatever memories one relives, it seems as if some commonality of experience is required to tune into them although LSD subjects eventually seem to be capable of becoming one with virtually anything imaginable. Recall that Aurobindo pointed out that all of our imaginations and fantasies are themselves based on deeper aspects of Reality of which we are not aware in our normal state of existence. Although some of these experiences may be largely fantasy, even if the fantasy is based on some subtle order of Reality, the LSD subject appears to be able to gain access to knowledge about entities which she or he would not otherwise have been expected to know. Grof claims to have produced independent confirmation of some of the claims made by LSD subjects in regard to natural phenomena or past events[41,182]. Thus if the experience of oneness with more familiar entities seems to have such a basis in Reality, we cannot so easily dismiss the claims of experiencing oneness with other entities more far-removed from our everyday realm of perception as pure fantasy. Various psychological or psychosomatic problems have been traced by LSD psychotherapy to traumatic experiences from childhood, birth or transpersonal so-called past-life memories. I mentioned above in regard to *pratiprasava* that these problems were usually resolved by the subject allowing these memories to surface and reliving these seemingly incomplete psychological gestalts which seemed to demand completion through such surfacing into consciousness. Talbot[15] notes that the psychiatry textbook, *Trauma, Trance and Transformation* warns those learning hypnotherapy that such past-life memories may arise spontaneously and also notes that they may have remarkable healing effects. Grof states that confronting the underlying experience is usually considerably more difficult and painful than living with the symptoms it generates[41].

Reincarnation phenomena and parapsychological approaches to 'Afterlife Survival'

Seemingly the most startling evidence related to the notion of reincarnation comes from studies like those of Ian Stevenson, a psychiatry professor, who has carefully documented nearly three thousand cases of seeming reincarnation. Stevenson[15] has often managed to verify the assertions made by children claiming to be reincarnations of other people by checking autopsies and various other sources of information relating to the deceased person. Interestingly, Stevenson states that he finds no compelling evidence for 'retributive *karma*', i.e. any punishment for our 'sins'. However, he does find that psychological traits like moral conduct, interests and aptitudes are shared by the deceased and the living person claiming to be their reincarnation. Most interestingly, Stevenson has found that the children may have unusual physical features in common with the deceased such as deformities, facial features and skin pigmentation. More frequently, the child bears scars or birthmarks which correspond to knife wounds, bullet-holes or other injuries responsible for the death of the seemingly reincarnated personality. Stevenson suggests that such evidence indicates that some sort of 'extended body' which acts as a template for the physical body has been carried over, bearing the imprints of the fatal wounds; a view resembling that of Grof's aforementioned belief that an immaterial organizing principle survives or the widely held folklore views that some sort of *astral* or *subtle* body is the transmigrant.

Parapsychologist Hoyt Edge finds the concept of an astral body difficult to make intelligible[150]. Indeed, J.B. Rhine called for the abandonment of parapsychological research into afterlife survival in 1960 because clairvoyant channeling and similar paranormally derived information could not be adequately distinguished from ESP information obtained from living people[183]. Edge notes the enormous difficulties presented by the concept of personal survival and focuses on parapsychological theories assuming impersonal survival of aspects of consciousness. C.D. Broad, Edge notes, suggested that, just as radio waves can persist as possible sounds after the station has gone off the air, the dispositional basis (or the potential for) consciousness may survive, having no experience unless picked-up by an appropriate organism. Edge states that he finds Broad's view emotionally unsatisfying, asking of what use is the survival of the bare dispositional basis of consciousness. He also asserts that there doesn't seem to be any evidence for this view[150]. Edge's emotional response seems very strange to me as such survival of the bare dispositional basis (which sounds very much like a modern reinterpretation of *saṃskāra,* the dispositional traces) may just occur as a natural consequence of the way the world manifests. The Buddhist notion of Dependent Co-origination asserts that all individual phenomena are interdependent and mutually condition each other as, for instance, is found in Nāgasena's view of potentials of acts remaining like shadows to influence the causal stream of life. In response to Edge's question of what use such survival of the dispositional basis of consciousness might serve, one may postulate that such surviving potentials may act as Nature's learning mechanism operating through resonance of form type effects allowing for transgenerational transfer of instinctual patterns and perhaps other forms as has been suggested by Sheldrake with his notion of morphic resonance. In response to Edge's point about evidence, I suspect that Edge's view of what constitutes *evidence* would preclude the yogic knowledge of *saṃskāra,* the *ākāśa* and related facts which lie beyond the scope of parapsychology which aims to emulate the methods of positivistic science which has excluded consciousness altogether.

A more popular theory of non-personal survival, notes Edge, is the field theory associated with Gardner Murphy and, more recently, William Roll. It seems as if the key consideration inspiring this view has been that situations involving ego-dissolution (or loss of a sharp sense of individuality) facilitate paranormal events thus indicating that loosening of individuality allows the field aspects of consciousness to come to the fore. Following on from this, it is argued that when the biological individuality disintegrates, the field aspects of consciousness may survive. Roll argues that evidence such as the fact that the supposedly-dead communicator in a channeling session may turn out to be alive, or perhaps to have never existed, from psychometry where the clairvoyant picks up 'traces' which seem to be left in a physical object, and from hauntings, which are localized in particular spaces, indicate that field relations are involved. In putative cases of reincarnation such as Stevenson's reports, the purported reincarnations tend to occur in the same geographical area, again indicating that consciousness establishes field relations with physical systems and that such fields may survive. Edge points out the positive features of this view as it moves away from the old dualistic separation of 'mind' and 'matter' which imbued parapsychology but he notes that it remains to be seen if it can prove to be of any real use[150]. I am not sure what exactly Edge means by "real use". It may be that he means something along the lines of predictive capability along the lines of a scientific hypothesis. It has been argued, as I noted above, that it may be more worthwhile to attempt some sort of understanding of these phenomena without attempting to derive scientific-style models for them which may be wholly inappropriate when considered from the broader perspective beyond scientific limitations. I would also point out that the linkage between consciousness and physical systems, as suggested by Roll, is also apparent in the studies of psychokinesis by Jahn and Dunne who tend to refer to the wave aspect of consciousness in regard to such paranormal phenomena as opposed to its particulate aspect. Jahn and Dunne, unlike Roll, stress the space and time transcending nature of parapsychological phenomena which cannot be accounted for in terms of conventional field theories (i.e. such as electromagnetic fields).

Edge, like J.B. Rhine before him, points out the difficulty in distinguishing supposed afterlife survival from ESP. The view that afterlife phenomena are merely manifestations of ESP phenomena is referred to as the 'this world ESP hypothesis' or the 'super-ESP hypothesis' (in Germany it is known as the 'animistic hypothesis')[150]. Klimo, who favours personal survival, refers to it disparagingly as the 'Grand Unified ESP hypothesis'.[183] Edge notes a famous case in which a medium gave accurate information about a psychic researcher's friend who was supposedly killed in a war but who, it later transpired, was still alive. Edge states that various attempts have been made to distinguish Survival from ESP including Stevenson's work which Edge claims cannot be distinguished from cases of mere fantasy. Edge also points out the difficulty in falsifying the 'super-ESP hypothesis' which could be moulded to fit any of the phenomena[150]. It is not clear if Edge accepts the possibility that information from real people who actually have died is obtained by ESP or whether he holds the hypothesis to entail just some sort of telepathy between living people. Stevenson's data, especially with the verified cases of birthmarks corresponding to actual fatal wounds, must clearly be distinguished from cases of mere fantasy and cannot be interpreted by telepathic communication amongst the living. Indeed, even the *Journal of the American Medical Association* carried a review of one of Stevenson's books which stated that "the evidence for reincarnation is difficult to understand on any other grounds".[15]

A consistent interpretation of past-life memories, 'liberation' and supposed reincarnation phenomena

In fact it is possible to interpret the evidence relating to *karma* and supposed rebirth, including the birthmark and scar evidence found by Stevenson, without having to postulate reincarnation. It is clear from my discussion of yogic knowledge and of Buddhist views of *karma* that the actual empirical basis of karmic doctrine involves the formation of memory traces or subtle mental reverberations associated with terms like *saṃskāra, bīja* and 'potentials' continuing in the stream of consciousness. Clearly, I have rejected the existence of any sort of permanent *jīva* or soul which could function as the transmigrant in any sort of rebirth. As I have stated previously, my views support the Buddhist doctrine of *Anatta* (*anātman*) which holds that there is no permanent soul-like entity. I also reject the notions involving some sort of astral body or immaterial organizing principle as the transmigrant. I have mentioned above that there may indeed be some sort of *etheric body* associated with the organization of the physical body but this seems to be closely tied to the physical body. The reader will recall that various other auric bodies and the notion of a so-called subtle body, which vary from tradition to tradition, have been rejected. I would thus sympathise with the seemingly contradictory Buddhist view that, in a sense, there isn't really a transmigrant but what seems to transmigrate may be viewed, simplistically, as something akin to a 'stream of consciousness' or more aptly described as some sort of subtle memory trace reverberations. Such memory trace reverberations need not have anything to do with death. Rather, they are probably the subtle vibrations emanating from the manifestation of all phenomena which persist at some deeper level of Reality corresponding to what Aurobindo called the *Ākāśa-lipi* (the Akashic Writing) or what is nowadays popularly called the Akashic Records. All manner of information about the past seems to be available to psychics, yogis, LSD subjects and others which has nothing whatsoever to do with traditional views of *karma* and rebirth. Indeed, a number of archaeologists have fruitfully employed psychics to reveal information about the past at archaeological sites; information which has often been confirmed by digging. The famous Sutton Hoo ship burial site discovered in England in 1938 was only excavated because a friend of the landowner kept seeing visions of Anglo-Saxon warriors performing a ritual dance around the mound and persuaded the landowner to allow excavation.

The claim in the *Tibetan Book of the Dead* that failure to attain liberation at the basic Clear Light experience results in a reawakening into the karmic forces resulting in rebirth is most interesting. We may take liberation to mean actual death here, the realization of one's true nature as the Light of the Buddha Mind entails acceptance of death whereas a recoil from the Light and reawakening suggests some sort of deep coma-like existence. This interpretation of so-called *liberation* as simply death is supported by the traditional Indian doctrine of *videhamukti* which asserts that true liberation can only occur at death, even if enlightenment has been attained during life[45]. This doctrine is opposed to that of *jīvanmukti* (liberation in life) with its problematic status of eliminating all karmic patterns whilst maintaining a body. Shankara, whilst accepting the *videhamukti* doctrine, attempts to account for the continued existence of the body in the *jivanmukta* by claiming that *Brahman* realization destroys all the *sañcita* and *kriyāmạn karma* whereas the *prārabdha karma*, which has to be worked out during this lifetime, cannot be eliminated until death and that this *prārabdha karma* continues to motivate the body of the *jīvanmukta* although he remains immersed in *Brahman* realization (or 'fruition enlightenment' as Brown[23] calls this state which is developed after the initial 'basis enlightenment') and detached from bodily activity[45]. Indich notes that the likes of Plotinus and Christian mystics, including Eckhart, held that salvation or the highest freedom is not attainable in life[45]. Sānkhya philosophy holds that eternal and absolute *kaivalyam* ('isolation' of *puruṣa* from *prakriti*) is not attained until death.[65] Thus we can see that the concept of liberation in life is a problematic one requiring *ad hoc* justifications and that true liberation, if indeed we are to take this rather quaint concept seriously, can only be attained through death. Bear in mind that Shankara also holds that the realm of *karma* is coextensive with that of *avidyā/māyā,* the 'illusory' realm of phenomenal superimpositions. Furthermore, the original meaning of *saṃsāra* is 'the ceaseless flux of the phenomenal world' rather than the supposed cycle of rebirths. Thus it seems as if the realm of *karma* is equivalent to the phenomenal world and supposed 'rebirth' stems from some sort of persistence of one's vibrations (or reverberations from one's manifestation) which subtly influence the manifestation of the phenomenal world. This is consistent with Nāgasena's interpretation of Dependent Co-origination involving shadowy potentials left by past acts which can influence the ongoing stream of life. My deeper Self seems to have known this when I wrote in the verse:

When into Thee I am reabsorbed
Sun's rays no more shall catch my face
Amidst the ocean of *saṃsāra*
How faint the ripples of my trace

Returning to the *Tibetan Book of the Dead,* we thus find that so-called 'rebirth' is the consequence of remaining in a deep coma-like state. Revealingly, Rinpoche notes that clairvoyant activity is experienced in this state. This claim is consistent with the testimony of modern Near-Death Experience cases. We have seen that Garrett described clairvoyant reality to be one of fundamental unity of all things where time is undivided and whole with past, present and/or future perceived in abruptly swift successions. Thus in the so-called *bardo* state the subject seems to be at the verge of death in a state of consciousness equivalent to clairvoyant trance. In this time/space transcending plane of consciousness, where the world is experienced as an undivided whole, the authoritative yogic traditions describe acausal, relativistic connections between events underlying the apparent causality of the space-time order[23]. Thus it seems as if the so-called 'rebirth' caused by the 'reawakening' of the subject into the forces of *karma* involves some sort of clairvoyant projection of life history memories into the deeper level of Reality associated with the so-called Akashic Records from where such memory information may be retrieved by psychics or yogis performing the *siddhis*. In rare cases this memory information seems to become amplified and takes over the mind of another individual resulting in cases of spirit possession which are misinterpreted as reincarnation.

The flashback of memories is very frequently described in NDEs and seems to correspond to the *bardo* experience of being blown to all the places you have been in life. There seems to be some confusion as to the level of detail in this flashback experience with some reports seeming to suggest that one's life is relived in incredible detail although at great speed relative to normal time. We have seen that the experience of time speeding up is a common part of yogic experience in Insight Meditation where the yogi seems to bring attention to focus on preconscious processes operating with rates of change much faster than in normal consciousness. We have also considered notions such as *process time* which involves relativistic time frames between autonomous process systems. Talbot cites a number of NDE reports indicating the 'holographic' characteristics of this life review experience which indicate that memory storage may indeed involve holographic/holonomic type processes as Pribram has suggested[15]. The holographic metaphor is also of special interest in regard to *karma* in that the holographic method of information storage allows for the generation of composite images created by the superimposition of numerous similar images. Both Grof and Talbot, as I have mentioned previously, note the significance that such composite holographic images may have in understanding the 'archetypal' (syncretic) memories which appear to be the collective, composite memories of numerous individuals experiencing similar emotions. It would at first appear that all such memories should blend together into a collective, composite blur. Indeed, Jung, whose notion of *archetypes* was strongly influenced by by Indian karmic notions, at first only accepted collective *karma* rather than both collective and personal *karma*. Jung even equated his collective 'archetypes' with *saṃskāra*. Patañjali Yoga, however, held that most *saṃskāra* were not collective but came from the individual's past lives[28].

Grof finds it astonishing that Jung overlooked past-life memories[41] but Jung did apparently change his attitude toward personal memories late in life[28].

If it were not for the fact that people clearly seem to relive memories from other individuals and that reincarnation-like spirit possession occurs, one would be tempted to stick to a Jungian 'collective unconscious' to account for such transpersonal experiences. Satprem claims that, at death, the aggregate of mental vibrations amalgamated around us due to habitual repetition forming our mental ego disintegrates into the universal Mental plane and other layers of vibrations disintegrate into their respective planes such as the Physical and the Vital. Satprem asserts that only the 'psychic centre', which is eternal, remains carrying its memories from one life to another. It carries only the *essence* of all its experiences, certain general tendencies which have stood out strongly. These self-perpetuating imprints of acts (*karma*) carried into another life result in special predispositions, innate tastes, irresistable attractions etc. Only those activities which are 'psychicised', says Satprem, participate in the immortality of the psychic. The psychic level has to participate in the more superficial levels in order to remember them, i.e. in profound moments of inner revelation or in tragic moments, we may feel a presence behind us which guides us. The details of the scene may become imprinted but a spontaneous mechanism effaces the precise memories and only the essence of scenes in which the depth of being comes forward transmigrates[52]. Satprem's view that only a deeper 'psychic centre' transmigrates bears some resemblance to the *Sānkhya* view, as discussed by Larson[184]. Dualistic *Sānkhya* (the theoretical side of the *Yoga Sūtra* or Patañjali Yoga tradition) distinguished between *puruṣa* (contentless, passive witness consciousness) and *prakriti* (gross and subtle matter and all contents of consciousness). Only *prakriti* in its various forms transmigrates. The individual in *Sānkhya* consists basically of two levels. There is a deep level which is devoid of ordinary experience and which is like a predispositional set of possibilities. There is also a surface level of projections constituting ordinary awareness. The deep 'core' determines the place of the individual in the scheme of things and stores the traces generated by the surface projections which in turn determine the future placement of the deep core. It is this deep core of essential traces determining the character of the surface personality which transmigrates in a supposed transmigrating subtle body.

Satprem's assertions tie in with the view that what actually transmigrates is a set of memories and his emphasis on the role of the psychic centre (the centre of the individual being, beneath the physical, mental and vital layers) again indicates a link to 'clairvoyant reality' in that this deeper level would correspond to the mind in a clairvoyant trance. His assertion that it is only the essence of profound or traumatic experiences which transmigrate ties in with Rajneesh's views about spirit possession amongst those in great fear or those in deep prayer and also seems to suggest that, if the details are removed, such experiences should be much the same for everyone leading to a merger into the collective essences of various types of experience as is found in transpersonal LSD resonances with syncretic, archetypal memories. Indeed, Satprem's assertion that, upon transmigration, these general tendencies bring about special predispositions, innate tastes etc. seems to resemble Jung's notion of archetypes which involved such psychic heredity. Although the *Sānkhya* philosophy postulates a transmigrating subtle body which I have rejected, if we let this pass and consider the notion of a deep core of essential predispositional traces determining the character of the surface personality, we see that it is generally dealing with the same sort of process as is discussed by Satprem. What appears to transmigrate is some subtle deeper aspect of our mental constitution which are seed-like in that, placed in another body, they influence the character of the surface projections which constitute the personality.

It seems to me that individual past life memories are perhaps the result of unusual circumstances involving great trauma or other emotions resulting in activation of deeper mental processes associated with psychic phenomena. The fact that Stevenson's cases often involve fatal wound marks, that Rajneesh, Grof and Satprem mention incomplete gestalts or unresolved problems, and that exorcism seems to involve bringing 'peace' or 'absolution' to 'restless souls' which have not fulfilled some necessary process, indicates that there may well be some truth in the popular views that 'earth-bound spirits' have some sort of 'unfinished business' which requires resolution. Moments of trauma or deep emotional crisis may trigger altered states of consciousness generating some sort of memory projection process which results in a 'strong signal' which differentiates itself from the collective, syncretic blur of reverberations. It seems that the recipient of such 'reincarnated' individual memories tends not to be your average person but either someone naturally endowed with the capacity to function psychically or a child in whom it seems these faculties are less likely to have been repressed by the processes of cultural indoctrination. As I have stated in regard to LSD-induced experiences, the 'pick-up' of such memories seems to be based on resonance of form relations, with the recipient having something in common with the emotional tone of the memories that possess them. Such resonance of form relations determining such memory transfers has resulted in the karmic myths of types of souls choosing suitable embryos and the recurrence of encounters with the same personalities or the same unresolved problems through a series of lives. It could well be that all of us pick-up such collective and perhaps also individual memories, some of which may become imprinted in our brain subtly influencing us without ever surfacing into our attention. It is also possible that the neuronal patterns laid down in the developing embryo which form our instinctual pathways are partly determined by collective morphic resonances from the past as indicated in Coward's discussion of *karma* above and as has been suggested by the likes of Sheldrake, with processes similar to our later learning from our experiences operating in our brain even before we have left the womb.

In the case of a friend of mine who had been possessed by memories from some person living seventy to one hundred years previously, she was not even aware of the name of the person whose memories possessed her. As she was blessed with some psychic abilities, she had probably brought to attention memories with which she had subconsciously resonated. Her case shows that it is not always complete personalities which become 'reincarnated' but rather some fragmented memories may come to possess another person. Thus one can hardly argue that it is some sort of 'soul' which is transmigrating. Where possession involves the taking over of a body by a full-blown personality claiming to be someone who has died, this is easily explained on the same basis. Our own sense of personal identity at any time depends on the 'possession' of the self-organizing mind-field by memories from our life history which maintain our sense of self-continuity when the mind-field is regenerated after annihilation in deep sleep. Similarly, our dreaming self, having access to the same life history memories, maintains our sense of personal identity. Given this situation, were the memories of some other person to intrude upon these processes within our brain and become imprinted and amplified so as to create their own activated complex, which like an alter personality in multiple personality disorders, seized control of the body, then this alien complex would identify with the body which generated the memories giving it its sense of ongoing personal identity. Thus, once such alien memories are amplified in a brain, the actual 'possession' of the body does not pose a great mystery as this involves the same processes of personal identity creation and dissociation as found in a normal individual. The problematic question is how these memories are transferred from one person to another in the first place.

Stevenson's documented evidence of birthmarks, wound scars, physical resemblance etc. are not some sort of unique, isolated phenomenon suggestive of the transmigration of some body-organizing astral body but the same mind-body interaction phenomena as found in normal individuals, multiple personality disorder cases, stigmatics etc. Indeed, Stevenson's first book on such issues *Twenty Cases Suggestive of Reincarnation*, published in 1966, also included evidence that the thoughts of pregnant women might influence their babies' development[185]. If the mother's thoughts seem capable of influencing the development of the embryo, then it is also conceivable that the memories from others can play a role. We have seen that the transmission of instinctual pathways in the brain may in fact be partly dependent upon morphic resonance with collective reverberations from the species. I have also noted that Hunt asserts that past-life memories are maintained in the auric energy field which she also associates with the development and organization of the body. The evidence from stigmatics suggests that unusual transformations of the body involve deep belief and persistent visualization of the stigmatic forms and prayer. This may be related to my suggestion above that deep emotional crises trigger some sort of memory projection process responsible for reincarnation-like processes. Whereas stigmatics project countless 'thought-forms' or images over a long period of time which subtly influence the organizing fields of their own bodies, the person in trauma or emotional crisis may activate processes which send out repeated memory reverberations in a rapid burst which stand out against the collective, syncretic blur of reverberations. It is interesting to note in this regard that Hunt asserts that most thoughts never leave the auric field of their creator. Only those firmly structured and vitalized by emotion have sufficient power to be broadcast[146].

The general meaning of Karma

Leaving aside these unusual cases of possession by memories from another individual, it would seem that such phenomena point to a more general truth relating to the Buddhist karmic doctrine of Dependent Co-origination and the interconnectedness of all individual phenomena. As we have seen such notions are related to Jung's notions of archetypes, psychic heredity and the collective unconscious and Rupert Sheldrake's notions of morphic resonance through transcendental morphogenetic fields. I have mentioned that Sheldrake has linked his ideas to those of Jung's and I have pointed out that both of these sets of ideas show the strong influence of Indian notions involving *karma* or the *ākāśa.* Tarnas[27] notes that Jung's 'middle period' conception of archetypes was one of inherited structures or dispositions that preceded human experience and determined its character. Later on Jung, in relation to his study of synchronicities, began to conceive archetypes as autonomous patterns of meaning that appear to structure and inhere in both psyche and matter thus dissolving the modern subject-object dichotomy and resembling more the Platonic and Neoplatonic conception of archetypes. Grof says that, in studying synchronicities, Jung concluded that archetypes must in some way influence the very fabric of the phenomenal world. As archetypes were thus a link between matter and the psyche Jung referred to them as 'psychoids'. Grof asserts that archetypes should be understood as phenomena *sui generis,* cosmic principles woven into the fabric of the transcendent order[41]. This again sounds like fixed Platonic Forms. I would concur with Bohm and Sheldrake that there are no immutable Platonic Forms, rather the archetypal patterns arise spontaneously and evolve. At the interface of mind and cosmos, the yogi realises that both microcosm (mental phenomena) and macrocosm manifest according to the same vibratory principles (*saṃskāra*). This leads to the realization of the possibility for paranormal interactions through karmic resonances in the *ākāśa*.

Although the likes of Goodwin would suggest that we need not look beyond the physical forces operating within the embryo for our 'morphogenetic fields', which as we have seen are non-transcendental in Goodwin's models, the existence of past-life memories, archetypal images, mind-body interactions and remote healing etc. do suggest the persistence of influences from the past which in some subtle manner shape the processes around us. Homoeopathy also indicates the existence of subtle influences from the past. The studies by Benveniste mentioned in the introduction aroused much debate about the possibility of water retaining some sort of memory of the active solute's presence even after repeated dilution had removed all of these solute molecules. Becker[21] notes in this regard that, although a beaker full of some solution appears placid to us, it is actually teeming with unimaginable activity at the atomic/molecular level. We have seen that the likes of Aurobindo and Sheldrake would argue that the regular patterns of behaviour we think of as laws are but habits that Nature has acquired, the persistence of patterns of behaviour which arose spontaneously and have been repeated countless times becoming more or less fixed like habits. I noted above that Bohm, expressing ideas which resemble the yogic experience of acausal connections in the undivided wholeness beyond the time/space matrix of perception, argues that, since the (transcendental) implicate order is non-local, similar forms resonate and are thus connected without regard to Space and Time. Through resonance, certain forms are reinforced and become stable manifestations. Herein lies the true meaning of *karma*, the transcendental resonances of past phenomena subtly influencing and stabilising the mani-festation of the present as is indicated in the notion of Dependent Co-origination (note Pauli's Exclusion Principle). Such karmic processes allow the *Brahmalīlā*, the spontaneous creativity of the Divine Ground, to maintain the Creation whilst evolving new forms out of old without disintegrating the Creation into chaos.

2(n). SOME CONCLUDING REMARKS

In this essay I have attempted to bring together the highest knowledge from yogic mysticism and modern science in order to glean something of the underlying Reality which both interpret in their limited ways. Of course, I am limited by the fact that I have relied upon the written testimony of yogis having no personal experience of yoga. Furthermore, the deeper yogic phenomenology, as the yoga-derived philosophies repeatedly state, cannot be expressed properly in words. We have noted that languages are imbued with the spatio-temporal categories of mundane existence and conceptual abstractions of limited features of Reality cannot possibly capture Reality as it is in itself. Given that such limitations will affect any philosophical interpretation and acknowledging that I have been constrained by time and access to resources, I hope that the reader will appreciate that I have shown that yogic mysticism and modern science can be directly linked together through my identification of the physical correlate of the Divine Light/*chit*/Pure Consciousness experienced by advanced mystics with a process well-known to modern science although usually conceived only within the limited referential frame of electroencephalography. I hope that the reader will also appreciate my attempt to show that the essential core truths underlying the various yogic philosophies do converge with the speculative considerations of the deeper levels of Reality beyond the extremely limited abstract models put forward by scientific specialists in order to predict the behaviour of various limited aspects of Reality. As previously stated, we find that where the various scientific frameworks break down in regard to questions relating to consciousness, paranormal phenomena, mind-body interactions, biology, quantum mechanics, cosmology and other questions which they were not formulated to deal with, the resolution of the paradoxes which arise tend to converge upon the common factors of psychophysical non-duality, space-time transcendence, differences arising from levels of perceptual focus, subtle vibratory activity, resonances of form etc. which are some of the components of the essential core of the yogic understanding of Reality.

I am not pretending that all the problems have been clearly resolved. Obviously there are a number of questions which remain problematical but as, overall, things have begun to fall into place, we may pass over such troublesome issues for the time being recognising that such problems are likely to be indicative of our epistemological limitations in trying to synthesise frameworks which once seemed so disparate. Such problematical issues include the fact that the content of our cognitions seems to be correlated with energetic activations in the brain whilst the complex physical structure of the brain deduced by modern science appears transparent to our consciousness. Another such question is the difficulty in coming to terms with consciousness energy as a sort of continuous 'substance' and the yogic vibratory picture of a pulsating plenum which creates the emergent manifest forms which we abstract from the underlying Reality. In regard to such perplexing questions it is worth keeping in mind the seemingly unimaginable concepts utilised by modern mathematics and physics which, it turns out, can be realised in experience in altered states of consciousness. We are often told that the yogi in the deepest realizations experiences that everything in the world is as it should be, transcending our mental projections of suffering, right and wrong and other human attributes onto Reality. These problematical issues are products of our relative minds and their limited constructions failing to harmonise with each other whereas Reality remains forever harmonious.

The glaring absurdity of Materialism

Various thinkers have asserted that the 'worlds' of Science and Mysticism are incommensurable. I hope that the reader appreciates that this is not so even though the two cannot be smoothly synthesised for the time being. I have tried to present the overall picture of human knowledge grounded upon *Brahman,* the Ultimate Reality or the Ground of all Being which, through its myriad modes of subtle energetic vibrations manifests the entire emergent universe of limited spatio-temporal forms and the coexistent experiences in the individuated forms of this Great Spirit, this eternal Light of Consciousness. In contrast, the scientific picture is one of an insentient realm of abstractions, whose components interact according to mechanical laws, completely at odds with the basic facts of our experience which materialists are forced to deny because their abstractions can only account for such limited aspects of Reality. The epistemological absurdity of

Materialism is glaringly obvious to anyone who analyses the metaphysical assumptions but the naïve projections of technological constructions onto Reality remain appealing in a society dominated by technology where the mind is encouraged to remain in the lowest, sensorimotor planes of existence traditionally associated with the simple commoner who, knowing nothing personally of deeper realms, asserted that such spiritual realms were just lies conjured up by manipulative priests. It is illuminating to point out here the fact that Science now accepts without question the existence of spectacular, large-scale electrical discharge phenomena in the Earth's upper atmosphere occurring above the storm clouds which we can normally only see from below. The processes generating such phenomena remain a mystery. In fact 'sprites' and related phenomena had been witnessed by a number of pilots flying high-altitude aircraft before the existence of such phenomena was recognised. These pilots kept quiet for fear of being grounded as mentioning such seemingly fantastic displays of electrical activity stretching for tens of kilometres would have been interpreted as hallucinations by the air force authorities. Today such strange phenomena in the mysterious world of the higher planes of the atmosphere are commonly witnessed by astronauts in the space shuttles.

To put the difference between the Neo-Brahmanical view presented here and Materialism into perspective, one has to reiterate that Materialism holds consciousness to be a rarified product of the abstractions structured through mechanical projections (the so-called 'physical world') which it holds to constitute the actual Reality. In contrast, the yogic picture holds the 'physical world' itself to be but a product of our minds, a limited picture abstracted from the whole Reality through a selective perceptual focus and denial of all contradictory evidence and considerations. Although the Materialist accuses the yogi of primitive magical and animistic thought, it is the Materialist who is magically conjuring up a supposed 'consciousness' into his picture of small-scale spatio-temporal patterns of energetic activity generating ever more complex spatio-temporal patterns which has no scope to admit any sort of awareness whatsoever as no amount of complex pattern formation, however cleverly phrased, amounts to actual conscious experience. Science's animistic projection of laws and its projection of technological mechanisms onto Nature denies the basic creative freedom of consciousness underlying the emergent habitual patterns which Science abstracts as supposed laws. Thus the only consistent picture available to the materialist is that of eliminative materialism, a nonsense of an insentient universe in which we ourselves have to be insentient automatons devoid of any experience. Any attempt at sneaking in consciousness only when brains have evolved to a certain degree of complexity involves invoking magical dualistic worlds of mind and matter. Materialists also put forward nonsensical arguments about evolution of complex inanimate and animate forms through blind chance in this insentient universe which suddenly appears out of absolutely nothing. Contemplation of such a picture is intuitively unsatisfying as the essence of our Self is one with the essence of the universe and we begin to realise that the same urge for exploration of creative possibilities must exist in the universe at large. Being and Consciousness are one and the materialists' insentient, mechanistic universe operating by sheer chance without any awareness of its own existence or any will to fulfil its potential is but a fantasy constructed from abstractions by minds which cannot break free from their entrapment in mechanistic models to contemplate the whole picture.

The collective delusion of the modern materialists faced with the undermining of their naïve physicalist pictures by the most simple metaphysical analysis must rank alongside the collective madness that seemed to plague the German nation at the height of Nazi power. If enough people repeat the same nonsense enough times then the herd begins to believe that this nonsense is true. Indeed, many of the great physicists have themselves recognised the inadequacy of Materialism and the likes of Newton wisely refrained from extrapolating from the predictive models to making metaphysical statements ('framing hypotheses') about Reality. The loudest advocates of modern materialistic views tend to be lesser minds who, like religious zealots, dogmatically appeal to the authority of great physicists whilst ignoring the fact that many of the great physicists did not hold the naïve views that the lesser minds have projected onto them.

We have seen that the distinction of having been awarded a European Nobel Prize in one of the sciences does not prevent one from complete misapprehension of the metaphysical problems posed by consciousness even though any reasonably educated person can usually see through the flimsy tissue of pseudo-logical subterfuge that materialists put forward in regard to consciousness. Even that icon of modern materialist society Albert Einstein, upon whom many have projected prophet-like attributes of privileged access to some sort of cosmic archetypes, could not free his mind from the subtle dualistic indoctrinations of Western society even though he was a follower of the panpsychist Spinoza. I have noted that whilst he failed to recognize the validity of panpsychism, Einstein also failed to rid himself of Spinoza's determinism. The likes of Bergson and Whitehead pointed out how Einstein's space-time continuum conception has led to a picture of a 'block universe' which has completely distorted the modern understanding of the perennial view of Time as relating to the world-creation process or 'Becoming'.[55] For instance the goddess Kālī, a personification of (Mother) Nature (whom the modern materialist 'worships' in the abstract form of 'Matter'), gets her name from the Sanskrit *kāla* which means Time although the popular mythology focuses on the other meaning of *kāla*, black. In regard to Einstein, it is worth pointing out here that the writings of the likes of Heisenberg (who has been largely ignored due to his role as the head of Hitler's atom bomb project), Schrödinger, Bohr, Pauli and Eddington reveal that they were more broadly educated than the prodigious Einstein and thus more capable of placing the mathematical abstractions of physics into their proper context within the whole of human understanding. The wise would realise that a mathematical genius resembles more an *idiot savant* than an all-knowing prophet in that a specialized skill has been developed to an extraordinary level of proficiency. As the modern mind has forgotten the spiritual roots of all insight and creativity, let us remember that the word *whole* shares its roots with the word *holy* in the Old English *hal (hael)* from which we have also derived the modern word *heal*.

The modern West's subliminal Christian legacy

I have attempted to heal the rift between the spiritual and the natural which has been a lingering sore in Western thought from the time of the origin of the Christian myth of Creation *ex nihilo* onwards, exacerbated by the political accommodation between the Church, given authority over the realm of Spirit, and the 'natural philosophy' of modern science as became crystallized in

Descartes' psychophysical dualism. Western misunderstanding of the spiritual realms is highlighted by the projections of the medieval alchemists of the philosophers' stone and the philosophers' gold (the mind/'soul' and the Divine Light) onto the external world and the attempted transmutation of metals into gold. Such activities contributed, of course, to the birth of modern science which consolidated the Western focus on the external world. We can see that the mistake of the early European alchemists manifested itself in the medieval myths surrounding the alchemical notion of the 'Elixir of Life', resulting from the projection of the *prāṇa* aspect of the Divine Light or Godhead. The medieval myths of some external 'Fount of all Wisdom' were the projection of the Divine insight (gnosis, *vijñāna*) aspect of the Godhead as experienced in the highest yogic realizations. My identification of the Divine Light or Godhead with the brainwaves of the Reticular Activating System again accords with this notion of a fount or fountainhead welling up with supreme insights. Such alchemical ignorance in the medieval West arose as a product of the closed systems of Christianity and Islam which both asserted on pain of death that they alone held the one and the only 'Truth'. Gnosticism, from which the later alchemy had secretly developed had been branded a heresy by the early Christians who suppressed its practice and dissemination. Prior to the rise of this mass religion, Gnostics and Neoplatonists had flourished in the Hellenistic world's great centres of learning, especially Alexandria which had been visited by Ásoka's Buddhist missionaries and itinerant yogis. It is easy to forget after over two thousand years that India was once the neighbour of the Hellenistic world and that Megasthenes, the Seleucid ambassador, lived in the court of Chandragupta Maurya at Pātaliputra. It was no surprise that Plotinus had attempted to reach India. We have seen that both Aristoxenus, a pupil of Aristotle (as was Alexander himself), and Diogenes Laertius testified that Socrates had met with an Indian at Athens before Alexander's incursion into India. There were of course indigenous spiritual traditions in the pagan West. Both Plato and Aristotle were acquainted with the Eleusinian and Orphic mysteries, the former allegedly having been an initiate into the Eleusinian sect[41]. However, in medieval Europe Pātaliputra remained only as Tribalibot, a name for India (derived from the Latin word for the people of Pātaliputra) in the Parzival legend and the story of Buddha's Great Renunciation had become the legend of the 'Christian prince' Josaphat (derived from *Bodhisat*) whom the Christians actually made into one of their saints[186].

Although the barriers between 'East and West' have largely disappeared, the subliminal Christian legacy remains, as we have seen, deep within Western culture and vestiges of Christian mythology remain at the very heart of modern science even though most scientists hold that Science has made a clean break from the superstitious Christian past. We have come across a few of these myths such as God as the Roman governor laying down the laws and also across the more general Western attitude, developed in the ignorance of Yoga, that supreme insights are available only to a privileged few, like the prophets of the Semitic religions. It is interesting to note that modern scientists coming from countries whose cultures have sustained yogic traditions, such as India, China and Japan, are often far more aware of the deficiencies of the Materialist picture than their counterparts in the West. However, Western scientists, steeped in Western cultural arrogance, often perceive such views as indicative of retention of primitive superstitions as with their own spiritual traditions. In regard to Christianity, it appears as if Indian Buddhism and Yoga influenced early Christianity just as it influenced Gnosticism and Neoplatonism, both of which played significant roles in the early development of Christianity. The popular myths created about the life of the Buddha, long after his death, in the *jātakas,* such as the virgin birth, the walking on water and the feeding of many people with a little food are all rehashed in the mythology surrounding the life of the historical character Jesus. Deeper similarities between Buddhist and Christian teachings have been pointed out by a number of scholars and, of course, we have seen that medieval Christianity mistook the legendary Josaphat for an ideal Christian. Interestingly, on a recent visit to Sri Lanka, the current Roman Catholic Pope made some disparaging remarks about Buddhism and was duly snubbed by Sri Lanka's Buddhist hierarchy. This incident goes to show the highly Eurocentric attitudes permeating the highly Eurocentric (if not 'Italocentric') Roman Church which still holds universalist pretensions even though it was the Greek Church which focused on the spiritual message of the apostles rather than the spiritually immature Roman focus on the personality cult of Christ. It is worth remembering that until the 1960s the Roman Church held the Jews responsible for the 'death of God'. In contrast, as Odajnyk noted, Buddha was the first person known to history (unlike the anonymous Upaniṣadic *riṣis*) to describe Self-realization in primarily psychological and non-religious terms when most of humanity was still very deeply involved with primitive deities. It should also be noted that Christianity came to India perhaps as early as the second Christian century, existing to this day as Nestorian Christianity in South India, but made no serious impact in such a spiritually sophisticated country. In regard to mass religions, as with mass culture, we should keep in mind that appealing to large numbers of lowly educated followers are no substitute for serious critical assessment of issues. Given the increasing trend towards universal literacy, if not education, worldwide, the time for the high *jñānamarga* for the educated and the low *bhaktimārga* for the masses, has passed and the essential core of the once-secret yogic teachings can be made available to everyone.

The Western religious focus on symbols rather than Reality is paralleled in Western science's focus on mathematical abstractions. Any educated person can find out that the Biblical story of Cain and Abel, for instance, is a mythological account of the transition from the primitive, dreamlike 'mindfulness' state of consciousness to the highly developed ego-consciousness and sharp self-other distinction underlying the rise of civilised societies[69]. A similar interpretation can be given for the Christian doctrine of Original Sin which we have seen has been reformulated by the religion-bashing Richard Dawkins in his 'Selfish Gene' mythology. The revelations given to Moses in his encounter with the burning bush that the first name of God is 'I am that I am' and the second name is 'I will be what I will be' are poetic ways of stating the nature of the divinity as Being and Becoming[69]. The Christian practice of baptism was originally a secret initiation ritual whereby an out-of-body experience was induced (to 'prove' the existence of the spiritual world) by holding the head under water for a much longer period of time than in today's ceremonial baptisms[69]. The Book of Revelation, taken by many uneducated people to hold historical prophecies, actually contains a series of elaborate puzzles symbolically referring to Gnostical knowledge about spiritual energies corresponding to the Indian *Kuṇḍalinī* and the *chakras.*[187] Thus we find some elements of the Perennial Philosophy mixed up with all the historical folklore of the Israelites although the mainstream Christian interpretations focus on the superficial symbolism rather than the actual snippets of perennial wisdom hidden underneath.

The incompatibility of theistic religion and the perennial wisdom

The fact that Christianity contains elements of the perennial wisdom is often seized upon by zealots as a justification of the 'truth' of Christian dogma. The fact is, as we have seen in this work, that if we analyse *any* system of human knowledge we will begin to discern the underlying structure which reflects the perennial wisdom as the perennial wisdom itself reflects the construction of the human mind. To illustrate the incompatibility of Christianity and the Perennial Philosophy, it is useful to consider the case of one of the great scholarly mystics, whose teachings, as scholars of perennial mysticism like to point out, correspond with the essential core structure of the yogic philosophies and other mystical traditions from around the world. Early in the Fourteenth Christian century, leading Christian theologian Meister Eckhart, who had held the same Chair at Paris occupied by Thomas Aquinas, discovered in his meditations that, from the point of view of the Godhead beyond the vantage point of the mind/'soul', all dualism disappeared and there was no distinction between the seeming God and the individual. The distinctions of the Trinity, Eckhart pointed out, are *our* attributions which barely cover the essential oneness[188].

> *Here God's ground is my ground and my ground is God's ground.*
> *The knower and the known are one. Simple people imagine that they should see God as if he stood there and they here. This is not so. God and I, we are one in knowledge.*
>
> Meister Eckhart[189,190]

Forman's[188] interpretation of Eckhart's descriptions of his realizations, which involve a unique terminology, closely resemble the traditional Indian yogic insights as described in modern times by Aurobindo and quoted above. As Erwin Schrödinger commented in regard to Aldous Huxley's *The Perennial Philosophy*, the significant point about the various mystical realizations described was that these mystics lived in different parts of the world in different periods of history and, usually, did not even know of the existence of the other mystics described by Huxley. And yet, across the world, throughout human history mystics have over and over again independently rediscovered the great truths which Huxley, following Leibniz, called the Perennial Philosophy.

Little minds, envious of Eckhart's popularity instigated an inquisition against Eckhart. The Roman Church, which in Eckhart's time was steeped in brazen nepotism and corruption, ignored Eckhart's pleas that he had no intention of challenging the Church's authority and the inquisitional tribunal held in Cologne in 1326 found his remarks heretical. Eckhart appealed against the decision but died before the outcome of the appeal. The papal commission which heard his appeal in Avignon in 1327 did not condemn the already deceased (and thus not a threat) Eckhart personally as a heretic but, none the less, found his propositions heretical. This is in fact was what Eckhart had hoped to achieve by appealing[188]. Thus we see that the Christian Church condemns as heresy the testimony of mystics who affirm the great yogic truths just as Christianity branded Gnosticism, which resembled yogic knowledge, to be heresy. Christianity, as with any religion, has to base its theistic mythology on what in India is called the *bhakti* experience of loving embrace of the soul by the deity, corresponding to the Christian 'Passion with Christ'. We have seen that *Advaita Vedānta* equates this experience of the *Īśvara* (Lord) aspect of *Brahman* with the yogic *savikalpa samadhi* which is not the Ultimate Realization. This experience corresponds to lucid deep sleep or the Near-Death experiences where simpler people describe encounters with their culture's deity. Aurobindo notes the paradoxical co-existence of the personal and impersonal aspects of *Brahman* which precede the Ultimate Realization of identification with the impersonal Absolute. The dualistic experience of a personal God is simply the experience of the penultimate state of consciousness prior to enlightenment in which the mind, stripped of everything except basic individuality and intentionality, floats in the Divine Light which it experiences through projection of its own individuality, as a separate mind-like supreme individual with personal attributes. From this experience arises the dualistic, theistic myth of God and the soul as completely separate entities. Eckhart's realization of the ultimate oneness of the ground of God and the ground of the I is essentially a restatement of the *Upaniṣadic mahāvākya* (grand pronouncement) *tat tuam asi.* As Romain Rolland[191] told Freud, "religious sensation . . . is entirely different from religions and much more durable". Religious experience, Roland asserted, referring to Rāmakrishna and Vivekānanda, was, "independent of all dogma . . . of all organization of the church, of every holy book".

It should be clear to any educated person that the exoteric paraphernalia of any religion is nothing more than the 'ritual trappings' that the Jesuits themselves recognised in their own religion when faced with Vedāntic philosophy. Although the esoteric knowledge of the initiates may involve aspects of the perennial wisdom, these insights are subjected to the 'superstitious distortions' of the creed which are dogmatically defended with counter-evidence and counter-argument treated as heresy. Indeed, the arguments put forward by anti-perennialist scholars of religions that all mystical experiences are mediated by doctrinal expectations have an element of truth in them especially in regard to the 'lower planes'. However, such scholars, as well as using Kantian epistemology which denies the existence of mystical experiences in the first place, tend to be keen to defend religion against the challenge of the perennial wisdom and thus bring in their own subliminal distortions to disguise the glaring similarities between various mystical testimonies at the deeper planes and especially in regard to what Brown referred to as 'basis enlightenment'. The existence of such experiences, although testified to repeatedly in all cultures throughout history, are dismissed as impossible by these word-worshipping scholars of religion.

The early Christian Church had to revise its doctrine relating to the 'Holy Spirit' as it did not want individuals claiming to be possessed by the 'Holy Spirit' challenging their dogma and thus their authority. In the original Christian community the Holy Spirit had been given prominence and members of the community sought to experience the presence of the 'living' spirit within themselves but the spontaneous outbursts of healing powers, speaking in tongues, ecstasies, charismatic personalities, prophecies, and varying revelations led the Church to deny the authority of the Holy Spirit, reducing its status to the third component of the Christian 'trinity' and to select a limited number of apostolic statements as the dogma, thus rejecting any independent claims to divine authority[27]. By rejecting the authority of the Holy Spirit within, the priest retained his status as the medium between the supposed God and the layman. We have seen that the scientific establishment maintains such dogmatic traditions associated with the Semitic religions.

Any educated person can easily identify the numerous social factors informing the pronouncements of the holy men and the social functions of the religious organization which purports to hold divine authority. We have seen how the Buddhist appeal to the lay majority resulted in the projection of ethical superstitions onto karmic knowledge and we all know of the misuse of such interpretations of the term *saṃsāra* in support of the very caste system which the Buddhists challenged. Such projections are equally apparent in the Western religions. The claim that Christ is the *Messiah* is taken by Christians to confer unique historical status upon this historical character when in fact the *Messiah* is actually supposed to be the 'redeemer' of the nation of Israel which is presumably how the character Jesus himself conceived it. Indeed, the Cult of Christ was seen by many of its early members to be exclusive to Jews and not to be universalized as the Romanised Paul attempted to do. As Jung noted, such myths of the 'redeemer', wherein an individual becomes possessed by the collective affliction tormenting his people's 'psyche' are found all over the world. The individual, thus possessed, internalises his people's collective affliction and seeks to formulate a creative solution or a way out of the problem situation. As Jung pointed out, the phenomenal growth of the Christian Cult in the Roman world had to do with the growing antipathy throughout the Empire with the Roman infatuation with hedonism, power and greed with which the Christian message struck a chord. The rise of Islamic fundamentalism today in countries like Egypt where a Westernised elite lives in hedonistic luxury whilst the masses fester in poverty reflects similar social processes. Whilst the challenge to ego-driven elites through the awakening of collective identities and related phenomena can have beneficial socio-economic effects, the need to appeal to, or mobilise, the masses leads to the superficial anthropocentric projections by the mass religions onto the politically motivated or simply superstitious distortions of the founding holy men and their followers.

The 'Eternal Truth' of the Sanātana Dharma

The true 'Perennial Philosophy' has nothing to do with mass religions and their socio-political ideologies claiming undisputed spiritual authority. Such organizations have more in common with Stalinistic bureaucracies or even Mafia-style cliques than with open-minded spiritual enquiry. Nor is the Perennial Philosophy the simplistic utterances of uneducated holy men, ancient or modern, who assert that they have unique access to the Divine Reality, especially those who assert that everyone should follow the strictures revealed to them. Rather it is the collective wisdom gained from the testimony of countless, largely anonymous, seers gleaned over thousands of years, subjected to repeated personal testing by yogis and other contemplatives and to rational scrutiny by highly educated philosophers.

> *As Kumarila, a well-known leader of orthodox thought, has remarked . . . a 'vision' that has unfolded itself to but one single person may after all be an illusion . . . To avoid this possible defect of subjectivity orthodox thinkers postulate in the place of testimony, based upon the intuition of a single sage, another, viz. 'revelation'.*
>
> M. Hiriyanna, *The Essentials of Indian Philosophy*[192]

As Arvind Sharma[193] elaborates:

> *the Hindu tradition may be seen as relying on a plurality of both the experiencers and the respondents to authenticate the experi-*

> *ence. Hinduism has no single founder; its foundational scriptures, the Vedas, are based on the collective experience of the ancient sages. Within Hinduism the condition has also 'sometimes' been laid down as "essential to all 'revealed' teaching, viz. that it should have proved acceptable to the best minds (mahājana) of the community".*

This is the true spirit of the *Sanātana Dharma*, the 'Eternal Truth' that lies at the core of the Indian pagan traditions which Westerners have conceived as 'Hinduism'. It is this *Sanātana Dharma* which needs to be universalized to incorporate the insights from all reasonable, educated *riṣis* from all over the world and to offer itself to scrutiny before the best minds across the whole world. This is of course what I have been attempting to move towards in this essay.

The *Sanātana Dharma*, transcending all cultural constructions, combined with modern scientific knowledge will provide the essential basis of the universal metaphysics for the future universal civilisation. This fusion of spirituality, metaphysics and science which can absolve the differences between all systems of knowledge is India's great gift to the world. I look forward to a future in which the age of mass religious mythology and the modern age of materialist mythology are looked back upon as projection systems of immature societies. Already we have John Horgan, a writer for *Scientific American*, putting forward the thesis in his *The End of Science* that Science has been reduced to mere theory twiddling, tinkering with existing theories like the scholastics of old who debated the proverbial issue of the number of angels on a pinhead. There is much truth in this view when looked at from within the limited perspective of the West encountering the limits of its scientific approach but, from the Indian point of view, Horgan's attitude that there are no new great horizons for exploration is just Eurocentric narrow-mindedness. As the great civilisations of India and China flower again they will begin to modernise their modes of interpreting the world making use of the amazing developments that have occurred in the modern West to go well beyond the closed world of Western science towards a truly universal understanding of Reality. It should be clear from the limitations of this essay that we have a very long way to go before we can say the Science and Mysticism have been synthesized such that there is no longer much need to distinguish between the knowledge gleaned by either approach. None the less, it should be apparent to the reader that such a synthesis is not impossible and that the approach taken in this work has begun to show the various domains of human knowledge in something like their proper relationship to the Whole.

What am I and why am I here ?

Leaving aside such historical issues of false dualisms between Spirit and Nature and between the individual and the Absolute, let us consider briefly what I have stated about what we are and our place in the scheme of things. I have pointed out that the 'field' notion is intrinsically vague. As Bohm has stated, it is a pragmatic concept, nobody really knows what the mathematical concept of a field represents. It may be possible, however, to realise such intrinsically paradoxical concepts in altered states of consciousness as has been reported by LSD subjects. We exist as a sort of transforming field in the brain generated by certain parts of the overall brain activity. I have mentioned above the paradox regarding the transparency of the complex structure of the brain, deduced by Science, to our awareness even though we, as the mind-field, coexist with all of this incredibly complex activity. Some insight into this paradox appears to come from after-images such as those produced by staring directly at a light bulb filament which is glowing brightly. The pattern of the filament remains in the 'mind's eye' for some time and gradually begins to disintegrate. Contemplation of such experiences indicates to me that the image is being generated by a pattern of hyperactivated neurons which persist in attention through the hyperactivity exceeding some sort of energetic threshold. In 1994, I attempted for a brief period to try to meditate with little success. I occasionally found a purple cloud, rising through my field of visual attention eliciting a sense of exhiliration. This phenomenon seemed to me to be the psychical correlate of some sort of chemical discharge and diffusion in some part of the brain given the movement of the cloud and the sense of exhilaration.

Thus the complex physical structure/activity of the brain seems to manifest in our awareness as cloud-like blurs of colour or glowing patterns of light emerging from presumed physical formations co-existing with such phenomena, invisible to our awareness. This accords with the concept of *closure* which I put forward in 1983, in that our awareness resembles somewhat the materialist notion of an emergent phenomenon in that the information within the lower-level, smaller-scale, substructures such as cells and molecules appears transparent to our awareness or, in my 1983 terminology, is *closed.* I have shown that consciousness cannot be explained by such simplistic notions of emergent materialism and that the closed substructures must be sentient entities in themselves individuated from a panpsychic Reality. This was the essence of my vision of living brain cells in 1983 which led to my rudimentary panpsychist model of consciousness.

I have argued that our minds resemble closed 'fields' such as cells and molecules, in that the mind is a self-organising process within the brain's electromagnetic field activity. I have utilised the metaphor of the whirlpool to try and capture something of this paradoxical coexistence of individuated, 'closed' fields within the all-embracing plenum of Consciousness-Energy. It is not possible to give some sort of logical or mathematical reasoning for such assertions, one can only point to the evidence such as the yogic experience of enlightenment with the difficulty of attainment caused by the 'throwing back' into the subtle 'vehicles' of individual existence, the Zen Buddhist experiences with the ego and meditation complexes as "closed" energy fields, the evidence from Multiple Personality Disorders and the therapeutic integration of the subpersonalities, dissipative structure notions and so on to substantiate such assertions. Our conscious experiences seem to be correlated with the gross activity in this closed field although more subtle activity seems to exist which we experience as subconscious influences subtly coexisting with our gross experiences. The differences between the visual sensory mode and the other sensory modes appears to arise from the energetic dominance of the former. Colours and forms have nothing intrinsically to do with the biologically evolved mode of information reception called human vision, it is simply that our visual mode dominates the activity of our brain and thus disrupts the Light of Pure Consciousness into its myriad gradations of colour. The other sensory modes appear to act, metaphorically, like shadows within the field of experience dominated by vision. Evidence from synaesthesia indicates the interchangeability of these modes. The non-spatiality of our thoughts may indicate that conceptual activity is not structured by the spatial aspects of the time/space matrix of perception although it is clearly sequenced with the flow of the so-called stream of consciousness. I have mentioned notions such as quantum coherence and phase locking which indicate the cotemporality of phenomena coëxisting within a single cycle of a process which generates an internal time frame. Similarly, the subject/object distinction appears to reflect some sort of 'straddling' of planes with the 'lower' planes constituting the contents or object of perception in relation to an ethereal subject associated with our thoughts, and occasionally subtle bodily experiences, which retains a degree of imaginative freedom relative to the fixed behaviour of the perceptual constructions existing in the lower plane of gross sensorimotor activity. I have mentioned the yogic knowledge of the subject/object relationships existing between higher/lower planes of consciousness.

In a very real sense we are Spirit trapped within 'matter', the creative freedom of the Spirit, the Consciousness-Energy, intermingling with the lawlike activity of its material crystallizations which is in itself Spirit subject to even greater levels of self-imposed constraints. Our consciousness is, in essence, no different from that of any individuated entity, however different they may appear to us. It is our existence within the human brain which gives our consciousness its sense of distinctness through the meaningful organization imposed upon it in relation to the organism's world and the control of the body through our influence upon the very brain activity that generates us. All of the capacities of our consciousness are pale reflections of the supreme powers inherent within *Brahman,* the Absolute Spirit which is everpresent as the background essence of our existence beneath the superficial constructions of perceptions, conceptions and any other contents of experience. *Brahman* is in fact omnipresent as the underlying substratum of the entire universe; its world-creating power subjecting it to self-limitation within its multiform created entities.

The yogi who learns to hold the superficial fluctuations of

mentation in abeyance through exercise of our limited power of free will, resisting the outflow of the pranic energy into the lower planes of material existence, begins to experience the deeper levels of the mind. Through remarkable exercise of the will, it is possible to strip the mind of all contents of mentation and experience oneself in one's naked individuality, still equipped with the limited choosing power of the will which seems to accompany individuation or closure, floating in the all-embracing Light of Pure Consciousness, the Fount of all Wisdom, or the Godhead. In this state, corresponding to lucid deep sleep or the theist's ultimate experience of loving embrace of the soul by a supreme personality, the naked individuality gains access to a bewildering array of realizations which confound attempts to truly describe them within the limited frames of representation available to us in our mundane existence and the extreme limitations of languages. Some of these realizations have been mentioned above both in regard to yogic experiences and the experiences of LSD subjects such as the purported simultaneous identification with atoms and galaxies resembling the Upanisadic pronouncements of *Brahman* being greater than the greatest yet smaller than the smallest. Realizations of the underlying karmic interconnectedness of all phenomena in the universe, resulting in doctrines such as Dependent Co-origination, also occur in such deep states where the normal perceptual filters which filter out the reverberations of the Past and the play of forces creating the Future have been deactivated. Here in this indescribable Fount of all Wisdom, where the secrets of the Creation are revealed through mysterious identity experiences beyond the limitations of Space and Time in the underlying cosmic oneness, we discover what it is to be a true 'philosopher', a lover of wisdom.

Yet even these miraculous realizations have to be held in abeyance to attain the true Ultimate Realization, the dissolution of individuality and the identification with the true Self, the impersonal *Ātman*, the microcosmic Light within which is one with the macrocosmic *Brahman* from which arises the entire universe. Perhaps it is the state of flux which exists at the brink of enlightenment, where the naked mind, the causal body, is spontaneously reconstituted against its will (the yogi 'thrown back into the vehicles' of the *māyā* world) which allows the yogi to capture something of the character of the impersonal Absolute within the limitations of individual existence. In this state of flux between naked individuality and the indescribable oneness with the supreme Ground of all Being, the yogi realises the truth of the *mahāvākyas, tat tuam asi* and *sarvam idam Brahma eva,* that the individual is in Reality, a limited expression of this Divine Ground from which all things arise. Realizations, paradoxical to our limited frame of existence, occur revealing the Unmoved Mover character of the impassive, distinctionless Ground which is 'simultaneously' pulsating and vibrating, 'boiling and seething' into the manifest Creation. Reality transcends our conceptual categories which find contradictions in opposites which, in Reality, can coexist.

In such encounters with the Light and realizations of oneness with all manner of created forms, the yogi realises that matter is but a stable manifestation of this intense vibratory activity, the individuated forms being nothing more than self-repeating, self-sustaining patterns of activity within the underlying 'ocean', the plenum of Consciousness. The phenomena of both microcosm and macrocosm are revealed to be created through the same vibratory principles leading to the possibility for paranormal interactions through karmic resonances. The Pauli Exclusion Principle cannot be explained by Science yet if it did not operate there would be no orderly chemistry or evolution. Pauli said that it operated like synchronicities. Synchronicities are in fact expressions of karmic resonances of form and so the Exclusion Principle operates through the resonances of stable forms emerging out of the *Brahmalīlā,* creating order from the chaotic fluctuations. What we loosely refer to as 'energy' appears to be the less restricted activity, in relation to matter, of this paradoxical, underlying Reality. Although I have spoken of 'energy' as if it were the substance of Reality, one should recall Rāmakrishna's description of the relationship between the Pure Consciousness and the Divine Energy as being like that between the snake and its smoothly flowing motion. Thus although we tend to conceive of 'energy' as a substance, it appears to be only the activity (*kriyā*) abstracted from within the impassive Ultimate Reality of Pure Consciousness, the Unmoved Mover, which creates and sustains the universe through such activity. This paradox relates to the notion of *Māyā,* the illusory nature of the created world as realised from the level of the Divine Ground, although the created forms appear solid and substantial from our limited perspective within the world of forms.

And this Creation, the enlightened yogi realises, comes to be through *Brahmalīlā,* the sheer aimless sport, the spontaneous creativity of the Ground of all Being which in itself contains all possibilities, imaginable or unimaginable to humans, which it can actualise through its *Māyā* power. Hence, the macrocosmic cycle, the *kalpa* literally means 'the imagination' for, in a sense, the entire material universe crystallizes out of this imaginary exploration of possibilities within the transcendent *Brahman.* The self-limitation into the multitudinous forms appears to be part of this *līlā,* this playful exploration of creative possibilities as does the evolution of ever more complex living forms. We have seen that Life, far from being the mere replication of genetic information, primarily involves the spontaneous play of Consciousness-Energy, which brings about the self-organization, integration, creative evolutionary transformations and, in higher mammals, the creative mental functions of the organism. We exist as limited expressions of *Brahman* within the living forms of the human organisms, Spirit emerging within the created forms in the material plane. Although constrained by the limitations of the material plane, we retain the essential freedom and creativity of *Brahman* to explore possibilities and to actualise them. And as humans with highly developed individualities, curiosity, powers of conceptualization, linguistic communication, and civilised cultures we exist in a new world of conceptual meaningfulness where we can begin to overcome the 'self-forgetfulness' with which we are created and reflect upon our very creation, creating ever more complex representations of the macrocosmic order within our microcosmic existence. Of course, the commoner remains engrossed in the sensorimotor activity of the lowest plane developing little in the way of an intellect or even a simplistic theistic spirituality. But the wise, having developed their intellects, remain unsatisfied as intuitively they realise that the knowledge of the intellect is not the whole Truth and they yearn for more. Often they realise that, within them, exists another self which may communicate to them as the Inner Voice and may even reveal to them glimpses of their destiny. It is this deeper Self, the second 'bird' in classical Indian symbolism, which connects us to our greater beings through the countless resonances which transcend the spatio-temporal limitations of our mundane perceptions. Through such transcendental connections our deeper Self, the *Ātman,* attuned to the play of forces shapes our destiny, reveals to us insights and guides and inspires us to transcend our limited selves in our greatest achievements (When me they fly, I am the wings). And it is in these connections to our greater beings that our microcosmic existence has its meaning for as I stated in the verse:

No monad in itself has meaning
For meaning lives within the wholes
Its meaning is its greater beings
In which it plays so many roles

And those who persist in seeking the Truth, the meaning of it all, may eventually come to realise that to know the Truth, they must become one with their true Self, the *Ātman-Brahman,* for in Truth all this is *Brahman.*

AUM Shanti, Shanti, Shanti

REFERENCES

1. Lott, E. (1980) *Vedantic Approaches to God*. MacMillan.
2. *Evening Standard*. London, March 1993.
3. Storr, A. (1980) *Jung: Selected Writings*. Fontana.
4. O'Neil, L.T. (1980) *Māyā in Śaṅkara: Measuring the immeasurable*. Motilal Banarsidass.
5. Harvey, A. (1991) *Hidden Journey: A spiritual awakening*. Bloomsbury.
6. Katz, S.T. (ed.) (1983) *Mysticism and Religious Traditions*. Oxford U.P.
7. Eadie, B.J. (1994) *Embraced by the Light: What happens when you die?* Harper Collins.
8. Morse, M. with Perry, P. (1992) *Closer to the Light: Learning from the near-death experiences of children*. Bantam.
9. Odajnyk, V.W. (1993) *Gathering the Light: A psychology of meditation*. Shambhala.
10. Forman, R.K.C. (ed.) (1990) *The Problem of Pure Consciousness: Mysticism and philosophy*. Oxford U.P.
11. Tsung-mi. Cited by Gimello, R.M.(1983) Mysticism in its contexts. In Ref.6.
12. Smith, J.E. (1983) William James' account of mysticism: A critical appraisal. In Ref. 6.
13. St Bonaventure. From *The Mind's Road to God*, cited in Ref. 12.
14. Potter, D.D. in Dialogue on Buddhism, neuroscience and the medical sciences. In Goleman, D. and Thurman, R.A.F. (eds) (1991) *MindScience: An East-West Dialogue*. Wisdom Publications.
15. Talbot, M. (1991) *The Holographic Universe*. Harper Collins.
16. Coombs, A. and Holland, M. (1990) *Synchronicity: Science, myth and the trickster*. Paragon House.
17. Orme-Johnson, D.W. (1977) Higher states of consciousness, EEG coherence, creativity and experiences of the *siddhis*. *Electroencephalography and Clinical Neurophysiology*, **4**:581.
18. Blackmore, S. (1991) Is meditation good for you. *New Scientist*. London. 6th July.
19. West, M.A. (1987) Traditional and psychological perspectives on meditation. In West, M.A. (ed.) *The Psychology of Meditation*. Oxford U.P.
20. Taylor, E. (1994) Radical Empiricism and the conduct of research. In Harman, W. and Clark, J. (eds) *New Metaphysical Foundations of Modern Science*. Institute of Noetic Sciences. Sausalito, CA.
21. Becker, R.O. (1990) *Cross Currents: The promise of electromedicine. The perils of electropollution*. Tarcher Putnam.
22. Wilber, K., Engler, J. and Brown, D.P. (eds) (1986) *Transformations of*

Consciousness: Conventional and contemplative perspectives on development. Shambhala.

23. Brown, D. (1986) The stages of meditation in cross-cultural perspective. In Ref. 22.
24. Wilber, K. (1984) *Quantum Questions: Mystical writings of the world's great physicists.* Shambhala.
25. Sri Aurobindo (Aurobindo Ghose) (1914-21) *The Synthesis of Yoga.* Fourth Edition. 1970. The Aurobindo Ashram Trust.
26. Murphy, M. (1992) *The Future of the Body: Explorations into the further evolution of human nature.* Tarcher Putnam.
27. Tarnas, R. (1991) *The Passion of the Western Mind: Understanding the ideas that have shaped our world view.* Ballantine Books.
28. Coward, H. (1985) *Jung and Eastern Thought.* State University of New York Press.
29. Segal, R.A. (1992) *The Gnostic Jung.* Princeton University Press.
30. Matt, D.C. (1990) The concept of Nothingness in Jewish mysticism. In Ref. 10.
31. Sheldrake, R. (1988) *The Presence of the Past: Morphic resonance and the habits of Nature.* Harper Collins.
32. Nelson, L.H. (1994) On what we say there is and why it matters: A feminist perspective on metaphysics and science. In Harman, W. and Clark, J. (eds) As for ref. 20.
33. Goodwin, B.C. (1994) Towards a science of qualities. In Harman, W. and Clark, J. (eds) as for ref. 20.
34. Laughlin, C.D. (1994) On the relationship between science and the life-world: A biogenetic structural theory of meaning and causation. In Harman, W. and Clark, J. (eds) as for ref. 20.
35. Heisenberg, W. (1962) *Physics and Philosophy.* Harper and Row.
36. Goswami, A. (1994) *Science within Consciousness: Developing a science based on the primacy of consciousness.* Institute of Noetic Sciences. Sausalito, CA.
37. Goodwin, B.C. (1987) A science of qualities. In Ref. 54.
38. Capek, M. (1986) The unreality and indeterminancy of the future in the light of contemporary physics. In Ref. 55.
39. Friedman, N. (1990) *Bridging Science and Spirit: Common elements in David Bohm's physics, the Perennial Philosophy and Seth.* Living Lake Books.
40. Jahn, R.G. and Dunne, B.J. (1987) *Margins of Reality: The role of consciousness in the physical world.* Harcourt Brace.
41. Grof, S. (1985) *Beyond the Brain: Birth, death and transcendence in psychotherapy.* State University of New York Press.
42. Perovich, Jr, A.N. (1990) Does the philosophy of mysticism rest on a mistake. In Ref. 10.
43. Woodhouse, M.B. (1990) On the possibility of pure consciousness. In Ref. 10.
44. Rothberg, D. (1990) Contemporary epistemology and the study of mysticism. In Ref. 10.

45. Indich, W.M. (1980) *Consciousness in Advaita Vedānta.* Motilal Banarsidass.
46. Deikman, A.J. (1966) Deautomatization and the mystic experience. Psychiatry Vol. 29, excerpted in Ornstein, R. (1986) *The Psychology of Consciousness.* Penguin.
47. Clarke, J.J. (1994) *Jung and Eastern Thought:* A dialogue with the Orient. Routledge.
48. Sheldrake, R. (1981) *A New Science of Life.* Blond and Briggs.
49. Sheldrake, R. (1994) *Noetic Sciences Review.* Summer 1994. Excerpted in *Noetic Sciences Review.* Winter 1996. Institute of Noetic Sciences. Sausalito, CA.
50. Ellison, A.J. (1987) Western science and religious experience. In Singh, T.D. (ed.) *Synthesis of Science and Religion.* Bhaktivedanta Institute.
51. Padfield, S. Cited in Ref. 16.
52. Satprem (1968) *Sri Aurobindo or The Adventure of Consciousness.* Sri Aurobindo Ashram Trust.
53. Wolf, F.A. (1994) *The Dreaming Universe.* Simon and Schuster.
54. Hiley, B.J. and Peat, F.D. (eds) (1987) *Quantum Implications: Essays in Honour of David Bohm.* Routledge.
55. Griffin, D.R. (ed.) (1986) *Physics and the Ultimate Significance of Time.* State University of New York Press.
56. Ferguson, M. (1978) Karl Pribram's changing reality. Reprinted in Wilber, K. (ed.) (1982) *The Holographic Paradigm and Other Paradoxes.* Shambhala.
57. Pribram, K. cited in Ref. 56 and Ref. 76.
58. Pribram, K. (1978) What the fuss is all about. In Wilber, K. (ed.) (1982) as for ref. 56.
59. Rosen, S.M. (1986) Time and higher-order wholeness: A response to David Bohm. In Ref. 55.
60. Harman, W. The new science and holonomy. Excerpted in Wilber, K. (ed.) (1982) as for Ref. 56.
61. Nunez, P.L. (1990) Physical principles and neurophysiological mechanisms underlying event-related potentials. In Rohrbaugh, J.W., Parasuraman, R. and Johnson, Jr, R. (eds) *Event-Related Brain Potentials.* Oxford U.P.
62. Fenwick, P. (1987) Meditation and the EEG. In West, M.A. (ed.) as for Ref. 19.
63. Mavromatis, A. (1987) *Hypnagogia: The unique state of consciousness between wakefulness and sleep.* Routledge.
64. Griffiths, P.J. (1990) Pure consciousness & Indian Buddhism. In Ref. 10.
65. Chapple, C. (1990) The unseen seer and the field: Consciousness in *Sānkhya* and *Yoga.* In Ref. 10.
66. Benson, H. with Stark, M. (1996) *Timeless Healing: The power and biology of belief.* Simon and Schuster.
67. Crick, F. (1994) *The Astonishing Hypothesis: The scientific search for the soul.* Simon and Schuster.

68. Pribram, K. cited in Ref. 76.
69. Lancaster, B. (1991) *Mind, Brain and Human Potential: The quest for an understanding of self.* Element.
70. Swami Satyananda Saraswati cited in Roney-Dougall, S. (1993) *Where Science and Magic Meet.* Element.
71. Wilber, K. (1990) Are the chakras real?. In White, J. (ed) *Kundalini: Evolution and enlightenment.* Paragon House.
72. Iyer, K. (1991) *Vedanta or the Science of Reality.* Adhyatma Prakasha Karyalaya. Bangalore.
73. Koestler, A. (1978) *Janus: A summing up.* Hutchinson.
74. Quinton, A. (1987) speaking on *The Great Philosophers.* BBC Television.
75. Edgar, W.J. (1976) Continuity and the individuation of modes in Spinoza's physics. In Wilbur, J. B. (ed.) *Spinoza' s Metaphysics: Essays in critical appreciation.* Van Gorcum.
76. Ferguson, M. (1980) *The Aquarian Conspiracy.* Harper Collins.
77. Jantsch, E. (1980) *The Self-Organizing Universe.* Pergamon Press.
78. Pribram, K. (1991) *Brain and Perception: Holonomy and structure in figural processing.* Lawrence Erlbaum Associates.
79. Bohm, D. and Peat, F.D. (1987) *Science, Order and Creativity.* Routledge.
80. Briggs, J. and Peat, F.D. (1989) *Turbulent Mirror: An illustrated guide to Chaos theory and the science of wholeness.* Harper and Row.
81. Lansner, A. and Liljenstrom, H. (1994) Computer models of the brain: How far can they take us? *Journal of Theoretical Biology.* 171: 61-73. (Special Issue on Mind and Matter)
82. Haken, H. (1994) A brain model for vision in terms of synergetics. *Journal of Theoretical Biology,* 171: 75-85.
83. Laughlin, Jr, C.D., McManus, J., d'Aquili, E.G. (1990) *Brain, Symbol and Experience: Toward a neurophenomenology of consciousness.* Columbia U.P.
84. Potter, K. (1980) The Karma theory and its interpretation in some Indian philosophical systems. In O'Flaherty, W.D. (ed.) *Karma and Rebirth in Classical Indian Traditions.* University of California Press.
85. Taimni, I.K. (1961) *The Science of Yoga.* Quest Books.
86. Jenkins, M. (1997) American therapy that could blow your minds. *The Independent on Sunday.* London. 9th February.
87. Putnam, F.W. (1989) *Diagnosis and Treatment of Multiple Personality Disorder.* Guilford Press.
88. Hurley, III, T.J. and O'Regan, B. (1985) Multiple personality: Mirrors of a new model of mind. Excerpted in McNeill, B. and Guion, C. (eds) *Noetic Sciences Collection: 1980 to 1990. Ten Years of Consciousness Research.* Institute of Noetic Sciences. Sausalito, CA.
89. Harman, W. (1994) *The Scientific Exploration of Consciousness: Toward an adequate epistemology.* Institute of Noetic Sciences. Sausalito, CA.
90. Griffin, D.R. (1985) Bohm and Whitehead on wholeness, freedom, causality and time. Reprinted in Ref. 55.
91. Ho, M.W. (1994) Towards an indigenous Western science: Causality

in the universe of coherent space-time structures. In Harman, W. and Clark, J. as for ref.20.

92. Deloria, Jr, V. (1994) If you think about it, you will see that it is true. In Harman, W. and Clark, J. (eds) as for Ref. 20.
93. Stapp, H.P. (1986) Einstein time and process time. In Ref. 55.
94. Chaudhuri, H. (1974) The psychophysiology of Kundalini. Excerpted in White, J. (ed.) as for Ref. 71.
95. Long, B. (1980) The concepts of human action and rebirth in the *Mahābhārata*. In O'Flaherty (ed.) as for Ref. 84.
96. Sirag, S.P. (1993) Energy. In Kane, B., Millay, J. and Brown, D. (eds) *Silver Threads: 25 Years of parapsychology research.* Praeger.
97. Isaac Newton, quoted in Ref. 41.
98. Taylor, A.M. and Taylor, A.M. (1993) *Science and Causality: A historical perspective.* IONS, Sausalito, CA.
99. Dyczkowski, M.S.G. (1987) *The Doctrine of Vibration: An analysis of the doctrines and practises of Kashmiri Shaivism.* State University of New York Press.
100. Panda, N.C. (1995) *The Vibrating Universe.* Motilal Banarsidass.
101. Jordens, J.F.T. (1967) *Prāṇa* and libido: *Prajñā* and consciousness. Reprinted in Ref. 28.
102. Chennakesavan, S. (1980) *Concept of Mind in Indian Philosophy.* Motilal Banarsidass.
103. Kaplan, S. (1987) *Hermeneutics, Holography and Indian Idealism: A study of projection and Gauḍapāda's Māṇḍūkya Kārikā.* Motilal Banarsidass.
104. Borchert, B. (1994) *Mysticism: Its history and challenge.* Weiser.
105. Scriven, M. (1994) The psycho-physical foundations of modern science. In Harman, W. and Clark, J. (eds) as for Ref. 20.
106. Capra, F. (1988) *Uncommon Wisdom: Conversations with remarkable people.* Century Hutchinson.
107. Penrose, R. (1994) *Shadows of the Mind: A search for the missing science of consciousness.* Oxford U.P.
108. Josephson, B.D. (1987) Science and religion: How to make the synthesis? In Singh, T.D. (ed.) as Ref. 50.
109. Goswami, A. with Reed, R.E. and Goswami, M. (1993) *The Self-Aware Universe: How consciousness creates the material world.* Simon and Schuster.
110. Thompson, R. (1987) God and the laws of physics. In Singh, T.D. (ed) as Ref. 50.
111. Finkelstein, D. (1987) All is flux. In Ref. 54.
112. Rubinstein, R.A.C., Laughlin, C.D. and McManus, J. (1984) *Science as Cognitive Process.* University of Pennsylvania Press.
113. Laughlin, C.D. (1992) *Scientific Explanation and the Life-World.* IONS, Sausalito, CA.
114. Harman, W. (1994) Toward a science of wholeness. In Harman, W. and Clark, J. (eds) as Ref. 20.
115. Hawking, S. cited in Weber, R. (1986) *Dialogues with Scientists and Sages: The search for unity.* Routledge.

116. White, J. (1990) *The Meeting of Science and Spirit: Guidelines for a New Age.* Paragon House.
117. Hiley, B.J. and Peat, F.D. (1987) General introduction: The development of David Bohm's ideas from the plasma to the implicate order. In Ref. 54.
118. Bohm, D. (1986) Time, the implicate order, and pre-space. In Ref. 55.
119. Finkelstein, D. cited in Talbot, M. (1993) *Mysticism and the New Physics.* Arkana.
120. Prigogine, I. (1986) Irreversibility and space-time structure. In Ref.55.
121. Penrose, D. cited in Ref. 80.
122. Bohm, D. cited in Ref. 80.
123. Bohm, D. cited in Ref. 15.
124. Roberts, R. (1993) *A Seth Reader.* Vernal Equinox Press.
125. Herbert, N. (1993) Quantum reality and consciousness. In Kane, B., Millay, J. and Brown, D. (eds) as Ref. 96.
126. Neufeldt, R. (1986) In search of Utopia: Karma and rebirth in the Theosophical movement. In Neufeldt, R. (ed.) (1986) *Karma and Rebirth: Post-classical developments.* State University of New York Press.
127. Monroe, R. cited in Ref. 15.
128. Aurobindo Ghose cited in Ref. 15.
129. Eddington, A. (1929) *The Nature of the Physical World.* Excerpted in Ref. 24.
130. Wilber, K. cited in Ref. 39.
131. Dyczkowski, M.S.G. (1992) *The Stanzas on Vibration.* State University of New York Press.
132. Wilber, K. (1986) The spectrum of development. In Ref. 22.
133. Dixey, R. (1994) Man, matter, and metaphysics: Can we create a total science? In Harman, W. and Clark, J. (eds) as Ref. 20.
134. Bohm, D. cited in Weber, R. (1986) as Ref. 115.
135. Goodwin, B. (1994) *How the Leopard Changed its Spots: The evolution of complexity.* Wiedenfeld and Nicolson.
136. Sperry, R. (1994) Holding course and shifting paradigms. In Harman, W. and Clark, J. (eds) as Ref. 20.
137. Goldstein, K. (1933) (Reprinted 1995) *The Organism: A holistic approach to biology derived from pathological data in man.* Zone Books.
138. Searle, J. (1984) *Voices.* Conversation with Geoffrey Hinton. Channel 4 Television. London.
139. Prigogine, I. and Stengers, I. (1984) *Order out of Chaos: Man's new dialogue with Nature.* Bantam.
140. Gauss, K.F. cited in Ref. 142.
141. *Horizon.* BBC Television. 6th March 1997.
142. Kautz, W.H. (1993) Parapsychology, science and intuition. In Kane, B., Millay, J. and Brown, D. (eds) as Ref. 96.
143. Paracelsus, quoted in Ref. 21.
144. Vigier, J.P. (1983) Louis de Broglie: Physicist and thinker. Reprinted as, Causality and the physical laws of Nature. In Singh, T.D. (ed.) as Ref. 50.

145. Rush, J.H. (1986) Physical and quasi-physical theories of psi. In Edge, H.L., Morris, R.L., Palmer, J. and Rush, J.H. (1986) *Foundations of Parapsychology*. Routledge.
146. Hunt, V.V. (1989) *Infinite Mind: The science of human vibrations*. Malibu Publishing Co.
147. Persinger, M.A. (1979) ELF field mediation in spontaneous psi events: Direct information transfer or conditioned elicitation. In *Psychoenergetic Systems* Vol. 3 No. 1-4.
148. Bell, J.S. (1987) Beables for quantum field theory. In Ref. 54.
149. Rush, J.H. Parapsychology: A historical perspective. In Edge *et al.* as Ref. 145.
150. Edge, H.L. Survival and other philosophical questions. In Edge *et al.* as Ref. 145.
151. Thomson, S. (1993) Truth and science: The ethical dimensions of psi research. In Kane *et al.* as Ref. 96.
152. Kautz, W.H. (1993) The dilemma of parapsychology. In Kane *et al.* as Ref. 96.
153. Targ, R. (1991) from *Journal of Parapsychology* 55: 59-83. Reprinted in Kane *et al.* as Ref. 96.
154. Rauscher, E.A. (1993) A theoretical model of the remote-perception phenomenon. In Kane *et al.* as Ref. 96.
155. Weil, A. (1983) cited in Vilenskaya, L. (1993) Firewalking: A new look at an old enigma. In Kane *et al.* as Ref. 96.
156. Walker, E.H. (1979) The quantum theory of psi phenomena. In *Psychoenergetic Systems*. Vol. 3 Nos. 1-4.
157. Sirag, S.P. (1993) Hyperspace reflections. In Kane *et al.* as Ref. 96
158. Burns, J.E. (1993) Time, consciousness and psi. In Kane *et al.* as Ref. 96.
159. Locke, S. and Colligan, D. (1986) *The Healer Within: The new medicine of mind and body*. E.P. Dutton.
160. McClelland, D. cited in Ref. 159.
161. Stent, G.S. and Calendar, R. (1978) *Molecular Genetics: An introductory narrative*. Second Edition. W.H. Freeman.
162. Becker, R.O. (1979) Electromagnetic fields and life. In *Psychoenergetic Systems*. Vol. 3 Nos. 1-4.
163. National Federation of Spiritual Healers (UK) (1994). Information Leaflet.
164. Rush, J.H. (1986) Findings from experimental PK research. In Edge *et al.* as Ref. 145.
165. Hunt, V.V. cited in Ref. 15.
166. Bohm, D. cited in Ref. 15.
167. Brennan, B. cited in Ref. 15.
168. Thurman, R.A.F. (1991) Tibetan psychology: Sophisticated software for the human brain. In Goleman, D. and Thurman, R.A.F. (eds) as Ref. 14.
169. Benson, H. (1991) Mind-body interactions including Tibetan studies. In Goleman and Thurman (eds) as Ref. 14.

170. McDermott, J.P. (1980) Karma and rebirth in early Buddhism. In O'Flaherty, W.D. (ed) as Ref. 84.
171. Creel, A.B. (1986) Contemporary philosophical treatments of karma and rebirth. In Neufeldt, R.W. (ed.) as Ref. 126.
172. Anand, K.K. (1982) *Indian Philosophy: The concept of Karma.* Bharatiya Vidya Prakashan.
173. Halbfass, W.. (1980) Karma, *apūrva,* and "natural" causes: Observations on the growth and limits of the theory of *Saṃsāra.* In O'Flaherty, W.D. (ed.) as Ref. 84.
174. Obeyesekere, G. (1980) The rebirth eschatology and its transformations: A contribution to the sociology of early Buddhism. In O'Flaherty, W.D. (ed.) as Ref. 84.
175. Coward, H. (1986) Karma and rebirth in Western psychology. In Neufeldt, R.W. (ed.) as Ref. 126.
176. Matthews, B. (1986) Post-classical developments in the concepts of karma and rebirth in Theravāda Buddhism. In Neufeldt, R.W. (ed.) as Ref. 126.
177. Schmithausen, L. (1986) Critical response. In Neufeldt, R.W. (ed.) as Ref. 126.
178. Rinpoche, S. Survival of consciousness: A Tibetan Buddhist perspective. In McNeill, B. and Guion, C. (eds) as Ref. 88.
179. Stablein, W. (1980) The medical soteriology of karma in the Buddhist Tantric tradition. In O'Flaherty, W.D. (ed.) as Ref. 84.
180. Gussner, R.E. (1986) Teachings in karma and rebirth: Social and spiritual role in the Rajneesh neo-samnyāsin movement. In Neufeldt, R.W. (ed.) as Ref. 126.
181. Grof, S. and Harman, W. (1994) *The Survival of Consciousness.* (Audiotape) New Dimensions Tapes. IONS, Sausalito, CA.
182. Grof, S. with Bennett, H.Z. (1990) *The Holotropic Mind: The three levels of human consciousness and how they shape our lives.* Harper Collins.
183. Klimo, J. (1993) Channeling. In Kane et al. as Ref. 96.
184. Larson, G.J. Karma as a "sociology of knowledge" or "social psychology" of process/praxis. In O'Flaherty W.D. (ed.) as Ref. 84.
185. Thompson, K. (1996) In *Noetic Sciences Review.* No. 40., IONS, Sausalito, CA.
186. Rawlinson, H.G. (1975) Early contacts between India and Europe. In Basham, A.L. (ed.) *A Cultural History of India.* Oxford U.P.
187. Pryse, J.M. (1907) *The Restored New Testament.* Excerpted in White, J. (ed.) (1990) As for Ref. 71.
188. Forman, R.K.C. (1991) *Meister Eckhart: Mystic as theologian.* Element.
189. Meister Eckhart cited in Ref. 188.
190. Meister Eckhart cited in Ref. 26.
191. Romain Rolland cited in Ref. 188.
192. Hiriyanna, M. (1949) cited in Ref. 193.
193. Sharma, A. (1990) *A Hindu Perspective on the Philosophy of Religion.* MacMillan.

BIBLIOGRAPHY

Indian History and Culture - Selected titles related to this book

NB. Motilal Banarsidass Publishers have a huge list of scholarly titles covering all aspects of Indology.

Basham, A.L. (ed.) (1975) *A Cultural History of India.* Oxford University Press. Oxford and Delhi.

Bose, M. (1982) *The Lost Hero: A Biography of Subhas Bose.* Quartet Books, London.

Chatterjee, P. (1986) *Nationalist Thought and the Colonial World.* Zed Books, London and Oxford University Press, Delhi.

Dutta, K. and Robinson, A. (1995) *Rabindranath Tagore: The myriad-minded man.* Bloomsbury, London.

Fay, P.W. (1993) *The Forgotten Army: India's armed struggle for independence 1942-1945.* The University of Michigan Press, Ann Arbor, Michigan.

Feuerstein, G., Kak, S. and Frawley, D. (1995) *In Search of the Cradle of Civilization: New light on Ancient India.* Quest Books, Wheaton, Illinois and Madras.

Frankel, F.R. and Rao, M.S.A. (eds) *Dominance and State Power in Modern India: Decline of a social order.* Volume 1 (1989), Volume 2 (1990), Oxford University Press, Delhi.

Heehs, P. (1989) *Sri Aurobindo: A brief biography.* Oxford University Press, Delhi.

Hixon, L. (1992) *Great Swan: Meetings with Ramakrishna.* Shambhala, Boston. Indian Edition, Motilal Banarsidass, Delhi.

Klostermaier, K.K. (1989) *A Survey of Hinduism.* State University of New York Press, Albany, NY.

Nandy, A. (1994) *The Illegitimacy of Nationalism: Rabindranath Tagore and the politics of self.* Oxford University Press, Delhi.

Nandy, A. (1983) *The Intimate Enemy: Loss and recovery of self under colonialism.* Oxford University Press, Delhi.

Prabhavananda, Swami (1979) *The Spiritual Heritage of India.* Vedanta Press. Hollywood, California, USA.

Radhakrishnan, S. (1953) *The Principal Upaniṣads.* Centenary Edition

(1989) Unwin Hyman, London. Also published in India presumably by Oxford University Press.

Raychaudhuri, T. (1988) *Europe Reconsidered: Perceptions of the West in Nineteenth Century Bengal.* Oxford University Press, Delhi.

Selected works on Indo-European Cultural Exchange and Orientalism

Alvares, C. (1979) *Homo faber: Technology and Culture in India, China and the West 1500-1792.* Allied Publishers, Bombay.

Amin, S. (1989) *Eurocentrism.* Zed, London and Monthly Review Press, New York.

Bernal, M. (1987) *Black Athena: The Afroasiatic roots of classical civilisation: Volume 1. The fabrication of Ancient Greece 1785-1985.* Free Association Books, London.

Clarke, J.J. (1994) *Jung and Eastern Thought: A dialogue with the Orient.* Routledge, London.

Coward, H. (1985) *Jung and Eastern Thought.* State University of New York Press, Albany, NY. Indian Edition (*c.* 1995) Sri Satguru Publications, Delhi.

Halbfass, W. (1988) *India and Europe: An essay in philosophical understanding.* State University of New York Press, Albany, NY. Indian Edition (1990) Motilal Banarsidass, Delhi.

Inden, R. (1990) *Imagining India.* Blackwell Publishers, Cambridge, Mass., and Oxford, UK.

Joseph, G.G. (1991) *The Crest of the Peacock: Non-European Roots of Mathematics.* Penguin Books, London.

Kejariwal, O.P. (1988) *The Asiatic Society of Bengal and the Discovery of India's Past 1784-1838.* Oxford University Press, Delhi.

Nandy, A. (1995) *Alternative Sciences: Creativity and authenticity in two Indian scientists.* [Jagadis Chandra Bose and Srinivasa Ramanujan]. Second Edition. Oxford University Press, Delhi. [Jagadis Chandra Bose and Srinivasa Ramanujan—Nandy mentions Bose's hope of creating a new Indian Science by synthesizing European science and Indian Philosophy].

Schwab, R. (1984) *The Oriental Renaissance: Europe's rediscovery of India and the East 1680-1880.* Columbia University Press, New York.

Versluis, A. (1993) *American Transcendentalism and Asian Religions.* Oxford University Press, New York.

Indian Philosophy: Selected titles relating to this work

NB. Motilal Banarsidass Publishers have the largest and most comprehensive list of titles in Indian Philosophy (including Buddhism).

Sri Aurobindo (1914-1918) *The Synthesis of Yoga.* Ninth Book Edition, 1992, Sri Aurobindo Ashram Trust Publication Department, Pondicherry.

Dyczkowski, M.S.G. (1987) *The Doctrine of Vibration: An analysis of the doctrines and practices of Kashmir Shaivism.* State University of New York Press, Albany NY. Indian Edition, Motilal Banarsidass, Delhi.

Indich, W.M. (1980) *Consciousness in Advaita Vedanta.* Motilal Banarsidass, Delhi.

Lott, E. (1980) *Vedantic Approaches to God.* MacMillan (Library of Philosophy and Religion), London. US Edition, Harper and Row Inc., Barnes and Noble Import Division, New York.

Neufeldt, R.W. (Ed.) (1986) *Karma and Rebirth: Post Classical Developments.* State University of New York Press. Albany, NY. Indian Edition (1995) Sri Satguru Publications, Delhi.

O'Flaherty, W.D. (ed.) (1980) *Karma and Rebirth in Classical Indian Traditions.* University of California Press, Berkely and Los Angeles, CA and London, UK. Indian Edition, Motilal Banarsidass, Delhi.

Satprem (1968) *Sri Aurobindo or the Adventure of Consciousness.* Sri Aurobindo Ashram Trust Publication Department, Pondicherry.

Taimni, I.K. (1961) *The Science of Yoga.* (The *Yoga Sūtras* of Patañjali in Sanskrit with transliteration in Roman, translation in English and Commentary). Quest Edition (1992) The Theosophical Publishing House, Wheaton, Illinois, USA; Madras, India and London, UK.

Selected Titles relating to Science and Mysticism and to Mysticism and Philosophy

Becker, R.O. (1990) *Cross Currents: The perils of electropollution; the promise of electromedicine.* Tarcher/Putnam, New York.

Bohm, D. (1980) *Wholeness and the Implicate Order.* Routledge and Kegan Paul, London.

Bohm, D. and Peat, F.D. (1980) *Science, Order and Creativity.* Bantam, New York. UK Edition (1989) Routledge.

Deikman, A.J. (1966) Deautomatization and the Mystic Experience. *Psychiatry,* Vol. 29. Excerpted in Ornstein, R. *The Psychology of Consciousness.* Second Revised Edition, Penguins Books, New York and London.

Eddington, A. (1929) *The Nature of the Physical World.* MacMillan, London and New York.

Edge, H.L., Morris, R.L., Palmer, J. and Rush, J.H. (1986) *Foundations of Parapsychology: Exploring the boundaries of human capability.* Routledge and Kegan Paul, London. US Edition, Methuen, New York.

Forman, R.K.C. (ed.) (1990) *The Problem of Pure Consciousness: Mysticism and philosophy.* Oxford University Press, New York.

Friedman, N. (1990) *Bridging Science and Spirit: Common elements in David Bohm's physics, the Perennial Philosophy and Seth.* Living Lake Books, P.O. Box 16145, St Louis, MO63105, USA.

Griffin, D.R. (ed.) (1986) *Physics and the Ultimate Significance of Time: Bohm, Prigogine and Process Philosophy.* State University of New York Press, Albany, NY.

Grof, S. (1985) *Beyond the Brain: Birth, death and transcendence in psychotherapy.* State University of New York Press, Albany, NY.

Hameroff, S., Kaszniak, A. and Scott, A. (eds) (1996) *Toward a Science of Consciousness: The First Tucson Discussions and Debates.* MIT Press, Cambridge, Mass.

Harman, W. and Clark, J (eds) (1994) *New Metaphysical Foundations of Modern Science.* Institute of Noetic Sciences, 475 Gate Five Road, Suite 300, Sausalito, CA94965, USA.

Heisenberg, W. (1962) *Physics and Philosophy.* Harper and Row, New York. Reprinted 1989, Pelican Books. UK (1990) Penguin Books, London.

Hiley, B.J. and Peat, F.D. (eds) (1987) *Quantum Implications: Essays in honour of David Bohm.* Routledge, London and New York.

Ho, M-W. (1993) *The Rainbow and the Worm : The physics of organisms.* World Scientific, Singapore.

Hunt, V.V. (1989) *Infinite Mind: The science of human vibrations.* Malibu Publishing Co., P.O. Box 4234, Malibu, CA90265, USA.

Jahn, R.G. and Dunne, B.J. (1987) *Margins of Reality: The role of consciousness in the physical world.* Harcourt Brace, Orlando, FL.

Jantsch, E. (1980) *The Self-Organizing Universe: Scientific and human implications of the emerging paradigm of evolution.* Pergamon Press, Oxford.

Kane, B., Millay, J., Brown, D. (eds) (1993) *Silver Threads: 25 Years of parapsychology research.* Praeger Publishers, Westport Connecticut. UK: Greenwood Publishers, London.

Kaplan, S. (1987) *Hermeneutics, Holography and Indian Idealism: A study of projection and Gaudapada's Māṇḍūkya Kārikā.* Motilal Banarsidass, Delhi.

Laughlin Jr, C. D., McManus, J., d'Aquili, E.G. (1990) *Brain, Symbol & Experience: Toward a neurophenomenology of human consciousness.* Columbia University Press, New York.

LeShan, L. (1974) *The Medium, the Mystic and the Physicist.* Ballantyne, New York.

Mavromatis, A. (1987) *Hypnagogia: The unique state of consciousness between wakefulness and sleep.* Routledge and Kegan Paul, London.

McNeill, B. and Guion, C. (eds) (1991) *Noetic Sciences Collection 1980-1990: Ten years of consciousness research.* Institute of Noetic Sciences. 475 Gate Five Road, Sausalito, CA94965, USA.

Murphy, M. and Donovan, S. (eds) (1997) *The Physical and Psychological Effects of Meditation.* Second Edition. Institute of Noetic Sciences. 475 Gate Five Road, Sausalito, CA94965, USA.

Odajnyk, V.W. (1993) *Gathering the Light: A psychology of meditation.* Shambhala, Boston.

Peat, F.D. (1987) *Synchronicity : The bridge between matter and mind.* Bantam, New York.

Panda, N.C. (1995) *The Vibrating Universe.* Motilal Banarsidass. Delhi.

Pribram, K.H. (1991) *Brain and Perception: Holonomy and structure in figural processing.* Lawrence Erlbaum Associates, Hillsdale, New Jersey, USA.

Prigogine, I. and Stengers, I. (1984) *Order out of Chaos: Man's new dialogue with Nature.* Bantam, New York and Heinemann, London.

Putnam, F.W. (1989) *Diagnosis and Treatment of Multiple Personality Disorder.* The Guilford Press, New York.

Rubinstein, R.A., Laughlin Jr, C.D. and McManus, J. (1984) *Science as Cognitive Process.* University of Pennsylvania Press, Philadelphia.

Sheldrake, R. (1988) *The Presence of the Past: Morphic resonance and the habits of Nature.* HarperCollins, London.

Stace, W.T. (1960) *Mysticism and Philosophy.* Lippincott, New York.

Stevenson, I. *Twenty Cases Suggestive of Reincarnation* (1974); *Cases of the Reincarnation Type* (1974) Vols 1-4; *Children Who Remember their Past Lives* (1987). University Press of Virginia, Virginia, USA.

West, M.A. (ed.) (1987) *The Psychology of Meditation.* Oxford University Press, Oxford.

Wilber, K. (ed.) (1982) *The Holographic Paradigm and Other Paradoxes: Exploring the leading edge of science.* Shambhala, Boulder, Colorado (now at Boston).

Wilber, K., Engler, J., and Brown, D.P. (1986) *Transformations of Consciousness: Conventional and Contemplative Perspectives on Development.* Shambhala, Boston.

INDEX